Social Inequality

Social Inequality

Patterns and Processes

Second Edition

Martin N. Marger

Michigan State University

Boston   Burr Ridge, IL   Dubuque, IA   Madison, WI   New York
San Francisco   St. Louis   Bangkok   Bogotá   Caracas   Kuala Lumpur
Lisbon   London   Madrid   Mexico City   Milan   Montreal   New Delhi
Santiago   Seoul   Singapore   Sydney   Taipei   Toronto

McGraw-Hill Higher Education

*A Division of The **McGraw-Hill** Companies*

1 2 3 4 5 6 7 8 9 0 MAL/MAL 0 9 8 7 6 5 4 3 2 1

Library of Congress Cataloging-in-Publication Data

Marger, Martin.
   Social inequality : patterns and processes / Martin N. Marger.—2nd ed.
     p. cm.
   Includes bibliographical references and index.
   ISBN 0-7674-2086-1
     1. Equality. 2. Social classes.   3. Social structure. 4. Marginality, Social. I. Title.
   HM821.M37 2001
   305--dc21   2001030609

Sponsoring editor, Serina Beauparlant; signing representative, Joe Hanson; production editor, Holly Paulsen; manuscript editor, Deborah Fogel; design manager, Susan Breitbard; art editor, Emma Ghiselli; text designer, Detta Penna; cover designer, Joan Greenfield; illustrator, Joan Carol; manufacturing manager, Randy Hurst. The text was set in 10/12 Palatino by Carlisle Communications, Ltd., and printed on 45# Scholarly Matte by Malloy Lithographing, Inc.

www.mhhe.com

■ Contents

Preface   xiii

Chapter 1:   An Introduction to the Study of Social Inequality   1

Major Issues in the Study of Social Inequality   2
Key Questions in the Study of Social Inequality   2
A Comparative Approach   4
Examining Inequality in a Sociological Mode   4
The Sociological Mode   4
Objectives of Inquiry   9
Individuals and Social Forces   10
Some Basic Terms and Concepts in the Study of Inequality   12
Social Differentiation   12
Social Stratification   12
Stratification Forms   15
Structured Inequality   16
Life Chances and Inequality of Opportunity   16
Stability in Systems of Inequality   19
Change in Systems of Inequality   20
Equity versus Liberty   22
Summary   22

Chapter 2:   The American Class System   25

Social Class: A Two-Dimensional Picture   25
Economic Class   26
Class as Lifestyle   26
Popular Notions of the American Class Structure   27
The Reality of Class in the United States   28
The Six-Part American Class Structure   29
The Distribution of Income   34
The Distribution of Wealth   38

v

Change and Continuity in Economic Inequality   41
Trends in the Distribution of Income and Wealth   41
Looking Beyond   44
Economic Inequality: A Comparative Perspective   45
Summary   47

Chapter 3:   Poverty and the Poor   49

Defining Poverty   49
Absolute Poverty   49
Relative Poverty   50
Official Poverty   50
Who Are the Poor?   52
The Poor and Those at Risk   52
Poverty Trends   55
The Working Poor and the Underclass   58
The Working Poor   58
The Underclass   60
Why Are the Poor Poor?   62
Individual-Focused Explanations   62
Structure-Focused Explanations   66
Popular Views of Poverty   70
Public Policies and Poverty   70
Welfare Programs   71
Poverty in Comparative Perspective   76
Summary   79

Chapter 4:   The Middle Classes and the Changing Economy   81

Historical Development of the Middle Classes   82
Formation of the Middle Classes in the United States   82
Industrialization and the Changing Class Structure   83
Post-Industrialism   84
The Classes in the Middle and the Occupational Structure   85
The Upper-Middle Class   85
The Lower-Middle Class   86
The Working Class   87

The Changing U.S. Economy and the Classes in the Middle 89

The Growth of the Middle Classes 90

The Shrinking Middle 91

Economic Restructuring and the Classes in the Middle 96

Technological Changes 96

Globalization 97

The Decline of Labor Unions 105

Downsizing 106

Demographic Factors 108

Public Policies and the Shrinking Middle 109

The Middle Classes and the New Consumerism 109

Lifestyles, Desires, and Debt 109

Two-Tier Marketing 111

Summary 112

Chapter 5:   The Upper Class and the Power Elite 114

The Upper Class 114

Income 114

Wealth 116

The Rich: Old and New 118

The Privileges of Wealth 123

Inheritance, Effort, and Wealth 124

The Power Elite: Patterns and Theory 125

The Relationship between the Upper Class and the Power Elite 126

Social Class and the Power Elite 131

The Social-Class Origins of U.S. Elites 132

Paths to Power 136

The Elite Recruitment Process 136

The Systemic Nature of Elite Recruitment 138

Power Elites in Other Societies 140

Summary 140

Chapter 6:   Stratification Systems and Social Mobility 142

Systems of Stratification 143

Slavery 144

Caste 147

Estate 151

Class Systems 154

Patterns of Social Mobility in Modern Societies   155
  Measurements of Mobility   155
  Mobility Trends   156
  Mobility in Historical Perspective   158
Determinants of Social Mobility   160
  Structural Mobility   160
  Individual Mobility   161
Education and the Process of Mobility   165
  Education: The Key Life Chance   166
Summary   171

Chapter 7:   Public Policy and the Class System   172

The Political Economy   172
  Capitalism, Democracy, and Inequality   175
  Macroeconomic Policy   177
Taxation: How Much, from Whom   177
Government Spending: On What, for Whom   181
  Categories of Government Spending   181
  Welfare for the Poor, the Middle, and the Wealthy   182
The U.S. Welfare State in Comparative Perspective   187
  The Scope and Impact of the U.S. Welfare State   187
  Accounting for the Difference   188
  Public Perceptions of Government Spending   191
Government Regulation   191
  Regulatory Agencies   191
  Efforts to Influence the Business Cycle   192
Partisan Differences in Public Policy   194
  Demand-Side Policies   194
  Supply-Side Policies   195
  More or Less Inequality? Policy Choices   196
Summary   196

Chapter 8:   Theories of Class and Social Inequality   198

Marx's Theory of Social Inequality   199
  The Economic Foundation   200
  The Class Division   201

Class Conflict and Societal Change 203
Marxian Theory in Summary 205
The Failure of Marx's Vision 205
Enduring Points of Marx's Theory 207
Revising Marx 208
Weber: The Inevitability of Inequality 210
Class 210
Status 211
Party 212
Weber on Power 213
Weber's Contribution to Inequality Theory 214
Michels's Iron Law of Oligarchy 215
Dahrendorf: Neo-Weberian 216
Functionalism and Conflict Theory 217
Functional Theory: The Need for Inequality 218
Conflict Theory: The Dysfunctions of Inequality 219
Lenski's Synthesis 221
Summary 224

Chapter 9:   Ideology and the Legitimation of Inequality 225

Legitimation 226
The Nature of Ideology 227
Dominant Ideologies 228
Ideology and Reality 230
The Dominant American Ideology 231
Individual Achievement 231
Equality of Opportunity 234
Meritocracy and Universalism 235
The Work Ethic 238
Liberal Capitalism 239
Ancillary Beliefs 241
Changing Ideologies 243
Legitimation, Ideology, and Socialization 243
Socialization 243
Legitimation, Socialization, and the School 244
The Mass Media in the Legitimation Process 247
Summary 253

Chapter 10:   Racial/Ethnic Differentiation   255

Ethnicity and Race   256
  Ethnicity   256
  Race   257
Changing Ethnic Patterns in the United States   259
  Ethnic Categories   259
  The American Ethnic Configuration   261
The Shaping of American Ethnic Diversity and Inequality   263
  Native Americans   263
  Euro-Americans   264
  African Americans   268
  Hispanic Americans   272
  Asian Americans   274
The Newest Immigrants   276
  Issues of the Newest Immigration   277
Summary   279

Chapter 11:   Racial/Ethnic Stratification   280

Majority and Minority   280
  Minority Groups   280
  Dominant Groups   283
  The Relativity of Dominant Status and Minority Status   283
  The Origins of Ethnic Stratification   284
  The Intersection of Class and Ethnicity   286
The American Ethnic Hierarchy   287
  Ethnicity and the Economic Hierarchy   288
  African Americans   292
  Explaining the Economic Gap between Whites and Blacks   293
  Hispanic Americans   295
  Asian Americans   296
  Native Americans   298
  Ethnicity and Power   299
  Prejudice and Discrimination   302
  Social Integration   305
Stability and Change in the American Ethnic Hierarchy   306
  Efforts at Changing the Hierarchy   306
  Affirmative Action   307
Summary   312

Chapter 12:   Gender Inequality   314

Gender Differentiation   316
Sex and Gender   316
Gender Stratification   317
Why Gender Inequality?   317
Sexism and Sexist Stereotypes   319
Gender Inequality in the Workforce: Continuity and Change   320
Labor Force Participation   321
Occupational Concentration   323
Earnings   325
Authority   328
Work and the Family   329
Patterns of Gender Inequality: Politics, the Corporation, and Education   330
Gender Inequality in the Political World   330
Gender Inequality in the Corporate World   332
Women and Education   334
The Status of Women in Global Perspective   336
Discrimination and Abuse   336
Women and Power   340
The Feminist Movement   340
Feminism   342
The Feminist Ideological Spectrum   343
Summary   345

Chapter 13:   Political Inequality   346

Political Stratification   346
The Scope and Dimensions of Power   346
Elites and Masses   348
Three Models of Power in America   349
The Class Model   350
The Power Elite Model   352
The Pluralist Model   354
The American Power Structure: Unity and Division   356
Power in America: An Integrated Model   357
The Role of Masses in the System of Power   360
Political Participation: A Key Life Chance   360
The Effective—and Costly—Forms of Participation   362

Political Participation and Social Class   368
Participation and Elite Accountability   369
Mass Participation and the Class Structure   371
Noninstitutional Forms of Participation   372
Summary   375

Glossary   377
References   384
Index   416

◤ Preface

At the outset of the twenty-first century, nothing has detracted from the historically consistent observation of social scientists and philosophers on the ubiquity of inequality in human societies. This book is intended to serve as an introduction to the patterns and processes of social inequality in its major forms—class, racial/ethnic, gender, political—in the United States and other contemporary societies. Its objective is also to help develop an awareness of how inequality impinges on virtually all facets of individual and group life. It is designed primarily for an undergraduate student audience and assumes little prior exposure to the social sciences.

Inequality has long been a staple of sociological inquiry but has held an important place among the topical concerns of other social science disciplines as well. In recent years its traditionally prominent status among the foci of social scientists has been raised higher. In the United States, issues of economic inequality, particularly the widening gap between rich and poor, have not only become standard points of social science discourse but are also an increasingly salient part of political debate. Racial/ethnic inequality has always served as a focal point of American sociology, but it has grown even more compelling with the emergence of several ongoing societal trends: a persistent economic gap between Euro-American groups and racial/ethnic minorities, a public debate that has arisen in response to efforts to deal with that gap (namely, measures subsumed under the rubric of affirmative action), and the influx of new immigrants who have created a more pluralistic ethnic mélange. Gender issues are a fundamental component of the social inequality mix, and particular attention in recent years has been paid to the manner in which they impact class and ethnic issues. The political dimension underlies all other forms of social inequality, and the ability of citizens to hold leaders accountable and to affect public policies is an abiding concern in all contemporary societies, regardless of the presence of democratic institutions.

In teaching an interdisciplinary undergraduate course in social inequality during the past decade, I have discovered that most texts either narrowly focus on one or another form of inequality or they analytically conflate these forms, making it difficult to distinguish them. Although the major dimensions of inequality are obviously interwoven, they do not fall neatly together in a coherent package, either for individuals or for whole societies. Accordingly, I have treated different forms of inequality in self-standing chapters, although the interrelationships among them are discussed throughout. I do consider the class dimension to be most basic, however, and it is there that the book is primarily focused. In discussing racial/ethnic, gender, and political inequalities, emphasis is placed on how they relate to and overlap with class inequalities.

Perhaps no other area of inquiry in the social sciences better lends itself to an interdisciplinary approach than does social inequality. Although sociology has usually taken the lead, economics, political science, and anthropology all focus in various ways on this universal phenomenon. As social scientists have acknowledged the interweaving and overlapping nature of the major dimensions of social inequality, courses in this field have become more integrative and comprehensive. I have tried to design this book to conform to such an interdisciplinary and inclusive perspective.

I also believe that American students of social inequality can acquire a more profound understanding of patterns and processes in their own country through comparative analysis. Too often undergraduates enter social science courses with an inflated view of the United States vis-à-vis the rest of the world; unfortunately, they often leave with a similar view. One of the objectives of this book, therefore, is to inform readers of how the nature of social inequality in the United States is both distinct from and common with social inequality in other contemporary societies. Although all chapters emphasize conditions in American society, each contains discussions of U.S. inequality in a cross-national context, drawing illustrations and data from other comparable societies.

Chapter 1 sets the tone of the book, exploring the unique ways in which sociologists deal with issues of inequality and establishing a lexicon of key terms and concepts utilized throughout the book. It also explains the extant forms of inequality in modern societies and provides a preview of succeeding chapters.

Chapter 2 describes the American class system, presenting a bird's eye view of the class hierarchy and an examination of the distribution of income and wealth. Chapters 3, 4, and 5 deal with the three major class divisions—the poor, the rich, and the classes in the middle—emphasizing socioeconomic issues and patterns. Chapter 5 also discusses the power elite and the ways in which power relates to wealth. Chapter 6 begins with a description of the major systems of stratification, explaining the provisions for mobility in each, and then looks at the nature of social mobility in the United States.

Chapter 7 examines the ways in which government affects the distribution of wealth and power. An underlying assumption of this chapter is that public policies play a fundamental role in determining the shape and depth of inequality in all modern societies. Much discussion centers on how the U.S. welfare state differs from those of other post-industrial societies.

Chapter 8 explores theories of social inequality, particularly those that seek to explain social class. Theoretical issues are discussed here rather than nearer the beginning of the book for two reasons. First, in my own classroom experience I have found it more effective to move sequentially from a description of class systems to an explanation of those systems, framed within different theoretical perspectives. Some instructors, I am sure, will prefer a converse order of coverage, discussing theory antecedent to describing class systems. The order of Chapter 8, as well as most others, can be easily rearranged to accommodate different pedagogical approaches. Second, much theoretical discussion is contained in other chapters that deal with particular issues, such as poverty, the elite structure, and mobility, or with racial/ethnic, gender, and political dimensions of inequality. The purpose of this chapter is to examine class theories in a more general context.

Chapter 9 is devoted to ideology and the legitimation process. The basic objective is to explore the function of ideology in solidifying and sustaining social inequality. The features of the prevailing American ideology are discussed along with the role of major institutions in communicating that ideology.

Chapters 10 and 11 focus on issues of racial/ethnic inequality. Chapter 10 describes the ethnic makeup of American society and the development of its ethnic diversity as a prerequisite to explaining the U.S. ethnic hierarchy in Chapter 11. Over the years I have discovered a disturbing lack of awareness on the part of U.S. students, as well as the general public, of the most elemental features of the American racial/ethnic system, particularly the historical processes of its formation and the demographics of specific groups and categories. Essential to a meaningful analysis of racial/ethnic inequalities is a basic understanding of the concepts of race and ethnicity and of the society's racial and ethnic composition.

Chapter 12 focuses on the gender dimension of inequality. With the enormously wide range of issues that today comprise gender studies, coverage of gender as part of a comprehensive introduction to social inequality must be selective. Among gender issues, it is changes in the occupational role of women, in my view, that have rendered the most far-reaching societal effects during the past several decades. Much of this chapter, therefore, concerns patterns and processes of gender inequality in the workplace, though other institutional areas are discussed, including politics and the family.

Chapter 13 examines political inequality. The first part of this chapter covers the more prominent theories and debates about the U.S. power structure and the role of political elites. The second part deals with the role of masses, exploring how and to what degree they can effectively impact the political system.

Although I did not set out deliberately to frame these chapters thematically, as I wove together the various topics, a leitmotiv seemed to emerge: the discordant societal currents of *liberty* and *equity*. In all societies various forms of social inequality, the efforts and policies that address them, and the theories that seek to explain them appear to revolve around the clash of these two overarching values. This ideological confrontation is particularly evident in the United States, where the sanctity of individual freedom within capitalism conflicts with notions of democracy and equality. This is an age-old philosophical battle, of course, not limited to the contemporary world or to capitalist democracies. As the nineteenth century essayist Walter Bagehot put it, "There is no method by which men can be both free and equal."

Changes to the Second Edition

While the core of the first edition has been retained, all chapters have been updated with the latest statistical data available. Several new tables and figures have been added, and many of the tables presented in the first edition have been converted to bar graphs, line graphs, and other more easily readable forms. This edition also includes several new cartoons.

New sections have been added to several chapters. Chapter 3 examines the impact of the welfare reform measure of 1996. Chapter 4 includes a section on the new consumerism and explains how this accelerating phenomenon has particularly affected the middle classes in American society. Chapter 4 also contains a section that updates the discussion of the state of inequality in America in light of the surging economy of the late 1990s. A discussion of modern-day forms of slavery is new to Chapter 6. A new section on sociopolitical movements in Chapter 13 presents a somewhat extended discussion of the role of unconventional, sometimes noninstitutional, political behavior on the part of masses, and how and why such behavior occurs.

Accompanying Test Bank

Kevin Everett of Radford University, who served as an academic reviewer of the manuscript, has written a test bank to accompany the text. The test bank includes multiple-choice, true-false, and short-answer/essay questions.

Test Bank Items on Disk

In response to adopters' requests, test items from the printed test bank are now available on disk.

Acknowledgments

The completion of a text is never the product of the efforts of the author alone. At Mayfield, Serina Beauparlant believed in the project from the outset and gave me the encouragement and incentive to bring the first edition to fruition. Her support remained unwavering for the second edition. Others at Mayfield who contributed their assistance and expertise are Holly Paulsen, Susan Breitbard, Randy Hurst, Emma Ghiselli, and Cristin Yancey. Deborah Fogel did an outstanding job of copyediting. I appreciate the thoughtful reviews and critical suggestions offered by those who read all or parts of the manuscript of both first and second editions: Chat Ballard, Valdosta State University; Linda Liska Belgrave, University of Miami; Sally Bould, University of Delaware; Penelope Canan, University of Denver; Mona Danner, Old Dominion University; Lelah Dushkin, Kansas State University; Daniel Egan, University of Massachusetts–Lowell; Kevin Everett, Radford University; Kathryn M. Feltey, University of Akron; Nicole T. Flynn, University of South Alabama; Elizabeth Hartung, California State University, Fresno; Linda C. Majka, University of Dayton; Rebecca Matthews, University of Iowa; Steve B. McConnell, University of Toledo; Joan M. Morris, University of Central Florida at Orlando; Charles W. Mueller, University of Iowa; David E. Redburn, Furman University; Stephen J. Scanlan, Ohio State University; Scott Sernau, Indiana University at South Bend; Pamela J. Smock, University of Michigan; Victoria Sturtevant, Southern Oregon University; Eleanor Townsley, Mount Holyoke College; and Amy S. Wharton, Washington State University. Finally, in this, as in other projects, my wife Connie has been an unfailing source of confidence and, when needed, consolation.

1

An Introduction to the Study of Social Inequality

[F]or centuries and over almost the whole of the globe, it has been a basic assumption in societies of any size or complexity that some men are born to power and luxury, others to toil and poverty.
PHILIP MASON

Equality would be a heaven, if we could attain it.
ANTHONY TROLLOPE

In 1989, Malcolm Forbes, the publisher of *Forbes* magazine, celebrated his seventieth birthday by gathering his friends at Kennedy Airport in New York and flying them to Tangier, Morocco, for the weekend. There they dined in Arabian tents erected on terrace gardens overlooking the sea. Luxury also extended to the portable sanitary facilities, which were designed with black-and-white tile floors, sinks, and toilets that flushed. Forbes's date for the affair was Elizabeth Taylor.

Just a few miles from where the Forbes party was getting ready to board three chartered jets (including a Concorde) to attend the birthday party to end all birthday parties, a husband and wife and their four children were living in two small rooms at the Kenmore Hotel, a run-down apartment house where the toilets did not work, the mice ran free, and the hallways were used by prostitutes and drug dealers.

Although the contrast in these two cases could not be more stark, it is not one that is particularly uncommon or surprising. The gap between rich and poor in the United States is wide and in recent years has been continually expanding. In this, however, the United States is far from unique. Although there are relative differences among them, all contemporary societies have a significant disparity between those at the top of the social hierarchy and those at the bottom. Moreover, the gap between whole nations, rich and poor, is also great and in most cases shows little sign of closing.

How can we explain these inequalities? Are inequalities within and between human societies natural and inevitable? Is equality ever more than a chimera, an ideal that can never be realized? Social scientists have been wrestling with those questions since the nineteenth century. This book is about social inequality: its origins, its scope, the ways in which it is sustained, and the ways in which humans seek to reduce it.

No sphere of inquiry is more fundamental in the social sciences, whether we are studying sociology, economics, or political science. Each of these disciplines deals most basically with human inequalities, specifically, differences in income and wealth, differences in social standing and prestige, and differences in power. In one way or another, all questions and issues in the various social science disciplines ultimately involve, directly or indirectly, matters of inequality. Indeed, we would not be stretching the matter to declare quite simply that inequality is the transcendent issue of all social science.

Major Issues in the Study of Social Inequality

Our concern is with different types of social inequality. This entails the exploration of many specific questions and issues. We can summarize our investigation of inequality, however, by posing a few very basic and broadly conceived questions, which form the essential structure of the chapters that follow.

Key Questions in the Study of Social Inequality

1. *What is social inequality?* In pursuing this question, we will look at how social inequality is conceived by sociologists and other social scientists and how they go about studying this phenomenon. Social inequality, it is clear, has been one of the central concerns of sociology from its very beginnings. We will then look at the various forms of inequality and the dimensions of society in which inequality is most evident and deep-seated. We will also see how social inequality is structured, that is, built into the culture and institutions of the society and not the result of chance or even entirely of individual actions.

2. *Why is there social inequality? Is inequality inevitable in all societies? And what, if any, functions does inequality serve?* These are interrelated questions that compel us to investigate different theories that have been developed by sociologists. Inequality is surely one of the most primary, if not the most basic, issues of sociology. As a result, it is a phenomenon that has been dealt with extensively by the major sociological theorists. Karl Marx and Max Weber, two of the most prolific and influential, have left a gigantic legacy of thought on issues of social inequality, and much of our attention will focus on their theories.

3. *What is the nature of economic inequality today in American society and in other societies like it?* One of this book's central objectives is to present a picture of the actual condition of social inequality in the United States and in advanced capitalist societies of the contemporary world. Differences in economic standing constitute only one dimension of inequality, but it is, arguably, the most significant and consequential. The essential query here is

"who gets what?" As we will see, in the United States and other modern societies like it, income and wealth are distributed in a highly inequitable manner, with enormous differences among those who receive a huge proportion, those who receive some, and those who receive little or none.

4. *What is "power" and who are the powerful in society?* As we will see, differences in power underlie all forms of inequality. Thus, power is implicit in all of our queries. Our concern is institutional, or societal, power, where actions and decisions affect much or perhaps all of the society. Such power lies within the major economic and political institutions, like the federal government and giant corporations. In the United States and other democratic societies, it is assumed that individuals, regardless of their social station, can have some say over how they are governed and can influence those who shape public life. We will investigate whether this belief has much basis in reality or whether the few always exert power over the many.

5. *What is the nature of racial and ethnic inequality?* In modern multiethnic societies, like the United States and Canada, people's ethnic and racial identities have much social significance and weigh heavily in determining their opportunities for acquiring the society's valued resources, such as jobs, housing, and education. We will analyze the concepts of "race" and "ethnicity," examine inequality among various American racial and ethnic groups, and look at how race and ethnicity impact on other forms of inequality.

6. *What is gender inequality?* In addition to inequalities based on economic wealth and race and ethnicity, gender is a factor in how people are treated. Quite simply, as we will see, in no society do men and women receive the same rewards. Why this is so is an essential question with which we will deal. We will also look at the actual nature of inequality between men and women in various areas of social, economic, and political life in the United States and similar societies and will examine how those patterns are changing.

7. *How is social inequality sustained and, conversely, how do societies move toward greater social equality?* Social inequality is evident in all societies; some groups and individuals always get more of the society's valued resources than do others. Moreover, the patterns of distribution are structured and thus remain firm for long periods of time. Powerful groups and individuals, through their actions and decisions, are able to sustain the system of inequality, but we will discover that people's beliefs about the system and how it works—ideology—also help to uphold it. Prevailing patterns of inequality, however, are often challenged by those who receive less and believe they are entitled to more; hence, efforts arise to equalize the distribution of valued resources. In the United States, as in all modern societies, government plays a central role in stabilizing the system of inequality but also in providing the tools for change. This, we will see, is a result of different public policies.

A Comparative Approach

In exploring these essential questions, our focus will fall mostly on the United States. Keep in mind, however, that although American institutions and events are often the focal point of the rest of the world, the United States is not the *world;* it is one society among many, increasingly linked to others in global institutions and structures. This necessitates a more international perspective and requires that we incorporate comparisons with other societies on matters of social inequality. Are the patterns and dimensions of social inequality in American society radically different from those of other contemporary societies? Or are there similarities and common features?

Ironically, a comparative approach not only exposes us to the nature of inequality in other societies but also provides us with a sharper insight into inequality in the United States. It has often been observed that we cannot truly understand our own society without some knowledge of others. Comparing ourselves with others forces us to adopt a perspective that often yields not only new understandings but also curious and intriguing surprises.

Examining Inequality in a Sociological Mode

Before we can begin to explore social inequality, we need to become aware of how sociologists analyze social phenomena and how their perspective differs from other ways of interpreting the social world. Approaching social inequality using the sociological mode will yield a more accurate and reliable picture than can be obtained by relying on conventional or popular modes of inquiry and sources of information. We can conceptualize the difference between these two modes as encompassing a few components.

The Sociological Mode

Going beyond the Obvious   To begin with, sociology questions ideas that are often accepted as "true," or simply "common sense." The basic assumption of sociology, as sociologist Peter Berger has so poignantly put it, is "Things are not what they seem" (1963:23). The basic objective of sociology, therefore, is to explain how society really works, not how it seems to work or how we think it ought to work. Simply stated, sociologists seek to explain what *is,* not what *appears* to be or what *should* be.

To illustrate, let us consider how people formulate their views of economic inequality. For middle-class Americans, a superficial view of poverty or wealth might lead to the conclusion that the poor are few and the rich, similarly, are few. Middle-class people are not likely to maintain much contact with either the rich or the poor. The United States, therefore, would seem to be, from this perspective, a thoroughly middle-class society. Relying on one's personal experience is a common and logical way of substantiating a belief and might be employed as a way to begin one's investigation. One might question the assertion of economists and sociologists that there are vast differences in income and wealth in American society because one rarely sees any poor people or, conversely, any extremely wealthy people.

To explore this issue sociologically, however, would require that we go beyond our own very limited social worlds. We may have seen few poor or rich people because our daily interactions are confined to a constricted social sphere, limited to our personal experience. Those with whom we go to school, work, and interact closely are generally people whose levels of income and wealth (that is, their social class) are similar to our own. Consider your personal social environment. How much time is spent among people who are fundamentally different from you in social class? Probably not a great deal. What most people know of society usually derives from their particular niche of society. Hence, they tend to generalize from their own social experiences. Movie director Martin Scorsese tells of growing up in New York's Little Italy in the 1950s, watching television shows like *Leave It to Beaver* and *Father Knows Best*. The families in these shows depicted a suburban way of life that was completely alien to Scorsese and those in his neighborhood. "They existed on some other planet. We couldn't understand those people. . . . We'd ask ourselves, Who are these people? Why are they speaking to us? What do they want us to think? *That's* not America. *This* is America. Little Italy is America" (Lyman, 1998:B14).

Obviously, basing one's beliefs on only a limited range of interactions is apt to lead to a distorted and inaccurate picture. Therefore, we need to extend our range of thought and perspective to encompass other social groups in what are, comparatively speaking, other social worlds. Sociology forces us to do this. To begin to understand inequality from a sociological perspective, then, requires more than reliance on one's personal experience.

Turning to journalistic accounts—television news, newspapers, books—takes us one step beyond personal experience, but these, too, are not always reliable sources of information. Increasingly, all mass media, whether electronic or print, aim to entertain, not necessarily inform, the viewer or reader. Most TV news programs and newspaper articles are designed to present a simplified, easy-to-understand story line that can be conveyed quickly and that requires a minimal intellectual challenge. There are always elements of validity in these chronicles, but they are usually oversimplified pictures that do not take into account the complexities that ordinarily are involved. Moreover, the presentation of numerous news items and stories in rapid-order succession, as is characteristic of the modern media, does not enable us to carefully absorb and process this information, considering different points and perspectives. Sociologists, by contrast, study social issues, such as inequality, in a more rigorous fashion, looking at every possible angle and nuance. It is a much slower, deliberate process and one that, in the end, is more frustrating, for it does not always yield a clear-cut conclusion.

Looking through the Lens of Sociology   Few political issues of our time do not concern inequality in some fashion or another. Wages, jobs, welfare, taxes, social security, health care, affirmative action, criminal justice, education—all of these are most essentially issues of inequality, concerning who will get what portion of the society's wealth, prestige, and power. They are the major issues that politicians debate, that commentators speak and write about, and that citizens ponder. Inequality, then, is not a social phenomenon that can be explored without evoking strong opinions and, at times, burning emotions. We would be less than human if we did not maintain some views and preferences on these matters. But the approach taken by politicians, commentators, or citizens in addressing issues of inequality is ordinarily not the same as the approach taken by sociologists. How do they differ?

Politicians and commentators consider issues of inequality within a value-laden framework. This means that their views are shaped essentially by their beliefs and opinions about what constitutes the "good society" and about how people, as members of society, should behave. Should the poor receive more or less welfare? Should taxes be raised or reduced? Should special preference in employment and educational access be given to racial minorities and women? On such issues, politicians base their actions on views that reflect their political philosophies or that seem expedient to win elections. Similarly, commentators are paid to interpret these issues according to their views. Their objective is to persuade us or, at minimum, to present an argument that is convincing enough to make us think about an issue and to think about it with a view the commentator feels is correct.

All of us, of course, including sociologists, have opinions and perhaps strong feelings about these issues. But using the sociological approach compels us to hold those opinions and attitudes in abeyance as we go about the business of examining forms and processes of social inequality. This approach, ordinarily referred to as *objectivity*, is a cardinal principle of all rational pursuits, whether in sociology or any other human endeavor.

This does not mean, however, that as sociologists we need to divest ourselves of our values; indeed, we could not do this even if we wanted to. The ability to conceptualize values—ideas of right and wrong, good and bad, beautiful and ugly, and so on—is one of the principal features that distinguish humans as a species. All that is necessary is that we be prepared to accept what may be surprising and perhaps even displeasing to us if our findings do not support what we strongly believe or hold dear. It is analogous to sharpening our vision by wearing glasses with corrective lenses. Metaphorically, to observe social inequality using sociological lenses, then, gives us a view quite different from that which we would ordinarily maintain with the naked eye. It provides us a truer vision.

Using the Tools of Sociology   How do you know what you believe is true? This may sound like a question designed to puzzle or to evoke a philosophical debate, but it addresses the root of the difference between the thinking of sociologists and laypersons on most basic issues of society, including inequality. To maintain, as I suggested above, that the gap between rich and poor is very wide and even expanding might be questioned by those who would like to believe that the United States is a more egalitarian society and that differences in wealth are exaggerated by those who want to bring about change. How can we be certain that the gap is in fact wide and getting wider?

The basis of sociologists' assertions is *empirical substantiation.* This means that they are subject to inspection and investigation. They are founded on data collected through research, which can be verified by others. This, too, is a fundamental principle of the scientific approach, with which all of us are familiar, having been exposed to it in almost all of our schooling.

In the case of the rich-poor gap, the sociological approach would entail a careful examination of income and wealth data gathered by various social scientists and organizations. Sociologists might pour intensively over statistics gathered by census takers and other agencies, looking for patterns among the mass of numbers, or they might collect data on their own by questioning people through surveys and in-depth interviews. In investigating issues of social inequality, journalists and even laypersons might, of course, also employ these techniques, and to that extent, they are operating in a sociological mode. Usually, though, only sociologists and other social scientists are prepared to invest time, energy, and other resources into such study. This reflects their professional training and demonstrates the slow pace at which sociological investigation takes place. Journalists need answers quickly; they have deadlines to meet. Laypersons do not have the time or inclination to engage in tedious and time-consuming research. Sociological inquiry, however, is deliberate and laborious, requiring huge investments of time and energy, which, incidentally, do not always yield useful results.

Seeing Probabilities, Not Certainties   Not only does the sociological mode require us to set aside our values and to invest much time and effort that may not guarantee rewards, but it is apt to create frustrations. To employ the sociological approach is to invoke a principle of *skepticism.* In science, no belief is absolute. Sociologists and other social scientists, therefore, must be prepared to question not only the conventional wisdom, what "everyone knows to be true," but even their own findings and conclusions. Social science, like physical or biological science, seeks discovery of "truth." But truth, in any scientific field, is ephemeral—that is, it is short-lived and thus subject to change and reformulation. We might say that, in science, there is no truth with a capital T. There are no final answers.

This is especially the case in sociology, where the subjects under scrutiny are humans, not physical elements or even lower animal species, and where predictability and generalization are therefore far more difficult to produce. Sociologists repeatedly discover, much to their chagrin, that humans are not always rational, and that models and theories that appear solid on paper turn out to be applicable only in selective cases. Economists, too, often build models of economic processes based on the assumption that people will act rationally in the market—that is, they will seek out the most profitable alternatives in their consumer choices and other financial decisions. These models do not always hold up, however, because people's spending patterns are not based entirely on purely rational factors. Consumers may purchase one brand of cereal over another not because the quality is superior or the cost is lower, but because they like the shape or because it is endorsed by their favorite basketball player. Advertisers know very well that price and quality are not the only bases of consumer decisions and they commonly play on those irrational tendencies.

Hence, in sociology we must be content to deal with *probabilities*, not certainties. But this in itself should not detract from the value of the sociological approach. We cannot predict the behavior of any single individual or event. But we can make predictions about aggregate behavior, that is, about collectivities of people and events. In studying human physiology, for example, no one would question the assertion that men are generally taller than women, despite the fact that some men are shorter than some women. Similarly, in studying inequality and its various aspects, we would not be off base if, for example, we were to assert that upper-class Americans generally support Republicans and working-class Americans generally support Democrats, despite the fact that some rich people support Democratic candidates and some workers support Republicans. Again, we must think in terms of probabilities, not airtight certainties. When we are aware of what people of particular social categories (women, Catholics, urban residents, Mexican Americans, teenagers, farmers, welfare recipients, bowlers, etc.) usually do, and we have observed this behavior repeatedly and over long periods of time (observing "aggregate regularities"), we are then able to make reasonable generalizations about people in those categories.

As an example, consider occupation. As we will see, occupation is a key element of social class, and knowing this single feature enables us to predict with some accuracy many other characteristics of a person's social identity and behavior. If you meet a woman and learn that she is a physician, can you not make a good estimate of her income? What kind of house and neighborhood she lives in? Even what kind of leisure activities she prefers? You could assess all of these things, not necessarily with 100 percent accuracy, but with a high degree of probability.

Thinking in terms of probabilities rather than certainties, however, can bring about discomfort and frustration. All of us want to think that our beliefs and views are valid and free of ambiguity. Operating on the basis of faith is a way of avoiding such uncertainty. In sociology, however, uncertainty is unavoidable. Sociologists, like scientists of all fields, are naturally skeptical. But skepticism in science is a virtue and not to be resisted. To question what is "tried and true" is, in fact, what sociology, or any science, is about. Here we need to reiterate Berger's principle of sociological thinking, that "things are not what they seem." Sociologists are often accused of telling us in high-blown fashion what we already know. But in fact sociologists more often tell us that what we know is not always true. Sociologists may have few unassailable answers to problems and issues of inequality, or any other social phenomenon, but they can inform us of and lead us to the paths of inquiry we need to travel in seeking answers.

This book may challenge many orthodox ideas about social inequality in its various forms. Its intent is to expose you to different views and to stimulate new ways of thinking about the distribution of income, wealth, and power; about the impact of class, ethnicity, and gender on that distribution; and about the role of major groups and institutions in creating, sustaining, and perhaps changing those patterns. Sociology is, in many ways, an inherently iconoclastic discipline: it calls into question venerable and often unchallenged beliefs and ideas. As such, it can sometimes seem hypercritical of dominant institutions and social structures. This is especially the case in the study of social inequality. But if the use of sociological knowledge is to provide some of the intellectual bricks and mortar in building a more informed society, we need to consider Thomas Hardy's reminder: "If way to the better there be, it exacts a full look at the worst."

Objectives of Inquiry

In examining inequality in societies, sociologists pursue questions that involve description, explanation, and prescription.

Description   At times, sociologists simply try to describe the characteristics of a particular social phenomenon or group. Regarding social inequality, some questions they might pose, for example, are: How much of the society's wealth is owned by what percentage of the population, and how much of the society's total income is earned by what share of all American families? Have those of the upper class reached the top of the social ladder through their work efforts or through inheritance? How do patterns of inequality change over time? Do the wealthy stay wealthy? And what are the chances that those born into poverty will be able to achieve a higher social position? These are all questions whose answers involve descriptions of "what is."

In describing inequality—or any social issue—sociologists rely on rigorous empirical data, use precise terminology, and frame their descriptions in theories. Journalists and others examining inequality may often operate similarly, but ordinarily they do not dig as deeply, nor are they as precise and rigorous in their procedures of gathering information.

Explanation   At the explanatory level, efforts are made to explain various aspects of social inequality. The objective is to go beyond merely describing the extent and nature of inequality and try to account for it. This calls for "why" questions. Why is inequality evident in all societies? Why are the poor poor and the rich rich? Why do patterns of inequality remain stable over many generations? Why do Euro-Americans enjoy higher status in American society than members of racial and ethnic minorities? Why do men seem to hold the majority of power positions in all societies?

Here, sociologists use the scientific method or, at minimum, subscribe to the scientific spirit. They perform empirically based studies and, in order to make their explanations more generalizable, try to place their findings into theoretical schemes. Journalists and commentators may emulate this process in some fashion, but their analyses are usually more speculative in nature. Moreover, rarely are their explanations guided by theory, as sociologists' are.

Prescription   In pursuing prescriptive questions, the concern is with strategies of change. The prescriptive approach essentially involves policy applications of sociological knowledge. This level of inquiry addresses issues of what should be done to bring about social change. Although it is the role of the sociologist to describe and explain the structures and patterns of social inequality, it is decision makers in both public and private realms who may implement sociological findings in changing those structures and patterns. Any attempt to determine what "should be done" involves the application of the political beliefs and preferences of those making the proposal. Social scientists may offer their views on policy issues, but in the end, social prescriptions are actually applied by policymakers. Should taxes be raised or cut? Should welfare be reformed? Should affirmative action continue to give special preference to some over others? How one weighs such issues and reaches decisions on them may involve sociological insight, but those decisions should not be confused with description and explanation.

Individuals and Social Forces

Americans are firmly committed to the notion that people are shaped mainly by their individual actions. Indeed, as will be shown in Chapter 9, this is the essence of the American ideology. Social inequality, therefore, is most commonly interpreted as a product of individual differences. Most people, if queried about why some individuals have achieved great wealth and fame while others are penniless and forgotten, why some are esteemed and others held in disrepute, why some have achieved great political power while others merely follow or observe the actions of others, would respond that these differences are the result of personal effort and ability. Achievement, in other words, makes for inequality.

Sociology, however, compels us to look not simply at how individuals act but at the social forces that shape their actions. People's fate is determined by structural factors, in addition to individual effort. By structure is meant those social institutions, organizations, and groups in which we act and are acted upon. Take, for example, occupation. We might assume that people reach a particular position in their place of work on the basis of their individual achievement, and in the same way, we might conclude that those who lose their jobs do so because they have insufficient ambition or skills. Their job fate, in short, is a product solely of their personal actions. This, of course, can readily be seen as a fatuous explanation. It is true that people are often hired and fired on the basis of their individual skills and performance. But people are hired and fired for any number of reasons that have nothing to do with their personal characteristics or abilities. If your favorite uncle lost his job, would you conclude that he "simply didn't try hard enough," or that "he lacked what it takes"? Probably you would look for an explanation that goes beyond your uncle's individual efforts. Did his company replace his job with a machine? Did the company need to eliminate jobs because of continued low profitability? Did the company move his plant abroad, where the cost of labor is considerably cheaper? Here we can begin to see that larger forces, part of what sociologists call social structure, set limits and impose constraints on people, regardless of their individual abilities and attitudes.

Inequality, then, is the result not merely of people's personal actions. It is determined by structural forces of the society and even global structural forces. Political leaders in Washington make decisions regarding tax policy, educational loans, welfare, tariffs, and countless other issues, all of which impact in some manner on the economic and social fate of individuals. Similarly, corporate executives have much power in shaping the U.S. labor market as well as the consumer market. Moreover, we live in a time in which we are subject to the dynamics of markets not only in the United States but in the world as a whole. Giant transnational corporations make decisions about how many jobs will be created, where they will be located, and how much workers will be paid. And, it is on such decisions—about which individual workers have virtually no say—that people's economic fate hinges. At this level—the structural level—individual effort and achievement have no consequence.

C. Wright Mills, an influential American sociologist writing in the 1950s, referred to the "sociological imagination" as the ability to recognize the difference between "troubles" and "issues." Personal troubles, Mills explained, are mostly personal in origin whereas public issues are social in origin. Thus, one person unemployed is a "trouble" that can be explained in terms of that person's character, skills, or ambition. But the unemployment of 5 or 6 percent of fully able workers in the United States is an "issue" that can be explained only as part of the workings of the society's economic and political institutions. Using the sociological imagination enables us to understand our place on the larger social stage as more than simply the product of our personal drama acted out on our personal stage, that is, our limited social environment.

This is not to deny the significance of individual differences in talent, ambition, and effort in creating social inequality. Those are undeniably factors of great importance. But they come into play only within the context of a much wider societal—and global—structure that is far outside the realm of the individual.

Some Basic Terms and Concepts in the Study of Inequality

Precision in the use of terms is one attribute of social science analysis that separates it from casual explanations of social issues or from the reporting of journalists. The following section examines some concepts and terminology that will arise repeatedly throughout this book.

Social Differentiation

All societies are diverse in some regards. Biology imposes some of this diversity. Males and females obviously differ, as do people of various ages and physical characteristics. All but the most technologically primitive societies, however, also exhibit diversity on certain social bases. All people do not perform the same economic functions, for example, and therefore a set of diverse occupational roles is evident. Distinguishing individuals on the basis of their occupations creates an occupational order. We might think of this as the horizontal dimension of social structure. Let us suppose that society X has a simple occupational order, made up of six specific roles: doctor, teacher, soldier, toolmaker, farmer, and laborer. Arranging those who fill these six occupations horizontally simply demonstrates that people in this society perform six different tasks (Figure 1-1a). It tells us nothing about how people in each of these occupations are rewarded (who gets more of the society's wealth and who gets less) or how much prestige is attached to each occupational position. It does not necessarily imply a rank order, only an order of differentiation. However, differentiation does establish the basis for inequality and stratification.

Social Stratification

If societies were divided only along horizontal lines, there would be little social conflict, for although people might be assigned to different groupings and perhaps even be segregated, there would not necessarily be invidious differences among them. That is, there would be no basis for envy or feelings of injustice so long as no differential rewards were accorded the different groupings. Clearly, however, in all societies people receive different shares of what is valued and scarce, that is, what is desirable and what members of the society strive for. These can be referred to as **social resources.** People are, in other words, differently rewarded.

This unequal distribution of the society's resources creates a system of stratification. Stratification, as sociologists use the term, is akin to the geological concept. Geologists describe the different layers of subsoil—strata—as having different properties. Digging beneath the ground at a particular location,

a. Differentiation

Laborers	Farmers	Toolmakers	Soldiers	Teachers	Doctors

b. Stratification

Doctors

Teachers

Soldiers

Toolmakers

Farmers

Laborers

Figure 1-1 ■ Social Differentiation and Stratification, by Occupation

we might find a layer of soil, then rock, shale, water, perhaps even oil. The sociological meaning of stratification is essentially the same as the geological meaning, except it is human groups that are arranged in a vertical order.

If we take the graphic depiction of the occupational order of society X and tip it on its side, we then have a hierarchy of occupations (Figure 1-1b). Now we can see that doctors are at the top of the structure, laborers at the bottom, and the others between them in relative order. This is no longer simply diversity or differentiation, but stratification. **Social stratification,** then, is the ranking of persons and groups on the basis of various social, and sometimes physical, characteristics. It is the vertical dimension of social structure. Concentrations of people with roughly similar amounts of societal resources form points on this hierarchy, and this rank order ordinarily remains fixed from generation to generation.

Stratification Dimensions   Sociologists, following Weber, have usually explained social stratification as comprising three dimensions: wealth, prestige, and power. Individuals rank differently on each dimension, depending on their accumulation of social resources or rewards.

Wealth refers to economic resources. In capitalist societies, these comprise people's market capacity, that is, their ability to purchase the material things that they want and need. People receive different amounts of income and other sources of wealth and thus enjoy more or less of the society's benefits. Economic inequalities are a function primarily of people's occupations. Doctors generally earn more than truck drivers, who earn more than dishwashers, and so on.

Prestige is the deference that people are given by others. It is, essentially, social esteem. Important positions in the society's major institutions usually carry with them a great deal of prestige, and people who occupy those positions are therefore treated with much respect and deference. The president of the United States, for example, would never be referred to by his first name by anyone but his family and closest friends. Social custom would dictate that others address him as "Mr. President" or, at minimum, "Sir." We need not look at such an extreme case, however, to understand prestige. A worker would interact with his manager quite differently than with a co-worker; he would accord his manager greater deference. In modern societies, prestige, or what Weber referred to as status, derives, for the most part, from one's occupation. Doctors have more prestige than teachers, who, in turn, have more prestige than factory workers, and so on. Other important bases of status, in addition to occupation, are age and ethnicity. The latter is particularly critical in multiethnic societies.

Power underlies all forms of inequality. As a social resource, power refers to people's authority in groups and organizations. Some have the power, as a result of their positions, to command others, to get them to do things, as Weber described, even against their will. The more important and broadly based the position, the greater the scope of one's power. The president of the United States has greater political power, as a result of his position, than a state governor, who, in turn, has greater power than a county sheriff. In the corporate world, the chief executive officer has greater power in the company than a regional manager, who, in turn, has greater power than a local salesperson. These power differentials are evident in all spheres of social life, but are particularly critical in economic and political realms.

Inequalities in wealth, prestige, and power are usually closely related. Thus, those who have a disproportionate share of economic resources will likely be accorded a similar degree of prestige and will have comparable power. This consistency across the three dimensions of inequality, however, is not always evident. Teachers, for example, are accorded more occupational prestige than their salaries would seem to warrant.

In sum, not only are people differentiated in their social roles, but they are rewarded unequally as well. Some get more of the society's scarce and valued items than others. Some are treated with more esteem than others. And some have more power than others. Subsequently, people are grouped on the basis of how much of the society's rewards they receive, and these groups, or strata, are arranged in a rank order, or *hierarchy.* Those at the top receive the most of what there is to get, and those at the bottom the least.

Stratification Forms

All societies rank their members on the basis of some characteristics. In societies with low levels of technological development, those typical of the premodern world, stratification systems are quite simple, with only a few bases of differentiation and an equally few bases of ranking. Usually sex and age are the only two sources of social difference. Each man of a particular age plays a role similar to that of other men of that age, and the same is true of women. Moreover, there are minimal differences in rewards. This is because almost all that is produced is used immediately to provide the basic needs (food, clothing, shelter, and so on) to all members of the society. There is little in the way of a surplus to be divided and thus no basis for competition. Hence, everyone is rewarded pretty much the same.

Modern societies, with high levels of technological development, are far more complex, and as a result, there are numerous bases of differentiation. Think, for example, of the thousands of occupations that make up the labor force of an industrial society. And, with high levels of production, there is a huge surplus for which people are in competition. This creates the conditions for stratification. Thus, there are many social hierarchies, each based on some social characteristic. The most important, however, are hierarchies of class, race and ethnicity, and gender.

Class   Social class is a concept that has been the focus of much sociological debate and theorizing. Essentially, however, it refers to groupings of people with approximately similar incomes and occupations. Class hierarchies are characteristic of all modern societies, and they are enormously consequential. Much of our analysis of social inequality, therefore, will focus on them.

Race and Ethnicity   In societies comprised of a variety of racial and ethnic groups, such as the United States and Canada, people's race and/or ethnicity become the basis of categorization and, subsequently, of inequality. In no multiethnic society are these racial and ethnic divisions of no consequence. On the contrary, in almost all cases, race or ethnicity becomes a major differentiating characteristic and distinct racial/ethnic hierarchies are formed.

Gender   In no society do men and women perform identical functions, but, more important, in none do they rank equally and, thus, in none are they treated equally. A gender hierarchy is part of all societies regardless of their level of technological development or the complexity of their social structure.

Age   All societies differentiate people on the basis of age, and they subsequently rank them as well. People of different age groups are expected to play particular roles and are given more or less of the society's power, wealth, and prestige. Children are not expected to do what adults do, and they don't have the same powers as adults; the elderly have certain privileges that younger people do not have, and so on. In each case, people receive unequal shares of the society's wealth, are given differential amounts of prestige, and are able to exert different degrees of power over others.

Structured Inequality

Societies may comprise any number of hierarchies based on various social characteristics (income, occupation, ethnicity, gender, age, and so on), but in all cases, this system of inequality is **structured.** This means that stratification is not random, with groups and individuals occupying different positions by chance; rather, social institutions such as government, the economy, and education operate to assure the position of various groups. Those who comprise the upper class do not lose their high position from one year or even one generation to another. The rich remain rich, the poor, for the most part, remain poor, and those in the middle tend to remain in the middle. Likewise, ethnic minorities do not lose their minority status and receive the same treatment as dominant group members without great struggle over long periods of time. The same is true of the relationship of men and women. Moreover, the system of stratification in all societies is legitimized by an ideology that justifies inequality. The pattern of stratification in a society therefore remains in place for many generations.

Life Chances and Inequality of Opportunity

Social resources, as noted earlier, are those things that people strive for, things material and nonmaterial that are valued and scarce. The uneven distribution of social resources produces **inequality of condition**—variations in people's actual living standards or life conditions. This is not the same as **inequality of opportunity,** however, which means differences in people's chances at acquiring social resources. Weber referred to the opportunities that people have to acquire social resources as **life chances.** Among the most basic life chances in modern societies are education, physical and mental health, residence, and justice.

To illustrate life chances and the creation of inequality of opportunity, consider two children. One is born into a family in which the father is a medical doctor and the mother an attorney. We can predict with a good deal of certainty that this child will be exposed to opportunities that will almost automatically assure her social success as she proceeds through life. As a result of her parents' high-status occupations and the correspondingly high income they earn, she will enjoy the opportunity to acquire a superior education, enjoy the best in health care and, if needed, the best in legal aid. These, in turn, will assure that she, like her parents, will most likely work in a high-paying and rewarding occupation. Compare her life chances with those of a child born into a family in which the parents (or, more likely, parent) are high school dropouts and possess hardly any occupational skills. Just as the probabilities of social success for the child from the more well-to-do family are extremely high, for this second child, the probabilities of social failure are equally high.[1]

All of our life chances are determined by our position, or as children, the position of our parents, in the various stratification hierarchies, particularly the class hierarchy. Take health, for example. We might assume on the face of it that health is mainly a product of genetic inheritance. To a great extent that is the case. We have no say in whether we will be born with healthy bodies or with genetic defects that may handicap us. Some of us will need to wear

---

[1]Here is a good example of the idea of probabilities. We could not predict social success or failure for any particular child. One from a well-to-do-family might fail miserably in life, just as one from a poor family might overcome all the handicaps imposed by poverty. But the probability of either of these occurrences is not great.

glasses all our lives, whereas others will enjoy 20/20 vision. Statistics indicate, however, that those in the lower classes have higher rates of illness and lower life expectancy than those higher in social class. Differences in health care may explain some of this, but medical sociologists suggest that environmental and psychosocial conditions probably play a larger role (Williams, 1990; Charlson et al., 1993). Poor people live and work in more toxic, hazardous, and nonhygienic environments. More stressful family and work conditions may also lead to unhealthy lifestyle characteristics, like excessive use of tobacco and alcohol or poor nutrition. Although it is not yet fully understood, the relationship between health and social class has been apparent for generations (Blackburn, 1991; Critser, 2000; Syme and Berkman, 1997).

The same is true of another basic life chance, justice. Again, we might assume that all people in the United States or societies like it, where there are constitutions and other legal protective mechanisms, are equal before the law; that justice, therefore, is "blind," distributed with no undue preference to any group or individual. If we conducted a census of prisons, however, we would find that they are filled mostly with people from the lower social classes. Is this because the poor commit most crimes? The answer is both yes and no. Crime knows no class bounds; middle- and upper-class people commit crimes just as people lower in the class hierarchy do. But the kinds of crimes committed by the poor are usually those that are defined as socially threatening and are pursued arduously by the police. They are the kinds of crimes with which the criminal justice system is designed to deal. Crimes committed by the nonpoor, in contrast, are most often less starkly menacing and more deceptive; therefore, they are not viewed as harshly or treated by the police and the courts as severely as crimes committed by the poor.

Even if there were no differences in the types of crime committed, the nonpoor are in a better position to defend themselves within the criminal justice system. Most simply, they can purchase more and better legal assistance. It is true, of course, that the nonpoor who are accused of crimes are not always acquitted and, if guilty, do not always receive lesser sentences than poor criminals, but their chances of winning favor in this way are increased enormously by their ability to pay for more and better justice.

Life chances are acquired, then, as a result of factors that are only partially in the control of individuals. Obviously, our class position at birth is ascribed; over this we can exercise no control. People's initial class position and, therefore, the dimensions of their opportunities and future prospects are essentially an "accident of birth." Certainly, people may subsequently enhance their life chances through individual effort, but those of lower social origins will need to overcome many socially imposed handicaps to do so. Again, it is important to think in terms of probabilities. Obviously some born into wretched social environments are able to escape and go on to a significantly higher social standing. But we cannot use the experiences of these relative few as examples of typical patterns followed by the many, since most do not escape. Tongue-in-cheek, people might be advised that if they want to assure themselves a comfortable and secure future, they should choose their family carefully!

Although inequality of condition is not the same as inequality of opportunity, the two are closely interdependent. Debate on public policies regarding issues of inequality often revolves around the question of whether people should be afforded greater equality of opportunity or equality of condition.

Stability in Systems of Inequality

Social hierarchies are ordered. They are arranged in a systematic way and do not change radically over long periods of time. How is this order and stability of inequality, in class, race and ethnicity, and gender, maintained?

The Society's Culture   A society's cultural norms and values may support inequality. This is particularly the case in capitalist societies. The basic objective of behavior within a capitalist system is to maximize personal interests, that is, to acquire as much as one can even at the expense of others. Competition within the market is the central operating principle of a capitalist economy. This automatically produces inequality; it can be no other way. Competition yields winners and losers. Capitalism, then, encourages, indeed requires, inequality.

In capitalist societies, ownership of property is sanctified. Private property is, in other words, a fundamental societal value. Children learn early on to respect others' property and to protect their own. Elaborate bodies of law spell out the rights of property, and crimes against property are enforced rigorously.

Inequality in noneconomic realms is also supported by the society's culture. Consider education. Students are expected to compete against each other for grades. This competition and the resultant inequality is such a basic part of Americans' perception of the educational environment and so ingrained that most students would recoil at the thought of a collective classroom effort, one that would reward high grades to everyone regardless of their individual contribution.

Individual and Organizational Power   Inequality is stabilized through the efforts of powerful individuals and organizations. Power, as earlier explained, is the foundation of all forms of inequality. Differentials in power, therefore, create and sustain inequality in other forms. Those who possess power are not apt to voluntarily relinquish it.

Effective power in modern societies is wielded by individuals, but they act within the context of organizations and institutions. In the United States and advanced capitalist societies like it, power is essentially an interplay of government and business. The consequences of the actions of business and government leaders affect all people; the far-reaching issues of inequality—jobs, prices, public services, education, and so on—are settled by them. Thus, it is in large measure through the decisions of leaders within these institutions that the distribution of wealth, prestige, and power is both upheld and changed.

Ideology and Legitimation   It is not only through cultural expectations and the power of groups and individuals that stratification systems are stabilized. For a system of inequality to endure, people must come to see the inequalities in power and wealth as natural and even socially beneficial. When this is accomplished, social inequality acquires legitimacy, and ruling groups need not resort to coercion to maintain their power and privilege. Such long-range stability and popular acceptance require the development of an effective ideology and its communication through socialization. Sociologists refer to this process as *legitimation.*

An *ideology* is a set of beliefs and values that explains and justifies a society's system of power and privilege, that is, structured inequality. Although a number of competing ideologies may be evident, a dominant ideology emerges that explains and justifies the status quo. This becomes the prevailing or generally accepted belief system of the society. Chapter 9 discusses the dominant ideology in American society; for the moment we can describe it simply as comprising the belief that people are responsible for their fate and that their social position is essentially a product of their personal efforts and talents. The American ideology is, in a word, *individualism.* The opportunity structure is presumed to be open, and as a result, equality of opportunity provides everyone an equal chance at rising to the top. Positions are awarded on the basis of merit, and thus people earn their ultimate fate in the social hierarchies. The system of inequality, then, is fair and just. To the extent that people subscribe to these beliefs, they are disinclined to question, let alone challenge, the prevailing system of inequality. Obviously, this is a far more effective means of sustaining a hierarchical order than is the coercive power of a ruling class or an authoritarian leadership.

Change in Systems of Inequality

Although patterns of social inequality are structured and endure for very long periods of time, they are not static. Individuals do change their place on the stratification hierarchies and even entire social categories may change their rank.

Individual Mobility   The ability of individuals to change their position on a social hierarchy is referred to as *mobility.* Generally, individual mobility is limited to one's economic class. In societies with class systems, such as the

United States, theoretically there are no impediments to movement up or down. Thus, one born into poverty may advance upward without limit, just as one born into wealth may experience a free fall into the ranks of the poor.

Neither of these cases is typical. Here we need to reapply the idea of structural factors. Although one's individual mobility may be theoretically unlimited, in fact there are numerous obstacles that hinder people's movement. To move up the occupational ladder, for example, requires that good jobs be available. Thus, individual occupational mobility is very much dependent not simply on one's personal achievement but on the state of the labor market.

Also, the social position of a person's family of birth will influence that person's mobility chances more than his or her individual efforts will. The resources accumulated by parents are inherited by their children, and the prevailing patterns of inequality are thereby perpetuated from generation to generation.

Nonetheless, individual mobility is not uncommon, especially in societies like the United States, where the economic and political systems place few impediments before people. Also, despite the overarching importance of structural factors—and of luck—we should not think that personal efforts are of no consequence in people's quest for higher social positions. In fact, there is a great deal of individual mobility in American society, though most people who move do so only in small steps, not in great leaps. Rags-to-riches stories are rare (and riches-to-rags stories are even rarer).

Group Mobility   Although stratification systems are stable for long periods, they are not immune to change. In fact, social hierarchies are at times challenged successfully by lower-ranked groups. American workers in the late nineteenth century, for example, launched a movement that led to the creation of trade unions that forced employers to recognize their rights and modify the conditions of work. Again in the 1930s, a workers' movement produced a greatly expanded system of labor unions that effectively challenged the power of industrialists.

Ethnic and gender hierarchies are also successfully challenged at times by lower-ranking groups. The civil rights movement, beginning in the 1950s, led to a fundamental change in the social and economic status of African Americans. Similarly, the women's movement of the 1960s and 1970s yielded basic changes in the status of women. In these cases, a group's hierarchical position vis-à-vis others changed, and the extent of inequality among them was modified in some degree.

These institutional challenges are usually supported by corresponding changes in ideologies. Workers' movements were undergirded by the belief that workers had certain basic rights in the workplace that employers could not violate. The so-called "muckrakers" of the latter nineteenth and early twentieth centuries described conditions of capitalism that led to a greater awareness of injustices and the need for institutional reforms. People's ideas of what was a "just" and "fair" work environment began to change, creating public support for workers' rights. Similarly, changes in the perception of racial and ethnic minorities accompanied the demands for black rights. Until the 1930s, few in American society, including social scientists, questioned the assumption that black people were intellectually and morally inferior to white people. As that belief was effectively challenged, greater impetus was given to the demands for black rights, and public support was strengthened.

Equity versus Liberty

Capitalist democracies, like the United States, constantly struggle with the conflicting forces of equity and liberty. On the one hand, they honor the principle of democracy, which dictates adherence to **equity**—that is, distribution of the society's rewards in a just manner. If all citizens see themselves as part of a unified nation, they are thereby required to engage in some collective acts, such as paying taxes, in order to bring about a fairer apportionment of resources than would occur if they acted only on the basis of personal interest. Collective interests, in other words, tend to take precedence over individual interests.

On the other hand, as capitalist societies, they are committed to the principle of **liberty**—that is, freedom to pursue one's interests as one desires and to reap the benefits of one's efforts. Such personal freedom naturally produces inequality; in a competitive, free-market system, some are bound to get more than others. Where liberty prevails, however, individual interests are expected to take precedence over collective, or societal, interests.

The distribution of the society's rewards, therefore, always hinges on a delicate balance between these two forces. At certain times equity outweighs liberty and at other times liberty takes precedence. The latter has certainly been the case in the United States throughout most of its history, but it has been exceedingly prevalent in the past twenty years. In western European societies, by contrast, equity has seemed to outweigh liberty. The conflict between the forces of equity and liberty is a theme that will resurface at various points in the chapters that follow.

Summary

The major issues in the study of social inequality concern what forms it takes, why it exists, how it is sustained, and whether it is inevitable in all societies. Focusing specifically on the United States, key questions involve the nature of economic inequality, inequalities in power, racial and ethnic inequality, and gender inequality. Studying social inequality in American society requires comparisons with other societies, looking at how the United States is both different and similar.

Using the sociological mode in examining inequality entails going beyond the obvious, that is, questioning ideas that are often accepted as conventional wisdom. The sociological approach also compels us to set aside our values and to examine issues objectively. Using sociological tools requires the use of empirical substantiation, subjecting assertions to inspection and investigation. To employ the sociological approach in looking at inequality is to invoke a principle of skepticism, questioning not only commonly held ideas but also scientific findings. Predictability and generalization are more difficult to produce in sociology than in the hard sciences, forcing us to be content with probabilities, not certainties.

In looking at social inequality, sociologists work at three different levels of analysis. At the descriptive level, they describe the actual nature and extent of inequality: what share of the society's resources is acquired by which groups. At the explanatory level, efforts are made to explain why various forms of social inequality exist and why the processes that produce inequality occur. At the prescriptive level, policy applications of sociological knowledge are made. This level of inquiry addresses issues of what should be done to bring about social change.

Sociology compels us to look not only at how individuals act but at the social forces that shape their actions. Inequality is thus seen as the result not only of people's personal actions but of the way social institutions are structured and function, over which people have little control.

Social differentiation refers to the diversity of a society's groups; social stratification, by contrast, refers to the division of society into a hierarchical order of groups. In all societies, people receive different shares of wealth, prestige, and power.

The major forms of stratification in modern societies are social class, race and ethnicity, gender, and age.

Differences in social resources produce inequality of condition, that is, differences in people's actual living standards or life conditions. Life chances, such as education, health, and justice, are opportunities that people have to acquire resources. Differences in life chances produce inequality of opportunity.

Systems of inequality, arrangements of "who gets what," remain stable for long periods of time. A society's cultural norms and values ordinarily support inequality. This is especially so in a capitalist society. Inequality is stabilized as well through the efforts of powerful individuals and organizations who seek to protect their privilege and through the development and communication of an ideology that explains and justifies the structure of inequality.

Individuals do change their positions on the social hierarchy, a process called social mobility. Individual mobility is common in the United States and other advanced industrial societies, though the distance moved is ordinarily slight. Groups also may change their position in the structure of stratification by successfully challenging powerful institutions and prevailing beliefs and ideologies.

In democratic capitalist societies, liberty and equity are conflicting objectives. As a result, the distribution of the society's rewards is always contingent on the shifting balance between the two.

2

The American Class System

Exploration of the major dimensions of inequality in the United States and other advanced industrial societies begins with studying class structure. Some argue that social class is the most consequential form of stratification, exceeding ethnicity, gender, and all others. Following a discussion of how social classes are conceptualized, this chapter presents a broad picture of the American class hierarchy, showing the socioeconomic characteristics of the different strata. Then it looks at the distribution of income and wealth, demonstrating through statistical data "who gets what." Finally, the chapter shows how patterns of inequality have changed during the past several decades.

Social Class: A Two-Dimensional Picture

Few people are unfamiliar with the idea of social class. Like race, ethnic group, and gender, class is a sociological concept that most of us make reference to from time to time. Early in life, we come to understand that this is one of the ways in which societies are divided. We are also apt to acquire some perception of our own social-class standing. But beyond this very general understanding, most Americans have only a vague notion of what social class entails or implies. To add to the confusion, sociologists themselves are often in disagreement about what social classes are and how they should be measured. To begin with, we need to understand that class can be seen in two dimensions—economic and behavioral.

Economic Class

As an economic concept, **social classes** can be understood most simply as groupings of people who share roughly similar incomes and wealth, similar occupations, and similar levels of education. These three aspects of class— income and wealth, occupational prestige, and educational level—are closely intertwined and together create economic commonality. Income is, for most people, dependent on their occupation, which, in turn, is largely dependent on their education. Occasionally, of course, the three do not coincide. For instance, a truck driver with only a high school diploma may, through an extremely long and arduous schedule, earn over $100,000 a year, placing him among the society's highest income earners. Conversely, college professors with Ph.D.'s, obviously among the society's elite in terms of educational attainment, may sometimes earn less than factory workers. But cases such as these are not common. For the vast majority of people, income, occupation, and education coincide.

Sociologists often refer to a combination of these three social characteristics not as social class but as **socioeconomic status,** or simply SES. In a purely economic sense, classes are merely statistical units, and the lines of division between them can be drawn somewhat arbitrarily. Although this would seem to prompt an endless debate—where does one class begin and the other end?—there are roughly discernible divisions between economic classes, especially as they extend out from the center to the top and bottom poles of the class hierarchy.

Class as Lifestyle

There is a second dimension of social class that goes beyond a simple division of the society into socioeconomic units. Classes may be thought of as groupings in which people share not only similar occupations, incomes, and levels of education but also similar lifestyles. We recognize, for example, that upper-class people generally use different patterns of speech; maintain different tastes in music, fashion, and cuisine; decorate their houses differently; and prefer different forms of leisure than do either middle-class or lower-class people. Social classes, then, are more than simply statistical units. They are real divisions of society that are manifested in people's behaviors.

This is not to imply that there is no correspondence between economic class and class as lifestyle. Indeed, as Max Weber so clearly pointed out, the two are very much interdependent.[1] To maintain a particular lifestyle requires a certain income. One might prefer to drive a Mercedes, dine on pheasant, and vacation on the French Riviera, but to support such an upscale standard of living would necessitate a commensurate income. Thus, people's

---

[1]Weber's theory of stratification will be discussed in Chapter 8.

lifestyles generally conform to their economic level. Moreover, those preferring to live a particular lifestyle will likely associate with people of similar tastes and preferences. Thus, what Weber referred to as **status groups** emerge among people with similar incomes, occupations, and educations. It is in this sense that classes become subcultures, in which similar patterns of behavior and beliefs are expressed. Beginning in early childhood, individuals learn class-based norms and values, and although these may change somewhat with social mobility, for most people they are quite enduring.

A story is told about a conversation held between F. Scott Fitzgerald and Ernest Hemingway, two of America's great twentieth-century novelists. While sitting in a Paris cafe in the 1920s, Fitzgerald, whose novels often depicted life among the wealthy, is reputed to have remarked to Hemingway, "You know, Ernest, the rich are different from you and me." To which Hemingway replied, "Yes, Scott, they have more money." What Hemingway was referring to was the economic conception of classes—groupings of people with similar amounts of socioeconomic resources. Fitzgerald, however, was referring to classes as groupings of people who practice different lifestyles, or, in Weber's terms, status groups.

Popular Notions of the American Class Structure

Class Consciousness   Although most Americans have a vague awareness of class, their own as well as others, they have a low level of class consciousness—that is, an understanding of how social class impacts on their lives and how the political, economic, and social interests of different classes conflict. Most Americans simply do not frame their perspective of politics and their social lives within class lines. In short, although they are implicitly aware of the fact that the United States is divided by class, they don't pay close attention to these class divisions and the issues raised by these divisions, and they rarely think of themselves in class terms.

Americans, however, do pay close attention to other lines of division in U.S. society, particularly race and ethnicity. Indeed, Americans are extremely conscious of the racial and ethnic differences between themselves and others. Ethnicity remains an important part of most people's self-identification. Moreover, people are aware of what they perceive as their ethnic interests, and as a result, political issues in American society often revolve around race and ethnicity rather than around social class.

Americans are also keenly aware of how ethnicity commonly impacts sharply on various spheres of social life. People may not consciously consider class differences in choosing a neighborhood in which to reside, for example, but they carefully consider its racial and ethnic makeup. Of course, people always implicitly choose their neighborhoods on the basis of class, too, if for no other reason than that their income and occupations dictate that they live among those who are economically like themselves. This creates a society that is even more tightly segregated by social class than it is by race

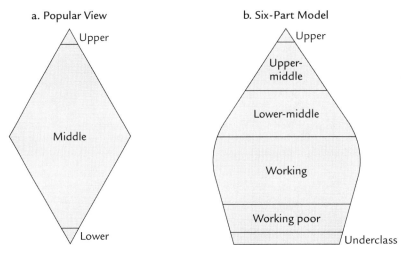

Figure 2-1 ■ Two Views of the U.S. Class Structure

and ethnicity. Similarly, in dating and, ultimately, marriage, people ordinarily are implicitly aware of the social class of their partner even though they consider more consciously his or her race or ethnicity.

"America Is a Middle-Class Society"   Given their low level of class awareness, most Americans picture the U.S. class system in overly simplistic terms. The most popular conceptualization of the class hierarchy is a diamond-shaped structure with tiny upper and lower classes and a gigantic middle (Figure 2-1a). The fact that most people self-identify as somewhere in the middle seems to reflect this image. In social surveys conducted over the past forty years, almost all people, when asked to identify themselves in terms of class, consistently respond with "middle" or "working" class (Heath, 1998; Jackman and Jackman, 1983).

Another way of oversimplifying class divisions is to entirely dismiss the class structure, to thereby portray the United States as a "classless" society. Conservative politicians will often denounce any effort on the part of political opponents to point out sharp differences between the wealthy and other classes and will accuse these rivals of "exploiting the issue of class" or creating "class warfare." The idea is to deny that classes have any significance in the United States or even that class divisions exist at all.

The Reality of Class in the United States

The reality is that there are sharp differences in income and wealth, educational levels, and occupational status among the American population. These differences translate into a highly inequitable distribution of life chances and societal resources. They also produce strikingly different lifestyles.

The Six-Part American Class Structure

Dividing the population into class units is imprecise simply because there are no "natural" divisions, or breaking points, of the class hierarchy in terms of income and wealth, occupational status, and education. Any division of the society into a conceptualized hierarchy, therefore, is bound to be somewhat arbitrary. If, for example, one sociologist draws the line dividing middle and working classes at $20,000 annual income, another might draw it at $25,000. The boundaries of social classes are abstractions and thus do not lend themselves to precision.

Despite such inherent difficulties in clearly delineating the different units of the class hierarchy, there is general agreement among analysts regarding its basic shape. Although it is not possible to demonstrate exact points at which one class begins and the other ends, there are sufficient commonalities among people in terms of income, occupation, and education to draw a picture of the class system (Figure 2-1b). If those lines of division were not already apparent, people would be unable to distinguish themselves from others in terms of class. But of course they do make such distinctions. Both the very wealthy and the abject poor are easily recognized. It is the groups within the central portions of the hierarchy—the middle, or intermediate, classes—that are not so readily distinguished. Here, too, the divisions, though often hazy, are clear enough to be able to fill in the nuances of the American class hierarchy. Using the three major components of SES (income, occupation, and education), we may divide the hierarchy into six specific strata as depicted in Table 2-1.[2]

Table 2-1 is not intended to present a precise picture of the American class structure. The percentage of each class as part of the total class structure should be seen only as an approximation. Moreover, many families will not be consistent on all of the indicators of social class. For example, the income of a family's major breadwinner may not reflect his or her level of education. Nonetheless, the table provides a bird's-eye view of the class system as a whole, the details of which will be discussed in Chapters 3, 4, and 5.

The Upper Class   At the top of the structure are those whose share of income and wealth far exceeds those in other classes. Most important, they generally derive the bulk of their income not from wages and salaries, as do most people, but from returns on investments, such as stocks and bonds, real estate, and other forms of property. This is why those at the top of the class hierarchy are sometimes referred to as the *capitalist* class. Some are corporate executives who have enormous ownership shares in their companies. Others have inherited wealth and may play no direct managerial role. All are highly educated, often at the most prestigious prep schools, colleges,

---

[2]This six-part depiction of the U.S. class structure draws heavily from the model suggested by Dennis Gilbert and Joseph A. Kahl (1993).

Table 2-1 ■ Model of the American Class Structure

Class	Percent of Families	Approximate Family Income Range	Major Source of Income	Typical Occupations	Level of Education
Upper or "capitalist"	<1	>$1,000,000	Assets	Investors, corporate executives	At least 4 years college
Upper-middle	18–20	$75,000–$1,000,000	Salaries	Upper-level managers; professionals; some business owners	At least 4 years college; postgraduate training for many
Lower-middle	25–30	$35,000–$75,000	Salaries and wages	Lower-level managers; semiprofessionals; small business owners; craftspersons	At least high school graduate; often some college
Working	25–30	$25,000–$40,000	Wages	Operatives; clerical, retail sales workers	High school graduate
Working poor	12–15	$12,000–$25,000	Wages	Lower-level service workers; unskilled operatives	Some high school
Underclass	8–10	<$12,000	Public assistance; underground economy	Unemployed	Some high school

and universities. The upper class represents a very tiny percentage of the general class structure, no more than 1 percent.

Members of the capitalist class also enjoy maximum prestige and ordinarily occupy positions of great authority, giving them much societal power. Often it is difficult to distinguish between the capitalist class and those who comprise the higher range of the upper-middle class. Many of the truly wealthy may be professionals, such as doctors and lawyers, occupations typically held by the upper-middle class. Most important, however, is the fact that members of the capitalist class derive their income not primarily from their occupations, like the upper-middle class, but from their assets.

The Upper-Middle Class   Facetiously, it might be said that if the capitalist class "owns" the society, then those who comprise the upper-middle class "run" the society. While the upper-middle class is certainly distinguishable on the basis of income and wealth—well above average—these are the people whose skills and expertise are critical to the functioning of the society's major institutions: government, corporation, mass media, education, medicine, and so on. They are the executives and professionals who occupy the managerial and technical positions where important, far-reaching societal decisions are made. Their occupations influence what we buy, eat, see on TV, and teach our children. Their decisions help set the agenda of government and determine the state of the economy.

More than any factor, education sets apart members of the upper-middle class from other classes and creates a common lifestyle. To be part of the upper-middle class is almost automatically to be college-educated. The nature of upper-middle-class occupational positions makes higher education imperative. Managers must be trained in the skills of business and economics; doctors cannot expect to practice medicine or attorneys law without professional training. Similarly, engineers, scientists, and educators all require formal training at the highest levels.

Members of the upper-middle class derive their income not only from wages and salaries, which are high compared to other class groups, but also from investments. Moreover, the occupational positions of the upper-middle class rank high in terms of prestige, and members of this class are commonly among the most esteemed in the society. Studies have shown repeatedly that Americans accord greater prestige to people in professional positions (e.g., doctors, attorneys, and professors) and to top corporate managers than they do to those engaged in most other occupations. Obviously, these are also positions of significant authority and thus, as already noted, often carry with them substantial power to influence people's social and economic lives.

The upper-middle class has expanded more than any other during the past several decades as the occupational structure of the society has changed. In 1940 less than 15 percent of the workforce comprised managers, technicians, and professionals, but today more than 30 percent are part of these categories (U.S. Census Bureau, 1975, 1997d).

The Lower-Middle Class   The lower-middle class is probably the least clearly definable and most diverse among the various class strata. Occupationally, these are middle managers, semiprofessionals (e.g., nurses and technicians), craftspersons, and many service workers (such as nonretail salespersons), police and firefighters, and other government employees. Also part of the lower-middle class are proprietors of small businesses, the petty bourgeoisie, who employ only a few people and whose business assets are modest by comparison with large corporate firms.

Those in the lower-middle class can be expected to earn incomes close to the society's median. As to education, almost all are at least high school graduates and many have attended college, though the percentage of college graduates is far below that of the upper-middle class.

Although those of the lower-middle class may be esteemed, they do not enjoy the level of prestige of the upper-middle class nor do their positions afford them authority beyond their rather circumscribed social roles. Nonetheless, they share many of the attributes and values of the upper-middle class and aspire to upward mobility.

If there is a stratum that corresponds to the familiar description of "middle America," it is the lower-middle class. Conservative in their politics and in their social values, these are people who subscribe strongly to the basic beliefs of the American ideology, especially self-reliance.

The Working Class   Traditionally, the working class comprised those occupying manual laboring jobs. The term "blue collar" was attached to this stratum, denoting the physical nature of their work. The stereotypical blue-collar worker dressed in coveralls, carried a lunch bucket, and stopped at the corner bar for a beer on the way home from work. Today, the working class comprises a broad range of occupations, from skilled manual workers to retail sales clerks.

In the past few decades, the economies of modern industrial societies have changed from primarily production of goods to the provision of services. As that change has occurred, blue-collar jobs have declined and been replaced by service jobs. Many of these service jobs are only semiskilled, and the wages they pay are relatively low. As many traditional working-class jobs have been phased out, it is the occupants of these lower-skilled and lower-paying service jobs that today make up a growing part of the working class. The working class, then, comprises both blue- and white-collar workers. The jobs of both, however, are apt to be highly routinized, with little opportunity for creativity or innovation, and they entail little authority.

Occupations in this stratum usually require a high school diploma, but an increasing number of working-class people have completed some college, and a small, but growing, percentage are even college graduates. In line with these educational requirements, working-class incomes fall generally below the society's median. Although many among the working class may work for a salary, most are paid an hourly wage. Working-class people are thus able to maintain a standard of living that is adequate to provide the basic necessities of life but few of the amenities that the middle classes take for granted. Moreover, the expectations of upward mobility, so vital a part of the middle-class perspective, are much less evident. This is a result of the limited educational qualifications of working-class people as well as their more tenuous job security.

The upper-middle, lower-middle, and working classes are less distinct from each other than are those at the two extremes of the class hierarchy, the rich and the poor. Accordingly, they can be referred to as "classes in the middle," or the "intermediate classes." Certainly, there are vast and obvious differences between upper-middle-, lower-middle-, and working-class people. The point, however, is that the divisions among these middle classes are not discrete; rather, they blend into each other. Moreover, most of the social mobility that occurs in American society is experienced by people in these classes, moving from one stratum of the middle to another. Also, changes in the occupational structure of the society have been most evident within this intermediate segment of the class system, creating a picture that is mixed and in flux.

The Working Poor   Defining poverty is a highly debatable issue, as shown in Chapter 3. For now, the poor may be defined simply as those families who fall below the official U.S. government poverty line or are only slightly above it. Essentially, the poor can be broken down into two categories: the working poor and the abject poor, or underclass.

The working poor comprises those who are poor but are part of the working population. They may drift in and out of poverty as they experience unemployment periodically, or their wages may be so low that they are unable to rise above the poverty line. The jobs performed by the working poor are at the very bottom of the occupational hierarchy, those least desirable, least skilled, and requiring the least education. Correspondingly, these jobs pay the lowest wages, often the minimum wage, and have few or no benefits. Increasingly, people at this level work on a temporary or part-time basis, further contributing to their inability to rise above poverty, despite the fact that they may be employed. Many of the occupational handicaps faced by the working poor derive from their generally low educational level—few advance beyond high school and many do not even finish high school.

The Underclass   A second element of the poor comprises those who are abjectly poor, that is, who remain chronically in poverty and who are, for the most part, dependent on government welfare of one kind or another. This component of the poor has been referred to as the underclass. To all intents and purposes, these are people outside the social and economic mainstream. They possess few skills that would enable them to function as part of the workforce, and many engage in petty crime or operate on the margins of the mainstream economy.[3] As sociologist Peter Saunders has described it, the underclass is permanently marginalized:

> It seems surplus to economic requirements, and high rates of long-term unemployment make it difficult to argue that its members are essential to the efficient functioning of a capitalist economy, for there are many who will never find work again. (1990:120)

The underclass, though comprised of a variety of ethnic groups, is disproportionately African American and is confined primarily to inner-city ghetto areas. It has come to serve for the nonpoor as a kind of symbol of the social ills that afflict American society. And, as sociologist Herbert Gans (1996) and others have suggested, the underclass is commonly seen as the "undeserving poor."

The Distribution of Income

For most people, their income is the single most significant determinant of their social class. Income is, most simply, monetary gain from any of a variety of sources. Most of it derives from wages and salaries, but dividends and interest payments are also forms of income. In order to begin to understand the structure of inequality in American society, it is necessary to look carefully at how income is distributed. The simple question is "Who gets what?"

Family Income   Income statistics are most commonly stated in terms of family or household, rather than personal or individual, income. As defined by the U.S. Census Bureau, **families** consist of two or more persons who live in the same housing unit and are related by marriage or blood, whereas **households** consist of both families and persons who live by themselves, with roommates, or with unmarried partners. The figures and tables in this chapter use the family unit of measurement. A family's income might include the wages of two income earners, husband and wife, and perhaps even the wages of a child who is contributing to the total income. It would also include whatever interest and dividends the family members earned on their financial investments, such as savings accounts or stocks. A family income of, say, $60,000 might be broken down as follows:

Husband's wages	$36,000
Wife's wages	21,000
Dividends from bank accounts	2,500
Dividends from stock holdings	500
TOTAL	$60,000

---

[3]The term "underclass" has become an issue of controversy in recent years. Some maintain that it is a pejorative term used to describe a group whose behaviors are disapproved by the nonpoor. Others, however, consider it simply a description of the socioeconomic position of those who experience long-term poverty. I use the term here in the latter sense.

Table 2-2 ■ Percentage of Families by Income, 1999

Income	Percentage
Under $10,000	5.7
$10,000–$14,999	4.8
$15,000–$24,999	12.0
$25,000–$34,999	11.9
$35,000–$49,999	16.5
$50,000–$74,999	21.2
$75,000–$99,000	12.7
$100,000 or more	15.2

Source: U.S. Census Bureau, *Money Income in the United States: 1999.* Current Population Reports P60-209, Table B-4.

How is family income actually distributed in American society? Table 2-2 indicates that it is apportioned in a sharply unequal way: 5.7 percent of families earn less than $10,000. At the other end of the income hierarchy, slightly more than 15 percent earn over $100,000.

Median Income   An important statistic in looking at income inequality is median family income. The median is a figure that indicates the mid-point of a distribution, where 50 percent fall above and 50 percent below. This is a more accurate indicator of a central point or "average" than is the mean, since the latter can be distorted by a few very extreme cases at either end. In the case of income distribution, the mean family income will be pushed up by the enormous incomes of a very small percentage of families at the top of the hierarchy. The median, however, gives the exact "middle" point. The median can then be used as a base point from which to observe deviations.

Figure 2-2 shows the median family income from 1947 to 1999 in both current and constant dollars. Looking at changes in the median family income in current dollars would not tell much about how this figure had changed over time, because the value of the dollar changes from year to year. It is therefore necessary to convert yearly figures into constant dollars, that is, the equivalent of the value of the dollar at the present time. Figure 2-2 shows that when measured in current dollars, annual income has increased enormously since 1970. However, when measured in constant dollars, the increase has been quite modest. Indeed, annual income actually declined between 1990 and 1995 and in 1999 was only moderately higher than in 1990.

Keep in mind that Figure 2-2 shows family income, not household income. The median family income for any year is higher than the comparable median household income because persons living alone—considered household units—usually earn less than family units.

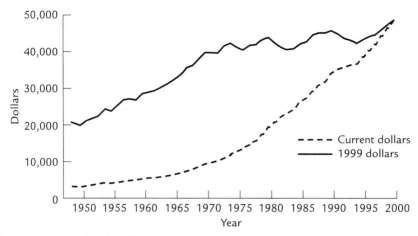

Figure 2-2 ■ Median Family Income

Income Quintiles   As a way of viewing the overall distribution of income, sociologists and economists commonly divide the population into income fifths, or quintiles, each with the same number of families. These income quintiles are arranged in the order of family income, from highest income earners to lowest. The income received by all families in each of the quintiles is expressed as a percentage of total family income. Thus, there is the highest 20 percent of income earners, the second highest 20 percent, and so on. The best way to conceptualize this is to think of a pie divided into five pieces. If income were distributed equally, with all families earning the same, each piece (or 20 percent) would receive 20 percent of the society's total income. To the extent that income is distributed unequally, the pieces of pie will be larger or smaller.

As Figure 2-3 shows, rather than proportionately divided, the income pie is immensely maldistributed. Table 2-3 provides some historical perspective on the distribution of income, showing its changes from decade to decade. To begin with, looking at any particular year, we can see that the richest 20 percent of families earned a highly disproportionate share of total income. In 1999, for example, the richest quintile earned almost half of all income. Also obvious is the enormous discrepancy between the richest and poorest quintiles. While the richest 20 percent of families earned 47.2 percent of total income, the poorest 20 percent earned only 4.3 percent. The income of the top 20 percent, in other words, was almost eleven times greater than the bottom 20 percent.

Concentrating on the discrepancy between the top and bottom fifths actually understates the extent of income inequality in the United States. Included in the top fifth are many families who are hardly among the very affluent. In 1999, for example, all families earning at least $88,000 were part of that top quintile. Thus, we need to move closer to the peak of the income

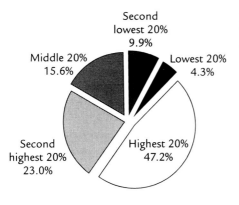

Figure 2-3 ■ The American Income Pie
Source: U.S. Census Bureau, *Historical Income Tables—Families*, 2000, Table F-2.

Table 2-3 ■ Percentage of Shares of Income Received by Each Fifth (20 Percent) of Families

Category	1950	1960	1970	1980	1990	1999
Highest 20 percent	42.7	41.3	40.9	41.1	44.3	47.2
Fourth 20 percent	23.4	24.0	23.8	24.4	23.8	23.0
Middle 20 percent	17.4	17.8	17.6	17.6	16.6	15.6
Second 20 percent	12.0	12.2	12.2	11.6	10.8	9.9
Poorest 20 percent	4.5	4.8	5.4	5.3	4.6	4.3
Top 5 percent	17.3	15.9	15.6	14.6	17.4	20.3

Source: U.S. Census Bureau, *Historical Income Tables—Families*, 2000, Table F-2.

hierarchy, that is, the richest 5 percent of families. As is seen in Table 2-3, in 1999, that top 5 percent earned more than 20 percent of all income. This was considerably more than the total income of the bottom two quintiles—40 percent of all families!

The data in Table 2-3 do not reveal the impact of other dimensions of inequality on the distribution of income. In American society, race and ethnicity relate closely to family income. This means that those of a particular racial or ethnic category will disproportionately fall at some point on the income hierarchy. For example, African Americans and Hispanic Americans collectively rank considerably below Euro-Americans in family income, whereas Asian American family income, on average, is highest of all. This does not mean that all African American and Hispanic American families earn less than all Euro-American families. It only means that African Americans are more likely to rank lower in the income hierarchy. (Remember the idea of "probability.") The same is true of women in comparison with men. Chapters 11 and 12 look more closely at how ethnicity and gender influence income distribution. There are also regional disparities in income. The median household income in West Virginia, for example, is about half of what it is in Maryland. Even within particular states, there are often sharp contrasts from county to county and between rural and urban areas.

The Distribution of Wealth

Having now looked at the distribution of income in American society, it should be apparent that the notion of the United States as a thoroughly middle-class society, in which there are no sharp class divisions, is largely fantasy. Income is distributed in a highly inequitable fashion and has been so for many decades. Wealth is even more grossly maldistributed between those who have much, those who have some, and those who have little.

What Is "Wealth"?   Wealth is not the same as income, and the distinction between them is important. Whereas income is monetary gain, wealth is the value of one's assets, or property. Economists have distinguished income and wealth by describing the former as a flow of money over time and the latter as a stock of things owned that have market value (Dowd, 1993; Atkinson, 1975; Inhaber and Carroll, 1992; Keister, 2000). Wealth is most commonly measured in terms of "net worth." In modern capitalist societies, wealth is ordinarily thought of as income-producing assets, not simply as one's material possessions (clothes, cars, etc.), though the latter are certainly assets. The major forms of wealth are stocks, bonds, and other financial instruments, cash, real estate, and business equity. Wealth, then, produces income in the form of dividends on investments or profits from business assets.

Inequalities in wealth are more consequential than inequalities in income because, as the old adage goes, "it takes money to make money." Although high income can lead to a comfortable standard of living, only through wealth can great riches be amassed. Usually, people use their wages—that is, their regular income—for living expenses. What they save from those wages and invest then becomes wealth. Few people, however, can ever save enough of their wages alone to amass a fortune. Even if they were to save regularly for their entire lifetime, it is unlikely that they would accumulate a sufficient amount to enter into the ranks of the truly wealthy, who earn their income primarily from their investments. But if wealth is acquired through investments, we have a kind of catch-22: investments require wealth. As economist Lester Thurow has put it, "Once wealth is acquired, opportunities to make more money multiply, since accumulated wealth leads to income-earning opportunities that are not open to those without wealth" (1996:243). Moreover, as Thurow points out, there are limitations to what one can earn through wages since there are just so many hours that one can work. Wealth, however, is not limited in the same way; wealth generates wealth, and there is no constraining force, like time or energy, to inhibit the process.

Economist Edward Wolff has explained that wealth is not only a source of income but also a kind of security for those who own it, who understand that even if their income is not forthcoming steadily, their assets will enable them to continue to live at a level to which they are accustomed. Thus, in times of economic crisis, such as the loss of one's job, a marital breakup, or a serious illness, wealth provides the means of consumption. "The very knowledge that wealth is at hand," notes Wolff, "is a source of comfort for many families" (1995b:6).

Wealth more than income contributes to the perpetuation of the class hierarchy. This is because wealth can be passed down from generation to generation. Children usually inherit the wealth amassed by their parents, perhaps enhancing its amount further in their lifetimes and then handing it down to their children. Consider two college graduates entering their initial jobs: One knows that he will inherit $100,000 when his parents die; the other begins only with debts incurred from student loans that helped him pay his tuition. The first graduate can purchase some luxuries, like a new car, or rent an expensive apartment. More important, he can afford to take financial risks and perhaps invest some of the salary he will earn where it will yield dividends and thus quickly earn him more income. The second graduate, however, will have to budget carefully, will not be able to take chances with his money, and unless his salary increases sharply in a short time, will have little left over to save after his bills are paid. It will be several years before he will be able to begin to save enough for any kind of substantial investment. By that time, his fellow graduate's investments will have put him many steps ahead in the competition for the society's rewards, not because of any superior effort or ambition, but mainly because of the wealth his parents amassed. And once he marries and forms a family of his own, *his* children will likely be assured of some of the same advantages.

It is in this way that the rich stay rich and that the distribution of wealth does not change radically. Several years ago, the late Malcolm Forbes (whose seventieth birthday party was described in Chapter 1) appeared on the *Late Show* with comedian David Letterman. In a serious moment, Letterman asked Forbes how he had acquired his fortune. With a perfectly straight face, Forbes replied, "My father died." Only if strict and formidable taxes on inheritance could be effected might we see a lessening of the continuation of wealth from one generation to the next. So long as the bulk of one's wealth can be passed on, the continuation of class inequality is virtually assured. Thus, the places on the class hierarchy of the rich, the poor, and those in the middle do not change much from one generation to the next. Entrance into the ranks of the wealthy occurs mainly through inheritance or, for the uncommon few, the ability to amass a fortune through extraordinary business success or through achievement in professional sports or the entertainment world.

Wealth in American Society: "The Rich and the Rest of Us"   Although income and wealth are not the same, there is an evident relationship between

Table 2-4 ■ Family Net Worth, 1995

Family Income	Median Net Worth ($1,000s)
Less than $10,000	4.7
$10,000–24,999	30.0
$25,000–49,999	53.4
$50,000–99,999	121.1
$100,000 and more	482.0

Source: U.S. Census Bureau, *Statistical Abstract of the United States 1999,* Table 771.

them. Not surprisingly, those who *earn* the most are *worth* the most. This is shown in Table 2-4.

The breakdown of total wealth by family income, however, is actually an understatement of how much is owned by just a few. We can get a better idea of the extreme concentration of wealth by looking at the top 10 percent and, even more specifically, the top 1 percent. Wolff has referred to the top 1 percent on the wealth hierarchy as the "Super Rich," the next 9 percent as the "Rich," and the remaining 90 percent as "Everybody Else."[4] The wealthiest 10 percent, a combination of the Super Rich and the Rich, own more than 70 percent of all wealth. But the top 1 percent, the Super Rich, alone own almost 40 percent. If we consider only financial assets—a concept of wealth that leaves out the value of owner-occupied housing—the concentration of ownership is even more stark: 1 percent own more than 47 percent, and the top 10 percent own almost 80 percent of total financial wealth (Table 2-5).

Looking at specific forms of wealth, we can further see how much is owned by so few. Take stock ownership, for example. Many like to extol the virtues of contemporary capitalism by exclaiming the great dispersion of stock ownership. No longer are corporations and banks owned by wealthy individuals or families, they point out, as stock ownership in these firms has become widespread among millions of ordinary people. The distortion in this assertion, however, is that among individually owned shares, the rich hold almost 90 percent. Most of the remainder of the stock-owning families own shares in retirement accounts. The same pattern is evident for other forms of wealth. The top 10 percent also hold almost 90 percent of all bonds, 90 percent of business equity, and 80 percent of all nonhome real estate. In short, the top 10 percent of families own the majority of significant forms of wealth, such as stocks, bonds, real estate, and cash; most of the remaining 90 percent

---

[4]Even looking only at the wealthiest 1 percent understates the concentration of wealth at the top. The majority of wealth owned by these families is actually owned by only a fraction of the families that make up the top 1 percent (Keister, 2000).

Table 2-5 ■ Distribution of Wealth, 1998

Wealth class	Net worth	Net financial assets
Top 1% (The super rich)	38.1	47.3
Next 9% (The rich)	32.9	32.4
Bottom 90% (Everybody else)	29.0	20.2

Source: Mishel et al., 2001.

of families own little more than their homes and cars. It is not an exaggeration to refer to the distribution of wealth in America as "the rich and the rest of us."

Change and Continuity in Economic Inequality

Stratification systems are not static. This section examines how the American class structure has changed over the past few decades. Specifically, how has the distribution of income and wealth been modified? Have income and wealth been shared more equitably over the years, or has the tendency been in the opposite direction?

Trends in the Distribution of Income and Wealth

Extremes of income and wealth should not be surprising in the United States, where capitalism has been more unfettered and less regulated than in almost any other society. Throughout most of American history, however, various segments of the society—farmers, workers, women, immigrants, blacks—were enabled to share in relative prosperity. Although the process was slow and tortuous for most, these aggrieved groups were increasingly provided with the life chances, like education, to compete more fairly in the market system. In all of these cases, the power of the state was used to rectify the inequality stemming from the excesses of capitalism left to its own forces. Despite periods of economic hardship, then, the capitalist economy, tempered by government, seemed to present opportunities for the advancement of each generation further up the class hierarchy. This tendency reached a high point following World War II.

The Post–World War II Boom   In the 1950s the United States embarked on a period of economic growth unprecedented in its history. Unburdened by war, the economy turned to the production of consumer goods—houses, automobiles, refrigerators, electronic goods, and the like. This stimulated job creation and higher wages, which, in turn, enabled families to enjoy a rising standard of living. Workers and management entered into an informal agreement in which both sides could realize advantages: Workers would remain loyal and support their companies in exchange for continued higher wages and benefits. The result was a significant expansion of the middle class. More and more people realized their piece of the American Dream—owning a home, sending their children to college, and earning enough to envision retirement with at least a modest degree of comfort.

Family income grew almost continuously from 1949 through 1973. Optimistically, Americans came to take for granted that this steady upward movement would continue indefinitely. Each generation, it was assumed, would exceed the economic level of the previous one. There was good reason for people to express such optimism. The growth in productivity gave a boost to family income in all social classes. Moreover, the gap between top and bottom, rich and poor, began to close. Looking again at Table 2-3, it can be seen that the income of the poorest quintile rose between 1950 and 1970 at the same that the income of the top quintile declined. Thus, the income pie, though still grossly maldistributed, was becoming less so.

The Post-1973 Era and Beyond   Changing conditions in the early 1970s, however, brought an abrupt end to what had seemed like a never-ending expansion of affluence. Economic growth began to decline, and as it did, the previously recorded wage and income gains ended. Median family income from 1973 on showed about as many year-to-year declines as increases (Danziger and Gottschalk, 1995). By the late 1970s, families, for the first time since the Great Depression of the 1930s, were on average worse off than families of a decade earlier. Median family income grew again during the 1980s, though at a rate far slower than in the 1960s, and then declined again in the early 1990s. By 1993, median family income was about the same as it had been twenty years earlier. For the first time in the post–World War II era, the middle class was not expanding but, on the contrary, seemed to be contracting. Those among the higher income groups continued to prosper, but those at the lower ends of the middle, particularly those among the working class, fared more poorly than at any time since the Great Depression.

As is seen in Table 2-3, the trend toward narrowing the gap between rich and poor now reversed itself: The richest 20 percent increased their share of total income, while the poorest 20 percent lost much of theirs. Whereas the richest quintile in 1980 received 41.1 percent of all income, by 1999 it received over 47 percent. At the other end of the hierarchy, the poorest quintile received 5.3 percent of total income in 1980 but only 4.3 percent in 1999. Regardless of how it is measured, inequality in income and earnings increased between the mid-1970s and mid-1990s (Danziger and Gottschalk, 1995; Yellen, 1998).

Moreover, during the 1980s and 1990s the growing inequality in distribution of income occurred in a period of renewed economic expansion. Almost all the fruits of this expansion, however, went to the top 20 percent. As economist Richard Freeman explains, "If divided evenly, the $2 trillion increase in the GDP from 1980 to 1994 would have been enough to give roughly $2,000 more to each American family" (1996:120). Instead, however, only the top 20 percent received any significant gains in income, while the proportion going to the other 80 percent fell. Most of the gains, in fact, went to the top 5 percent, whose share rose from 14.6 percent of total income in 1980 to 20.7 percent in 1997.

As Americans entered the twenty-first century, the U.S. economy seemed more prosperous than at any time since the 1960s. Family income and workers' wages were again on the rise, and unemployment was at its lowest level in many decades. Even poverty was on a downward slope. This general prosperity, however, failed to translate into a more equitable distribution of income. Although the income gap between top and bottom was no longer expanding as it had done during the previous twenty years, neither was it growing narrower. As economists Jared Bernstein and Lawrence Mishel report, in 1999 income inequality remained "at about the same historically high level that prevailed in the early 1990s when the current recovery got underway" (2000:1). Aside from the top 20 percent, most families were simply holding their ground, and doing so primarily because more family members were working more hours. In fact, had it not been for the extra hours of work contributed by working wives, the average income of middle-income, married families in the 1990s would have fallen (Mishel et al., 1999). For them, the income and wage gains of the late 1990s were not great enough to offset the long-term losses of the previous two decades. As Danziger and Reed (1999) point out, it would require many years of continued economic growth to bring income inequality back to its level of the early 1970s.

Growing Inequalities in Wealth   In recent times, trends in the distribution of wealth have paralleled those in income. Inequalities in wealth, however, are much greater, and the gap between the very wealthy and everyone else has grown enormously in the past two decades. From the mid-1960s through the late 1970s, America experienced a decline in the maldistribution of wealth, just as income inequality declined during that period. This trend reversed itself sharply in the 1980s, however. In 1965 the richest 1 percent of Americans held 37 percent of the nation's wealth; by 1979 their share had dropped to 22 percent. But after 1979 it rose precipitously, so that by 1992 they held 42 percent of all wealth (Wolff, 1995b).

With increasing productivity, much new wealth was created in the 1980s. However, most of it went to those at the very top of the class hierarchy, with very little filtering downward. Between 1983 and 1989, the top 20 percent received virtually all (99 percent) of the total gain in marketable wealth. But even this figure does not reveal the extreme concentration of wealth expansion at the top. The richest 1 percent alone received 62 percent of all the new wealth.

Economic and political analysts have shown that the rate and extent of the rise in wealth inequality during the 1980s is almost unprecedented in American history. Not since the 1920s had there been a comparable upsurge of riches for those at the top (Barlett and Steele, 1992; Phillips, 1990; Wolff, 1995b). And never before had such a proliferation of millionaires and billionaires occurred in such a short time. As Kevin Phillips (1990) explains, by the late 1980s millionaires were almost commonplace. *Forbes* magazine, which each year publishes a list of the wealthiest people in the United States, reported in 1988 that the estimated number of billionaires in that year—fifty-one—was double the number from 1986. By 1992 the *Forbes* list of American billionaires had grown to seventy-one (*Forbes*, 1988, 1992).

Throughout the 1990s, the trend toward greater wealth inequality continued. With a booming stock market, investors increased their wealth enormously. As before, however, those below the higher classes generally did not become richer. Between 1989 and 1997, the share of total wealth held by the top 1 percent of households grew from 37.4 percent to almost 40 percent. At the same time, the share of wealth held by the middle 20 percent of the population dropped from 4.8 percent to 4.4 percent. And, the share of those in debt (i.e., with negative wealth) increased to 18.5 percent of households. By the middle of the decade, almost 90 percent of the value of all stock was owned by the richest 10 percent of households; on the other hand, almost 60 percent of households owned no stock at all or at most held very small investments. The upshot of this skewed distribution of ownership was that almost 86 percent of the benefits of the surging stock market of the 1990s went to the richest 10 percent of households (Mishel et al., 1999).

Looking Beyond

Looking at the class system overall, by the early 1990s, it seemed that, in a very real sense, the rich had gotten richer and the poor poorer, while most in the middle classes had struggled to keep pace. Those at the top of the income and wealth hierarchies had, as Danziger and Gottschalk put it, "never had it so good" (1995:9). For most others, however, their economic condition seemed to be either stagnant or declining.

During the late 1990s and extending into 2000, the American economy seemed to be functioning at its peak, with rising wages and incomes, an upsurge in the creation of wealth, and poverty on the decline. Yet this extraordinarily robust economy has had little effect on the distribution of income and wealth. The income gap continues to grow, though not as much as in the previous twenty years, and, perhaps most important, wealth remains as concentrated as ever among the rich and the super rich. The beneficiaries of the booming American economy of the past few years, then, have primarily been those at the very top of the class system and, secondarily, many among the upper-middle class. The current period shows that propitious economic conditions do not assure a more equitable distribution of income and wealth. The problem of inequality, then, is a problem not of economic expansion and the production of wealth, but of the distribution of the society's economic resources.

At the outset of the twenty-first century, the American class structure appears to have evolved into a three-part configuration, with the rich taking the bulk of income and wealth, the poor receiving little, and those in the middle scrambling to maintain their standard of living. In Chapter 4, we will look more closely at the factors that have contributed to these shifting lines of division in income and wealth. Briefly, however, much of the continued inequality of the past quarter century has been the result of economic restructuring, both in the United States and abroad. Those with critical occupational skills have fared well in the new economy, while those with few skills have lost out. Also, new industries have emerged, revolving around new technologies—especially computers and communications—creating in the process wide opportunities for the creation of instant fortunes and for those with capital to increase their wealth enormously.

Economic Inequality: A Comparative Perspective

In no contemporary society are economic resources distributed equitably. In all, there are rich, poor, and those in the middle. What does differ among societies, however, is the relative gap between the classes, particularly between those at the top and those at the bottom. How does the United States compare to other countries in this regard? Is economic inequality more or less severe?[5]

Comparing the United States with developing countries yields a truly astounding picture. Whereas the income ratio of the richest 20 percent of families to the poorest 20 percent in the United States is about 11 to 1, it is, for example, 32 to 1 in Brazil, a country in the process of industrializing (Passell, 1996). Huge portions of the Brazilian population live in severely depressed conditions, while a wealthy elite take a grossly disproportionate share of the society's wealth. In countries that are poorer and less developed than Brazil, the spread between the few rich and the many poor is sometimes even greater.[6]

But comparing the United States, the world's largest economy, to developing societies provides only a comparison in absolute, not relative, terms. It is hardly meaningful to contrast the level of inequality in Brazil, for example, to that in the United States, whose per capita income is almost ten times

---

[5]It needs to be cautioned that making comparisons of the United States with other countries is risky since economic data do not always coincide precisely from one country to another. However, the data do provide for at least rough comparisons.

[6]Considering the world as a whole, the discrepancy between rich and poor is glaring. In 1993 the poorest 20 percent of the world's population received 1.4 percent of global income whereas the richest 20 percent received 85 percent, a ratio of 61 to 1 (UNDP, 1993). By 1997, the ratio had risen to 74 to 1 (UNDP, 1999).

Table 2-6 ■ Gini Index for Selected Countries

Country	Gini Index
Japan	24.9
Sweden	25.0
Italy	27.3
Germany	30.0
Canada	31.5
Netherlands	32.6
France	32.7
Australia	35.2
United Kingdom	36.1
United States	40.8

Source: World Bank, 2000. *2000 World Development Indicators.* Washington, DC: The World Bank, Table 2-8.

larger. A more significant comparison would lie between the United States and other societies with comparable levels of economic development and resources, that is, other advanced industrial societies. When such comparisons are made, the United States is shown to be markedly more unequal in its distribution of income and wealth. Indeed, since the 1980s, the United States has had no peer in economic inequality. A study by the OECD, an international economic research organization, reported that the income spread between rich and poor during the 1980s was greater in the United States than in any other large industrialized country. And, the study concluded, these inequalities persisted in the 1990s (Bradsher, 1995). "The United States," writes economist Richard Freeman, "has now cemented its traditional position as the leader in inequality among advanced countries" (1999:3).Table 2-6 shows the concentration of income in the United States compared to other Western industrial societies using the Gini index. This is a statistical measure that indicates the difference between the actual distribution of income and a perfectly equal distribution. If the latter were the case, each 20 percent of the population would receive 20 percent of income. The Gini index ranges from 0 (perfect equality) to 100 (complete inequality); thus, the closer to 100, the greater the inequality of income.

Even in some newly industrializing societies, such as those of East Asia, the difference is striking. In South Korea, for example, the ratio of top 20 percent to bottom 20 percent is less than 6 to 1 (Passell, 1996), a gap considerably narrower than in the United States.

Another way of comparing U.S. inequality with that of other societies is to look at the average hourly pay of workers. In 1992 men in the top 10 percent of wage earners in the United States earned 5.6 times as much as those in the bottom 10 percent. By comparison, the ratio in Britain was 3.4; in France, 3.2;

in Japan, 2.8; and in Germany, 2.7 (*Business Week,* 1994). Moreover, those at the low end of the wage scale in the United States are significantly more depressed relative to other parts of the workforce than those in other countries. Low-paid German workers, for example, earn over twice what low-paid U.S. workers earn (Freeman, 1996). These differences are exacerbated when consideration is made of the much smaller safety net provided by the U.S. government in the form of health insurance and other welfare benefits.

A number of studies have also shown that there is a much larger income gap between managers and workers in the United States than in any other advanced industrialized country. And that gap has grown enormously in the past twenty years. In 1962, the typical CEO made about 20 times more than the average worker; by 1999, the typical CEO made 107 times more (Mishel et al., 2001). Also, CEOs' wages are vastly higher in the United States than in other developed societies (Thurow, 1999).

Other data indicate that wealth inequality in the United States is also more extreme than in any other advanced industrial society. Whereas 1 percent of U.S. households own almost 40 percent of the society's wealth, the top 1 percent in Britain own only about 18 percent of total wealth (Wolff, 1995b).

Many of the same forces that drive the gap between rich and poor in the United States are at work in other advanced industrial societies as well. They have not been immune to the effects of economic restructuring, corporate downsizing, immigration, and changing demographics. However, in most, inequality has been held in check to a much greater degree. Part of the explanation for this lies in the more liberal social programs of these societies, where minimum wages are considerably higher and worker benefits, like unemployment insurance and child-care payments, are more numerous and comprehensive. Labor unions are also far more potent, thereby helping to protect workers' wages. Governments, too, require companies to reassign workers or reduce hours before they institute pay cuts or layoffs.

Summary

Social classes can be conceived in two ways. As an economic concept, classes are simply groupings of people who share roughly similar incomes and wealth, occupations, and levels of education. Classes may also be thought of as groupings in which people share not only similar socioeconomic standing but similar lifestyles. The economic and behavioral dimensions of social class are closely interdependent.

Contrary to popular views, the United States is a society in which the class system is highly developed. There are marked differences in income and wealth, educational attainment, and occupational status among the American population. Specifically, the U.S. class system is a six-part structure, consisting of an upper, or capitalist, class, an upper-middle class, a lower-middle class, a working class, and a poverty population made up of two components: the working poor and the underclass.

Inequality in the distribution of income and wealth in the United States is very apparent. The richest 20 percent of families earn almost half of all income and own almost 80 percent of all wealth. Income and wealth inequality has always characterized American society, but it has become evident that economic inequality expanded throughout the 1980s. That trend was not reversed in the 1990s; rather, the gap between those at the top—the upper and upper-middle classes—and the rest of the class hierarchy continued to widen.

Comparisons with other advanced industrial societies reveal a more inequitable distribution of income and wealth in the United States. Measured in various ways, the gap between rich and poor in the United States is wider than in any other society with comparable economic institutions and standards of living.

3

Poverty and the Poor

Wealth can be concealed, but not poverty.
FINNISH PROVERB

Lack of money is the root of all evil.
GEORGE BERNARD SHAW

As noted in Chapter 2, most Americans identify themselves as part of the middle classes, and most people do fall in the middle range of the class hierarchy. Nonetheless, there are certainly identifiable upper and lower classes. This chapter focuses on the latter, those at the bottom—the poor—and on the general phenomenon of poverty. The questions explored here are Who are the poor? and Why are they poor?

Defining Poverty

Defining those at the bottom would seem to be easier than trying to divide the various parts of the middle or to distinguish those at the top, but this is not the case. In large part, the imprecision of delineating the poor stems from the fact that there is much debate about what actually constitutes **poverty.** People who see great injustices in the class hierarchy are apt to draw a broader, more inclusive boundary around those classified as poor, whereas people who defend the basic fairness of the class system will enumerate the poor in less sweeping terms. Moreover, poverty can be a contentious political issue when seeking explanations of why people are poor and how best to address their problems.

To help clarify the issue, poverty can be conceptualized in three different ways: absolute, relative, and official.

Absolute Poverty

The least complicated way of defining poverty is to conceptualize it in absolute terms. This means that there are certain measures of poverty about which there are no disagreements. It is generally accepted that the poor in society are those who are unable to acquire the necessities of life. No one would argue that a basic diet, shelter from the elements, access to minimal health care, and a few articles of personal property such as clothing are essential, that anything less constitutes a state of poverty. Moreover, from society to society this formula for defining poverty would hold up. Those whose incomes caused them to fall beneath this absolute standard would comprise the poor, and the same criteria would apply to all countries. In an absolute sense, then, poverty is simply a socioeconomic condition in which people are unable, for whatever reason, to meet their fundamental human needs: "Subsistence or absolute poverty implies that there is a fixed basic minimum income below which physiological efficiency cannot be maintained" (Walker and Walker, 1995:655).

Relative Poverty

Defining poverty as an absolute standard, however, is not so simple. What constitutes "necessity"? In a modern society like the United States, is a telephone a necessity or a luxury? What about an automobile? Or, at the beginning of the twenty-first century, a computer, equipped with a modem? Moreover, what comprises a "minimal" level of health care or a "basic" diet? Arguments can be made on all of these points.

Poverty, therefore, is more rationally defined in relative terms—relative, that is, to the standards and expectations of people in a particular society at a particular time. A basic diet in the United States, for example, would not be the same as a basic diet in Bangladesh or Bolivia. In the United States or a society of comparable economic development, a telephone and an automobile have become necessities, though in the past these were luxury items enjoyed by only a select few. Today, a computer is fast becoming a necessity merely to keep pace, let alone to advance, in the educational or occupational worlds and to supply vital information regarding all facets of social, economic, and political life.

Poverty, then, is contextual, subject to changing standards as situations change. Poverty is not the same everywhere, and it is not the same in any society from one historical period to another. Thus, we cannot easily impose our standards on other societies, nor can we impose past standards on current times.

Official Poverty

Unfortunately, neither absolute nor relative definitions permit us to actually make a count of the poor or to measure poverty. Even if, using either of these conceptions, there were no disagreement regarding what the general state of poverty is, there is no way of implementing that standard and enumerating the poor without imposing some measurable criteria. Government, in a sense, settles the argument about who is poor and what conditions actually constitute poverty by applying a uniform yardstick for counting the poor and measuring poverty. This is the official definition of poverty.

"No, those people aren't anorexic. Those people are starving."

In 1964, as part of President Johnson's War on Poverty, the U.S. Department of Labor was asked to create a standard of living that would serve as a threshold of poverty. That standard would then constitute the poverty line, with those falling beneath it labeled by the federal government as "the poor" and thus eligible for various public assistance programs. It was determined that families spent about one-third of their income on food. The poverty line, therefore, was set at three times the cost of a nutritionally adequate diet. The initial formula for determining the official poverty count has not been altered.

In 1999 the official poverty line was $17,029 for a family of four. The poverty line, however, is a sliding scale, which changes with the number of people comprising a family. For a larger family the threshold is higher, and for a smaller family it is lower. Thus, for a family of five, the poverty line was set at $20,127; for a family of three, at $13,290; and so on (U.S. Census Bureau, 2000a). Also, the official poverty threshold is adjusted each year to account for increases in the cost of living.

Obviously, the official poverty line is somewhat arbitrary. If a four-person family earned $17,500 in 1999, would it be "safely" above poverty? Moreover, people live at different standards, regardless of what they earn. A family of very modest tastes that spent little on anything but basics might survive on an income below the official line. Similarly, one accustomed to a higher standard might find itself unable to function below a figure well above the official poverty line. Also, the cost of living varies from region to region, from city to city, and between rural and urban areas. Families in U.S. cities on the east or west coast would find it difficult to live at a comparable level to families with similar incomes in southern or midwestern cities. Finally, an official poverty standard accounts only for money income and neglects consideration of other aspects of poverty such as poor schools, health care, and the like. For example, income statistics alone would fail to reveal that the poor are twice as likely as the nonpoor to be victims of violent crimes (Federman et al., 1996). We can easily see how the line is a convenient cutoff point, but it is hardly one that corresponds to the realities and vagaries of economic life.

Moreover, counting the poor by establishing an official poverty line is a highly political issue. Policymakers can choose to measure the extent of poverty from a number of competing definitions of poverty, depending on their policy intentions (Walker and Walker, 1995). Those who approach the issue of poverty with a conservative political perspective point to the fact that the value of some welfare payments, such as food stamps, is not included when creating the poverty line, and that therefore the size of the poverty class is overstated. They argue that if these benefits were added, the number of poor would decline—that is, some would simply be "defined out" of poverty by being pushed over the official poverty cutoff point.

On the other side of the issue, those who subscribe to a more liberal view of poverty argue that the number of poor is actually understated when the official definition is applied. The poverty line, they point out, is determined on the basis of pre-tax income. Since taxes on wages reduce income available for consumption, using after-tax income as the standard would increase the number calculated as poor. Also, they note that the poor ordinarily must spend more than one-third of their income on food. In this view, then, the official poverty line is not high enough. In 1993, for example, whereas 8.4 million families were below the poverty line, redefining poverty as 125 percent of the current threshold would have increased the number of poor families to almost 11 million (U.S. Census Bureau, 1996). If the poverty line were set at one-half the median family income (as is done in most European Union countries), it would have raised the number even more substantially.

Who Are the Poor?

Given the relative nature of poverty and the politics of actually counting the poor, the dividing line between the poor and the rest of the class hierarchy will always be subject to debate. In examining the dimensions of poverty in the United States, however, we need a working definition and so must use the official standard. Moreover, the data that government agencies collect, based on that standard, are the most complete and reliable available to us.

The Poor and Those at Risk

In 1999, 11.8 percent of the U.S. population were living below the official poverty line. This translated into 32.3 million people (U.S. Census Bureau, 2000a). Table 3-1 presents a more precise look at the U.S. poverty population. It shows that most of the poor (about two-thirds) are white, not black or His-

Table 3-1 ■ Number of Americans in Poverty, 1999

Category	Number (millions)
All Persons	32.3
Race/Ethnicity	
White	21.9
Black	8.4
Hispanic	7.4
Asian	1.2
Family Structure	
In families	23.4
In families with children under age 18	11.5
Age	
Children (under 18 years old)	12.1
Adults (18 to 64 years old)	17.0
Elderly (65 years old and over)	3.2

Source: U.S. Census Bureau, *Poverty in the United States: 1999.* Current Population Reports P60-210. 2000.

panic, as is often assumed. The poor are also disproportionately children, with almost 40 percent below the age of eighteen and a large number in single-parent, female-headed families.

Merely enumerating the poor in absolute figures yields a somewhat distorted picture. It does not reveal what the risk, or chances, of being in poverty are. From which social groups are the poor most apt to come? That is, what are the probabilities of being in poverty? A truer portrait of the poverty population is provided in Table 3-2, which shows the percentage of each social category that falls below the poverty line. Looking at poverty among different racial and ethnic groups, for example, we see immediately that although there are many more whites in poverty, the poor are disproportionately black and Hispanic. Whereas less than 8 percent of whites are in poverty, almost one-quarter of blacks and one-quarter of Hispanics are in this stratum. Thus blacks and Hispanics are almost three times as likely as whites to be in poverty.

Table 3-2 also reveals that children are far more likely to be in poverty than either adults (between 18 and 64) or the elderly (those over 65). Almost 17 percent of children are poor, compared to 10 percent of adults and less than 10 percent of the elderly. Also noticeable in Table 3-2 is that the at-risk poverty population is more concentrated in the central cities of metropolitan areas than in the suburbs. The poverty rate for those in central cities is twice the suburban rate.

Another common feature of the at-risk poverty population is a truncated family structure. Where families are dual-headed, that is, with two parents present, the incidence of poverty is far lower than in families with

Table 3-2 ■ Percentage of Each Category of Americans in Poverty, 1999

Category	Percentage
Total Population	11.8
Race/Ethnicity	
White, non-Hispanic	7.7
Black	23.6
Hispanic	22.8
Asian	10.7
American Indian*	25.9
Family Structure	
Married-couple families	4.8
Families with female householder, no husband present	27.8
Age	
Children (under 18 years old)	16.9
Adults (18 to 64 years old)	10.0
Elderly (65 years old and over)	9.7
Nativity	
Native-born	11.2
Foreign-born	16.8
Residence	
Reside in metropolitan areas	11.2
Inside central cities	16.4
Outside central cities	8.3
Reside outside metropolitan areas	14.3

Source: U.S. Census Bureau, *Poverty in the United States: 1999.* Current Population Reports P60-210. 2000.
*Three-year average, 1997–1999

only one parent. The latter are almost always headed by females. Since women generally earn less than men, this exacerbates the rate of poverty among single-parent families. In 1999 the median income of married-couple families was $56,676, but for female-headed families with no husband present, it was only $23,732 (U.S. Census Bureau, 2000c). When family structure is combined with race and ethnicity, black and Hispanic female-headed families display the highest incidence of poverty. The continuing rise in the number of single mothers has created a trend referred to as the **feminization of poverty.**

The social characteristics with the strongest relation to poverty, then, are ethnicity, age, gender, and family structure. The profile of poverty that emerges is a population disproportionately made up of racial and ethnic minorities, females, young people, and those living as part of female-headed families.

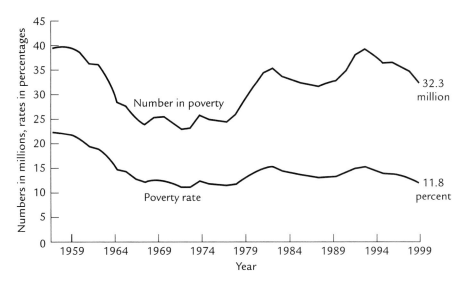

Figure 3-1 ■ Number of Poor and Poverty Rate: 1959 to 1999
Source: U.S. Census Bureau, *Poverty in the United States: 1999.* Current Population Reports
P60–210. 2000.

Poverty Trends

How has the incidence of poverty in the United States changed in recent times? Have the number and proportion of the poor increased or declined, and have the characteristics of the at-risk population varied or stayed the same?

Figure 3-1 shows the trend of poverty over the past four decades. Several dips and rises are evident. The poverty rate dropped quite significantly in the late 1960s and early 1970s. What had been a poverty population of over 22 percent in 1959 was reduced to 11.6 percent by 1973. The rate began to climb again in the 1980s, however, and appeared to stabilize at around 14 percent by the mid-1990s. In 1999, the poverty rate dropped below 12 percent, making a twenty-year low.

How can these peaks and valleys in the poverty rate be explained? Some understanding of these fluctuations can be captured by considering the general economic condition of the society during the post–World War II era and the introduction of particular public policies aimed at addressing poverty.

The Rediscovery of Poverty   As a result of what seemed like a continuing rise in prosperity, poverty in the years immediately after the end of World War II was viewed as a receding problem that would soon disappear entirely. However, poverty in America was "rediscovered" in the early 1960s. A significant book of that time, which, many maintain, was largely responsible for alerting policymakers to the fact that poverty was not disappearing, was Michael Harrington's *The Other America* (1962). In it Harrington showed that poverty was a continuing phenomenon in American society but had become more difficult to discern because of its obscured nature. The poor, he explained, were now more concentrated in urban and rural ghettos where they were less visible to the nonpoor. They were, in a sense, out of sight and out of mind.

Poverty's rediscovery, in conjunction with the black civil rights movement, set off an ambitious government effort to address the issues of the lingering poor and to put an end to what seemed like an anomaly in the context of a robust economy and an expanding middle class. President Lyndon B. Johnson announced an "unconditional war on poverty," prompting the creation of new antipoverty programs and agencies. These efforts were continued during the early years of the 1970s, despite the more conservative political perspective of Johnson's successor, Richard Nixon. The impact of these expanded welfare programs was a general reduction in the number of poor, but the effect was especially great on reducing the elderly poor. Many who had previously faced old age with financial insecurity were lifted above poverty by the expansion of Social Security and the creation of Medicare, a health insurance system for the elderly. By 1973 poverty was at its lowest rate since such statistics had been collected.

The New Poverty   In 1984, two decades after *The Other America* had sparked the War on Poverty, Michael Harrington wrote a sequel called *The New American Poverty*. In it he explained that despite encouraging statistics, little had actually changed in the intervening years. Much of the decline of poverty in the late 1960s was simply the result of the booming U.S. economy, providing jobs and rising wages. Moreover, despite the enactment of many new government programs aimed at alleviating poverty, Johnson's War on Poverty had been feebly supported by comparison with the other— shooting—war being waged at that time in Vietnam.

The 1980s brought a new category of the poor to the public consciousness: the homeless. Although homeless people had continually been part of the American urban landscape, in the early 1980s their numbers increased and their presence was magnified. Today, rare is the city, large or small, that has no homeless population. During the daylight hours, these people may visually blend into the surrounding environment, but at night they can be seen sleeping in doorways, bus stations, and abandoned buildings, on park benches and even on sidewalks. Others, less visible, sleep in homeless shelters. Jennifer Toth (1993) studied homeless people in New York and found that at least five thousand were living in abandoned underground tunnels throughout the city.

The poverty that reemerged in the 1980s seemed even more intractable than in earlier decades, given the structural changes that had occurred in the American economy. Many of the low-skill jobs that had previously been occupied by the poor had been phased out of existence or had been moved abroad to countries with more pliant and docile workers prepared to work for wages that, to Americans, were unthinkably low. Thus, a new class of the poor had emerged, made up of those whose jobs had been eliminated or exported.

In addition to these structural changes, the 1980s brought to power an administration with a sharply divergent view of the poor and of how they should be dealt with. Ronald Reagan espoused a strong market-oriented approach to public policy and sought to reduce the role of government in all spheres of social and economic life. As a result, measures enacted in the 1960s and 1970s that were designed to benefit the poor were now viewed skeptically, even disdainfully, and were seen not as solutions to poverty but as problems themselves that had created a culture of welfare dependency (Murray, 1984). Many public assistance programs for the poor were now slashed as the poor were seen in a new light: "deserving" or "undeserving." The latter were thought to be beneficiaries of a welfare system that was far too generous and easy to exploit. Reagan, in his 1980 campaign, spoke frequently of "welfare queens who drive Cadillacs."

American Poverty Today   What accounts for the seemingly persistent level of poverty in the United States? What is puzzling to many is that during most of the 1990s, policies were revised in such a way as to adjust some of the extreme inequalities in the tax burden that were imposed by the Reagan and Bush administrations. Nonetheless, poverty has not seemed to abate. Also baffling is the persistence of poverty in the face of an economy that continues to grow and to produce more and more wealth.

There are structural factors that account in major part for this continued pattern. The labor market in the United States and other advanced capitalist societies has undergone fundamental changes in the past three decades and in the process has eliminated many of the manufacturing-sector jobs that had been held by those on the lower rungs of the class hierarchy. These were jobs that enabled workers with limited skills and education to earn a livable wage. As those jobs are terminated or moved to areas or countries with cheaper labor, the remaining manufacturing jobs require higher skills for which most of the poor do not qualify. Hence, no longer can those with a low level of education expect to find a decent-paying entry-level job, as was the case in the past.

To make matters worse, low-level jobs in the expanding service sector for which the poor might qualify rarely pay a wage that can vault them above the poverty line. Hourly wages fell for the majority of the workforce from 1970 to 1999, but they fell further for the lowest-paid workers. For example, women workers in the bottom tenth percentile (that is, the percentile that earned less than the remaining 90 percent of women workers) earned on average $5.77 an hour in 1999, down from $6.36 in 1979. And workers with minimum education continued to fall further behind. In 1979 a high school graduate entering the workforce earned an hourly wage of $12.19; by 1999 it had fallen to $9.27 (Mishel et al., 2001).

In sum, as those on the higher rungs of the occupational hierarchy thrive in an expanding economy, the ranks of the poor are increasingly filled by those who cannot find work or who can only find work that does not pay a viable wage. As sociologist William J. Wilson has put it, "economic growth today does not necessarily produce good jobs" (1996:153). Government policies designed to alleviate poverty are mostly ineffective since it is in the private sector—businesses large and small—that most jobs are created. (Government strategies that address the plight of the poor are discussed later in this chapter.)

The Working Poor and the Underclass

The poor are not a homogeneous category in terms of either economic class or lifestyle. The most important division among them is between those who have been referred to as the working poor and those who have been called an underclass.

The Working Poor

Many workers in American society are caught in an economic vise. On the one hand, they are poor to the extent that their economic status is extremely precarious. They literally live from paycheck to paycheck. These are workers who commonly work on a part-time or temporary basis, rarely employed at any one job long enough to establish themselves solidly and build some economic security, unlike those in classes above them. Their wages are usually low, and therefore even if they do work regularly, they have difficulty making financial ends meet, let alone saving a portion of their income.

But at the same time that they are sufficiently stressed economically to qualify as poor by almost any definition, they are usually not poor enough to be eligible for public assistance. That is, their income, though low, may be adequate enough to push them above the official poverty line. Failing to qualify for welfare programs such as Medicaid makes their economic status especially unstable, perhaps even more so than the abject poor below them, who are chronically un- or underemployed and who therefore qualify for government benefits. Since they do not work enough hours to qualify for medical insurance or they work in a job that does not provide such benefits, a serious illness among working-poor families can be catastrophic.

The working poor are those who occupy the bottom rungs on the occupational ladder, filling jobs that are lowest not only in wages but in prestige and power as well. Kitchen workers, unskilled factory operatives, migrant farm laborers, and laundry workers are typical of this category. These are jobs that pay at or close to the minimum wage. In 2000, at the minimum wage rate ($5.15 an hour), even if they had worked a full workweek (forty hours), their pay would have been only $206. Assuming that they worked fifty weeks during the year, their annual income would have been $10,300, considerably below the official poverty line. This is a hypothetical case, of course, since most of the working poor do not work a full forty-hour week nor do they work for the entire year.

To illustrate the working poor, consider two cases. Diana K. is a thirty-four-year-old single parent of three children. Her run-down apartment is sparsely furnished; its plumbing is in serious disrepair; and when it rains, the ceiling leaks. Diana works as a nurse's aide and is paid on an hourly basis, just above the minimum wage. At one time she was dependent on welfare, but now that she is working she is no longer eligible for cash assistance. She does continue to receive food stamps, however, and is trying to move into a government-subsidized house that will cost her about the same as her apartment rent. Interestingly, Diana lives not in the inner-city of Chicago or Philadelphia or in an impoverished rural area of the South—environments that are commonly believed to breed poverty. Rather, she and her family live in a midsize city in Iowa, where the population is virtually entirely white and non-Hispanic (Kilborn, 1992).

Melonise W. is twenty-two, a high school graduate, and lives in Detroit with her mother. She is supporting two young daughters. She earned the minimum wage when she began to work at her present job—stuffing fifty pounds of finished rags into cardboard boxes and labeling them for shipment—but two years later, she is earning somewhat more. Despite the fact that she lives with her mother and works as much overtime as she can, her income simply does not permit her to make ends meet. For baby formula, she relies on a federal food program (Meredith, 1996).

There are some common features of the working poor in these two cases. Most important, both Diana and Melonise are raising their children alone, although in Melonise's case, her mother is helping. As shown in the previous section, family composition is a critical element of poverty. Single-parent, female-headed families are more likely than any others to be poor. Furthermore, both women have a minimum of education and thus lack the skills that would enable them to qualify for a better-paying job. Diana would like to become a registered nurse, which would more than triple her wages. But to do that would require a couple of years of full-time schooling. This would mean giving up her present job and going back to relying almost entirely on welfare. Thus, she is caught in a dilemma.

Often the working poor are those who are temporarily in a poverty condition, either between jobs or experiencing a cut in wages. Workers whose jobs may be lost as a result of corporate downsizing, for example, and who are for a time unable to find work may suffer a sharp drop in income and in their standard of living, throwing them into the ranks of the poor. Changes in their employment or education may boost them out of poverty, just as sudden or unforeseen circumstances may push them back down. Thus, they should not be thought of as a permanent class of poor people.

The Underclass

In recent years, Americans have become accustomed to viewing the poor not as people who may drift in and out of poverty because of changes in their jobs or other personal or societal circumstances, but rather as a population that remains more or less permanently impoverished. The majority of the poor do not correspond to this popular view; they are working but simply do not always earn enough to boost them over the poverty threshold. However, there is a segment of the poverty population that does seem to fit the popular description: They have few occupational skills, are undereducated, are rarely employed, and are ordinarily dependent on some form of public assistance. Sociologists and others have referred to this element of the poor as an **underclass.** Two essential characteristics define this stratum: poverty that is chronic, not temporary or short-term, and social and economic isolation. Perhaps more than anything else, it is the fact that they are largely cut off from the mainstream society and its major institutions that makes the plight of this part of the poverty population so intractable.

The Makeup of the Underclass   The dividing line between those who drift in and out of poverty and those who remain mired permanently in that condition is by no means clear-cut. What seems to be the key differentiating factor, however, is the loose connection of the underclass to the mainstream labor force. The working poor often live below the official poverty line, but they are usually employed, at least for a portion of the year. They are in a precarious situation, of course, and are always in danger of falling further into poverty. Unlike the working poor, the underclass, for the most part, does not participate in the general labor force. Most depend to some degree on government welfare, and some may engage in illegal activities.

Much of the economic activity among the underclass is part of what is called the **underground economy.** This covers a wide range of economic activities that occur outside the mainstream economy where activities are regulated through licensing and other requirements and where earned income is taxed. Activities within the underground economy are ordinarily "off the books"—that is, exchanges are made only in cash with no record of transfer of money. Hence, earnings are not reported to the government, and no taxes are paid on them. Many activities in the underground economy are legitimate, such as selling goods on the street or bartering services, but many are illegal, like drug dealing, prostitution, and gambling.

Trying to enumerate the underclass is difficult. More than other classes, those who comprise this stratum are apt to slip through the cracks of census counts. The underclass resides mostly in inner-city ghettos that characterize almost all large U.S. cities. This, by itself, serves as an effective isolating mechanism. Some of these areas are treated as "no-go zones" by all but those who have obligations to enter them, like police or social workers. People living in concentrated ghettos are not likely to talk to census takers or to fill out census forms. Also, since they are not active in the mainstream labor market, they do not earn enough to pay income taxes; hence, there are no IRS statistics on this group, as there are for other classes. Their numbers, to all intents and purposes, can only be guessed at.

Because the underclass is confined mainly to ghetto neighborhoods of urban areas, it has been seen as essentially a black population, though its racial and ethnic composition is varied. Nonetheless, it is true that the underclass in American society today is disproportionately African American.

The urban ghettos in which the underclass is found have been chronicled widely by social scientists and journalists (Kotlowitz, 1991; Kozol, 1995; Wilson, 1987, 1996). In a real sense, those who make up this part of the poverty population constitute "a separate America" in that they are virtually detached from the remainder of the U.S. population. Moreover, the conditions of life in these areas are so alien to the more affluent neighborhoods and suburbs that surround them that they could just as well exist on another continent. Consider Wards 8 and 3, two neighborhoods of Washington, D.C., only a few miles apart. Ward 8, in the city's southeast area, is a largely black area where the median household income is a little more than $21,000. One-quarter of all households in this neighborhood are below the poverty line, and only 8 percent of adult residents are college graduates. In Ward 3, a largely white area in the northwest corner of the city, the median household income is $49,000. Here only 6 percent are below the poverty level, and 70 percent of adults have four or more years of college. But the differences in income and education are only part of the story, for these class differences translate into shockingly contrasting social conditions. In Ward 8, only 26 percent of children are living in two-parent homes and most are born out-of-wedlock; but in Ward 3, 84 percent of children—few of them born out-of-wedlock—are living with both parents. Moreover, the rate of violent crime in Ward 8 is over thirteen times higher than in Ward 3 (Clines, 1996; Terry and De Witt, 1996). Nothing better illustrates the growing bifurcation of the class system in the United States today than comparisons such as these, juxtaposing those in urban areas who are relatively well-off with those who are in a constant struggle for survival.

The Underclass Debate   Sociological debate has arisen in recent years regarding the underclass. Some contend that the chronically poor are behaviorally flawed, maintaining a degraded and dysfunctional lifestyle, and that this is the major cause of their condition. Lawrence Mead, for example, defines the underclass as "a disorganized group unable to get ahead because of a lack not so much of opportunity as of personal organization" (1992:29). Only by adopting mainstream norms and values, therefore, can they hope to alter their predicament.

Others hold that the condition of the underclass is the result of structural forces outside their control. The most critical of these is the basically restructured urban economy, creating an exodus of jobs and industry from inner cities (Wilson, 1987, 1996). This has left the urban underclass a redundant population whose labor is no longer needed. Without jobs, a panoply of attendant social problems—drugs, crime, welfare dependency, out-of-wedlock childbirth, and so on—has arisen. In this view, only through the restoration of jobs with livable wages can the underclass be expected to advance out of its current state.

The debate, then, boils down to a view of the underclass as either cultural or structural in its formation and continuation. In the cultural view, underclass people are not only economically deprived but culturally deficient, their lifestyle and general values antithetical to the mainstream society. In the structural view, members of the underclass are ill equipped in skills and education and thus unable to enter the mainstream workforce; they are victims of a restructured economy. The very term "underclass," in this view, is pejorative (Gans, 1996).[1]

Sociologist Christopher Jencks (1993) points out that much of the controversy swirling around the notion of an underclass stems from the fact that, like most class terms, this one is ambiguous. He suggests that there are at least four ranking schemes, each of which implies a different definition of the underclass: an impoverished underclass, a jobless underclass, an educational underclass, and an underclass that violates middle-class values. Hence, there are significant differences among people within the so-called underclass.

The underclass debate is part of a larger theoretical clash that consists of contrasting views of the causes of poverty in general, which are discussed in more detail in the next section.

Why Are the Poor Poor?

Explanations of poverty, like explanations of inequality in general, differ in several ways. They may focus on individuals or on social structures. They may interpret poverty as inevitable—perhaps even necessary—or as the product of the efforts of the powerful and wealthy to protect their own interests. Let us look at some of these explanations, keeping in mind that, despite their differences, each may contain elements of validity and therefore may offer at least a partial answer to the question of why some people are poor.

Individual-Focused Explanations

In explaining poverty, individual-focused theories stress the personal responsibility of people in determining their place in the social hierarchy.

---

[1]Some favor dispensing with the term "underclass," given its pejorative connotations. Substitute terms, however, like "ghetto poor" suggested by Wilson (1991), seem hardly more flattering. As Morris (1996) has pointed out, the real issue is not terminological but rather whether the underclass is cultural or structural in nature.

These theories fall closely in line with the popular thinking about the poor in America. This is because they complement well the dominant ideology of individualism. The essential idea is that if people are poor, it is mainly because of their own actions or inactions, as well as their personal traits. The source of poverty, in other words, lies with the poor themselves. The two major individual-focused theories emphasize either biological traits or cultural traits.

Biological Explanations   A theory once widely held maintains that people are poor because of inherent deficiencies in their character or mental makeup—that is, they are biologically less "fit" than others. Because they are genetically handicapped, they are bound to be poor.

This biological deterministic explanation was popular earlier in this century and was a basic part of the notion of **social Darwinism.** Some social scientists and commentators held that one's wealth or poverty was a demonstration of one's inherent capabilities. This idea was put forth by those such as British social scientist Herbert Spencer, who asserted that the emergence of the poor, as well as the emergence of an elite at the top of the social hierarchy, was a natural development. Spencer drew an analogy to Darwin's notion of survival of the fittest among animal species. Applying the idea to human societies, Spencer maintained that through a process of free and natural competition, the most able would rise to the top and the least able would sink to the bottom. In this way the social Darwinists rationalized the extreme inequality that typified the newly industrialized societies at the turn of the century, like Britain and the United States.

If the poor were a natural development, so the theory went, there was nothing that could be done to alleviate their condition. Giving assistance to the poor would only extend their inevitable decline. Indeed, the most desirable occurrence would be the rapid extinction of this element of the society. Calls for social welfare programs of one kind or another to help lift the poor from their condition were therefore met with the argument that these were fruitless and wasteful efforts.

Social Darwinism in its most crude form is an idea that no longer holds much weight among social scientists or even the general public. Yet, there are remnants of a genetic explanation for poverty that occasionally surface. In 1994 psychologist Richard J. Herrnstein along with sociologist Charles Murray authored a controversial book, *The Bell Curve,* in which they proffered a theory of poverty that is well within the tradition of social Darwinism. The essence of their position is that IQ is the most significant factor in determining people's place in the social hierarchy. Herrnstein and Murray posit that intelligence, as measured by IQ, is in large part genetic. They see strong relationships between IQ and various social pathologies. Those with lower IQs have a greater proclivity toward poverty, crime, illegitimacy, poor educational performance, and other social ills. Because IQ is mostly genetic, they argue, there is no way to change the condition of those with low intelligence through educational reforms or welfare programs. Because lower-intelligence people are reproducing much faster than higher-intelligence people, the society is faced with the possibility of a growing underclass, increasingly dependent on the more intelligent and productive classes. Herrnstein and Murray hold that such an underclass is apt to remain in a state of dependency on the nonpoor and continue to engage in antisocial activities. Thus, they question the value of welfare payments, remedial educational programs, affirmative action, and other efforts designed to raise the social and economic levels of the poor.

Herrnstein and Murray's arguments have been countered by most mainstream sociologists, who claim that their methods are flawed and their reasoning specious (Fischer et al., 1996; Fraser, 1995; Jacoby and Glauberman, 1995). Moreover, many consider *The Bell Curve* as much a statement of the political leanings of the authors as a work of social science. Specifically, Herrnstein and Murray have been challenged on a number of points: For one, IQ has been shown to measure only certain kinds of intelligence. Furthermore, IQ is not fixed but is subject to variation within one's lifetime and, for groups, subject to change over generations. Perhaps most important, the authors failed to place sufficient weight on the environmental factors that enable people, regardless of IQ, to express their intelligence.

Certainly *individuals* differ in terms of their natural abilities and these differences will affect their socioeconomic positions. But that does not mean that there are differences among *groups* that ultimately determine their position in the social hierarchy. Theoretical views like Herrnstein and Murray's have appeared periodically, but the understanding that environment, not inheritance, is the key influence in shaping social behavior remains the dominant perspective in social science, as it has for many decades.

Public policies often reflect the philosophies and ideologies of those in power at any particular time. The policies of the Reagan administration in the 1980s regarding social welfare and inequality were put forth much in the tradition of social Darwinism. Administration officials believed that the public assistance programs of the 1960s and 1970s were self-defeating and had actually exacerbated poverty. It was suggested that the poor were discouraged from taking responsibility for their condition by welfare that was too generous. The seemingly chronic condition of the underclass was interpreted as the result of government policies that had disinclined people from seeking work and rewarded them for idleness. In 1984, Charles Murray (coauthor of *The Bell Curve*) authored *Losing Ground,* a book that became a primer, of sorts, for Reaganites and conservatives in general on why the poor were poor and why they seemed to stay that way. Murray suggested that programs of the Great Society, begun by the Johnson administration in the 1960s, were responsible for creating the urban underclass. The AFDC (Aid to Families with Dependent Children) program was a prime example, according to Murray. He argued that giving welfare payments to poor mothers only in cases where a male was not residing with the family was a way of encouraging the breakup of poor families and perpetuating their poverty.

The Culture of Poverty   Few today subscribe to biological theories like social Darwinism. A more compelling individual-focused theory, however, is what has been called the **culture of poverty.** Essentially the idea is this: Poverty is the result of a set of norms and values—a culture—that is characteristic of the poor. Because those norms and values are not compatible with the society's dominant culture, its practitioners are unable to function in and adapt to the mainstream. The poor, then, are attuned to a dysfunctional culture. Although poverty is not seen as biologically based, it is nonetheless attributable, in this view, to personal characteristics of the poor.

The idea of a culture of poverty was first put forth in the early 1960s by anthropologist Oscar Lewis, who studied poor families in Mexico City, San Juan, Puerto Rico, and New York City. Lewis lived among these families and concluded that there were basic behavioral traits and attitudes that typified the poor everywhere, which together constituted a coherent "culture of poverty." Some of the key features of this culture, Lewis explained, were a present orientation (rather than the future orientation typical of the middle class), a fatalistic view of the world and one's place in it, a tendency toward female-headed families, authoritarianism within the family, a high rate of abandonment of wives and children, frequent use of violence in settling disputes and in disciplining children, a high rate of alcoholism, a belief in male superiority, and a martyr complex among women (Lewis, 1961, 1965, 1966).

Lewis maintained that these values and behaviors are responses to the conditions of poverty but that in the process they become well-entrenched cultural traits that are passed on from one generation to the next. "By the time slum children are age six or seven," Lewis wrote, "they have usually absorbed the basic values and attitudes of their subculture and are not psychologically geared to take full advantage of changing conditions or increased opportunities which may occur in their lifetime" (1965:xlv). Lewis explained, however, that not all poor people necessarily live in or develop a culture of poverty.

A related view of poverty and the poor is held by political scientist Edward Banfield (1968, 1974). Banfield asserted that the plight of the urban poor was a result of their failure to adopt conforming, specifically middle-class, social values. He focused primarily on the urban black poor, claiming that their situation and their behaviors must be seen not as a product of racial discrimination but as class behavior. European immigrants of earlier decades, he pointed out, were also mostly poor and manifested high crime rates, unstable families, and low school performance, but they eventually assimilated to the dominant culture and improved their economic standing. Poor blacks are therefore simply experiencing the same process of transition to a higher class position. The problems of the urban black poor, in this view, will abate once they are solidly part of the middle class and have embraced middle-class values and lifestyles.

As part of the culture-of-poverty thesis, structural factors and the "accident of birth" may be acknowledged, but these are not seen as unconquerable obstacles. People may not choose to be poor, but through their personal efforts, the road out of poverty is open to them. They need only subscribe to the mainstream culture.

Critics of this cultural explanation of poverty have pointed out that the basic argument blames the poor themselves for being poor. That is, their condition is essentially a product of their failure to adopt middle-class norms and values rather than of a restructured economy or ethnic discrimination (or both) that makes escape from poverty, for most, difficult at best (Ryan, 1975; Valentine, 1971). Moreover, much debate has centered on the culture-of-poverty concept itself. Some sociologists and anthropologists took issue with Lewis's conceptualization of the poor as a "culture." Are the behaviors and values of the poor a culture in the sense of a way of life consciously passed on from one generation to the next, or are these traits simply adaptive mechanisms that would be discarded once the material conditions of poverty were removed (Gans, 1968; Lewis, 1967)? Critics of the culture-of-poverty thesis suggest the latter and contend that its exponents confuse cause and effect.

Structure-Focused Explanations

In contrast to individual-focused theories, structure-focused theories stress factors that lie outside the realm of individual behavior. In this view, it is structural forces stemming from the workings of the major societal institutions that impact on people and contribute to their poverty. Through the accident of birth or through social and economic circumstances over which they have little control, individuals are thrust into poverty with few resources to disengage from that situation. The explanation for poverty, therefore, is found in how the society's institutions, especially the economy and the government, operate so as to either create opportunities or to lodge people in deprived conditions. Structural explanations hold sway among sociologists on issues of poverty.

The Cycle of Poverty   The idea of a **cycle of poverty** is that the array of societal institutions sustains a poverty class through a kind of circular process. When individuals find themselves enveloped by this institutional web, they face daunting obstacles to overcoming their circumstances.

It is primarily within the society's economic institutions that the cycle is most compelling, but the effect extends well beyond the economy into other institutional realms. By definition, the poor are those at the bottom of the class hierarchy. This means that their income, their occupational opportunities, and their educational achievement are all at the lowest levels. These have devastating effects on all aspects of social life. And the effects of low income, occupation, and education operate in a kind of circuit, making it improbable that individuals can break the cycle and either move out of poverty themselves or enable their children to do so.

If we start with education, it is obvious that those with the fewest years and the poorest quality of schooling will take their place at the end of the job queue. As a result of their low educational level, they will have the fewest skills. Thus, they will qualify only for jobs that are the least challenging and that offer no opportunities for advancement. In a word, they are dead-end jobs. Many, of course, will be unable to find even these low-level jobs. Thus, just as low education assures a correspondingly low level of work, the poor jobs assure a low income since these are the jobs that pay minimally. Low income forces people to live in the poorest neighborhoods, where schools are ill equipped and where few highly educated people who might serve as positive role models live. The result is a disincentive for children to value education and a tendency to drop out of school. The cycle, then, is complete: Low education leads to low occupational level, which leads to low income, which leads, in the succeeding generation, back to low education.

This is a cycle that operates perpetually. Unless a breakout can occur at some point by having a family member acquire more and better education or earn a more substantial income, nothing will change. It is a kind of catch-22: Without more income, one cannot acquire more education, but without more education, one cannot acquire more income. Moreover, the same cycle will ensnare the children. Unless they can be afforded more education, the likelihood that family poverty will be sustained in their generation is very great.

At various points in this cycle, other aspects of social life such as health care, housing, and criminal justice are affected, which reinforces the negative effects of low income and education. Take housing, for example. Where people live, that is, their neighborhood or community, usually determines the quality of schooling they receive. Suburban communities in which middle- or upper-middle-class families reside will be able to support their schools more amply than poor inner-city neighborhoods. Thus, moving poor families to more affluent areas might result in breaking the cycle of poverty for many. But poor families are prevented from moving to these areas mainly because they cannot afford the price of housing.

In addition, the effects of racial and class discrimination further reduce the opportunities to move out of impoverished neighborhoods with inferior schools. Efforts to build public housing—occupied mainly by the poor—in suburban communities are almost always resisted strongly by the residents of those communities and by the politicians who represent them, for fear of the infestation of crime, drugs, and other social pathologies that, they assume, will follow. The poor, then, are confined to self-contained communities not only by their place in the economic structure but also by political action and by social discrimination.

The Political Economy of Capitalism   A second structural theory focuses on the uneven economic development that results from capitalism. As a capitalist system works, business enterprises seek to maximize their profits. This is true whether the enterprise is as massive as General Motors or as diminutive as Harry's Hot Dog Stand. In the United States and other industrialized societies, it is large corporations that are the major capitalist enterprises. It is they who control the rate of economic development in communities because it is they who create jobs and generate economic activity generally. Through their decisions, the fate of workers is largely determined. Given the capitalist principle of profit maximization, these firms will move their capital, and thus employment opportunities, from location to location as their interests dictate. If a manufacturing firm located in community X can secure its labor more cheaply in community Y, it will be inclined to move its production facilities to community Y. In the process of such corporate decisions, some communities win and others lose. This capitalist rationale is not limited to local communities within a particular country but is extended beyond national borders. Thus, if workers in Milwaukee lose their jobs because of cheaper wages in Mexico, workers in Mexico will be the temporary beneficiaries of this flow of capital. But if workers in Malaysia can perform the same tasks at an even cheaper wage, then Mexican jobs may begin to flow to that country.

Deindustrialization is a term that has been used to describe the flight of capital and industrial jobs from communities where they have been traditionally located. Many cities in the U.S. Northeast and Midwest have been especially impacted by this shift in recent decades (Bluestone and Harrison, 1982). As a result, many communities have been left with few, if any, jobs for workers who are unskilled and poorly educated. Between 1967 and 1987, Philadelphia, for example, lost 64 percent of all its manufacturing jobs (Kasarda, 1995). Similar losses were experienced by other industrial cities like Chicago and Detroit. Neighborhoods and communities dependent on those jobs are transformed into blighted areas, where much of the population is unemployed and welfare-dependent. As businesses and middle-class residents leave, they take with them their wealth and the taxes they pay to support public services, such as police, transportation, and schools. Those left behind are the poor who are not economically capable of moving but who now live in a community that is deteriorating. The lack of jobs, and thus income, leads to an even lower tax base and further deterioration.

Sociologist William J. Wilson (1987, 1996) has been the most influential exponent of this explanation of the poor in America, specifically the urban poor who are trapped in inner-city ghettos. As he explains, changes in the society's economic structure have made lower-class, unskilled people an excess labor force that is becoming a permanent underclass. The labor market today calls for jobs requiring technical and educational skills, for which such persons cannot qualify. Moreover, industry has moved to areas on the urban

fringe so that those low-level jobs still available are outside t
central-city residents. The result is a semipermanent state of une
The lack of job opportunities creates a vicious circle in which
forced to remain in inner-city ghettos, attending inferior schools and ᴜᴏ.
reinforcing their disadvantaged position in the labor market. Wilson further
explains that the problems of the urban underclass—high rates of joblessness, school dropouts, crime, teenage motherhood, and so on—have been
exacerbated by the exodus of middle- and working-class families from
ghetto neighborhoods, removing vital role models and a support system of
basic institutions.

Poverty as "Functional" Sociologist Herbert Gans has suggested that poverty
can be explained as a social phenomenon that serves certain societal functions.
That is, it is beneficial to some elements of the society, namely the nonpoor, and
thus it endures so long as it serves those purposes.

Gans explains that it is particularly those who are labeled the **undeserving poor** who are used by the nonpoor. The "undeserving poor" are those
who appear to be able-bodied but who are unemployed and who are receiving welfare benefits of one kind or another. Gans explains that labeling some
of the poor "undeserving" creates a number of positive functions for those
who are not poor, or, at least, for some groups and institutions. These functions are unintended and unrecognized, but nonetheless they serve to benefit the nonpoor in some fashion.[2]

The undeserving poor, for example, can be used as ideal scapegoats and
thus "blamed for virtually any shortcoming of everyday life which can be
credibly ascribed to them" (Gans, 1994:274). The undeserving poor also
serve as suppliers of illegal goods—drugs, for example—to the nonpoor.
They create jobs for many in the better-off population, such as social workers who attend to them, police and others in the criminal justice system
who deal with them, and even social scientists who study them. Moreover,
the undeserving poor contribute to the reinforcement of mainstream
norms and values: "If the undeserving poor can be imagined to be lazy,
they help to reaffirm the Protestant work ethic; if poor single-parent families are publicly condemned, the two-parent family is once more legiti-
mated as ideal" (276).

What can be seen in this explanation is a focus away from individuals
themselves and upon the social institutions that give support to poverty and,
in some ways, are actually dependent on it. Eliminating poverty, in this view,
would require that poverty become dysfunctional for the people who most
benefit from it: the affluent and powerful (Gans, 1971).

---

[2]Gans is among those who feel that the term "underclass" has been used pejoratively to describe
the undeserving poor. He sees it as a term applied not simply to those who are chronically poor
and unemployed but also to those who choose not to work or to engage in crime and thus do not
deserve public aid.

Popular Views of Poverty

Although few laypersons think of poverty in systematic and formal terms as sociologists do, almost all have some explanation, simple though it may be, for why people are poor and why so few seem to rise from that position. In general, the prevailing public view of poverty is that it is largely self-imposed—that is, it is mostly the fault of the poor themselves. In terms of the theories we have considered, it is the individual-focused explanations that seem most persuasive to the American public. Structural factors—the changing economy, lack of jobs, poor educational opportunities, and so on—are not discounted, but they are secondary to individual shortcomings. This stress on individualism has basically shaped government policies toward the poor. There is little disagreement regarding the belief that the needy should be helped. However, the belief is equally strong that if they are able, they must first make efforts to help themselves. Surveys have confirmed repeatedly this individualistic view of poverty in America (Davis and Smith, 1994; Kluegel and Smith, 1986).

Surprisingly, even the poor themselves are not in sharp disagreement with the dominant view. Wilson, in his study of Chicago's inner-city poor, found that a substantial majority agreed with the idea that opportunities are plentiful and that people are rewarded on the basis of their efforts. Typical were the observations of one poverty-area resident: "Life is what you make it. . . . If you want something from life you have to go for it. Everybody can go for it, you see, but there's nobody that's gonna give you somethin' for nothin': you gotta work for what you want" (1996:180).

A basic premise of the dominant American ideology is that opportunities are unlimited. If people want to work, they can work. No one need be in a situation of helplessness and dependency if they simply make the effort to better themselves. So, as the ideology explains it, people get what they deserve, and in the case of the poor, they merit their poverty. More precisely, however, Americans tend to separate what they see as the **deserving poor** from the "undeserving" poor. The former are those who are poor through no apparent fault of their own: the disabled, the elderly, widows, children, and those who work steadily but do not earn enough. The undeserving, on the other hand, are people who lack ambition, are irresponsible, are morally weak, and so on. These are men and women who "should" work regularly but don't, and who are poor as a result (Jencks, 1993).

Public Policies and Poverty

All societies in the modern world acknowledge that poverty is a public issue and that efforts should be made to ameliorate the plight of the poor. But as to the strategies for attaining the agreed-upon societal objective of minimizing poverty, there is wide disagreement among policymakers, social scientists, and the general public.

As a public issue, poverty is also a political issue. Thus, people of varying political persuasions will respond to poverty and the poor in different ways. At one extreme are those who would leave the plight of the poor to the market, essentially removing government entirely from the picture. This is almost always a minority view, however. Even those who are political conservatives recognize that the existence of poverty impedes the smooth functioning of the society and its economy. It is beneficial to aid the poor in some fashion, therefore, if only to assure that the poor do not upset the peace and security of the nonpoor. Conservatives, however, do not look kindly on ambitious programs aimed at succoring the poor.

At the other end of the political spectrum are those who see the desirability of government playing a major role. For them, an advanced welfare state offering the indigent maximum assistance is the proper objective. This, too, appears to be a minority view among citizens of most industrialized societies. Even those who strongly favor public assistance recognize its limits and insist that the poor make at least some efforts to help themselves.

Public policy issues regarding poverty evoke the societal values of liberty and equity and the balance between them. Those favoring the liberty side of the equation contend that people should be free to rise or fall on their own efforts. For them, the market naturally and fairly sifts out society's winners and losers. On the other side, those who favor equity insist that all members of society are part of a community, and as such, it is the social obligation of the "haves" to make sure that the "have-nots" receive their share of the society's wealth. In this view, there should not be gaping disparities between rich and poor; rather, economic differences, ideally, should be minimized. The difference in the two views, then, boils down to a vision of the good society as one in which either equality of *opportunity* or equality of *condition* is the proper goal. The problem, then, is finding the acceptable equation between these two ideals.

Welfare Programs

Social welfare in the United States consists of a broad variety of programs designed to assist people in need. Some are basically **social insurance programs,** like Social Security and Medicare, and are financed through payroll taxes. All people in the society regardless of their economic status are the beneficiaries of these programs. Others are what are called **public assistance programs** and are financed through general government revenues. They are "means-tested," requiring that recipients demonstrate a need in order to qualify for them. It is the public assistance programs that constitute what most people think of as "welfare."[3] Until 1996, four programs made up the bulk of public assistance: AFDC (Aid to Families with Dependent Children), SSI (Supplemental Security Income), Food Stamps, and Medicaid.

---

[3]In Chapter 7 we return to the issue of welfare and examine its different forms. Here the focus is specifically on public assistance programs designed to ameliorate poverty.

AFDC had been the most expensive of these programs and also the most controversial. Indeed, few government programs have been as thoroughly vilified. For several decades, this had been the primary family assistance program of the federal government. Originally enacted during the Great Depression of the 1930s, it was designed to provide temporary assistance to families who had suffered the loss of a parent, particularly through death or incapacitation of a father or mother. By the 1960s, however, its recipients had become mostly young unmarried women with children; in 1993, it was helping to support 5 million single-parent families. As a result, AFDC became the special target of those who strongly opposed the welfare system as it had traditionally functioned. It was a symbol for all of the negative assumptions made about public assistance programs and had come to represent "welfare" in the minds of Americans.

Opponents of AFDC assumed that the program was the cause of high rates of illegitimacy. Young mothers were having children, they believed, in order to collect more welfare. AFDC, then, perfectly represented the cause of the "culture of dependency" that had formed around welfare recipients. Another common belief regarding welfare was that most of its recipients were permanently welfare-dependent, unable or unwilling to ever assume financial responsibility for themselves. Welfare was also seen in racial terms, the assumption being that it was benefiting primarily blacks. Finally, popular views of welfare assumed that payments were generous, providing recipients with luxuries at taxpayers' expense.

In fact, most of the assumptions regarding AFDC and welfare programs generally were faulty. Studies found that most teenage pregnancies were unintended and that families receiving welfare were, on average, no larger than most. Sociologists pointed out the lack of evidence to support the belief that welfare causes illegitimacy and single parenthood, noting that the rate of single motherhood in western European countries was lower than in the United States despite their far more generous welfare programs (Sandefur, 1996; Sidel, 1996). Also, single motherhood had increased throughout the 1980s and early 1990s despite the fact that AFDC benefits had declined. Furthermore, single motherhood had grown among *all* social classes, not only the poor. Regarding the permanency of welfare, research showed that most recipients did not stay dependent but drifted in and out of welfare as they drifted in and out of the workforce (Wilson, 1996). As to the racial connotations of welfare, more whites than blacks were the recipients of public assistance (including AFDC), though blacks did represent a disproportionately large percentage. Less than 10 percent of whites were receiving some form of welfare, compared to one-third of blacks. Finally, to assume that families could live comfortably on welfare was a gross exaggeration. AFDC payments varied from state to state, but in 1993 the average monthly payment was $377. Even with the addition of other forms of public assistance, total payments were hardly sufficient to push recipients above the poverty line. Furthermore, until it was abolished in 1996, the benefits provided by AFDC had dropped consistently for the previous twenty years.

Welfare Reform   Despite misunderstandings of welfare and misperceptions of its recipients, the federal welfare changes enacted in 1996 seemed motivated primarily by these popular assumptions. The welfare system had come to be seen as a giant bureaucracy providing assistance but not demonstrating the capacity to actually lift people into a productive life in the mainstream economy. Recipients, therefore, were portrayed as welfare-dependent and the system as broken and ineffective. The prevailing view had come to be that simply being poor should not automatically entitle an individual or family to public assistance. In the 1990s, spurred by an unusually conservative U.S. Congress, political support was strong enough to, as it was popularly expressed, "change welfare as we know it." These changes in the welfare system represented a fundamental shift in government policy.

Chief among the basic changes in the welfare system contained in the 1996 legislation was a mandate that welfare recipients be working if they are able-bodied. Failure to work within two years after the start of receiving welfare would result in a loss of benefits. In no case, however, were families to receive welfare benefits for longer than five years. Under the legislation, the federal government agreed to give to individual states block grants that they could then use to shape their own welfare programs. Thus, each state now had the power to tailor its welfare program as it saw fit, providing state-specific requirements for people to qualify and varying levels of benefits. To encourage states to implement programs that put welfare recipients to work, the legislation provided that in order to receive federal money, states must ensure that half of all adults receiving welfare would be working by the year 2002.

The revised welfare rules evoked mixed reactions from policymakers and social scientists. Although some believed that they would vault the chronically poor into the mainstream labor market and impose more personal responsibility, others contended that they would impose even further hardship on needy families. What do we know of the results of the 1996 welfare reform measures?

Because the new requirements have been in place only a few years, there is not yet a solid data base from which to draw hard conclusions about their long-term effects. A few trends, however, are clear. First, there is no debate regarding the fact that the number of people on welfare has declined sharply. Whereas 5.1 million families were receiving welfare in 1994, less than half that number were still on the welfare rolls in 2000 (Pear, 2000). Second, as the reform measures intended, many former recipients have been placed in the workforce. The first to leave the rolls were those with the most job skills, but even many with limited skills were able to find jobs in the surging economy of the late 1990s.

Despite these apparent successes, a number of problems have been brought to light by the new system, leaving some basic issues in dispute. The key question is whether welfare reform has led to a decline in poverty, not simply a reduction of the welfare rolls. Although millions of former welfare recipients have found work, it appears that most have been unable to earn wages sufficient to boost them above the poverty level. In Wisconsin, for example, after a year in the workforce, only 36 percent of former welfare recipients were earning more than they had received while on welfare. Only a quarter had lifted themselves above the poverty line (DeParle, 1999). In Florida, a survey of former welfare recipients reported that over 40 percent could not, at some point, put food on the table (Yearwood, 1999). A national study of mothers who had left welfare found that they were entering the low end of the labor market, working in much the same circumstances as low-income mothers who had not been on welfare (Loprest, 1999). Another study of poor single-mother families found that their income actually declined after changes in the welfare system took effect, despite the strong growth in the economy. The reduced benefits exceeded increases in earnings, thus causing these families to lose ground (Primus et al., 1999).

Another problem stems from the fact that not all who have been taken off the welfare rolls have blended into the mainstream labor force. Some stripped of welfare may simply have been thrust into an even more desperate and helpless state, as many critics of the new welfare measures feared. Some may be working only part-time, while others may have found employment in the underground economy. Moreover, an increasing number of those who remain on the welfare rolls are children whose parents do not quality for public assistance and in many cases are being raised by grandparents or other relatives (Vobejda and Havemann, 1999). For them, programs aimed at getting people into the workforce are meaningless.

In sum, welfare reform may have succeeded in reducing the welfare rolls, but it is not evident that it has reduced poverty (Lerman, 1999; Stoesz, 1999). The responsibility for welfare has been shifted largely to the states, which have handled reform in a variety of ways. Some have set up programs such as child care, wage supplements, and tuition for job training and education. The emphasis in most, however, has been on reducing case loads, not in placing people in jobs that pay a living wage and offer long-range opportunities. Accomplishing that goal entails providing the poor with hard skills as well as a combination of other forms of assistance like child care, expanded income tax credits, and a higher minimum wage. Moreover, addressing the issue of poverty must take into account the fact that the poor are not a homogeneous collectivity. Some are in need of only a slight push to boost them into the ranks of the working class or even lower-middle class. Others need more assistance, and still others may be incapable of ever competing independently in the job market. For those in this latter group, it is questionable whether they can overcome a lack of social skills (what sociologists sometimes refer to as "cultural capital") and prolonged separation from the worlds of education and work to make a successful transition into the mainstream labor force (Havemann, 1996).

The debate continues regarding which approach to welfare reform is likely to be most effective. Some emphasize that getting people into the occupational world, regardless of the type of job or its pay, is more important than providing education and job training (Mead, 1996). "Forcing welfare parents to get even modest jobs can contribute to giving new hope and motivation to their children," notes economist Gary Becker (1996:22). Others, however, stress that without developing skills, it is unlikely that people can earn enough to significantly affect their economic status and enable them to escape the conditions of dependency. As sociologist Christopher Jencks has put it, the essence of the welfare trap is not that it makes people pathologically dependent but that "although welfare pays badly, low-wage jobs pay even worse" (1993:225).

The arguments on either side of this debate hinge on the creation of jobs. Unless there are decent-paying, long-term jobs into which those who have been receiving welfare up to now can be placed, the debate about how to get them into the workforce is not meaningful. As noted earlier, this is an issue on which government policymakers can have only a limited impact, since it is within the private sector that the creation of most jobs occurs. In the robust economy of the past several years, placing many former welfare recipients in low-level jobs has been relatively easy because of high labor demand. It is not at all certain, however, whether many of these jobs will survive an economic downturn. The great test of welfare reform will come when the economy slows and jobs are not so plentiful.

Public Views of Welfare   Even before the 1990s, welfare for the poor had always been controversial in the United States. Moreover, as a society more thoroughly committed to a laissez-faire style of capitalism, welfare seemed to be at odds with individualistic values. Given the American ideology's emphasis on self-reliance, those who are able-bodied but who are not employed are seen not as the victims of structural economic and social changes but as individual failures. The same is true of those who find themselves as single mothers. Their plight, in this view, is their own doing, and therefore they do not merit taxpayers' assistance.

Americans, however, are not consistent regarding welfare. Although most evince a strong distaste for it in any form, most also recognize the social responsibility for caring for those who are unable to provide for themselves. But public opinion polls indicate an even stronger belief that adults who are able to work should be required to do so to earn welfare. Mead argues that it is the willingness to work that, in the public mind, basically separates the "deserving" from the "non-deserving" poor (Mead, 1992).

Although welfare has been the focus of most public policies in attempting to deal with the issues of poverty, alternative strategies have been suggested. One that has been given some prominence in recent years is the idea of reestablishing a public works program, similar to the Works Projects Administration (WPA) and the Civilian Conservation Corps (CCC) introduced by President Franklin D. Roosevelt in the 1930s when almost a quarter of the entire workforce was unemployed. The WPA put people to work building thousands of projects, such as roads, bridges, schools, post offices, and other public facilities. Those who have proposed bringing back something like the WPA contend that such a program would get people out of socially isolated environments, would instill a work ethic, and would possibly give them some occupational skills. At the same time, the entire society would benefit from the improvements such an agency would make on an American infrastructure in serious disrepair (Kaus, 1995; Wilson, 1996).[4]

Poverty in Comparative Perspective

How does the United States stand in comparison with other societies in its rate of poverty and in the level of living of its poor?[5] Using an absolute definition, it is clear that there are fewer poor in the United States than in most other societies. There is a destitute population of homeless people that can be found in almost all large American cities and the conditions of the underclass are indisputably wretched. But such groups represent only a small proportion of the general population. In short, a smaller percentage of Americans lack sufficient food and shelter to maintain their lives than do people in much of the rest of the world. Consider the conditions of life in the Democratic Republic of Congo (formerly Zaire), for example, a country of 45 million in east central Africa. In Kinshasa, the capital, 60 percent of working-age people are thought to be unemployed. Thousands scavenge garbage dumps in search of food that will keep them alive another day. As one resident describes her family's plight, "I wake up every morning not knowing what we will eat that day" (French, 1996).

    Defining poverty in a relative fashion, however, gives us a different perspective. Comparing American poverty with poverty in a developing society like Congo is hardly meaningful in light of the very different social and economic resources of the two countries. A more valid comparison, therefore, would be the United States with other societies of approximately similar economic and social development, that is, other First World, or highly advanced, societies. As noted in Chapter 2, the United States today exhibits the most un-

---

[4]Unintentionally, welfare reform may have a negative impact on the working poor. Welfare recipients, now required to work, are doing jobs ordinarily done by low-wage workers not on welfare—the working poor. This may result in the displacement of many of the working poor and, with more low-skilled people in the labor market, may hold down wages (Uchitelle, 1997).

[5]Here it should be reemphasized that comparing class systems, especially particular parts of those systems—such as the poor—is not without problems. Standards of living are not the same from one society to another, and cultural systems dictate different ways of dealing with inequality. Moreover, definitions of poverty may vary from society to society.

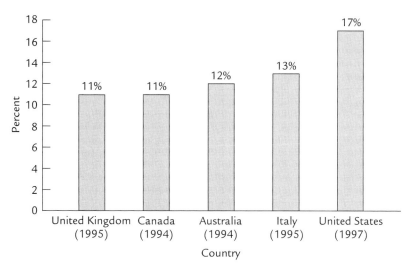

Figure 3-2 ■ Percentage Living below Poverty Line*
*Because poverty is defined somewhat differently from one society to another, a uniform poverty line for these five societies was set at 50 percent of equivalent median disposable household income.
Source: United Nations Development Programme (UNDP). *Human Development Report 2000* (New York: Oxford University Press, 2000).

equal distribution of income and wealth among advanced industrial societies. The rate of American poverty is consistent with that finding. Comparative rates of poverty are shown in Figure 3-2.

Not only is the rate of poverty higher than in other advanced industrial societies, but the extent of poverty is more severe. A study that compared children in eighteen highly developed countries found that childhood poverty is worse in the United States than in all but two (Figure 3-3). The study attributed the lower American standing to an appreciably wider gap between rich and poor, as well as to the United States' more miserly welfare programs. What is seen in Figure 3-3 is that rich families in the United States were the richest and poor American families were the poorest except for those in Ireland and Israel. The average income in 1991 for an affluent family of four was $65,536, whereas it was $10,923 for a poor family of four. The difference between the two—$54,613—was considerably greater than between rich and poor in any of the other seventeen countries. These findings belie the notion that the poor in the United States are better off than the poor of other countries. While that assumption may be true in comparison with underdeveloped societies, it is plainly not the case when the United States is placed beside countries with comparable standards of living.

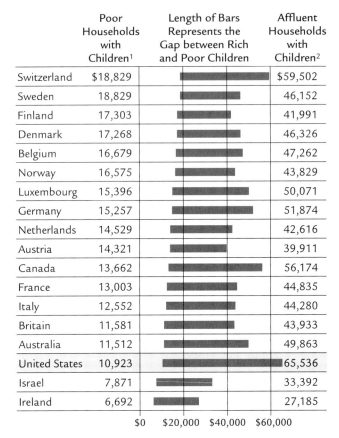

	Poor Households with Children[1]	Length of Bars Represents the Gap between Rich and Poor Children	Affluent Households with Children[2]
Switzerland	$18,829		$59,502
Sweden	18,829		46,152
Finland	17,303		41,991
Denmark	17,268		46,326
Belgium	16,679		47,262
Norway	16,575		43,829
Luxembourg	15,396		50,071
Germany	15,257		51,874
Netherlands	14,529		42,616
Austria	14,321		39,911
Canada	13,662		56,174
France	13,003		44,835
Italy	12,552		44,280
Britain	11,581		43,933
Australia	11,512		49,863
United States	10,923		65,536
Israel	7,871		33,392
Ireland	6,692		27,185

$0 $20,000 $40,000 $60,000

[1] After-tax income, including government benefits like food stamps or the Earned Income Tax Credit, for a family of four that includes children and that is poorer than 90 percent of the households in the country and more affluent than 10 percent of the households.

[2] After-tax income, including any government benefits, for a family of four that includes children and that is more affluent than 90 percent of the households in the country and poorer than 10 percent of the households.

Figure 3-3 ■ The Gap between Rich and Poor Children
Source: Data from Luxembourg Income Study, art from *New York Times* (August 14, 1995), A7.
Copyright © 1995 *The New York Times*. Reprinted by permission.

The approach to solving problems of poverty also is markedly different in most western European countries than in the United States. The welfare states of those countries are far more comprehensive and generous and thus provide a much broader and deeper safety net for those who are economically in need. For example, among advanced industrial societies, only the United States has no universal preschool, child-support, or parental-leave programs. This places poor children in the United States at an almost automatic disadvantage in their educational quest and puts onerous burdens on single mothers who must work while raising their families. Economist Lester

Thurow (1999) has explained that for the United States to eradicate poverty would be an accomplishment that the most advanced societies in the world (Scandinavia, Germany, Japan) have already achieved. Americans have simply failed to adopt public policies that would lead to a similar outcome.[6]

Comparing the problem of poverty in the United States with that of other industrialized countries is important, for it broadens our perspective and forces us to dismiss assumptions of equality that are often based more on ideology than reality. Those assumptions often blind us to the number of poor in our midst and to the severity of their condition. If we ourselves are not among the poor, in many ways we can lose sight of their presence or simply choose to ignore them, going about our daily lives confined to our immediate social environments. Moreover, poverty is more than an economic condition. For the poor it is also a social condition that creates a stigma and a psychological state that erect further barriers separating them from the remainder of the population. Paradoxically, then, only by looking at American poverty in comparison with other societies can we begin to more fully perceive and, ultimately, understand its character and dimensions.

Summary

Poverty may be conceptualized in three ways. In absolute terms, it is a condition in which people are unable, for whatever reason, to meet their fundamental human needs. Relative poverty means that poverty is contextual, subject to different standards as societal conditions change. Official poverty is the government-defined measure delineating the poor.

About 13 percent of the U.S. population falls below the official poverty line. Disproportionately, the American poor are found among racial and ethnic minorities, females, young people, and those living as part of female-headed families. The poverty rate has fluctuated over the past four decades, dropping in the late 1960s and early 1970s but climbing again in the 1980s with no significant subsequent decline until the late 1990s.

The poor may be divided into two relatively distinct components: the working poor and the underclass. The former ordinarily work but do not earn sufficient wages to lift them over the poverty line; the latter are chronically unemployed and socially isolated. Much debate has centered on those who constitute the underclass. Some see them as culturally deficient and, in large measure, victims of their own behavior; others view them as the victims of structural changes in the economy.

Individual-focused and structure-focused theories offer varying explanations of why the poor are poor. Among the former are biological theories,

---

[6]Mayer (1995) suggests that the American poor may not be worse off compared to the poor of other advanced industrial societies if living conditions, rather than income, are used as a measuring rod.

such as social Darwinism, and the culture of poverty. These attribute poverty to the actions and values of the poor themselves. Structure-focused theories include the cycle of poverty, the political economy of capitalism, and the functions of poverty. These posit the workings of the economy and other institutions as the sources of poverty.

Measures aimed at alleviating poverty have been standard public policies in all modern societies. There is wide disagreement, however, regarding the strategies for dealing with issues of the poor. In the United States, public assistance programs have traditionally constituted what most people think of as "welfare" for those in poverty. Though never as extensive as popularly believed, most of the major public assistance programs have been radically reformed in recent years, resulting in major cutbacks.

Comparisons with other advanced industrial societies reveal that the U.S. poverty rate is higher and the gap between rich and poor is wider in the United States. Other countries also provide a broader and deeper safety net for those who are economically in need.

4

The Middle Classes and the Changing Economy

The most perfect political community is one in which the middle class is in control and out-numbers both of the other classes.
ARISTOTLE

The general feeling in America is that you are middle class if you say so.
ALAN WOLFE

"America is a middle-class society." Countless chroniclers of U.S. society have made that observation almost from its very founding. The middle-class nature of American society is both an objective fact and a subjective mood. As to the former, most people are neither at the top of the class hierarchy nor at the bottom. Three-fifths of American families have incomes between $23,000 and $88,000. While this certainly represents a broad range, it is a range whose components are clearly separated from the top 10 percent who own most of the society's wealth and the poor, who hover below or near the poverty line. In an economic sense, then, it is quite accurate to describe the United States as a society in which most people are "in the middle."

But the middle-class idea is also a state of mind; it is how people see themselves, regardless of their actual economic position, and it is reflected in their attitudes and values. The level of class consciousness in the United States is markedly lower than in most other contemporary societies. National surveys for many decades have consistently shown that almost all Americans, when asked to classify themselves in the stratification system, almost reflexively answer "working class" or, more commonly, "middle-class" (Heath, 1998). Even those of very low or high income tend to identify as part of the great American middle. As one observer of the middle class has put it, "The widely perceived class *un*consciousness of the American people is a consequence of a class psychology characteristic not only of actual members of the middle class but of aspirants to that status, and overall, therefore, of the great majority of the nation" (Baritz, 1982:xii).

It is important to understand that there is no cohesive middle class, as such, but rather several classes that constitute neither the rich at the top nor the poor at the bottom. As described in Chapter 2, the classes in the middle consist of at least three specific categories—the upper-middle class, the lower-middle class, and the working class.

It seems logical to analyze these intermediate classes together for several reasons. First, despite the significant differences among the three in income, occupation, education, and lifestyle, they are all clearly set apart from those at the top and bottom of the American class hierarchy. The very affluent and the decision-making elite are, in both financial and lifestyle terms, far distant from other classes. And by the same token, those at the other end of the hierarchy, especially the underclass, are equally divorced from the mainstream. This leaves the "classes in the middle" or the "intermediate classes" as the bulk of the American population.

It is also the case that most of the mobility that occurs in the class system occurs within and between the units of this middle range. Rare are the rags-to-riches cases, with individuals moving from the bottom of the class system to the top. The most common forms of mobility are short-range, incremental moves that occur mostly within the working, lower-middle, and upper-middle classes.

Finally, and perhaps most important, the American economy has been restructured in the past three decades with the emergence of a global economic system. It is the classes in the middle that have been most seriously affected by that process.

Historical Development of the Middle Classes

Although the classes in the middle are seen as the backbone of American society and other economically developed societies, the emergence of these classes is a historically recent occurrence. Prior to the advent of industrial capitalism, agrarian societies consisted essentially of two classes: the landed aristocracy who controlled most wealth, and the remainder of the populace who worked the land as poor peasants, living in degraded and deprived conditions. As commercial activities and industrial production replaced agriculture as the major economic pursuits, a merchant class, or **bourgeoisie,** gradually replaced the landowners as the most powerful class, and their wealth increased commensurately.

Formation of the Middle Classes in the United States

Nowhere else in the Western world did the middle classes develop as thoroughly and as early as in the United States. Although colonial leaders did constitute an aristocratic elite, an American landed gentry never really existed. There was no sharply divided system of aristocracy and peasantry, which had typified European societies. Hence, it was the classes in the middle, made up of independent farmers and entrepreneurs, that seemed to predominate almost from the outset. As French politician and writer Alexis de

Tocqueville observed in the 1830s, ". . . the social state of America is a very strange phenomenon. Men there are nearer equality in wealth and in mental endowments, or, in other words, more nearly equally powerful, than in any other country of the world or in any other age of recorded history"(1966:49).

From the beginning, farmers, who were the numerically dominant group until the end of the nineteenth century, owned their land. They were joined by small business owners—producers, tradesmen, merchants—who formed another part of the American middle. The most important fact linking farmers and merchants was their possession of property. As owners of their enterprises, they worked for themselves. Moreover, the ownership of property was widespread rather than characteristic of just a small portion of the society. The middle class that arose in the latter eighteenth and early nineteenth centuries, then, was comprised basically of entrepreneurs. This class of entrepreneurs epitomized the American ideology of individualism and free enterprise (Mills, 1951).

Industrialization and the Changing Class Structure

Growth of the Working Class   The predominance of farmers and farm laborers as part of the workforce began to change as the society moved more fully toward industrialization. By the end of the nineteenth century, the shift toward an industrial workforce was clear and irreversible. Automation drove many farmworkers from the land, where their labor was no longer needed. Machines could do the work of men more efficiently and more cheaply. Moreover, the lure of better-paying jobs in factories in the urban areas was very strong, serving as an additional push of workers off the farms. In 1880, 20 man-hours were required to harvest an acre of wheat; by 1916, only 12.7 man-hours were needed; and by 1936, only 6.1 (Rifkin, 1995).[1]

Karl Marx described **capitalism** as a system marked by a social division between those who owned the means of production—the factories and machines of the newly emergent industries—and the workers, whose labor produced the wealth of capitalism but who were dispossessed of power since they were not owners. Marx saw a continuing drop in the standard of living of industrial workers who, he felt, would be increasingly exploited by the capitalists. For many decades, the conditions of industrial Europe and the United States seemed to confirm Marx's dismal picture. The new industrial owners expanded their empires while their workers worked long hours under degraded and often unsafe conditions. Steelworkers employed in the great Carnegie steel mills in western Pennsylvania, for example, labored

---

[1]As Jeremy Rifkin explains, despite the fact that nearly half of all people on earth still farm, we are rapidly moving toward a world without farmers as technological changes in the production of food continue to advance. Consider that one farmworker in 1850 produced enough food to feed four people. Today, one farmer produces enough to feed seventy-eight people.

twelve hours a day, seven days a week, constantly exposed to workplace hazards and debilitating injuries. For their toil, they earned about $10 a week, just above the poverty line of $500 a year. The annual earnings of Andrew Carnegie, by comparison, were the equivalent of the wages of almost four thousand steelworkers (*The American Experience,* 1997).

The New Middle Class   By the 1920s the United States had become a thoroughly industrialized society, and its workforce reflected that transformation. In addition, white-collar jobs, those in the service sector, began to grow with increasing speed. This contributed in great measure to the emergence of a large middle class in the mid–twentieth century. This new middle class was made up mainly of salaried white-collar workers working not for themselves but for employers, often as part of large, bureaucratic organizations. This was a worker's category, the development of which Marx had not anticipated.

The emergence of a large white-collar sector of the labor force was brought about by the increasing concentration of the means of production into fewer and fewer large corporate enterprises. No longer were small, family-owned and -operated firms the dominant form of business. Production and distribution became more complex and national in scope. As a result, smaller firms, with fewer resources, were unable to compete against large corporate enterprises, which were organized in bureaucracies with hundreds, perhaps thousands, of workers occupying highly specific work roles and led by a managerial elite.

Post-Industrialism

Starting in the 1960s, a service economy began to emerge, in which most workers no longer labored in factories but instead provided services of one kind or another. The United States and other advanced industrial nations entered into what has been called post-industrialism (Bell, 1973). Unlike a traditional industrial society, **post-industrial society** is characterized by the production mainly of services and information rather than finished goods. This means that the majority of workers are white-collar rather than blue-collar, and many are professional, managerial, and technical workers. Post-industrial society is driven by knowledge, not so much of a practical kind, as was the case in industrial society, but of a theoretical or abstract nature. Thus, scientists, engineers, and academics play a critical role in maintaining the socioeconomic system.

As service workers became numerically dominant, industrial workers began to decline as a part of the labor force. In 1959, 40 percent of American workers were in the service sector and 60 percent in manufacturing; by 1985, the ratio had reversed itself, with almost three-quarters in the service sector (Newman, 1988). This change was brought about by a shift in consumer patterns. Today, Americans spend more on services, including health care, education, and food service, than on manufactured goods, such as housing, appliances, and automobiles. In 1990, three times more was spent on health and medical care, for example, as was spent thirty years earlier (Farley, 1996). As personal services have become a greater proportion of consumer spending, a correspondingly greater need for service rather than production workers has developed.

The Classes in the Middle and the Occupational Structure

It is not an exaggeration to claim that nothing influences a person's life more than his or her occupation. Occupation not only determines the economic, power, and prestige aspects of social class but generally defines the parameters of a person's social life, cultural style, residential patterns, and consumer preferences. It is also the main cue that others use to view and make judgments about individuals. In looking at the three classes in the middle, perhaps the major distinguishing feature separating them is their different place in the occupational structure.

The Upper-Middle Class

Sometimes referred to as the "new class," the upper-middle class is made up of those who hold the key decision-making positions in various institutions. They are the doctors and lawyers, engineers, technicians and scientists, university professors, media editors and producers, corporate executives, financial managers, high-ranking government bureaucrats, and, at the lower end, schoolteachers who Barbara Ehrenreich (1989) refers to as the "professional middle class."

As Ehrenreich describes them, the two major subgroups of this stratum—professionals and managers—have largely interchangeable skills and often move back and forth from one category to the other. Moreover, the two categories occupy the same part of the social landscape, living in the same neighborhoods, functioning in the same social circles, and intermarrying. Above all, among those of the upper-middle class there is an emphasis on formal education, for themselves and their children, and on the establishment of a stable career leading eventually to a comfortable retirement.

As **white-collar workers,** members of the upper-middle class, like many others in the intermediate strata, do mental work. But they are at a level of power and authority that clearly sets them apart from the other classes. They enjoy much autonomy in their jobs and are able to make independent decisions rather than to respond routinely to the commands of others. Moreover, their jobs require, almost by definition, a college degree, which in itself gives them a higher social standing and presents them with substantial economic advantages.

Common occupational and educational experiences create a lifestyle and a set of consumer preferences that distinguish the upper-middle class from others. For example, professionals and managers at the upper end of this stratum will typically own spacious suburban homes and drive upscale cars. They are apt to dine in restaurants serving trendy cuisine and purchase clothes with carefully chosen designer labels.

Politically, the upper-middle class is characteristically liberal on social issues such as abortion and civil rights but is generally conservative on economic issues of taxation and wages. Those of the upper-middle class are more politically active than other classes. They vote more consistently and are more apt to participate in the electoral process in other ways as well, such as contributing money to political campaigns.

Studies have also shown that the upper-middle class is more active in voluntary associations (Smith, 1980). Moreover, much of the social life of upper-middle-class families is an outgrowth of their occupational lives, and the two are commonly combined. The country club or the dinner party often becomes a setting in which clients are entertained or colleagues consulted.

The Lower-Middle Class

As part of the intermediate strata, the lower-middle class is the most difficult to precisely define since it is made up of so many disparate elements. It is a collection of occupational categories consisting mainly of small business owners and white-collar workers, including middle-level managers in the business world, paraprofessionals (e.g., nurses and legal workers), middle-level government bureaucrats, non–retail sales workers, secretaries and clerks, and medical technicians.

In terms of income, those of the lower-middle class span a broad range, according to specific occupation, but what is common to all is their relative lack of significant wealth. They are dependent primarily on their jobs for income and ordinarily do not own substantial assets aside from their homes.

Workers of the lower-middle class—with the exception of small business owners—exercise little power in their jobs. They ordinarily respond to the authority of managers and professionals of the upper-middle class.

Most within the lower-middle class have more than a high school education, but a college degree is not necessary to meet the qualifications of most of their occupations. Junior college or vocational training may therefore be the more common form of post-secondary schooling in this class. As with the upper-middle class, relatively common incomes and occupational statuses, along with common educational experiences, create a distinct lifestyle for the lower-middle class, along with corresponding consumer preferences.

Those of the lower-middle class are politically active, but not in the same way as the upper-middle class. Participation, though strong and common, does not usually extend much beyond voting. This is quite different from the political activism of the upper-middle class, who are participants at a higher level and who are more directly engaged in the political process.

The Working Class

What has traditionally characterized the working class more than anything else is the nature of its occupational role: **blue-collar work,** that is, work involving manual or physical labor. The skills of the working class, however, vary widely. At the top are skilled tradespeople and craft workers, such as carpenters, electricians, and plumbers. In the middle are those with mechanical skills, who, like most of the working class, work for an hourly wage. Tool-and-die makers, machinists, repair persons, and the like constitute this sector. At the bottom of the working class are those with few or no skills, who perform routine, perfunctory roles in factories or shops. These workers are usually referred to as operatives and constitute the largest element of the working class. Although the working class is still comprised in large part of factory workers at different skill levels, starting around the 1960s, certain economic and technological forces began to emerge that led to a decline—which continues—of blue-collar occupations.

The educational level of the working class is limited by comparison with the lower-middle class and especially with the upper-middle class. Predictably, members of the working class possess little in the way of productive property, ordinarily owning only their homes and cars. Income, however, can vary among the different categories within the working class. Those at the top, the skilled tradespeople, may own their own businesses and thus exhibit some of the characteristics of the lower-middle class. Those at the bottom, the unskilled, may be one short step from the poverty class and may in fact drift in and out of the working-poor category.

The working-class subculture has been the subject of many studies, and the picture that emerges is one in which members marry younger (a result of the fact that education is usually curtailed earlier than among the upper- or lower-middle classes) and families are strongly patriarchal (Sennett and Cobb, 1973; Shostak, 1969). That traditional structure is breaking down, however, as working-class wives are now commonly part of the labor force, contributing their wages to family income. Indeed, like families in the other intermediate classes, working-class families today more often than not consist of two wage earners. As that has occurred, wives have asserted more family power (Rubin, 1994).

The consumer, housing, and leisure patterns of the working class are quite distinct from the other intermediate classes. Although these are often stereotyped and subject to a kind of upper-middle-class ridicule ("Joe Six-Pack," for example), there are identifiable features of the working class that may be said to constitute, roughly, a working-class lifestyle. As part of urban communities, working-class neighborhoods are clearly recognizable, made up of modest single-family dwellings or perhaps mobile homes. Leisure activities are also likely to differ noticeably. Whereas the upper-middle class and, increasingly, the lower-middle class may play golf or tennis, the working class will more often bowl and hunt. Vacations among the working class are not likely to include foreign travel, as vacations frequently do for the upper- and even lower-middle classes, but will more typically consist of excursions in a recreational vehicle.

Work, for the working class, is separated from other spheres of life. Unlike the upper-middle class, where work and leisure are often combined, people "leave the job at work." Rather than realizing much personal fulfillment from one's occupation, as is typically the case among professionals and managers of the upper-middle class, working-class people, particularly the unskilled, ordinarily engage in boring and routine tasks, not those that present personal challenges.

In their politics, working-class people are a kind of mirror image of the upper-middle class: conservative on social issues but liberal on economic issues. Except among union members, however, they tend to be less politically active than either of the other two intermediate classes. Moreover, American working-class people are less politically active than their counterparts in almost all other contemporary industrial societies (Marger, 1987). There is no major socialist or labor party in the United States catering primarily to working-class interests, as there is in most western European societies, as well as Canada and Japan. One explanation of this phenomenon is that American workers are no less committed than classes above them to the idea of individual achievement. And, as has been pointed out many times, workers generally have hopes of eventually establishing their own business and becoming their own boss. Thus, there is little sympathy among them for socialist ideas. There is no gainsaying the capitalist system among workers so long as most see themselves as future capitalists.

The Blurring of Traditional Occupational Categories   Today the blue-collar/white-collar distinction is no longer as meaningful as it once was, and as a result, the division between the lower-middle and working classes is, at times, hazy. It is not at all clear where the lower end of the lower-middle class begins to diverge from the higher end of the working class. Many white-collar jobs that in previous times would have been clearly distinguishable from blue-collar ones have been downgraded in skills and wages.

Some have referred to a "proletarianization" of white-collar workers, implying that there is no longer a significant difference between many blue- and white-collar jobs (Braverman, 1974; Glenn and Feldberg, 1977; Judis, 1994). White-collar jobs at the lower status levels have been deskilled, that is, reduced to repetitive, routine tasks that involve little brainpower. Consider a cashier in a fast-food restaurant or a department store. Little more is involved than taking the customer's money, punching a few keys on a computer-connected cash register, and giving customers their change. Cashiers needn't even calculate the change since the cash register will do it for them. These routine tasks are not essentially different from unskilled blue-collar jobs, where workers perform a simple function repeatedly. Bank tellers are another illustration of deskilling—in handling commercial transactions today, they do little more than operate computer keyboards, entering a few items of information. Indeed, machines have brought bank tellers to the point of eventual extinction. Consider that their numbers dropped by 41,000 between 1985 and 1995, and that most of those who remained were converted to part-time positions. The first ATM (automatic teller machine) was installed at a bank in 1971; by 1995, almost 10 billion transactions were processed at 123,000 ATMs (Morisi, 1996).

At the same time, the rise of a category of technicians has further blurred the distinction between white- and blue-collar workers. As Robert Reich (1994) describes them, "These workers often wear ties or dresses (as did their white-collar predecessors). But they also often work with their hands, use tools and monitor machinery (as did their blue-collar predecessors)." These are the people who design and test computer systems, repair copy machines, operate hospital equipment, and so on. In fact, as the nature of blue-collar jobs shifts toward the service sector, an increasing number of people with college experience are filling them. In 1985, about 17 percent of factory workers had some college training; by 1995, that figure had risen to 25 percent, and almost 20 percent of factory workers had college degrees (Baker, 1996; Hershey, 1997; Holusha, 1995).

As Herbert Gans (1988) has pointed out, even the lifestyle differences of the lower-middle and working classes are no longer sharply distinct:

> Working- and lower-middle-class people usually do not live in separate neighborhoods or speak and dress differently. The once sizable gulf in education, ways of raising children, furnishing dwellings, and spending leisure time have also declined. As long as note is taken of the remaining differences such as job security and working conditions, the two populations can often be described as middle Americans (8).

The Changing U.S. Economy and the Classes in the Middle

In recent years the intermediate classes have been profoundly affected by what has been referred to as **economic restructuring.** Jobs, income, and wages are all being impacted by the advent of a global economy and by what has been called a third industrial revolution, in which occupations and the very nature of work itself are being transformed by new technologies. These changes have affected each of the intermediate classes in different ways. Those in the upper-middle class have generally prospered, while those in the working class and, to a lesser degree, the lower-middle class, have been the losers. To better understand the current status of these classes, we need to briefly trace the major developments of the American economy and its workforce over the past few decades.

The Growth of the Middle Classes

The Great Depression   During the 1930s, the United States, along with most other industrial societies in the world, experienced the most severe economic depression in its history. Capitalist economies had traditionally experienced periodic swings in which an era of prosperity was followed by recession, which, in turn, was followed by recovery. This pattern did not hold up in the 1930s, however, and the result was an inability to stimulate demand. Falling prices led to falling wages and extremely high unemployment. Some saw this as the beginning of the end of the capitalist system. Efforts of the Roosevelt administration to jump-start the economy through massive public spending programs did put many people back to work, but these measures were, in the end, not effective in ending the depression.

Not until the United States entered World War II did the economy finally recover from this most serious economic crisis. Starting in 1941, jobs became plentiful as the society prepared for the war effort. Workers were needed to man factories that were converted into war production facilities. Plants that previously had made automobiles and kitchen appliances now produced tanks, jeeps, and airplanes. The recruitment of hundreds of thousands of men into the armed forces led to a labor shortage at home. This stimulated a migration of thousands from the rural South to northern industrial cities to work in the plants. Moreover, women were now recruited into the industrial labor force, filling jobs that ordinarily had been occupied only by men. The image of "Rosie the Riveter" became a morale booster for the home front workforce.

The Postwar Years   Following the war, it was feared that the United States would once again be plunged into an economic depression. With the end of the conflict and the return of soldiers and sailors into the domestic workforce, images of an oversupply of labor resurfaced. What emerged instead, however, was a thriving economy that gave rise to a twenty-year period of great prosperity. The demand for consumer goods that had been denied people during the depression and the war stimulated the economy and led to a tremendous industrial expansion. Returning to civilian life, men and women married in record numbers, giving rise to the so-called baby boom. These new families created a demand for new housing. The old housing stock of the central cities could no longer support the expanding population, which sought a more placid environment in which to raise their families. This they found in the suburbs. The movement to the suburbs was boosted as well by the construction of a superhighway system in which expressways now enabled workers, whose jobs were still located mostly in the central cities, to commute back and forth.

Another factor that prevented a return to economic depression was the maintenance of a strong military. The army and navy had been disbanded after World War I; but at the end of World War II, the perceived threat of the Soviet Union and the onset of the Cold War provided the rationale for the continued support of a huge military establishment. The manufacture of weapons, therefore, became a mainstay of the American economy, providing jobs and income to thousands and generally providing a society-wide economic stimulus.

American prosperity was also the result of the fact that the United States had emerged from the war as the only advanced society with its industrial infrastructure still in place. Americans at home had been unaffected by the fighting, unlike the Europeans and the Japanese, whose industrial bases were left in shambles. The United States, as a result, became an economic superpower unchallenged by any nation. It would be many years before Germany, Japan, and others would be able to present serious economic competition.

The upshot of this great economic boom was a substantial expansion of the middle classes. Rising productivity in the 1950s led to rising wages and higher family incomes (Danziger and Gottschalk, 1993; Levy, 1995, 1998). Many now entered the middle class for the first time, gaining their piece of the American Dream: a secure and well-paying job, a relatively comfortable home in which to raise a family, and the availability of an unprecedented variety of consumer goods. No image better reflected the American optimism of the 1950s than the television sit-com of that period, *Ozzie and Harriet*. Here was the prototypical middle-class family: station wagon parked in the driveway of their suburban home, where their teenage boys were growing up in a world that promised nothing but continued prosperity. That was the prospectus not only of the general public but also of economic and social forecasters. Economic expansion seemed unlimited, and Americans had every reason to believe that prosperity and economic supremacy in the world would continue not only for their generation but for their children and grandchildren as well.

The Post-1973 Period of Economic Restructuring   The unrelenting optimism of the 1950s and 1960s (the latter decade was one of great social turmoil, but economic prosperity for the middle classes did not abate) was halted by events and economic developments starting in the early 1970s. The year 1973 is often used as a historic watershed. The OPEC oil embargo occurred in that year, and the American economy was forever changed afterward. The oil-producing nations, mostly of the Middle East, imposed for a time an embargo on oil shipments to the United States and subsequently placed limitations on the amount of oil for American export. Suddenly, the United States discovered that it was heavily dependent on outside sources for its economic well-being; no longer could it assume that its huge domestic market was unthreatened and its dominant place atop the world's economies unchallenged. In a sense, this marked the introduction to Americans of the global economy.

The Shrinking Middle

Since the mid-1970s, new socioeconomic patterns have led to profound changes for the intermediate classes. Economists, sociologists, policymakers, and commentators have begun to speak of the U.S. stratification structure as "shrinking" in the middle. The basic idea is that those in the middle classes are being pushed either up into the professional and managerial category, or they are being pulled down into the ranks of low-level service workers, many of whom are now part of the working poor.

This **middle-class squeeze,** or bifurcation, can be seen in the development of a two-tiered wage structure and in family income patterns.

Income and Wages   As pointed out in Chapter 2, inequality in American society is growing. The gap between those at the top and those at the bottom has been widening for the past two and a half decades, and those in the middle are finding it more difficult simply to keep pace. In effect, the working and middle classes are falling behind. As some have described it, the United States is increasingly emerging as a two-tiered society: those who are doing very well and are enriching themselves, and those who are falling further behind the successful people. Work itself is no longer a guarantee against poverty or downward mobility. Most of those who find themselves in a declining economic position are in fact employed.

Regardless of the definition applied or the unit measured—households, families, or individuals—the proportional size of the middle has been steadily decreasing for over two decades (Duncan et al., 1993; Kacapyr, 1996; Thurow, 1999). Looking at wages is one way to track the middle-class decline. While workers' wages increased consistently from the 1950s to around 1973, from that point forward not only were increases not forthcoming, but, given the rate of inflation, wages actually declined somewhat. During the 1980s, a general downward shift occurred in the wage structure in which proportionately fewer workers were in the middle- and high-wage groups. The only exception was a modest expansion of the share of the workforce at the very highest earning level (Mishel and Bernstein, 1993).

By the early 1990s, the paychecks of full-time male workers had 10 percent less purchasing power than they did twenty years earlier (Farley, 1996). A turnaround began in 1997, when real wages (that is, the inflation-adjusted purchasing power of people's paychecks) began to rise. Nonetheless, the median wage of workers in 1999 was still substantially below its 1973 level when the downturn in wages began (Economic Policy Institute, 2000).

The stagnation of wages for most of the past twenty years among the working class and part of the lower-middle class has created a growing fissure between them and the upper-middle class. Although the latter may also depend on their salaries for income, they are ordinarily able to supplement them with interest, dividends, capital gains, and other nonwage sources (Kacapyr, 1996).

Some of the gap between high- and low-wage workers is explained by education. Workers at the high end of the occupational hierarchy, whose jobs require higher education, have increased their income at the same time that those with only a high school diploma or less have suffered a sharp decline in wages (Levy, 1995, 1998). In the 1970s, earnings for men fell in all educational categories, including those with college degrees. In the 1980s, however, while earnings continued to decline for male high school graduates, they increased for those with college educations. College-educated men earned 36 percent more than men with high school diplomas in 1980, but earned 60 percent more in 1990. This trend continued throughout the 1990s (Farley, 1996; Gottschalk, 1997). By 1998, male college graduates were earning 68 percent more than those with only high school diplomas (Danziger and Reed, 1999).

Not only has the wage gap widened, but merely keeping pace demands greater effort. Two-wage-earner families have become increasingly common, and thus family income, though hardly changed from 1973, is now often the product of two workers (Mishel, 1995; Mishel and Bernstein, 1993). Indeed, Thurow has proclaimed that "The one-earner middle-class family is extinct" (1996:33). Many families in the middle have discovered that two incomes are essential merely to keep pace with the standard of living to which they have become accustomed. With both parents working, a new context for raising children has been created, placing especially great pressures on women. Anthropologist Katherine Newman has referred to "the great middle-class experiment of the late twentieth century, the working mother" (1993:100).

Although a small gain by those in the middle was apparent by the late 1990s, there was no reversal of the growing gap between top and bottom in the American workforce. The curious side of polarization in the 1990s is that it occurred at the same time that productivity was rising, corporate profits soared, and the stock market gained enormously. Furthermore, inflation was steadfastly under control, and unemployment was lower than at any time in several decades. The American economy, in brief, appeared to be functioning perfectly. None of this affected the precarious economic position of workers, however. Nearly a third of all workers in 1997 were in lower-skilled jobs paying less than $15,000 a year (Bernstein, 1997). These developments demonstrated that a productive and growing economy does not necessarily translate into improved living standards for most workers and their families (Mishel, 1995). A popular metaphor describing the effects of a growing economy is "a rising tide lifts all boats." The 1990s, however, seemed to show that only the yachts were rising; the other boats were trying hard to simply stay afloat.

The Decline of Middle-Income Jobs   Much of the explanation for the increasing bifurcation of income is attributable to the fact that the workforce is becoming more of a two-tiered structure—those whose jobs are in demand and who earn a good wage, and those whose jobs are insecure and who earn a wage that often is not enough to support a family. What has occurred is an expansion of jobs at the top of the occupational hierarchy, particularly among professional, managerial, and technical workers, and at the bottom among service workers performing low-skill jobs that pay correspondingly low wages. Jobs in the middle of the occupational hierarchy have, as a result, declined.

During the 1980s and 1990s, the economy provided jobs for more and more people, including large numbers of women and immigrants who entered the workforce. But the increase in jobs occurred at the same time that wages declined. In an analysis of census data, sociologist Reynolds Farley (1996) shows that many, perhaps most, of these new jobs were low-skill and low-paying, but that there has also been a rapid growth of new jobs at the high end of the wage scale. What has seemed to develop, then, is a growing gap between high-paid, high-skilled workers on the one hand and low-paid, low-skilled workers on the other (Rosenthal, 1995).

This occupational bifurcation has been especially evident in the service sector, where over two-thirds of Americans now work. Service occupations are extremely varied, ranging from unskilled workers at the bottom, to clerical workers and salespersons in the middle, to highly trained professionals like doctors and lawyers at the top. Obviously, these jobs are considerably different in pay, skills, and prestige. In recent years, the most significant growth has occurred among the bottom portion of the service sector, those jobs requiring few skills, paying minimum wages, and offering little opportunity for upward mobility. The low end of the service sector includes such jobs as fast-food workers, kitchen workers, hospital workers such as orderlies and nurse's aides, nursing-home workers, maids, and child-care workers. However, significant growth has also occurred in the top portion of the service sector, including professionals and managers—hence the growing split between those at the top and those at the bottom, leaving a reduced middle.

The decline of jobs in the middle range and the growth of jobs at the two extremes of the workforce have been particularly noticeable for men. Women have fared better, experiencing "modest growth of jobs in the low-wage range, and rapid increases for jobs in the middle and upper ranges" (Farley, 1996:102). This is reflective of the growth of occupations and industries where women are well represented (like health care and retail) and the decline of those more typically male-dominated (like machine operators).

The effects of a declining middle have hit well-paid blue-collar workers especially hard. Many have lost their jobs as a result of downsizing, mechanization, or globalization and now work precariously at jobs that pay a fraction of what they were previously earning. Take Craig Miller, a former sheet-metal worker for a large airline. In the summer of 1992, he was laid off. When he started to look for a job, he discovered that someone with his skills and educational level was unable to earn much more than minimum wage. He works behind the counter at a McDonald's, drives a school bus, and has started a small business changing furnace filters. His wife also works part-time. Between the two, they hold four different jobs, but their total income is about $18,000, less than half of what Craig had earned as a union sheet-metal worker. They had acquired a piece of the American Dream, which they now find slipping away. Craig's former work buddies have experienced a similar fall in income and status. One has taken a job as a school janitor. Another, unable to find a job paying more than $6.00 an hour, has been forced to move back home with his parents at age thirty-nine. He is no longer confident that he will ever marry and start a family of his own. "Women are just like me; they want security," he says. "What are they going to see in me?" (Johnson, 1994:A9).

In addition, many workers today are temporary or part-time employees, hired or fired on the basis of seasonal or contingent needs where there is a built-in time limitation to the work (Polivka, 1996). As the labor needs of employers change, the status of workers is thrown into jeopardy. Hence, the regularity of work is no longer assured. Retail sales personnel, for example, may be asked to work only those hours during which they are most needed. Employers commonly prefer to hire workers on a contingent basis so they can adjust their wage costs to the utmost efficiency. This provisional nature of work has affected not only those workers nearer the bottom of the occupational hierarchy but also many at the higher end, even professionals. Some estimate that up to 30 percent of all U.S. workers are now contingent workers— part-timers, temporaries, or subcontractors (Heath, 1998).

In short, the middle-class squeeze does not appear to be slowing down. The future of the classes in the middle is likely to be one of a continuing gap between workers who are part of the New Economy (information industries like software, financial services, and media) and those attached to the Old Economy (Mandel and Gutner, 1999). Workers in the former are experiencing a rapid and substantial rise in wages, whereas those in the latter are, by comparison, losing ground. Higher productivity and bigger profits enable New Economy companies to pay higher salaries than Old Economy firms. This is not simply a reflection of the skill or educational levels of workers. Many college-educated workers, for example, today find themselves with stagnant or even declining wages.

The intermediate classes, then, are increasingly being pushed either upward or downward in terms of jobs, skills, and income. Economic insecurity not only threatens the traditional working class but is a concern of the lower-middle class and even, to some degree, the upper-middle class. Americans at all points within the intermediate classes are apprehensive about economic issues. Will their income enable them to maintain their lifestyle? How secure is their current job? What will be their occupational future?

The United States and Other Societies: A Comparison   Have the changes of the past two and a half decades in American society been evident in other advanced industrial societies? To a certain extent they have, but the decline in the middle seems to have been more severe in the United States. In the early 1990s, the average American worker earned less than his counterpart in other advanced industrial societies; for example, hourly wages were 60 percent higher in Germany and 50 percent higher in Sweden. In addition, low-paid workers in the United States were further below the average than low-paid workers in other countries (Freeman, 1994). At the other end, higher-paid U.S.

workers earned more than comparable workers in other countries. What is evident, then, is the wider split in the American workforce in terms of earnings.

The trade-off for American workers has been a lower rate of unemployment by comparison with western European countries. Because of higher wages and stronger unions in societies such as Germany and France, there has been less incentive on the part of employers to hire new workers. As a result, unemployment rates in those countries in the late 1990s were as much as twice as high as in the United States.

Economic Restructuring and the Classes in the Middle

What accounts for the changes in the American economy that have led to shifting patterns among the intermediate classes in recent years? During the past three or so decades, the United States has been engaged in economic restructuring—the radical shift from what had been a manufacturing-based economy to a service-based economy. Increasingly, fewer workers are needed in the traditional blue-collar sector. Moreover, many white-collar jobs have been and continue to be eliminated. At the same time, highly skilled jobs, particularly technical, professional, and managerial, have expanded. These developments have been the result of two major factors: the emergence of new technologies and the development of a global economy.

Technological Changes

Each historical period has produced new innovations in production that have displaced workers. The development of mechanical forms of labor forced workers out of jobs that machines could perform more efficiently and cheaply. The notorious Luddite movement of the early nineteenth century in England, for example, was a response to the fears of workers that machines would replace them and thus divest them of their livelihood. The Luddites were bands of workingmen in England's industrial centers, especially textile manufacturing, who rebelled against the introduction of knitting machines, power looms, and wool-shearing machines (to which they attributed their low wages and high unemployment) by wrecking the machinery.

Today, it is workers in the manufacturing sector who have experienced the most serious decline as a result of new technologies. Increasingly, computers and robots do what workers once did. On automobile assembly lines, where workers once welded body parts together, robots now do the same tasks, only more efficiently. This trend has affected not only unskilled and semiskilled workers, but also skilled production workers. Jeremy Rifkin has put the matter quite simply: "By the mid-decades of the coming century, the blue collar worker will have passed from history, a casualty of the Third Industrial Revolution and the relentless march toward ever greater technological efficiency" (1995:140).

Computers have changed the very nature of industrial production. Indeed, "computers," writes economist Sheila McConnell, "may be the most profound technology since steam power ignited the Industrial Revolution" (1996:3). In the past, large-scale industries made for low production costs. That is no longer the case. As a result of computer technology, the flow of materials, their quality, and changes in them can be managed more easily and efficiently. Moreover, manufacturers can deliver a larger variety of goods more quickly. Sales data can be gathered more rapidly and with less effort, making it possible to transmit such information to manufacturers, who can respond quickly with finished goods. Workers, too, can be managed more effectively (Garson, 1988). Unlike the impact of changing technologies of the past, which affected only specific industries, computers affect all industries and job categories.

During previous periods of mechanization and the development of new industries, old jobs that were destroyed were usually replaced by new jobs into which displaced workers could move. Thus, as blue-collar workers were phased out, the service sector usually absorbed them. Some, like Jeremy Rifkin (1995), believe that the computer revolution, however, has rendered some workers permanently superfluous—that is, they have been displaced but there are no jobs for them to take in replacement, even in the service sector. Increasingly, technological advances have made obsolete many categories of jobs there, too. Telephone operators and receptionists are replaced by voice-mail systems, electronic scanning machines replace cashiers and retail clerks, and so on. This has led to dramatic cuts in the workforce. Even professionals and artists are not immune to the impact of technological advances. Synthesizers, Rifkin notes, reduce musical sounds to digitized form, save them, and reproduce them in various combinations, thereby replacing live musicians.

Rifkin has posited that we are now at a point in the development of technology that may spell the end of work itself: "The road to a near-workerless economy is within sight" (1995:292). Whether this will open new opportunities and freedoms for people or lead to unemployment and depression is, in his estimation, contingent on how equitably the productivity gains of this new economy are distributed.

Others forecast a more sanguine future for the U.S. workforce. Technological innovations, they believe, will continue to create new jobs that will be filled by more highly educated working-class and middle-class people (Farrell et al., 1998).

Globalization

Perhaps the most important change that has occurred in the American economy during the past three decades is the globalization of production and distribution. In a real sense, the American economy is today part of a world economic system in which the economies of various politically independent countries are loosely tied together. This is what has been called the **global economy.** The emergence of the global economy has contributed in large measure to the changes now being experienced by the classes in the middle.

Development of a Global Economy   Although today we take for granted the global economy, in fact it is a relatively recent development. No more than fifty years ago, the notion of a world economic system was unimaginable (Bloom and Brender, 1993). Several factors have contributed to its growth. One concerns technological changes in communications and transportation that have effectively reduced the geographic and social distance between countries. Travel from America to Europe, for example, that might have taken weeks by ship in the early part of the century now takes only hours. Reducing distance generates frequent contact among people and organizations. And it facilitates the delivery of goods to literally every corner of the globe. Items produced in Germany can be shipped for sale in Los Angeles as quickly and as easily as if they were produced in Chicago. Trade, then, has become increasingly internationalized.

The production process itself has been globalized. Although a Ford automobile may roll off the assembly line in Dearborn, Michigan, or Atlanta, Georgia, its various parts may have been manufactured in any number of locations throughout the world. To call it an "American" car, therefore, is something of a misnomer; in fact, it is a "world" car, as are most others, regardless of where they are actually assembled. This decentralized global production process increasingly typifies many products. An IBM computer manufactured in the United States, for example, may be made up of components manufactured in Taiwan, Singapore, Mexico, Thailand, and Korea.

Management, along with actual production, has been internationalized. Electronic communication systems, including telephones, computers, and interactive television, make it possible for organizations to conduct their business *from* anywhere *to* anywhere. As a result, vast resources in different parts of the world can be managed from a home base. At the Nike offices in Oregon, executives can instantaneously keep track of their supply of shoes in plants in Thailand or Indonesia. They can also keep account of what is occurring in those plants and can direct the plant managers without ever leaving the Oregon offices.

Most important, financial capital can be moved around the globe at the press of a key. People and organizations in one country invest in others. Capital may be moved almost at will wherever it can yield the greatest return on investment. International flows of capital thus continue to grow.

The result of all these technological changes is a world, as economist Lester Thurow has described it, in which "for the first time in human history, anything can be made anywhere and sold everywhere" (1996:115). American businesses and their workers consequently find themselves in competition with businesses and workers in other countries.

Transnational Corporations   The major units of the world economy are corporations whose operations span the globe. These are massive companies whose scale far exceeds that of other economic units. The wealth of corporations like General Electric, Bank of America, and Exxon Mobil exceeds the wealth of many nations of the world. These **transnational** (or multinational) **corporations** are spread out like octopus arms, with manufacturing and sales dispersed in numerous world locations. Most of the largest U.S. corporations operate as much abroad as they do in the United States. Consider some of the corporate names that we think of as "quintessentially American." Procter and Gamble—most Americans use a product of this company on a daily basis, from toothpaste to soap to toilet paper—today derives over half of its revenue from outside the United States. Two-thirds of the sales of Coca-Cola, perhaps the most widely known of all American consumer goods, are made abroad (*Forbes,* 1997b). MTV has had regional production centers in Europe, Brazil, Japan, and India since 1987 (*Newsweek,* 1995). Nike, the largest American shoe producer, manufactures almost all its products in Asian countries. Even American service corporations, such as banks, are essentially global. Consider that Citigroup, one of the largest U.S. banks, operates in virtually every country and derives over 60 percent of its revenues from non–U.S. operations (*Forbes,* 1997b). These and hundreds of major corporations like them may fly the American flag in front of their world headquarters located in the United States, but they are "American" only in their origins. They are world firms.

American corporations are not alone in this globalizing trend. Japanese, German, French, British, Korean, and other transnational firms have become familiar global names. Honda, a Japanese company, manufactures cars in Ohio, which are then exported to and sold in Japan. Almost all electronic appliances bought by Americans, such as TVs, microwave ovens, and stereo equipment, are manufactured by Japanese or Korean firms whose factories are in East or Southeast Asian countries. Nestlé, a Swiss firm best known for chocolate, derives 97 percent of its revenue from outside Switzerland (Heilbroner and Thurow, 1994). Whether we buy gasoline from Shell (Dutch/ British), film from Fuji (Japanese), aspirin from Bayer (German), CD players from SONY (Japanese), or shoes from Nike (American), we are participating in the global economy. The fifty largest transnational corporations are shown in Table 4-1.

In their international role, large corporations maintain few national loyalties. Their primary objective, as for all capitalist enterprises, is maximizing their return on investment. If that can be accomplished by producing in the United States, Mexico, China, or any other country, that is where it will be done. The global, not national, loyalties of transnational corporations were poignantly demonstrated in 1994 at the World Cup, the most important event in the sport of soccer, when it was held in the United States. Each country's best teams competed for several weeks in different venues. The various sports gear manufacturers each had "their" teams, that is, teams that were

Table 4-1 ■ The Fifty Largest Transnational Corporations

Rank	Company	Business	Country	Revenue ($mil)	Net Income ($mil)	Assets ($mil)	Market Value ($mil)	Employees (1000s)
1	Citigroup	financial svcs	United States	82,005	9,994	716,937	209,613	173.5
2	General Electric	elec & electron	United States	111,630	10,717	405,200	520,686	316.5
3	Exxon Mobil	energy	United States	160,883	7,910	144,521	290,023	115.0
4	Bank of America	banking	United States	51,632	7,882	632,574	91,903	163.4
5	Royal Dutch/Shell Group	energy	Netherlands	105,366	8,584	113,883	224,265[1]	99.0
6	Ford Motor	automobiles	United States	162,558	7,237	276,229	59,344	364.6
7	HSBC Group	banking	United Kingdom	39,348	5,408	569,139	94,105	146.9
8	General Motors	automobiles	United States	176,558	6,002	274,730	57,498	392.0
9	International Business Machines	computer systems	United States	87,548	7,712	87,495	190,359	299.2
10	American International Group	insurance	United States	40,656	5,055	268,238	173,503	52.3
11	Toyota Motor	automobiles	Japan	120,697	3,812	149,309	170,080	214.6
12	Wal-Mart Stores	retailing	United States	165,013	5,575	70,245	258,963	1,025.0
13	BP Amoco	energy	United Kingdom	83,566	5,008	89,478	206,692	88.1
14	ING Group	financial svcs	Netherlands	59,276	4,976	493,806	58,138	86.0
15	AT&T	telecom	United States	62,391	5,450	130,973	130,913	141.1
16	DaimlerChrysler	automobiles	Germany	151,632	5,809	172,520	54,665	463.6
17	SBC Communications	telecom	United States	49,489	6,573	83,215	148,614	202.5

18	Allianz Worldwide	Germany	insurance	70,305	2,258	376,830	89,018	113.6
19	Fannie Mae	United States	financial svcs	36,969	3,921	575,167	60,569	3.9
20	Morgan Stanley Dean Witter & Co	United States	financial svcs	33,928	4,791	366,967	81,094	50.5
21	Chase Manhattan	United States	banking	33,710	5,446	406,105	61,556	73.8
22	TotalFina Elf[2]	France	energy	75,859	3,534	81,012	114,709	127.3
23	AXA Group	France	insurance	83,069	2,043	509,815	54,352	92.0
24	Credit Suisse Group	Switzerland	banking	47,705	3,298	450,593	50,999	62.8
25	Deutsche Bank Group	Germany	banking	52,317	2,554	838,324	47,705	78.2
26	Philip Morris Cos	United States	bev & tobacco	61,751	7,675	61,381	60,008	140.5
27	WorldCom	United States	telecom	37,120	3,950	87,053	107,568	77.3
28	UBS	Switzerland	banking	26,968	3,979	613,173	56,275	49.1
29	Zurich Financial Services	Switzerland	insurance	39,962	3,260	221,178	41,735[3]	68.8
30	Intel	United States	computer peripherals	29,389	7,314	43,849	417,580	67.4
31	Bell Atlantic	United States	telecom	33,174	4,208	62,614	81,727	142.9
32	ABN-Amro Holding	Netherlands	banking	36,433	2,598	459,014	33,673	108.7
33	Fortis	Netherlands	financial svcs	41,381	2,342	407,565	31,780[4]	61.1
34	Lucent Technologies	United States	telecom	38,467	3,477	38,634	186,406	153.0
35	Siemens Group	Germany	elec & electron	72,074	1,697	64,121	88,580	440.2
36	Lloyds TSB Group	United Kingdom	banking	22,608	4,057	284,576	60,287	76.1
37	Merrill Lynch	United States	financial svcs	34,879	2,618	328,071	37,671	65.5
38	Merck	United States	personal care	32,714	5,891	35,634	171,726	57.3
39	BNP Paribas	France	banking	37,871	1,500	700,178	40,852	77.5

(continued)

Table 4-1 ■ The Fifty Largest Transnational Corporations (concluded)

Rank	Company	Business	Country	Revenue ($mil)	Net Income ($mil)	Assets ($mil)	Market Value ($mil)	Employees (1000s)
40	Wells Fargo	banking	United States	21,795	3,747	218,102	73,597	90.4
41	Hewlett-Packard	computer systems	United States	43,808	3,325	33,911	119,855	84.4
42	Bank of Tokyo-Mitsubishi	banking	Japan	34,041	1,199	651,336	58,552	18.2[5]
43	British Telecom	telecom	United Kingdom	29,566	3,246	59,957	94,876	132.1
44	Microsoft	computer software	United States	21,855	8,746	45,093	329,207	31.4
45	Deutsche Telekom	telecom	Germany	35,859	1,267	94,546	190,008	204.4
46	Bank One	banking	United States	25,986	3,479	269,425	38,170	88.7
47	Procter & Gamble	food, household	United States	39,188	3,727	36,001	86,975	108.2
48	France Telecom	telecom	France	27,532	2,799	52,009	150,382	174.3
49	Nestlé[6]	food, household	Switzerland	47,158	2,984	35,413	73,592	230.9
50	Pfizer[6]	health care	United States	27,601	4,959	31,379	280,503	95.0

[1]Combined market value for Royal Dutch Petroleum and Shell Transport & Trading.

[2]Pro forma for the merger of Totalfina and Elf Aquitaine.

[3]Combined market value for Zurich Allied AG and Allied Zurich Plc.

[4]Combined market value for Fortis (NL) and Fortis (B).

[5]Not fully consolidated.

[6]Pro forma for the merger with Warner-Lambert.

The table ranks the 50 largest U.S. and foreign firms on a composite score based on each company's best three out of four rankings for sales, profits, assets, and market value. Using these criteria, Citigroup is both the largest U.S. corporation and the world's biggest company. Royal Dutch/Shell Group is the largest company outside the U.S. Source: *Forbes*, July 24, 2000, p. 289. Copyright © 2000 Forbes, Inc. Reprinted by permission of *Forbes Magazine*.

Reprinted with permission of King Features Syndicate.

outfitted with the manufacturer's brand of shoes and uniforms. Outfitting professional and college sports teams with specific brands of equipment has, of course, become standard practice for these companies. Nike, an American-based company, has been one of the most aggressive in promoting its name in this manner. Few people in the world do not recognize the Nike "swoosh" logo, prominently displayed on sneakers, football jerseys, and the like. During the World Cup, Nike outfitted the Brazilian team. Adidas (a German firm) outfitted the American team. Phil Knight, CEO of Nike, talked of a natural evolution in the shoe and apparel industry as "dividing the world into their athletes and ours. And we glory ours." Knight was not referring to American athletes versus other countries' athletes, however. He was talking of Nike-sponsored athletes versus those endorsing other brands. "When the U.S. played Brazil in the World Cup," he explained, "I rooted for Brazil because it was a Nike team. America was Adidas" (Lipsyte, 1996:B7).

The globalization of economic processes has led to a tremendous expansion of labor mobility. All firms in a capitalist system seek a common end: maximization of profit. This is accomplished in large measure by lowering the costs of production. An important cost is labor, which is held in check by minimizing wages.

Today, labor costs are controlled by transnational corporations through the easy movement of capital. If a U.S.-based automobile manufacturer pays its workers an average of $20 an hour to produce engines in Detroit but could produce the same engines in Mexico where it need pay workers an average of only $3 an hour, obviously, it will be in the company's interest to move its engine production to Mexico. Of course, other factors are involved in the decision of where to produce. Workers in Mexico may not be as efficient and thus not as productive as American workers, for example, which may cause the company to reconsider making the move. But the cost of labor is a critical factor in production and will be a strong incentive for the company to transfer its engine operations to Mexico. In seeking out the cheapest cost of labor, firms gravitate to low-wage areas, moving their facilities from location to location. The upshot of this movement is that some workers win new jobs while others lose them (Bluestone and Harrison, 1982).

Reich's Model   Economist Robert Reich, the former U.S. secretary of labor, has offered a model of how the U.S. workforce has been restructured as a result of the world economy. The model helps in explaining how the dynamics of globalization have impacted the American classes in the middle.

Reich suggests that traditional occupational classifications (white-collar, blue-collar, professional, managerial, etc.) no longer make sense in the context of the global economy. American workers (and workers in other countries as well) are today increasingly subdivided into three distinct categories: symbolic analysts, routine production workers, and routine personal service workers. Each has been affected differently by the emergence of an internationalized labor market.

Those whom Reich refers to as *symbolic analysts* are professional and managerial workers, who make up much of the upper-middle class. Reich calls them symbolic analysts because they are workers who "solve, identify, and broker problems by manipulating symbols" such as scientific formulas, legal arguments, and marketing strategies (Reich, 1992:178). They are highly trained and possess valued skills, making them adaptable to changing conditions. As a result, they are strongly competitive and can command high salaries in the international labor market. They have generally prospered in the global economy. Doctors, lawyers, engineers, publishers and editors, investment bankers, financial consultants, and top-level managers are typical occupations that fall into this category. They make up no more than 20 percent of U.S. jobs, according to Reich.

Routine production workers are the traditional blue-collar workers, whose work consists of repetitive tasks and who are usually paid on an hourly basis. As noted earlier, many white-collar workers' jobs also have become increasingly routinized as a result of computerization. Obviously, the skill level of routine production workers is much lower than that of symbolic analysts and their educational requirements are correspondingly reduced. Most important, routine production workers are in competition with similar workers worldwide and are therefore apt to be most negatively affected by the vagaries of the global economy. They constitute about 25 percent of the American workforce, but their numbers are declining and their standard of living is declining as well.

Those whom Reich calls *routine personal service workers* are, like production workers, doing simple and repetitive tasks. They too are usually paid on an hourly basis, and their skill and educational level is low. The major difference between them and routine production workers is that they are not in competition with similar workers in other countries. Their jobs involve personal services, which cannot be supplied from abroad. In a sense, they are in competition against machines rather than against foreign workers. Restaurant workers, hospital workers, janitors and maids, secretaries, auto mechanics, and security personnel are among the typical occupations of this category. They constitute around 30 percent of the workforce, and their numbers are increasing rapidly. Reich points out that during the 1980s, over 3 million such jobs were created in fast-food outlets, bars, and restaurants, more than all the routine production jobs still in existence in the auto, steel, and textile industries combined (Reich, 1992). Routine personal service workers are disproportionately women and ethnic minorities and, in some areas, illegal immigrants. And unlike the wages of symbolic analysts, the wages of these workers have declined.

The split in the intermediate classes, then, can be seen as one in which the upper-middle class, consisting mostly of symbolic analysts, drifts further away from the other two sectors, whose economic status becomes increasingly tenuous and whose occupational prestige declines.

The Decline of Labor Unions

In a capitalist market, business owners try to keep wages in check or to drive them down, while workers seek to do the opposite. Where labor unions are strong, wages are driven upward. Unions put pressure on employers to keep wages high and to improve the conditions of work. It is the threat of a strike that serves as the unions' weapon in this struggle. The 1950s and 1960s represented the apex of U.S. labor union strength. In the mid-1950s, about 40 percent of private sector workers and 5 percent of public sector workers were union members (Freeman, 1994). In 1970, unions still represented 31 percent of the workforce. By 1983, however, the percentage had declined to 20, and by 2000, less than 14 percent of workers were union members; among private sector workers, union members accounted for less than 10 percent (Bureau of Labor Statistics, 2001; Katz and Krueger, 1999). As labor economist Richard Freeman explains, short of a sharp reversal of what has been a continuing downward trend, "the United States will enter the twenty-first century with its work force having less collective representation than all other countries in the developed world" (1994:18).

Several factors account for the decline. Unions lost their strength as the educational attainment of workers went up and manufacturing employment declined (Farley, 1996). As the American workforce has shifted from manufacturing to service, it has shifted from what had traditionally been the most heavily unionized sectors of the economy: automobiles, steel, and transportation. When those industries were at their peak after World War II, wages increased and inequality in income generally declined. With the turn toward service industries and the increasing movement of production abroad, the power of labor unions began to decline. Although unions gained membership among some service workers, especially state and local government employees and health care workers, they lost far more in shrinking manufacturing industries.

In addition to the loss of jobs in the manufacturing sector, antilabor policies and actions of the Reagan administration during the 1980s further weakened labor unions. In 1981, the Professional Air Traffic Controllers Organization (PATCO) attempted to strike in response to what they saw as inadequate working conditions and benefits. As government employees, the air traffic controllers had to bargain with the federal government. The Reagan administration not only rejected their demands but fired those controllers who went on strike, vowing not to rehire them. This action set the tone of labor relations in the 1980s (Ehrenreich, 1989).

A combination of high unemployment, automation, overseas production, and an unsympathetic administration reduced the threat of strikes, the traditional union weapon, as workers suffered job insecurity. Their major concern was simply holding on to their jobs, rather than fighting for higher wages. As a result, they were disinclined to strike and more apt to accept concessions in their bargaining with companies. Whereas during the 1960s and 1970s work stoppages averaged almost 300 per year, in the 1980s they averaged only 83, and during the early 1990s, less than 40 (U.S. Census Bureau, 1995b).

Some hold that it is the decline of American labor unions, more than anything, that has contributed to the continued wage decline of the past two decades (Freeman and Katz, 1994; Judis, 1994). During the years of high labor union membership, all workers benefited from union power, even those who were not organized. In order to avoid unionization, companies would often pay nonunion workers as much as their union counterparts or at least would keep wages competitively high.

It is of note that in other advanced industrial countries, the precipitous decline of union membership has not paralleled that of the United States. In Canada, for example, union membership remains more than double that of the United States (Laxer, 1998). This has translated into a greater voice for workers in matters of public policy and has been an important factor in explaining the much more generous social welfare policies of these countries, as well as tougher regulations governing plant closings and worker retraining.

Downsizing

Downsizing is a popular term referring to the tendency for large corporations to cut their workforce, with the objective of becoming more efficient and profitable. In large measure, this has occurred in response to the global economy, in which American firms must now compete on a worldwide basis, no longer unaffected by economic trends in other countries. From 1979 to 1996, more than 43 million jobs were abolished in the United States (Uchitelle and Kleinfield, 1996). Lost jobs have been mostly in manufacturing, that is, typically blue-collar occupations. But downsizing has also affected the high-status jobs of upper-middle-class managers and professionals. In a global economy, downsizing is practiced by all companies, even those that are profitable (Thurow, 1999). Although replacement jobs are usually found for displaced workers, they are often not comparable in salary or prestige. For many, then, downsizing has meant downward social mobility. Managers or professionals with what had been secure and well-paying jobs may find themselves with jobs paying half of their former salary with fewer benefits and virtually no security. Lower-middle- and upper-middle-class people have therefore begun to more fully comprehend the economic insecurity that has always plagued the poor and some elements of the working class (Newman, 1999).

Consider two workers, one blue-collar, the other white-collar, both affected by the downsizing phenomenon. Robert Muse was laid off from his job as a machinist with Northrop Grumman Aircraft, in southern California. For twenty-two years his blue-collar job paid well and provided good benefits. Following his layoff, the best he could secure was a job as a maintenance worker, earning half the $20 an hour he used to earn. What he now makes is the equivalent of what he earned when he was young and had no family to support. Obviously, his family's lifestyle has been downgraded. Moreover, there is no expectation that he will ever get called back to his old job (Bragg, 1996a).

At age fifty-one, James Sharlow suddenly found himself without a job. Unlike Muse, Sharlow was no ordinary worker. He had been a senior manager at Eastman Kodak earning $130,000 a year. When Kodak decided to close the plant he managed, he was dismissed after twenty-six years of service to the company. Abruptly, his and his family's life was thrown into disarray. They were now in jeopardy of losing their house, their comfortable lifestyle, and their expectations of retirement (Bragg, 1996b). Cases like Sharlow's demonstrate how even some upper-middle-class families have had to deal with the effects of economic restructuring.

Much of the downsizing phenomenon is a result of the technological changes discussed earlier. General Motors, for example, can make as many cars with 315,000 workers today as it made in the 1970s with 500,000 (Uchitelle and Kleinfield, 1996). U.S. Steel, the largest producer of steel in 1980, once employed 120,000 workers; by 1990 it employed only 20,000 but was producing about the same amount of steel (Rifkin, 1995). Similarly, in almost every other area of the workforce, companies can do as much or more with fewer workers. Between 1990 and 1995, ten of the largest corporations in the United States (including GM, Boeing, General Electric, IBM, and Sears) laid off almost 850,000 workers, 29 percent of their entire workforce; yet, productivity rose dramatically among these ten (Koretz, 1997). Globalization has also contributed to downsizing. By sending work abroad, transnational corporations cut their need for workers in the United States.

Demographic Factors

Immigration   In the past three decades, immigration to the United States has increased greatly. So great have the numbers been, in fact, that the flow has reached proportions resembling the classic period of immigration to America of the late nineteenth and early twentieth centuries. Let's examine how these newest immigrants have impacted on the labor market and, in particular, on the place of the working and middle classes.

Social scientists have debated the economic effects of immigration. Whereas some argue that immigrants constitute an added burden to an already swollen labor pool, others contend that the jobs they typically hold are those that native workers shun and, furthermore, that they create as many jobs as they take. Similarly, while some maintain that the new immigrants overburden the social welfare system, others hold that they pay in taxes more than they collect in benefits (Beck, 1996; Borjas, 1994; Bouvier, 1992; Simon, 1991).

The newest immigration appears to favor some sectors of the economy and harm others. Most of the immigrants from Mexico (the largest single group) and the Caribbean are unskilled and take their place at the lowest occupational levels. They benefit employers in labor-intensive industries, such as clothing manufacturing or other work areas calling for cheap labor, but they depress the job opportunities of native low-status workers, especially African Americans. A report of the National Academy of Sciences in 1997 concluded that immigration produces substantial economic benefits for the society as a whole but does have a slightly negative impact on the wages and job opportunities of low-skilled U.S. workers, especially high school dropouts (Pear, 1997).

Not all the new immigrants come as unskilled workers, however. A large segment of some groups, particularly Asian Indians, Chinese, and Filipinos, are highly trained professionals and managers whose economic impact is far different from that of those who enter with few occupational resources. Many immigrant doctors, for example, staff large city hospitals, which would find it difficult to operate without them. The United States has also increasingly relied on immigrant engineers and other highly trained scientific workers (Muller, 1993; Suro, 1989; Szabo, 1989). Consider that almost a quarter of U.S. residents holding Ph.D.'s in science and engineering are foreign-born (Gleckman, 1998).

Regarding the economic impact of immigration, labor unions and political groups that support workers generally oppose increasing immigration on the grounds that immigrants are a potential threat to jobs and wages. Employers, on the other hand, usually favor more liberal immigration policies, seeing immigrants as a means of containing wages. The intensity of the immigration debate waxes and wanes depending on the state of the U.S. economy. When unemployment is low and jobs are plentiful, as was the case in the late 1990s, arguments against immigration are muted. The debate becomes more shrill, however, during times of economic dislocation.

Women in the Workforce   Women have entered the workforce in massive numbers during the past three decades, usually as a matter of necessity. Two income earners have become crucial in families trying to maintain a standard of living that most Americans have come to expect. Moreover, the rise of single-parent families has meant that women in such contexts must support their families through their work.

   The entrance of women in the world of work in substantial numbers has affected not only women but also the labor market as a whole. Women have often been prepared to accept lower wages than men, and this has contributed in some part to the failure of wages to rise in recent years.

   Some claim that the entrance of large numbers of women into the labor force in the 1970s was, in itself, a contributing factor in wage declines. Walter Russell Mead, for example, notes that "when one woman went to work, the household income rose; but as millions of women went to work, labor became cheaper" (1998:34). Others such as Robert Reich, however, assert that Mead has it backward. Rather than women helping to bring down wages, it was low wages that prodded women into the workforce in order to maintain family incomes (1998).

Public Policies and the Shrinking Middle

In addition to economic restructuring, globalization, and demographic trends, public policies have contributed significantly to the shrinking middle classes. Government policies in the 1950s and 1960s—decades that marked the greatest expansion of the American middle classes—moved the class structure toward greater equality. That the share of income going to the top 20 percent of families declined in the 1950s and 1960s while the share going to the bottom 20 percent increased was due in large part to changes in tax policies and other government actions that benefited those at the lower end of the class hierarchy more than those at the top end. Many of those policies were reversed in the 1980s and early 1990s, exacerbating the bifurcation that had been brought about as a result of economic restructuring in the global economy.

The Middle Classes and the New Consumerism

Lifestyles, Desires, and Debt

The American economic boom of recent years has created a puzzling phenomenon among the intermediate classes: Despite rising family prosperity, particularly for those of the upper-middle class, many find themselves unable to satisfy their material needs and thus teeter precariously on the brink of economic disaster, living from paycheck to paycheck. How can this paradox be explained?

Economist Juliet Schor (1998; 1999; 2000) has written extensively on this issue and has offered several explanations. First, she describes a national culture of upscale spending, which she calls the "new consumerism." Increasingly, in this view, people acquire their consumer aspirations not just from their colleagues and peers, but also from what they see on television and movies and in various forms of advertising. Rather than comparing their status and lifestyle with their neighbors and "keeping up with the Joneses," as in previous decades, "people are now more likely to compare themselves with, or aspire to the lifestyles of, those far above them in the economic hierarchy" (Schor, 1999:43). This higher standard is introduced primarily by the mass media, which expose people to upscale lifestyles. The new consumerism is also founded on the endless introduction of new products and on continually raising standards: "What we want grows into what we need, at a sometimes dizzying rate" (1998:6).

What is most curious about the new consumerism is that it affects not, as might be expected, only the poor and those families with limited incomes, but rather those that are solidly part of the lower- and, especially, upper-middle class. Schor explains that 27 percent of all households making more than $100,000 and nearly 40 percent of those earning between $50,000 and $100,000 a year say they cannot afford to buy everything they really need. The important word here is "need." As people earn more money, they compare their status not with others like themselves but with those who have even more. Hence, to try to keep up they are constrained to buy more, fueling the cycle of consumerism. Social essayist Roger Rosenblatt has written that "if one were to ask a couple making $40,000 per year before taxes and a couple making a pre-tax $200,000 what class they were in, both would answer (honestly and persuasively) not only that they belong to the middle class but also that they are just scraping by" (Rosenblatt, 1999:16). Economist Robert Frank has described this paradox as middle-income families "experiencing unprecedented levels of economic distress, largely because they are trying to keep up with a living standard they cannot afford" (Frank, 2000:64).

With upscale competitive consumption has come a steep rise in consumer borrowing and credit card spending. Families in the 1990s ran up debt in record proportions. Moreover, the largest increases in debt occurred not among low-income families but among those in the lower- and upper-middle classes. The amount of money owed by the average household rose by 42 percent between 1995 and 1998, from $23,400 to $33,300 (Russell and Mogelonsky, 2000). Almost three-quarters of U.S. households are now in debt, and personal savings are at an all-time low.

Another result of the new consumerism is the emergence of a "work and spend" cycle. When given the choice between shorter hours and longer hours with more pay, workers almost always opt for more pay. That increase in income is usually spent on more material goods, but these are unable to provide long-term satisfaction, leading to further spending and, consequently the need to continue working longer hours. To pay for the material goods that are increasingly seen as essential, major breadwinners have often lengthened their workdays and families have required a second income earner. As noted earlier, Americans are working longer hours today than they were twenty years ago. Moreover, they work considerably more hours than Europeans and as many hours as Japanese workers (Schor, 1992; Freeman, 1998). Americans, then, continue to acquire more material possessions but find themselves with insufficient time and, therefore, less opportunity to enjoy them.

To Schor and others who share her view, the paradox of the current American economy—arguably the most prosperous in history—is that its major beneficiaries remain unfulfilled. People are caught on a "positional treadmill," continually pressured to maintain consumer parity with others. They must work harder and longer and often go into debt simply to keep pace, despite the fact that they consume more and more. As Schor argues, "We should be articulating an alternative vision of a quality of life, rather than a quantity of stuff" (2000:29).

Some argue that increasing levels of consumption are the product not of emulation of the wealthy and celebrated, but of the nature of the contemporary market system, which impels people to continually redefine themselves by changing experiences and lifestyles through their purchases (Holt, 2000; Thompson, 2000). Others suggest that Schor and similar critics of the new consumerism are implicitly imposing their ideas of what is socially desirable consumer behavior on others, who may actually find meaning and pleasure in continual consumption. James Twitchell (1996) maintains that the consumption ethic is nothing new, but merely the latest expression of a human desire to amass things.

Two-Tier Marketing

In response to the emergence of an increasingly bifurcated class structure, producers and retailers have begun to cater to what they see as a two-tier market: those at the top end of the income hierarchy and those at the bottom. The middle part of the consumer market is seen as declining, in contrast to its predominant place in past decades (Leonhardt, 1997). Consumer goods are now increasingly designed, advertised, and sold in a strikingly different manner than in the past. Rather than targeting the middle, as in the past, products and services are focused on those who can afford high-priced, top-of-the-line items and those who can afford only low-priced, low-end items. Thus, upscale retail stores, such as Tiffany, report an upsurge in sales, as do low-end retailers like Wal-Mart. Midscale chains like J. C. Penney, in contrast, report weak sales. The same pattern is apparent in other parts of the consumer market. In automobiles, for example, midrange models are no longer the best-selling cars. At the high end of the income hierarchy, however, there are more people who are prepared to purchase an upscale vehicle. This is a result in large part of what Schor describes as the pressures experienced by the intermediate classes to consume increasingly expensive items, in emulation of those more affluent than themselves.

As David Leonhardt (1997) explains, marketers have realized that as a group, low-wage earners represent a very significant market. Many companies therefore now target them with goods that are simulations of more upscale items. Check-cashing centers and even pawnshops, typically the "banks" of the poor and even the working class, have begun to look and act more like conventional banks and are used by an increasing number of people who don't have checking accounts at a regular bank. Meanwhile, conventional banks cater to clients with large capital investments and must compete with brokerage firms like Merrill Lynch. A similar split in the market is apparent in telecommunications. Whereas Motorola offers worldwide satellite phone service at $3,000 a phone and $3 per minute, AT&T and other companies offer prepaid phone cards and calling arcades where banks of telephones are used by those who do not have a credit card or cannot afford their own telephone.

Summary

The middle, or intermediate, classes comprise three fairly distinct components: the upper-middle, lower-middle, and working classes. Each differs in income, occupation, education, and lifestyle, but together they are far apart from those at either the upper or the lower extreme of the American class hierarchy.

The emergence of the middle classes is a relatively recent historical phenomenon, but nowhere did they develop as thoroughly and early as in the United States. The American middle classes have experienced significant changes during the past two hundred years. Until the mid-nineteenth century, the majority of Americans were farmers and small business owners. The industrial revolution gave rise to a blue-collar workforce, which remained numerically dominant until the 1970s when white-collar workers predominated. In the current post-industrial economy, most workers are providing services, not producing things, but the service sector comprises a wide range of occupations, extending from high-status to low-status.

The upper-middle class is comprised of those who occupy high-status jobs with much power and authority that sets them apart from the other classes in the middle. The lower-middle class is a diverse stratum, consisting mainly of small business owners and white-collar workers such as middle-level managers, clerks, and bureaucrats. The working class are blue-collar workers who occupy a range of skills. Increasingly, the blue-collar/white-collar distinction is less meaningful as the character of work becomes similar for many of the occupations in these two sectors.

The 1950s and 1960s marked a period in which the classes in the middle expanded greatly. Rising wages and general prosperity led to the fulfillment of the American dream for many. Starting in the 1970s, however, the working and middle classes in the United States began a backslide, the effects of which continue to be felt. Millions of jobs in the manufacturing sector were eliminated and replaced by jobs in the service sector. The former paid well, whereas most of the latter, by comparison, paid little. This shift was brought about by a combination of the emergence of a global economy in which American workers now had to compete with foreign workers, new technologies that facilitated the replacement of workers with machines and computers, and the decline in numbers and power of labor unions. At the same time, the upper-middle class thrived in the new economy, thereby distancing itself from the other two components of the intermediate classes. This bifurcation continues to characterize the middle part of the American class structure.

One of the curious aspects of the intermediate classes is that, despite rising family prosperity, particularly for the upper-middle class, many families find themselves in a precarious economic situation. This is a result of what has been called the "new consumerism," in which people's material standards and aspirations continually rise as they observe the lifestyles—mainly through television—of those more affluent than themselves. This, in turn, produces pressures to consume ever more.

5

The Upper Class and the Power Elite

If you can actually count your money then you are not really a rich man.
J. PAUL GETTY

So far as men may do as they will with the property that they own or that they manage for owners, they have power over other men.
C. WRIGHT MILLS

This chapter examines those of the upper class and the power elite, exploring their identities, the sources of their wealth and power, and the path they follow to the top. It also considers the relationship between wealth and power. Certainly, the probabilities are great that the rich will be powerful and the powerful will be rich, but wealth and power are not the same and it is important to keep the two analytically separate. The upper class are those who hold great wealth, and the power elite are those who occupy positions of great importance and whose decisions have profound impact on the society.

The Upper Class

Where do we draw the line between the upper class and the rest of society? As with other parts of the class hierarchy, the separation is largely arbitrary, but in purely financial terms, it is clear that the rich are apart from others.

Income

One way of separating those at the very top of the American class hierarchy from others is to use income as a guide. Andrew Hacker, in his analysis of income and wealth in the United States, defines the rich as all individuals and households that have an annual income of at least $1 million (Hacker, 1997). This comprises a tiny portion of U.S. households, about one-twentieth of 1 percent.

A key group among those whose incomes surpass $1 million are top-ranking corporate executives. The average income in 1999 for a chief executive officer (CEO) of one of the 362 largest and most powerful American corporations was $12.4 million, including salary, bonuses, and other benefits, such as gains on stock options. The top twenty CEOs averaged almost $113 million each and the top five executives together earned $1.2 billion (*Business Week*, 2000). Clearly, in terms of income, corporate executives are in the highest class. Moreover, their income has climbed considerably over the past several decades. Between 1989 and 1997, compensation for the average CEO grew 100 percent. It is noteworthy that American corporate executives outearn their counterparts in other developed societies. In Germany, for example, the typical CEO of a large blue-chip company earns about a half million dollars in salary and bonus. The American model is being increasingly adopted, however, as stock options become a more common element in European executives' compensation (Kroll, 1998).

Some who are among the American rich may be considered the "celebrity rich"—entertainers and professional athletes whose names are easily recognized and who earn fabulously high incomes. Consider the earnings of a few prominent stars in a single year, 1999: Pop singers Shania Twain and Celine Dion each earned almost $50 million, the Backstreet Boys earned $60 million, and at age eighteen, Britney Spears earned $15 million. Talk show hosts

David Letterman and Jay Leno earned $20 million and $17 million respectively, and Oprah Winfrey earned $150 million from a range of enterprises. Coming from opposite ends of the political spectrum, radio personalities Rush Limbaugh and Howard Stern were among the top-paid entertainers, Limbaugh receiving $22 million and Stern $18 million. In the sports world, basketball star Shaquille O'Neal was in the third year of his seven-year $120 million contract and another basketball player, Kevin Garnett, signed a six-year contract for $126 million. Golfer Tiger Woods earned $47 million and Michael Jordan, even in retirement, earned $40 million simply from product endorsements. Boxer Mike Tyson fought only twice but still earned $33 million (*Forbes,* 2000b). These figures represent only the earnings from salaries and endorsements and don't include millions more that may derive from business investments. The earnings of some Hollywood stars are even more phenomenal. Actors like Tom Cruise, Jim Carrey, and Julia Roberts earn about $20 million per film plus a percentage of the film's gross earnings. In 2000, Cruise reportedly netted about $70 million for *Mission: Impossible,* and another $65 million for *Mission Impossible 2.*

Some may be able to enrich themselves merely from having occupied a prominent position or from having a publicly recognizable name. Former political officials perhaps best exemplify this category. Several months after he left the presidency, Ronald Reagan was paid $2 million simply to give a speech in Japan. Indeed, the speaking fees of politicians, noted authors, or newscasters can be enormous. In 1999, Colin Powell, having retired as chairman of the Joint Chiefs of Staff, earned several million dollars from speaking engagements, mostly before business groups; his price for a one-hour delivery was $80,000 (*Forbes,* 2000b). In the same fashion, former House Speaker Newt Gingrich garnered an estimated $2 million in less than a year, charging $50,000 per speech (Woellert, 1999). And poet Maya Angelou earned more than $3 million at $40,000 for each performance (*Forbes,* 2000b).

Wealth

Although high income is certainly a mark of great economic status, what distinguishes the rich from others is that the majority do not derive most of their income from their occupations. Most of those who earn over $1 million each year derive only a third of that from actual employment; the rest is derived from assets. By contrast, among those with income below $75,000 (the vast majority of American households), 90 percent is earned through their work (Hacker, 1997).

Perhaps the value of assets is the best indicator of the division between the rich and the remainder of the population. For this reason, the upper class has been referred to by some as the capitalist class. Industrialists and entrepreneurs own capital, that is, shares in companies, which typically grow in value over time and produce income in the form of dividends. Entertainers or athletes, by contrast, must continue to perform to maintain their flow of income. Their talent cannot be transferred to someone else and their income-earning years may be few. To assure their lofty status and lifestyle, they must wisely invest the money they earn through their performances. As Hacker explains, although the rich are a sociologically diverse stratum, what is common among them is that "the dominant share of the group's income comes via their brokerage accounts" (1997:84).

To comprehend the rich in American society, therefore, we need to look more closely at wealth, that is, the ownership of assets, not simply income. It is primarily through assets—stocks and bonds, real estate, cash accounts and other financial instruments, and business investments—that the rich have acquired their high economic status. "As they have been for centuries," observes sociologist Lisa Keister, "the truly rich are still separated by their wealth rather than their income" (2000:83).

As noted in Chapter 2, a relative handful of individuals and families hold an enormously disproportionate share of the society's wealth. To reiterate a couple of compelling statistics, the richest 1 percent of American families own over 40 percent of all assets, and the richest 10 percent own almost 70 percent. It is important to also recall the relative stability of the unequal distribution of wealth in American society. Although wealth inequality has accelerated in the past two decades, it has been a fundamental characteristic of the United States since the mid–nineteenth century (Dowd, 1993; Soltow, 1984; Williamson and Lindert, 1980).

In 1989, 1.25 million people in the United States owned assets in excess of $1 million (U.S. Census Bureau, 1996). Although this is a large number, these individuals represent, like millionaire income earners, a very tiny percentage of the total population: less than one-half of 1 percent. Consider that less than 3 percent of American families have net assets of more than a *half* million dollars. Moving up the hierarchy, the numbers shrink considerably. There are only 150,000 to 200,000 families with assets of $10 million or more (Phillips, 1995)."Even among the wealthy," notes Thurow, "wealth is very unequally distributed" (1999:200). At the very top of the wealth hierarchy, the assets of the richest people and families stagger the imagination.

One way to begin learning about the truly wealthy is to examine the annual issue of *Forbes* magazine that lists the 400 richest Americans. Therein lies a trove of fascinating information about the rich: In 2000, most were men, though 46 of the 400 were women. The average age was 61, though they ranged from 28 to 92. Three-fourths were college graduates, many with advanced degrees, though a few never even finished high school. Included on the *Forbes* list were a few recognizable names (Ted Turner, Bill Gates, Donald Trump), but only one was an entertainer (Oprah Winfrey, also the only

African American) and there were no sports stars. Most of those whose wealth is of truly great magnitude are not celebrities whose names are household words.[1]

As to the actual wealth of the richest Americans, the numbers are quite astonishing. The average net worth of the *Forbes* 400 in 2000 was $3 billion. Individuals worth at least $1 billion numbered 298. The two richest people in the United States (who also happened to be the richest in the world) were Bill Gates, the founder of Microsoft, who was worth $63 billion, and Larry Ellison, whose $50 billion derived mainly from Oracle, a computer software company (*Forbes,* 2000a). Table 5-1 shows the 25 wealthiest Americans listed in the *Forbes* 400.

The Expansion of Wealth   During the 1980s and 1990s, the wealth of the rich increased at a phenomenal pace. In the past when Americans thought of "rich," they usually used "millionaire" as a standard. As political commentator Kevin Phillips (1990) explained, by the late 1980s, "millionaire" had become a term that could be applied to so many people that it no longer was meaningful as a measure of true wealth. To understand what "rich" means in American society today, one must think in terms of billions, not millions. To be placed on the *Forbes* list of the 400 richest Americans in 1982 required $91 million; in 2000 it required $725 million (*Forbes,* 2000). Whereas in 2000 there were 298 billionaires in America, in 1982 there had been only 13 and in 1978 only 1 (*Forbes,* 1997a; Phillips, 1990).

The Rich: Old and New

The rich are different, as F. Scott Fitzgerald put it, and it is not only that they have more money, as Ernest Hemingway retorted. More than other classes, the upper class, particularly those who comprise the "old rich," is distinguished by its singular and exclusive style of life. The lives of upper-class families revolve around select social clubs, prep schools, prestigious Ivy League universities, debutante balls, and other social and cultural institutions that promote an upper-class lifestyle. Their relative separation from the rest of society and their close interrelations produce a class awareness that is missing among the other social classes. Even within the ranks of the wealthy, however, there are divisions, particularly between the "old rich," whose wealth is family-based and descended from several generations, and the "new rich," who have earned their wealth more recently, usually in their own lifetimes.

---

[1]The *Forbes* list, or any other similar to it, is, in the end, only an approximation of how much wealth the rich actually possess. Most of the truly wealthy do not reveal their assets to magazine reporters. Even if they did, as Inhaber and Carroll point out, "the financial affairs of the wealthiest are often so complicated and convoluted that reporters would have to have advanced degrees in finance or accounting to interpret them adequately. Few do" (1992:68). These figures, then, are estimates, a fact not disputed by *Forbes.*

Table 5-1 ■ The Twenty-Five Wealthiest Americans

Name	Amount of Wealth	Source of Wealth
William H. Gates III	$63 billion	Computer technology
Larry Ellison	$58 billion	Computer technology
Paul Allen	$36 billion	Computer technology
Warren Buffett	$28 billion	Stock market
Gordon E. Moore	$26 billion	Computer technology
Philip F. Anschutz	$18 billion	Communications
Steve Ballmer	$17 billion	Computer technology
Alice Louise Walton	$17 billion	Retailing (Wal-Mart)
Helen R. Walton	$17 billion	Retailing (Wal-Mart)
Jim C. Walton	$17 billion	Retailing (Wal-Mart)
John T. Walton	$17 billion	Retailing (Wal-Mart)
S. Robson Walton	$17 billion	Retailing (Wal-Mart)
Michael Dell	$16 billion	Computers
Sumner Redstone	$14 billion	Media
John W. Kluge	$13 billion	Media
Rupert Murdoch	$11 billion	Media
Charles Ergen	$11 billion	Satellite television
Barbara Cox Anthony	$10 billion	Media
Anne Cox Chambers	$10 billion	Media
Abigail Johnson	$10 billion	Mutual funds
Henry T. Nicholas III	$10 billion	Computer technology
Henry Samueli	$10 billion	Computer technology
Charles Schwab	$10 billion	Stock brokerage
Sanjiv Sidhu	$9.8 billion	Computer technology
Ted Turner	$9.1 billion	Media

Source: *Forbes,* 2000a.

The upper class is the social stratum least studied by sociologists, in large measure because it is so underexposed and relatively secluded. Few besides those who are actually part of the upper class have access to the institutions that are the foundation of upper-class life. As a result, we know far less about the rich than about the poor. This is particularly the case with many of the old rich, who prefer relative anonymity to celebrity.

Sociologist E. Digby Baltzell, himself a member of the upper class, presented one of the few intensive studies of the structure and formation of the American upper class. In his study, Baltzell (1958) pointed out a number of features of the upper-class subculture that distinguish it from the remainder of the population. Whereas the average American tends to stress the future and to deemphasize the past as well as other forms of traditionalism, the upper classes "more or less revere the past, especially the past accomplishments of their ancestors" (52). Family life revolves around a complete set of activities:

> Even the most socially secure families . . . place a high value on belonging to the correct clubs and associations, and making an appearance at the fashionable balls, dancing assemblies, weddings, and funerals; and where their children are concerned, the right summer resorts, dancing classes, schools and colleges, and finally, their daughter's debut, are each and severally of vital importance. (54)

All of these activities contribute to a sense of social cohesion and the formation of an upper-class community. As Baltzell noted, "More than at any other social class level . . . the upper class in America has many of the aspects of a caste" (69).

Although the difference between old and new wealth may no longer carry the kind of significance it once did, the inheritors of upper-class status may still look askance at the wealth and lifestyle of the newly enriched. Wealth, fame, and even political power are not, by themselves, always sufficient to gain entrance into the old upper class. One must be born to the "right" family and must possess the proper pedigrees. Moreover, the source of one's wealth is ordinarily of critical importance. Some who have made their fortunes in their own lifetime through business success or in the entertainment or sports worlds may find that they still do not qualify to enter the social circles of the old upper class. The new rich also may spend their money ostentatiously, calling attention to their wealth, whereas the old upper class traditionally spend their money in a muted fashion.[2] It is ironic that members of the old upper class today are the progeny of those who were similarly looked upon by the old rich of their time as parvenus whose displays of wealth were seen as crude and vulgar.

Development of the Old Upper Class   The old-line families of great wealth in the United States emerged during the latter part of the nineteenth century as a product of the formation of the great industrial empires of that age. The major entrepreneurs of the time—Rockefeller, Carnegie, Vanderbilt, Frick, Morgan, Ford, and others—acquired fortunes that became the basis of their family wealth (Allen, 1987). A few had established their

---

[2]The tendency for those of the old upper class to often look askance at the new is illustrated by the fact that entertainers Madonna and Cher, despite their wealth and fame, were refused permission to buy apartments in exclusive co-op buildings on Central Park East in New York City (Mason, 1996).

wealth even earlier. The du Pont fortune, for example, stemmed from the production of gunpowder starting in the late eighteenth century, and the Astors', from fur trading. These families became the old, established upper class, whose scions inherited their wealth with each succeeding generation. It was these families that formed the core of the American upper class and emerged as the closest the United States has come to an aristocracy.[3]

During the Gilded Age, at the end of the nineteenth century, an upper-class lifestyle and class consciousness began to develop, with ostentatious displays of wealth by the new industrial millionaires. New York became the heart of this emergent upper-class society. Great mansions were built, along with opera houses and museums, that catered to the tastes of the nouveau riche. The *Social Register,* a book listing the families of this would-be aristocracy, was published in New York and other large cities. Having one's family name listed in the *Social Register* served as a kind of official recognition of upper-class status. Exclusive associations and institutions began to replace the family as important socializing agents and as meeting places for the upper class. Children were sent to New England boarding schools and then to Ivy League colleges, which were financially supported by the wealthy industrialists. Exclusive men's clubs and country clubs became places where business and social affairs of the rich were joined. All of these developments had the effect of creating a national upper class, linking families from various localities (Baltzell, 1958).

The New Rich   While the old established families of wealth are still evident, their position at the top of the class hierarchy has been challenged in recent decades by newly enriched individuals and families who have acquired great wealth in their own lifetimes and done so through enterprises that they themselves either founded or nurtured. Political scientist Thomas Dye (1995) has referred to these mostly western and southern new rich as "cowboys" and contrasts them with the older established eastern "yankees." The differences between the two, Dye explains, lie in the sources of their wealth and in the recency of the cowboys' entrance into the top echelon. Whereas the old rich have a long line of money that extends back over several generations, the new rich are, if not self-made, people who have made their money in a rapid fashion in new industries, such as oil, aerospace, and discount merchandising, that have become predominant in the U.S. and global economies.

An even more recent element of the new rich attributes its wealth to emergence of the knowledge and information industries. Computers and related technologies and telecommunications and other media are more typical of

---

[3]The antebellum southern planter class, however, displayed some of the characteristics of a landed aristocracy.

the sources of wealth of the most recent rich. In 2000, 121 of the Forbes 400 derived their fortunes from technology, computer software, or media. Many of the newly wealthy have benefited from the surging values of their companies' stock, which they acquired through stock options (Sloan, 1997). The process by which the new rich have amassed their fortunes is comparable to the way in which fortunes were made in the past: radical changes in technology—steel, railroads, electric power, for example, in past ages, computers in the present—create opportunities for great wealth to emerge. Thurow describes the process:

> New technologies mean change. Change means disequilibrium. Disequilibrium conditions create high-return, high-growth opportunities. The winners understand the new technologies, are lucky enough to be in the right place at the right time, and have the skills to take advantage of these new situations. They become rich (1999:33).

A prime example of the new rich of the knowledge-based economy is H. Ross Perot, the Texas billionaire who ran for U.S. president in 1992 and 1996 as an independent candidate, funding most of the costs of the campaigns himself. Perot's family was not wealthy (his father was a horse trader), but he won an appointment to the U.S. Naval Academy. After four years of active military duty, he sold computers for IBM for a time and then decided to form his own software company, EDS (Electronic Data Systems). Through lucrative government contracts, EDS became the major subcontractor providing computer software for processing Medicare and Medicaid claims. Perot made other investments in oil, gas, and real estate that prospered greatly. In 1984, he sold EDS to General Motors for $2.5 billion (*Forbes*, 1996).

It is also in the computer and telecommunications industries that the ability to capitalize on an idea in a rapid and spectacular fashion has been so evident. For example, Mark Andreessen, while an undergraduate at the University of Illinois, conceived a software program, Netscape Navigator, that became a standard Internet tool. He became a multimillionaire at age twenty-four (Thomas, 1997).

Many among the computer entrepreneurs of today exhibit a similar precipitous rise to great wealth. Perhaps the best case is Bill Gates, founder of Microsoft, the computer software giant. Gates's story is no poor-boy-makes-good epic. His mother was from a wealthy and prominent banking family, and his father was a senior partner in one of Seattle's most politically influential and prestigious law firms. In addition to the wealth acquired from his parents, a trust fund was left to him by his grandparents. After attending an exclusive prep school, Gates, a brilliant student, enrolled at Harvard, though he never graduated. In 1974, Gates and a friend, Paul Allen, were convinced that they were on the cutting edge of a computer revolution. Gates was nineteen at the time; Allen was twenty-one. They started a company, Microsoft, and the rest, of course, is history (Wallace and Erickson, 1992). So rapid and profound was Microsoft's success that in less than twenty years, Gates's net worth had made him the second-wealthiest person in America, soon to be the wealthiest. Allen also was made a billionaire as a result of their enterprise. Microsoft today thoroughly dominates the computer software industry, and dozens of people who invested in the company in its early years have become fabulously wealthy.

The Privileges of Wealth

There are unique privileges that attach to great wealth. Obviously, the rich can partake of whatever the society offers in the way of material things; it is in that sense that money can buy almost anything. Steve Hilbert, a corporate CEO and one among the *Forbes* 400, wanted to play basketball for Indiana University but wasn't good enough. So he built a $5.5 million replica of Indiana's arena, Assembly Hall, where, as he explains, "On Saturdays I hit the winning shot to beat everyone from UCLA to Michigan to whomever in my own fantasy [while] playing by myself" (quoted in Pappas, 1997). Sociologist Thorstein Veblen, writing at the turn of the century, described the wealthy of that time in his classic work *The Theory of the Leisure Class* (1899). In it, he used the terms *conspicuous consumption* and *conspicuous leisure* to denote how people sought to demonstrate their wealth through styles and quantities of material goods and leisure activities. Such demonstrations of style and quantity are not relics of the past. Obviously, the need to flaunt one's wealth in an ostentatious and, as Veblen described it, wasteful way continues to drive much of the consumption behavior of the wealthy.

The privileges of wealth reach beyond consumption, however. The rich are able to avoid many of the inconveniences and chores of everyday life that most of us must endure: shopping at the grocery store, going to the bank, driving to work, filling the car with gasoline, waiting to be seated at a restaurant, filling out forms, caring for one's children. "The ultimate perk of the ruling class," notes Eric Konigsberg, "is no longer merely money or power, but the ability to be free of hassles" (1993:22). The rich accomplish this by having others do these mundane things for them. Konigsberg describes how this works for a few of the rich and famous. Movie star Demi Moore, for example, "has six assistants: one for her clothes, one for her hair, one for makeup, a bodyguard, a nanny and a general-purpose personal assistant, who has her own personal assistant, who is thinking of hiring one of her own"(22). But this does not even come close to the entourage of her (then) husband, actor Bruce Willis, who, on the set of a film he was shooting, required twenty-two assistants "including four or five bodyguards, a driver, a personal chef, a personal trainer, a masseuse and a hair and makeup stylist" (22). Not to be bothered by shopping, Saudi Prince Bandar bin Sultan, while vacationing in

Aspen, purchased one of every item in stock at the local Banana Republic (a retail clothing chain). As Konigsberg describes the event, the prince wasn't even in the store—he'd sent an assistant.

The rich and celebrated are also subject to different standards of conduct than others. Readers and viewers of supermarket and TV tabloids are fascinated by the various sexual exploits and love affairs of wealthy movie stars and entertainers, the kinds of behavior that they would look at scornfully if practiced among middle-class and, especially, poor people. These different standards often extend to the not-so-famous rich as well. Stock market tycoon Warren Buffet, currently America's fourth-wealthiest person, has remained married to his wife, whom he escorts to various public functions, but he lives happily with another woman (Lowenstein, 1995).

In addition to material privileges, wealth provides social esteem, or, as Max Weber referred to it, status. Moreover, wealth is ordinarily convertible into power in various social spheres. Most important, of course, is the fact that the life chances of the wealthy reach far beyond those of ordinary people.

Inheritance, Effort, and Wealth

Several years ago, actor John Housman appeared in a TV commercial for Smith Barney, a Wall Street investment firm. In the commercial, Housman, looking the part of a stodgy banker, grumbled that "at Smith Barney we make money the old-fashioned way—we *earn* it!" How do people get to the top of the class system today? Do they do it "the old-fashioned way," or do they inherit it, acquiring wealth through little effort of their own? In getting to the top, does the idea of the "self-made millionaire" (or billionaire, as the case may be) have much validity in the United States at the dawn of the twenty-first century?

Studies of the sources of wealth of America's richest individuals and families often seem to diverge. Some find that there is a continual renewal of names and faces among the super wealthy, whereas others contend that inheritance remains critical. Among the *Forbes* 400 in 2000, 137 attribute their wealth to nothing more than inheritance. Many others on the list, of course, are the scions of successful entrepreneurial families of the past that made the financial success of future family members all but a certainty. In a major study of the effects of inheritance on wealth accumulation, economist John Brittain found that gifts and bequests, on average, accounted for half or more of the net worth of the very wealthy. He concluded that the transfers of wealth from one generation to the next were "a major force in the perpetuation of wealth inequality" (1978:22). Other studies underscore the importance of inheritance in the accumulation of wealth (Keister, 2000; McNamee and Miller, 1998; Oliver and Shapiro, 1995).

Some, like Thomas R. Dye, maintain that there is much more mobility at the top than is commonly assumed. Dye asserts that despite the inheritance of much wealth through family channels, such family-based wealth "gradually dissipates over the generations, spreading more thinly among ever more heirs" (1995:91). Moreover, the energy and business skills that originally built family fortunes are rarely demonstrated by later generations. Most important, according to Dye, is the fact that each generation produces a new crop of successful entrepreneurs who emerge as self-made tycoons. What is of major significance to Dye and to others who view wealth inequality in America in a similar fashion is not the degree of inequality itself, which has always been evident, but rather the opportunity to enter into the ranks of the rich and the super rich. Some support for Dye's assertion is *Forbes's* claim that 220 members of the 400 richest Americans in 1997 were self-made (1997b).

What can be concluded from these seemingly conflicting accounts of how great wealth is acquired? Obviously, the surest (and most effortless) path to great wealth is simply to be born into it. This, in fact, characterizes the path followed by a large segment of the upper class. Moreover, even among those who earn their riches through their own enterprise and skill, family influences are apt to be hugely important. Nonetheless, the confines of the super wealthy are never entirely closed and limited to inheritance. New technologies and marketing innovations (like computer technology) can yield windfall returns on investment, as can the ownership of businesses in growth industries, providing the basis for the acquisition of great wealth within one's lifetime.

In any case, of course, those at the top of the wealth hierarchy will always number a relative few. Furthermore, however much circulation among the wealthy few occurs, there need be no effect on the inequality of wealth distribution. Indeed, as we have seen, despite the expansion of wealth in American society in recent decades, the distance between the wealthy and the rest of the society has widened enormously. By the early 1990s, the share of wealth held by the top 1 percent of the population (40 percent) was essentially double what it had been in the mid-1970s, comparable to where it had been in the late 1920s (Thurow, 1995).

The Power Elite: Patterns and Theory

This section looks at the social characteristics of the power elite and at their relationship to the upper class. As noted at the beginning of this chapter, the **power elite** are those who occupy top organizational positions, whose decisions have wide-ranging impact on the society.

In the United States, as in all modern societies, societal power is most essentially a synthesis of the actions of government and the economy. It is within these two institutional spheres that authority and influence are most crucial for the society as a whole and where societal resources are most highly concentrated. To examine the power elite in society therefore requires that we look at those in important decision-making governmental and corporate positions.

The Relationship between the Upper Class and the Power Elite

It would seem logical to assume that the wealthiest persons and families are also the most powerful. But consider whom you would select if you were asked to name the few most powerful people in the United States today. The president of the United States? The chief justice of the Supreme Court? The Speaker of the House? The chairman of the Federal Reserve Board? These are positions that immediately come to mind as "most powerful." They are, in fact, all positions of great power, but none of their incumbents is today among the truly wealthy.

There are others, outside the realm of politics, whose power is equally great but who are also not necessarily among the society's wealthiest persons. The top executives of General Motors or any of a few dozen giant corporations, the editors of the *New York Times* and a few other major newspapers, and the producers of the ABC, CBS, and NBC nightly news programs all hold positions that carry with them great societal power, but that (with the exception, perhaps, of top corporate executives) are not generally at the pinnacle of the income and wealth hierarchies. Moreover, unlike the familiar figures of the political world, they are rarely known to the general public.

The most wealthy in society, then, are not necessarily also the most powerful. It is true nonetheless that the association between wealth and power is strong. Since wealth is the most important resource in a capitalist society, it can be converted into various forms of power. Wealth, power, and prestige generally move in a circular flow. As in the proverbial chicken-and-egg dilemma, it is often difficult to determine which is the initial component in the cycle; but once one is established, the others tend to follow (Lenski, 1966).

Money is the driving force behind the political system, and the wealthy do play a disproportionately major role in the electoral and policymaking processes. Nonetheless, as already explained, wealth and power are not the same, and the relationship between them is not always neat and uncomplicated. We need to examine, therefore, the extent to which the upper class is also a *ruling* class, that is, a group that exerts societal power commensurate with its economic position. Sociologists and political scientists have studied this issue intently. Let's look at some of their major theories and research findings.

Mills's "Power Elite"   More than any other social scientist, C. Wright Mills is responsible for generating the study of the structure of power in the United States. Writing in the 1950s, Mills was a maverick among sociologists of that time, disputing the generally accepted depiction of the American power structure as a plurality of various interest groups lacking social cohesion. He concluded instead that a relatively unified power elite, made up of top political, corporate, and military officials, made key societal decisions:

> By the power elite, we refer to those political, economic, and military circles which as an intricate set of overlapping cliques share decisions having at least national consequences. In so far as national events are decided, the power elite are those who decide them. (1956:18)

Mills investigated the power elite's sociological characteristics and found that its members were quite similar in general outlook, interests, and social background. They attended the same schools, exhibited similar career patterns, and were, for the most part, exposed to common socialization experiences. They were, as a result, a socially cohesive group.

Given their similar social background, the members of the power elite shared the same outlook regarding the society's needs. In addition, the overlapping interests and functions of their institutions caused them to come together in a working relationship, further strengthening their common social and psychological orientations. They thought and acted the same, Mills contended, because their social and career environments were the same. Within the power elite, it was the business leaders, in Mills's estimation, who wielded the greatest influence. And, by implication, the business elite was integrally tied to the upper class.

Domhoff's "Governing Class" Theory   For the past three decades, G. William Domhoff has researched the relationship between the American upper class and the power elite more extensively than any contemporary sociologist. Domhoff, far more directly than Mills, asserts the close ties between the upper class and the power elite. He concludes that the upper class is essentially a ruling class (Domhoff, 1967, 1979, 1983, 1998). Domhoff posits that there is a readily apparent relationship between those who own or control a disproportionate share of the society's wealth, those who exercise control over major corporations, and those who greatly influence the governmental elite. Significant societal wealth is found within the corporation, and those who dominate this key economic institution through ownership or management maintain maximum influence in the public policy–forming process. Domhoff (1967) calls this group a "governing class":

> A governing class is a social upper class which receives a disproportionate amount of a country's income, owns a disproportionate amount of a country's wealth, and contributes a disproportionate number of its members to the controlling institutions and key decision-making groups in that country. (142)

Domhoff's essential thesis is that top corporate owners and managers are the major power figures in American society. Their views dominate government, particularly the federal government. His conclusion is that "a corporation-based capitalist class—manifesting itself most obviously as a social upper class—dominates the American government" (1993:171). The federal government, Domhoff concludes, "is dominated (which does not mean complete and total control) by a power elite rooted in the upper class and the corporate community" (177). He defines the power elite as "active, working members of the upper class and high-level employees in institutions controlled by members of the upper class, thereby making it the leadership group of the upper class" (172).

Domhoff (1998) emphasizes the social nature of the dominant corporate ownership and managerial class. The cohesiveness of this ruling group is largely a product of their common upper-class ties. "They belong to the same exclusive social clubs, frequent the same summer and winter resorts, and send their children to a relative handful of private schools. Members of the corporate community thereby become a *corporate rich* who create a nation-wide *social upper class* through their social interaction" (2). Through these common points of social interaction, the upper class consolidates a consciousness of purpose and effectively controls the power process.

The corporate rich, Domhoff (1974, 1998) explains, sponsor a network of policy-formation groups that strongly influence government policy. According to Domhoff, it is chiefly through elite men's clubs and through policy-planning organizations that the upper class formulates its policy preferences and communicates them to political decision makers. These clubs and organizations thus become major locations of upper-class interaction, not only for social purposes, but for functional or working purposes as well.

Many of Domhoff's basic conclusions seem well founded. The social interaction of members of the corporate elite and top-ranking political officials is easily verified empirically. Domhoff has also shown that even though political leaders may not be found as frequently as corporate leaders on upper-class club rosters, their presence is felt in other ways. More important, he demonstrates upper-class participation in influential policy-formation groups as well as the overrepresentation of members of the upper class in significant political positions.

Dye's Institutional Model   Political scientist Thomas Dye has also closely observed the American power elite. Although he conceptualizes the power elite in much the same terms as Mills and Domhoff, some of his conclusions are markedly different.

Dye (1995) defines the power elite as approximately six thousand individuals in seven thousand positions who "exercise formal authority over institutions that control roughly half of the nation's resources in industry, finance, utilities, insurance, mass media, foundations, education, law, and civic and cultural affairs" (244). Though a tiny fraction of the total population, it is still a larger figure than that posited by Mills or Domhoff.

Unlike Domhoff and Mills, Dye does not subscribe to the notion of a close relationship between the wealthy and the powerful. He sees institutional wealth as more important than personal wealth and, thus, control of institutions as most critical. He points to people who are among the society's billionaires who wield little or no societal power: widows, retirees, and other inheritors, as well as independent entrepreneurs, none of whom has ever played a significant role in the corporate world. Dye also does not see the upper class as a key recruiting ground for top political leaders. The link between the corporate elite and the political elite, in Dye's opinion, is tenuous at best.

Also, in contrast to Mills and Domhoff, Dye discounts the significance of common social institutions, such as exclusive clubs and schools, among the wealthy as the basis of a dominant class. Although he does not deny the importance of prestigious private clubs, he maintains that members of such clubs are mainly from the corporate elite and do not interact with governmental leaders. As far as the exercise of power is concerned, the clubs, according to Dye, "merely help facilitate processes that occur anyway" (1995:193). Perhaps more important, even if there may be a strong presence of political and economic elites in upper-class organizations, what remains questionable is the extent to which their interaction within these organizations helps to promote control of public policy. As political scientists Kenneth Prewitt and Alan Stone point out, "The overrepresentation of a social upper class no doubt gives some common tone and style to the elite circles, but it does not begin to explain what is politically critical about those circles (1973:159).

Like Mills and Domhoff, Dye does see a concentration of economic power in American society among a relatively small group of corporate managers. He identifies an "inner group" within the power elite who combine their corporate power with influence among important foundations, universities, and cultural and civic organizations. He also sees this inner group as socially cohesive. They not only come together at corporate board meetings but attend similar cultural and civic events, foundation meetings, and university trustee and alumni gatherings and are members of the same exclusive social clubs (Dye, 1995).

Also like Mills and Domhoff, Dye sees members of this inner group as links between the corporate world and government. It is corporate and personal wealth that "provides both the financial resources and the overall direction of policy research, planning, and development" (1995:220). And, it is within these policy-planning groups that leaders from various societal institutions are able to come together in shaping national policies.

Baltzell: The Conservative Elitist View   Further evidence of a strong overlap between the upper class and those who head the powerful institutions
of American society is provided by E. Digby Baltzell (1958, 1964). Baltzell's
conclusions regarding the interrelations between the upper class and the society's chief power wielders are similar to Domhoff's: Essentially, there exists a ruling class. But in contrast to Domhoff, Baltzell sees a ruling class as
socially beneficial and its special privileges justified.

Baltzell distinguishes three groups at the top of the social hierarchy.
First, there is what he calls simply the "elite," made up of top functional leaders of various spheres of social activity. These are the important decision
makers of the corporation, the government, education, the media, and so on.
Second, there is an "upper class," composed of families of established wealth
whose members are descendants of elite members of one or more generations ago and who make up a social upper class with a distinct style of life
and primary group solidarity. When this class combines its wealth and status with functional power—that is, when its members are simultaneously
elite members—there exists a ruling class, or what Baltzell calls an "establishment." This conceptualization of the power structure closely resembles
Domhoff's.

Baltzell sees the need for a society to maintain a system of power that
combines the traditional authority deriving from the past with the infusion
of new groups into positions of functional power: "The most difficult and delicate problem faced by democratic societies is that of balancing the liberal
need for the continuous circulation of individual elites with the conservative
need for maintaining a continuity of family authority" (1964:72). Ideally,
then, the establishment is made up of individuals whose power and prestige
are inherited; but it remains open to the newly powerful, those recruited into
the elite on the basis of talent and ability. This requires that members of the
elite be accepted into the upper class regardless of ethnic origin or religion.
Baltzell emphasizes that without the infusion of new blood from the elite, the
upper class will degenerate into a group that neglects its leadership duties
and concerns itself only with its rights to privilege. In a sense, Baltzell views
the establishment as a "noble aristocracy," socialized into accepting its leadership role and conscious of its societal obligations.

Baltzell finds much overlapping of the upper class and the elite throughout American history. Those who have occupied positions of power in government, the corporation, and other societal institutions have been overwhelmingly representative of those of wealth and prestige. In recent decades,
however, the upper class has become more narrow in its social composition,
excluding those of diverse ethnic and religious origins who have penetrated
the society's functional elites. As more Catholics, Jews, and other ethnic and
religious minorities have come into positions of power in government, the
economy, education, and other areas, they have not been absorbed into the

upper class, as they were in past generations. Baltzell thus sees an open class system operating in the society's functional institutions, with upward mobility from the lower social ranks, but an increasingly caste-like status system, closing off entrance into the upper class for the new occupants of power positions.

Baltzell, then, does not see a close interrelationship of upper class and power elite in modern times. Although it did so in past eras, the upper class, according to Baltzell, no longer constitutes or even necessarily controls the power elite. Those of non-upper-class origin are able to enter into top positions of power and may exercise their power independently of the upper class, which is increasingly concerned only with protecting its status and privilege, not with exercising power. Baltzell, however, views this development apprehensively. A closed upper class creates the possibility that power will be wielded by those who lack socialization to upper-class values and who therefore have little understanding of their larger social responsibilities. Their legitimacy may thus become questionable and force them to resort to coercion and deception to govern effectively.

Social Class and the Power Elite

In considering who gets to the top of the power hierarchy, the American ideology suggests that there are no built-in impediments. With sufficient effort and perseverance, the lowliest person can rise to the greatest heights. Anyone, therefore, can be the CEO of a major corporation or the owner of a broadcasting empire or even president of the United States.

In the latter decades of the nineteenth century, an American writer, Horatio Alger Jr., authored a hundred novels that almost perfectly reflected the belief that hard work, thrift, and honesty lead to economic and social success. The leitmotiv of each of Alger's books was the same: Even those of humble origins can make it to the top. Through adherence to the work ethic, along with a bit of luck, any adversity might be overcome. And in the Alger stories, the hero always conquers what seems overwhelming odds. Alger's novels were aimed primarily at a juvenile audience, particularly young boys who, he hoped, would use the stories as inspiration for living a good life. From Alger's novels came what has been called the **Horatio Alger myth,** essentially the idea that anyone, regardless of social standing, can reach the pinnacle of wealth and power with enough effort and perseverance. This has become a basic belief, held at least in the abstract, of Americans in explaining how people get to the top. To what extent does the idea of an essentially open system of elite recruitment hold true?

Former President Bill Clinton would seem to validate in some part the Horatio Alger myth. Rising from seemingly ordinary beginnings, neither poor nor rich, Clinton displayed many of the characteristics of an inspired overachiever. He excelled academically as an undergraduate at Georgetown University and won a Rhodes scholarship to study at Oxford. He went on to Yale Law School where he again earned outstanding grades. Clinton was determined to succeed in the political world and before his thirtieth birthday had been elected attorney general of Arkansas. By the age of thirty-two, he was elected Arkansas's governor, the youngest person ever to hold that office (Ifill, 1992). In 1992 he gained the Democratic Party's nomination for the presidency and subsequently won the election, despite imposing political obstacles (Allen and Portis, 1992).

Is Clinton's rise to political power, however, typical of those who hold high office? The path followed by both his predecessor and his successor in the White House, George Bush and his son George W. Bush, could not present a stronger contrast. Indeed, the Bushes' stories personify the upper-class, patrician model. The elder Bush's father was a U.S. senator who had been a partner in one of the largest Wall Street investment firms. Bush himself attended Phillips Andover, one of the most exclusive and prestigious prep schools, and then went on to Yale. Rather than joining his father's investment firm, Bush senior started as vice president of a Texas oil-drilling equipment company, of which his father was a director. With financing from his uncle, he formed several oil companies and while still in his thirties became a multimillionaire. Having succeeded in business, he then turned to the political world (Dye, 1990). The junior Bush, like his father, attended exclusive private schools and Yale University. His subsequent business ventures were financed in large measure by friends and relatives and were undistinguished until he parlayed a $600,000 investment in the Texas Rangers baseball club into a $14 million profit when he sold his share of ownership (Kristof and Bruni, 2000; Ratcliffe, 1998). Through the accident of birth, there was certainly a high probability, if not a guarantee, that the Bushes would take their place among the wealthy and powerful.

Which of these two types, then, typifies the quest for places in the power elite? The answer is a mixed picture. Although the linkage between wealth and power is usually very strong, there are nonetheless opportunities for those from less eminent origins who are determined and ambitious.

The Social-Class Origins of U.S. Elites

Examining the correlations between societal power and social variables such as class, ethnicity, gender, and age provides one means of determining the extent to which the society's power structure is open or closed. Do people of different social origins commonly enter powerful decision-making and influential groups, or do top leaders remain tightly knit in self-sustaining units? Chapters 11 and 12 examine the extent to which race, ethnicity, and gender affect entrance into positions of institutional power. The analysis in this section is limited to the significance of social class.

Almost all studies of top leaders of government and of the corporation conclude that the majority do not reflect the population as a whole in terms of social class. Specifically, they come from upper- or upper-middle-class families and have displayed such backgrounds since the founding of the nation.

Charles Beard, in a well-known historical study (1913), found that the members of the Constitutional Convention of 1787 were mostly the economic and social notables of their time. They were professional men, merchants, and landowners who, according to Beard, benefited economically from the adoption of the Constitution as it was written. The privileged status of these early political leaders is evident in their educational backgrounds. Philip Burch (1980) found that at a time when only a tiny element of the population attended college (about 0.2 percent), 87 percent of the major cabinet and diplomatic appointees of the George Washington and John Adams administrations had done so.

Studies of government leaders indicate that the predominance of those with privileged backgrounds has not been limited to the early eras of American history. Mills (1956) showed, for example, that the 513 men who occupied the top political offices of president, vice president, Speaker of the House, cabinet member, and Supreme Court justice between 1789 and 1953 were mainly from well-to-do professional or business families (see also Burch, 1980). Sociologist Lloyd Warner and his associates (Warner and Abegglen, 1963) studied 11,000 top federal executives and found that well over half had fathers who were professionals, business owners, or executives; only 15 percent were the sons of laborers. A study of the Supreme Court showed that of the 92 men who served in that body up to 1959, only 9 were not from families of economic importance, social prestige, and political influence (Schmidhauser, 1960). And, a study of 180 members of the U.S. Senate who served between 1947 and 1957 concluded that, with few exceptions, they were selected from "near the top of the society's class system" (Matthews, 1973:44). A later study (Zweigenhaft, 1975) found no basic differences through the mid-1970s. The occupational backgrounds of members of the 107th U.S. Congress are shown in Table 5-2. As can be seen, those from the business world and the legal profession predominate. Moreover, with the inflated campaign funds that are now commonplace in national elections, the tendency for the wealthy to attain high elective positions has grown stronger. By the mid-1990s, over one-quarter of the Senate and at least fifty members of the House were estimated to be millionaires (Simpson, 1994).

As to the presidency, the notion that most men who have held the highest office have been of humble origins does not hold up under careful historical examination. In his study of the social origins of U.S. presidents, Edward

Table 5-2 ■ Occupations of Members of the 107th Congress*

Occupation	House	Senate	Total
Actor/Entertainer	1	1	2
Aeronautics	1	1	2
Agriculture	25	6	31
Artistic/Creative	2	0	2
Business or banking	159	24	183
Clergy	2	1	3
Education	92	16	108
Engineering	9	0	9
Health care	4	0	4
Homemaker/Domestic	2	1	3
Journalism	9	7	16
Labor	2	1	3
Law	156	53	210
Law enforcement	10	0	10
Medicine	14	3	17
Military	2	1	3
Miscellaneous	6	0	6
Professional sports	3	1	4
Public service/Politics	126	28	154
Real estate	24	4	28
Secretarial/Clerical	2	0	2
Technical/Trade	3	0	3

*Because some members have more than one occupation, totals are higher than total membership. Source: Hirschfeld, 2001.

Pessen (1984) reveals that most were born to families of unusually high social status and economic well-being, quite unlike the socioeconomic circumstances of most American families of their time. Pessen does see some change in recent decades in that presidents born into the upper class have become less common in favor of those born into the upper-middle class. The poor and the lower-middle class, however, continue to be bypassed. "Despite slight changes in the patterns of the presidents' social origins," Pessen concludes, "from one period in our history to another, the central fact, now as earlier, remains the almost total exclusion of men born to poor or modest stations" (72).

In short, throughout American history, top political leaders have been drawn from a narrow social base, not typical of the general populace. They have been and remain, as political scientist Donald Matthews put it over forty years ago, "far from common men in either their origins or their achievements" (1954:23–24).

If top-ranking political leaders generally display class origins higher than average, leaders of big business are even more clearly from privileged backgrounds. Knowing the class backgrounds of economic leaders is often a question of judgment, for we must rely mostly on what business executives themselves choose to reveal. Their perceptions of the extent of their upward mobility may exceed their actual experience. The image of the poor boy who has made it to the top—the Horatio Alger notion—is more publicly favorable than the image of an executive whose place at the top was never in doubt. Hence, business leaders may sometimes exaggerate the humbleness of their origins. Although this is also true of political leaders, their pasts are subject to much greater public exposure than is true of top officials of the business world; it is therefore more difficult to sustain a "born in a log cabin" image if that is not actually the case.

Despite these methodological difficulties, it is a basic conclusion of most studies of the corporate elite of the United States and other advanced capitalist societies that their members usually come from the top or near the top of the social hierarchy. One important study done in the 1960s concluded that "whatever our national hopes, the business leaders of America are a select group, drawn for the most part from the upper-ranks" (Warner and Abegglen, 1963:14). Other studies have confirmed the upper- or upper-middle-class origins of the business elite since the emergence of the United States as an industrial society (Diamond, 1970; Newcomer, 1955; Keller, 1953; Lipset and Bendix, 1959).

Dye (1995) sees U.S. power elites as somewhat more varied in social-class background. He concludes that approximately 30 percent are of upper-class origins, having attended private prestigious prep schools and having parents who were high-ranking corporate, political, or other institutional officials. Thus, 70 percent appear to be middle class in family origin. On that basis Dye finds it illogical to conclude, as Domhoff and others have, that the upper class "dominates" the American power elite. Nonetheless, Dye recognizes that "even those who climbed the institutional ladder to high position generally started with the advantages of a middle-class upbringing" (246). Moreover, half are graduates of prestigious private universities.

It is quite apparent, then, that the top leaders of government and business in the United States, as well as other modern capitalist societies, are, in terms of social class, not typical of the general populace. Prewitt and Stone (1973) estimated that the wealthiest one-fifth of American families contributed about nine of every ten leaders of the political economy, and the next wealthiest fifth contributed most of the remainder (Figure 5-1). When elites of education, the military, and the media are combined with those of government and business, the same general pattern is evident.

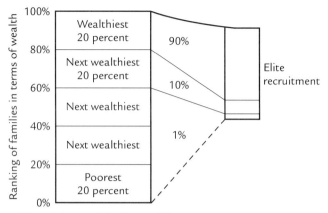

Figure 5-1 ■ Class Origins of the Power Elite
Source: Kenneth Prewitt and Alan Stone, *The Ruling Elites,* 137. Copyright © 1973 Harper & Row. Reprinted by permission of Addison Wesley Educational Publishers, Inc.

Paths to Power

The Elite Recruitment Process

Although the historical patterns of elite recruitment seem to show that ascription is critical, cases such as Bill Clinton's and a plethora of others who have risen in class and power indicate that there are opportunities for those who are not born into privilege. In the corporate world, entrance into the elite does not ordinarily occur without merit. This means that an individual cannot step into an executive position simply because his or her father was a high-ranking official of the company. To a lesser degree, the same is true in the political world. Government leaders must deal with a wide range of issues that often require specialized skills and expertise. The question, then, is how those born into lower social classes may be afforded the opportunities to acquire and subsequently display their skills and perhaps enter the power elite.

The Talent Pool   The elite recruitment process can be pictured as a system in which individuals are chosen from a potential talent pool. In this reservoir of possible leaders are the people with the skills, education, and other qualifications needed to fill elite positions. It is here that competition does exist, that the highest achievers do display their abilities, and that the best-qualified do generally succeed. Hence, what is most important is *entering this reservoir of qualified people* (Figure 5-2).

Many from sub-middle-class origins may have leadership potential, but unless they can gain entrance into the elite pool, their abilities will go unnoticed. Those of higher-class origins enter more easily into this competition, since they have been afforded greater opportunities to secure the needed

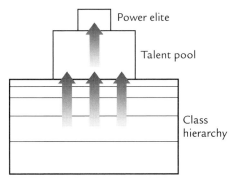

Figure 5-2 ■ The Process of Elite Recruitment
Source: Martin N. Marger, *Elites and Masses: An Introduction to Political Sociology,* 2d ed.
Copyright © 1987 Wadsworth Publishing Co. Reprinted with permission of Wadsworth, an
imprint of the Wadsworth Group, a division of Thomson Learning. Fax 800-730-2215.

qualifications. They not only acquire college and professional degrees, but often acquire them from the most prestigious institutions.

Social Connections   Following the acquisition of skills necessary to compete for elite places, one must then display them. There is, in a sense, a stage upon which potential elite members must audition their qualities. Having access to that stage means not only achieving the formal requirements for entering the talent pool (education above all) but also interacting within social circles where incumbent elites are likely to take notice of a talented individual. These are the social connections that come more naturally to those of higher-class families and that further filter out otherwise qualified persons from the competition. The familiar adage that "it's not what you know but who you know" is quite applicable in the process of elite recruitment.

Often, attendance at an elite university not only provides individuals with a prestigious degree but gives them an opportunity to nurture personal friendships and affiliations that will serve them well in the occupational world. To illustrate, assume that four individuals are born into the working class. They all have pretty much the same personal characteristics and are exposed to similar social environments. All are academically outstanding students. There are a few key differences among them, however. One is extraordinarily ambitious and talented; most think he will go far once he graduates from high school. A second has a very high IQ and, like the first student, her teachers and peers expect her to go far. A third is very confident and assertive; he is known as someone who will not stop short of achieving whatever it is he attempts. The fourth has none of the extraordinary personal traits of the other three but has a good enough academic record and sufficient financial assistance to attend Harvard. The first three, for personal reasons, go on to a state university near their home community. Who among these four has the best chance of entering into the power elite? Remember the idea of probability in social science analysis. We cannot predict who among them will actually enter the elite, but the probability is greatest that the fourth student will do so. Harvard and other Ivy League schools are favorite recruiting grounds for top corporations and prestigious law firms, but in addition, at Harvard she will have formed personal relationships that will give her entree to networks of the powerful and influential.

The reservoir of qualified people is larger than the number of positions to be filled. Hence, knowing the "right" people and being able to connect with them becomes critical. In addition, of course, are other ascriptive factors—race and ethnicity, gender, even physical attractiveness—that further filter out candidates at this point in the selection process.

Self-Selection   In addition to formal qualifications and social connections, there are less obvious social-psychological factors that tend to further narrow the potential elite pool. These involve a subtle process of self-selection by which those of higher social standing assert themselves, and by which those of lower social standing eliminate themselves from the competition for elite positions (Prewitt and Stone, 1973). For example, a young man or woman whose family has been active in politics, who has attended an elite university, and who has established a network of connections to the economic and political power establishments would not be starry-eyed in aspiring to a high position in the corporate or political world. Consider again the case of the Bushes, described earlier.

By comparison, consider that a young person from a less prestigious family, who has no connections and has earned only a high school diploma or perhaps a college degree from a second-rate state university, would probably not visualize a future place for himself or herself at the top. As Prewitt and Stone explain, such an individual "has few models to emulate, no contacts to put him into the right channels, and little reason to think of himself as potentially wealthy or powerful" (1973:140). Thus, self-selection aids in filtering out those of lower social class from the pool of potential elites. Most eliminate themselves from the competition early in the game.

The Systemic Nature of Elite Recruitment

As should now be obvious, elite recruitment is mostly a process in which the cards are heavily stacked in favor of the society's affluent and highest-status groups. The structural forces of class, ethnicity, and gender, as well as the more subtle social-psychological forces of self-selection, tend to perpetuate the place of dominant groups in key power positions.

This need not be seen, however, as a conscious conspiracy on the part of a ruling class to preserve its power. Rather, the system of elite recruitment is largely self-directing. The fact that the social composition of elites tends to be consistent from one generation to another reflects the structural nature of societal power. Those who are upper- or upper-middle-class, white, Protestant, and male need not conspire to protect their favored social positions; they are automatically afforded easier access to the wealth, education, and social connections needed to qualify for power positions. And by the same token, a cumulation of disadvantages automatically works to the detriment of those of lower-class, working-class, and ethnic and gender minority groups. Recall the notion of the accident of birth and the way in which social resources are accumulated. Thus, top power-holders in almost all institutional spheres quite naturally continue to come predominantly from the same social groups.

Moreover, these repetitive patterns of elite recruitment come to be commonly expected, thereby further strengthening the hold of dominant social groups on top positions. Most people simply do not expect those of low-income or even working-class origins, for example, to head giant corporations, to be nominated for the presidency, or to be five-star generals. Social expectations of who should occupy power positions are reinforced by widely held negative stereotypes regarding the capabilities of sub-middle-class groups, helping to make their underrepresentation in power elites a self-fulfilling prophecy (Marger, 1987).

It should be remembered, however, that because the system is not tightly closed, some individuals of lower social origins do work their way into the elite. There is always room at the top for those few who overcome social handicaps, manage to enter the talent pool, and, once there, excel. Incumbent elites, in other words, are not able to totally frustrate the entrance of lower-status individuals into positions of power. As sociologists Seymour Martin Lipset and Reinhard Bendix note,

> No elite or ruling class controls the natural distribution of talent, intelligence, or other abilities, though it may monopolize the opportunities for education and training. As long as many of those with high abilities belong to the lower strata (and many contemporary studies suggest that this is so), there will be leaders who come from those strata. The chance for potential leaders to develop the skills which will take them up from the ranks may be small, but sooner or later some will break through. (1959:3)

The penetration of a few from lower social ranks, however, should not be mistaken as commonplace. On the contrary, such cases are clearly exceptional.[4] *The outstanding fact of elite recruitment in the United States and other industrial societies is that leaders are chosen overwhelmingly from socially dominant groups and have been for many generations.* The entrance of the few from more

---

[4]It should also be obvious, of course, that those who are not qualified to run corporations or governments will not be selected even if they are of privileged class and status origins.

humble backgrounds, however, reinforces the traditional belief that the process of elite recruitment accommodates all, regardless of class and status.

Power Elites in Other Societies

In the predominance of those of higher social classes in elite positions, the United States is not unique. A similar pattern holds in virtually all other industrial societies.

In the realm of government, leaders are rarely below the middle class in social origin (Keller, 1963; Miliband, 1969; Porter, 1965; Putnam, 1976). One political scientist has explained that the British House of Commons, for example, like the U.S. Congress, is "anything but a microcosm of the nation" (Guttsman, 1963:373).

As to economic elites, the predominance of upper- and upper-middle-class men in top decision-making positions is even more pronounced in other industrial societies than in the United States (Hall et al., 1969; Fidler, 1981). This is the case even in societies in which the class structure is less sharply stratified. In Canada, for example, Porter (1965) and Clement (1975) found that few of the Canadian economic elite came from sub-middle-class origins. And in Japan, top executives come principally from the urban upper class, with only a tiny percentage from the working class or even the lower-middle class (Mannari, 1974).

Summary

In terms of income and wealth, the upper class in American society is far removed from other social classes. A relative handful of individuals and families earn multimillion-dollar salaries and, more important, possess wealth in even higher amounts. Moreover, the separation between the rich and the remainder of the U.S. population has widened during the past two and a half decades. In a real sense, the rich have become richer.

The upper class of past generations consisted of families that acquired their wealth through the burgeoning heavy industries of the late nineteenth century. Most of today's new rich derive their wealth from the emergent knowledge/information industries of post-industrial society.

Although the upper class are those at the top of the class hierarchy in terms of income, wealth, and lifestyle, the power elite consist of those who occupy the society's most important institutional positions of authority. It is particularly in the corporate world and in government that these positions are found. Although the relationship between the upper class and the power elite is very strong, the two are not the same. Therefore, some individuals may be part of the upper class but not the power elite, and vice versa.

The recruitment process into the power elite is one in which those from privileged social backgrounds have great advantages. Even though the process is technically open and some persons of modest social origins do penetrate the elite, those from the upper and upper-middle classes tend to disproportionately occupy the major leadership positions of the corporation and government.

In all societies, correlations between certain social characteristics and power positions are quite evident. No matter how accessible the power structure may seem, the social backgrounds of leaders tend to remain relatively consistent for long periods of time. Those who hold leadership positions are generally replaced by individuals of similar social origins, and these repetitive patterns of replacement come to be commonly expected. However, the critical importance of ascribed characteristics, especially family of origin, do not rule out individual ability and effort as factors in elite recruitment. Individual talent and achievement do become important determinants in the selection of institutional leaders, but only after the competitive field has been thinned out.

6

Stratification Systems and Social Mobility

Any organized social group is always a stratified social body. There has not been and does not exist any permanent social group which is "flat," and in which all members are equal.
PITIRIM A. SOROKIN

For Americans, to aspire to a higher social position is looked upon as natural and expected. Indeed, striving to improve one's social status is, in American society, recognized as a very positive personal characteristic. It is a basic part of the socialization process, and as a result, most young people believe that they will improve their social standing as they move through their careers. Most of them also believe that they will exceed their parents in acquiring income and wealth.

As common as the belief and expectation of changing one's social status may be in the United States and other modern societies, it is a relatively recent phenomenon in the longer span of human development. In most societies throughout history, the presumption was that people would stay in the social position into which they were born. To aspire to a higher place was not only seen as unrealistic but was disapproved and perhaps even considered heretical.

This chapter looks at the phenomenon of **social mobility,** that is, the movement of people up and down the society's various hierarchies. How much mobility is there in the United States and similar societies, and what are the factors that promote or repel it? As noted in Chapter 1, although patterns of social inequality are structured and endure for long periods, they are not unchangeable, either for individuals or for social groups. The accident of birth is a powerful force in determining people's social standing, but some do overcome economic and social disadvantages to rise in the class system and some born into families of high status may drop despite their relative advantages.

Whatever mobility occurs is dependent on the limitations presented by the society—specifically, the manner in which stratification is arranged. Depending on the society, stratification systems are structured to either impede or facilitate movement from one stratum to another. In some cases, like the United States, the class system is open and provides opportunities for mobility, but the stratification systems in some other societies make mobility rare. Before examining the forms and extent of social mobility in American society, first we look at different systems of stratification and how they both induce and obstruct movement.

Systems of Stratification

The extent to which people move up or down the society's hierarchies always rests most basically on the opportunities presented by the stratification system. Either stratification systems are porous, providing for free and perhaps even frequent movement between strata, or they are rigid, with strata relatively sealed, making it difficult for people to change their status.

Closed societies are those where mobility is uncommon and where political and cultural norms and values dictate against it. People are assigned a status at birth, which ordinarily does not change during their lifetime. Individuals may have the ambition and skills to move upward, but they are locked in to their hereditarily acquired position. Similarly, people do not move downward, regardless of their failures.

In traditional societies, where closed stratification systems prevail, custom rules the social order. People look to the past to solve current problems and do not believe that they are capable of changing their circumstances. They rarely question their status since the prevailing social and religious institutions validate social inequality. The predominant view is that inequality is a product of deities, not humans, and therefore it is not within human capacity to change that system or anyone's place in it. As Philip Mason has described such societies, "Everywhere, the top classes made some kind of alliance with the belief that the world was divinely ordained and persuaded their subjects that it was by divine intention that they must work so hard for so little" (1970:7).

Open societies, by contrast, theoretically present few impediments to mobility. People move up and down the class hierarchy on the basis of desire, merit, and talent. This form of stratification typifies the class systems of modern societies. Individuals compete for positions in the social hierarchy and gather resources that enable them to move upward. Downward movement can occur as well, of course, as people fail for lack of skills or because of circumstances over which they may have little control.

Stratification systems, whether open or closed, are never perfectly fluid on the one hand or rigid on the other. Some degree of competition for social positions is always evident, as is some degree of ascription. Thus, the systems of inequality found among different societies are mixed, with both open and closed features. Societies, however, may be much closer to one side or the other of this scale. Let's look at the different types of stratification systems that have characterized human societies.

Slavery

Slavery has been a persistent form of inequality throughout most of recorded human history and even remains in evidence today. Moreover, it has existed in all regions of the world. In some societies, slaves were captured in war; in others, slavery was the result of unpaid debts; and in others, enslavement was a form of punishment for crimes (Patterson, 1982). In the southern United States, Brazil, and the West Indies, Africans were captured and sold into slavery through a thriving slave trade that started in the fifteenth century (Rawley, 1981).

Slavery in the United States   When blacks first entered American society in 1619, their status as servants was not essentially different from that of many others, including some Europeans. Various forms of bondage had been prevalent in all the colonies almost from the founding of the society (Handlin, 1957). Perhaps the most common was voluntary, or indentured, servitude, in which a person was bound by contract to serve a master for a certain length of time, usually four to seven years (Jordan, 1969). In exchange, the servant's passage was paid to the colonies. A great number of people, particularly those from Scotland and Ireland, entered the country in this manner. By the 1660s, however, most southern states had enacted laws defining blacks as slaves rather than as indentured servants.

The evolution of slavery in the United States was primarily a consequence of economic rationality, prompted above all by the demand for cheap labor in the underpopulated colonies. "The use of slaves in southern agriculture," explains historian Kenneth Stampp, "was a deliberate choice (among several alternatives) made by men who sought greater returns than they could obtain from their own labor alone, and who found other types of labor more expensive" (1956:5).

The American brand of slavery operated as a system of paternalistic domination, resembling, in a way, a parent-child relationship between master and slave (Elkins, 1976). The slaves' lives on American plantations were controlled totally by the master, his power legitimized by the slave codes of the various slaveholding states. Slaves lacked almost all legal rights. They could not own property, testify in court, inherit property, hire themselves out, or make contracts. Moreover, slave laws held that marriage between slaves carried none of the legal rights of marriage between free people. As a result, families could be broken up in trade, with no consideration given to keeping husband, wife, and children together. Since slave laws prohibited slaves from learning to read and write, their dependence on their masters was virtually total.

Because slaves represented a significant financial investment, their treatment, though cruel and inhumane in the extreme, would ordinarily not extend to the point of rendering them unable to perform their work. Historians

Robert Fogel and Stanley Engerman (1974) explain, for example, that although slave marriages were not legally recognized, masters still encouraged their slaves to marry and establish families in order to ensure an atmosphere of stability. Hence, slave families were kept intact if possible.

During the 1830s, slavery came under serious attack from abolitionists, who argued that blacks should be free to develop their capacities to the fullest. In response, pro-slavery theorists developed a racist belief system that held that fundamental physiological differences existed between blacks and whites that naturally rendered blacks mentally and physically inferior to whites. Also stressed in these new racist theories was the failure of blacks to develop what Westerners considered a "civilized" life in Africa and the dangers of miscegenation, leading to racial degeneracy. After the 1830s, almost all whites of whatever persuasion agreed that blacks were inferior to whites in certain fundamental qualities, especially intelligence and initiative, and that those differences were essentially unchangeable. Because of those presumed differences, subordination of blacks was deemed natural and necessary (Fredrickson, 1971).

In a paternalistic system like American slavery, strict segregation of masters and slaves is not required. Rather, it is the *social* distance between them that is of greatest importance. Everyone knows his or her place in the social arrangement and sticks to it. In the South, in order to enforce this stratification, a well-understood racial etiquette developed in which physical contact was not uncommon but the social places of whites and blacks were not violated. Social intimacy might often be seen in the form of black women serving as mistresses to white slave masters or of the raising of white children by black "mammies." Such intimate personal contacts in a paternalistic system, however, are always relationships between unequals.

Slavery in the United States ended in 1865, but not long after, a new stratification system emerged that reinstalled the subordinate status of blacks and their economic dependence on whites. The new system, called "Jim Crow," is discussed later in this chapter.

Slavery in Brazil   The slave system in Brazil exceeded U.S. slavery both in numbers and in duration. The Portuguese began importing African slaves into their Brazilian colony as early as the late sixteenth century, after the indigenous population, used as slave laborers, was decimated. Slavery in Brazil was not abolished until 1888, over two decades after it ended in the United States. As in the American system, it was designed to supply an agricultural labor force, mainly for Brazil's sugar plantations, but in its actual administration, Brazilian slavery differed in a number of ways from its American counterpart.

Some have argued that the Brazilian form of slavery was typified by less brutal treatment of slaves. The Brazilian historian Gilberto Freyre maintained that the Anglo-Saxon and Portuguese cultures differed sufficiently to produce divergent patterns of master-slave relations. Freyre held that the Portuguese came to Brazil with a more tolerant attitude toward people of color.

Portugal had experienced contact with Africans in its colonial ventures as early as the fifteenth century and had endured a long period of rule by the Moors even earlier. The Portuguese sense of racial difference, therefore, was not as absolute as that of the Anglo-Saxons, who had had little contact with nonwhites. As a result, sexual relations between Portuguese slave masters and their slaves were far more commonplace and socially accepted than in the American system. This, Freyre contended, was evidence of a more compassionate and essentially altruistic master-slave relationship (1956, 1963).

Historian Frank Tannenbaum (1947) argued that the Brazilian slave system was more humane as a result of the difference between the Portuguese and Anglo-Saxon legal and religious concepts of slavery. The Portuguese did not perceive Africans as nonhuman, but simply as unfortunate people who wound up as slaves by accident of fate. Slavery was understood as a necessary evil and therefore was not defended on the basis of religious or biological notions of racial inferiority and superiority, as in the United States.

Brazilian slaves also retained certain legal rights and were not considered simply chattel. They could own property, marry freely, seek out another master, and even buy their freedom. Thus there were greater opportunities for manumission (release from slavery) than in the U.S. system. This in itself, Tannenbaum held, was evidence of a milder form of slavery. Also, once slaves were freed, they were afforded full and equal rights in Brazilian society. In the United States, by contrast, even if slaves gained their freedom, they did not acquire full citizenship but continued to suffer the economic, social, and legal handicaps that attached to their racial status.

Although certain differences from the U.S. and Caribbean patterns of slavery are indisputable, more recent historical accounts of Brazilian slavery have questioned whether it was in fact a more humane system. Humane slave owners may have been the exception, not the rule (Davis, 1966; Graham, 1970). Historian Charles Boxer (1962), for example, has described the brutish and often sadistic cruelty used by the Portuguese planters to keep slaves in line. To tie a slave to a cart, flog him, rub his wounds with salt, lemon juice, and urine, and then place him in chains for a number of days was not considered excessive. Runaways were dealt with by branding for the first offense, cutting off an ear for the second, and, usually, death for the third. That such punishments did not prevent slaves from continuing to run away on a large scale would seem to indicate the desperation to which they were driven.

Although slavery in both Brazil and the United States was a tightly closed system of stratification, there was always some movement of people upward into a higher rank, exceptional though such cases may have been. As noted, slaves could occasionally attain freedom (more commonly in Brazil) and thus change their status. The freeing of some slaves has typified slavery in most societies where it has been practiced (Meltzer, 1971).

Slavery in Modern Form   Slavery is not simply a historical peculiarity that has no modern counterpart. Reports of slavery in Mauritania and Sudan, poor Arab-dominated countries in Africa, bear a striking resemblance to its older, classic form. Black Africans are bought and sold as property, to be used by their owners as servants or laborers. In Mauritania, slaves are estimated to number in the tens of thousands in a country whose population is between 2 and 3 million. Although technically abolished several times, no legal framework has been established to actually put an end to the practice. Moreover, in underdeveloped societies, secular law often takes second place to custom, which in the case of Mauritania, has upheld the property rights of slaveholders (Finnegan, 2000; Jacobs and Athie, 1994).

Another form of modern-day slavery is the trafficking of people, mainly women and children, for forced labor in the sex industry, as sweatshop workers, and as domestic servants. This is a flourishing international activity carried out mainly by organized crime rings. In Asia, impoverished young girls are lured into the sex trade by strangers, kidnapped off the street, or sold by their families to pay off debts. In eastern Europe, women are seduced by promises of legitimate jobs in Germany, Belgium, and the Netherlands, but are then forced to work as prostitutes. This trade is prevalent in the United States as well. As many as fifty thousand women and children, mostly from Southeast Asia and Latin America but increasingly from eastern Europe as well, are trafficked each year to all regions of the country (Richard, 2000).

Unlike past forms of slavery, these modern-day examples are not legitimized. To hold people against their will to be used as laborers or prostitutes is today universally recognized as morally reprehensible. The slave trade, therefore, is always conducted surreptitiously. Even in Mauritania and Sudan, where slavery takes on features of the past, it is officially denied. Slavery in the Americas, by contrast, was rationalized, justified, and socially approved.

Caste

Caste is the purest type of social stratification in which mobility is severely constrained. The term **caste** has been commonly used to describe any system in which the different strata are rigidly fixed. The caste system of India is the most noted example, but the pre-1960s segregated American South and the apartheid system of South Africa are also instances of caste. In the Indian case, strata are divided not by physical distinctions between groups but by people's social descent (Béteille, 1969). As it is used in non-Indian settings, the idea of caste more generally refers to "a major dichotomous division in society between pariahs and the rest of the members of the society" (Berreman, 1966:292). Pariahs are those who are stigmatized on the basis of some physical or cultural characteristic.

All caste systems display certain common features. Perhaps the most basic is the hereditary nature of a person's position in the social hierarchy.

Membership in a caste is inherited and thus fixed for life; the individual is unable to change his or her social position through achievement. Second, castes are endogamous, with marriage restricted to other members of the caste. Segregation between castes in various areas of social life is also evident, particularly as it pertains to residence and other forms of social intercourse. Finally, a caste system of inequality is ordinarily based on either civil or religious law.

Caste in India   Caste has prevailed in India for centuries, well predating the Christian era (Kolenda, 1985). Members of each caste are guided in their social lives by a set of regulations that pertain to marriage, work, recreation, and most other social spheres. Each caste is assigned different rights and obligations, and the system is undergirded by a rigid set of rules governing social interaction, based on the Hindu principle of purity-impurity. The lower castes are considered unclean, and physical contact with them is avoided by the higher castes (Lannoy, 1971).

The ancient classification of the Indian caste system consisted of a structure of four *varnas* (or castes), each occupying a specialized occupational role: *Brahmans* (priests), *Kshatriya* (princes), *Vaishya* (merchants), and *Shudra* (ordinary people). All of those not part of the castes were considered polluted outsiders, referred to as "untouchables." The top three *varnas* were the privileged, and it was from among them that those with education and political and economic power came. These were referred to as the "twice-born" (Leach, 1967). *Shudras* comprised a peasantry whose members could not hope to better their position. Untouchables (*Harijans*), outside the *varna* system, performed jobs that were deemed unclean in Hindu principles, such as collecting garbage and working with leather. The four traditional *varnas* were actually overlaid by virtually thousands of distinct subcastes (*jatis*) in different regions and communities (Mayer, 1955).

The stability of this extreme system of inequality stems from the idea of reincarnation. The most essential moral duty is to accept one's place and to fulfill one's tasks according to caste principles. The rewards for virtue come in the next life. With the idea of reincarnation, one's place in the current caste system reflects one's past life. To have been born an untouchable signifies a more sinful previous life than to have been born a *Brahman* (Kolenda, 1985).

Although traditional caste in India appears to be an extremely closed stratification system, its inflexibility is an ideal picture and cannot be taken literally. Some mobility and social change in the system have always been evident (Rudolph and Rudolph, 1967). Moreover, entire castes might raise their collective position in the hierarchy over several generations through control of power or land and the purification of ritual symbols (Sinha, 1967).

Today, caste in India has been officially repudiated and with industrialization is giving way to a more class-based system of stratification. Barriers to mobility for the untouchables have been eliminated, and government measures have been put in place to help improve their occupational and educational status. It is now possible, therefore, to attain different economic and political positions despite one's birth into a particular caste (Béteille, 1996).

It is foolish, however, to think that a stratification scheme in operation for several thousand years could be eliminated so quickly and easily. Caste remains in evidence in rural and traditional parts of the country and, in subtle ways, even in urban areas. The specialization of occupations by caste has declined, but caste still sets limits on occupational choice (Béteille, 1996). Moreover, political factions may form around caste on particular issues (Srinivas, 1962). And caste attitudes continue to influence people's views of each other, thus affecting to some degree the distribution of life chances.

Caste in South Africa   Another illustration of caste is the former apartheid system of South Africa. In no other modern multiethnic society has stratification been so clear-cut, and in no other so fixed and rigidly enforced. Until very recently, the boundaries between strata were, by law, relatively impermeable.

The South African system of inequality was essentially "whites at the top and nonwhites at the bottom." More accurately, however, the society was divided into four officially designated categories, based on perceptions of racial difference: whites, Coloreds, Asians (mostly Indians), and Africans. The allocation of justice, health care, jobs, education, living quarters, and so on all depended, to some degree, on one's racial classification. Whites received the bulk of the society's resources; Africans, the least. The distance between the whites and the other three racial categories was so great, however, that the hierarchy was essentially a dichotomy—whites over nonwhites.

The South African caste system, called **apartheid,** was maintained by an elaborate arrangement of law and custom ensuring white dominance. Apartheid provided specific legislation mandating the social separation of the racial groups, the maintenance of separate social institutions for each, and, as it was envisioned, the eventual formal division of South Africa into separate and independent white and black nations. Indeed, so blatant and uncompromising was the South African system that the very term apartheid has, in recent times, come to be applied commonly outside the South African context, signifying any rigid and durable aspect of ethnic separation and inequality.

Under apartheid, each person in South Africa was classified by race and placed into one of the four official racial categories. Africans, Asians, and Coloreds were required to carry passbooks, identifying them by their official classification. Physical contact between nonwhites and whites was minimized through a system of petty apartheid, consisting of dozens of laws and mandates created to maintain racial separation in almost every conceivable area of social relations (van den Berghe, 1967, 1978).

As in other caste systems, the extreme inequality of apartheid was legitimized by an ideology that claimed the superiority of the dominant caste. South African whites, particularly Afrikaners (those whose ancestors had been among the first European settlers), believed themselves to be natural overseers of primitive Africans. The view that it was necessary to maintain white rule, based on the understood cultural superiority of whites, was thoroughly incorporated into all institutions.

The apartheid system was dismantled starting in the 1980s and was officially abolished in 1994. Blacks voted in a national election for the first time in 1994 and elected a black-dominated government led by Nelson Mandela. The end product of the radical changes that have occurred in South Africa as part of the abolition of the racially based caste system is still uncertain. Though the official system of racial inequality has been abandoned and blacks now dominate the political system, the major components of white economic domination remain in place. Moreover, in residence and social interaction, the society remains rigidly segregated along racial lines. The key issues of South Africa's immediate future, therefore, concern the manner in which the tremendous economic and social gaps separating whites and blacks will be reduced.

Caste in the United States   Not long after the American slave system was abolished, a system of white control reemerged in the southern states. The system was called **Jim Crow,** and it essentially consisted of a set of relations between blacks and whites that constituted a caste-like form of stratification. Although blacks were no longer held in slavery, their dependence on their former slave masters was reestablished by the denial of their voting rights and by the adoption of the sharecropping system.

Unlike slavery, the Jim Crow system called for the segregation of blacks and whites in almost all areas of social life: housing, work, education, health care, transportation, leisure, and religion. Most important, this social segregation was based in law. Although the presumption was that facilities for the two races would be equal, in fact they were inherently unequal; those reserved for blacks were grossly inferior or inadequate, usually by design (Woodward, 1974).

In addition to physical separation, there was the need for a system of racial etiquette, for blacks and whites obviously could not be totally isolated from each other. The etiquette was intended to make clear the caste positions of dominant and subordinate groups. Whites could not shake hands with blacks, for example, nor would blacks be addressed as "mister" but rather as "boy" or by the person's first name. And most important, racial endogamy was strictly enforced. Indeed, the prohibition of interracial marriage was one of the first formal measures enacted by southern states in the formation of the Jim Crow system.

The racial caste system was abetted by a racist ideology. Popular ideas of racial superiority and inferiority were given additional credence by scientific thought of the time. That blacks were innately inferior to whites was a belief unquestioned by most people (Fredrickson, 1971).

Some sociologists have equated the color bar between whites and blacks in the Jim Crow era with aspects of the Indian caste system. Berreman (1961), for example, points out that in both situations caste membership was inherited and membership was unalterable. Those of the lowest caste were deemed inferior and relegated to the least desirable occupational positions. Moreover, as in the Indian system, there existed rigorous rules of avoidance between castes, and certain types of contact were defined as contaminating.

Caste in Japan   An interesting case of caste exists in Japan, where a pariah group, the Burakumin, experiences extreme discrimination based on beliefs that portray them as a separate race. Although the Burakumin are physically indistinguishable from the rest of the population, there is a commonly shared social myth that they "are descendants of a less human 'race' than the stock that fathered the Japanese nation as a whole" (De Vos and Wagatsuma, 1966:xx). The Burakumin are considered mentally inferior, basically immoral, and unclean.

In the past, Burakumin were required to wear unique identifying garb, were strictly segregated residentially, and were limited to low-status occupations (Aoyagi and Dore, 1964). Although today they are not as stigmatized as in the past, their social and economic standing remains low (Kristof, 1995). Legal measures have been enacted to discourage discrimination against the Burakumin, but their outcast status remains evident. Japanese take great care to avoid marriage with a Buraku individual. A family may research in great depth the background of a potential mate to assure that there is no trace of Burakumin ancestry.

Estate

Another closed type of stratification is feudalism, sometimes referred to as the **estate system.** Although feudalism typified European societies in the Middle Ages, prior to the ascendancy of capitalism in the eighteenth century, it has also existed in other areas of the world, including Asia and Latin America. Indeed, most agrarian societies have experienced some form of feudalism. This is a system of stratification that is linked closely to land and is therefore more typical of agriculturally based societies. The owners of land, the most critical economic resource in such societies, are the dominant stratum, or "estate."

In the European system, the nobility were referred to as "lords," and although they comprised only a tiny portion of the population, they controlled not only most of the society's productive land but other resources, including, most importantly, an army. A peasantry, or "serfs," who were thoroughly dependent on the landowners for their livelihood, made up the bulk of the society's population. The lord offered protection to serfs in return for their labor and for a portion of what they produced on his land. Similar to caste, marriage was usually endogamous among those in the same social position. Moreover, people could not remove themselves from their assigned position without violating mutually understood rights and duties. The inequalities inherent in this system were based essentially on custom, but as the many feudal states began to consolidate, legal justifications became more important.

The nobility, though clearly the most privileged and powerful stratum, was in itself varied on the basis of land and wealth. Most often, the noble was a vassal, who held his land as a grant from the king or from another noble in return for military service or other obligations. Gradually, however, nobles began to assume their position as a hereditary right (Mayer, 1955).

At the bottom of the feudal hierarchy were the serfs, who worked the land and served as soldiers when needed. In all cases, serfs were obligated to pay a substantial portion (not uncommonly as much as half) of what they produced to those who owned the land. In almost all agrarian societies, living conditions for the peasantry were extremely primitive, "at, or close to, the subsistence level" (Lenski, 1966:271). The serfs were not slaves, but as Robert Heilbroner has described them, they were in many respects "as much the property of the lord as were his (or their) houses, flocks, or crops" (1993:28).[1]

As with other systems of stratification, an ideology explained and justified the feudal system. This was supplied by the Catholic Church, which endorsed social inequality and deemed it divinely ordained. This gave rise to a third major estate, the clergy or priestly class. Like the nobility, it enjoyed opportunities to accumulate wealth, especially in the form of land. The clergy was internally stratified, however, with those at the top of the clerical order constituting a kind of nobility in its own right (Mayer, 1955). The priestly class was important to rulers because, as religious leaders, priests were able to confer legitimacy on a system that generated such enormous inequalities. Since no ruling group was able to rule by force alone, the priestly class served to induce acceptance of the regime among those who least benefited by its actions (Lenski, 1966).

The stratification system of agrarian societies was made up of more than simply nobility, clergy, and peasants, however.[2] A governing class, the small number who shared the responsibilities of government, also enjoyed the right to share in the economic surplus that was produced by the peasant masses and the urban artisans. A retainer class, made up of officials, professional soldiers, household servants, and others that were basically in service to the ruler and governing class, served as a kind of mediator between the top stratum and the common people. A merchant class, though low-ranking on the social hierarchy, nonetheless often managed to acquire a significant portion of the society's wealth. Small populations fell even below the peasantry in social status. These included artisans, usually working for the merchant class; unclean or pariah classes; and those who were expendable, such as petty criminals, beggars, and prostitutes.

Figure 6-1 shows the relationship among strata in agrarian societies.

---

[1]Despite their commonly servile conditions, there were differences among the peasantry of medieval Europe, with some enjoying greater privileges than others (Bennett, 1969).

[2]The following description is based on Lenski, 1966.

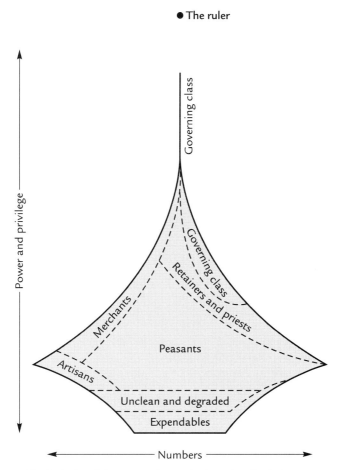

Figure 6-1 ■ The Relationship among Strata in Agrarian Societies
Source: Gerhard Emmanuel Lenski, Jr., *Power and Privilege: A Theory of Social Stratification.* Copyright © 1984 by the University of North Carolina Press. Used by permission of the publisher.

As with caste systems, feudal or estate systems dictate that people do not move from their ascribed position in the social hierarchy. Lenski (1966), however, has suggested that mobility in agrarian societies was not as uncommon as is usually believed. Downward mobility was far more common than upward mobility, though, due to the surplus of manpower. More offspring were produced, in all stratification groups, than could fill the available positions. But even upward mobility was, if not commonplace, certainly possible. For example, an ambitious and talented serf might rise to a position in the clergy, or a warrior might attain a position of nobility. In addition, serfs in medieval Europe who escaped and evaded capture for more than a year could be declared "free." Sometimes people filled new positions, as in the rising merchant class, as trade and commerce expanded. More frequent, however, were cases in which positions were vacated by the death of men who left no heirs or where people vacated their positions because they lacked the skills needed to hold them.

The merchant class, or bourgeoisie, increasingly assumed a greater importance in the economies of medieval societies and as their influence grew, they were recognized as a major estate, beside the nobility and the clergy. With urbanization and the expansion of trade and commerce, the interests of the bourgeoisie came into conflict with the landed nobility. The dye was cast for the emergence of capitalism and the end of feudalism in Europe.

Class Systems

By comparison with other forms of structured social inequality, class systems are the most open, affording individuals opportunities to earn their social place rather than being assigned to it at birth. Class systems emerged in Europe with industrialization, beginning in the eighteenth century. A more fluid form of stratification was required by the new industrial system of production, which called for a mobile workforce. With skills needed in a variety of occupations, social placement could no longer be left primarily to ascription.

Class systems characterize most societies of the modern world. People are not formally blocked from rising in social class, nor are they guaranteed that they will not drop from a high social standing. An individual born into a poor or working-class family can, with talent, ambition, and luck, rise in the class hierarchy, just as upper- or upper-middle-class individuals may lose their wealth and status and drop to a lower rank. Laws or customs do not preclude such movement in either case. The divisions between classes, then, are quite permeable, with no one permanently locked into a social position. Indeed, most people expect upward mobility and are encouraged to do better than their predecessors. Consider how American society judges those who do not maintain or exceed the status of their parents—such persons are seen, to some degree, as failures.

The description of stratification systems as open or closed should not be taken literally. As discussed earlier, no system, even caste in India, ever completely constrains mobility on the one hand or provides unhindered mobility on the other. In all cases, there are at least some opportunities for changing one's status. And similarly, in class systems where mobility is theoretically unhindered, in fact people are not completely free to move up or down. Where people ultimately end up in the class system is never simply a product of their individual achievement but is very much a function of the accident of birth.

Descriptions of societies as open or closed merely point out the most egregious differences among them. What is unmistakable, however, is that modern industrial societies are more open than developing or traditional societies, where agrarianism still predominates. In the latter, the clash between open and closed systems is often starkly evident. As these societies industrialize and urbanize, there is a push toward social placement by achievement; at the same time, traditional forces remain strong, and people's occupational and social status is therefore determined to some extent by their family of birth.

Patterns of Social Mobility in Modern Societies

Sociologists Seymour Martin Lipset and Reinhard Bendix have explained that, with industrialization, a large proportion of the population of a society find themselves in occupations that are quite different from those of their parents. "These changes in the distribution of occupations from generation to generation," they write, "mean that no industrial society can be viewed as closed or static" (1959:11).

Measurements of Mobility

Although social mobility seems to be a constant feature of industrial societies, the dimensions of mobility (how much, in which direction, and so on) may differ both within and between societies.

Generation   Social mobility may be observed and measured either from one generation to another or within one's own lifetime. In the first form, **intergenerational mobility,** a person's class position is compared to his or her parents' position. A son, for example, may be a middle-level manager, whereas his father had been an unskilled factory worker. This indicates upward mobility for the son, occupying, as he does, a higher occupational position than his father.

The second form is **intragenerational mobility,** in which a person's movement is observed and measured during his or her lifetime. A woman, for example, begins her working career as a hamburger flipper at a fast-food restaurant, and by age forty, she owns several fast-food franchises. She has experienced upward mobility, then, as measured by her markedly improved socioeconomic status.

Direction   The movement of people up or down the class hierarchy is **vertical mobility.** Although this needs little explanation, remember that not all mobility is upward in direction. So focused are we on upward mobility and so common is it in American society, we sometimes forget that in class systems it is possible for people to lose their socioeconomic status and move downward. During the Great Depression of the 1930s, for example, many people did just that, suffering not only economic losses but psychological deprivation as well. This was an experience that would forever frame their social perspectives. Anthropologist Katherine Newman (1993) describes this generation:

> As the depression passed from view, to be replaced by the war and the good times that followed, it never faded from the consciousness of the generation that lived through it. It remained their leitmotif and continues to be the central, defining experience of their lives. (63)

As noted in Chapter 4, during the past two decades, many within the working and middle classes have experienced downward mobility as industries have internationalized and downsized their workforces. Lillian Rubin (1994) describes how one working-class family, in which the husband had been laid off, experienced the reality of downward mobility:

> [My husband] was out of work so long that even he finally got it that he didn't have a choice. So he took this job as a dishwasher in this restaurant. It's one of those new kind of places with an open kitchen, so there he was, standing there washing dishes in front of everybody. I mean, we used to go there to eat sometimes, and now he's washing the dishes and the whole town sees him doing it. He felt so ashamed, like it was such a comedown, that he'd come home even worse than when he wasn't working. (219)

Horizontal, or **lateral, mobility** is movement sideways, involving a change of position that, in terms of socioeconomic status, is neither better nor worse than the previous position. A person might move, for example, from one company to another, maintaining the same occupational position. Corporate managers often engage in this kind of lateral movement, looking for new challenges or for a more compatible work environment. Or a person might change occupations, resulting in little or no difference in socioeconomic status. A lawyer, for example, might become a corporate manager; an electrician, a plumber; or a teacher, an educational consultant. None of these occupational switches entails much change in income, prestige, or power.

Mobility Trends

On the basis of empirical studies conducted by sociologists over the past three or so decades, several observations can be made regarding individual mobility trends in the United States and other contemporary industrial societies.

The Rate of Mobility   First, as earlier noted, upward mobility becomes more common as societies industrialize. A number of factors seem to account for this. Education becomes more accessible to greater numbers of people. As this occurs, more people acquire the qualifications to enter higher-status jobs. Job qualifications have also been standardized, and this, in combination with greater accessibility to education, has made it possible for people to rise despite the handicaps of birth into a less-well-to-do family. Most important, however, are the greater opportunities brought about by structural changes that occur with the movement from agrarianism to industrialism. Shifts in the occupational structure create more well-paying and high-skilled jobs and eliminate more low-level jobs.

Sociologists Peter Blau and Otis Dudley Duncan, in one of the most comprehensive studies of mobility ever conducted in the United States, showed that mobility is in fact quite common in American society. They found that from one-third to one-half of all people achieve an occupational status at least one level higher than their fathers. Blau and Duncan's findings were subsequently confirmed by other studies in the United States as well as in other industrialized countries (Hauser et al., 1975; Lipset and Bendix, 1959; McClendon, 1977; Grusky and Hauser, 1984; Slomczynski and Krauze, 1987). It is important to remember, however, that even though these studies confirm much mobility, they indicate that more than half the population does *not* experience upward mobility. Most people, then, do not change their place on the class hierarchy throughout their lifetime, and some may even experience downward mobility. This basic finding has been confirmed by many studies (Gottschalk and Danziger, 1998; Nasar, 1992; Thurow, 1999).

Is there greater mobility in the United States than in other societies? Although it is popularly believed that American society provides more opportunities for upward movement and, therefore, a higher rate of mobility, this belief is not confirmed by comparative studies. Economic mobility in other advanced industrial societies is, for the most part, similar to mobility in the United States (Smeeding, 1998; Gottschalk, 1997).

Direction of Mobility   A second conclusion that can be made about mobility in the United States and other comparable societies regards direction: Clearly, most social mobility is upward. One of the reasons for this is, again, the provision of higher levels of education to more and more people. But structural factors are of even greater significance. More skilled jobs have been created at the same time that jobs requiring fewer skills have declined. The most significant increases in the occupational system over the past several decades have occurred in the professional-managerial categories—doctors and other medical personnel, lawyers, engineers, teachers, and managers. At the same time, unskilled blue-collar jobs—factory production workers, for example—are gradually being phased out. Each generation has thus entered a labor market in which there are more high-status jobs than when the previous generation entered.

Trends of the past two decades, however, indicate that the traditional optimism regarding upward mobility in American society may be illusory. Recall the "middle-class squeeze" discussed in Chapter 4. We only need to reiterate that this pattern reflects increasing downward mobility for many Americans. Some occupying what seemed to be secure places in the middle classes have, in recent years, found themselves struggling to keep pace, let alone move upward.

The tendency toward widening income inequality and reduced opportunity seems to be especially evident among young people. One study found that 60 percent of men who had turned twenty-one before 1980 had attained a middle-class income by age thirty; for those turning twenty-one after 1980, only 42 percent had done so (Duncan et al., 1996).

Range of Mobility   Despite the commonness of upward mobility, the distance most people move is only marginal. This means that intergenerational mobility involves movement incrementally, that is, in short steps (Blau and Duncan, 1967; Gottschalk, 1997). Broad leaps from one class to another are not common. Moving from the working class into the lower-middle class is more typical than movement from the working class into the upper class or even the upper-middle class. The rags-to-riches cases, about which we so often hear, are relatively rare; thus, the Horatio Alger notion remains more a myth than a reflection of reality. Certainly, some do experience spectacular leaps in mobility, moving from poverty into the ranks of the truly wealthy. But such cases are exceptional and do not represent the span of mobility for most people.

Also, in general, the lowest levels of mobility are found in the highest and lowest classes, whereas the highest levels of mobility are found in the middle classes. In a sense, the rich stay rich and the poor stay poor while most mobility occurs within the middle, or intermediate, classes. Moreover, the tendency for the poor to stay poor and the affluent to stay affluent appears to have become stronger in the past two decades (Duncan et al., 1996). This is shown in Figure 6-2.

Mobility in Historical Perspective

In studying mobility, we need to carefully consider how the parameters of social classes and occupations change over time. For example, the conceptualization of the "rich" in American society may be quite different today from what it was forty or fifty years ago. In the 1950s, having a million dollars was the defining mark of great wealth; today, as mentioned in Chapter 5, millionaires number in the hundreds of thousands. Being rich has changed meaning. The same changing standards apply to occupational titles. Being a sales clerk or a mechanic, for example, carried greater prestige in past times than it does today. Even the extremely high status of doctors may be undergoing change as they increasingly become paid employees of health care companies or practice as part of HMOs rather than independently (Lau and Ferguson, 1998).

Furthermore, class lines themselves may blur over time. Chapter 4 noted the hazy distinction, for example, between those who comprise the lower-middle class and those who are part of the upper levels of the working class.

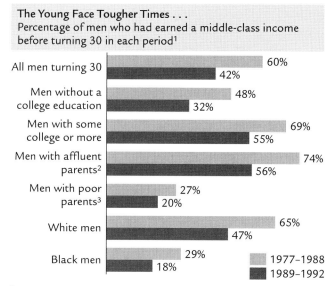

The Young Face Tougher Times . . .
Percentage of men who had earned a middle-class income before turning 30 in each period[1]

All men turning 30 — 60% / 42%

Men without a college education — 48% / 32%

Men with some college or more — 69% / 55%

Men with affluent parents[2] — 74% / 56%

Men with poor parents[3] — 27% / 20%

White men — 65% / 47%

Black men — 29% / 18%

1977–1988
1989–1992

[1]At least $23,042 in 1993 dollars, or twice the poverty level for a family of three.
[2]Household income equal to four times the poverty line or more.
[3]Household income equal to one and a half times the poverty line or less.

. . . And the Poor Move Up More Slowly
The poor are more likely to stay poor and the affluent are more likely to stay affluent.

Income level

| 1967–1979 | | 1980–1991 |

AFFLUENT
about 10% of population
– – – – – $72,000 – – – – –
in 1994 dollars[4]

1967–1979: 31.1% / 6.3%
1980–1991: 27.1% / 7.5%

Average percentage crossing income boundaries

MIDDLE CLASS
about 70% of population

Average percentage crossing income boundaries

$24,000
– – – – in 1994 dollars – – – –

1967–1979: 6.2% / 35.5%
1980–1991: 8.5% / 30.4%

POOR
about 20% of population

[4]All figures are for household after-tax income, including wages, salaries, and some government assistance programs like food stamps.

Figure 6-2 ■ Patterns of Upward Mobility
Source: Data from Greg Duncan, Northwestern University, and Timothy Smeeding, Syracuse University; art from *New York Times*, June 4, 1995, p. 4E. Copyright © 1995 The New York Times. Reprinted by permission.

Determinants of Social Mobility

Structural Mobility

Although Americans like to think that upward mobility is the result primarily of people's individual efforts—their talent, ambition, and perseverance—in fact, most mobility is the result of structural factors, namely, changes in the society's labor force and economy and innovations in technology.

The most critical aspect of structural mobility involves changes in the number and types of occupations relative to the number and qualifications of workers available to fill them. We might think of this as the **opportunity structure.** For individuals to move upward in the class system necessitates the presence of opportunities that will accommodate such movement. This means that the opportunity structure must provide new jobs into which people can move. At different times, the labor market has expanded or contracted, thereby affecting the rate, extent, and frequency of mobility.

As societies have industrialized, greater opportunities for improved occupational status have arisen naturally. With the technological changes that came with industrialization, new occupations were created, many of them calling for a labor force more skilled than was needed in an agrarian economy. These were jobs, therefore, not available to previous generations. Also, as jobs emerged requiring more skills, increased educational opportunities were made available to more people. This further stimulated upward mobility. At the same time, some elements of the labor market suffered job losses as a result of industrialization. New techniques for growing crops and the mechanization of farm implements, for example, reduced the need for farmworkers. Technological changes, then, rendered a dual effect, both closing as well as opening new occupational opportunities.

A similar process appears to be occurring today as computer technology ushers in the "information society." Dozens of new job categories related to computers and satellite industries have developed as computers play an increasingly basic role in the production and distribution of goods and services. At the same time, of course, computers have displaced many workers from their traditional jobs.

Only if and when opportunities present themselves can people move into jobs that represent an improvement in their socioeconomic status. As mentioned in Chapter 4, during the two decades following World War II, for example, the American economy expanded enormously, creating millions of jobs that enabled people to move into the middle classes. By contrast, during the Great Depression of the 1930s, the labor market contracted and millions of jobs were eliminated, driving people downward. In a similar way, in the 1980s and 1990s many companies cut their workforces, causing a shrinkage in certain segments of the labor market.

Another factor that may affect the opportunity structure is immigration. Currently and in the past, a large proportion of immigrants to the United States and other industrialized countries have been unskilled workers. The effect of such a population inflow is to push native workers upward into higher-status jobs as immigrants fill low-status jobs.

Individual Mobility

Knowing that changes in the society's economy and other structural forces create the opportunities (or lack of opportunities) for people to change their class position does not tell us which individuals are more likely to actually make the most of these opportunities. Certainly, the desire to rise in status is basic to those lower in the social hierarchy; individuals will therefore seek to improve their status when they have the opportunity to do so (Lipset and Bendix, 1959).

If the American ideology were translated into reality, we could assume that those who work hardest, have the most ambition and perseverance, and possess the most talent will eventually rise in the class hierarchy, regardless of the circumstances into which they are born. Research has shown, however, that certain social and economic factors outside the control of individuals are most critical in affecting the process of upward mobility. What are the factors that influence individual mobility?

The Accident of Birth   Perhaps the most significant single factor in raising the probability of upward mobility is the class position of one's family of birth. Quite simply, it is a combination of the occupational and educational levels of one's parents and the extent of their wealth that is the best predictor of mobility. Those born into well-to-do families automatically possess resources that give them opportunities to rise in social class. The accident of birth sets in motion a kind of vicious circle in which life chances reinforce each other. Those born into affluent families receive good educations, which lead to good jobs, which, in turn, provide good incomes. The same applies in reverse for those born into less affluent families. Moreover, those life chances are passed on from one generation to the next.

It is because inheritance of one's class position remains the most common condition in modern societies that family of birth is so critical. Class inheritance is most direct in the upper class, where wealth and prestige are passed down from generation to generation. For those of other classes, inheritance is more indirect, resulting from different opportunities in education and occupation. In any case, the influence of family cannot be underestimated. Consider, for example, the advantages enjoyed by those whose parents and grandparents contribute to their homes, cars, college expenses, and so on. This support constitutes a form of inheritance, which in the long run may be even more valuable than what is transferred at the parents' or grandparents' death. In a study that compared the variation of economic status among brothers to its variation among all men, John Brittain (1977) found that the degree of inequality among brothers was substantially less than among all men. He concluded that from one-third to two-thirds of the overall variance

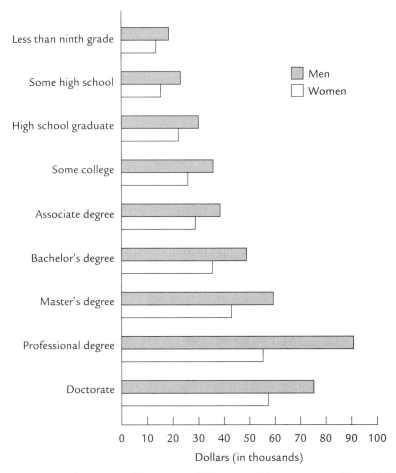

Figure 6-3 ■ Median Annual Income, by Educational Attainment and Sex, 1998
Source: U.S. Department of Education, *The Digest of Education Statistics: 1999.*

of economic status was accounted for by family inheritance. Moreover, Brittain found that much of the remainder of the explanation of inequality was accounted for by unmeasured parental influences, as well as by luck and other random factors. He concluded that the remarkable stability of economic inequality over many decades in many countries is in large measure the result of the tendency for economic status to be transferred from parents to children.

Education   The second most critical factor (and, some would argue, the *most* critical factor) in individual mobility is education (Featherman and Hauser, 1978). The relationship is quite simple: The higher the number of years of education, the greater the probability of upward mobility. A higher credential

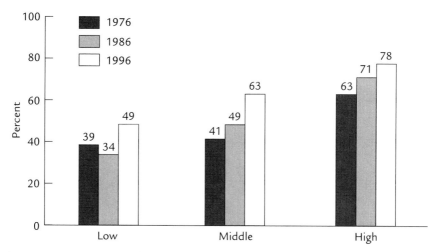

Figure 6-4 ■ Percentage of High School Completers Who Were Enrolled in College the October after Completing High School, by Family Income:* 1976, 1986, and 1996
*Low income is the bottom 20 percent of all families; high income is the top 20 percent; and middle income is the 60 percent in between.
Source: U.S. Department of Commerce, Census Bureau, Current Population Survey, October (various years).

translates into higher earnings over one's lifetime. Those with four-year college degrees therefore will usually earn more than those with only high school diplomas but not as much as those with graduate degrees. This is illustrated clearly in Figure 6-3.

Because a college degree is so critical to upward mobility, the question is, who goes to college? That is, what are the class backgrounds of those who enter colleges and universities and who ultimately graduate? Nothing could better illustrate the close relationship between education and social class than college attendance. As shown in Figure 6-4, as family income rises, college attendance rises. This means that upper- and upper-middle-class high school graduates are most apt to go to college and, beyond the bachelor's degree, to graduate and professional schools.

In an era in which many attend and graduate from college, however, merely having a bachelor's or even a master's degree is, in itself, no guarantee of upward mobility. It is not only a college degree per se, therefore, but also the perceived *quality* of one's college education that counts. There is a tiered prestige structure in the American university system, with highly selective private universities and colleges ranked highest, followed by top state universities and then by regional state universities. Given these perceived differences, a degree from a more prestigious university usually means higher earnings. For example, a survey of fourteen hundred senior executives found that those with undergraduate degrees from Ivy League universities annually earned 30 percent more than those with degrees from non–Ivy League universities (*USA Today*, 1994).

Because education is so critical to social mobility, it is discussed in more detail later in this chapter.

Ethnicity   Although blatant forms of discrimination no longer typify the workplace and the job market, indirect institutional forms of discrimination continue to have an impact on the mobility paths of members of ethnic minority groups, such as African Americans, Hispanic Americans, Asian Americans, and Native Americans. Many of the disadvantages in the labor market suffered by these groups are the result of lower educational and job skills, which, to some degree, can be traced to continued negative stereotyping and, in some cases, to residential segregation.

Gender   Gender continues to render an impact on the mobility paths of women. Much has been accomplished in the past three decades in creating a more equitable opportunity structure for women, yet structural impediments remain in place, making it more difficult for women to enter certain occupational fields, particularly those that are quite high in status.

For married women, the class position and prestige of their husbands have an impact on their own ultimate class position. This does not seem to work in reverse—that is, married men are not affected by the class and prestige of their wives.

Social Networks   Having skills, talent, education, and all the other requirements for upward mobility may be outweighed by one's ability to access key social networks. Consider, for example, how people acquire their jobs. Ideally, many apply and one or a few are chosen through a relatively objective, blind process. But more often than not, jobs are obtained through more informal processes such as word-of-mouth, knowing the "right" people, or knowing those who know the "right" people. Having access to influential social networks, then, is a decisive factor in accounting for why some rise and others do not, despite comparable qualifications (Granovetter, 1974).

Enhancing one's career often depends on being able to demonstrate one's talents and skills for those who control the selection process. To illustrate, think of the thousands of extremely talented and well-trained people in the performing arts—music, acting, dance—who seek to rise in their profession. There is usually only a nuance of difference among them in terms of talent, yet only a few are ever able to attain huge success in the music world, the theater, or the movies. Being seen or heard by those who are able to steer their careers in the right direction becomes key. This often means knowing who the selectors are and where and when such staging opportunities occur. A similar kind of network access operates in the careers of people in the business world and in academia. Understanding the selection process and having connections to those who regulate it become critical.

Luck   One might scoff at the idea that luck plays some part in the mobility process, but it cannot be so easily dismissed. All of us are familiar with the expression "being in the right place at the right time." Many Texas oil millionaires made their fortunes as wildcatters, gambling by drilling for oil in areas not known to be oil rich. They were successful because they were lucky enough to sink their drills at precisely those places where oil did in fact lie beneath the earth. We do not hear about the thousands who were unsuccessful because they had the misfortune to drill in unproductive sites. In addition, consider those who strike it rich in the stock market, subject to highly unpredictable trends (Sherden, 1998).[3]

As noted in Chapter 5, luck always plays a huge role in the formation of great fortunes. Those who find themselves in a position to capitalize on opportunities that arise out of technological or social change have the greatest chance to enter the tiny ranks of the fabulously rich. In addition to possessing the requisite skills, they are in the right place at the right time. The idea that one can rise to great wealth through personal savings or through diligence and hard work (à la Horatio Alger) is pure fiction. Thurow characterizes the sudden acquisition of great wealth as a "conditional lottery," where luck is critical. "Ability by itself," he notes, "is not enough" (1999:205). Many people may have the entrepreneurial skills and talents to excel in the business world—to "enter the lottery"—but few will become instantaneously wealthy.

Sometimes individuals find themselves in fortuitous situations through no design of their own. In 1935, an influential Hollywood publisher spotted an attractive fifteen-year-old girl in the drugstore across the street from her high school. When he asked her the hackneyed question, "How would you like to be in pictures?" in this case, it was more than a glib line. The publisher introduced her to an agent who subsequently took her to one of Hollywood's top directors. Without a day's experience as an actor, Lana Turner was signed to a movie contract and went on to become one of the top stars of her time (*Current Biography*, 1943).

Education and the Process of Mobility

In the United States and other societies with open systems of stratification, education becomes the primary means by which individuals equip themselves to move upward in the social hierarchy. Moreover, education, in the

---

[3]Winning the lottery is obviously one way in which luck is the path to upward mobility, but sometimes simply being in the right place at the right time yields a tremendous payoff. Consider Dan Jones, a salesman who happened to be in a particular seat in Camden Yards Stadium, watching the Baltimore Orioles play. He caught Eddie Murray's five-hundredth home run and was paid a half-million dollars for the ball (*New York Times*, 1996).

American ideal, creates equality of opportunity. Regardless of where people start out in the quest for the society's rewards, educational opportunities presumably create a common starting line. Given its focal place in the mobility process, let's look more carefully at the functions and effects of education.

Education: The Key Life Chance

Schools perform a variety of functions in modern societies. Some of these functions are manifest, or intended, whereas others are latent, that is, not intended, designed, or even acknowledged. Among their manifest functions, schools traditionally have been responsible for contributing to the development of students as workers and citizens by communicating social, political, and occupational skills. Another intended function of schools is to foster upward mobility.

In American society, there is also a more egalitarian attitude and approach to education than in most other societies. Beginning in the early nineteenth century, public education was recognized as a necessary component in a society that was founded so fundamentally on ideas of equality. Education, including higher education, was, in this view, not for an elite class only, but was to be made available to all. The notion of "equal educational opportunity" has historically supported the commitment to an open society. It is the popular belief, therefore, that the effects of class of origin (or of ethnicity or gender) are canceled out by education.

Despite their role in fostering upward mobility and creating a more equal opportunity structure, schools, ironically, play a major role in sustaining the structure of *in*equality. The relationship between education and socioeconomic status operates in a cycle that is perpetuated from one generation to the next: The higher the income and occupational status of the parents, the greater the amount and quality of the children's education. In turn, the greater the amount and quality of the children's education, the higher will be their income and occupational status as adults. Several factors operate to assure the continuity of this relationship.

Access to Quality Education   If access to quality education were the same for all students, regardless of their family's socioeconomic status, the school would in fact serve as a kind of leveling mechanism. All students would be able to start at the same point, and the competition among them would be relatively equal. However, this is not the case. There are vast differences in the quality of education from community to community and from neighborhood to neighborhood. This is a result primarily of the way in which education is funded in the United States. Public schools are financed mainly by property taxes. This creates a system in which school districts where property values are high will have more money available to support their schools, and school districts with low property values will have less. Upper-

and upper-middle-class communities therefore have greater resources to invest in their schools—more money to pay teachers' salaries, finance buildings and laboratories, and supply educational materials. More affluent suburban school districts may spend several times more per pupil than inner-city or rural districts.[4]

Jonathan Kozol, who has studied and written widely about American schools, argues that educational inequality created by the reliance on property taxes to finance public schools has produced a kind of caste system. The quality of a child's education locks that child into a place in the social hierarchy that cannot be easily rearranged at a later point in life:

> We are children only once; and after those few years are gone, there is no second chance to make amends. In this respect, the consequences of unequal education have a terrible finality. Those who are denied cannot be "made whole" by a later act of government. Those who get the unfair edge cannot be later stripped of what they've won. (Kozol, 1991:180)

This educational inequality is abetted by the fact that people with high levels of education are more likely to support higher property taxes to support schools. Thus communities with the best-educated populations will generally have the best schools. This is another reflection of the class-education relationship: The best educated are ordinarily those of the upper and upper-middle classes. As Sidney Verba and Garry Orren (1985) explain, in the United States,

> people who are better educated, more affluent, and higher in occupational status are more likely to participate in politics. The politically active are more concerned about education, as both a personal and a community need, than are the less active or the inactive citizens, whose highest priority is immediate economic problems. Consequently, public officials, attuned to the concerns of politically active Americans, perceive far more public support for educational programs than for other social policies. As the government responds to this support by strengthening education, the cycle of inequality begins anew." (17–18)

In addition to the fact that public schools are better financed in more prosperous communities, those same communities can augment state and local tax funds with moneys they can raise independently through parent groups and foundations. In a well-publicized case, parents at New York's Public School 41, located in a relatively affluent Manhattan neighborhood, raised

---

[4]One state, Michigan, recently adopted a new system of financing public education, abolishing its traditional reliance on property taxes and securing most funding for schools through a raised sales tax and a higher tax on cigarettes. A per-student spending floor was established, with no school district permitted to fall beneath it. The long-term result, presumably, will be to assure that poor districts receive approximately the same as rich districts. Several other states, faced with court orders to find a more equitable formula for financing public schools, are debating new ways to raise tax dollars.

$46,000 in a few weeks. Their objective was to offer to pay the salary of a teacher who was to be reassigned to another school. Losing the teacher would have raised the number of fourth-graders in each class from twenty-six to thirty-two, a change that the parents saw as detrimental to the school's quality (Hammonds, 1997).[5] Another advantage held by more affluent families is that, in the end, they have the option of sending their children to private schools if they are dissatisfied with the public system.

The issue of school financing reflects clearly the ideological conflict between liberty and equity. Conservatives, concerned with liberty, argue that they should be free to use whatever resources they possess or can marshal to assure their children the best education. In this view, the most affluent school districts are perfectly justified in raising as much money as they can and in using their tax money as they see fit. This, of course, perpetuates the discrepancy between rich school districts and poor ones. Liberals, by contrast, are most concerned with creating equity among different class groups. Regarding school financing, this means distributing tax revenue more equally among both rich and poor school districts. In the process, however, this option infringes on the liberty of local school districts to spend their money as they choose.

As the Internet (and computer technology in general) becomes a more basic component of education, those who have easy access to computers will extend their advantage over those who do not. And, as with other aspects of education, the relationship between computer ownership and class is very evident. Lower-income families are less likely to own computers and are less likely to have access to them (Hoffman and Novak, 1997). In 2000, 43 percent of U.S. households had computers and Net access, up from 35 percent in 1999. But the gap between those with and without access (the "digital divide," as it has been called) was not closing. Whereas 62 percent of households earning $50,000 to $74,999 and more than 70 percent of those earning over $75,000 were online, only 11 percent of those with incomes under $15,000 were (Crockett, 2000). "The great divide, in the coming age," writes Jeremy Rifkin, "is between those whose lives are increasingly taken up in cyberspace and those who will never have access to this powerful new realm of human existence" (2000:14).

Student Placement   Another way in which schools perpetuate class inequality is by the use of tests and tracking. IQ and other placement tests geared to middle-class children are critical devices used by schools in which students are sorted out by cognitive ability. Often this results in a self-fulfilling prophecy. Those who, as a result of scores on placement examinations, are labeled "smarter" or "more talented" are tracked into particular programs, apart from others who do not score as high (Jencks et al., 1972). At all levels, the presumed superior students are dealt with differently by teachers and ad-

---

[5]The city did not accept the parents' offer, but the teacher was retained.

ministrators, creating for these students a better quality of education. Thus the initial evaluation becomes a reality. Again, however, there is a clear relationship between placement examinations and social class—those from families of higher socioeconomic status tend to perform better than those from poorer families. For example, children whose parents are college graduates score 18 to 20 points higher on math and verbal tests than children of non–high school graduates, even after taking into account differences in income, race, and other factors (Bronfenbrenner et al., 1996).

Teachers also have higher expectations of students from more affluent families than of those coming from low-income families. This, too, often creates a self-fulfilling prophecy. Expecting that students they identify as high achievers will perform better than others, teachers are apt to devote more personal time and effort to present these students with more intellectual challenges. Conversely, teachers will expend less effort on students they identify as underachievers. The result is the higher academic achievement of those initially classified as "better" students and the lower achievement of those classified as "poorer" students.

Tracking students is another means by which schools perpetuate the class system. In American society, high schools commonly channel students into different academic programs, depending on their past performance as well as the evaluations of advisers and teachers. Some are placed into college preparatory curricula, and others are tracked into vocational programs. Social class is often a criterion in deciding where students will be placed. Low-income students, for reasons explained above, will likely have already demonstrated less academic promise and will be placed into vocational tracks. Once placement is made, the direction students will follow after high school is a foregone conclusion: College prep students will go to college and vocational students will look for jobs.

Family Environment and Educational Inequality   The family environment of students provides another clue to explaining the relationship between social class and education. Generally, the higher the social class of the parents, the higher will be their expectations for their children's education. This means they will provide them with more psychological and material support in their school efforts and activities. They will stress the importance of education and instill in their children values that are compatible with achievement. Poorer families, on the other hand, may undervalue education and fail to convey to children the long-range value of investing time and effort into educational pursuits. They may encourage children to enter the workforce rather than spend time and money on higher education.

Families of higher class are also apt to create an environment for their children that subtly and indirectly instills educational values. At an early age, these children are likely to be introduced to books and educational toys, for example, and exposed to cultural events such as concerts, plays, and museum exhibits. This equips the child with what has been called "cultural capital," providing valuable preparation for formal schooling.

All of this cultural training is reinforced by the child's peers. Children grow up with others who are generally of their same social class. Thus, peer pressure further stimulates middle- and upper-class children to do well in school. Children of lower-income families, by contrast, often find themselves pressured to perform poorly in school (Fordham and Ogbu, 1986).

These factors, it must be remembered, are external to the school itself. The material status of the school may therefore have less influence on student success than is generally believed. In a highly influential study of American schooling, sociologist James Coleman and his associates (1966) discovered that, rather than the physical facilities of the schools, the most important factor in determining students' educational achievement was their home environment, that is, the extent to which they had been exposed to educational and intellectual values by parents and other elders.

In sum, there are significant class differences in access to quality education and in the educational process itself. Regarding social mobility, this creates an irony: Since the educational system in American society has been the main channel for upward mobility, "it is a source of economic inequality rather than equality" (Verba and Orren, 1985:12).

Summary

Social mobility is movement upward or downward in the stratification system. Different types of stratification systems either limit or encourage mobility. In closed systems, cultural norms dictate against mobility, making it relatively uncommon,whereas open systems allow people to move up and down the class hierarchy on the basis of desire, merit, and talent. In reality, closed systems are never entirely rigid, and open systems are never perfectly fluid.

Slavery has been a historically persistent form of inequality throughout most of human history. In the United States, Brazil, and the Caribbean, slavery was a vital component of plantation economies. Caste is a type of social stratification in which people acquire their social position at birth and remain in that status for life. The caste system of India is the most noted example, but the pre-1960s American South and the apartheid system of South Africa are also cases of caste. The estate system, or feudalism, typified European societies of the Middle Ages, but it has been a common form of stratification in all agrarian societies. Class systems, in which the opportunities for mobility are greatest, emerged with industrialization in the eighteenth century and have been prevalent in modern industrial societies.

Intergenerational mobility is movement up or down from one generation to another; intragenerational mobility is movement within one's lifetime. Mobility may be vertical or lateral. Mobility in the United States has been frequent and mostly of an upward nature; however, the distance moved is usually quite limited. Horatio Alger success stories are uncommon.

Social mobility in industrial societies is determined to a large degree by structural changes such as shifting labor markets and occupational trends, accessibility to higher education, and changing demographic patterns. These operate in such a way as to push people up or down the class hierarchy from generation to generation as well as within their own lifetimes. The determinants of individual mobility include family of birth, educational attainment, ethnicity, gender, situational opportunities, and luck.

Modern societies are open in some regards but relatively closed in others. On the one hand, socioeconomic status is, to a significant degree, self-perpetuating. A cumulation of advantages or disadvantages makes it difficult for individuals to modify their status: Birth into a high-income family leads to quality education, which leads to a better job, which leads to a high income. On the other hand, despite the existence of this vicious circle, a significant minority in all industrial societies do move upward or downward in the class structure.

Education is an extremely critical aspect of the mobility process. Access to higher education is the primary means by which individuals equip themselves to move upward. There are vast differences, however, in the quality of education from one local community to another, in the educational process, and in the family environment, guaranteeing that those from more affluent families receive more and better education, thereby assuring the continuity of social inequality.

7

Public Policy and the Class System

. . . a more equitable distribution of income must be a fundamental tenet of modern public policy in the good society, and to this end progressive taxation is central.
JOHN KENNETH GALBRAITH

Only the little people pay taxes.
LEONA HELMSLEY

Although inequality is characteristic of all societies, the nature and extent of inequality are not fixed. They vary from society to society, and they change within societies. In modern societies, such changes take place primarily through public policies, carried out by the state, or government.[1]

This chapter examines how public policies help determine the distribution of societal resources. What, in other words, does government do that helps to shape social stratification? The state is not a neutral observer of the class system, and almost all of its actions affect the distribution of income and wealth, prestige, and power, whether intended or not. The political scientist Harold Lasswell (1936) described this relationship in his classic definition of politics as "who gets what, when, how."

The Political Economy

To understand how public policies affect the class system, we need to consider the central role of government in the economy. The study of how government relates to and affects the economy is called **political economy.** Government can impact on the economy in various ways, helping to stimulate economic development in one area or another, thereby creating (or abolishing) jobs and revenue and thus affecting the general level of prosperity. The economic and social opportunity structures within which people must operate, therefore, are fundamentally shaped by public policies. If the differential between the top and bottom income fifths in Germany, for example, is less

---

[1]Although *the state* and *government* are technically not synonymous, I use the terms interchangeably.

discrepant than it is in the United States, that difference is in large measure the result of different public policy choices. Both are capitalist societies, but in Germany the state is more actively involved in assuring a more equitable distribution of the society's resources.

Throughout American history, government has enacted measures that have benefited one class or another. As discussed in Chapter 4, most people identify with the middle classes, and the classes in the middle do in fact represent the vast majority of the American populace. What is often overlooked, however, is the role of government in promoting the growth and expansion of the middle classes during the course of U.S. history. This has occurred as a result of policies that at different times created new economic opportunities and distributed resources in ways that improved the condition of workers and other previously deprived groups, bringing them into the socioeconomic mainstream.

- The creation of compulsory public schools, starting in the early nineteenth century, is the first and, some would argue, the most important of these policies. Those who are not born into fortunate economic circumstances can nonetheless improve their position by acquiring, through public education, skills that qualify them for better jobs and improve their market capabilities. Indeed, a basic American belief is that public education provides the basis for an equal opportunity structure.

- In the mid–nineteenth century, the federal government went further in providing economic opportunities for those who were not privileged by legislating a system of land-grant colleges and universities. The Morrill Act of 1854 provided for the establishment of colleges and universities in all states, offering higher education to the children of farmers and workers, who before then had been effectively denied this opportunity.

- The Homestead Act of 1862 opened the West to settlers by giving land to those who promised to farm it. As a result, thousands became property owners through the largess of the federal government.

- At the turn of the nineteenth century, giant corporations, led by the so-called robber barons, attempted to extend their power by creating great trusts and huge industries that maintained inordinate control over their markets. In response, the federal government enacted antitrust legislation that provided for the regulation of railroads, oil, steel, and other major industries. The intent was to check the power of a few over the many in a capitalist economy.

- In 1913 the United States instituted an income tax for the first time. Most important, it was a *progressive* income tax, which promised to tax people on the basis of their ability to pay. The mechanism was now in place to make a direct impact on the distribution of income and wealth.

- The 1930s brought forth a spate of social legislation spurred by the disastrous economic circumstances of that decade and designed to provide people with economic security. Among the most significant was the

Social Security system, which mandated a safety net for those who were beyond their working years and no longer capable of earning a living. Unemployment insurance was another such measure giving workers some security against injury and incapacity.

- The Wagner Labor Relations Act of 1935 fundamentally changed the place of workers in American capitalism. This legislation made it possible for industrial workers to organize into labor unions. Prior to 1935, employers could fire workers for promoting unions. Now industrial workers were given some countervailing power.

- Following World War II, the federal government provided important new measures that greatly contributed to the expansion of the middle classes in the 1950s and 1960s. One was the G.I. Bill of Rights. Through this measure, returning veterans were given the opportunity to attend colleges and universities with the federal government picking up the cost of tuition and books. As a result, thousands who otherwise would never have seen the inside of a college classroom availed themselves of higher education.

- Home ownership was also made affordable to hundreds of thousands of families as a result of the G.I. Bill. The federal government guaranteed mortgages for returning veterans, stimulating the housing industry and marking the advent of the great movement of families from the cities to the suburbs.

- When President Lyndon Johnson announced his Great Society in 1964, many public assistance measures were introduced for the first time and others, established earlier, were expanded. The elderly poor were among the key beneficiaries. Social Security was strengthened; and Medicare, a health care system for the elderly, was instituted. Largely as a result of these policies, poverty plummeted among the elderly.

- Johnson's War on Poverty instituted many welfare programs aimed at giving the poor greater competitive opportunities. Medicaid, for example, now provided health care for the very poor. These measures in total lowered the rate of poverty substantially in just a few years.

- The passage of civil rights and voting rights legislation in the 1960s gave many African Americans the opening they needed to establish themselves solidly within the middle classes. Before this time, blatant discrimination had prevented them from entering into better-paying occupations and had held them out of positions of political importance. As a result of protection now provided by the federal government, a huge segment of the African American population was able to move upward in the class system.

- Affirmative action, starting in the 1960s, gave first to African Americans and then to other minorities and women access to jobs and educational opportunities that they had previously lacked. Although these groups were already beginning to make inroads into jobs at the higher levels and were entering institutions of higher education, their progress was accelerated by affirmative action measures.

All of these policies can be seen as stimuli for the reduction of inequality and the expansion of the middle classes. Groups that had been previously excluded or had been disadvantaged in the quest for the society's rewards were now given a boost in life chances. Keep in mind that these measures were aimed not at creating equality of results but rather at equality of opportunity.

Of course, government can also act in ways that perpetuate or even enhance *in*equality. For example, it can tax in a way that will benefit the wealthy at the expense of those in the middle and working classes. Or it can provide benefits to those groups and individuals who are already powerful, thus creating an even wider gap between classes.

Capitalism, Democracy, and Inequality

American society is both capitalist and democratic. These two features, however, create a dilemma: How can capitalism, an economic system that generates and assures inequality, coexist with democracy, a political system that encourages equality? Let's look more closely at how the political economies of democratic capitalist societies deal with this dilemma.

The Capitalist Framework   To understand how capitalism as an economic system creates and assures inequality, we need to consider the capitalist framework. The two most basic characteristics that shape economic activity in capitalist society are the competitive pursuit of profit and the private ownership of property.

That profit maximization is the motivational underpinning of capitalism needs little discussion. Most simply, people seek to enhance their wealth by competing with one another for the society's product within a free and open market. Business owners try to sell their goods at the highest price, while consumers try to buy them at the lowest price. Capitalists, big or small, try to contain the cost of labor while, on the other side, workers try to maximize their wages.

Pursuing self-interest is certainly common in all societies, but in capitalist societies such activity is considered socially beneficial and morally correct. Moreover, wealth and the means by which it is produced are primarily private. This means that profits generated are private profits. Most basically, capitalism is driven by liberty, the idea that people should be free to pursue their self-interests as they wish and to possess the fruits of their efforts. But individual liberty generates inequality—it can be no other way. In a capitalist system, then, there are winners, but there are also losers. Capitalism is a competitive system, remember, which means that not all can win. Quite simply, in the competition of the market, some are bound to get more than others.

The United States as a Political Democracy   Along with capitalism, the United States is defined most basically as a political democracy. Indeed,

Americans commonly think of the United States as the quintessential democracy, emulated but rarely equaled by other societies of the world. The essential components of political democracy have been debated as far back as the Greek city-states over two thousand years ago. But there is widespread agreement that the fundamental objective of a democratic system is to maximize the power of each individual citizen. People are to be afforded equal political rights in their pursuit of the good life; all are given the vote and all can participate in the political process. Unlike capitalism, democracy generates equality: the more democracy, the more equality.

The Contradiction of Democracy and Capitalism   The confluence of capitalism and democracy thus seems to create a contradiction. Capitalism is founded on *liberty*, which creates inequality; democracy is founded on *equity*, that is, fairness for all.[2] In an ideal capitalist system, a truly equal opportunity structure would exist, wherein all citizens have the same life chances to acquire the society's rewards. As we have now seen, of course, that is not the case in the United States or in any other capitalist society. In all capitalist democracies, however, the state intervenes in the market with a variety of programs that are intended to promote greater equality; in other words, the state attends to the needs of those who do not win in the capitalist competition and provides public goods and services used by all citizens.

Consider what we expect government to do: to assist those who cannot work or who cannot adequately care for themselves and their families; to protect people against foreign threats and to control crime domestically; to maintain public schools, from kindergarten to graduate schools; to build and maintain an infrastructure—roads, airports, water lines, and the like. All of these activities, along with thousands more, have economic implications that bear on who gets what.

In addition to providing these goods and services to its citizens, all national governments today recognize that certain economic problems and issues cannot be left entirely to the market. We expect government to help assure as low a rate of unemployment as possible and to contain the rate of inflation. We also assume that government will regulate trade and commerce both at home and within the global economy. A capitalist economy, based as it is on the fluctuations of the market, experiences swings, upward and downward. Government is expected to play a major part in minimizing the negative effects of those business cycles. In the past half century, these economic functions of government have grown enormously.

----

[2]Thurow (1975) points out that Americans often use the words *equity* and *equality* as if they were synonymous, though they are not. Equity has to do with the just distribution of economic resources. Justice may or may not require equality, however.

Macroeconomic Policy

The role of government in managing the national economy is called **macroeconomic policy.** Government acts in three ways to influence the society's economy and thus affect the distribution of income and wealth: it *taxes*, it *spends*, and it *regulates*. Each of these processes is subject to intense debate among competing political interests. Each also affects the balance between liberty and equity, and it is the contest between these two that constitutes the essence of national politics in America.

Taxation: How Much, from Whom

Through taxes, government finances all of its activities. Nothing that government does, whether building roads or missiles, operating universities, or providing police and fire protection, is done without cost. To finance these things requires that government raise revenue. This is done primarily through taxation. Government may also borrow to pay its bills, but borrowed moneys must be paid back, along with interest—and they are paid back, of course, with tax dollars. Although few cheerily make their tax payments, in the end, this is the only way that government can function. Often people take for granted what government provides, but it is tax dollars that pay for these public goods and services. We sometimes need to be reminded that, as the jurist Oliver Wendell Holmes put it, "taxes are what we pay for civilized society."

In the early nineteenth century, people paid taxes mainly locally and then only minimally. Gradually, however, government, especially at the federal level, expanded enormously. In the twentieth century, it became the supplier of goods and services that the market could not or would not provide. As people came to expect more from government, the need for more revenue grew correspondingly. Two things occurred in the United States and in other advanced industrial societies that especially propelled the emergence of an active government requiring massive revenues: wars and the development of a welfare state.

The two world wars created a need for armed forces that had been unprecedented. After World War II, with the onset of the so-called Cold War, the defense establishment grew enormously and became one of the major areas of public spending. Although the military portion of the federal budget has been reduced since the 1960s, it remains a major government expenditure, about 15 percent.

More than military spending, however, the emergence of a welfare state changed the role of government fundamentally. The **welfare state** refers to government insurance, public assistance, education, and medical programs designed to maximize the economic and social welfare of the society's population (Greenberg and Page, 1995). In the United States, Social Security, Medicare, family allowances, unemployment insurance, and support to educational and other related institutions are all part of the welfare state. Thus, the entire range of the citizenry is covered in one form or another. Although, by comparison with western European societies, the welfare state was relatively late in coming to the United States, most of its programs have come to be expected by Americans of all social classes.

Fiscal Policy and the Distribution of Income and Wealth   The rate at which people are taxed determines, in some measure, how much disposable income they will have. In effect, taxation has a redistributive influence, and policymakers can affect the distribution of income and wealth by deciding who is taxed at what rate. How government spends the tax dollars it collects has a similar effect. Taxation and public expenditures are together referred to as **fiscal policy.**

How Government Collects Taxes   There are different ways of taxing people and, depending on the method, different effects may be created. Essentially there are three types of taxes: progressive, regressive, and proportional.

   Progressive taxes require that as one's income rises, one's tax payment rises proportionately. This means that those with higher incomes will pay a greater percentage. The federal income tax is the best example of a progressive tax. The effect is to redistribute wealth downward, that is, from the richer classes to the poorer. As economist John Kenneth Galbraith has put it, "The only effective design for diminishing the income inequality inherent in capitalism is the progressive income tax" (1992:179).

   Regressive taxes impose a heavier relative burden on the lowest income earners. As income rises, the proportion one pays in taxes declines. This causes an upward redistribution of income, increasing the level of inequality. Social Security taxes, for example, are regressive. The Social Security tax is 6.2 percent of income up to a ceiling amount. That ceiling in 2000 was $76,200. Thus, if you earned, for example, $40,000, you paid 6.2 percent of that amount, or $2,480; if you made $120,000, you paid only on the first $76,200, that is, $4,724. So, your effective Social Security tax rate was not 6.2 percent but about 3.9 percent.

   Proportional, or flat, **taxes** levy the same percentage rate on all income earners and leave income distribution unaffected. Sales taxes, for instance, are proportional. Everyone pays at the same rate regardless of their income. In practice, however, sales taxes have a regressive effect. Wealthier people need to spend less of their income on consumer items and so a lesser proportion is paid in taxes. Someone earning $100,000 may only need to spend $50,000 (50 percent) on living expenses. A person earning $25,000 will have to spend much more of his or her personal income, perhaps as much as 75 percent, and thus will pay proportionately more in sales taxes. Governments usually try to modify this effect by exempting fundamental needs from taxation, like groceries or drugs.

   The impact of tax policies on the distribution of income and wealth can be seen during the post–World War II decades. In the 1950s and 1960s, the tax code was steeply graduated, with high income tax rates imposed on the top income earners. During these years, the bottom half of taxpayers paid less than 10 percent of their total income in taxes while the top bracket was 91 percent (Kuttner, 1996).[3] The gap between top and bottom of the class hierarchy, as a result, began to close.

Changes in the tax code in the early 1980s resulted in a reversal of that trend, contributing to substantial redistribution of income upward. During the 1980s, taxes paid by workers on their wages and salaries rose while the tax obligation of the wealthy and the corporations was reduced. The result was a sharp rise in after-tax income for the top classes and a concomitant loss for the middle and working classes. From 1977 to 1989, the average after-tax income of the top fifth of families grew by 28.1 percent. But the most dramatic growth occurred among the top 1 percent, the families at the very apex of the class system, whose average income grew by 102.2 percent. By contrast, the after-tax income of families in the bottom 80 percent fell by 2.3 percent, with the largest declines occurring among the poorest (Mishel and Bernstein, 1993). These changes in income distribution were not the result only of changes in the tax structure, of course, but they contributed significantly.

The regressive changes in the federal income tax that began in the early 1980s were arrested somewhat with further modifications to the tax code in 1993. Nonetheless, the long-term rise in untaxed corporate profits and an increasingly greater dependence on regressive state and local taxes precluded the tax system from contributing to greater income equality (Mishel et al., 1999).

Who Pays What in Taxes?   Everyone is familiar with the saying that the only sure things in life are death and taxes. No one completely escapes the tax burden. Even if one were to pay no income tax (the poor not earning enough, for example, or the rich employing tax attorneys to find tax loopholes), state governments impose sales taxes on most consumer goods and services. Also, excise taxes must be paid on such things as gasoline, liquor, and cigarettes. At the federal level, the income tax is the major source of government revenue. Most state governments also impose income taxes of their own. Put simply, individuals as well as corporations must pay taxes on their earnings, but as is seen in Figure 7-1, it is the individuals—the working men and women—who bear the major income tax burden.

Focusing on the income tax shows how changing policies can create a greater or lesser burden for both corporations and individuals. In the 1980s, corporations paid less, and individuals made up the difference. As shown in Figure 7-1, the corporate share of total U.S. income taxes collected in the 1950s was 39 percent, but during the 1980s that share had been reduced to only 17 percent. Hence, from the 1950s to the 1980s, taxes paid by corporations

---

[3]Very few wealthy taxpayers actually paid at the rate of 91 percent, however. Abundant loopholes in the tax code made it possible for most to pay at a substantially lower rate.

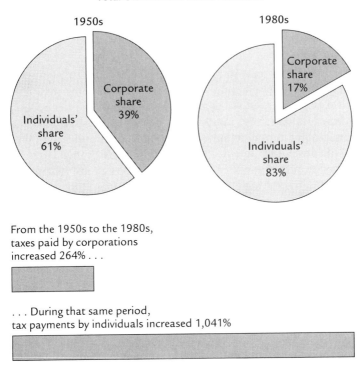

Figure 7-1 ■ Income Taxes Collected from Individuals and Corporations
Source: Data from Internal Revenue Service; art from Donald L. Barlett and James B. Steele, *America: What Went Wrong?* (Andrews and McMeal, 1992).

increased 264 percent, but during the same period, taxes paid by individuals rose by over 1,000 percent (Barlett and Steele, 1992). Today, about 10 percent of the federal budget is financed through corporate taxes, with most of the remainder financed through income and payroll taxes paid by individuals.

In addition to *how* governments tax, the distribution of income and wealth is affected by *what* is taxed. In the United States, there is a capital gains tax, for example, which is applied to earnings from the sale of assets. Sales of stocks and bonds that result in a profit are subject to capital gains tax, as would be profits earned through the sale of a house or any other asset. Because most assets are held by those at the top of the class hierarchy, this tax falls most heavily upon them. Taxes on wages and salaries (like Social Security), however, impact most heavily on the middle and working classes, whose income derives mainly from their jobs.

The United States and Other Societies: A Comparison   Most Americans, if asked their feelings about taxes, would claim that they pay too much. And few politicians voice a contrary opinion. But this view, popular as it is, does not

Table 7-1 ■ Tax Revenues as Percentage of GDP, 1998

Country	Percent
Sweden	63.0
France	50.9
Netherlands	46.5
Italy	46.4
Germany	44.8
Canada	43.4
Poland	41.9
United Kingdom	40.6
United States	34.4
Australia	33.4
Japan	30.8

Source: U.S. Census Bureau, *Poverty in the United States: 1999.*

reflect what is actually the case. Not only are Americans not overtaxed, but their overall tax burden is markedly lower than that of citizens of almost all other industrial societies (Mishel et al., 1999). This can be seen in Table 7-1.

Government Spending: On What, for Whom

Governments do not collect revenue and then stash it away. Nor do tax dollars fall into a bottomless pit, as is cynically claimed by many taxpayers. What governments collect in tax revenue, they spend on goods and services that are returned, in some form, to citizens. As the largest consumer of everything from paper clips to airplanes, the federal government has an automatic impact on the entire economy. State and local governments also spend tax dollars and have a similar, though less widespread, economic impact. Beyond their general economic impact, government spending policies affect specific parts of the class structure. As it turns out, all social classes, from top to bottom, are beneficiaries of government spending in some form.

Categories of Government Spending

There are three general areas in which government spends: First, it supplies public goods, such as defense and highways. These are goods that everyone in the society derives some benefit from, either directly or indirectly. Here, there are no intended class biases. In constructing highways, for example, there are not special superexpressways for the wealthy, two-lane highways for the middle classes, and unpaved roads for the poor. People of all classes make use of public highways. Government also provides institutions, like the public school system, that serve everyone, regardless of class position.

These public goods theoretically have the effect of maximizing equality of opportunity, but some groups benefit more than others from them. For instance, upper-middle-class commuters who drive from their suburban homes to the inner city and back each day make much greater use of expressways than do inner-city residents, who rely more on public transportation than on private automobiles.

Second, government provides services of various kinds and distributes transfer payments to people. There are virtually thousands of such programs provided by federal, state, and local governments. Some, like public assistance ("welfare"), provide minimal resources to those who do not prosper in the market system. Others, like Social Security and Medicare, focus on the elderly. Still others, such as home mortgage insurance and low-cost loans for college students, benefit working- and middle-class families.

Third, government pays interest on the debt it accumulates. When the federal government cannot pay for its purchases with tax revenues, it borrows, just as a family might borrow money to purchase a house or a car. The interest paid on those accumulated debts amounts to a significant part of the federal budget (Figure 7-2), currently around 11 percent.

It is the second part of government spending—payments and services to individuals and groups—that has the greatest direct impact on the class system. Obviously, *who* government spends its revenue on and *what* it spends it on will benefit different groups in different ways. Let's look in more detail at this part of government spending.

Welfare for the Poor, the Middle, and the Wealthy

Welfare supplied by government takes several forms. First, there is welfare in the popular sense—*public assistance*—programs designed mainly for the indigent. A second form is *social insurance,* payments in cash or kind to all eligible citizens. A third form of welfare is not easily recognized or even acknowledged—welfare for the well-off and the corporations, referred to by some as "upside-down welfare" or "corporate welfare" (Huff, 1992). The implication is that these are welfare programs designed to benefit those who would seem to need them least.

Welfare for the Poor: Public Assistance   Welfare for the poverty classes was discussed in Chapter 3, but we need to review it briefly and place it into the context of the overall tax system. A number of myths have surrounded public assistance. Never has it been as widely applied or as generous as is commonly believed. At no time has public assistance to the poor ever been a major component of the federal budget. Indeed, efforts to alleviate poverty through government benefits have been and remain less substantial in the United States than in any other advanced nation (Fischer et al., 1996; Noble, 1997).

Welfare for the poor reached a peak in the late 1960s with the Great Society programs of the Johnson administration. The average annual AFDC (Aid to Families with Dependent Children) payment in 1996, when the program

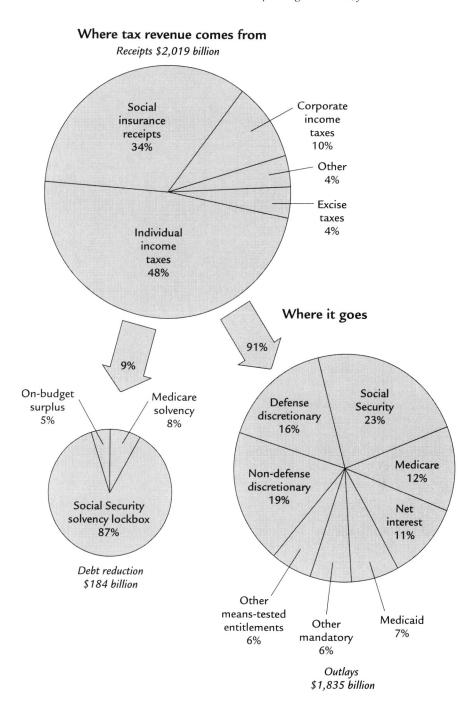

Where tax revenue comes from
Receipts $2,019 billion

Social insurance receipts 34%

Corporate income taxes 10%

Other 4%

Excise taxes 4%

Individual income taxes 48%

9%

91%

Where it goes

On-budget surplus 5%

Medicare solvency 8%

Social Security solvency lockbox 87%

Debt reduction $184 billion

Defense discretionary 16%

Social Security 23%

Non-defense discretionary 19%

Medicare 12%

Net interest 11%

Other means-tested entitlements 6%

Other mandatory 6%

Medicaid 7%

Outlays $1,835 billion

Figure 7-2 ■ The Federal Budget, Fiscal Year 2001
Source: Executive Office of the President, *Budget of the United States Government, Fiscal Year 2001.*

was abolished, was around 40 percent of the official poverty line. Adding in noncash programs like food stamps and Medicaid still did not enable families to rise above the poverty line. What's more, even before the radical welfare reform measures of 1996, the most costly public assistance programs— AFDC, food stamps, and Medicaid—had been declining as part of the federal budget. Even during their peak years of the 1960s, these traditional welfare programs constituted a relatively small part of the federal budget. Today, all of them have been either abolished or severely reduced in scope and content.

Welfare for the Middle Classes: Entitlements and Tax Expenditures   The classes in the middle of the stratification system, not the poor, are the major recipients of government welfare. This takes the form of programs that are often referred to as **entitlements.** Unlike public assistance, these are not means-tested programs wherein recipients must prove their need. So long as one has reached a particular age, as in the case of Social Security, or otherwise qualifies under the law, one is "entitled" to a benefit.

The two largest entitlement programs are Social Security and Medicare, both social insurance programs that benefit primarily the elderly middle classes. Social Security is a program originally instituted in the 1930s that provides old-age insurance. Wealthy individuals and families are usually able to provide for their long-term security through the accumulation of assets, but this is not the case for the working- and lower-middle classes and even for many of the upper-middle class. Hence, it is the intermediate classes that are most dependent on Social Security, and they are its chief beneficiaries. The same is true of Medicare, the government-funded health insurance program for the elderly. Unemployment benefits constitute another entitlement. All these programs are of aid primarily to working people who are dependent mainly on wages and salaries.

A public benefit afforded mostly middle-class families, though rarely seen as a form of welfare, is state-supported higher education. Although students and their families may often grouse about the rising costs of tuition, in no public university does students' tuition pay the full costs of operating the institution. The balance is financed through taxes, paid by all citizens, not only those who attend or send their children to state universities.

Those in the middle and upper income brackets receive a number of "hidden" welfare benefits, referred to as **tax expenditures.** These are tax breaks that amount to large subsidies for the middle and upper classes. The largest and certainly the most popular of these tax breaks is the deduction that families are allowed to take for interest paid on their home mortgages. This has been of significant benefit to homeowners of all classes and has encouraged home ownership. The poor, however, are less likely to be homeowners than are those in the intermediate classes. Obviously, the more expensive the home, the more substantial the tax break. Thus, the wealthy get an even larger benefit than those in the middle.

It is not difficult to see how such hidden welfare has a redistributive effect. When people, or corporations, are relieved of some of their tax burden, this provides them with more disposable income. Moreover, tax dollars not collected as a result of tax breaks must be collected from another source. The deduction allowed for mortgage interest for homeowners, for example, cost the government over $55 billion in 2000 (U.S. Census Bureau, 1999). To finance these benefits, then, may require cuts in other forms of social welfare for other groups.

Corporate Welfare   Perhaps the least obvious form of welfare is that which goes to the giant corporations in the American economy. This has sometimes been facetiously referred to as "wealthfare."

First, large corporations have been particularly adroit at avoiding taxes on income through a complex system of corporate tax laws enacted over many decades. Some of the more striking inequities are reflected in the extremely low or, for some, nonexistent tax bills incurred by the largest and most profitable firms. Between 1996 and 1998, twelve large corporations, including Goodyear, Texaco, Colgate-Palmolive, and MCI WorldCom earned more than $12 billion in profits, yet paid no income taxes over that period. In fact, together these companies received $535 million in tax credits or refunds (Johnston, 2000). Tax loopholes are massive when applied to large corporations. For example, the Corporate Foreign Tax Credit lets U.S.-based transnational corporations reduce their U.S. taxes dollar-for-dollar for foreign tax obligations, saving them billions of dollars. A similar tax break is given to the oil and gas industries, which receive tax credits by the federal government for depletion of reserves.

In addition to tax breaks, much corporate welfare comes in the form of subsidies and loans. Subsidies are payments made for the support of the economic health of certain industries or companies. Among the more highly subsidized industries over the years have been airlines, defense contractors, and commercial agriculture. As to the last, the bulk of agricultural subsidies such as price support payments are paid not to small farmers but to large corporate farm operations (Moore and Stansel, 1995).

Another subsidy is the exploitation of public property by private corporations. A classic example is the 1872 Mining Act—still in effect—that permits mining on federal land for the nominal charge of $5 an acre. This means that mining companies (as well as the timber industry, which cuts trees on federal land) earn profits by mining what belongs to the public. Many of the items produced and sold by large corporations are initially developed largely at public expense. The computer industry is a good example. Much of the early work done by scientists in developing computer technology was related to military projects financed by the Defense Department. The same is true of the aviation industry. The Boeing 707, for example, one of the most successful commercial airplanes, was originally developed at government expense as a military aircraft, the KC-135, for the U.S. Air Force. Boeing took the design and used it to produce the 707, from which it derived billions of dollars in profit. All of these programs reflect the socialization of investment and costs of production. At the same time that government subsidizes capital investment of large corporate enterprises, profits earned on that investment remain private.

State and local governments routinely induce companies to locate facilities in their states or communities by helping to finance their projects or by awarding them tax abatements. In 1993 the state of Alabama, for example, gave $253 million in economic incentives to Mercedes-Benz to build an automobile assembly plant near Tuscaloosa that would employ 1,500 workers. This amounted to a subsidy of $169,000 for each job (Barlett and Steele, 1998a). Similar economic gifts are given to the owners of professional sports franchises when state and local governments build stadiums and arenas for their teams at public expense (Rosentraub, 1999).

One of the more blatant (though relatively insignificant) illustrations of corporate welfare in recent years is the program that subsidizes huge transnational corporations to advertise their products abroad. In 1991 Sunkist received $10 million to promote its oranges and Pillsbury received almost $3 million to advertise its muffins and pies (Moore and Stansel, 1995).

Indirect forms of subsidization to corporations are of even greater significance. The trucking industry, for example, is subsidized by highway construction, as are airlines and shipping companies by the building of airports and harbors. Many of the costs of cleaning up environmental damage created by industry, such as oil spills and water pollution, are borne by consumers and ordinary taxpayers, not only through higher prices of goods but also through government environmental programs. Most industries also benefit from state-supported education, particularly colleges and universities, which train their workers at public expense.

Trade restrictions are another indirect subsidy to corporations. Some industries have been successful in getting the federal government to enact protections against foreign imports through tariffs. This enables U.S. corporations to keep the prices of their products artificially high. The U.S. automobile industry, for example, has lobbied the federal government to restrict the number of foreign-made cars that can enter the United States each year. And for many years the sugar industry has been able to effectively limit sugar imports, thereby keeping the price of sugar inflated (Barlett and Steele, 1998b).

Another form of corporate welfare is the protection government provides to especially large corporations or industries when they face financial difficulties. Several times in the past three decades, the federal government has come to the rescue of a large corporation when it was threatened with bankruptcy (Kraar, 1977). Perhaps the most notorious, and surely the most costly, case of corporate welfare in this form came in the late 1980s as a result of the collapse of the savings and loan industry, brought about in large measure by mismanagement and a failure of government oversight. This bailout will eventually cost taxpayers hundreds of billions of dollars (Waldman and Thomas, 1990).

The U.S. Welfare State in Comparative Perspective

As noted at the outset of this chapter, no capitalist democracy fails to ameliorate in some degree the inequalities that are naturally created by a capitalist economy. The welfare state provides a safety net—that is, a minimal standard of living that no one is expected to fall below. But societies differ in the extent of their welfare states; some are more comprehensive and generous than others. Where does the United States stand in this regard?

As with levels of poverty and wealth, the United States must be compared with societies in which the standard of living is not significantly different—the societies of western Europe, Canada, and Japan.

The Scope and Impact of the U.S. Welfare State

On most measures, the American welfare state is *less comprehensive* and *less generous.* Despite common public complaints about its size and cost, in reality it is, by comparison, a rather limited and stingy system, particularly as it affects the poor (Fischer et al., 1996). Compared to western European societies, the U.S. welfare state appears minuscule. Consider maternity leave, for example. In the United States, there is no societywide provision for paid leave. The best that women having children can hope for is to work for a company that offers its workers such benefits. By comparison, Norwegian women automatically receive forty-two weeks of fully paid maternity leave, as well as virtually full reimbursement for all medical costs and annual stipends of more than $1,600 for each child under seventeen (Ibrahim, 1996). Hungary gives twenty-four weeks of paid maternity leave, Italy gives five months, and Canada, seventeen weeks (Grimsley, 1998).

Perhaps the most noticeable shortcoming of the American welfare state is its lack of a universal health care component. Medical care, except for Medicare and Medicaid, is a primarily privatized system. Those who can afford to purchase medical insurance or who work for employers who provide it have most of their medical expenses covered. But today about 40 percent of Americans at some time in their lives lack medical insurance. Moreover, more than 43 million people have no medical insurance of any kind. Remember that health care is among the basic life chances.

In addition to its less comprehensive form, the American welfare system *covers fewer people* than others. The most highly developed systems blanket their entire populations with benefits. Family allowances in Austria, the Netherlands, or Canada, for example, go to all families with children, regardless of their economic status. Medical coverage, as already noted, is universal in most. The U.S. system, by contrast, is a patchwork in which many of those in actual need are not covered.

The U.S. welfare state is *less redistributive* than others. This is one of the major factors that contributes to the wider gap between top and bottom income earners in the United States. A key function of the welfare state in other countries is to redistribute wealth so that the extremes of the class system are reduced. Where there is a more advanced welfare state, there is a less acute class hierarchy. Certainly, there are rich and poor in these societies, but the gap between them is narrower than in the United States. Thus the poor are less poor and the rich less rich. It is, in large measure, the provision of public benefits that narrows the differential.

Accounting for the Difference

Several factors seem evident in accounting for the difference between the United States and other capitalist industrial societies in their welfare states, including the American traditions of individualism and self-reliance, American-style capitalism, a basic distrust of government, the power of business, and the weakness of labor.

Individualism   First, as we will see in Chapter 9, individualism and its correlate values are in no other society as overarching as they are in the United States. As a result, people are not overly sympathetic to those who are not able to succeed in the capitalist system on their own efforts. Self-reliance is a slavishly adhered-to principle. Thus, welfare in the traditional sense is viewed as appropriate only for those who are physically unable to earn a living or care for themselves. So long as one is able-bodied, no matter the social circumstances, one is expected to be able to support oneself and one's family. Americans are simply less inclined to see government as responsible for caring for the presumably "undeserving" poor. Europeans and Canadians, by comparison, have come to expect major welfare benefits from government.

Capitalism American-Style   Second, capitalism in the United States is more unfettered than in other contemporary capitalist societies. This, too, is in large measure an outgrowth of the primacy of individualism. The United States provides greater opportunities than most societies to rise as far as one can go on individual efforts. But it also provides the same kind of individualistic freedom to fail. And in a capitalist system, there are winners and losers—people may be able to climb higher in the United States, but they are also free to fall lower, with no guarantee of a social safety net to catch them. In other countries where capitalism is not so unencumbered, there is a higher limit below which people cannot fall; and by the same token, of course, there are lower limits to what people can earn. Thus, societies make choices in public policies that result in greater or lesser inequality.

Also as part of the firmer commitment to a more free-wheeling, laissez-faire style of capitalism, Americans seem more willing to accept a higher degree of risk than other societies. While Americans commonly live beyond their means, building up large debts, Europeans seem less prone to gamble in this fashion. They do not carry much consumer debt, do not play the stock market as commonly as do Americans, and even buy homes with less mortgage debt (Nash, 1995).

Distrust of Government   Third, Americans traditionally have expressed a basic distrust of government. As economists Robert Heilbroner and Lester Thurow have put it, "Americans have always been disposed to regard government as an interloper, not as an integral part of a society" (1981:57). And in recent years, this antigovernment bias has grown stronger (Lipset, 1996). Ronald Reagan rode to the presidency in 1980 with the message that the best government is the least government. The belief that "government is the problem, not the solution" became a mantra of the Reaganites, and it continues to characterize the major philosophical position not only of Republicans but of many Democrats as well. That idea has seemed to resonate strongly with the U.S. public in the past couple of decades. There is, however, a long history of suspicion of government that derives from the purer form of capitalism that has always guided the American political economy.

In other societies, although government may be viewed with some suspicion, there is a perception of the state as a necessary and beneficent institution. It is, if not the "solution," at least that institution responsible for finding solutions. Consider the Canadian case in this regard. As political commentator Richard Gwyn has written, "Canadians don't lobby and fight for their rights against government, because, in the collective perception, their government is *theirs*. They assume it is working for them. And it is enough of the time to continue being trusted" (1985:194).

Americans' attitude toward taxes is also noticeably more negative, despite the much lower rates they pay in comparison with those in other societies. The welfare state in European societies, by contrast, is understood as a necessary component of government that can only be financed with taxes. A German worker, for example, explains that Germans feel secure knowing that if they or their parents become ill, they will be cared for and that their children will receive a good education. "To Americans, these can be financially disastrous," he states. "But we don't fear them. That is why we keep paying. That is why we say we don't like it but the taxes are necessary." He says this despite the fact that his own tax rate is approaching 60 percent! (Nash, 1995:A4).

Norway's commitment to egalitarianism through the tax system would seem utterly astonishing to most Americans. Consider that, in addition to income tax rates that can exceed 50 percent, the Norwegian government imposes a 23 percent sales tax, and taxes on some items, like gasoline and alcohol, can drive their costs to astronomic figures (Ibrahim, 1996). Norwegians, however, seem prepared to tolerate this situation as the price of having a stratification system in which there are comparatively only slight differentials between top and bottom classes. American values simply do not seem to support such a public attitude. Americans, in short, are more firmly committed to equalizing the opportunity structure rather than assuring greater equality of condition.

Business Power and Labor Weakness   Business power is another factor that accounts for the more limited American version of the welfare state. Business in the United States has historically opposed the creation of a larger and more comprehensive welfare state along European or Canadian lines. It has, instead, been a voice for lower taxes, limited benefits, individual effort over government support, and limited responsibility on the part of private enterprise (Noble, 1997). In a striking comparison, the strength of the Norwegian commitment to greater social equality is attested to by the lack of resistance, even from business owners, to that society's extremely generous welfare state. The chief executive of Norway's largest supermarket chain, for example, declares "We are a very social democratic society, and we don't know another system. It may be costly, but there is social peace. There are no poor people in Norway and I don't want to see any. There are no strikes, and no high demand for salary increases. I want to adjust the system, but only to preserve it" (Ibrahim, 1996).

Along with the resistance of big business, the weakness of labor has been another contributing factor to the reduced size and scope of the U.S. welfare state. American labor unions have never had the kind of power and influence that labor unions have had in Europe or even in Canada (Lipset, 1996). Neither of the two major political parties identifies itself with labor unions or identifies itself as a working-class party, though Democrats, to some extent, did this in the 1950s and 1960s. In countries with strong welfare states, there has always been a socialist or social democratic political party, committed to creating greater economic equality and redistributing societal wealth. There have been no effective American counterparts.

Public Perceptions of Government Spending

The welfare state in the United States, despite its comparatively limited form and content, is grossly misconceived by much of the American public. Most people wildly overestimate what government currently spends and has spent in the past on welfare for the poor, a consistently unpopular government expenditure. By contrast, Americans seriously underestimate what is spent on hidden or indirect welfare that goes mainly to the middle and upper classes. A national survey conducted in 1996 asked respondents whether more of the federal budget was being spent on Medicare or on foreign aid. Fifty-eight percent answered "foreign aid," 27 percent answered "Medicare" (Morin, 1996). In fact, almost twelve times as much was spent on Medicare.[4]

Government Regulation

The state regulates the capitalist market by setting and enforcing the rules by which it operates. It does this through regulation of the monetary system and through various government regulatory agencies. As with taxation and spending, regulatory policies affect the class system.

Regulatory Agencies

Government regulates almost all industries in some fashion, either directly or indirectly. Virtually every business activity in the United States is linked to some government agency. The intent is to assure a more competitive and fair market system. To the extent that powerful industries are able to influence these agencies, however, this objective is sacrificed and power and wealth continue to flow to the top.

Particularly important government-business ties are found in the independent regulatory commissions. Beginning with the Interstate Commerce Commission in 1887, a succession of agencies has been created by Congress to regulate various parts of the society's commercial life. For example, new foods and drugs that are marketed must meet standards established by the Food and Drug Administration (FDA); the broadcasting industries are regulated by the Federal Communications Commission (FCC), which grants new licenses and maintains broadcast standards; and so on. Even those industries

---

[4]Respondents were asked how much of the federal budget went to foreign aid. The median estimate was 15 percent; in actuality, foreign aid comprised less than 1 percent.

that do not come under the purview of a specific regulatory agency are covered by general-purpose agencies such as the Federal Trade Commission (FTC). The regulatory bodies, then, serve as a key bridge between government and business.

In theory, these agencies have the potential to play a powerful controlling role over big business. It is therefore not surprising that they have become prime targets of corporate influence in government. Moreover, their ability to accomplish real control is often frustrated by the fact that the personnel who occupy the decision-making positions of the regulatory agencies commonly come from the very industries that they are regulating or are sympathetic to their interests.

Antitrust laws are another theoretical means of controlling excessive corporate power, but their ineffectiveness and lack of enforcement are well understood. The continued concentration of market power in almost every industry in the American economy affirms this. Hundreds of mergers of industrial corporations occur each year in the United States, but only a few are ever seriously challenged by the government (Barnet and Müller, 1974). Almost $1 trillion worth of corporate mergers and acquisitions have taken place since 1998 (Uchitelle, 2000).

In sum, government regulation, in theory, holds powerful economic institutions under control and forces them to act in the public interest. In effect, however, the very opposite is often glaringly evident. In such cases, government regulation of big business acts to solidify the power of large economic enterprises by stifling competition and providing the corporate elite steady access to government policymakers. This leads not to a fairer distribution of societal resources, but to a reinforcement of the stratification system.

Efforts to Influence the Business Cycle

A capitalist system operates, in theory, through the dynamics of the market. The laws of supply and demand dictate prices, costs, and other key decisions, all of which are decided by the natural workings of the market. Individual responsibility and the rational pursuit of self-interest, curiously, are balanced, making it impossible for any one firm to dominate the system. Adam Smith, in his famous treatise on capitalism, *The Wealth of Nations*, written in 1776, called this the "invisible hand." In this classic view, the success of capitalism is contingent on the market operating in a condition of laissez-faire—without interference by government. Through competition, individuals will advance or fall back on their own initiative and ambition. The free market, it is believed, provides a neutral competitive setting. Government, therefore, is not to interfere with these natural market processes. Individuals must be assured unhindered movement in the labor market and absolute freedom to buy and sell what they choose. Such competition is bound to create inequality, of course, but what is of utmost importance is not true equality—which, in this view, is a chimera—but equal opportunity for all to compete in the marketplace.

This classical view of the way the market works has never reflected reality. In fact, the state always plays a significant role in the capitalist economy. In the United States over the past hundred or so years, efforts to influence the market through state intervention have occurred in various ways.

Although the laissez-faire conception of business-government relations was never more than a figment of capitalist ideology, in the United States an unregulated market was most fully realized during the period of industrial growth following the Civil War. Big business strongly resisted attempts at government control or regulation, successfully in most cases. Furthermore, the industrial expansion that marked the age of enterprise was characterized by the unrelenting efforts of big business to assure the enactment of favorable government policies and to maximize its exploitation of government-controlled resources such as land, mining, and timber. Business involvement in government in the 1880s often featured the active role of corporate leaders themselves in politics. The U.S. Senate in 1889 was known as the "Millionaire's Club," since it included numerous industrial magnates of the day (Epstein, 1969:26).

The early part of the twentieth century, known as the Progressive Era, saw the emergence of a reform movement that was based in large part on the belief that the giant corporations had amassed enormous and potentially dangerous powers. As a result, government regulatory agencies were established and antitrust legislation enacted. However, corporate power and influence were not seriously diminished (Kolko, 1967; Weinstein, 1968).

The 1930s marked a major change in the relationship of government and business. The most serious economic depression in American history gave rise to the active role of government in shaping as well as influencing economic trends. Government controls became more direct in nature, and the fiction of laissez-faire was finally put to rest. Influenced most strongly by the economic theories of John Maynard Keynes, the federal government under the administration of Franklin D. Roosevelt instituted a sweeping series of measures, the basic purpose of which was to stabilize the business cycle.

Economists had traditionally argued that each economic recession or depression would reverse itself naturally, and this had generally been the case until the 1930s. The depression of that era, however, simply did not turn about, and the economy continued to stagnate. Keynes argued that during periods when private industry was unable to generate consumer demand, there was no necessary upswing and the level of production and employment might continue to remain low indefinitely. Keynes's solution was for the government to step in and stimulate demand through its own spending programs and through tax cuts. In the same manner, if consumer demand were excessive and inflation was threatening economic stability, government could reverse its policies by cutting its expenditures and raising taxes. With these policies, government assumed unprecedented responsibility for monitoring the economic system.

Despite the more active role of government in the economy, the basic capitalist system was upheld. But the fear of another depression of the severity of the 1930s created a general acceptance of the idea that government had at least some role to play in managing the capitalist economy.

The most forceful convergence of state and corporation took place in the era after World War II. The rise of big government and its intervention in the economic process was viewed by big business not as a countervailing threat but as a guarantor of a stable economy as well as a vital customer for its products and services. Likewise, government came to accept the inevitability, and indeed the necessity, of the large corporate enterprise as the dominant form of business in the society (Barber, 1970). Those views have continued to prevail even with the advent of the global economy.

Partisan Differences in Public Policy

Both major American political parties in the modern period have aimed for economic growth, and Keynesian policies were generally accepted by both until the 1980s. There have been long-established differences between Republicans and Democrats, however, in the philosophies and strategies employed in assuring economic prosperity.

The most essential difference lies in what is viewed as the proper role of government in the political economy. Republicans have traditionally advocated a less active state; solutions to economic problems, they believe, lie in the workings of the market. Thus, the public sector is to play only a minimal role. Democrats, on the other hand, have traditionally favored a more proactive government in the economy; they also see solutions in the market, but with more state intervention. These differences in philosophy and strategy have led to traditionally different public policies on the part of the two parties.

Demand-Side Policies

Demand-side policies, traditionally favored by Democrats, derive from Keynesian ideas. The problem of the economy, in this view, is that producers try to limit supply in order to maximize their profits and reduce inflation. In limiting supply, however, people lose their jobs; unemployment, therefore, is the major demand-side problem (Froman, 1984).

The solution is to put money in the pockets of workers—that is, consumers—who will spend it and thus generate economic activity, creating demand and keeping people working. To accomplish this, policies might be adjusted to give workers tax breaks and to pass more of the tax burden to the rich and the corporations. Similarly, increasing social welfare programs would leave more money for workers to spend in the consumer market. During the Great Depression, government became the employer of last resort, putting people to work on public projects in its efforts to create consumer demand and lift the economy out of the doldrums. Since that time, almost all administrations have adopted some form of the Keynesian strategy, acknowledging the important role of government in minimizing unemployment. These policies tend to shift wealth downward as the rich receive less of a return on their tax dollars and the middle, working, and poverty classes receive more.

Supply-Side Policies

Supply-side or "trickle down" **policies** aim for the same general objective as demand-side policies: keeping the economy growing and prosperous. The strategy for accomplishing this, however, begins from the opposite direction when compared to demand-side policies. Supply-siders maintain that it is suppliers (that is, producers) who must be given incentive to produce more, which, in turn, will eventually create demand. In this view, normal investment activities of the private sector can generate sufficient demand that, in turn, can generate sufficient growth without having the government intervene (Heilbroner and Thurow, 1994). This has been the traditional Republican perspective on the political economy.

The essential function of the state in the political economy, in the supply-side view, is to stimulate business investment and production in order to create jobs and generate economic activity. Rather than putting more money into the pockets of workers, therefore, more money is made available to the wealthy and to the corporations who, it is hoped, will invest it in productive projects, like new machinery and factories. To accomplish this, the tax burden is shifted from the top to the middle and bottom of the class system. Tax breaks and lower marginal tax rates are put into place. A reduction of corporate taxes and taxes that impact most heavily on the wealthy (capital gains, for example) is also employed. With the same objective in mind, welfare is shifted from the bottom of the social hierarchy to the top. This is what was earlier referred to as "upside-down welfare" (Huff, 1992). The short-term redistributive effect, as a result, is the opposite of demand-side policies. Rather than lifting those in the middle and lower income groups, more wealth flows to those at the top.

This supply-side strategy was adopted most zealously by the Reagan administration in the 1980s. Corporations and the wealthy were given huge tax breaks, while taxes on wages rose. Deregulation of banks and other financial institutions also was put into place, freeing them to make investments in projects that presumably would generate economic activity.

The outcome of these policies was to help create the widest discrepancy between the top and the bottom of the class hierarchies since the 1920s (Phillips, 1990, 1994). Recall the statistics noted in Chapter 2 regarding the expansion of inequality during this decade, a reversal of the trend in the 1950s and 1960s. Average wages declined, even though new jobs were created. The expected investment in productive projects, moreover, did not materialize, and rapid and substantial industrial growth did not result. Also, because of the reduction in federal revenue as a result of lowered income taxes, government had to borrow to pay for a huge increase in military spending. The result was a tripling of the national debt.[5]

More or Less Inequality? Policy Choices

When and where public investment in education, health care, housing, and other key life chances is great, inequalities are ameliorated; where it is low, inequalities are sustained and even intensified. Class differences, then, are in large measure the product of public policies. But these differences in public investment from society to society, and within societies from one historical period to another, are the result of choices made by citizens in choosing their governments and leaders. That investment will vacillate: In the United States, at times, like the 1950s and 1960s, it was substantial and resulted in inducing greater equality. At other times, like the 1980s, it was constricted and resulted in greater inequality. In any case, however, public investment has always been lower in the United States than in other industrial nations (Fischer et al., 1996).

What distinguishes American society from other advanced capitalist societies is not the domination of its capitalist economy by a small number of giant corporations—that is characteristic of western Europe, Canada, and Japan as well. What *is* strikingly different is the distribution of resources and power among government, business, and labor. The United States stands out clearly as the society most thoroughly dominated by private power—the business sector—with relatively underdeveloped public institutions and a historically weak labor movement. This influences all parts of the American political economy, especially the distribution of income and wealth and the public policies aimed at altering that distribution.

Summary

All contemporary capitalist societies make attempts to ameliorate the inequalities that are naturally generated by a capitalist economy. To affect the distribution of income and wealth, government acts in three ways: It taxes, it spends, and it regulates. The first two functions are called fiscal policy.

Progressive taxes have the effect of redistributing income downward. Regressive taxes have the opposite effect. Proportional taxes leave income distribution unaffected. The income tax is the major source of government revenue. Although individuals as well as corporations pay taxes on their earnings, the bulk of income taxes are paid by individuals. Despite popular beliefs to the contrary, Americans pay less in taxes than citizens of all other Western industrial societies.

---

[5]Some suggest that the creation of great national debt was purposeful: to "starve" the federal government so that it would be forced to reduce the welfare state, to which the Reaganites were philosophically opposed. In any case, the deficit became a force in its own right in reducing social welfare expenditures (Galbraith, 1994).

There are three general areas in which government spends its revenue: It supplies public goods, which benefit everyone regardless of social class; it provides services of various kinds and distributes transfer payments to people; and it pays interest on the national debt. The first two, especially the provision of various benefits, directly affect the class system.

Various government welfare policies benefit different classes. Public assistance is welfare for the poverty classes. This is what is commonly understood by the general public as "welfare." Welfare for the middle classes— namely, entitlements and tax expenditures—constitutes a much greater percentage of government spending; Social Security and Medicare are the two major entitlement programs. Corporate welfare takes several forms, including tax avoidance, direct and indirect subsidies by government, and government assistance to corporations in financial difficulty.

In the United States, public spending policies of the 1950s and 1960s had equalizing effects. Social Security and Medicare, for example, made it possible for millions of elderly Americans to escape poverty and to avoid the insecurity of old age. The federal government provided relatively inexpensive home loans, enabling millions to own their homes for the first time. Government subsidies to education, like the G.I. Bill, made it possible for millions to earn a college degree who would never have had the opportunity without such assistance. And the War on Poverty, comprising numerous public assistance programs, helped to reduce the poverty class. These spending policies were reversed in the 1980s and early 1990s as assistance programs were slashed and government spending was redirected to defense industries and other activities that benefited higher social classes.

The U.S. welfare state is less comprehensive and generous than that of other Western industrial societies. It is also less redistributive than others. These differences are accounted for by a stronger American belief in individualism, a more unfettered form of capitalism, a public distrust of government, and stronger business power combined with a weaker labor movement. Most Americans seriously overestimate the dimensions of the welfare state, particularly as it affects the poor.

Through regulation of the economy, the state tries to maximize fairness and equity in the distribution of societal resources. It does this through regulatory agencies that, in theory, have the potential to play a strong role in checking the power of big business. In reality, however, regulation often functions as a means of solidifying the power of large corporate enterprises by stifling competition and providing the corporate elite steady access to government policymakers. Government also seeks to keep the economic system functioning smoothly by influencing the business cycle. Since the 1930s, the U.S. government has adopted Keynesian policies in some degree, in which consumer demand is influenced by fiscal and monetary policies. In regulating the economy, Democrats traditionally have favored demand-side policies, whereas Republicans have favored supply-side policies.

8

Theories of Class and Social Inequality

No real observation of any kind of phenomena is possible, except in so far as it is first directed, and finally interpreted, by some theory.
AUGUSTE COMTE

Describing the "who and what" of inequality, as done in the previous chapters, is only the first step in exploring this seemingly universal social condition. As explained in Chapter 1, social scientists go beyond merely describing a social phenomenon—they seek to explain *why* it exists. This chapter focuses on some of the major theories of inequality.

If you were asked to give your view of why some people are rich whereas others are poor, or why some dutifully accept their place in society whereas others rebel, or why women and men differ so noticeably in their occupational roles, you would probably not hesitate to respond. Your answers would be based on your intuition, your past observations, what you have read and heard from various sources, and perhaps what you have learned through formal education. This is not unlike what social scientists do in beginning their search for explanations. Where they differ from laypersons, however, is in erecting a framework within which to organize their observations, insights, and data. This framework is a theory. Some theories are quite specific, whereas others are more encompassing and less formalized. The latter are theoretical perspectives, sometimes called models or paradigms, that comprise a set of general assumptions concerning various aspects of society.

All theories of class and social inequality focus on two basic issues: (1) *Why is there inequality in societies?* and (2) *Is inequality inevitable*, part of the human condition? Other issues (for example, Is inequality necessary? or Who benefits from inequality?) stem from these fundamental questions.

Much of this chapter is devoted to the theories of Karl Marx and Max Weber because of their influence and importance. The strength of their theories is attested by their endurance. Many of the basic notions that Marx and Weber presented in the nineteenth and early twentieth centuries remain vibrant and continue to be applied and debated by contemporary social scientists. Following an exploration of Marx's and Weber's ideas regarding social inequality, a few theories with more contemporary roots are presented.

It is important to consider at the outset that even though they may seem hopelessly at odds, different theoretical views of social inequality are not necessarily "either-ors." It is not a question of which theory is correct and which is incorrect. Theoretical explanations may overlap one another in some ways, and each may simply focus more sharply on one or more specific aspects of inequality.

Marx's Theory of Social Inequality

To call Marx one of the founding fathers of modern social science, as many have, would not be overstating his significance. Though he lived and wrote in the mid– and latter nineteenth century, his theories remain relevant and form part of the foundation not only of contemporary sociology but also of the other social sciences. So sweeping was the range of his thought that few areas of social life were untouched by his analysis. As a result, Marx would be hard to categorize in the context of modern-day academic disciplines. Sociology, political science, and economics can each claim a Marxian tradition. Indeed, it has often been remarked that all social science since Marx's time has, in one form or another, involved a response to his ideas. This is surely true in the case of stratification and inequality. Others before Marx had dealt with issues of social class, but Marx gave these issues a primary place in social analysis and offered related ideas and concepts that today remain basic points of inquiry in studying social inequality.

It is not possible in just a few pages to attempt a detailed examination of Marx's contribution to the study of social inequality. Many scholars have devoted their entire careers to such a task and have compiled literally thousands of volumes containing analyses, critiques, defenses, and refutations of his works. In fact, one of the difficulties in any study of Marx is this extremely wide range of interpretations. French sociologist Raymond Aron reminded us that "if only there were not so many millions of Marxists, there would be no question at all about what Marx's leading ideas are or what is central to his thought" (1968:145). We might take comfort in knowing that the dilemma is not new in our era. The many different interpretations and applications of his work, even in his own time, prompted Marx to declare that he was "not a Marxist" (Lewis, 1972:9).

One factor that has contributed to the proliferation of interpretations of Marx is the rather unsystematic manner in which his writings were presented. Friedrich Engels, a wealthy factory owner, was a close working associate of Marx and organized much of Marx's work, in the process supplementing it with ideas of his own. Furthermore, Marx's extremely broad scope of social analysis has undoubtedly helped to open the door to conflicting views of his thought.

As well as an explanation of inequality in societies, Marx's work encompassed a sweeping theory of sociohistorical change, a full explanation of the capitalist economic system, and a Utopian vision. Each of these units of thought is, of course, essentially interrelated and cannot be considered independently. Furthermore, within the context of the Marxian perspective—Marx saw societies as *total*—one cannot isolate any single aspect of society. The specific elements can be understood only in relation to the whole. What is of paramount importance to the study of inequality, however, is how Marx's analysis addresses the two key theoretical issues: Why is there inequality? and Is inequality inevitable?

The Economic Foundation

Fundamental to the Marxian theory of inequality is the pivotal role of a society's economic institutional structure. The predominance of economic institutions is so overwhelming, in Marx's estimation, that they are the determinants of the entire system of society. He saw the dynamics of society originating in economic, or productive, activity—securing food, shelter, and all the other necessities: "Life involves before everything else eating and drinking, a habitation, clothing, and many other things. The first historical act is thus the production of the means to satisfy these needs, the production of material life itself" (Marx in Tucker, 1972:120).

It is out of this economic reality, the process by which people fulfill their material needs, that a society's culture arises—its various structures of law, religion, education, and politics and the belief systems attached to these structures. In short, the manner in which people organize to produce their needs and the relations that develop out of these activities determine all other aspects of social life.

This system of production by which people provide for their material existence is the society's economic foundation or, as Marx put it, the **mode of production.** As the economic foundation changes, so do people's ideas, but it is fundamental that the former impel the latter. In a famous passage Marx explained this process:

> The mode of production of material life conditions the social, political and intellectual life process in general. It is not the consciousness of men that determines their being, but, on the contrary, their social being that determines their consciousness. (Marx and Engels, 1968:182)

The idea of economic reality, how people solve the problem of survival, is, then, the basic starting point for understanding the nature of power and inequality in societies.

The primacy of the economic mode cannot be overemphasized. For Marx, the central fact of all human history is the necessity for societies, in every epoch, to provide the necessary goods and materials for sustenance. How do people in society organize in order to provide these things? That is the fundamental question with which any societal analysis must begin. To understand social inequality, then, one must look not to the dominant philosophy of a historical period but to the dominant economic form. It is this *historical materialism* that is the cornerstone of Marxian thought.

Economic Base and Superstructure   Whatever form the economic base, or substructure, takes requires a whole superstructure of noneconomic activity and thought. This superstructure of noneconomic institutions—the family, religion, education, the state—necessarily reflects the foundation on which it is raised. The economic activity of an agrarian society, for example, is centered on the land. What the society produces for survival derives primarily from the soil, and most people will engage in occupations that relate to agriculture: farming, maintaining agricultural tools, and so on. To complement this mode of production, a set of noneconomic institutions will develop that helps sustain an agrarian economic system. The family will be large in order to provide as many hands as possible to work the land; religious rites will coincide with planting and harvesting times; the legal system will be concerned primarily with the ownership rights and the inheritance of land; and the political system will be designed to protect the economic and social interests of those who own the land and the tools with which it is worked.

All of these institutions are shaped to fit the needs of an agrarian society; they would not accommodate an industrial mode of production. As a society's economic base changes, therefore, the form and content of its noneconomic institutions must also change. Marx thus explains societal change as the result of changes in the mode of production:

> In acquiring new productive forces men change their mode of production, and in changing their mode of production, their manner of gaining a living, they change all their social relations. The windmill gives you society with the feudal lord, the steammill, society with the industrial capitalist. (1920:119)

The Class Division

Marx's answer to the first key theoretical question—Why is there inequality?—follows from the core place of economic activity in a society: Inequality arises as a result of control of productive resources, those things that are necessary to supply the society's economic needs. Marx referred to these as the **means of production.** And the division of the society is relatively simple: One element of the population owns these basic material resources, whereas the other owns no productive property and can offer only human labor in exchange for material needs. Thus, the latter is forced to work for the former. Although the workers are responsible for the production of economic wealth through their labor, it is the owning class that garners the bulk of the society's wealth.

A social class, for Marx, comprises those who stand in a common position with regard to the productive process. There are, then, essentially two classes in all societies: the owners of the means of production and the workers. All types of societies at different stages of human development and with different productive systems give rise to these two opposing classes, whether masters and slaves in slave societies or lords and serfs in feudal societies. In capitalist societies, these two classes are the **bourgeoisie,** or **capitalist class,** and the **proletariat,** or industrial working class.

The Hegemony of the Capitalist Class   This two-part division of society into owners and workers produces gross inequality. Capitalists, the dominant class, receive the bulk of societal rewards and workers get very little. The capitalist class is able to maintain its power as a result of the possession of three key assets: the means of production, control of the state, and control of ideas and values.

First, workers must submit to the rules established by the capitalists, because, in the end, they have no other choice. Without control of the means of production, they must sell their labor to the capitalists and must accept what the capitalists will pay. Workers do not get the full value of what they produce through their labor; they get only what the capitalist is prepared to pay them: enough to keep them alive and to make certain that they will return to work the next day. The remainder is taken by the capitalist as profit. Under these conditions, there is little likelihood that workers can save enough to eventually possess productive property and become capitalists themselves. Thus, Marx felt that any basic changes in the class structure could be realized only by a revolutionary movement that would divest the bourgeoisie of its control of the means of production.

Second, the capitalist class is a **ruling class** in the sense that it controls the state, that is, government. Marx's view of the state is neatly summarized in *The Communist Manifesto:* "The executive of the modern State is but a committee for managing the common affairs of the whole bourgeoisie" (Marx in Tucker, 1972:337). Thus, even if capitalists themselves may not be in key governing positions, they are represented by those who act in their interests. Political institutions and the actions of political leaders are outgrowths of the class structure and therefore function to protect the property and privileges of the bourgeoisie. Instead of Who governs the society? the more telling question is, Who owns and controls the means of production? Answering that question is tantamount to identifying those who dominate the state, that is, those who govern.

Third, control of ideas and values by the bourgeoisie is perhaps as important as control of the means of production and the state in assuring compliance with the social order of capitalist society. Marx asserted that "the ideas of the ruling class are in every epoch the ruling ideas: i.e., the class which is the ruling *material* force of society, is at the same time its ruling *intellectual* force" (Tucker, 1972:136). In this view, the rules and values of the sociopolitical system are created, disseminated, and enforced by the dominant class and are ultimately accepted by the society as a whole.

The institutions of education, religion, and the state aid in socializing people to the dominant values. They are merely reflections of ruling-class interests. And by controlling the means of communication (the press and, in modern societies, electronic media), the capitalist class is able to stifle opposing ideas effectively. Lacking class consciousness—that is, being unaware of their own class interests—members of the proletariat regard the ideas of the ruling class as "natural." The prevailing sociopolitical system is thus seen as just, fair, and working in the interests of all social classes, not simply the capitalists. Engels referred to this as **false consciousness.**

It is important to understand that Marx saw the breakdown of society into two opposing classes as a structural phenomenon. The class system is just that: a *system.* The personal identities of the capitalists or the workers are of no relevance. Whether they are good people or bad, kind and generous, or nasty and stingy is of no consequence. All are part of a system. In their role in this system, capitalists are obliged to exploit workers. To give their workers a share of their profits or to pay workers more in wages would only undercut their position vis-à-vis other capitalists and eventually force them out of business. They therefore have no choice but to pay their workers as little as necessary. To see capitalists as avaricious is to miss the point: They are simply doing what they are expected to do as capitalists. Workers likewise have no choice but to continue to work for less than their fair share of the product; it is the only way they can keep themselves and their families alive. So capitalists and workers may come and go. A few workers may even eventually amass enough resources to become capitalists themselves. But this does not change the nature of the system. New capitalists will act like capitalists and exploit their workers. That is the system's logic.

Class Conflict and Societal Change

Marx believed that classes become political groups in the sense that individuals eventually recognize their common socioeconomic interests and are prepared to engage in struggle to protect and enhance them. It is this power struggle between opposing classes that produces social change. Class conflict, Marx explained, is a certainty in societies as long as private ownership of property is sanctioned, thereby enabling one class to control the productive process, the distribution of wealth, and the communication of ideas. But class conflict generates social change, eventually giving rise to a new mode of production and thereby creating a new ruling class. Thus the feudal system, with its ruling class of nobles and lords who owned the land, replaced the slave system. In the same way, feudalism gave way to capitalism, bringing to power a new ruling class of capitalist owners. In each case, irreversible historical and economic forces led to the change and to the ascendance of a new dominant class.

By this logic, then, capitalism will give way to a more advanced form of social and economic organization as the relations of capitalist society are no

longer capable of supporting new productive forces. Just as capitalism replaced feudalism, the demise of capitalism and its replacement by a socialist
productive system in which the means of production are collectively rather
than privately owned was felt by Marx to be an unavoidable future development. The momentum behind the passing of capitalism and the emergence of
socialism is the conflict between capitalists and workers. Once the workers
become conscious of their true class interests, they are transformed into a political group, a *klasse für sich* (literally, a "class for itself"), as Marx described
it, prepared to engage in revolutionary confrontation with the bourgeoisie.
And just as irresistible historical and economic forces previously favored the
capitalist class in its conflict with the landowning class, they now favor the
working class.

As to the nature of the revolutionary struggle, Marx was not certain. Advancing industrialization and increasing worker exploitation, he felt, would
eventually propel such a movement. But the organizational details of the revolution were left to practitioners such as Lenin to clarify and carry out, well
after the deaths of Marx in 1883 and Engels in 1895.

The nature of post-capitalist society was also left largely to speculation, and
it is here that Marx was more a visionary than a social scientist. The broad outlines of post-capitalism, however, were well-formulated thoughts. Following
the revolution, two stages were envisioned, ultimately climaxing in a classless
society. The first phase, *socialism,* was seen as an indeterminate transitional period in which the workers would control the means of production. By this fact
alone, power relations would be radically changed, bringing worker exploitation to an end. The state would necessarily still be present, but it would now be
a proletarian state, which Marx called the *dictatorship of the proletariat.* The details
of this workers' government were not made clear by either Marx or Engels, but,
as noted, Lenin fashioned its actual working order, at least in the Soviet Union.

It is only with the total abolition of social classes that the final stage of
post-capitalism—communism—would emerge. The classless society is man-
ifestly Utopian, characterized by the complete socialization of the productive
system, the end of all economic exploitation, and the appearance of individuals no longer impelled by acquisitive and individualistic values. It is at this
point that the well-known dictum "from each according to his abilities, to
each according to his needs" is fulfilled. With these conditions in place, the
state withers away, since there are no more class interests to protect and no
need to impose social controls.

In the end, then, Marx was optimistic about the possibilities for the elim-
ination of inequality. Regarding the second key theoretical question, whether
social inequality is inevitable, Marx answers a qualified "no." Although it
would certainly be a long-term affair, the creation of a classless—and thus
equitable—society was possible.

We should keep in mind that capitalism, to Marx, was a very beneficial
productive system when compared with previous ones. It had created the
technology and material abundance that made it possible for people to enter

into a social condition in which poverty, both material and psychological, would no longer exist. But to make that condition a reality required the organization of society into a socialist productive system. Capitalism had had its place; indeed, it had been a necessary step in societal development. But its utility, Marx felt, was ended by the middle of the nineteenth century.

Marxian Theory in Summary

The essence of the Marxian theory of stratification and inequality can be distilled into a few simple premises.

- Reality consists of the constant production of basic life needs—food, clothing, shelter. Through work, people in society realize themselves, and it is around this productive process that history unfolds.

- Societies in different stages of social and technological development create different productive systems. Economic institutions (that is, the productive system) shape the general nature of beliefs and practices in all other areas of social life.

- In all societies, a class division evolves. Those who own or control the society's productive resources (the *means of production*) are inevitably in conflict with those who do not. In this conflict, the owning class controls key economic, political, and ideological institutions, all of which therefore reflect and protect its interests.

- Class struggle is a contest between these two primary and opposing classes, and it is here that the dynamic forces of society lie. Class struggle is the generator of societal change.

- All productive systems, with their attendant classes, give way to more advanced systems. This will occur with capitalism, too, as it gives way to socialism, wherein workers will control the means of production. Eventually, a communist society will emerge in which there will be no classes and thus no exploitation.

One might ask, of what relevance is a theory constructed in the mid–nineteenth century to conditions and issues of our time? Many specific Marxian propositions are clearly not germane to contemporary societies. Others, however, have had lasting impact and remain meaningful.

The Failure of Marx's Vision

Although parts of it are pertinent to the whole course of human social development, Marx's analysis is concerned primarily with the structure and dynamics of capitalist industrial societies. It is in such societies that Marx foresaw the occurrence of the workers' revolution. Obviously this has failed to materialize, especially in the West, where Marx believed the social and economic conditions were conducive to such a movement. Why did the Marxian vision not take shape?

To begin with, class struggle in advanced capitalist societies did not become more acute, as Marx predicted. Instead, the working classes of these societies seemed to settle for an accommodation with the capitalist system. As industrial capitalism thrived, the fundamental objective of workers became a more sizable share of the capitalist product, not a change in the productive system itself. Labor unions, for example, became less political organizations than groups designed to operate on behalf of workers within the accepted rules of union-management relations. Particularly in the United States, unions became forces of stabilization, not of radical change. Marx had seen workers' organizations as mobilizing agents, designed to instill consciousness and alter the prevailing power structure, rather than simply as bargaining agents that would represent labor's interests vis-à-vis the capitalist class. Rather than destroy capitalism, workers have sought to gain a bigger share of the product.

Further invalidation of Marxian theory is shown in the changing class structure itself. Serious class conflict was averted in advanced capitalist societies because the polarization of classes did not progress as Marx felt it would; rather, the very opposite occurred—an increasingly complex and diverse class structure. The Marxian formula called for a growing contraposition of the two major classes, capitalists and workers. The former would become smaller and more concentrated, and the latter would swell in size, gradually absorbing more and more of the marginal capitalists, mainly small entrepreneurs. Instead, the middle class grew, dimming the split between the two extremes. Moreover, as discussed in Chapter 4, automation and the emergence of a global labor market continue to eliminate traditional working-class occupations. Accompanying the decline in blue-collar occupations has been the growth of the professional-managerial and service sectors, the largest elements of the workforce of post-industrial societies. The place of these classes was not well defined or overly important in Marx's analysis. As will be discussed later in this section, some contemporary Marxist theorists have tried to deal with this issue by constructing a more complex model of the class system.

Another change in the class structure concerns the place of the capitalist class. Today it is difficult to clearly discern a "capitalist" class in the Marxian sense, that is, those who actually own the means of production. Stock ownership, though still very concentrated, is far more dispersed than in past times. Many workers, therefore, own stock in the companies for which they work or hold retirement funds that are invested in the stock market. Moreover, effective power in giant corporations lies with a professional managerial class, who may not necessarily be among the major owners of the corporations they manage. It is true, of course, that the top-ranking executives do typically own large amounts of stock in their companies.

In addition to the increasing complexity of the class system, the workers' material state did not deteriorate but improved markedly from the degrading conditions typical of Marx's time. These improvements were the result of various social forces and institutions, chief among them the intervention of the state in dealing with the vacillations of a capitalist economy and the formation of strong labor unions. Neither of these developments seemed possible to Marx. As a result, class conflict in the United States and other advanced capitalist societies did not intensify.

The Marxian idea seemed to have failed as well in those societies that did experience a so-called socialist revolution. Paradoxically, socialist revolutions of the twentieth century occurred in societies in which the economic and social conditions required for the kind of movement Marx forecast were least present. Russia in 1917, China in 1948, and Cuba in 1959 were societies in which capitalist development was not great. However, it is unlikely that the socialist systems of these societies, as they took shape, ever represented Marxism in anything but ideology. In many ways, they were aberrations of the Marxian legacy and must be seen as unique social orders. On few of their essential problems did Marx's theory shed any light (Harrington, 1973). Indeed, the political, economic, and social policies of these regimes could have been the same had Marx never lived.

Finally, Marx's assertion that class is the most fundamental and consequential form of social division has been shown to be questionable in societies with diverse racial and ethnic populations. Marx assumed that people everywhere will identify with others who have similar class interests and that such self-conscious class units would eventually come together as a potent political force. But in the United States and other ethnically diverse societies, class identity and action has seemed to take a back seat to racial and ethnic identity and political action. Racial and ethnic conflict has been more severe and frequent in the United States than has class conflict, and ethnic identities have proven themselves far more effective as a source of collective action than have class interests. Most internal conflicts in all countries today revolve not around issues of class inequality but around ethnic nationalism and the desire of ethnic groups to maintain their cultural and political autonomy. Gender divisions, too, have been extremely potent in affecting life chances and the distribution of society's wealth, power, and prestige, irrespective of class differences.

Enduring Points of Marx's Theory

Though the details of Marx's model of inequality and his vision of the future are certainly refutable in light of modern history, his theoretical contribution is, in a more general sense, of lasting and fundamental significance.

First, and perhaps most important, Marx proffered the idea of social class as the key ingredient in the process of societal conflict and change. Starting with Marx, class became a basic idea of social science that would henceforth enter into any and all societal analyses. Moreover, Marx established a perspective that linked economics and politics, *political economy,* that forces us to recognize the meshing of these two basic institutions in modern societies and the manner in which they operate to create and sustain the class system.

Second, the Marxian perspective demonstrates the way in which our social and political worlds are ideologically created. As shown in Chapter 9, we are attuned to a certain way of thinking about and seeing society. This is a highly one-sided process, however. The prevailing modes of social, political, and economic thought are not "natural" in the sense that they produce themselves without input from the social environment. Most simply, we *learn* to perceive our world in a particular way. And our learning is confined to that which we are offered by the society's socializing agents—the family, the state, the school, the media—all disseminators of the dominant ideology. Social and political behavior and attitudes we consider "normal" or "just" are, in fact, defined for us through this ideology. As Michael Harrington explained, the Marxian perspective "asserts that the common sense of any given society is a rationalization for that society, that vocabularies normally conceal as well as communicate, particularly when they speak of anything that has to do with power" (Harrington, 1976:192).

Our concepts regarding right and wrong, good and bad, then, do not simply come upon us. Rather, the ideas and values of the dominant class generally become those of the society as a whole, creating a legitimacy for the structure of power and contributing to its perpetuation. As sociologist Frank Parkin noted,

> Dominant values are in a sense a representation of the perceptions and interests of the relatively privileged; yet by virtue of the institutional backing they receive, such values often form the basis of moral judgements of underprivileged groups. In a way, dominant values tend to set the standards for what is considered to be objectively "right." (1971:83)

This being so, it should not surprise us that those who are seemingly oppressed by a socioeconomic system often are among its staunchest defenders.

Revising Marx

Neo-Marxist theorists have acknowledged the very different forms and conditions of modern capitalism from Marx's time and thus the need to revise Marxian theory in order to make it more relevant to contemporary issues. In doing so, however, they have retained the essence of the Marxian perspective.

A theoretical point of particular focus concerns the emergence of an extraordinarily more complex workforce, calling for a more elaborate model of the class structure than the two-part Marxian scheme. Although Marx did forecast an increasingly complex division of labor as capitalism evolved, he could not foresee the enormity of that complexity (Grimes, 1991). A related point with which modern Marxist theorists have dealt is the changed role of capitalists and workers in the productive system. Erik Olin Wright's work has most clearly addressed these issues.

Although accepting the basic Marxian class scheme, Wright delineates classes not on the basis of property ownership but on the basis of control of economic resources. In capitalist society, people may control financial capital, the physical means of production (such as factories), or labor (authority over workers). Major capitalists—the bourgeoisie—control all three whereas the working class controls none. Members of a third class, the petty bourgeoisie (independent, self-employed producers), have economic ownership and possession of the means of production but, since they employ no one, lack authority over workers (Wright, 1978). Thus, Wright accepts the fundamental Marxian idea of the division of capitalist society into opposing classes based on their relation to the means of production.

Wright recognizes, however, that many work situations do not fall neatly into this capitalist–worker–self-employed scheme. He suggests that in between these three classes are those who can control some, though not all, aspects of production. Wright calls these *contradictory class locations* (1979). For example, there are some who, in their class positions, exploit labor (à la capitalists) but who themselves are exploited (à la workers). Corporate managers occupy such a position. On the one hand, they are salaried workers themselves, but on the other, they have much control over workers whom they supervise. Professionals such as doctors, lawyers, and teachers may also be in such a contradictory class location. They have little or no control over the means of production but have much influence on the nature of their work as well as on that of employees who work at their direction (e.g., nurses, secretaries, and aides).

In later works (1985, 1997), Wright further refined this model so that it includes several additional class categories. In this more complex scheme, one's class location is based not only on control of financial assets, control of the means of production, and control of labor, but also on the possession of assets, including property, skills, and organizational position. This generates additional contradictory class locations.

Wright's theory, then, provides for changes in the class order of advanced capitalist societies while still retaining the basic Marxian notion that one's class is defined in relation to one's place in the society's productive system. His revised model, of course, does not speak to all of the problems of applying traditional Marxian theory to contemporary capitalism, but it illustrates how neo-Marxist theorists have tried to adapt the theory to modern conditions. It also demonstrates how Marxists continue to be confounded in their efforts to sort out and systematically arrange the property and power relations of modern capitalist societies.

All social scientists today recognize the utility of at least some aspects of Marx's analysis. But obviously some are more strongly committed to this approach than others. Among those who do lean more favorably toward this approach, however, Marx is not interpreted in an absolute or mechanical fashion. Instead, Marxian ideas are accepted primarily as a method for helping to understand society rather than as a definitive explanation. C. Wright Mills has referred to this group of scholars as "plain Marxists" who "are generally agreed that Marx's work bears the trademarks of the nineteenth-century society, but that his general model and his ways of thinking are central to their own intellectual history and remain relevant to their attempts to grasp present-day social worlds" (1962:98). Only among the dogmatic, or "vulgar," Marxists, then, should we expect to find attempts to apply Marxian ideas in a literal sense to societies of the present age.

In analyzing social inequality, Marx's theory is seminal. It is comprised of original ideas, providing the seeds from which further thinking about inequality grew. Just as Darwin's and Einstein's ideas changed the way people thought about certain areas of biology or about physics, respectively, so the ideas of Marx propelled social thinking in new directions. Others who followed him took his ideas and built upon them. It is the general thrust of the theory rather than its specific elements that remains most relevant to the study of inequality today.

Weber: The Inevitability of Inequality

Max Weber, a German sociologist whose writing spanned the latter years of the nineteenth century and the early decades of the twentieth, is considered, along with Marx, to be one of the most important contributors to sociological theory. Although not a contemporary of Marx, Weber was certainly influenced by Marx's ideas, as were most social thinkers of that time. Indeed, it has been said that all theorists who followed Marx engaged in a "dialogue with Marx's ghost." In some ways, Weber's approach to stratification and inequality is built upon Marx's analysis, but Weber went beyond the Marxian model, modifying and elaborating on it. Thus, Weber did not dispute Marx as much as he augmented his theory and made it more complete.

Whereas Marx's view of stratification—that classes are founded on economic criteria—was essentially unidimensional, Weber suggested a more elaborate, multidimensional model. People's class positions are based not simply on their relation to the means of production but also on a number of interdependent variables. In addition to a hierarchy based on economic factors, Weber denoted hierarchies based on status and on political power. Let's look at these three distinct dimensions of social inequality—class, status, and party.

Class

Weber's notion of class is, to some degree, similar to Marx's: A class comprises those who stand in a similar position with regard to their opportunities to acquire the society's economic rewards (i.e., life chances). Weber, however, saw a greater variety of factors that are important in class formation, such as skills and credentials. Marx, remember, conceptualized class essentially as one's place in the productive system: worker or owner. But Weber pointed out, for example, that although a doctor at a hospital is a worker, not an owner, he is in a very different class position from a hospital custodian. Moreover, even within the bourgeoisie there are distinctions. A landlord who acquires his income from rent or a stockowner who receives dividends is not the same as an entrepreneur who operates a small business. Each, Weber pointed out, will possess different life chances.

Weber's notion of class, then, is more complete than Marx's. Some people may possess greater life chances than others as a result of their ownership of property, as Marx suggested, but others may possess greater life chances as a result of skills or expertise in a profession, enabling them to command high salaries even if they do not own productive property. Occupation rather than ownership or nonownership of property is, therefore, the basis of the formation of classes. People with common occupations, earning approximately similar incomes, constitute a class.

Status

There is more to stratification, however, than occupation or income, Weber explained. **Status** refers to differences in prestige that derive from a particular lifestyle, not from purely economic factors. The status dimension, then, consists of groups that display a particular lifestyle and that are aware of differences between themselves and other status groups. Weber explains the difference between class and status:

> With some over-simplification, one might . . . say that "classes" are stratified according to their relations to the production and acquisition of goods; whereas "status groups" that are stratified according to the principles of their *consumption* of goods are represented by special "styles of life." (Gerth and Mills, 1946:193)

The concept of status, or prestige, is extremely important in analyzing social inequality because it elucidates the complexity of modern stratification systems. To illustrate, consider two individuals, a truck driver and a schoolteacher. In looking at their approximate incomes, we find that they are not too different. Moreover, neither is a self-employed worker. In terms of economic position, then, they earn pretty much the same and are both nonowners. But would we really consider the truck driver and the teacher to be part of the same social class? We probably wouldn't—because of differences in status, or prestige. Teaching is more prestigious than driving a truck. Also, to become a teacher requires extensive formal training, usually a college degree. Truck drivers ordinarily learn on the job and few possess college degrees. This automatically differentiates the two people, even though they are basically the same in terms of purely economic factors. (In fact, some truck drivers outearn some teachers.) Those who hold college degrees are held in higher esteem socially than those who are only high school graduates.

Not only are the truck driver and the teacher differentiated in terms of prestige, but they also consume differently. That is, they enjoy noticeably different lifestyles. Their preferences in music, entertainment, fashion, food, housing, cars, and numerous other aspects of social life will probably differ radically. Whereas the teacher may enjoy going to art museums in his or her leisure time, for example, the truck driver might prefer hunting and fishing.

When looking for a restaurant, the teacher might prefer nouvelle cuisine, whereas the truck driver may prefer a steak house. Because of the differences in how they live and spend their incomes, they can no more be considered part of the same social class than could a banker and a ditchdigger, despite their common economic standing.

These sharply different lifestyles make for the formation of what Weber called **status communities,** each made up of people who have similar cultural and social interests and common consumer patterns. As in the case of the teacher and the truck driver, each associates with people who have the same cultural tastes, lives in neighborhoods made up of people like themselves, and probably marries those of similar status. These status communities may become tightly closed, as is the case, for example, of the old rich. They may also be founded on social characteristics other than lifestyle, such as ethnicity. This is particularly the case in multiethnic societies, where people's social prestige is to a great degree based on their ethnicity.

Weber pointed out that status and class are by no means unrelated. To enjoy a particular lifestyle necessitates a certain economic standing. One might see oneself cruising the Mediterranean or sunning on the beaches of Tahiti in summer and skiing on Alpine slopes in winter, but to realize that vision will require the financial means to do so. Any style of life, therefore, will be based for the most part on occupation and income. Ordinarily, then, those who enjoy similar status will occupy a similar economic position. There are exceptions to that relationship, however, as the teacher and truck driver illustrate.

Delineating a status dimension of stratification is important, for inequality is not necessarily founded primarily on economic factors in all societies. Consider the Indian caste system, discussed in Chapter 6, in which inequality is based almost exclusively on one's status, with wealth playing no role. In modern, class-stratified societies, status may decline in significance but is nonetheless critical in some cases. Ethnic minorities and women, for example, commonly have been treated differently on the basis of their ethnic and gender status, regardless of their economic position.

Party

Weber's third dimension, *party,* denotes political rank—one's standing in a collectivity or organization whose "action is oriented toward the acquisition of social 'power,' that is to say, toward influencing a communal action" (Gerth and Mills, 1946:194). Such organizations may represent either class interests or status group interests or perhaps both. In addition to formal political organizations like parties, examples in modern societies include labor unions, consumer groups, business and professional associations, and ethnic organizations—in short, any group designed for or capable of involvement in political action. In modern societies, it is the state that people and groups try to influence, for it is the state that decides most public issues.

Differentiating a political dimension enables us to see that some may be very powerful yet not necessarily be part of the top class or status group. Many politicians, even at the national level, for example, are quite ordinary people in terms of class and status. Some who enter politics are small business owners or local lawyers or professionals, people who would hardly be considered (or who consider themselves) part of the elite.

Weber on Power

Weber responded to Marx in another way, by questioning the basis of ruling-class power that Marx had so vividly described. Whereas Marx saw the power of a ruling class as deriving from its economic ascendance and control of resources, Weber saw the fact of modern social organization as the most significant force compelling the formation of ruling groups. Weber's explanation stressed the nature of bureaucracy and how this uniquely modern organizational form created elite power.

Weber defined power as "the possibility of imposing one's will upon the behavior of other persons" (Weber, 1954:323). Power, Weber explained, is at the base of all forms of inequality—class, status, and party—and is a primary element of all forms of human interaction (Gerth and Mills, 1946). Although the relationship between power and wealth is undeniable, in modern societies, it is *organizational* power that is most critical. Power, then, stems not simply from the extent of one's income and wealth, but more importantly from one's organizational position.

Bureaucracy   With the modernization of society, government leaders and executives of large business firms become more and more dependent on organizations made up of specialists and experts to advise them and ultimately carry out critical decisions. This type of social organization takes the form of **bureaucracy.** A bureaucratic organization enables vast numbers of people playing specialized roles to blend into cohesive, well-functioning units. It is, in a sense, a social machine whose purpose is to instill efficiency, speed, and precision into organized human effort. "The decisive reason for the advance of bureaucratic organization," Weber noted, "has always been its purely technical superiority over any other form of organization" (Gerth and Mills, 1946:214). Indeed, it seems unlikely that the complex political, economic, and educational institutions of modern societies could be arranged in any other way.

Authority   In modern bureaucratic organizations there are clear distinctions of power. Think of the power hierarchy in government. Within the executive branch, for example, the president has more power than the attorney general, who in turn has more power than an FBI officer. But this is true of any social organization. In a school, teachers have more power than students, but both have less power than the school's principal.

Whether within government, businesses, schools, churches, or any type of social organization, some people have more power than others. Weber described this kind of organizational power as **authority.** By virtue of their position in the organization, they have the capacity to impose their will over others. Societal power, therefore, emanates not from ownership of the means of production (à la Marx) but from the control of administration. Executives and managers of huge corporations, for example, exert great power not through ownership but as a result of their control of corporate resources and the authority of their positions. The same is true of government leaders.

Weber saw the historical development of societies as a movement toward rational forms of organization, that is, groups organized not on the basis of the authority of personalities and traditions but on the basis of specific functions to perform or objectives to meet. Weber called this **legal-rational authority** and distinguished it from two forms of authority based on nonrational criteria. In **traditional** systems of authority, people obey out of a sense of tradition. In a monarchy, for example, the monarch inherits the throne and is recognized as the leader because "it has always been that way." In **charismatic authority,** people obey certain individuals who assume and maintain their positions on the sheer strength of personal appeal. In such cases, leaders assume their positions as a result of their ability to capture the allegiance of large numbers of people. Loyalty and compliance are given not to a rational system or even to custom but to a particular personality. Lenin, Hitler, Mao, Gandhi, and Castro are figures of modern history whose authority derived in large measure from their charisma.

As societies move toward legal-rational authority, greater and greater power is concentrated in bureaucratic organizations, which maintain control over vast human, material, and intellectual resources. Political and corporate bureaucracies exercise dominance even over elected officials in democratic societies or self-appointed leaders in autocratic systems. In turn, control over bureaucracies constitutes an immense power resource.

Weber's Contribution to Inequality Theory

Both the Marxian and the Weberian models of stratification are valuable, and they are necessary to fully understand structured inequality in societies. The basic difference between them, however, is that with Weber's multidimensional model, stratification can be seen as emanating from several sources, not simply one's place in the productive system. This is particularly important to racial and ethnic stratification and to stratification based on gender. In those cases, people are ranked on the basis of their ethnic group membership and their gender in addition to their economic position. Although there is generally a close correlation between these different dimensions of stratification, they do not always coincide.

Unlike Marx, who envisioned the possibility of a future society in which inequality was not a basic characteristic, Weber saw modern societies heading down a path of greater rationality and bureaucratization and, thus, more inequality and alienation. Even if socialism were to triumph, Weber felt, it would be a system characterized by bureaucracy, with its imposition of hierarchy and authority. It would thus be little different from capitalism in its depersonalizing effects on people. The result, then, would be an unavoidable subordination of the many to the dictates of the few (Giddens, 1975). Like Marx, Weber explained social inequality as rooted in power; but unlike Marx, Weber did not envision its eventual demise.

Michels's Iron Law of Oligarchy

Robert Michels, a contemporary of Weber, offered a related theory that traced the origins of social inequality to the way modern societies are organized. Also like Weber, Michels saw an unavoidable societal division between those who lead—an elite—and those who are led. Although Michels addressed specifically the issue of power in social organizations, his theory is more broadly applicable to all aspects of society for it demonstrates the inevitability of social inequality.

In his classic work *Political Parties* (1915), Michels demonstrated the seemingly natural emergence of elite rule created by the structure of modern social organizations. Michels saw the division among humans in modern societies stemming from differences in organizational power; essentially, societies are divided into elites (the few with power) and masses (the remainder of the population). Michels assumed that a craving for power and recognition is an inherent human psychological trait. But a few people always emerge as the powerful simply because of the nature of modern social organizations.

Oligarchy, the rule of the many by the few, is inevitable, even in the most democratic of organizations and societies. Michels posited that this development is a product of the size and complexity of modern social organizations. It is simply not possible for large numbers of people to make decisions in an efficient manner as a unit. The only realistic alternative is to invest officers with power to make decisions on behalf of the collectivity as a whole. With such delegation of powers, a stable—and eventually self-serving—leadership group is established. Thus Michels advanced his often-quoted dictum "Who says organization, says oligarchy" (1962:365).

When collectivities reach a certain dimension, a division of labor emerges, even among the leadership group. Positions are created that are held by people with special expertise, those who thereby become indispensable to the functioning of the organization:

> Just as the patient obeys the doctor, because the doctor knows better than the patient, having made a special study of the human body in health and disease, so must the political patient submit to the guidance of his party leaders, who possess a political competence impossible of attainment by the rank and file. (Michels, 1962:114)

This shows the similarity to Weber's view of bureaucracy and its effects on inequality. Because of their specialized expertise, elites are further enabled to perpetuate themselves in high positions. In pointing to the masses' lack of knowledge in any particular area, elites can assert that they must therefore be given the power to make important decisions. Furthermore, elites can control the training and recruitment process of their successors, thereby creating a self-reproducing class. The gulf between elites and masses then becomes increasingly wider. Once in power, elites devote more and more of their energies to maintaining their position.

It would seem that all of these developments would ordinarily be met with strong resistance from the masses. On the contrary, however, the masses seem content to turn over the affairs of the state (or any other organization) to elites. Michels blames apathy, insufficient time, lack of expertise, and, in some cases, a predisposition to be led. The masses, then, are not only incapable of ruling themselves but are indifferent about relinquishing decision-making power to elites. As Michels puts it, "Though it grumbles occasionally, the majority is really delighted to find persons who will take the trouble to look after its affairs" (1962:88). This indifference and incapability, of course, considerably strengthen the positions of the leadership and make more unlikely the development of countermovements among the masses.

Such movements stand little likelihood of success even if they do materialize, since elites have all the power cards stacked in their favor: information the masses do not have, control of the flow of that information, the credibility and prestige that automatically accrue to incumbent officeholders, and perhaps most important, cohesive organization. Through all of these power resources, the dominant leadership is able to carefully monitor the selection of new elites. Michels's theory is a compelling explanation of why there are low rates of political participation in many democratic societies, especially the United States.

We can see in Michels's theory of elites a response to Marx very comparable to Weber's: It is the means of *administration,* not the means of *production,* that are most critical in modern societies. Those who control organizations and their resources constitute the ruling class, not those who control the society's economic wealth. No matter who controls the means of production, the administration of capital and other vital resources will be necessary, and therein lies unavoidable bureaucracy and elite rule. And like Weber, Michels argued that the emergence of a socialist system would do nothing to reverse the inevitability of this development.

Dahrendorf: Neo-Weberian

Almost all contemporary sociologists have drawn upon the ideas of both Marx and Weber in their conceptualizations of class and their formulations of the class systems of modern societies. Ralf Dahrendorf (1959) has proffered a theory that is essentially Weberian, though it also rests in part on what are

Marxian notions. As a result, Dahrendorf may be considered both a neo-Marxian theorist as well as a neo-Weberian (Grimes, 1991).

Dahrendorf recognizes the Marxian division of society into two opposing and conflicting classes, one superordinate, one subordinate. But he rejects the idea that these classes are in conflict as a result of ownership or nonownership of property. Instead, it is different degrees of *authority* that make for class divisions and conflict.

In all spheres of social life—the economy, politics, education, the media, religion—modern societies are dominated by large, impersonal organizations. And all of these organizations have authority structures in which there are some people (a few) who have the right to issue authoritative commands, and other people (the majority) who must abide by those commands. Like Weber (and Michels), Dahrendorf sees the inevitability of bureaucracy and a structure of authority in such organizations. Dahrendorf adopts a Weberian notion to refer to these organizations: *imperatively coordinated associations.* It is differences in organizational authority, Dahrendorf contends, that lead to different interests and around which classes form. Hence, authority, not relationship to the means of production, is the most important basis of class and class conflict in modern societies, a view basically in line with Weber's theory.

Dahrendorf posits that the Marxian assumption that classes are based on ownership or nonownership of productive property is no longer meaningful in the context of contemporary capitalist societies. Large, bureaucratically organized corporations dominate the economy, and it is a professional managerial class that exerts essential control over the resources of these corporations. Hence, the question of who owns the means of production, so fundamental to the Marxian theory, is irrelevant. Corporate managers make decisions regarding the assets of these firms and direct the firms' workers, though the managers themselves are not the owners. What is most critical, therefore, is authoritative power: Who controls the decision-making apparatus of organizations? That, in Dahrendorf's view, is the basis of class division in modern societies.

Functionalism and Conflict Theory

In the 1950s a new theoretical approach emerged in the study of social inequality. It gave rise to a sharp debate among sociologists regarding the origins, inevitability, and social functions of inequality. The essential argument revolved around whether stratification was necessary in society. The two sides represented two general schools of thought in sociology, those who see the primary characteristic of societies as *order* and those who see it as *conflict*.

Order theorists, whose tradition is most heavily influenced by the early-twentieth-century French sociologist Émile Durkheim, view society as a relatively balanced system made up of differently functioning but interrelated parts. In this view, society is held together and social order maintained through a consensus of values among its groups and through the imperatives of functional interdependence. People generally agree on the basic rules of society, recognizing that only by abiding by such rules can they collectively survive.

In contrast, conflict theorists, beginning with Marx, see societies as held together not by functional needs and broad agreements among groups but by the power of dominant classes and ruling elites who impose their will on the majority. Stability and order are maintained through coercion, not consensus. People abide by the rules of society because they are coerced into doing so, not because they recognize some common survival purpose. Whereas order theorists stress the manner in which societies maintain cohesion and balance, conflict theorists emphasize the disintegrative aspects of societies and the manner in which they change.

Human societies are, of course, neither wholly ordered nor wholly in conflict; rather, there is always a combination of the two (Dahrendorf, 1959). Nonetheless, sociologists have favored one or the other of these broad theoretical perspectives in their analyses. Let's examine how these two approaches deal with the key issues of stratification and inequality; namely, Why is there inequality? and Is inequality inevitable?

Functional Theory: The Need for Inequality

In line with the order perspective, functional theorists begin with the assumption that all societies are made up of different and necessary roles that must be filled in order for the society to function. Society, in this view, is comparable to the human body, made up of various organs that must be working for the body to be in balance. A person cannot function as well with one lung as with two and, without at least one, cannot live at all. Roles in society, as in the body, must be filled. Some people must farm if the society is to eat; some people must work in factories if the society is to manufacture cars and refrigerators; some must teach if the society is to train its young; some must govern if there is to be order; and so on.

In this functional scheme, some roles are more vital than others; that is, some entail more important societal functions and require more expertise and training. In modern societies, for example, it would be hard to argue that medical doctors are not more critical to the society's well-being than are sanitation workers. Moreover, some positions require more extensive skills and training than others. Consider the time and effort involved in training a doctor, as opposed to a sanitation worker. Doctors must go through rigorous schooling that is costly in terms of time, energy, and money. It might require as much as six or seven years of training beyond a bachelor's degree before one qualifies to practice medicine. Sanitation workers, by contrast, can be trained to do their jobs in a matter of minutes.

So what we have is a situation in which certain positions, presumably more crucial and more challenging, must be filled. The question is, how are they to be filled and by whom? Obviously, they must be occupied by the most qualified people, that is, the smartest and most talented. How do societies assure that these "best and brightest" people will, in fact, fill the most crucial roles? How, for example, do societies persuade people to endure the hardships and sacrifices needed to train to be a doctor? The answer, according to these theorists, is to promise them more of the society's rewards. Kingsley Davis and Wilbert Moore, in an article that first articulated the functionalist theory, summarized this position: "Social inequality is . . . an unconsciously evolved device by which societies insure that the most important positions are conscientiously filled by the most qualified persons" (1945:243). In modern societies, this means paying them more than others. Inequality, then, is needed to induce the most qualified persons to fill the most important positions and, once filled, to ensure that they will continue to perform their duties in those positions.

Inequality, in this view, is inevitable. In no society can all roles be of equal importance. In addition, not all persons will be qualified to fill the more important positions. The functionalist theory not only posits that inequality is a built-in feature of all societies, but argues that it is beneficial. All members of a society need the most qualified people to fill the most important positions. Hence, it is in everyone's interest to reward them with a greater share of the society's wealth.

Conflict Theory: The Dysfunctions of Inequality

At first glance, the functionalists' argument seems convincing. How else to explain why doctors earn on average $200,000 a year, perhaps ten or fifteen times more than sanitation workers? Although the theory may explain such obvious cases, conflict theorists point out that it is flawed in numerous ways.

To begin with, if the functionalist assumption regarding the integrative nature of society is true—that various roles must be played in order for the society to function adequately—then aren't all roles critical? In 1965, sanitation workers in New York City went on strike. After several weeks, the heaping mounds of garbage piled on the city's streets posed so serious a threat to public health that the mayor requested the state governor to call up the National Guard to begin collecting the trash. Even sanitation workers, it was discovered, play a crucial social role.

How are the "most important" positions in society really identified? Although the case of doctors versus sanitation workers may be an extreme case, can we say that teachers are less important than doctors? Judging from the average income of teachers, one would have to conclude that they are considerably less important. If we accept the logic of the functionalist position— that people are rewarded according to the relative importance of their social role—we would also have to conclude that rock musicians earning hundreds of thousands of dollars for each performance or professional basketball players, whose average annual salary is $3 million, are even more important than doctors. Indeed, one could reverse the argument of the functionalists and offer the view that, logically, societies would pay more to people doing the more odious and unappreciated tasks—like collecting garbage—in order to induce them to play these roles.

What, then, makes it possible for some positions to emerge as presumably more important and thus more deserving? "Power" is the conflict theorists' answer. Those who are given the most rewards, it is argued, are able to apply the greater power resources they possess. Doctors can command great salaries because they can threaten to deny people their services. How long would society tolerate a doctors' strike? Moreover, doctors have the persuasive power to convince the society that their positions are in fact more important and thus merit more in rewards than many other positions. The American Medical Association (AMA), for example, is politically very influential and can sway public opinion with its views of medicine and public health. In a sense, doctors and other highly paid workers, in the conflict theorists' view, have convinced the rest of society that their positions are more important and thus warrant disproportionately high incomes.

Conflict theorists argue that there are no assurances that the most qualified individuals will actually occupy key societal roles. Assuming that the most important positions can be identified, how do societies discover the most capable people to fill them? If the society were one in which equality of opportunity were truly a reality, we could conclude that the only determining factors are people's skills and talents. But people start out in considerably different circumstances—for example, one child's father is a corporate executive earning several hundred thousand dollars a year; another child's father is an hourly paid factory worker. Both children dream of being doctors. Which one is more likely to realize that dream? The answer is obvious and has little to do with their innate talents, intelligence, or ambitions. Those from more-well-to-do families are not necessarily the best and brightest, but they are given the opportunities, the "stage," so to speak, in which to pursue and fully develop their aspirations. The system by which the "most capable" are chosen to fill the most important positions is rigged in favor of those closer to the top of the social hierarchy. Again, it is power—political, economic, and social—that is the key to understanding social inequality.

Another criticism offered by the conflict theorists concerns what seems to be the need to use material rewards to induce the presumably more qualified to fill the society's important positions. The assumption of the functionalist argument is that only by promising people a greater financial reward can they be induced to undergo the training and sacrifices needed to qualify for these positions. But this discounts the other rewards that people often acquire from their work, like prestige or self-gratification (Tumin, 1953). Many doctors, for example, will explain that high earnings are not the sole reason they were attracted to their profession. Perhaps they were genuinely interested in medicine or enjoyed the prestige that doctors are afforded or altruistically felt the need to work in a profession that helps people. These individuals might have studied medicine even if there had been no generous monetary rewards for doing so. Most college professors must train for years beyond their bachelor's degrees to attain Ph.D.'s, but in many cases they end up earning no more than factory workers. Why, then, do they undergo the rigor and hardship? Most professors would answer that they enjoy intellectual pursuits, desire the contemplative and independent lifestyle of scholars, and would not think of doing anything else, even if they were offered more lucrative opportunities.

Finally, conflict theorists ask whether the extreme differences in the distribution of rewards are really necessary, even if we accept the functionalists' basic argument (that some positions are more important and must be rewarded accordingly). Perhaps it is justifiable that doctors earn more than sanitation workers. But *how much* more is justifiable? Again, it is power, not societal need, that is the determining factor in explaining this discrepancy. Inequality, in this view, is neither inevitable nor functional but stems from the ability of the powerful to protect their privileges and to coerce the rest of society into accepting the stratification system.

In sum, the essence of this ongoing debate among sociologists is simply this: The unequal distribution of power, wealth, and prestige is the result of either (a) the need to induce those with necessary skills and talents to fill the most important societal positions by rewarding them unequally, or (b) the power of those at the top of the social hierarchy, who use their power and privilege to prevent others from securing a greater share of society's rewards.

Each of the arguments made by the conflict side was met with counterarguments by the functionalists, but the debate has never really been resolved. It is of some note, however, that on one point the two theories were never in disagreement: the universality of stratification. Tumin, in his famous response to the functionalists, acknowledged that "The fact of social inequality in human society is marked by its ubiquity and its antiquity. Every known society, past and present, distributes its scarce and demanded goods and services unequally" (1953:387). It is in their explanations of how and why that inequality arose and whether it is inevitable that the two sides have disagreed.

Lenski's Synthesis

Gerhard Lenski's theory of stratification and inequality is an attempt at a synthesis of the functional and conflict theoretical perspectives. Lenski holds that the distribution of societal rewards is based on the seemingly contradictory principles of both need and power. His theory suggests that inequality can be explained in terms of both.

The Distribution of Power, Privilege, and Prestige   Lenski begins by postulating that most human action is motivated either by self-interest or by the interests of one's group. Furthermore, most of what people strive for is

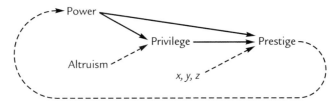

Figure 8-1 ■ The Relationship of Power, Privilege, and Prestige
Source: Gerhard Emmanuel Lenski, Jr., *Power and Privilege: A Theory of Social Stratification.* Copyright © 1984 by the University of North Carolina Press. Used by permission of the publisher.

in short supply. These conditions assure that there will be social conflict. Paradoxically, however, for people to attain their basically selfish goals requires cooperation. Thus, despite the predominance of self-interest, people in society will cooperate to the extent that they must in order to survive and to meet their objectives. From this, Lenski posits what he calls the first law of distribution: "Men will share the product of their labors to the extent required to insure the survival and continued productivity of those others whose actions are necessary or beneficial to themselves" (1966:44). This recognizes the functionalist tenet that societies are basically cooperative units.

Problems begin to arise, however, once societies are capable of producing a surplus, that is, more than is needed for survival. Who will get what share of this surplus? Although an element of altruism may enter into the formula, for the most part it is through power struggles that the distribution is decided. Hence, the second law of distribution: "Power will determine the distribution of nearly all of the surplus possessed by a society" (Lenski, 1966:44). Lenski refers to possession or control of part of this surplus as *privilege*. What follows is a third axiom: "Privilege is largely a function of power, and to a very limited degree, a function of altruism" (45). The third element of the distributive system, prestige, is essentially a product of both power and privilege.

Lenski's model (Figure 8-1) shows that privilege stems mainly from power and, to a very limited degree, altruism. Prestige, in turn, flows mainly from power and privilege, though other minor variables may enter the picture. The dashed line indicates that there is some feedback from prestige to power. It is power, however, that is the fount of social inequality in its various other forms, political, economic, and social.

Comparative Social Inequality   Lenski's theory seeks to explain not only why there is inequality in human societies but also why it varies in degree from one society to another. The keys to understanding the latter are two variables: the levels of technology and of power.

Human societies have advanced through stages differentiated by level of technological development. Where technology is very primitive and unchanging, the degree of inequality is low. This is because little in the way of a surplus can be produced, and as a result, there is minimal conflict over who will get what and how much. Moreover, the society's survival depends on co-operation. Consider a hunting-and-gathering society. Here each member must contribute to the goal of securing food. And because all hands are needed, everyone receives a proportionate share. Goods and services in these societies are distributed on the basis of *need*.

Once technology advances to a higher level, more than enough to consume at once is produced and the society is faced with the question of surplus distribution. Internal struggles arise over how the surplus will be distributed, and it is at that point that power enters the picture. The most powerful are able to take a greater share, and consolidating their economic resources reinforces and sustains their societal power. Thus, in societies that are in the initial stages of technological and industrial development (essentially agrarian societies), there is a high level of inequality. A small upper class or elite controls most of the society's wealth and is able to impose its will on the rest of the population. So goods and services in these societies are distributed on the basis of *power*. Contemporary global conditions seem to give weight to this idea. It is in societies that are usually referred to as "developing" or "Third World" that we see the most extreme gaps between the wealthy and the poor. A few affluent families or individuals own and control the bulk of the society's resources, and the massive peasantry remains relatively powerless and poor.

Although we might expect an even greater level of inequality as industrialism begins to emerge, modern industrial societies do not substantiate this. In fact, the very opposite seems to occur—extremes of inequality begin to decline. As Lenski explains, "The appearance of mature industrial societies marks the first significant reversal in the age-old evolutionary trend toward ever increasing inequality" (1966:308). In these societies, political inequality is reduced, and although the distribution of income remains markedly unequal, it is less so than in nonindustrial societies. Why does this occur when it would seem logical that even greater inequality would be the result of much increased productivity?

Lenski attributes a reduction in inequality to several factors. To begin with, industrial societies are much more complex than earlier societal forms, thus compelling those at the top of the hierarchy to rely more and more on lieutenants and underlings. Delegating authority to others makes for a diffusion of power and privilege. Second, by granting lower classes a share of the economic surplus, ruling groups can neutralize worker hostility and the economic losses that can be suffered from strikes and work slowdowns. Third, in a highly productive economy, elites are no longer interested solely in enriching themselves and so may be willing to share more with others. Finally, in modern industrial societies, democratic ideology takes hold, making it necessary for those with power to concede some of it to the masses in order to avoid serious challenges to their position.

Summary

Two key issues form the focus of theories of social inequality: Why is there inequality? and Is inequality inevitable in human societies?

Marx saw social inequality as a basic characteristic throughout human history. All societies break down into two opposing and conflicting classes: those who own the means of economic production and those who do not. The latter have no choice but to work for the owners. Inequality, then, is a product of ownership of the means of production. Those who control the society's productive resources are a ruling class. Their dominance is not only economic but political and social as well.

Inequality is not part of the human condition, according to Marx, but in capitalist society it is fundamental. Only through a workers' revolution, in which ownership of the means of production changes hands, can the capitalist system of inequality end. Although no specific formula or time frame was offered, Marx saw the end of capitalism as inevitable, just as other productive systems had passed and were replaced. Capitalism will give way to socialism, in which workers will control the means of production. Only with the development of an entirely new human being, one divested of personalistic and material values, can true social equality emerge in a communist society.

Weber saw modern forms of social inequality as emerging from the complexity of modern societies, and saw the power of ruling classes stemming from control of organizations, not ownership of property. Weber was more pessimistic than Marx, believing that so long as societies were large and complex, none could avoid the need to be bureaucratically organized, and that those bureaucracies would be controlled and directed by power elites. Michels drew similar conclusions in his theory.

A contemporary theoretical debate is rooted in the order and conflict perspectives pioneered by Durkheim and Marx. Functionalists posit that inequality is not only inevitable but necessary, ensuring that the most capable individuals wind up occupying the most important societal positions. Conflict theorists rejoin that argument by asserting that inequality, rather than inevitable and functional, is mainly the result of powerful individuals applying their resources to secure and sustain their places at the top of the hierarchy. Lenski has attempted to synthesize these two opposing views by suggesting that social inequality may, under different conditions, be both functional and conflict-inducing. In technologically simple societies, humans will share because they must in order to survive. Once a surplus is produced, however, inequality sets in. In societies less economically developed, the surplus is distributed primarily on the basis of power. As societies industrialize, the level of inequality declines.

9

Ideology and the Legitimation of Inequality

The surest method of social control is to induce subordinates to regulate themselves. To that end, the unmeditated weapon of choice is ideology.
MARY R. JACKMAN

A well-established ideology perpetuates itself with little planned propaganda by those whom it benefits most. . . . Systems of life which confer special benefits on the other fellow need no plots or conspiracies when the masses are moved by faith and the elites are inspired by self-confidence.
HAROLD LASSWELL

As we have now discovered, inequality of income and wealth is a basic characteristic of the United States and of all societies, past and present. Moreover, access to the resources of power is hardly the same for all groups and individuals, and power elites do not, in the main, resemble the general populace in their class origin and other sociological traits. And, as will be shown in Chapter 13, the democratic character of the American sociopolitical system is in many ways questionable. Given these facts, one might logically ask, How is a system in which privilege and power are so unequally distributed given legitimacy? Why, in other words, do those lacking great wealth and political influence—a decided majority—accept a system that remains so apparently inequitable?

What is perhaps even more puzzling is the fact that those with little wealth and power not only tolerate the prevailing socioeconomic system but, for the most part, consider it just and beneficial. In short, few ever question any of the basic assumptions of the society's major economic, political, and social institutions. People may recognize certain societal shortcomings from time to time and may acknowledge the realities of inequality, but the system as a whole is seen as fundamentally fair and the best that humans have yet devised.

The acceptance of inequality is not a recent occurrence; indeed, it is as old as human societies. And the extremes of inequality in societies of past ages were much greater than those found in most modern societies. Recall the feudal system that characterized Europe during the Middle Ages. Here was a socioeconomic arrangement that nicely illustrated Marx's notion of a two-part division of society into those who owned the means of production and those who were forced to work for the owners. The most puzzling aspect of feudalism was not its injustice and the degree of inequality it produced, however, but its duration. Until it was replaced by capitalism, feudalism in Europe lasted for several centuries. How could a system so unjust and unequal be sustained for such a long period?

Other systems of production in human societies have yielded as much or even more inequality than feudalism. And they, too, proved to be quite enduring and stable. The very idea of "equality" is a relatively new and unusual notion. It is essentially an idea that stems from the eighteenth-century philosophic movement known as the Enlightenment, or Age of Reason, which held that mankind, through the application of reason and science, could achieve increasing material and moral progress. Until relatively recently, the thought that people were to be seen as equals and that they were deserving of an equal share of the society's product was a radical idea. Even in the contemporary world, social inequality has not often been challenged by mass movements. Whereas political revolutions, in which one ruling group replaces another, have been numerous, social revolutions, in which the entire stratification system is radically reconfigured, have been rare. Put simply, most people at all times have accepted the system of inequality in the societies in which they live. The willing acceptance of the prevailing institutional system and its attendant social inequality by most members of the society is called **legitimacy,** and the process by which it is brought about is **legitimation.**

Legitimation

How is the enigma of mass acceptance of inequality to be explained? Might it be that support for the prevailing institutions is produced by force? Do the powerful and wealthy few induce the masses to obey on the basis of fear? Coercion is, in fact, always at the root of obedience to authority, and all states use force when the need arises. Coercive techniques are most common in societies in which the dominant system is not accepted by a significant part of the populace. In modern autocratic societies, such as China and North Korea, the powerful must often enforce their will through blatant forms of repression.

The stability of sociopolitical systems that rely primarily on coercion is, however, always precarious. Indeed, the use of raw force alone cannot be effective in prompting compliance over long periods. For government and related institutions to establish and sustain a system of inequality that is popularly supported over many generations requires that power be enforced in less repressive and direct ways. In protecting their privileges, dominant groups try to engender loyalty and respect in subordinates, not fear. Force and the threat of force, therefore, are to be avoided as much as possible (Jackman, 1994). People must come to see the exercise of power by the few as natural and socially beneficial. Only then does power become authority, that is, legitimate power. When this is accomplished, ruling groups need no longer resort to force as the principal means of assuring their will. Without creating legitimacy, the powerful in society would be continually faced with a rebellious population questioning the dominant institutions and the inequality they produce.

It is only when a society's economic, political, and social institutions are supported reflexively—almost unconsciously—by the masses that long-range stability is evident, as in the United States. Occasionally, there are signs of discontent and even mild rebellion (the urban riots of the 1960s, for example); but these unusual instances are generally squelched with a display of force or through minor concessions. The widespread and consistent support of the society's institutional system is not often seriously challenged. To assure legitimacy and thus to sustain the system's long-range stability requires the development of an effective ideology and its communication through the process of socialization. People must come to *believe* that the system is fair and deserving of their allegiance. Dominant groups, explains Jackman, therefore "work to engage subordinates in a common view of the world that rationalizes the current order" (59). The answer to the perplexing question of why the feudal system endured so long is, in great measure, that the serfs believed in the system; they accepted it as legitimate. Their view of the system as just and acceptable was founded on an ideology that explained that feudalism was divinely ordained. It was God who shaped society, and thus it was not to be questioned. If a serf were asked why he must toil in the fields each day, forever indebted to the lord of the manor, his answer would be simple: "Because God intended for me to be a serf." This belief, widespread and accepted by virtually all, contributed heavily to the legitimizing of the system, enabling it to endure for more than five centuries.

As shown in the following section, ideology plays a major role in legitimizing inequality.

The Nature of Ideology

An **ideology** is a set of beliefs and values that rationalizes a society's structure of power and privilege.[1] Most simply, it is both an explanation of how and why a society's major institutions work as they do, as well as a justification for the outcomes produced by those institutions. "Sets of beliefs or theories that are ideological," notes John Plamenatz, "purport to tell us how things are or were, and how they come or came to be so" (1971:75). Ideologies can

---

[1]As with other sociological concepts, ideology has been applied in a variety of ways. Some have used the term broadly to denote a society's entire belief system, and others have used it more narrowly to describe a specific program of action of a particular group or party. My use of the term is less extreme than either of these two. On varying definitions of ideology, see Shils (1968), Lane (1962), and Plamenatz (1971).

be propounded not only for the purposes of stabilizing and defending a prevailing system but also for changing it.[2] Ideology can therefore be an instrument for ruling groups or for those who oppose them. Ideologies are also used to provide support for various forms of inequality; for example, racism and sexism are specific sets of beliefs that have provided a rationale for racial/ethnic and gender inequality. This chapter discusses ideology as a force for stabilizing and perpetuating the general structure of power and privilege.

Dominant Ideologies

An ideology that explains and justifies the prevailing power and reward structures is called the **dominant ideology.** Since power and wealth are never distributed equally in any society, some justification and explanation must be provided not only for those at the top who gain the most from the way the system works but for those lower on the social ladder who get progressively less. As sociologists Joan Huber and William Form have put it, "Dominant ideologies function to comfort those whom the system rewards and to justify the system to those who fail" (1973:79). A society's dominant ideology, then, explains and rationalizes the great discrepancies in power and wealth.

It is not surprising that those at the top of the society's power and wealth hierarchies should believe in the justness of their position. But people across the entire class range pay allegiance to the ideology, including even those in the lowest social positions. Sociological theorists have offered several explanations for this paradox.

Marx and Ideology   As explained in Chapter 8, Marx was one of the first sociological theorists to deal with the issue of ideology. As he saw it, ideology was an important tool for assuring the interests of the few over the many. It was not so much the deliberate creation of a ruling class as the natural product of the society's productive forces. Recall that in the Marxian scheme, those who control the means of production are the ruling class. This class controls not only the means of economic production but also the means of *mental* production. This assures that the ideas of the ruling class regarding all aspects of social life—government, religion, family, and so on—become those of the entire society. Institutions such as the school and the media, which impart ideas about politics and economics, quite naturally disseminate ideas that reflect the interests of the ruling class.

This predominance of ruling class ideas is often referred to in Marxist writings as **ideological hegemony.** Hegemony is a term that refers to domi-

---

[2]In a classic work, Karl Mannheim (1936) termed ideologies that seek to change a social system "utopias" and those that seek to keep them as they are "ideologies" per se.

nance; ideological hegemony is therefore the prevalence of one group's ideology over all others. Antonio Gramsci, an Italian Marxist writing in the 1920s, described this phenomenon as

> the "spontaneous" consent given by the great masses of the population to the general direction imposed on social life by the dominant fundamental group; this consent is "historically" caused by the prestige (and consequent confidence) which the dominant group enjoys because of its position and function in the world of production. (1971:12)

Ideological hegemony is, in other words, a legitimation of the status quo wherein those values that favor the interests of the ruling group become the acceptable standards of subordinate groups as well. The predominance of the ruling group's standards is dependent on the development and maintenance of false consciousness. As explained in Chapter 8, false consciousness is a belief on the part of nonruling groups that the prevailing political and economic systems work in their interests, when in fact they work primarily in the interests of the ruling class. The power of the capitalist class, then, is enforced and perpetuated so long as the workers remain in a state of ignorance of where their true interests lie.

The Elitist View of Ideology   Some social scientists explain that ideology consists of ideas produced by elites themselves to justify their dominance. In this view, elites use ideology to support their power, similar to the Marxian idea, but they may claim their right to power through various rationales. The divine right of kings, the assertion that kings were rulers chosen by God, was an effective ideology during the Middle Ages in Europe. European colonialists of the nineteenth century claimed their right to power over indigenous peoples on the basis of biological and moral superiority, a rationale also employed by Euro-Americans in their dealings with African Americans and Native Americans. A common modern-day elitist justification for the maldistribution of power and wealth is the possession of skill or expertise in a particular field. A few see those at the top as meriting their positions as a result of a biologically based superiority in the form of high IQ (Herrnstein and Murray, 1994). In short, those at the top are thought to merit their positions because they have superior qualifications, talents, or skills.

Some elite theorists see the use of ideology by the wealthy and powerful as conscious manipulation of the masses. In this view, elites are fully aware of what they are doing and seek to enhance and protect their power through propaganda. Other elite theorists explain that elites believe in the ideology and see themselves as naturally taking their places at the top and being rewarded accordingly. In this sense, ideologies differ from propaganda, which, as Alvin Gouldner explains, "is not believed in—at least at first—by those spreading it." Ideologies, by contrast, "are intended to be believed in by those affirming them publicly and by all men, because they are 'true' and they thus have a universal character" (1976:33).

Functionalist Theory and Ideology   A third explanation of how and why people come to accept the dominant ideology rests on the functional theorists' notion of societal need. Unlike the Marxian and elite theories, this perspective does not postulate that ruling groups have the capacity to impose their version of social reality on the remainder of the society. Acceptance of the ideology, therefore, is based neither on false consciousness nor on elite manipulation. Rather, it arises from a general consensus of values among the society's people. The idea is that people abide by the prevailing system because they share the basic values on which the system rests (Parsons, 1953). There is, in this view, a fundamental consensus of values among a society's populace that creates stability and order. Without that consensus, society could not function and would exist in a constant state of turmoil and uncertainty.

The stress, then, is on the role that ideology plays in maintaining societal balance. Like the debate between functional and conflict theorists regarding the cause and inevitability of stratification, a similar disagreement is evident here. Functionalists maintain that people recognize the need for a common set of values, whereas conflict theorists hold that those values are created and imposed by the powerful in society.

Ideology and Reality

Although the beliefs that constitute ideology are held by the bulk of a society's population, they are not necessarily true descriptions of reality. People's *beliefs* about society do not always coincide with the conditions of social *reality*. Much of the dominant explanation of how social, economic, and political institutions work is not entirely or even in large part accurate. Much of ideology is oversimplification, distortion, and even myth. It comprises beliefs that, through constant articulation, become accepted as descriptions of the true state of affairs.

People may accept much or perhaps all of the ideology in the abstract, but when faced with their own situation, they may interpret it selectively, picking and choosing parts, often in an inconsistent or contradictory manner (Kluegel and Smith, 1986). "[E]veryone makes sense of his or her environment partly by applying beliefs about distributive justice to specific circumstances" (Hochschild, 1981:44). In addition, people's class position and racial identity commonly affect the degree of commitment to the ideology. In the United States, for example, not surprisingly, those higher in the class and racial/ethnic stratification systems more fervently subscribe to the dominant ideology (Huber and Form, 1973; Kluegel and Smith, 1986; Ladd, 1994; Mann, 1970; Swidler, 1992).

So although the dominant ideology may be hegemonic in the sense that it pervades all societal institutions, it is neither accepted in total by all people at all times nor universally interpreted. In short, the dominant ideology is not a set of beliefs that everyone accepts in the same way and in the same degree.

The Dominant American Ideology

Although it hardly resembles feudal societies of medieval Europe or contemporary developing societies, the United States is acutely unequal in power and privilege, more so, in fact, than most Western industrialized societies. Nonetheless, for its entire history the United States has never faced a serious challenge to its basic economic and social institutions. Even during the Great Depression of the 1930s, when as many as a quarter of the total workforce was unemployed, the capitalist socioeconomic framework was altered but not overthrown. What is perhaps most puzzling is that even the poor have not strongly supported political efforts aimed at redistributing income and wealth (Hochschild, 1981; Ladd, 1994).

What beliefs and values have contributed to the stabilization of this system? What is the societal rationale for the obvious facts that some get more than others and that the system of stratification has not changed substantially for most of American history? What, in other words, is the dominant American ideology regarding inequality, and why do most people subscribe to its basic components?

Because of the discrepancy between beliefs and reality, describing the dominant American ideology, as Huber and Form write, can be both simple and difficult:

> On the one hand, the stuff of the dominant ideology is embedded in political campaign literature, newspaper editorials, TV shows, civics textbooks, stories about Dick, Jane, and Sally, and Chamber of Commerce brochures. It is the sum and substance of what every child has learned about the way the American system works. It is what everybody *knows*. . . . On the other hand, what everybody knows sometimes turns out to be wrong. (1973:3)

Despite the facts that ideology and reality do not always coincide and that the dominant ideology is neither supported unquestioningly by all people nor interpreted in the same way, there is a recognizable body of interrelated beliefs and values that strongly guides most Americans' thoughts about inequality. Among the most essential of these are *individualism, equality of opportunity, the work ethic, meritocracy,* and *liberal capitalism.*

Individual Achievement

Perhaps the most basic component of the dominant American ideology, individual achievement is the belief that each member of society is responsible for his or her fate and that one's social position is a product of personal efforts and talents. The place of individualism as the most basic component of the American creed, and its pervasiveness throughout American culture has been recognized almost since the country's founding. Scholars and social commentators have repeatedly shown this aspect of American society to be truly exceptional in comparison with other societies (de Tocqueville, 1966 [1835]; Bryce, 1959 [1912]; Lipset, 1996).

With the stress on individual achievement, the effect of structural factors, over which the individual has little or no control, is seen as less critical. The accident of birth and the society's opportunity structure account for most of the inequality among people, but those factors are given short shrift by most people. This shows how ideology may mask reality. In extensive surveys, political scientists James Kluegel and Eliot Smith found that "Americans consistently strongly endorse individual reasons for economic position, particularly for poverty, and reject liberal and (especially) radical explanations emphasizing structural causes" (1986:100–101). In her research, sociologist Mary Jackman (1994) found a similar absence of support for income equality among people of all social classes, stemming from a belief in the principle of individualistic achievement. In the end, it is individuals themselves who control their economic and social destinies. And, it is individuals themselves who therefore are responsible for their class position.

The basic idea is that anyone can succeed with enough effort, whatever one's social and economic handicaps at birth. It all depends on personal effort, ambition, and talent. Differences in wealth and power are not denied, but they are seen as the product of individual factors rather than as the workings of a class system that favors success for the wellborn and failure for the poor.

Self-Reliance   As a corollary of individual achievement, self-reliance is the notion that people should pursue their objectives of success through their own efforts rather than rely on others. Social rewards, in this view, are earned by personal effort. "The 'success story' and the respect accorded to the self-made man," notes sociologist Robin Williams, "are distinctly American, if anything is" (1970:417).

Consider how fundamental this idea is in almost all areas of American social life. Children are taught from their earliest moments of life to be as self-reliant as possible. As they grow older and enter school, they are instructed in the correctness of doing their own work and of not relying on others. And they learn that their rewards are contingent on their individual efforts. Group or communal efforts in the school are sometimes encouraged but are usually limited to extracurricular events. The distribution of really meaningful rewards, namely grades and honors, is dependent on the student's own efforts, not on how much or how well he or she has contributed to the class performance.

The idea of self-reliance remains powerful throughout one's working career and extends even into old age. A national survey in 1997 asked people what they feared most about growing old. Sixty-four percent were "very worried" about spending their last years in a nursing home, and 48 percent, about becoming a financial burden on their families. Only 28 percent were worried about death (Morin, 1997). So potent is the self-reliance value that people who find themselves in dire economic straits will commonly balk at the idea of accepting welfare or handouts of any kind.

Table 9-1 ■   Percentage Saying They "Completely Agree" with the Statement "It Is the Responsibility of the State (Government) to Take Care of Very Poor People Who Can't Take Care of Themselves" (1991)

Country	Percentage
United States	23
Germany	50
Poland	56
Hungary	58
United Kingdom	62
France	62
Italy	66
Ukraine	69
Russia	70
Spain	71

Source: Everett Carll Ladd, *The American Ideology* (Storrs, CT: The Roper Center for Public Opinion Research, 1994), 79.

The power of this value accounts in large measure for the strong antiwelfare bias in American society. Those recognized as genuinely needy are viewed sympathetically. Thus Americans are willing to support measures like job training and education, but such compassion does not extend to those who seem unwilling to make the effort to support themselves and their families. It is the latter who are seen as welfare recipients (Ladd, 1994). Despite their acceptance of the notion that some of the poor are in need of help, there is a far weaker commitment to government assistance in this regard than in other industrialized nations (Table 9-1).

It is interesting to consider how persistent the belief in individual responsibility for one's social place seems to remain in American thought. In their classic study of a midwestern community in the 1920s, Robert and Helen Lynd (1929) asked high school students whether they agreed with the statement "It is entirely the fault of a man himself if he does not succeed." Forty-seven percent answered yes. In a replication of this study almost fifty years later, Caplow and Bahr (1979) asked the same question and got the same 47 percent yes response.

The individual responsibility model is adopted by a wide variety of class groups (Coleman and Rainwater, 1978; Lane, 1962; Sennett and Cobb, 1973). It would not be surprising to learn that people of higher social standing would subscribe to this notion. But even those lower in the social hierarchy accept it in some degree. In a national survey conducted in the 1960s, Free and Cantril (1968) found that whereas most affluent people attributed poverty simply to "lack of effort," a majority of the poor also agreed that they were at least partially to blame for their own condition.[3]

Even when individuals themselves are not totally faulted for their social disadvantages, their problems are seen not as deep-seated and widespread but rather as marginal and amenable to relatively quick and easy solution. Poverty, after its rediscovery in the 1960s, was seen not as a creation of the normal workings of a capitalist socioeconomic order but as a minor imperfection of an otherwise healthy system. Government leaders saw alleviation of poverty as requiring only a "mopping-up" effort, not basic institutional change. Today, efforts at addressing poverty continue to focus on changing the poor themselves, not on changing the institutional structure within which the poor are found.

The belief that individual achievement and initiative are most important in getting ahead in life is particularly strong in the United States, but it is predominant in all Western societies. Whereas in the United States and Canada "ambition" is viewed as critical, in Britain "hard work" is seen as the key to success, and in Germany it is "having a good education" (Pammett, 1996). Common to all these views, however, is the belief that people attain success mostly on the basis of their own ability. Other factors, like "luck" or "knowing the right people" are acknowledged as helpful, but they are not seen as primary. Sociodemographic factors, like race or gender, are believed to play only a minor role in handicapping individuals in pursuit of their goals.

Equality of Opportunity

If people earn their position and wealth through their own talents and efforts, the resultant inequality is fully justified. But the justification for inequality hinges on the condition that everyone is given the same opportunities to display their individual talents and fulfill their capacities. The competition must be unobstructed. Thus Americans are firmly committed to the principle of *equality of opportunity* (Ladd, 1994; Lipset, 1963; Williams, 1970). The society's opportunity structure is pictured as open, providing equal chances for all to achieve material success or political power regardless of their social origin. This being the case, each individual controls his or her social destiny. Political scientist Jennifer Hochschild (1995) has described the dominant American ideology as pursuit of the "American dream." A basic tenet of that dream is that everyone can pursue it.

Studies have repeatedly confirmed the acceptance of this principle among Americans of different social classes (Coleman and Rainwater, 1978; Jackman

---

[3]Most of the poor, however, combined "lack of effort" with "circumstances" in explaining poverty, unlike the affluent, who explained it more exclusively as a result of "lack of effort."

and Jackman, 1983; Ladd, 1994). This does not mean, however, that Americans do not recognize the advantages enjoyed by the wealthy. Kluegel and Smith, for example, concluded that "the American public has little illusion that the rich share the same opportunity for economic advancement as the rest of society." They found that 83 percent believe that the children of the rich have "a better or much better chance to get ahead than the average person" (1986:48).

The emphasis on equality of opportunity accounts for why Americans seem more prepared to invest public dollars in education than in most other areas. Overwhelmingly, Americans see education as the key to economic advancement (Kluegel and Smith, 1986). Providing individuals with opportunities through education is quite different from providing aid to the poor. Education, in this view, equips people with skills and enables them to compete on their own. Welfare assistance, on the other hand, is designed to improve people's actual living conditions. The contrast with western European societies in this regard is noteworthy. The United States spends proportionately more on education at all levels, whereas the Europeans devote far more public funds to welfare services (Lipset, 1996). This is perfectly in line with the contrasting social philosophies of the United States and most European societies: equality of opportunity, stressed in the United States, and equality of condition, stressed by Europeans.

Meritocracy and Universalism

As a corollary of the principle of equality of opportunity, **meritocracy** is a system in which rewards are yielded on the basis of performance and qualification. That is, people are expected to earn their social standing and property. These are not to be acquired through inheritance or through the influence of family and friends. So long as people are perceived to have the same chances to succeed or fail, those in the upper rungs of the social hierarchy deserve their positions (Turner, 1960).

Meritocracy is consonant as well with both individualism and the work ethic. We are told that in the competition for society's rewards, after taking into consideration individual ambition and hard work, those who succeed do so on their merits. They have demonstrated their superior skills and talents through performance. Ascribed factors like family of birth, race, ethnicity, or gender are not seen as critical.

The meritocratic idea assumes **universalism,** the notion that everyone should be treated the same regardless of ascribed personal characteristics. This social egalitarianism demands that there is a denial of social rank and any claim to precedence. As Everett Ladd describes this aspect of the American ideology, "Having a lot of money, for example, is O.K. But it's not O.K. to act as though you think you are better than someone else" (1994:9–10). More

"*Meritocracy worked for my grandfather, it worked
for my father, and it's working for me.*"

than a hundred years earlier, James Bryce, an Englishman who wrote a classic description of American society, made a similar observation:

> In America men hold others to be at bottom exactly the same as themselves.
> If a man is enormously rich . . . or if he is a great orator . . . or a great
> soldier . . . or a great writer . . . so much the better for him. He is an object
> of interest, perhaps of admiration, possibly even of reverence. But he is
> deemed to be still of the same flesh and blood as other men." (1959
> [1912]:520)

The stress on egalitarianism explains in some part the tendency for Americans to deny the importance of social class or, as discussed in Chapter 2, even to recognize the strong class divisions in their society.

Lowered Class Consciousness   Emphasizing the availability of opportunities in combination with individual achievement and meritocracy stabilizes the system by discouraging collective efforts that may turn into sociopolitical movements seeking to alter the society's major institutions (Ossowski, 1963). This accounts for the fact that there is not much sympathy among Americans for divesting the rich of their wealth. Anti-rich sentiment is diffused in large measure because Americans see the possibility that they themselves have a chance to be wealthy. In a 1990 Gallup survey, for example, over half said that people have a good chance to become rich if they are "willing to work hard."

Moreover, antipathy toward the wealthy is not as strong in the United States as in many other countries because Americans are more likely to perceive the rich as having earned their wealth. Consider the view of Maria, one of Hochschild's respondents, who lives in poverty and cleans other people's homes for a living. Does she feel that her wealthy employers are undeserving of their wealth? Although she resents them, she respects their right to be wealthy: "You work for it, it's fair. If I got a good education and I'm doing a different job [than you] and a harder job, I deserve more. But if you deserve it, you deserve it. I don't believe in this equal, all equal" (Hochschild, 1981:28). As economist Robert J. Samuelson has put it,

> Getting rich is the end point of economic opportunity, and faith in the self-made person is a central part of the national folklore. Americans believe in ambition and don't reject those who fulfill their ambitions. If the victors in the economic struggle were all suspect, then the ideals of hard work, risk-taking and self-improvement would be illegitimate. (1997:24)

Americans also do not see the rich as naturally antagonistic to their interests. In the Gallup survey cited above, over half indicated their belief that the United States had the "right number of rich," and two-thirds said that the country "benefits from having a wealthy class." The fact that conservative politicians can sometimes win election in districts where the poor or working classes predominate demonstrates this low level of class consciousness.

In line with this view of the wealthy and the belief in an open opportunity structure, few in the United States see government's proper role as equalizing income (Hochschild, 1981; Ladd, 1994; Lipset, 1996). This is in sharp contrast to citizens' views in other industrialized societies (Table 9-2).

Recall the difference between liberty and equity. In American society, liberty, in the sense of individual freedom to pursue one's objectives and to reap the profits of those efforts, is stressed over equity, the notion of a fair distribution of societal resources.

The belief in an open class system in which people can rise without limit on the basis of their own effort is strengthened by the few who actually do make spectacular leaps in class position. In fact, rising from poverty to great wealth is, and always has been, very exceptional in American society. But

Table 9-2 ■   Percentage Agreeing That "It Is the Responsibility of Government to Reduce the Differences in Income between People with High Incomes and Those with Low Incomes" (1985 and 1987)

Country	Percentage
United States	29
Australia	44
Germany (West)	61
United Kingdom	64
Netherlands	65
Italy	81

Source: Everett Carll Ladd, *The American Ideology* (Storrs, CT: The Roper Center for Public Opinion Research, 1994), 75.

the handful who, for whatever reasons, break out of poverty and rise to the top are widely heralded, whereas the vast majority of those who remain poor are ignored. These few exceptional cases "confirm" the reality of the American Dream, "proving" that success is mainly dependent on individual effort.

The Work Ethic

The **work ethic** is the notion that hard work is the key to success and is the most noble of man's activities. Social and economic success, in this view, is the result of one's willingness to work hard; failure is the result of lack of ambition or desire to improve oneself. Through sufficient effort, anything can be accomplished. The work ethic obviously overlaps with the tenets of individual achievement and self-reliance. It basically defines *how* one is to accomplish upward mobility or measurably change one's material condition.

There is much empirical evidence that demonstrates the continued belief in the Horatio Alger formula for improving oneself. Consider that in 1952, 88 percent of Americans agreed with the statement that "there is plenty of opportunity and anyone who works hard can go as far as he wants." Almost thirty years later, 70 percent still agreed with that statement (Kluegel and Smith, 1986). In 1993, when given a choice of which factors they felt were most crucial to success, 94 percent of Americans felt that "hard work" was the most crucial (Marsden and Swingle, 1994). The contrast between the United States and other Western industrial societies on this point is indicated in Table 9-3. Americans clearly believe that hard work is the route to success and, moreover, believe that the chances favor their own upward mobility (Ladd, 1994; Lipset, 1996).

Coleman and Rainwater (1978) asked their respondents what they thought was the most effective way for individuals to improve their social

Table 9-3 ■   Percentage Disagreeing with the Statement "Hard Work Offers Little Guarantee of Success"

Country	Percentage
United States	63
Italy	51
United Kingdom	46
France	46
Germany	38

Source: Everett Carll Ladd, *The American Ideology* (Storrs, CT: The Roper Center for Public Opinion Research, 1994), 79.

standing in America. They found that "ambition, energy, and application" were seen as the prime virtues; "dereliction" was the prime defect. In this view, victory in the quest for success goes to the vigorous, while defeat goes to the lazy. Coleman and Rainwater suggest that the most fitting name for this perceived system is "effortocracy":

> The people who rise in this system—in our respondents' idealized view— are those who have been the most determined to do so, who have put out the greatest efforts toward that end. The people who fall—again in this idealized view—are those who have lacked the character, the will, and the enterprise even to maintain the social position they inherited." (241)

This is a strongly held belief that cuts across class lines. "People can make money if they put their minds to it and get off their little rear ends. People get lazy, but I have no doubt that I will make out well. Because I'm very ambitious, so if there's something I want, I'll do it" (Hochschild, 1981:29). We would naturally assume that this is the view of someone occupationally successful and economically secure. But these are the words of an unemployed secretary living below the poverty line.

Liberal Capitalism

As components of the dominant American ideology, individual achievement, equality of opportunity, meritocracy, and the work ethic are woven together with the fundamental premises of **liberal capitalism,** that is, a democratic political system combined with a capitalist socioeconomic system. As the framework around the tenets of the American ideology, liberal capitalism is a reflection of the philosophy of classical liberalism.

As it emerged in Western thought, classical liberalism stems mainly from the writing of seventeenth-, eighteenth-, and nineteenth-century philosophers, including Adam Smith, John Locke, Voltaire, Jean Jacques Rousseau, Thomas Jefferson, and John Stuart Mill. All extolled the worth of individuals and their right to control their destiny. Liberalism challenged the notions of hereditary rights and privileges that had been part of the feudal system. In this view, humans are rational beings who, if left to their own efforts, will naturally pursue their self-interest. Indeed, self-interest is seen as the primary human dynamic. Liberty, therefore, is the most critical right of individuals in society. Government should be as limited as possible; its singular role should be the protection of individual rights, particularly property rights. *Classical* liberalism should not be confused with *modern* liberalism. Today, liberalism is associated with the philosophy that government should play an active economic role in assuring equitable social and economic opportunities. Paradoxically, many of the tenets of classical liberalism are today most consistent with modern conservatism (Marger, 1987).

Personal property and liberty, in the classical liberal view, are sacrosanct, and the two are not unrelated. These are natural rights, not to be violated by government. Locke, whose central ideas form the basis of most theories of democracy, proclaimed that property (broadly defined as life, liberty, and estate) was the chief motivation for people to establish governments and laws. Consequently, no government has the right to "take from any man any part of his property without his own consent" (Locke, 1960 [1690]:408).

Classical liberalism converges logically with capitalism in its advocacy of individual responsibility and the rational pursuit of self-interest. Through competition, individuals will succeed or fail on their own initiative and ambition. The free market, it is believed, provides a neutral competitive setting. Government, therefore, is not to interfere with natural market processes. Its role in economic affairs is reluctantly accepted as long as it remains minimal. Individuals must be assured unhindered movement in the labor market and absolute freedom to buy and sell what they choose. Such competition is bound to create inequality, of course, but what is of utmost importance is not true equality—which, in this view, is a chimera—but equal opportunity for all to compete in the marketplace.

In the political realm, the economic freedoms inherent in the capitalist market are related to the political liberties of democracy. In a sense, the free market is replicated in the competitive electoral system. The people as a whole must be free to choose and hold accountable their leaders through democratic elections. Hereditary monarchies and aristocracies, characteristic of feudalism, are contrary to liberal notions. In the political realm, inequality is not as readily accepted as it is in the economic. Americans, note political scientists Sidney Verba and Gary Orren, "have a stronger taste for political than for economic equality" (1985:2). The tolerance for economic inequality alongside the ideal of political democracy is indeed a curious paradox of the American ideology.

Both economic and political processes, in the classical liberal view, are seen as "free markets" in which the individual can choose from among competing products and businesses in the economic sphere and from among competing candidates and parties in the political.

Ancillary Beliefs

A set of ancillary beliefs undergirds the dominant American ideology. These are general ideas that complement and reinforce its basic components, that dispel contrary beliefs and strengthen people's commitment to dominant institutions. They are basic to the legitimation process.

Unchanging Human Nature   The prevailing stratification system is not likely to be questioned when people view it as founded on unchangeable human traits. For example, the political and economic relations of a capitalist system are based on avarice and competition. These can be explained and justified by declaring such behavior merely "human nature." Expressions such as "keeping up with the Joneses" are commonly voiced. Most Americans tend to believe that competition and the pursuit of personal interests are simply basic human qualities. They are, in this view, "natural." This, in turn, further deflates any ideas of change. If competition and the pursuit of individual interests are merely "human nature," the resultant inequality is, similarly, only natural. Efforts to bring about radical change are therefore futile. "What can you do? It's always been that way and always will be."

The Neutrality of Societal Institutions   Another way in which inequality is given legitimacy is by the depiction of societal institutions as neutral, serving the interests not of particular groups but of the society as a whole. Americans are inclined to see major institutions—school, government, criminal justice, the media, and business—as functioning in a neutral fashion, not favoring the interests of any particular class, ethnic group, or gender. Government agencies or legislatures, for example, are not pictured as representatives of special economic or regional interests but as objective public institutions. That certain interest groups are far more resourceful than others in fashioning and benefiting from these public institutions is not stressed. Similarly, law enforcement agencies are seen as disinterested crime-fighting organizations, not as politicized groups that enforce laws more or less vigorously depending on who the criminal is or what the crime may be. "Crime" is ordinarily understood as acts that are clearly visible and blatantly offensive, like street muggings and homicides, committed mostly by the poor. The criminal justice system and the media focus most of their attention on these types of crime. But crimes committed by those of higher social classes (such as embezzlement) or by powerful corporations (such as price fixing or the dumping of pollutants into the environment) are more silent and invisible. Hence, they are not treated with the urgency of crimes committed by lower-income groups and rarely engage the attention of the media. As a result, only in the most egregious cases do they become the concern of the general public.

Giant corporations are similarly portrayed as neutral organizations that provide people with goods and services they want and need. Corporate advertising and public relations are aimed at strengthening a belief in the naturalness and goodness of the prevailing economic system, of which the corporation is, of course, the chief element. That corporations are profit-seeking entities whose purposes are primarily to enrich those who own them is rarely brought to public consciousness. Occasionally, when corporations are seen as profiteering at public expense, there remains little question that no realistic alternative to the corporate economy exists.

The mass media are also generally understood to be objective in their presentations of news and entertainment. In the case of news, the media become reporters of events "as they occur"; in the case of entertainment, the public is given "only what it wants." That media elites select news events from among countless events of social significance and present them in a predesigned manner is not often considered. Nor is much thought given to the fact that the U.S. media are private business enterprises that rely for their revenue on commercial advertisers, who may have much to say about what will or will not be printed or broadcast.

Finally, schools, from primary to graduate levels, picture themselves and are generally seen by the public as nonideological institutions that train students in practical skills and impart a curriculum that is objective and fair. The curriculum is supposedly designed to enable students to think independently. Schools are not seen as "political" in function despite the constant enunciation and glorification of dominant political and economic values. Also, the popular picture of the educational system in the United States is one in which no particular class or ethnic group is favored over others. This neutral image prevails despite the fact that, as seen in Chapter 6, schools function in some ways as social placement agencies, assuring top places for those of higher class origins and making upward mobility for those at the opposite end of the social hierarchy difficult at best.

Fear and Doubt of Other Systems   A compelling aspect of the society's dominant ideology is that, as it is propagated, other systems based on different ideologies are seen as neither viable nor credible. Thus, even if there is doubt about prevailing values and the institutions built on them, there are no workable alternatives. "The American system may have its shortcomings," leaders admit, "but the shortcomings of other systems are much greater." Such an admission, along with its implicit warning of the uncertainties and insufficiencies of other systems, serves to defuse efforts at mobilizing people around counterideologies. Fear of other systems additionally serves to affirm and strengthen the belief in the American system, despite its inequalities. Communism, for many decades, served as an effective countersystem to American capitalism. Here was an alternative, it was held, whose economic failures and political repression demonstrated the superiority of American economic and political institutions.

In addition, when there is a recognition of institutional deficiencies in meeting social ideals, violence and serious social disturbances are averted by calling up the larger ideological principle that only within the prevailing political framework can changes eventually be realized. Groups calling for change are advised to "work within the system." The black civil rights movement of the 1950s and 1960s serves as an example. As white people became collectively conscious of the plight of blacks in all areas of social life, the movement was recognized as legitimate and justifiable. But only traditional methods of the political process—voting, lobbying, and so on—were deemed acceptable as part of the movement. Violence was not recognized as either legitimate or effective. Civil rights groups and leaders calling for direct and sometimes violent confrontations with the white power structure were denounced as radicals, and their tactics were labeled counterproductive.

Changing Ideologies

In considering the dominant American ideology, it is important to understand that it is not etched in stone. Like all ideologies, it is subject to challenge and thus to change. For example, in the United States in recent decades, a much greater realization of the impact of race and gender on the system of inequality has emerged among the general public. This has resulted from the successes of the civil rights and women's movements that put forth counterideologies, challenging the long-held explanations and justifications for racial and gender inequality. Although this has not led to a rejection or even to a deemphasis of the idea that individual achievement and self-reliance are the major determinants of social position, it has brought about an acknowledgment that inequality can be explained in some part as a result of ascribed factors. Similarly, although the classical liberal notion of liberty remains paramount, most Americans today, as noted in Chapter 7, expect government to regulate the market in some degree in order to reduce the gross inequalities produced by unfettered, laissez-faire capitalism.

Legitimation, Ideology, and Socialization

Having now looked at ideology and how it helps to legitimize inequality, we turn our attention to how the dominant ideology is transmitted and how loyalty to the system is infused. How do ideas about social inequality unfold? And what is the process by which people come to accept them?

Socialization

Socialization is the process through which people learn their society's culture. This involves not simply learning the rules and beliefs of the society but internalizing them, making them an integral part of one's way of seeing and making judgments about the world. Most simply, socialization consists of learning and accepting the socially defined rights and wrongs of thought and action. If successfully imparted by socializing agents such as the school, the family, and the media, the correctness of those beliefs is henceforth seldom questioned or even given much conscious thought.

In American society, for example, there is rarely any question regarding the desirability of applying democratic principles to power conflicts in all areas of social life. From choosing members of a neighborhood softball team to selecting members of Congress, the same basic notions of fairness and equality are assumed. From the time children begin to interact with peers, and particularly when the school begins socializing them, they learn the "rightness" of democratic practices in social relations.

Such beliefs and preferences are, like all other cultural values, imparted through various learning experiences. They are no more natural to the individual than is riding a bicycle or having a preference for chocolate rather than vanilla ice cream. People of different societies are exposed to different ideologies and thus learn different norms and values. What few people ever recognize, however, is that this learning process is aimed at acceptance of the dominant sociopolitical and economic systems. It is the subtle and essentially unconscious nature of the process that makes it so effective. The given system is accepted as seemingly natural; other systems become, in our minds, deviant or inadequate. As already noted, the effectiveness of socialization to the dominant ideology and to the system of inequality is revealed by the fact that even those who are severely disadvantaged by the prevailing institutional arrangement come to accept, at least in the abstract, most elements of it.

Let's look at the major transmitters of the dominant ideology and see how they function in the socialization process and in legitimizing the system of inequality. In examining the way these institutions work, remember that the extent of their effectiveness will differ from person to person. As explained earlier, ideology is not interpreted and accepted in the same manner or degree by all people. Some will accept the system almost blindly, whereas others will question some of its most fundamental features. Most fall at neither of these extremes. In any case, our focus here is on the socializing agents rather than the individual being socialized.

Legitimation, Socialization, and the School

Socialization takes place through the workings of many institutions, beginning with the family. But it is in the school that the process is most deliberate and systematic. Social critic Ivan Illich described the school in modern society as serving a purpose similar to that of powerful churches in past eras: "It is simultaneously the repository of society's myth, the institutionalization of that myth's contradictions, and the locus of the ritual which reproduces and veils the disparities between myth and reality" (1971:37). Schools do not turn out loyal and unquestioning citizens who act more like robots than humans; the educational system is never totally effective in perfectly reproducing a social consciousness in each new generation. But as one of the key agents of socialization in modern societies, the school must be viewed "as an instrument of power" (Spring, 1972:23). Socialization in the school occurs in deliberate as well as indirect ways.

Deliberate Socialization The school creates legitimacy and imparts the dominant ideology in a variety of ways, some of which are quite straightforward. Although educators proclaim a spirit of objectivity in the content and methods of their teaching efforts, it is apparent that at all levels of instruction, from kindergarten to college, there is little real competition of ideas. This is particularly the case in the social sciences and history where course content is heavily biased in favor of the prevailing political and economic institutions; alternative systems are rarely considered, much less studied intensively.

Some have pointed out that a distinction must be made between the political, or civic, education provided by the school and outright indoctrination (Coleman, 1965). The difference between these two concepts, however, is highly subjective and often difficult to discern. For example, teaching students principles of capitalism while ignoring other alternative ways of organizing an economy is viewed as "educational" by the dominant groups despite its indoctrinating character. In effect, education, no matter how seemingly neutral, is always political in nature. As political scientist V. O. Key observed, "In the American setting the schools are not so obviously seen as arms of governance; yet in the large they play a significant role in the perpetuation of the values of the culture, including those habits, patterns of action, norms, and outlooks that are fundamental to the political order" (1964:316).

Despite the common application of such direct techniques, research is inconclusive regarding their impact (Langton, 1969; Litt, 1963; Niemi and Sobieszek, 1977). Several studies indicate that their effects may not be very great in actually molding attitudes. High school civics courses, for example, appear to do little more than reinforce an already well-accepted ritual of the democratic creed (Dawson et al., 1977; Zeigler and Peak, 1970). In any case, however, these educational efforts complement those of other institutions in solidifying the legitimacy of the prevailing system in the minds of students (Hess and Torney, 1967).

What students are *not* exposed to may be as important as what they are exposed to. For example, students at the primary or secondary level are rarely given a realistic picture of the acute economic and political stratification of the society. Serious socioeconomic differences among class and ethnic groups and conflict among them are minimized. "The categories of exploitation, dominance, structure, repression, class, and socialist perspectives," notes Murray Levin, "are not only not transmitted to the young, they are presented as antitruth, intellectually shallow, irrelevant, or utopian" (1971:267).

Efforts to assure that only dominant values will be taught in the schools have led at times to very explicit policing measures. For example, during the hysteria of the "Red scare" following World War I and during the McCarthy period of the early 1950s, teachers were often required to sign loyalty oaths; those suspected of espousing "un-American" ideas were admonished and in some cases even dismissed (Caute, 1978; Murray, 1955). Such blatant tactics to assure educational conformity, however, are usually unnecessary. In most cases, teachers, school board members, and others who determine the content and direction of schooling conform naturally to acceptable standards since they, too, are products of the same socialization process.

Freer expression of ideas occurs at the college level, where the boundaries of tolerance imposed by authorities are much wider than in the public schools. Some, in fact, maintain that the content of higher education in the United States has a natural tendency to undercut rather than reinforce traditional ideologies, unlike primary and secondary schools (Milner, 1972). Yet, colleges and universities, though less constrained, also operate in a cultural, political, and economic milieu that dictates their conformity to dominant ideas. Most U.S. institutions of higher education are heavily dependent on federal and state governments for operating funds and on corporations for developmental and research programs. Therefore, they cannot stray too far from acceptable political and economic values and objectives.

Incidental Socialization   Direct forms of instruction may be less important than indirect ones in the school's socialization role. Sociologists refer to this as a *hidden curriculum.* Schools at all levels teach fundamentally individualist, capitalist values in a largely unintentional manner. Competition, for example, is an important incidentally imparted value of the classroom. From the first day of school to the conclusion of one's educational experience, competitive incentives are the chief tools used by the educational system—grades, promotion, awards, and so on. With few exceptions, these are individualized competitive situations in which the person rather than the group is held responsible for his or her success or failure. Collective efforts, particularly in academic matters, are not encouraged. This solidly reinforces the principle of individual responsibility, so basic a part of the dominant ideology.

Another theme emphasized by the American educational system is the practical usefulness of education as opposed to its intellectual or abstract value (Williams, 1970). Education is seen as training, leading to economic improvement. Students attend college mainly to acquire a better job rather than to raise their political awareness or to ponder social issues, such as inequality. As a result, utilitarian curricula stressing technical skills are more highly valued than are philosophy, the humanities, or the social sciences—fields of study that often force students to consider alternative systems of thought and social action. Preparing people for careers thus acts as an important mechanism in maintaining the status quo.

The Mass Media in the Legitimation Process

In modern societies, the mass media—television, radio, newspapers, magazines, books, motion pictures—serve a critical role in the legitimation process. First, they are the major sources of information, supplying citizens with knowledge about the society and especially about the political economy. Second, they function as propaganda mechanisms through which powerful units of the government and economy seek to persuade the public either to support their policies, as is the case with government, or to buy their consumer products, in the case of corporations. Third, they are primary agents of socialization, instructing people in the norms and values of their society. All of these functions contribute to the process of legitimation, generating mass belief in and acceptance of dominant political and economic institutions and acceptance of the system of inequality (Marger, 1993). In examining the role of the mass media in the legitimation process, consider their economic context, their content, and their effects.

The Economic Context of the Media: Control and Accessibility   As they are organized in the United States and, to some extent, in other modern societies, the mass media are mostly capitalist institutions. Today, the mass media are dominated by television and, to a lesser degree, newspapers, both of which are organized within a few giant media corporations. Viacom, for example, one of the largest of these conglomerates, earned revenues in 1998 of $14.5 billion. Among its holdings were several book publishing houses, including Simon and Schuster; Paramount Pictures (movies); numerous regular and cable television networks including MTV, Nickelodeon, Showtime, and UPN; eighteen U.S. television stations; home video chains, including Blockbuster; and five theme parks, including Kings Island (McChesney, 2000). The intent of these media corporations is to sell news and entertainment to advertisers, who in turn use them to sell products and services to the audiences they attract. This places constraints on the media and forces them to reflect the interests of those who support them—advertisers.

Today, publicly communicating views or ideas requires using the media. A critical concern, therefore, is not only who owns or controls the media but also who has access to them. In modern societies, only government and big business have the resources—money, authority, and influence—to employ the media regularly and effectively.

As privately owned enterprises, the major objective of the various media is to generate revenue. This objective requires that the media cater primarily to those who can pay to put their views on the air or into print: the major corporations, which use the media primarily to create demand for their products and services through advertising. Consider that a thirty-second television commercial on Super Bowl Sunday costs over $2 million; or that a full-page color ad in a national weekly magazine costs $135,000; or that Procter and

Gamble spends more than $2.5 billion each year on media advertising. Advertising not only serves to generate consumer demand but also provides corporations with a means of creating a positive public image. General Electric, for example, tells the public that "we bring good things to life." Most corporations convey similar messages in which they are portrayed not as profit-seeking enterprises but as compassionate, publicly responsible citizens.

The economic constraints of the media affect their accessibility. If you feel strongly about a social or political issue, how can you make it known? You can talk to your friends and relatives. You might even go so far as to write a letter to the editor of your local newspaper and have it printed. But how many ears or eyes will these efforts reach? Obviously, very few. Those who are able to communicate their messages to the society as a whole or to large segments of it are those who have the economic resources to buy the use of the media or who possess the authority and influence to command them. This means the corporate wealthy and the politically powerful.

Government access to the media is founded not on financial power but on the fact that the media are closely interwoven with government, particularly at the national level. Put simply, the relationship between government and media is symbiotic; neither can function effectively without the other. As a regulated industry in the United States, the media must take into account the interests of government elites. More important, however, the media are heavily dependent on government elites as their major source of political information, which is the core of news. Studies have indicated that not only are government officials the source of most news but most news stories are drawn from situations over which newsmakers "have either complete or substantial control" (Sigal, 1973). On the opposite side of this relationship, political elites need the media to communicate their views and actions to the citizenry and to maintain their public images. They can easily gain access to the mass media not only because they are the primary newsmakers but also because they possess credibility among the public as well as among the media elite. Accounts of events and policies given by political elites are more likely to be accepted and thus become part of the news format than accounts and interpretations provided by other sources (Gans, 1979).

In sum, given the way in which the media are organized in the United States and most other modern societies as well, it is the wealthy and powerful who have maximum access to them. It is those at the top of the power and wealth hierarchies, therefore, who can convey their messages to the public and help shape public opinion. Their views, objectives, and interpretations become those that most people see or read.

Media Content   Think, for a moment, about where you get your information about what is happening outside the confines of your immediate social world, that is, your family, friends, school, workplace, and neighborhood. To find out what is occurring in the larger society, or in the world, you rely on the mass media—specifically radio, newspapers, and, especially, television. Almost two-thirds of Americans claim that they get most of their news about current events from television (Thomas and Vistica, 1998). These mass media, then, act as gatekeepers of political, economic, and social information—what is ordinarily termed "news." As information gatekeepers, the media are your window on the world, and it is through them that you learn about key events and personalities. Since they define what is news or what is socially significant, the media, in a sense, have become a source of reality itself. As media expert Ben Bagdikian has put it, "For most of the people of the world, for most of the events of the world, what the news systems do not transmit did not happen. To that extent, the world and its inhabitants are what the news media say they are" (1971:xii–xiii).

Given the media's strong influence on the molding of political, economic, and social reality, a key issue concerns the decision-making process of news selection and presentation. Like major decisions of government and the economy, this process is essentially an elite function. Events become newsworthy, and thus of importance to the society, only after they have been selected by the communications elite—editors, journalists, and media executives (Cohen and Young, 1973; Epstein, 1974; Gans, 1979; Tuchman, 1978). It is the media elite, therefore, who are largely responsible for molding the public's conception of political, economic, and social events and conditions.

Given this concentration of control over the "shaping of reality," what is most critical is gaining access to or influence on the media elite. Because the major media operate as business enterprises, the media elite, when making decisions about what to present, must take into account the interests of dominant economic groups—the large corporations—that supply them with revenue. Second, in light of their symbiotic relationship with government, these decisions must be weighed against the interests of political elites. The result is that ideas of groups and individuals outside the political and economic mainstream receive little attention. In U.S. elections, for example, minor parties and candidates are generally treated by the mass media as curiosities, not as legitimate contenders, and are thus rarely taken seriously. So political debate is narrowly limited to the two major parties in the mainstream political arena. In short, parties, organizations, and individuals who advocate serious economic or political change but lack financial and political resources have a very difficult time communicating their messages through the mass media. Ruling business and political elites are best situated to exercise influence over the content of the mass media.

The emphasis on official perspectives results in limited public understanding of the nature of political, economic, and social problems and how they might be resolved. Rarely do the mass media subject the dominant political economy and the system of inequality to serious scrutiny and criticism. Moreover, even when attention is drawn to societal shortcomings by public affairs or news programs (such as *60 Minutes* or *20/20*) or by investigative journalists, it is done in the spirit of the dominant ideology. That is, problems are presented as the products of deviant individuals or groups within the context of an otherwise healthy social system. The *systemic* origins of chronic problems—like poverty—are rarely explained or even acknowledged. As David Paletz and Robert Entman have observed, "The mass media have never given powerless Americans the necessary information to link the ubiquitous rotten apples to the structure of the barrel" (1981:167). Questioning the structure and functioning of the dominant political and economic institutions is clearly beyond the capabilities of the mass media (Gans, 1979; Gitlin, 1980; Parenti, 1986).

The bias of mass media content toward the dominant system should not be seen, however, as the result of government and economic elites conspiring with media editors, journalists, and executives. The media elite express dominant values largely unconsciously: They see themselves as objective journalists, not bearers of opinion. As Herbert Gans has noted, "The values in the news are rarely explicit and must be found between the lines—in what actors and activities are reported or ignored, and in how they are described" (1979:39–40). Political objectivity, therefore, is not political neutrality. Critical information presented by the media in the form of news and public affairs is framed by dominant values and shaped by power elites, no matter how seemingly objective the presentation may be (Iyengar and Kinder, 1987).

The inability of the mass media to present issues to the public in a thorough and critical manner is largely a result of their commercial imperatives. News, like other aspects of mass media, must be sold as a consumer product. This requires that it be presented in an entertainment format and, as political scientist Lance Bennett (1988) has explained, be personalized, dramatized, fragmented, and normalized. It is personalized in the sense that it "gives preference to the individual actors and human interest angle in events while downplaying institutional and political considerations that establish the social contexts for those events" (26). Similarly, the media seek out dramatic events and personalities to which viewers and readers can relate, rather than events and personalities that may be more politically significant though less glamorous and fascinating. The entertainment format of news forces it to be presented in unrelated bits and pieces rather than as a meaningful whole. As a result, news becomes a series of what Neil Postman (1985) has called "decontextualized facts," comparable to background music. Finally, information presented as news is filtered through traditional themes and images of the society, thereby assuring the viewer or reader of the merit of dominant institutions and discrediting challenges to them.

In short, although they may engage in social criticism, the mass media frame their presentations in a way that legitimizes the prevailing political economy and the attendant structured social inequality. Although there is no blatant censorship of media content in the United States as there is in a totalitarian society, an implicit understanding exists on the part of the media elite regarding their role in upholding the status quo. Self-censorship by the media is reinforced when they anticipate the reactions of political and economic elites and alter their presentations in advance. At times, of course, more blatant attempts at censorship may arise, as when corporate advertisers exert direct pressure to influence the content of the media or when government elites pressure the media to "toe the line" (Gans, 1979). Although the media elite may resist these pressures, more often their ideological perspectives are fully compatible with those of political and economic elites, and they therefore have little inclination to follow a path not basically in line with those views. Moreover, although the media commonly present opposing sides of social and political issues, the two perspectives are only narrowly divergent, and the issues are presented in ideologically safe stereotypes. The irony of modern communications systems is that despite the profusion of messages with which the citizenry is bombarded daily, the absence of a thorough exploration of issues by the mass media results in an increasingly uninformed public (Marger, 1993).

Media Effects   Given the immense power of and the limited access to mass media in the United States and other modern societies, are we to conclude that they are simply propaganda tools for the wealthy and powerful? C. Wright Mills explained four decades ago that there is a growing tendency for mass media to be manipulative devices rather than channels for the interchange of opinion: ". . . in the mass society of media markets, competition, if any, goes on between the manipulators with their mass media on the one hand, and the people receiving their propaganda on the other" (1956:305). But concentrated media power does not necessarily guarantee that the media are always effective in molding public opinion and in shaping people's versions of political and social reality.

Although sociologists and communications experts are not certain about the precise effects of the mass media on socialization or how the media modify the influences of other socializing agents such as the family and the school (Comstock, 1980; Gerbner, 1967), it appears that the media are becoming the chief means through which people construct their versions of social reality. Well before the advent of television, Walter Lippmann (1922) explained how the mass media, by selectively reporting and interpreting events and personalities, determine the pictures in our heads (stereotypes, as he referred to them) that shape our social worlds. With the predominance of television, this "reality-shaping" function of the mass media has become much more complete. Television serves increasingly in this capacity because few can escape its influence. Only sleep and work occupy more of Americans' time than television viewing. Most important, the mass media serve as the primary organs of political communication, setting the framework of public discourse, solidifying the legitimacy of powerful institutions and elites, and transmitting the society's dominant ideology.

Early research led communications theorists to conclude that mass media had a direct and significant influence on public attitudes and beliefs.

Further research, however, concluded that such direct media power had been exaggerated. People's interpretations of media presentations, it was explained, were modified by social class, ethnicity, religion, and other social variables (Lazarsfeld et al., 1948). The same message, therefore, was unlikely to have the same effects on the shaping of attitudes among all people. Moreover, media messages might simply reaffirm people's prior beliefs and views (Gollin, 1988).

Later communications research pointed out that the emphasis on what media were doing to shape attitudes overlooked the more significant impact of mass media on creating a public *awareness* of issues (McCombs and Shaw, 1972). The idea is that although television and other mass media may not be overly effective in telling us *what* to think, they are extremely effective in telling us what and whom to think *about* (Shaw and McCombs, 1977; Iyengar and Kinder, 1987). Issues emphasized by the media become the issues regarded by viewers and readers as significant. As the media shift their emphasis to new issues, public perceptions change correspondingly.

In setting the framework of social discourse and describing events and personalities, the mass media convey the society's dominant ideology. It is in this sense that they are agents of social control, used by power elites not only to communicate and legitimize their policies and actions but to stabilize the political and economic systems by generating allegiance among the public. As sociologist Todd Gitlin has explained:

> The media bring a manufactured public world into private space. From within their private crevices, people find themselves relying on the media for concepts, for images of their heroes, for guiding information, for emotional charges, for a recognition of public values, for symbols in general, even for language. Of all the institutions of daily life, the media specialize in orchestrating everyday consciousness—by virtue of their pervasiveness, their accessibility, their centralized symbolic capacity. They name the world's parts, they certify reality *as* reality—and when their certifications are doubted and opposed, as they surely are, it is those same certifications that limit the terms of effective opposition. To put it simply: the mass media have become core systems for the distribution of ideology. (1980:1–2)

We should not assume that the presentation of news is the mass media's only way of creating support for the society's dominant ideology and institutions. In modern societies, news and public affairs represent only a small portion of all media fare, particularly of television. The remaining entertainment, and especially the advertising that constantly accompanies it, is no less reflective and supportive of the society's prevailing value system (Bagdikian, 1983; Goldsen, 1977; Parenti, 1986).

In recognizing the enormous power of mass media in modern societies to portray a particular version of reality, it should be understood that this is not consummate power. The ability of the media to propagate dominant values and shape political reality is by no means absolute. Acknowledging the less-than-total power of mass media to influence people's social and political worlds, however, should not lead to an underestimation of the power of this institution. In all modern societies, control of information is critical: Whoever controls the means of communication has great power. Marx posited that those who control the society's means of material production are the most powerful. It might be claimed that in modern societies great power hinges on control of the means of information—the media. This is the reason that political and economic elites make great efforts to dominate the media and to control the flow of information. Those who exert significant control over the media or who can freely gain access to them are able to exercise great influence in determining the views, images, and ideas that will become part of the public consciousness.

Summary

Legitimation is the process by which people come to accept the stratification system. As part of this process, ideology is a set of beliefs and values that support the major societal institutions and the unequal outcomes they produce. The dominant ideology in a society explains and justifies the prevailing power and reward structures.

Several explanations have been offered as to why most people in the society, including even those in the lowest social positions, give allegiance to the dominant ideology. Marxists explain it in terms of ideological hegemony and false consciousness. The ideas and values of the ruling (capitalist) class become those of the entire society, despite the fact that they work only in the interests of the ruling class. Elitist theorists explain ideology as ideas produced by elites themselves to justify their dominance. Functionalist theorists explain that people accept the dominant ideology because they share the basic values represented by the ideology; this consensus assures social stability.

The dominant American ideology consists of a number of basic beliefs and values that strongly guide most Americans' thoughts about inequality. The most essential of these are individual achievement and self-reliance, equality of opportunity, the work ethic, and meritocracy. These are framed within the context of liberal capitalism. Several ancillary beliefs give additional support to the ideology. These include the ideas that competition and inequality are natural and unchangeable human traits; that societal institutions operate in a neutral, objective fashion; and that there are no viable alternatives to the prevailing political and economic systems.

Legitimation occurs as part of the socialization process. The dominant ideology is transmitted primarily through the workings of two institutions: the school and the mass media. The school imparts dominant beliefs and values both deliberately and indirectly. School curricula that support the prevailing social, political, and economic systems are stressed overwhelmingly, with little attention paid to alternatives.

In modern societies the mass media are the chief sources of information for the public, and they strongly influence the molding of political, economic, and social reality. Ownership of the media is highly concentrated in a few major corporations, giving their owners, editors, and producers great power to determine their content. Because the mass media are profit-generating firms, they are dependent on corporate advertisers for their revenue. Also, through regulation and mutual dependence, they are strongly linked to political elites. Hence, regular access to the media is limited primarily to the wealthy and the politically powerful. This results in what is generally a media defense of the status quo, including the system of stratification.

10

Racial/Ethnic Differentiation

The hostility of one tribe for another is among the most instinctive human reactions. Yet, the history of our planet has been in great part the history of the mixing of peoples.
ARTHUR M. SCHLESINGER JR.

Driving on Interstate 75 in northwest Ohio, one is struck by the flat, drab landscape. A more nondescript vista would be hard to imagine. Ten miles south of Toledo, what appears to be a misplaced Disneyland castle pierces the horizon. As one drives closer, the minarets on the building become more distinct, and its true identity is revealed: a Muslim mosque, its towers pointed toward Mecca. Here in the midst of middle America is what seems a most incongruous religious facade. But it is perfectly reflective of what America has become in the past three decades: a society more ethnically diverse than at any time in its history.

Societies with a variety of ethnic groups are referred to as **multiethnic.** To point out that the United States is a multiethnic society is to state the obvious. Indeed, it is not exaggerating the matter to declare that no society holds a more ethnically varied population. Nor is ethnic diversity a recent development. Quite simply, the United States has, for almost its entire history, been a society comprised of people whose origins cover the globe.

The United States is by no means unique in the contemporary world in its ethnic heterogeneity; most societies, it appears, are moving in this direction, some at a very rapid pace. Worldwide immigration, in large part stimulated by the advent of the global economy, has made the movement of people from one society to another more evident than at any time since the early years of the twentieth century, creating, in the process, multiethnic national populations on virtually every continent. Nonetheless, no society today—or in the past—has attempted to accommodate as great a mix of peoples as has the United States. In that sense, it remains one of the great social experiments of human development.

In all multiethnic societies, people's wealth, power, and prestige are in many ways related to their ethnic identity. As a preface to examining ethnic inequality (Chapter 11 will describe how ethnic diversity translates into a hierarchical arrangement), this chapter's purpose is twofold: First, some terms and concepts are introduced that are basic to a study of ethnic relations and ethnic inequality. These terms and concepts are used commonly but inconsistently, and they often are seriously misunderstood. Second, as in previous chapters, the analysis of the ethnic dimension of inequality focuses primarily on American society. Therefore, an important prerequisite is to examine the current ethnic makeup of the United States and the historical development of its ethnic inequality.

Ethnicity and Race

We begin with two concepts that are among the most misunderstood and controversial in all of the social sciences: *ethnicity* and *race*.

Ethnicity

Ethnicity is the easier concept to deal with and the one less debatable. **Ethnic groups** are groups within a larger society that in some degree are set off from others by displaying a unique set of cultural traits, such as language, religion, diet, and so on (Marger, 2000; Tumin, 1964). Members of an ethnic group perceive themselves as a community, in a broad sense, and thus maintain feelings of "we" (group members) as opposed to "they" (those not group members). They share what they believe to be common historical roots and experiences and are therefore apt to feel a stronger affinity for each other than for those of other ethnic origins (Blauner, 1992). In American society, ethnic groups are usually identified by their national or regional origins (Irish Americans, Mexican Americans, African Americans, and so on).

Not all members of an ethnic group, of course, will feel as strongly as others about their ethnicity. Some are very conscious of their ethnic ties and make efforts to sustain them by choosing coethnics as friends, neighbors, and marital partners. Others may deemphasize ethnicity to the point where it is no longer a significant part of their personal identity and affects little of their social life. In immigrant societies, such as the United States, there is commonly a dilution of ethnicity with each successive generation. Ethnic identity and association progressively fade as people are more thoroughly assimilated into the larger society and its culture. Ethnicity declines in importance for many as they marry across ethnic lines and maintain social relationships devoid of ethnic content.

In most heterogeneous societies, however, ethnicity remains a fundamental source of identity and determines much of how a person thinks, acts, and is treated by others. Ethnic conflicts in Bosnia, Rwanda, Northern Ireland,

and a host of other contemporary societies demonstrate the intractability of ethnic boundaries and the power of ethnicity as a mobilizing force.

Ethnicity, then, is variable from society to society, from group to group within those societies, and from individual to individual. There are also other social categories in modern societies to which people feel a sense of attachment and that provide a source of identification: social class, gender, age, occupation, religion, and so on. Like ethnic groups, these other categories become bases of solidarity, social cleavage, and social hierarchies. But in multiethnic societies, ethnicity is an especially strong base of loyalty and consciousness for most people and thus serves as a catalyst for competition and conflict. In addition, ethnicity is usually interrelated and overlaps with these other sources of group identification and attachment. Most important, ethnicity is a basis of ranking, in which one is treated according to the status of his or her ethnic group. In this sense, ethnicity is a dominant force in people's lives whether or not they are strongly conscious of their ethnic identity and regardless of the degree to which ethnicity shapes their social relations.

Panethnic Groups   In the United States several ethnic groups are often lumped together into more inclusive categories, usually based on their world region of origin: Asian Americans, Hispanic Americans, Euro-Americans, and so on. Each of these broad ethnic categories actually consists of different specific ethnic groups whose only similarity may be the continent from which they originally came. Japanese Americans, Vietnamese Americans, and Asian Indians, for example, are all considered part of the Asian American category, even though in terms of language, religion, and even physical appearance they exhibit few commonalities.

Race

A case can be made that the concept of race is the most highly charged and contentious in the entire lexicon of social science. Without question, it is one of the most misconceived and misused ideas of the modern world, and rarely is it used dispassionately.

To begin with, "race" is not applied consistently and thus may mean different things to different people. In popular usage it has been applied to a wide variety of human categories, including people with roughly similar physical features (the white race), religion (the Jewish race), nationality (the English race), and even the entire human species (the human race). None of these applications is accurate and meaningful from a social scientific standpoint.

The best that can be said is that **race** crudely describes people who share a set of similar genetic characteristics or, as biologists refer to them, gene frequencies. Racial categories, however, must be understood as entirely arbitrary. Physical differences among people obviously exist, and these differences are statistically clear among groups. It is true that, through a high degree of inbreeding over many generations and as adaptations to different physical environments, groups with distinctive gene frequencies and pheno-typic traits (i.e., observable physical features) are produced. There are evident differences, for example, between a "typical" black person and a "typical" white person in the United States. People may therefore be said to fall into statistical categories by physical type.

These statistical categories, however, should not be mistaken for actual human groupings founded on unmistakable hereditary traits. Physical dif-ferences between groups are not clear-cut but instead tend to overlap and blend into one another at various points, forming a continuum, not a set of sharply demarcated types. Moreover, differences among individuals of the same group (or "racial type") are greater than the differences found be-tween groups (Marks, 1995). Even the most inattentive person can see that the skin color of many people who are considered "black" is as light as those considered "white," and vice versa. The popular division of the hu-man population into three major racial groupings—Caucasoid, Mongoloid, and Negroid—is thus overly simplified and essentially discretionary. More-over, this scheme excludes large populations that do not easily fit into such a simple arrangement. Where, for example, are East Indians, a people with Caucasian features but with dark skin, placed? Or groups thoroughly mixed in ancestry, like most Indonesians? Because all human types are ca-pable of interbreeding, there are simply too many marginal cases such as these that do not easily conform to any particular racial scheme, regardless of its complexity.

Races, then, are social creations. This can be seen easily when we compare different societies, each with numerous physical types. The same individual categorized as "black" in the United States, for example, might be catego-rized as "white" in Brazil. Brazilians do not see or define races in exactly the same way as Americans, nor do they necessarily use the same physical char-acteristics as standards with which to categorize people (Harris, 1964; van den Berghe, 1978). Each heterogeneous society takes whatever are perceived as important physical differences among people and builds a set of racial cat-egories into which people are placed. Different societies will use different cri-teria with which to assign people racially, thereby creating classification sys-tems that may have little or no correspondence from one society to the next (Marger, 2000).

Even *within* societies, the definition of races has never been consistent. Consider the United States, where many Euro-American ethnic groups— Italians, Jews, Poles, for example—were classified by the U.S. Census as "races" as late as 1900. Also, "mulatto," "quadroon," and "octoroon" cat-egories (neither "black" nor "white") existed in the 1800s but were later discarded.

Despite the dubious scientific nature of the term, societies and thus in-dividuals within them attach significance to the idea of race and consider it a real and important division of humanity. And, as long as people believe that differences in selected physical traits are meaningful, they will act on those beliefs, thereby affecting their interrelations with others. If one believes intelligence, criminality, or other behaviors are related to race, one will, accordingly, make judgments about people on the basis of their racial identity.

Some social scientists have suggested doing away entirely with the notion of race, using "ethnicity" instead to describe and subdivide the population of a multiethnic society (Montagu, 1974; Patterson, 1997). This seems most reasonable since it is to their ethnic group that most people declare an affinity, beyond the larger society, and it is cultural traits that set off groups more clearly than presumed physical traits. Polish Americans, Irish Americans, and Jewish Americans may all be "white," but they are culturally quite diverse. Likewise, it makes little sense to lump together African Americans with "black" West Indians from Haiti or Jamaica, whose culture and, in the case of Haitians, language are vastly different. The notion of race, however, is so venerable and commonly used that we are forced to recognize it and to deal with it.

Changing Ethnic Patterns in the United States

It is surprising how misinformed most Americans are about the ethnic makeup of their society. Despite the virtually unparalleled heterogeneity within which they live, the majority of Americans cannot describe the actual size of various ethnic groups with anything even approaching accuracy. This was made poignantly clear in a national poll conducted by the *Washington Post* in 1996. Respondents from different ethnic categories were asked what they believed to be the ethnic composition of the United States. On average, they believed Euro-Americans to be no more than 50 percent of the society's total population; in fact, they are over 71 percent. The size of minority ethnic groups—African Americans, Hispanic Americans, and Asian Americans— was *over*estimated in all cases, sometimes by as much as twice. The size of the largest ethnic category, then, was grossly underestimated, and the minority categories were seen as much larger than they actually are. This seriously distorted picture of the American ethnic configuration is bound to influence people's attitudes and actions regarding ethnic-related issues. Given this general public misperception, we need to carefully clarify the ethnic makeup of American society.

Ethnic Categories

Even before looking at the numbers, we must examine the categories used to divide the population by ethnicity. As earlier noted, "race" and "ethnicity" are commonly used in an inconsistent and often confusing fashion.

In 1977 the U.S. federal government, as a means of monitoring and enforcing civil rights legislation and affirmative action programs, adopted a set of ethnic categories by which people could be classified and counted (Wright, 1994). These were subsequently adopted by virtually all government agencies, including the U.S. Census Bureau, as well as by educational institutions, corporations, and the mass media. Five major categories were established, which have been changed only in minor form since then: white, black, Hispanic, Asian/Pacific Islander, and American Indian/Alaskan Native. These have become familiar categories, appearing, as they do, on various educational and employment applications, census forms, and surveys of one sort or another. Unfortunately, rather than clarifying the conceptual morass of race and ethnicity in American society, these categories have further confounded the issue and contributed to even greater confusion.

Let's start with "white" and "black." Obviously, as a basis for classifying people, white and black no more accurately describe people physically than do green and blue. And even if they did, what would those divisions really mean? The very idea of "race" is scientifically questionable, at best. Yet, here we have a classification system—endorsed by the U.S. government and other major societal institutions—that obligates people to identify themselves "racially" and thus subdivides the population into so-called racial categories. I prefer to conceptualize these as ethnic groups or, in some cases, panethnic groups. For the most part, I use the terms African American and Euro-American in place of black and white.

Next, let's consider the category *Hispanic*. The first two classifications, black and white, are "racial" designations, but here, alongside them, is an ethnic designation. Hispanic[1] refers to anyone whose ancestral origins are Mexico, Central and South America, Spanish-speaking islands of the Caribbean, and Spain. Hispanics can therefore be of any "race." More confusion! The Asian/Pacific Islander category might seem more straightforward than the others, but it, too, contains numerous inconsistencies and conceptual problems. Not only are a myriad of cultures combined into this single "racial" category, but it encompasses a broad range of physical types, extending from Middle Eastern people (who are virtually indistinguishable from Europeans) to East Indians (who have European features with generally darker skin), to Chinese, Japanese, Koreans, Filipinos, and other East Asians who resemble not at all the first two. Even Native Americans constitute neither a physically distinct group (given their widespread intermarriage, most are hardly distinguishable from Euro-Americans) nor even a culturally demarcated group, since they derive from literally dozens of different tribal cultures.

What the current U.S. classification system represents is an extremely crude and bewildering attempt to count the population by ethnicity. It also

---

[1]*Latino* is sometimes preferred to *Hispanic,* and I use these terms interchangeably.

demonstrates the arbitrariness of racial or ethnic classification. Remember, race—and ethnicity—are social constructs, not biologically fixed divisions of the human population or of the population of any particular society. The ways that societies choose to subdivide and classify their populations can and do change.[2]

Unfortunately, we are thoroughly reliant on data gathered by the U.S. Census Bureau, as well as by other public and private agencies and organizations, to understand the ethnic makeup of the society. Until sociologists and other social scientists can collaborate with policymakers to construct a more rational and meaningful way of conceptualizing ethnic boundaries, we are constrained to use the categories currently in place.

The American Ethnic Configuration

Table 10-1 shows the current U.S. ethnic breakdown and how it has changed since 1980. It also shows some projections for the future. As can be seen, almost three-quarters of the U.S. population is Euro-American. African Americans are the largest ethnic minority (12 percent) but are on the verge of being surpassed by Hispanic Americans. Asian Americans constitute only 3.8 percent, but their numbers are growing rapidly. Native Americans number slightly less than 1 percent of the total population.

Projections into the years 2030 and 2050 reveal the rapidly advancing ethnic heterogeneity of American society. The United States is being transformed into what some have called a "majority-minority" society. Euro-Americans, the society's dominant group, are declining as a percentage and may constitute less than half the total population by midcentury. African Americans are increasing, but only slightly. It is the Hispanic American and Asian American populations that are growing most rapidly and substantially.

These demographic probes into the future, however, must be looked at with some caution. To begin with, these are population projections, which means they are merely estimates demographers construct based on current and, what they assume to be, future demographic trends. But demographers

---

[2]The politics of racial classification are very obvious. The more people who can be counted as members of an ethnic category, the more political benefits and power that will flow toward those who comprise that category. Ethnic leaders will therefore usually resist any change in this classification system. A good example is the recent case of so-called mixed-race people. These children of racially mixed marriages have in recent years lobbied for the establishment of a mixed-race category, to be included with the other racial and ethnic categories by the U.S. Census. Many, particularly within the African American community, have resisted this, viewing it as a measure that could lead to a numerical decline of the African American as well as other minority ethnic populations. The 2000 U.S. Census did offer people the choice of identifying with more than one racial category, an option chosen by 2.4 percent of the population (Lee, 2001).

Table 10-1 ■ Ethnic Makeup of the United States

Ethnic Group	1980	2000	2030[*]	2050[*]
Euro-American	80.0%	71.4%	60.1%	52.8%
African American	11.5%	12.2%	13.0%	13.2%
Hispanic American	6.4%	11.8%	19.4%	24.3%
Asian American	1.5%	3.8%	6.7%	8.9%
Native American	0.6%	0.7%	0.8%	0.8%

Source: U.S. Census Bureau, *Population Estimates Program, Population Division.*
<www.census.gov/population/estimates/nation/intfile3-1.txt>
[*]Projected

have no way of predicting what kind of fertility and mortality rates might be unleashed by economic and social forces. Few predicted the post–World War II baby boom, for example. Nor can they know what immigration rates will be in the future, since these are determined mostly by federal legislation, making them a key political issue subject to the influence of all kinds of interest groups.

Even if demographers were capable of making accurate predictions, however, these estimates do not take into consideration that the categories currently being used to classify the population by race and ethnicity are likely to change in the future. There is much intermarriage occurring across racial and ethnic lines, the effect of which is to further blur these already fuzzy and politically influenced categories. Consider golf star Tiger Woods as an example. Woods has been touted as the newest black sports hero. But is he "black"? His father is African American, his mother is Asian American, and his ancestry also includes Euro-American and Native American. Woods himself explains that "Growing up, I came up with this name: I'm a 'Cablinasian'," a blend of Caucasian, black, Indian, and Asian (Fletcher, 1997).

As the population becomes more diverse, cases such as Tiger Woods's are becoming more commonplace. Indeed, Woods may be the exemplar of the United States' ethnic future. The result is that the familiar racial/ethnic categories—white, black, Hispanic, Asian—no longer make much sense (if they ever did) in classifying people and simply no longer work in accurately describing American society.

What emerges from all of this is one unmistakable fact: The United States continues to evolve into a more ethnically heterogeneous society. In the twenty-first century, America's ethnic character will be more culturally and physically diverse than it was in the twentieth century. And despite the efforts of many ethnic leaders to preserve their groups' social boundaries, the trend toward a fading of those ethnic lines seems irreversible.

The Shaping of American Ethnic Diversity and Inequality

With the exception of Native Americans, all ethnic groups in the United States trace their origins to other societies. American society is, to a degree unmatched by others, an "immigrant" society.[3] This section traces the socio-historical experiences of the United States' major ethnic groups.

Native Americans

When Europeans first crossed the Atlantic in the late fifteenth century, they found two continents inhabited by perhaps 75 million people (Thornton, 1995). These "Indians," as the Europeans called them, were by no means homogeneous but were practicing a vast array of cultures, some quite advanced in social organization and technology. Both the Indians themselves and their cultures were very different from the Europeans, and these physical and cultural differences were interpreted ethnocentrically by the invaders as proof of inferiority and lack of civilization.

In North America, conflict between European settlers and Indians centered mainly on control of land: Native people occupied it; settlers coveted it. Throughout the nineteenth century, Indian lands were ceded irreversibly by treaties, through fraudulent schemes, or by sheer force. Mostly, however, dispossession was accomplished through government policies (Wright, 1992).

In addition to dispossessing them of traditional lands, Indian societies were reduced physically through a combination of exposure to diseases, armed conflict, forced migration, starvation, and the breakup of cultural systems that had traditionally provided for social and material needs. Though Indians did make many cultural adaptations to the Euro-American presence, this did not prevent the eventual destruction of their social forms and the succession of Euro-American dominance (Wax, 1971).

By the end of the nineteenth century, the Indian population had been reduced to fewer than 250,000. Indians were now officially wards of the federal government, having been awarded full citizenship, and were thus no longer seen or dealt with as separate nations. Throughout the twentieth century, government measures toward Indians vacillated between, on the one hand, trying to assimilate them to the cultural ways of Euro-Americans and, on the other, viewing them as unassimilable and thus to be left alone. In either case, with few exceptions, gross neglect typified the attitudes of policymakers, and the severely impoverished condition of Indians did not change markedly.

The American Indian Population Today   The official Indian population today is 2 million, which is less than 1 percent of the total U.S. population

---

[3]Even Native Americans, of course, were "immigrants" in the sense that they migrated from Asia, perhaps ten thousand years ago.

(U.S. Census Bureau, 1997d).[4] American Indians are therefore among the smallest ethnic categories. Nonetheless, the Native American population has been growing for the past few decades. This is accounted for partially by the high birthrate among American Indians but also by a growing tendency for people to declare their Indian affiliation.

The American Indian population is split between those living on and those living off the 278 federal Indian reservations (U.S. Department of the Interior, 1991). Most of those who do not live on reservations are concentrated in large urban areas, particularly in the western states. Native Americans, whether on or off the reservations, continue to rank among the most impoverished of ethnic populations in the United States.

Euro-Americans

Americans of European descent, often referred to simply as "white" Americans or panethnically as Euro-Americans, are still the vast majority—about 75 percent—of the American ethnic mélange. To refer to Americans of European descent in such a collective fashion, of course, obscures the cultural differences among this extremely diverse collectivity of groups. Moreover, to lump together those whose ancestors came from Ireland, Germany, Poland, Italy, Russia, and literally every other European society is to disregard the different adaptations made by each group and the varied rate of mobility each experienced following its entry into the society.

The Anglo Core Group   Sociologist John Porter suggested the term *charter group* to describe an ethnic group that is the first to enter previously unpopulated territory and that subsequently "has the most say" (1965:60). This charter, or core, group retains many privileges and prerogatives, including decisions about what other groups are to be admitted to the society and what they will be entitled to do. In the United States, the charter group was British, and its major institutions would therefore reflect British social and cultural characteristics. English became the primary language, English common law became the basis of the legal system, and Protestantism was established as the dominant religion. Although other, smaller, European groups came to America in the early nineteenth century, most were culturally and racially close to this Anglo-Protestant core group and, as a result, were relatively quickly absorbed into it. It was this group, the defining ethnic features of which were its northwestern European and Protestant origins, that

---

[4]It is difficult to accurately count the Indian population since definitions of who is "Indian" are not clear and unquestioned. As with other ethnic categories, the U.S. Census counts anyone as Indian who declares himself or herself so. Within the Native American population itself, Indian identity is left to each tribe to define. Thus a variety of different criteria may be used in establishing a person's tribal membership.

set the cultural tone of the society and established its major economic, political, and social institutions.

Although the Anglo core group has been diluted by successive immigrant waves over many generations and its cultural imprint likewise colored by other groups, its social dominance has remained unwavering throughout American history. "The white Anglo-Saxon Protestant," notes sociologist Lewis Killian, "remains the typical American, the model to which other Americans are expected and encouraged to conform" (1975:16). The makeup of the dominant group itself, however, has changed somewhat as other white Protestant groups have blended almost imperceptibly with those of British origin. White (or Euro-American) Protestants, then, have varied national roots, but their common Protestantism and perceived racial character have neutralized any meaningful national differences among them.

The "Old Immigration"   The six decades between 1820 and 1880 mark the first significant period of non-British immigration to the United States. The two most sizable groups arriving during this era were the Germans and the Irish, though immigration from Britain and other northwestern European societies continued unabated. Between 1847 and 1854, about 1.2 million Irish immigrants came to the United States, and by the end of the Civil War, they constituted 7 percent of the Euro-American population. Germans came in two waves; from 1850 to 1857, almost a million arrived, and between 1865 and 1885, 2 million more. By the late nineteenth century, Germans were the second-largest ethnic group in the society, exceeded only by the British.

This period marked the entrance not only of non-British people in large numbers but also, for the first time, of significant numbers of non-Protestants. Most of the Irish were Catholic, as were about half the Germans. As a result, nativist activities, specifically anti-Catholic actions and rhetoric, became widespread. Catholics were seen by many as a subversive element, and Catholicism as basically incompatible with American ways (Dinnerstein et al., 1990). By midcentury, however, anti-Catholic nativism had begun to wane as national attention turned to the issue of slavery and as immigration was temporarily halted by the Civil War. Moreover, immigration generally was welcomed by industrialists and others of the business community who saw immigrants as a source of cheap labor and a growing consumer market.

Despite prejudice and discrimination toward the Catholics among them, especially the Irish, these northwestern European groups were, by comparison with groups that would follow them, advantaged in two ways: They were close enough culturally to the Anglo core group to assimilate within a relatively short time, and they were physically indistinct from the Europeans who had preceded them to America, thereby avoiding imputations of racial identity. Their integration into the mainstream society, therefore, was not severely constrained, and the resistance of the dominant group to them was relatively mild.

In many ways, these groups have melded with and are indistinguishable from the Anglo core group. Certainly there are differences among them, but their ethnic cultures have been, in large measure, erased with each passing generation. Who today can describe what it means to be German American, for example? There are few remnants of the origin culture in public view: There is no language that lives on, nor is there any real sense of community among those with common German ethnic origins. A further dissipation of a distinct ethnic culture for these groups has resulted from the great degree of intermarriage among them. If not thoroughly assimilated, groups of the old immigration have come very close to the point of total absorption into the larger society.

The "New Immigration"   Although substantial German and Irish immigration had presented the first real challenge to Anglo dominance, the polyglot nature of American society took shape most forcefully through what has been called the *new immigration.* During a period extending roughly from the early 1880s until the outbreak of World War I, almost 25 million European immigrants came to the United States. It is from this second great wave of European immigration that most of today's non-Protestant "white ethnics" are descended.

These new immigrants not only represented the numerical peak of European immigration to the United States but also changed radically the ethnic character of the society. To begin with, most were from southern and eastern European societies, whose cultures were alien to those of Britain and northwestern Europe. Most important, they were non-Protestant—primarily Catholic and secondarily Jewish. Although most of the earlier Irish had been Catholic, in other respects they were not so culturally distant from the Anglo-Americans. Likewise, the Germans may have spoken a different language, but over half were Protestant, and they were not looked on by the dominant British group as cultural inferiors. Another important distinguishing feature of the new immigrants was their class origins: in the main, lower than those of previous groups, except perhaps the Irish. They were chiefly peasants from the poorer states of Europe—southern Italy, Russia, Poland, and the many parts of the Austro-Hungarian Empire.

Their cultural and class differences brought forth a more strongly antagonistic reaction from the dominant group than previous entering groups had produced. Americans questioned how the immigrants would ultimately fit into the society and, abetted by notions of social Darwinism, widely assumed their cultural—and even biological—inferiority. Prompted by the continued influx, nativist feelings and racist theories reached a peak by the early 1920s, resulting in restrictive quotas that curtailed once and for all the large-scale immigration of southern and eastern Europeans.

Most who came as part of the new immigration were unprepared for life in an industrial, urban society. Many lacked the skills and education that could be converted into rapid occupational mobility and economic success in

Table 10-2 ■ Largest Euro-American Ancestry Groups

Ancestry Group	Median Family Income	Percent U.S. Population
German	$38,216	23.3
Irish	$38,101	15.6
English	$40,875	13.1
Italian	$42,242	5.9
French	$36,237	4.1
Polish	$41,700	3.8
Dutch	$43,415	2.5
Scotch-Irish	$39,816	2.3
Scottish	$43,293	2.2
Swedish	$40,459	1.9
Norwegian	NA	1.6
Russian	$58,826	1.2

Source: U.S. Census Bureau, *Ancestry of the Population in the United States, 1990*; U.S. Census Bureau, *Statistical Abstract of the United States 1995.*

America. As a result, they entered the labor force in unskilled jobs, where they and, more often than not, their children remained.

Despite their initial hardships, by all indications, ethnic groups of the second major immigrant wave may be seen as a great success story in American social history. Within three generations, most moved solidly into the intermediate classes and are today not easily distinguishable from first-wave (old immigration) groups. Indeed, overall, the differentials between various European ethnic groups in the stratification system have shrunk considerably (Table 10-2).

This is not to overlook the social class differences that remain apparent among them. Jewish Americans are among the most successful American ethnic groups, exceeding almost all others in median family income, educational level, and occupational prestige. What makes the case of Jewish Americans so remarkable is that their spectacular upward mobility occurred within only two generations (Glazer, 1958; Lipset and Raab, 1995). For Italian Americans, Polish Americans, and other second-wave Euro-American ethnic groups, upward mobility was slower and much less significant for the first two generations, but they now show solid evidence of middle-class status in terms of income, occupation, and education (Alba, 1990).

These groups have also exhibited a noticeable degree of assimilation to the core Anglo-American cultural patterns. By the third generation, most have substantially disposed of traditional ethnic cultural ways. More important, these groups have moved into the mainstream of American society structurally. This means that they have begun to enter positions of power within most institutional realms, including government, the corporate world, education, and the media (Alba, 1990; Alba and Moore, 1982).

Table 10-2 shows the major ancestry groups that currently make up the Euro-American population, which derives primarily from the two main periods, old and new, of immigration. Actually, the diversity of the European component of the American ethnic configuration is greater than is indicated in the table, because only the largest ancestry groups are shown.

African Americans

The experience of African Americans is unique among U.S. ethnic groups. This stems from the fact that no other group, no matter how severe the prejudice and discrimination it experienced, entered the society involuntarily as a slave population. In many ways, the vestiges of slavery continue to influence the adaptive patterns of the African American population. The history of African Americans is complex and subject to a variety of interpretations. There is no debate, however, that it is a history marked by the continued stress of accommodation to the culture and institutions of a Euro-American–dominated society.

Slavery   The cultural and physical differences of Africans were primary rationales for their enslavement, but in the end, the most critical factor was differential power (Geschwender, 1978; Noel, 1968). Although black skin and "heathenism" gave rise to white ethnocentrism, this did not predetermine the choice of Africans as slaves. Indeed, attempts to enslave the indigenous Indian population were made unsuccessfully. The difference with Africans was simply the lack of a viable community from which they might have mustered sufficient counterforce to resist slavery, as Indians were able to do. Color became the visible symbol of slave status, and a racist ideology was gradually developed to buttress the system.

Jim Crow   After the Civil War and the abolition of slavery, most African Americans remained in the southern states. For the brief period of Reconstruction, the future looked very bright for a rapid and significant improvement in their socioeconomic and political circumstances. Freed blacks began to acquire some of the power resources needed to enter the mainstream society. They exercised the vote and were even elected to high offices in state and federal governments. An educational system promised even greater potential opportunities. This period, then, marked the end of what had been a paternalistic system under slavery and established competitive relations between whites and blacks.

But it was this competition that eventually led to a system of segregation as a means of controlling the black threat to white economic and social advantage. The southern planter class gradually reestablished its traditional place of power, and the economic dependence of blacks on their former masters was revived with the advent of the sharecropping system. Once federal troops were removed from the South, the ability to prevent whites from re-asserting their power over blacks was removed. Blacks were subsequently disenfranchised, and the path was cleared for the enactment of a complex array of measures designed to separate blacks and whites in almost all areas of social life (see Chapter 6). With the 1896 Supreme Court decision in the case of *Plessy* v. *Ferguson,* the "separate but equal" doctrine was upheld, and the system of segregation known as Jim Crow was securely in place in the South.

Racial segregation was maintained by both force and ideology. As to the former, fear and humiliation were integral parts of everyday life for blacks in the southern states.[5] With the rise of vigilante groups such as the Ku Klux Klan, violence and physical intimidation became the order of the day. Lynching was the most extreme technique employed to maintain black subservience. From 1884 to the outbreak of World War I, over thirty-six hundred lynchings took place, most in the South and with most of the victims black (Franklin, 1980).

Conditions in the North, though not supported by legal mechanisms as in the South, were not significantly different. Although black civil rights were acknowledged, segregation in virtually all areas of social life prevailed (Woodward, 1974). In both the South and North, segregation was abetted by the fullest development of a racist ideology. Ideas of racial superiority and inferiority were now supported by scientific thought and were applied not only to blacks but to all non-Anglo-Saxon groups.

Northward Migration   Industrial expansion in the North in the early years of the twentieth century created an increased demand for labor, and with the cutoff of immigration from Europe following the passage of restrictive immigration laws in the mid-1920s, blacks from the South began to fill these places. If jobs were the key "pull" factor impelling black out-migration from the South, the declining cotton economy and the continued enforcement of Jim Crow were the chief "push" factors. The demographic changes involving the black populace were profound. In 1910, almost 90 percent of blacks were living in the South, but eighty years later, little more than half remained there. Moreover, this migration was almost wholly to the cities, making blacks an increasingly urbanized population (Lemann, 1991).

Movement of blacks to the urban North created a perceived threat to white workers, generating resentment and overt conflict. The upshot of the rising competition for work and housing was an increase in the frequency and severity of black-white hostilities. Serious race riots occurred in numerous cities

---

[5]A poignant description of the constant terror and degradation to which blacks were subjected is found in the works of Richard Wright, one of the great African American writers of the twentieth century, especially *Black Boy,* written in 1945, and *Uncle Tom's Children,* written in 1938.

throughout the first two decades of the century (Rudwick, 1964; Rudwick and Meier, 1969; Tuttle, 1970).

The Civil Rights Era   The three decades following World War II marked a period in which the acquisition of power resources by African Americans impelled the most forceful challenge to the American racist system.

As early as the 1930s, President Franklin D. Roosevelt had begun to appoint African Americans to nonpolicy-making government advisory positions (Franklin, 1980; Myrdal, 1944). African Americans also began to enter the labor movement, specifically the Congress of Industrial Organizations (CIO). Wartime conditions in the 1940s opened new areas of work to blacks and provided an even greater push to the northward migration that had been occurring since the early part of the century.

The cause of black rights was aided as well by a political dilemma faced by U.S. leaders: How could the United States support a racist system at home while it was at war abroad with Nazi Germany, the most flagrantly racist regime? This inconsistency was difficult to reconcile without a greater commitment to minority rights. Moreover, following the war, racist policies proved an international liability in dealing with the emerging nations of non-white Africa and Asia. As a result, the federal government now seemed more amenable to efforts at ending patterns of discrimination.

Perhaps the most momentous single government action during the 1950s that stimulated the push for African American advancement was the Supreme Court decision of 1954 in the case of *Brown* v. *Board of Education of Topeka.* In that case, the Court ruled invalid the separate-but-equal doctrine, which had been upheld in the famous *Plessy* v. *Ferguson* decision of 1896. The 1954 decision basically removed the legal foundation of segregation and thus marked the beginning of the end of the entire Jim Crow system. Influenced by the testimony of social scientists, the Court made clear in its ruling that separate schools were inherently unequal and imposed an inferior status on African American children, causing irreparable psychological damage. School segregation laws, the Court declared, therefore violated the equal protection clause of the Fourteenth Amendment to the Constitution. This clause stipulates that no state shall deprive people of life, liberty, or property without due process of law or deny them the equal protection of the law. The *Brown* ruling was subsequently used as the legal basis for court decisions that struck down other segregated institutions.

One year after the *Brown* decision was handed down, the civil rights movement was symbolically launched with the boycott by African Americans of the segregated bus system of Montgomery, Alabama. From the late 1950s to the mid-1960s, nonviolent protest and civil disobedience were the movement's chief tactics. The basic idea was that individuals had a moral duty to disobey the law when it was clearly unjust. Taking a cue from other nonviolent protest movements, the technique involved actively opposing the law but in a peaceful fashion. The proponents of nonviolent protest, Martin

Luther King Jr. in particular, emphasized that it was necessary to win over the opposition through friendship and understanding, not through defeat or humiliation (King, 1964).

The movement culminated in 1964 with enactment of the most comprehensive civil rights measure since the Civil War, prohibiting discrimination in voting, public facilities, schools, courts, and employment. And in 1965, the Voting Rights Act was passed, ending the systematic disenfranchisement of southern blacks.

Following the movement's success in the South, focus shifted to northern cities where economic inequities, not political rights, were the targets of action. The civil rights movement passed through a more militant phase, giving rise to the idea of "black power," which proposed not the use of nonviolent tactics but rather confrontation with white authorities and a black nationalist ideology (Jacoby, 1998).

The Post–Civil Rights Era   By the early 1970s, the legal infrastructure of the system of segregation in the South had been dismantled. No longer could state and local authorities prevent African Americans from entering public facilities previously reserved for whites. Unlike the first Reconstruction following the Civil War, white vigilante groups such as the Ku Klux Klan were limited in their influence and were not supported either materially or morally by the majority of whites. Of great significance was the fact that the federal government accepted the commitment to black civil rights and effectively countered state and local governments that sought to sustain segregation.

Economic opportunities expanded, giving rise to the emergence of a sizable African American middle class. Blacks accumulated much greater competitive resources, such as white-collar jobs, middle-level incomes, and higher education, than at any previous time. These resources, however, were not distributed equitably among the African American population. Thus, although the black middle class expanded considerably, the conditions of a significant black underclass, submerged mainly in urban ghettos, were not seriously affected. Economic and social gaps between Euro-Americans and African Americans also remained substantial.

Finally, if the decline of biological racist ideas was clearly on the horizon as early as the 1930s, by the 1970s their persuasiveness was further diminished. The notion of innate black inferiority was no longer given credence by the vast majority of white Americans (Schuman et al., 1985; Sniderman and Piazza, 1993).

Black Ethnic Diversity   Today African Americans have become a population quite varied in social class. As we will see in Chapter 11, these differences have created a sharp division between those who have established themselves as part of the intermediate classes and those who remain mired in poverty. In addition, the American black population is becoming ethnically more varied. African Americans are being joined by black immigrants from Caribbean countries such as Haiti and Jamaica and from African countries such as Somalia and Nigeria. Although these new immigrants may evince "racial" similarities, culturally they have little in common with African Americans. As a result, the American black population is evolving into a broader, more culturally diverse ethnic category.

Hispanic Americans

Hispanic Americans, or, as some prefer, *Latinos,* constitute several distinct ethnic groups linked by their region of origin and, in large part, their language. The most sizable groups are Mexican Americans—the largest—followed by Puerto Ricans and Cubans. The remainder are mostly from Central and South America and the Caribbean. Despite broad cultural similarities, in particular the Spanish language (even here there is no uniformity, for those from Brazil speak Portuguese), Hispanic American groups have each displayed distinct patterns of settlement in and adaptation to American society. Here are brief descriptions of the three largest Latino groups.

Mexican Americans   Most Americans are not aware of the fact that Mexicans were present on what is now U.S. territory long before Anglo[6] settlers came to what is today the American West. Mexico gained independence from Spain in 1810, and at that time, Mexican territory encompassed an area as far north as what is today Colorado. Following the Mexican War in 1848, the United States acquired what eventually became the states of California, Colorado, New Mexico, Nevada, Utah, and most of Arizona, in addition to Texas, which had been annexed earlier. Anglos displaced the few Mexicans who had been living in that region and firmly established themselves as the dominant group.

Except for those few who were incorporated through annexation, all Mexicans entered the United States as voluntary immigrants. Starting in the nineteenth century, Mexicans served as a cheap labor force in the building of railroads, in mining, and in agriculture (Camarillo, 1979; Tyler, 1975). In the early decades of the twentieth century, immigration reached enormous proportions with the expansion of the American Southwest and the corresponding inadequacies of the Mexican economy. Political destabilization brought about by the Mexican Revolution in 1910 further stimulated migration northward.

Mexicans in the Southwest were subjected to much discrimination in work and in housing. Indeed, in many areas, the social conditions were not unlike the Jim Crow system in the southern states, including segregated restaurants, churches, schools, and other public facilities (Burma, 1954; Grebler et al., 1970). The attitude toward Mexicans was dependent on their economic role. When their labor was needed, they were recruited; when their labor was no longer

---

[6]In areas with large Hispanic populations, the non-Hispanic population is commonly referred to as "Anglo."

deemed necessary, they were encouraged to return to Mexico, sometimes forcefully. Deportations and repatriations were carried out during the 1930s and 1940s, and in the 1950s a policy called Operation Wetback resulted in the deportation of almost 4 million people (Moore, 1975).

Today, Mexican Americans[7] constitute two-thirds of all Latinos and are also the country's largest immigrant group. As in past decades, economic conditions have been the chief stimulant of this migration. Although in recent decades they have dispersed throughout the United States, the Southwest remains the area in which Mexicans are most heavily concentrated, with almost 80 percent in California and Texas alone.

Puerto Ricans   Puerto Rico became a territory of the United States in 1898 following the Spanish-American War, and in 1917 the inhabitants of the island were given the status of American citizenship. Puerto Ricans, therefore, are not technically immigrants, even though they come to the mainland from a distinctly foreign culture. Their unique legal status enabled them to immigrate freely to the U.S. mainland with no restrictions, though the major immigration of Puerto Ricans did not occur until the 1950s.

Puerto Ricans inherit a racial background that is a combination primarily of European and African but also some Indian elements. The large African population originally brought to the island as slaves intermarried with whites over several generations, and today the Puerto Rican population is thoroughly mixed, covering the entire color spectrum. On the island, one's color is seen along a scale, or continuum, in contrast to the mainland where there are relatively fixed black and white racial categories, allowing for no "intermediate" cases (Fitzpatrick, 1987; Padilla, 1987; Rodríguez, 1989). Many who are "white" on the island may therefore find themselves classified as "black" when they come to the mainland. The differential treatment they subsequently receive on the basis of their darker skin (by American standards) is frustrating and problematic because interracial marriages are commonplace in Puerto Rico and social treatment of darker groups is more equitable than on the mainland. Their perceived racial features have often made Puerto Ricans the target of severe prejudice and discrimination in cities where they are a significant percentage of the population.

Cuban Americans   On all measures of socioeconomic status, Cuban Americans are well in advance of Mexican Americans and Puerto Ricans, despite their more recent arrival. Their income and educational levels are higher, their unemployment rates are lower, and they are well represented across the occupational spectrum. Their relative success can be attributed to a number of factors that relate to their class background, the conditions of

---

[7]Mexican Americans are often referred to as *Chicanos,* particularly in the Southwest.

their immigration, and their settlement patterns. All were quite different from those experienced by other Latino groups.

Cubans began to come to the United States in significant numbers in the 1960s, following the revolution in Cuba led by Fidel Castro. Because the revolution imposed a socialist system in Cuba, the power and economic position of most of the early immigrants—the majority of them middle-, upper-middle, or upper-class people—had been severely constricted (Portes, 1969). Cuban immigrants, then, were political refugees whose stay in the United States, they hoped, would be only temporary and who would return to Cuba as soon as political conditions changed (Portes et al., 1977).

Cuban immigration from 1960 onward was aided by American policies that, in effect, permitted the entrance of Cuban refugees without restriction. Cuba became a basic element in the Cold War and was portrayed as a "communist stronghold." The migration of large numbers of Cubans was seen as confirmation of this perspective, and the refugees were welcomed enthusiastically. In addition, the U.S. government provided them with financial and educational assistance, enabling many to reestablish their businesses and professions in the United States (Pedraza-Bailey, 1985). A second wave of immigrants—more than 125,000—arrived dramatically in 1980 in a flotilla of small boats. These immigrants were generally lower in social class than the original Cuban refugees, and many were racially mixed. As a result, they did not find the adjustment to American society as smooth or their reception as enthusiastic (Portes et al., 1985).

Much of the Cuban American economic success story is attributable to the higher class origins of most of the early refugees. Unlike Mexicans and Puerto Ricans, the Cuban immigrants were likely to have been occupationally successful and well educated before emigrating. These higher skill and educational levels translated into rapid upward mobility in the United States. The substantial economic success of many enabled them to offer jobs and other assistance to those who followed them (Portes and Manning, 1986). Also, most immigrant Cubans, unlike many Mexicans and Puerto Ricans, were perceived racially as "white" and therefore were not exposed to the added handicap of racial discrimination in the labor market.

In addition to a favorable context of reception, Cuban immigrants were aided by the strong family and kin support system they brought with them (Portes et al., 1977). Furthermore, Cubans have benefited from the creation of a tightly knit ethnic community in Miami, where the vast majority of Cuban Americans reside, with hundreds of businesses, as well as newspapers, radio stations, churches, and other institutions, providing for ethnic needs (Wilson and Portes, 1980).

Asian Americans

Asians have been in the United States since the early part of the nineteenth century. Only in recent decades, however, have they emerged as a sizable element of the American ethnic configuration. It is important to understand that the Asian American ethnic category is extremely diverse, including at least a dozen culturally and even racially distinct groups. Currently, the largest are Chinese, Filipinos, and Koreans, with substantial populations of Japanese, Asian Indians, and Vietnamese, as well as small numbers from other Asian and Pacific Island societies. To speak of Asian Americans as a whole is simply to create a panethnic statistical category that lumps together several disparate ethnic groups, enabling us to look at the general characteristics of the groups collectively, in comparison with other ethnic populations (Espiritu, 1992).

The Asian experience in the United States can be divided into two distinct and divergent parts. The first consists of the old Asian immigration, occurring roughly from the middle of the nineteenth century to the early years of the twentieth. The Chinese were the first to arrive, followed by the Japanese and, in much smaller numbers, by Koreans and Filipinos.

The first Asian immigrants were mostly unskilled laborers recruited for construction or agricultural work. Their entrance into American society produced severe antagonism and a set of stereotypes that eventually led to exclusionary measures, effectively barring future large-scale immigration from Asia. The intensity of early anti-Asian attitudes and actions seemed to hinge on the perceived threat of Asian immigrants to the jobs of native workers. Perhaps the most devastating aspect of anti-Asian stereotyping involved the notion of a "yellow peril." Chinese immigration, in this view, was an invasion of people who were loyal only to their country of origin and who, if not stopped, would eventually take over the United States (tenBroek et al., 1968). Many of the same attitudes and actions were cast on the later Japanese immigrants.

Anti-Asian sentiment, directed specifically at Japanese Americans, reached an apex at the outset of World War II. Following the Japanese attack on Pearl Harbor in 1941, almost the entire Japanese American population living in California, Oregon, Washington, and Arizona—120,000—were sent to internment camps further inland. They were detained in the camps for almost the entire war. No other series of events in American ethnic history, other than the enslavement of African Americans and the genocidal measures employed against Native Americans, were comparable to this action. Although the internment of the Japanese is the most infamous case of institutional discrimination, historically all Asian groups were subjected to various legal forms of discrimination at one time or another (Kitano and Daniels, 1995).

Following restrictive measures in the late nineteenth and early twentieth centuries, very few additional Asians entered the society until the revision of immigration laws in 1965. That marked the onset of the second period of Asian immigration to the United States, which continues to the present. The second immigration has been markedly different from the earlier movement in that many of the new immigrants have been noticeably higher in class origin, well educated, and occupationally skilled. On the other hand, another element, specifically from Southeast Asia, remains at the low end of the American ethnic hierarchy (Jiobu, 1988).

The new Asian immigration has also been considerably more diverse in national origin than the first one, made up of people from almost every contemporary Asian society. Although the Asian American population is a relatively small part of the total population, it is the fastest-growing U.S. ethnic minority (Pear, 1992). This rapid and sizable population growth is a result mainly of the fact that Asians now account for the largest element of immigration to the United States, more than 45 percent. Today, except for the Japanese, Asians in the United States are predominantly foreign-born (U.S. Commission on Civil Rights, 1992).

One of the salient features of the economic role played by Asian Americans today is the unusually large number who choose to own small businesses. Asian Americans have the highest rate of business ownership for all U.S. minority groups (Manning and O'Hare, 1988). Koreans have been especially prominent in small business in a number of large cities (Hoffman and Marger, 1991; Light and Bonacich, 1988; Min, 1988, 1995). In the New York metropolitan area, for example, where Koreans number about a hundred thousand, they run some nine thousand small business enterprises (Kim, 1981, 1987).

Several factors seem to account for the proportionately large numbers of Asian Americans in the small business sector. Family members commonly participate in the operation of the enterprise, reducing labor costs and capital requirements. In addition, operating a business of one's own allays the fears of many immigrants that their opportunities for advancement within the mainstream economy, dominated by big corporations, is limited, especially for those who do not speak English fluently.

The Newest Immigrants

The prominence of ethnic issues in American society today stems primarily from the continuing socioeconomic gap between the Euro-American population and large portions of minority ethnic groups. But it also derives from the large-scale immigration of diverse peoples in the past three decades. These latest immigrants have begun to have a significant impact on the ethnic flavor of the society and have introduced new problems and questions of ethnic relations.

Between 1960 and 1990, 15 million people either came to the United States as legal immigrants or were granted permanent residence. During the 1980s alone, 8.3 million entered the society. This approached the 8.8 million figure that was reached during the first decade of the 1900s, when immigration to the United States was at its peak.[8] During the 1990s, on average, almost 900,000 immigrants entered the society annually (U.S. Immigration and Naturalization Service, 2000).

---

[8]The proportion of immigrants to total population, however, was much greater in the early 1900s than it is today. The average annual number of immigrants admitted from 1981 to 1990 was 3.1 immigrants per 1,000 U.S. residents; from 1901 to 1910, the annual rate was three times as great. Further, the percentage of foreign-born as part of the total population was much greater in the earlier part of the century.

But numbers do not tell the whole story of this latest era of immigration to the United States. Most important, the character of immigration has changed radically from past eras. The vast majority of immigrants throughout the nineteenth and early twentieth centuries were from European countries. Today, most are from Latin America and Asia, though virtually every region and nation of the world is represented in the new immigrant wave. This has resulted from a fundamentally changed immigration policy. In 1965 legislation was enacted abolishing the discriminatory quota system that since the late 1920s had favored northwestern European groups and severely restricted the entrance of others. This policy change enabled groups to enter in significant numbers that had previously been effectively excluded. Few anticipated the profound impact that the 1965 reform would ultimately have on the ethnic composition of American society.

As with past immigrants, most of the new arrivals today have come to the United States in pursuit of economic betterment. The majority are coming from poorer nations whose economies and populations are not capable of providing the job opportunities and quality of life that the United States promises.

Most of the new immigrants have settled in large cities, especially Los Angeles, New York, Chicago, and Miami, but virtually no area of the country has been unaffected by the influx. A national poll conducted in 1997 indicated that nearly all Americans, regardless of where they lived, said they encountered new immigrants in their everyday lives, either while shopping, at work, in their children's school, as doctors and other professionals, or in church (Dewar, 1997).

Issues of the Newest Immigration

The large-scale entrance of immigrants in recent decades has created both economic and social issues that have become the focus of much public controversy.

Economic Issues   As noted in Chapter 4, the economic impact of the newest immigration is widely disputed. Do immigrants take jobs that native-born Americans would ordinarily fill? Or do they take their place in the labor market in jobs that Americans either cannot or will not fill? The debate is ongoing. This is an old issue, however, that has been evident during all previous periods of large-scale immigration. The debate seems to vacillate, depending on the health of the American economy and the rate of unemployment. When people are apprehensive about the security of their jobs, immigrants—who are often willing to work for lower wages and under more demanding conditions—are likely to be viewed as a menace; resistance is vocal and strident. When jobs are plentiful and the economy is productive, opposition seems to abate.

Social Issues   The fact that most are not European makes the newest immigrants highly visible, bringing to American society cultural and physical features distant from those of the Euro-American majority. Today's issues, therefore, concern not simply the new immigrants' economic integration but their social assimilation as well. These issues have a familiar ring, recalling those that raged at the turn of the century with regard to southern and eastern European immigrants.

The most vehement social issue of the newest immigration concerns language. Dispute centers on the use of non-English ballots in political elections, language proficiency standards for prospective citizens, and the use of non-English languages at work. Perhaps the most impassioned debate has focused on language use in schools. The controversy swirls around whether foreign-born students should be instructed in their native language or in English, and in what proportion. In New York City, for example, classes are now taught not only in Spanish but in Chinese, Haitian Creole, Russian, Korean, Arabic, Vietnamese, Polish, Bengali, and French. And in Los Angeles, almost half of all students have limited English proficiency. And the problem is not limited to large immigrant-receiving areas. Almost half of all U.S. school districts have at least some non-English-speaking children (Hornblower, 1995).

Those arguing for the exclusive use of English in schools and government maintain that without a common language, new immigrants will resist assimilation and the United States risks becoming linguistically divided. In response, critics charge that efforts to impose English are a backlash against the new immigrants and essentially a mask for ethnic antagonism. Moreover, they claim that unilingual policies do nothing to help promote the learning of English (Braverman, 1988; Crawford, 1992). Public opinion currently seems to favor the "English only" side of the controversy. A national poll revealed that almost two-thirds of Americans favor a law that would make English the country's official language (*Time*, 1995).[9] Moreover, in 1998 a referendum was passed in California striking down bilingual classrooms.

The issue may be moot in any case because studies indicate that the children of recent immigrants adopt English as their major language and gradually drift away from the use of the native language outside the home (Portes and Rumbaut, 1990; Saad, 1995). This inevitable shift to English has been characteristic of every previous immigrant group (Veltman, 1983; de la Garza et al., 1992; Portes and Schauffler, 1996).

The social issues of the newest immigration go beyond language, however. Some Euro-Americans see the entrance of large numbers of non-Europeans as a threat to what, in their view, is the essence of the American social fabric (Brimelow, 1995). The new groups, with their cultural and physical distinctness, are viewed as unassimilable and thus a continual drag on the society. African Americans have also reacted in some cases negatively to immigrants, perceiving the new groups as a threat to their traditional segment of the labor market (Beck, 1996; Portes and Stepick, 1993; Warren and Stack, 1986).

---

[9]By 1995 more than twenty states had passed legislation to that effect.

The absorption of immigrants has been a persistent issue of American social history. In one sense, the United States has always been regarded as a golden door, open to all seeking economic opportunity or political refuge. But the acceptance of new groups has been countered with a tradition of protectionism, which has manifested itself repeatedly in efforts to limit or exclude newcomers for both economic and ethnocentric motives (Marger, 2000). The current controversy is, therefore, only the latest in a long tradition.

Summary

Race and ethnicity are systems of classification in which statistical categories are created on the basis of perceived physical characteristics (race) or cultural characteristics (ethnicity). Ethnic groups are defined on the basis of shared cultural traits, a perception of community, and what is believed to be a shared heritage. Contrary to popular belief, races are not biologically fixed groupings but are socially constructed categories, subject to historical and contextual change.

The American ethnic configuration is extremely diverse and becoming more so. Currently Euro-Americans constitute the largest component (about three-quarters) with African Americans 12 percent. The two groups that are growing most rapidly are Hispanic Americans and Asian Americans. It is possible that by the middle of the twenty-first century, the United States will be a majority-minority society, with Euro-Americans making up less than 50 percent of the population.

Changing patterns of ethnic diversity and inequality have occurred over the course of U.S. history. The British established themselves as the dominant group, setting the cultural and political tone of the society. Euro-American, Hispanic American, and Asian American groups entered mostly as voluntary immigrants. Native Americans, by contrast, were conquered, and African Americans entered involuntarily as slaves. Entering groups experienced prejudice and discrimination in different degrees and displayed different patterns of social and economic adaptation.

The United States opened a new era of mass immigration in 1965 that continues to the present. Most of the new groups are non-European, mainly from Asia and Latin America. Their economic and social impact has been debated, much as the impact of previous immigrant waves was the subject of public controversy.

11

Racial/Ethnic Stratification

[T]he great social question of the new millennium is less likely to be "can we all get along?" than "can we all get ahead?"
CHRISTOPHER H. FOREMAN JR.

In no multiethnic society are ethnic groups unranked and rewarded equitably. The historical development of ethnic inequality in the United States, therefore, has a counterpart in all multiethnic societies. A hierarchical arrangement of ethnic groups emerges in which one establishes itself as the dominant group, with maximum power and prestige. Other, subordinate, ethnic groups exert less power and receive less of the society's rewards, corresponding to their place in the hierarchy, extending down to the lowest-ranking groups, which may wield little power and receive little in the way of rewards.

Group rank is determined mainly on the basis of distance from the dominant ethnic group in culture and in physical appearance. Those most like the dominant group are more highly ranked, and those markedly different are ranked lower. A system of **ethnic stratification** is a rank order of groups, each made up of people with presumed common cultural and physical characteristics, interacting in patterns of dominance and subordination. This chapter looks specifically at the American ethnic hierarchy and the way in which class stratification intersects with ethnic stratification.

Majority and Minority

Minority Groups

Ethnic stratification systems are made up of a dominant group (or groups) and minority groups. **Minority groups** are groups that, on the basis of their physical or cultural traits, exert less power and receive fewer of the society's rewards than does the dominant group. In a classic definition, sociologist

Louis Wirth defined a minority group as "a group of people who, because of their physical or cultural characteristics, are singled out from the others in the society in which they live for differential and unequal treatment, and who therefore regard themselves as objects of collective discrimination" (1945:347). Members of minority groups more commonly occupy poorer jobs, earn less income, live in less desirable areas, receive inferior education, exercise less political influence, and are subjected to various social indignities. These inequalities are, to some degree, the result of their social mark, that is, the physical or cultural features that distinguish them. And, as Wirth pointed out, minority group members are conscious of the fact that they are differentially treated.

It is important to understand that the sociological meaning of minority is not the same as the mathematical definition. Numbers have no necessary relation to a group's minority status. As mentioned in Chapter 6, for example, nonwhites in South Africa, though over 85 percent of the population, traditionally constituted a sociological minority. Essentially, minority groups are afforded unequal treatment because they lack the power to negate or counteract discriminatory treatment. Dominant or minority status is most clearly a result of differences in societal power.

Types of Minorities   In its sociological meaning, the term minority can be applied to a variety of social groups. In addition to ethnic traits, many other physical or behavioral characteristics are sufficient to set off groups from the society's mainstream, resulting in differential treatment. To equate minority groups only with highly visible ethnic groups fails to account for the many other types of minorities found in complex societies.

Sex, for example, is a distinguishable physical characteristic that in most societies serves to single out one group—ordinarily, women—for unequal treatment. Women throughout the world have rarely occupied positions of great political or economic power, have been barred from entrance into many occupations, and have been excluded from various areas of social life. Only in recent decades have these deeply rooted patterns of sex discrimination begun to change.

Physically challenged people—the blind, the deaf, those confined to wheelchairs, and so on—are another evident minority. Age, too, constitutes a physical feature that serves to set groups apart for differential and unequal treatment. In all societies, of course, certain limitations necessarily are placed on people according to their age; but in some cases, this differentiation and unequal treatment exceeds any rational explanation. Some workers are forced into retirement at age sixty-five, even if they remain capable of carrying out their occupational duties and wish to do so. Or certain occupations are denied those who exceed an arbitrarily selected age requirement. These are examples of age discrimination.

Groups might be singled out for differential treatment not on the basis of physical distinctions, but on the basis of their past or current behavior. Gays and lesbians are obvious examples, as are the mentally ill and ex-convicts. Those acknowledging homosexuality, past treatment for mental illness, or a prison record risk social exclusion and discrimination by employers, landlords, and law enforcement agencies (Sagarin, 1971).

For each of these groups, a belief system, or ideology, explains and justifies their differential treatment. They are deemed to be "inferior" in some way. These beliefs serve as devices to sustain unequal treatment.

Ethnic Minorities   Ethnic minorities are those groups singled out and treated unequally on the basis of their cultural or physical differences from the dominant group. In multiethnic societies, ethnic minority status is most significant because, more than any other minority status, it intersects most sharply with class. In the United States today, the groups that are especially prominent in terms of cultural and, in many cases, physical differences, are African Americans, American Indians, Asian Americans, and Hispanic Americans. These are the groups that have historically experienced the most serious forms of discriminatory treatment and about whom mythical belief systems have been created to justify such treatment.

For much of American history the belief system, or ideology, that has rationalized racial/ethnic inequality has been **racism.** This is essentially the belief that races are real (not social constructs) and that there are innate behavioral differences among members of each racial category. Groups can thus be ranked as superior or inferior (Nash, 1962; Montagu, 1972). The presumed superiority of some groups and inferiority of others is subsequently used to legitimate the unequal distribution of rewards.

Although applied most vehemently to African Americans, some variant of this ideology has been applied to other minority ethnic groups as well. Southern and eastern European groups (such as Poles, Jews, and Italians) who entered the society in large numbers during the late nineteenth and early twentieth centuries, for example, were commonly perceived as "races" and their innate inferiority was commonly assumed, often by social scientists.

Today, few in the academic world accept such beliefs, and they have waned significantly among laypersons as well (National Conference, 1995; Sniderman and Piazza, 1993). Most now view discrepancies in social achievement among ethnic groups more as cultural differences, not as biogenetic ones (Banton, 1970; Schuman, 1982). Nonetheless, racist ideology has proved tenacious, though modifiable in form and content, in multiethnic societies.

Although African Americans, Hispanic Americans, Asian Americans, and American Indians are the most noticeable ethnic minorities, remember that the treatment of minorities is relative and thus will vary from group to group and from time to time. Some groups may be consistently singled out and deprived of social rewards whereas others experience only minimal discriminatory treatment. Moreover, members of a particular group may encounter rejection and denial in some areas of social life but not in others.

Dominant Groups

The existence of minority groups logically implies a majority group. Most simply, the **dominant,** or majority, ethnic group is the group at the top of the ethnic hierarchy, with maximal access to the society's power resources, particularly political authority and control of the means of economic production.[1] This does not mean, of course, that all those classified as part of the dominant ethnic group enjoy equally great wealth and power advantages. It means only that members of the dominant ethnic group occupy *disproportionately* such positions. Consider American society, where Anglo Americans historically have been and, to a great extent, remain the dominant ethnic group. Obviously, not all members of this category are high-ranking officials of government or corporation executives. Nor are they all wealthy and holders of university degrees. They are, however, *disproportionately* holders of the most important positions in government and the economy and, compared with other ethnic groups, disproportionately attain more of the society's valued resources.

In addition to its greater economic and political power, the dominant group has much cultural power: Its norms and values prevail in the society as a whole and become the society's standards. Minority groups are expected to acculturate to the dominant group's customs and ideals. In American society, it is assumed that all groups will speak English, maintain Judeo-Christian ethics, abide by democratic principles, and accept capitalist values. Although specific facets of these cultural standards are transformed over the long run, such changes are slow, deliberate, and usually accompanied by controversy and open conflict. As noted in Chapter 10, the use of languages other than English in schools, businesses, and government, for example, is a hotly debated national issue.

The Relativity of Dominant Status and Minority Status

Group membership in a modern, complex society is rarely a simple matter of either-or but instead takes the form of combinations that often yield confusing and ambiguous statuses. Whether a person is part of the dominant group or a minority group depends in all cases on the social situation. In some instances, people will be part of one, and in other instances, they may

---

[1]I prefer the term *dominant* rather than *majority* since this avoids the tendency to think in numerical terms, especially in cases where the dominant group may be a numerical minority.

find themselves part of another. For example, Jews in American society are ordinarily designated a minority group. Yet from the standpoint of African Americans, who generally rank lower in economic class and prestige, Jews are part of the dominant Euro-American group.

The Origins of Ethnic Stratification

Patterns of dominance and subordination among ethnic groups characterize all multiethnic societies in the modern world. How does ethnic stratification arise, and why does it seem so inescapable?

Forms of Contact   Ethnic stratification systems are created by the movement of people across national boundaries bringing with them different languages and cultural systems, or by the establishment of new political boundaries. What may have been a relatively homogeneous society thus becomes more diverse. This can take place through several processes.

One group may establish dominance over others through *conquest*. European colonialism of the eighteenth and nineteenth centuries illustrates this pattern. Through greater military technology, the British, French, Spanish, Dutch, Belgians, and Portuguese conquered peoples in Asia, Africa, Australia, North America, and South America. Indigenous groups were brought under colonial rule and became economic appendages of the mother country. The ruling colonists became the dominant group, and the natives, the minority. The case of European settlers and North American Indians is an example of such contact and the subsequent establishment of dominant-minority relations.

Another means by which ethnic stratification can occur is *annexation*, a political occurrence in which a part or perhaps all of one society is incorporated into another. For example, after the transfer of territory at the conclusion of the war with Mexico in 1846, Mexicans living in those annexed areas became a minority, subject to the dominance of Anglo cultural and political institutions.

Voluntary immigration is the most common pattern by which ethnic groups come into contact with each other. This has traditionally been and remains the chief source of ethnic heterogeneity in all contemporary societies, including the United States and Canada. Each entering group finds its place in the ethnic hierarchy, with those furthest culturally from the dominant group starting at a lower level.

A recent instance of the emergence of dominant-subordinate relations as a result of voluntary immigration can be seen in western Europe. Following World War II, workers from southern European countries such as Italy, Portugal, Greece, Spain, Turkey, and Yugoslavia or from newly independent former colonies such as Algeria or Indonesia migrated to Germany, France, Switzerland, the Netherlands, and Belgium as these nations experienced their postwar industrial expansion. A similar voluntary immigration occurred in Britain with the entry of thousands of people from the newly independent countries of the British Commonwealth—India, Pakistan, Jamaica, and others (Castles et al., 1984). This population movement accelerated in the 1960s, leaving previously homogeneous western European societies with substantial ethnic communities made up of immigrants of vastly different cultures and physical characteristics. The upshot of the creation of these multiethnic societies has been the emergence of conflict and competition among ethnic groups and the development of dominant-minority relations. In Germany, for example, the foreign-born are 9 percent of the population, with Turks comprising the largest single group. Various forms of discrimination, not uncommonly involving violence, have been aimed at these groups, and obstacles to citizenship are daunting (Drozdiak, 1997).

Involuntary immigration involves the forced transfer of people from one society to another. The prime example is the slave trade starting in the seventeenth century that brought millions from Africa to work the cotton and sugar plantations of the United States, Brazil, and the West Indies.

Consequences of Contact   The way in which diverse ethnic groups initially come into contact has been shown to be a critical factor in the patterns of ethnic stratification that subsequently emerge.

Stanley Lieberson (1961) suggests two major types of contact situations. One involves the subordination of a native population by a more powerful migrant group. Here, long-term conflict is very likely. Native groups less powerful than the arriving colonials are left with few options other than resistance to the new social order imposed on them. The arrival of Europeans in North America, for example, ignited a continuous struggle between the indigenous Indian tribes and the more powerful settlers.

A second situation involves the subordination of a migrant population by an indigenous ethnic group. This typifies most voluntary and involuntary immigrations like those to North America; in such cases, the arriving groups are initially made subordinate to a resident dominant group. The arriving immigrants who followed the Anglo Americans were obligated to assimilate to that group's culture and to accede to its political and economic power.

Donald Noel (1968) has pointed out that there are additional factors following intergroup contact that give rise to and shape the eventual system of ethnic stratification. When they initially meet, divergent groups judge each other ethnocentrically, that is, in terms of their own culture. These judgements are usually negative, particularly if the groups are quite distant culturally or, perhaps, physically. *Ethnocentrism,* while a necessary precondition, is not by itself sufficient to bring about ethnic stratification. Groups may view one another negatively without dominant-subordinate relations emerging among them. What is further required is *competition* among the groups for the same scarce resources, like jobs and land. The more intense such competition, Noel points out, the greater the likelihood of ethnic stratification. Those with greater resources wind up higher on the ethnic hierarchy. The final prerequisite for the development of ethnic stratification is *differential power*. Unless one group can overpower another, there is no basis for a stable rank order of ethnic groups, even if there is competition and ethnocentrism among them. When there is a particularly wide power gap between competing and ethnocentric groups, the emergent stratification system is likely to be quite durable. Power breeds more power, and once established, the dominant group uses its power to obstruct the competition of other groups and to solidify its dominance.

In sum, Noel's theory postulates that competition for scarce resources provides the motivation for stratification, that ethnocentrism channels this competition along ethnic lines, and that differential power determines whether one group will be able to subordinate others (Barth and Noel, 1972).

The Intersection of Class and Ethnicity

Although ethnicity and class are distinct dimensions of stratification, they are closely interrelated. In virtually all multiethnic societies, people's ethnic classification becomes an important factor in the distribution of societal rewards and, hence, in their economic and political class positions. Put simply, power, wealth, and prestige are in some part a function of ethnicity. The ethnic and class hierarchies are largely parallel and interwoven. In all multiethnic societies, where people begin their quest for the society's rewards and what they ultimately achieve depend to a significant extent on their ethnicity.

If a person is a member of the dominant ethnic group, his or her way will not necessarily be unimpeded; being part of the dominant ethnic group as a result of the accident of birth does not, in itself, assure success. As noted earlier, obviously not all Anglo Americans, for example, are doctors, lawyers, corporation executives, and high-ranking politicians. Many people living in the hills of rural Appalachia who are Anglo Americans and whose ancestors extend back to the eighteenth century are among the poorest in the United States. What is important, however, is that for members of the dominant group, the ethnic factor is removed as an impediment to upward mobility; other factors, both individual and structural, will affect their fortunes, but ethnicity will not.

In the same way, of course, minority status does not mean that a person is automatically relegated to the bottom rungs of the class hierarchy. But the chances of winding up at the bottom are much greater for minorities. As we proceed down the ethnic hierarchy, we find increasing political powerlessness, lack of economic opportunity, and social discrimination and exclusion. The closer to the bottom of the hierarchy, the more difficult the path to social success in whatever form, regardless of other nonethnic social traits.

In short, the effect of ethnicity is that minority ethnic group members encounter barriers to the attainment of the various rewards of their society that dominant ethnic group members do not face.

This does not mean, however, that all minorities are affected to the same extent. For those who are members of low-ranking groups with high ethnic visibility—African Americans, for example—minority status may be the overriding determinant of their economic class. For other minorities more highly ranked and less visible—for example, Polish Americans or Irish Americans—ethnicity will be much less consequential. It is important to remember that there are *degrees* of minority status. The ethnic hierarchy in any society is rarely a simple two-part structure with a dominant group at the top and subordinate groups at the bottom. Minority groups occupy places on a continuum, and the impact of ethnicity varies among them. The question for minority group members is, then, "To what extent does ethnicity become a factor in the allocation of jobs, education, wealth, political influence, and all other life chances?"

Minority status does not necessarily indicate where in the class hierarchy a group's members *enter* the society but rather where they *remain* long after they have entered (Gans, 1967). Indeed, most groups, even those who immigrate voluntarily, enter collectively at or near the bottom. Some may rise very quickly, whereas others remain trapped at the bottom, generation after generation.

The American Ethnic Hierarchy

The American ethnic hierarchy today is broadly divided into three comprehensive tiers:

1. The top tier comprises Euro-American Protestants, for whom ethnicity has no real significance except to distinguish them from the remainder of the ethnic hierarchy.

2. The intermediate tier consists of Euro-American Catholics and Jews of various national origins and many Asians, for all of whom ethnicity continues to play a role in the distribution of the society's rewards and continues to influence social life, but in both instances, decreasingly so over time.

3. The bottom tier is made up of ethnic groups often defined in racial terms, for whom ethnicity today has the greatest consequences and for whom it continues to shape many of the basic aspects of social life. This includes African Americans, Latinos, Native Americans, and some Asians.

This ethnic hierarchy has remained essentially unchanged for the past century and a half. Although the distance between many of the groups has been reduced, their rank order has, with few exceptions, not been basically altered.

Perhaps the most important aspect of this three-part American ethnic hierarchy is that the gap between the bottom tier of groups and the other two is much greater than the gap between the top and intermediate tiers. In terms of socioeconomic status, prestige, and access to power, the division between tier one and tier two is fading. Differences in wealth, prestige, and power are far more steadfast, however, between tier three and the other two. The overriding issues of American ethnic relations, therefore, remain focused on the economic, political, and social disparities between these ethnic categories and the policies intended to reduce them. Some of these issues are addressed later in this chapter.

The Bases of the Hierarchy   Arranging ethnic groups in such a rank order, of course, masks the more specific class and cultural differences among them as well as the internal differences within each. But in a very general sense, each of the society's ethnic groups can be placed on this hierarchy on the basis of a combination of several factors:

- The place of the group on the society's economic hierarchy
- The place of the group in the society's political power structure
- The extent to which prejudice and discrimination remain significant for the group
- The extent to which group members have entered into full social participation with those of the dominant group[2]

Let's look at each of these factors.

Ethnicity and the Economic Hierarchy

Individual members of various American ethnic minorities will be found at all points on the occupation, income and wealth, and education hierarchies. Looking specifically at occupation, we find, for example, African American doctors, Jewish American construction workers, Mexican American engineers, and Anglo American kitchen workers. But these combinations of ethnicity and occupation are not typical. It would be more common to find Jewish American doctors, Mexican American construction workers, Anglo American engineers, and African American kitchen workers. Ethnic groups tend to concentrate in particular areas of work, especially as they enter the society, and these patterns may remain evident for several generations. In the United States in the 1830s and 1840s, Irish workers built the canal system. In

---

[2]Using a combination of these factors means that some will offset others. For example, although Jews and Asians rank higher than northwestern Europeans in their aggregate economic class position, they still do not fully interact at the primary level with those groups, and the extent of prejudice and discrimination directed against them is much greater. Hence, when all these factors are considered, Jews and Asians are part of the intermediate tier of groups rather than the top.

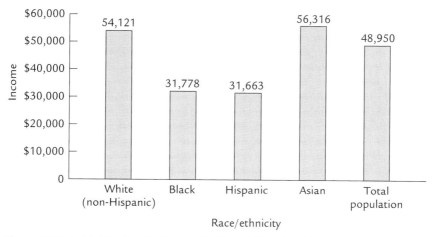

Figure 11-1 ■ Median Family Income by Race/Ethnicity, 1999
Source: U.S. Census Bureau, *Money Income in the United States: 1999*. CPR P60-209.

the second half of the nineteenth century and the early twentieth century, Italians were heavily represented in building construction, Jews in the garment trades, and Slavs in the steel industry. Racially defined ethnic groups such as African Americans remained overwhelmingly in the least advanced sectors of the economy, as agricultural and service workers. Though ethnic groups today are far more occupationally dispersed, the remnants of these earlier patterns are still evident. In the same way, newer ethnic groups display much occupational concentration.

In addition to occupation, other aspects of economic class—education, income, and wealth—are closely linked to ethnicity. Those most highly educated, those earning the highest incomes, and those possessing the greatest wealth are statistically more likely to be members of the dominant ethnic group or members of ethnic groups closest to the dominant group in culture and physical appearance.

Figures 11-1 through 11–4 as well as Table 11-1, show this relationship. They also demonstrate the economic gap referred to earlier regarding the place of the third-tier groups relative to the others. Figure 11-1 shows that median family income for African Americans and Hispanic Americans is less than 60 percent of white (non-Hispanic) income.[3] Table 11-1 shows that on average, black wealth and Hispanic wealth are each one-tenth the size of white wealth.[4] Recall that wealth is even more important as a key to upward

---

[3]Figures for American Indians are not shown because available data are not entirely comparable to those for other groups. In 1990, the latest year for which data are available, the median family income for American Indians was $21,619, about half the national median family income.

[4]In this chapter, the terms "black" and "white," rather than "African American" and "Euro-American" are sometimes used simply because those are the descriptive terms used by the U.S. Census Bureau in reporting socioeconomic differences among racial and ethnic groups.

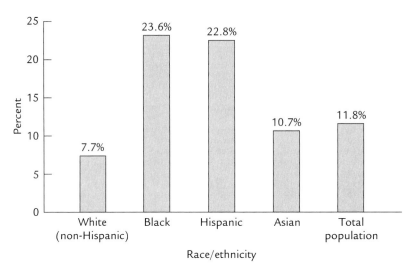

Figure 11-2 ■ Persons in Poverty, by Race/Ethnicity, 1999
Source: U.S. Census Bureau, *Poverty in the United States: 1999.* CPR P60-210.

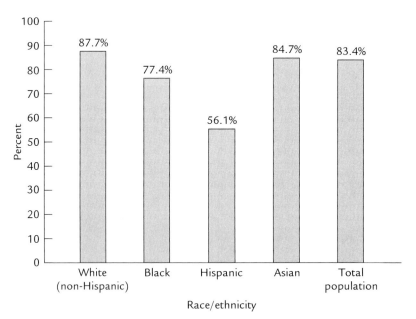

Figure 11-3 ■ High School Graduates, by Race/Ethnicity, 1999
Source: U.S. Census Bureau, *Educational Attainment in the United States: March 1999.*
CPR P20-528.

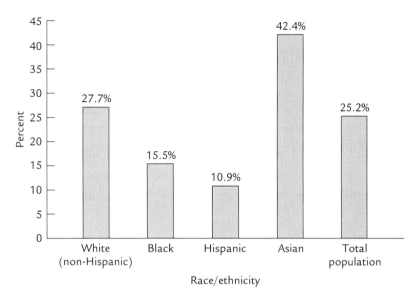

Figure 11-4 ■ College Graduates (Bachelor's Degree or More), by Race/Ethnicity, 1999
Source: U.S. Census Bureau, *Educational Attainment in the United States: March 1999.*
CPR P20-528.

Table 11-1 ■ Household Wealth, by Race/Ethnicity, 1993

	White	**Black**	**Hispanic**
Median net worth	$45,740	$4,418	$4,656
0 or negative net worth	9.8%	25.6%	24.3%

Source: U.S. Census Bureau, *Asset Ownership of Households: 1993.* <http//www.census.gov/hhes/www/wealth/html>.

mobility than is income. The possession of wealth, regardless of income, relieves families of dependence on others and furthermore can be passed on from parents to children. Thus, even if aggregate income between dominant and minority groups were not sharply different, white families would be at a significant advantage for they start with more in assets (Landry, 1987; Oliver and Shapiro, 1995). This also means that black middle-class families are in a more precarious financial state than are white middle-class families. Whereas the latter may be able to withstand a loss of job or a temporary layoff, given their assets, black families in a similar situation are apt to lose quickly much of what they have gained.

African Americans

The aggregate difference in socioeconomic status between African Americans and Euro-Americans is especially apparent: African Americans exhibit much higher rates of poverty, unemployment, and low income. They are also underrepresented in jobs at the top of the occupational hierarchy and overrepresented at the bottom. These discrepancies, however, must be viewed in a historical context. In some ways, despite the collective gap between whites and blacks, there has been a significant movement in the direction of greater equity over the past several decades. One must remember that until well into the 1960s, a system of direct and intentional discrimination effectively thwarted efforts of African Americans to compete with Euro-Americans for jobs and wealth. When considered in that light, there are grounds for both positive and negative views regarding the socioeconomic status of African Americans.

Regarding income, it is clear that the status of black families has improved markedly during the past five decades. And the enormous expansion of the black middle class is undeniable. The negative view arises, however, in considering the gap between median black income and median white income: It has remained relatively constant since 1950. In 1999 median black family income was 59 percent of median white (non-Hispanic) family income; in 1950 it was 54 percent. Similarly, the percentage of blacks below the poverty line remains three times greater than the percentage of whites.

Education, as discussed in Chapter 6, is a key life chance, arguably the most critical. Blacks have almost reached parity with whites in median years of schooling completed, and substantial gains have been made in black college attendance and graduation. In 1980, 8 percent of adult blacks had earned at least a bachelor's degree; by 1999, more than 15 percent had done so (U.S. Census Bureau, 2000b). On the negative side, however, the quantity of education is not necessarily commensurate with its quality. Despite the narrowing differential in years of schooling, black achievement continues to lag behind white achievement at all school levels and regardless of social class (Farley and Allen, 1987; Jencks and Phillips, 1998; Thernstrom and Thernstrom, 1997; U.S. Department of Education, 1992).

These aggregate figures should not obscure the fact that comparisons between black income and white income are subject to a number of factors, including region and urban location. In a few communities, black median income has actually surpassed that of whites (*New York Times*, 1994). More important, the African American population is polarized between relatively stable middle- and working-class families on the one hand and those in poverty on the other. The substantially greater percentage of blacks over whites below the poverty line accounts in large measure for the general differences between income patterns for blacks and whites. The gap between whites and blacks with higher education has diminished considerably, and for black women it has virtually disappeared (Farley, 1993).

Another important factor accounting for the income disparity between blacks and whites are changes in the African American family structure. Families that have experienced income increases have been dual-breadwinner families, among which only slight differences exist between blacks and whites. Similarly, the halt in the relative rise of black income from the late 1970s through the early 1990s is largely attributable to the increasing number of female-headed, single-parent families, who, as noted in Chapter 6, earn considerably less than husband-wife families (Farley, 1993).

Explaining the Economic Gap between Whites and Blacks

The lingering economic gap between whites and blacks (and, to some extent, between whites and Latinos) has prompted debate among sociologists: Is this persistent gap attributable to lingering racism, is there something unique about the African American experience that contributes to the group's continued plight, or are there deeper structural forces that impede the attainment of economic equality?

In considering this issue, remember that the black population is by no means homogeneous in terms of economic status. Indeed, some have suggested that there are really "two black Americas"—one that has established itself solidly within the middle and working classes, and one that is isolated and not fully part of the mainstream workforce (Gates, 1998). The latter is the black underclass, or ghetto poor, and constitutes perhaps one-third of the total black population (Hochschild, 1995; Kaus, 1995; Wilson, 1980). What is really being analyzed, then, is the persistence of a much larger low-income proportion of the African American population, compared to the Euro-American population.

Continued Prejudice and Discrimination   Some see the economic gap between whites and blacks as the result of continued discrimination in labor and housing markets (Hacker, 1995; Pinkney, 1984; Steinberg, 1995). Andrew Hacker, for example, takes this position: "To be black in America is to know that you remain last in line for so basic a requisite as the means of supporting yourself and your family. More than that, you have much less choice among jobs than workers who are white" (1995:110). The idea is that whites still harbor negative stereotypes of blacks, which prevents full acceptance of blacks into the workforce. Employers, for example, often see blacks as less dependable and less trustworthy than other ethnic groups and, even for low-skill jobs, prefer to hire immigrants (Wilson, 1996).

In a related argument, Douglas Massey and Nancy Denton (1993) point to the continuation of residential segregation as preventing the movement of blacks out of inner-city ghettos where decent jobs are scarce or where there is no accessible transportation to areas where jobs do exist. Residential segregation is sustained, they argue, by the continued intransigence of whites to accept more than a token representation of blacks in primarily white suburban neighborhoods.

Group Culture   Others see the continued high proportion of poor blacks as the product of a dysfunctional ghetto culture. This is a variant of the culture-of-poverty thesis, discussed in Chapter 6. The essential idea is that blacks living in a ghetto subculture find it difficult to thrust themselves out of that environment and to take advantage of available opportunities. The environment to which observers refer is one in which there are mostly families without fathers, neighborhoods infested with drugs and crime, and residents heavily dependent on welfare. Perhaps most important, the work ethic has disappeared. The underclass—not entirely, but primarily, black—therefore lacks the attitudes that lead to meaningful employment in the mainstream workforce (Kaus, 1995). The solution, in this view, is to instill a work ethic and a sense of personal responsibility and initiative among the underclass, suggesting a kind of self-help approach (Puddington, 1992).

Economic Restructuring   Still others see the lag of poor blacks economically as more structural than the result of either white racism or cultural failures. William Julius Wilson has addressed the issue most directly in this way. His position is that although discrimination based on race accounted for the denial of necessary economic resources to African Americans in earlier times, the traditional patterns of black-white interaction have been fundamentally altered so that class factors are today the dominant influence on African American life chances (1980, 1987, 1996). It is the poverty population, of which African Americans make up a disproportionate percentage, that has borne the negative consequences of economic restructuring. As explained in Chapter 4, the American economy has changed radically, tossing aside those who lack the skills necessary to compete in an increasingly high-tech workforce or forcing them permanently into dead-end, low-paying jobs. Thus, lower-class, unskilled African Americans have become a redundant labor force that is becoming a permanent underclass. The labor market today calls for jobs requiring technical and educational skills, for which such persons cannot qualify. Moreover, industry and commerce have moved to areas on the urban fringe so that any available entry-level jobs are outside the range of the central city where most low-income African Americans live. The result is a semipermanent state of unemployment.

The lack of job opportunities creates a vicious cycle in which blacks are forced to remain in inner-city ghettos, attending inferior schools and thereby reinforcing their disadvantaged position in the labor market. Moreover, high rates of joblessness, Wilson explains, "trigger other neighborhood problems that undermine social organization, ranging from crime, gang violence, and drug trafficking to family breakups and problems in the organization of family life" (1996:21).

Hispanic Americans

As part of the third tier of groups in the American ethnic hierarchy, Hispanic Americans rank well below average on all measures of class: income, occupation, and education. Keep in mind, however, that there are important differences among the three major Latino groups: Cubans are highest in socioeconomic status, followed by Mexicans in the middle, and Puerto Ricans at the bottom.

As seen in Figure 11-2, more than 20 percent of all Latino families fall below the official poverty line, three times the percentage for non-Hispanic white families. As with income, however, there is a range among the three major groups: 26.7 percent of Puerto Rican families and 24.4 percent of Mexican-American families were in poverty in 1999, compared to only 11 percent of Cuban families (U.S. Census Bureau, 2000f).

The low income and high poverty rates of Latinos, particularly Mexicans and Puerto Ricans, reflect their generally lower occupational levels. Except for Cubans, Latinos are underrepresented in the higher-status occupational categories and overrepresented in the lower ones. They also exhibit high unemployment rates.

Although employment discrimination has historically been a factor for particular groups, especially Mexicans in the Southwest and Puerto Ricans in New York, today low levels of education and their relatively recent entry into the labor force seem most critical in accounting for the relatively low levels of income and occupation of Latinos. Large proportions of all Latino groups have immigrated to the United States since 1950 (Massey, 1981). As latecomers to the American post-industrial economy, they have necessarily taken the least-skilled and lowest-paying jobs. Like African Americans, Latinos have become a disproportionately large part of the most expendable element of the workforce: those lacking the requirements for positions above the semiskilled or unskilled levels. Moreover, as an unusually young population, Mexican Americans and Puerto Ricans are most likely to lack marketable skills and work experience.

Education, however, appears to be an even more important factor in explaining the lower income and occupational positions of the Hispanic population. As the gap grows between those with higher education and those without, Latinos have been especially hard hit, given their relatively lower educational levels in general and the group's low proportion of members with a college education in particular (Carnoy et al., 1993). Language, too, is a critical barrier to upward mobility for Latinos, so many of whom are first-generation immigrants (Goldberg, 1997).

Despite their low aggregate economic standing, some see Latinos following a path toward upward mobility more in line with the past experience of
Euro-Americans, particularly those of the second wave of immigration, the
southern and eastern Europeans (Chavez, 1991).

Asian Americans

One of the most striking features of Figures 11-1 through 11-4 is the high ranking of Asian Americans compared to the other ethnic categories. Put simply,
Asian Americans rank higher than most ethnic groups in family income,
occupational prestige, and level of education. As is seen in Figure 11-1, Asian
median family income is substantially in excess of family income of other ethnic categories, even Euro-Americans. Asian Americans are more heavily represented in white-collar occupations and less represented in blue-collar occupations than are non-Hispanic white men. Especially noteworthy is the fact
that 37 percent of Asian American males are managers or professionals, compared with 32 percent of non-Hispanic white males (U.S. Census Bureau,
2000g).

Perhaps the most astonishing statistic regarding the socioeconomic status
of Asian Americans is level of education. Not only are they significantly
higher in number of years of education (Figures 11-3 and 11-4), but in terms
of academic achievement, Asian American students are above average on almost every measure. For example, Asian American high school students
score higher than students from any other ethnic category in mathematics
scholastic aptitude tests and are second only to whites on verbal aptitude
tests (U.S. Department of Education, 1992). Predictably, Asian students enter
top universities far out of proportion to their numbers.

In looking at the comparatively high class position of Asian Americans,
two caveats are in order. First, this is a diverse ethnic category, and as with
Hispanic Americans, there are differences among specific groups as well as
among members of the same group. Vietnamese and other Southeast Asian
groups are considerably lower in income, occupation, and education than
other Asian American groups. For example, although nearly half of employed Asian Indians are professionals or managers, less than 20 percent of
Vietnamese are in such occupations. The income and educational levels of
Southeast Asians are also considerably lower than those for other Asian
American groups. Almost half of all Cambodian families, for example, are below the poverty line (U.S. Census Bureau, 1993a). The Asian American population, then, appears in a kind of bipolar distribution on the class hierarchy,
well above average or well below.

Second, as noted in Chapter 10, the Asian American population consists
of two historical components, those who immigrated as early as the
mid–nineteenth century and those who have come since 1965. Many of the
more recent Asian Americans have come with class and educational back-

grounds considerably higher than those of earlier times. They have therefore raised the collective level of the entire Asian American category. Still, the contemporary Asian American experience has been marked by an unusual degree of high achievement.

Explaining High Asian American Achievement   Attempts to explain the extraordinarily high rates of Asian American mobility, educational attainment, and social adaptation take several different lines of thought. Some sociologists and psychologists point to cultural factors. Stressed in this explanation are values that emphasize the importance of education and the cohesiveness of the family. Studies that have taken this approach seem to converge on one point: Asian Americans are prepared to work arduously and, in turn, are able to instill in their children a great motivation to work hard (Kim, 1981; Light and Bonacich, 1988; Stevenson and Stigler, 1992).

That cultural factors are of key importance in explaining Asian American educational and economic success is suggested by a study conducted by University of Michigan researchers investigating the social and economic adaptation of Vietnamese refugees. At the time of their arrival in the United States, most of the subjects of this study had completed little formal education, few had any marketable skills, and only one in a hundred spoke fluent English. The researchers found that, despite these handicaps, many had achieved economic independence after only a few years. Furthermore, whatever success they had realized was almost entirely a product of their own efforts; the assistance of outside agencies had played a very limited role. The academic achievement of school-age children from these families was even more remarkable. Despite their severe language deficiencies and family poverty, after an average of only three years, they were experiencing success in American schools. This rapid educational success was found to be closely linked to a cluster of core values deriving from the Confucian and Buddhist traditions of East and Southeast Asia: education and achievement, a cohesive family, and hard work. These, the researchers found, were highly congruent with mainstream American values regarding the role of education in getting ahead (Caplan et al., 1989; Caplan et al., 1991).

A second explanation for high Asian American achievement recognizes the fortuitous fit between the opportunity structure of contemporary American society and the class background of the new Asian immigrants. Noted in Chapter 10 was the disproportionate number of highly skilled and educated individuals that comprise the Asian immigrant population. Hence, the existence of many doctors, engineers, and highly trained professionals among them is largely a function of their preimmigration class position. In some ways, then, today's Asian immigrants represent a select subset of the population of their origin societies. Such people recognize the more abundant opportunities to employ their skills and training in the United States and also the possibility of earning substantially more income. Many are not poor, underprivileged immigrants but are already imbued with achievement-oriented values and possess the class qualifications to implement those values. Structural opportunities, therefore, in addition to a cultural heritage compatible with American achievement values, are critical in accounting for the relatively rapid success of so many Asian Americans.[5]

Native Americans

Wherever Native Americans reside, on reservations or in urban areas, they are below the national average on most socioeconomic measures. Median family income is well below average, and the percentage of families in poverty is two and one-half times greater than average. The social and economic conditions on reservations are especially dismal and remain resistant to significant change. Three of the ten poorest counties in the United States are Sioux reservations in South Dakota.

Of particular consequence is the serious Native American unemployment rate. Inadequate educational preparation and, on reservations, geographical isolation have contributed to extremely severe employment problems. Native Americans commonly find themselves without the skills and qualifications to secure steady jobs. Thus the impoverished status of many Native Americans continues from one generation to the next.

Regarding education, Native American students have a relatively high dropout rate compared to other ethnic groups, and their achievement levels are among the lowest (U.S. Department of Education, 1991). More than any other factor, the low level of human capital among Native Americans, primarily in the form of education, accounts for the socioeconomic discrepancy between Indian and white populations (Waters and Eschbach, 1995).

Economic insecurity and low educational achievement translate into other forms of deprivation and long-term problems, including low health standards, high rates of alcoholism and suicide, and high crime rates (Garrett, 1994; Grobsmith, 1994; McCoy, 1994; Worsnop, 1992).

Although the differences between Native Americans and the remainder of the population are wide, progress has been made in recent years in closing the gap, particularly in improving health and educational standards. The numbers of Native American students attending college and pursuing graduate and other professional degrees, for example, have steadily risen. Nonetheless, there remains a glaring socioeconomic discrepancy between

---

[5]Some people even believe that Asians are innately superior to other ethnic groups. An eminent pediatrician, for example, suggests that Chinese and Japanese babies are more alert and sensitive at birth, making them faster learners (Butterfield, 1986). Few social scientists acknowledge the validity of such biological arguments, whether applied to seemingly high-achieving or low-achieving groups.

Native Americans and the larger society. One reason for this continued gap is that government policies and favorable court decisions aimed at improving the quality of life of Native Americans have mainly affected tribes living on reservations; left unaffected are the more than half of all Native Americans who live not on reservations but in urban areas (Nichols, 1992).

Ethnicity and Power

The power dimension of stratification entails the extent to which people are able to affect others through their actions in positions of authority. This kind of power ordinarily occurs within two realms: government and the corporation. In considering the relationship of power and ethnicity, then, we need to look at the extent to which members of different ethnic groups occupy top decision-making positions in these institutions.

Government   There is a lengthy U.S. history of resistance to the efforts of minority ethnic groups to attain political equality. Through immigration quotas and exclusionary measures, Indian-removal acts, slave laws, institutionalized segregation, antilabor regulations, voting restrictions, and an array of other measures, dominant interests have traditionally been protected. Throughout American history, of course, these policies have all generated great controversy and conflict, and minority challenges have often met with success. But concessions wrested from the dominant group have always been slow, costly, and incremental.

 To observe that Euro-Americans have dominated American political institutions in the past and continue to do so today overlooks the sharp differences within this panethnic category and the different pace by which members of its various groups have penetrated the highest levels of political power. Southern and eastern European groups, for example, mostly Catholic and Jewish, began to enter high governmental positions in significant numbers only in the years after World War II. Consider that a Catholic was not elected president of the United States until 1960. Indeed, until recent decades, Catholics traditionally were underrepresented in all of the highest offices of the three branches of American government (Alba and Moore, 1982; Mills, 1956; Stanley et al., 1967). Today, Catholics are represented in Congress approximately in proportion to their share of the total population and experience no evident impediments to their entrance into top positions in any sphere of government.

 Jewish Americans were also denied full entrance into the political world in past eras, but in their case, too, this situation has been rectified in recent decades. Indeed, in some spheres, Jews are actually overrepresented, considering their minor proportion of the general populace. In the U.S. Congress, for example, Jews make up 10 percent of the Senate and over 6 percent of the House, despite the fact that Jewish Americans consti-tute no more than 2 percent of the total population (Hirschfeld, 2001). Changing public attitudes toward Jews in high office are revealed by a 1987 Gallup poll that indicated that 89 percent of Americans would vote for a well-qualified Jewish presidential candidate; only 46 percent had felt that way fifty years earlier (Gallup, 1982, 1988). The acceptance of Jews in higher politics is demonstrated as well by the fact that Jewish candidates are today commonly elected by overwhelmingly non-Jewish constituen-cies. The selection of Joseph Lieberman, an Orthodox Jew, as the vice-presidential candidate on the Democratic ticket in 2000 symbolically shat-tered any remaining barriers to Jewish American participation at the very highest levels of government.

Asian Americans, another tier-two ethnic category, have been slower to penetrate the world of political power. This is due in largest part to the fact that most of the Asian American population has entered the society only since 1965. Thus, they have not had sufficient time to build a power base within the American political system. Second, their numbers have not been as large as other ethnic categories, and furthermore, they are highly concentrated in just a few large states. Nonetheless, as their population base widens and as the newer immigrants experience progressive assimilation, Asian Americans are likely to play a more active political role, especially where they constitute a sizable proportion of the population or where they are a significant minority. In 1996, for example, a second-generation Chinese American was elected governor of the state of Washington.

Among the tier-three groups, the substantial increase in the number of African American elected officials in the past two decades is an indication of expanding political power. This is particularly so when compared with the virtual absence of African Americans in national politics during the early part of the twentieth century. By the mid-1990s, over forty African Americans were serving in the U.S. Congress. At the local level, the election of African American mayors in cities throughout the United States had become com-monplace. What's more, an increasing number had won election from ma-jority white districts or communities. In addition to a growing presence in Congress, by the 1990s African Americans had served as governor of Vir-ginia, as national chairman of the Democratic Party, and as chairman of the Joint Chiefs of Staff, the nation's top military post. Perhaps most significant, several African Americans had been appointed to President Clinton's cabi-net. Moreover, for the first time, an African American had been given serious consideration as a presidential candidate.

Despite the increased number of African Americans elected and appointed to political office, it must be understood that they do not represent the numer-ical proportion of the U.S. black population or that of any individual state. African Americans still constitute less than 2 percent of all elected officials in the United States (Joint Center for Political and Economic Studies, 1994).

Hispanic Americans have not yet seemed to mobilize as effectively as African Americans, and their political power is still in its primary stages. As with Asian Americans, many are immigrants who are not naturalized citizens and thus cannot vote. Nonetheless, Latinos are a growing political force, especially in cities and states where they constitute a large portion of the population, like Los Angeles, Miami, New York, Chicago, and Houston (Maharidge, 1998). Nineteen members of the 107th U.S. Congress were Latinos, most of them representing heavily Latino districts (Hirschfeld, 2001). Hispanic political power at the national level seemed to reach a new high during the Clinton administration when two Mexican Americans were appointed to the president's cabinet.

The Corporate World Power in American society is certainly not limited to the governmental sphere. In the economic realm, key societal decisions regarding jobs, incomes, the standard of living, and the society's general economic condition are made by executives of the giant corporations. Here the dominance of Euro-Americans is much more thorough than in the political world. Clearly, the ethnic origins of American business leaders have been and remain primarily those of the tier-one groups (Alba and Moore, 1982).

In recent years, however, tier-two groups have begun to penetrate corporate elites in significant numbers. Jewish Americans, for example, were historically limited to high positions in the corporate world only through the growth of their own companies rather than by climbing the organizational ladder of well-established firms. Although some maintain that this traditional pattern of discrimination has not entirely ended (Korman, 1988), others indicate that it has changed significantly, with Jews increasingly entering the top executive positions of major corporations (Klausner, 1988; Silberman, 1985; Zweigenhaft, 1984, 1987; Zweigenhaft and Domhoff, 1998a).

For third-tier groups, entrance into corporate executive positions has been more limited. Few African Americans serve on the boards of directors or in top-level executive posts of the largest corporations, and these few are often token rather than bona fide decision-making appointments (Jones, 1986). Despite these limitations, African Americans continue to increase their presence in executive and managerial positions, small though their numbers are (Williams, 1995).

The role of Latinos in the corporate world has also been limited. Only a few dozen Hispanics are on the boards of directors of the largest firms, and fewer than two hundred are at the vice presidential level or above (*Hispanic Business*, 1995). Although Hispanic-owned firms are growing in number and economic significance, most of those owned by Mexican Americans or Puerto Ricans are small, family-operated businesses (Fitzpatrick, 1980; O'Hare, 1987). Cuban Americans play a very significant role in the Miami business world, where they have helped to develop trade and banking ties to Latin

American countries. Their economic power, however, remains a local phenomenon and does not translate into national influence within the corporate economy.

Asian Americans are underrepresented in corporate managerial positions despite their comparatively large numbers in professional and technical positions. And, at the very top of the corporate ladder, their numbers are as small as for African Americans and Hispanic Americans. In 1990, only 0.3 percent of senior corporate executives were Asian Americans (U.S. Commission on Civil Rights, 1992). Asian Americans have often spoken of a glass ceiling, referring to the limits to which they are able to rise in the corporate world (Pollack, 1992). Despite their small numbers at the executive level, the extraordinarily high level of education of most Asian Americans will likely accelerate their movement into top management positions at a faster rate than other minorities. Furthermore, as the number of Asian Americans in the general population grows, corporations will find it in their interest to seek out and place more Asian Americans into higher-ranking positions, much as they have done with African Americans and Hispanic Americans.

Richard Zweigenhaft and G. William Domhoff (1998a, b) have studied the socioeconomic backgrounds of top political and corporate leaders and conclude that executive positions of the corporate world and high-ranking political positions are in fact occupied today by a more ethnically diverse group than in the past. Nonetheless, regardless of ethnicity, the class requirements for membership in the power elite remain much the same: at least middle-class in origin and well above average in education, usually with a degree from a prestigious university.

Prejudice and Discrimination

Another basis of the ethnic hierarchy is the extent to which ethnic group members continue to be the targets of prejudice and discrimination. Widely held beliefs regarding the character and capacities of particular groups are necessary to assure the long-range maintenance of ethnic inequality. These beliefs and values take the form of **prejudices,** that is, negative ideas regarding subordinate ethnic groups and ideas expressing the superiority of the dominant group. These beliefs may come together in a cohesive ideology of racism, as was the case in the nineteenth and early twentieth centuries. At other times, however, they are applied to groups in a somewhat disparate, unsystematic fashion.

Perhaps more important than beliefs, the dominant group in an ethnic hierarchy applies actions against minority ethnic groups that create disadvantages for them in various areas of social, economic, and political life. These actions are collectively termed **discrimination.** Whereas prejudice is the attitudinal element in enforcing ethnic stratification, discrimination is the active, or behavioral, element. Although there is ordinarily a tendency for prejudicial attitudes to accompany discriminatory behavior, there is no necessary relation between the two (Merton, 1949).

The discriminatory actions that create disadvantages for minority group members may vary widely in both form and degree. Verbal discrimination, that is, using ethnic slurs or derogatory labels, is a relatively minor form. More serious forms with much greater consequences involve the denial of access to various life chances such as jobs, housing, health, education, justice, and political participation. The most severe forms of discrimination involve acts of aggression against ethnic minorities, ranging from isolated incidents of violence to *genocide,* the deliberate destruction of an entire group.

Individual and Institutional Discrimination   Discrimination is not always overt, nor does it always entail intentional actions of denial or aggression. Moreover, there is a vast difference between the isolated actions of individuals and the rational policies of institutions that create and sustain patterns of discrimination. The behavior of an apartment-building owner in refusing to rent to members of a particular ethnic group, for example, is hardly the equivalent of a corporation's policy of not hiring that group's members or of a government policy requiring separate public facilities for them. The first example is **individual discrimination**—actions carried out by individuals or small groups, usually in violation of the society's laws or norms. The latter examples illustrate **institutional discrimination,** which is the result of the policies and structures of organizations and institutions.

Individual discriminatory actions obviously continue to occur, particularly as they involve third-tier ethnic groups. In 1997, for example, skinheads in Denver, Colorado, beat to death a black person whom they encountered on the street, because, as they explained it, "he didn't belong there" (Murr, 1997). In the past, individual discriminatory actions against particular ethnic groups were commonly sanctioned by the society's normative code. To taunt with ethnic slurs, to harass, to threaten, or to commit violence against minority ethnic group members was simply a well-understood feature of the society. Today, however, such actions are no longer normative and those who carry them out are seen as deviants. Moreover, antidiscrimination laws are further disincentives to individual forms of discrimination.

Institutional discrimination occurs in more complicated and less easily understood forms. Such actions may be legal or customary, in which case they are not socially unexpected or disapproved but are legitimized. The Jim Crow system of the pre-1960s American South and the South African apartheid system, for example, were fully supported in law. The forced removal of Native Americans to lands west of the Mississippi in the nineteenth century and the internment of Japanese Americans in the 1940s are other historical illustrations of a consciously constructed policy designed to keep a minority in its subordinate place.

Sometimes institutional discrimination is unintentional and not the result of prejudicial beliefs or the deliberate establishment of rules seeking to withhold privileges or injure members of particular ethnic groups. Rather, it exists as a product of the normal functioning of the society's institutions. Because of past discrimination of an overt, intentional nature, or because of the spillover effect of intentional discrimination in one institutional area into another, certain groups find themselves perpetually at a disadvantage in the society's opportunity and reward structures (Feagin and Feagin, 1978). A large portion of the African American population, for example, is confined to inner-city areas. Because most new jobs are in the outlying suburbs and because of a lack of public transportation, these people find themselves at a disadvantage in the labor market. Note what has occurred here: No person and no organization has directly discriminated against inner-city African Americans, but residential segregation has produced a powerful discriminatory effect.

The most evident, persistent, and consequential form of institutional discrimination in American society occurs in the area of housing, and it affects groups of the third tier, particularly African Americans, more than others. What's more, the patterns of discrimination here are often deliberate, whereas in the areas of work and education de facto discrimination occurs indirectly as a result of spatial arrangements and demographic trends. It is well recognized that less progress in breaking down ethnic barriers has been made in housing than in other spheres of social life (Levitan et al., 1975; Massey and Denton, 1993; Pettigrew, 1979). Although the level of black-white residential segregation in the largest U.S. metropolitan areas has declined somewhat in recent years, the simple fact is that most African Americans, regardless of their social class or the geographic area in which they live, continue to reside in predominantly black neighborhoods (Farley and Frey, 1994). Although this pattern is partly the result of voluntary action, it has been well documented that much is the result of discrimination, both individual and institutional (Massey and Denton, 1993). In turn, residential discrimination produces, often unintentionally, institutional discrimination in other areas, like schools and jobs.

It is important to point out that the United States holds no monopoly on ethnic prejudice and discrimination. Comparable actions typify the history, current and past, of most multiethnic societies. Indeed, when looked at in historical and global perspective, the American experience at times seems mild. The nineteenth and twentieth centuries have witnessed occurrences of horrific ethnic violence and destruction in almost all world areas, including, among many others, the annihilation of native peoples in Australia and South Africa, the slaughter of over a million Armenians by Turks, the systematic murder by Nazi Germany of 6 million Jews, and, more recently, massacres of entire populations in Rwanda and Bosnia.

Social Integration

A final indicator of placement on the ethnic hierarchy concerns the extent to which groups remain socially segregated. Sociologists use the terms **assimilation** and **pluralism** to describe how completely members of particular ethnic groups interrelate with others in various spheres of social life. There are two dimensions of assimilation and pluralism: cultural and structural. **Cultural assimilation** refers to the adoption by the minority ethnic group of the dominant group's norms and values. **Cultural pluralism,** in contrast, refers to the retention of ethnic ways. **Structural assimilation** is the gradual integration of the minority group into the societal mainstream: entering into the workforce at all levels, occupying positions of political power, living in dominant-group neighborhoods, and, ultimately, intermarrying with the dominant group. The converse of structural assimilation is **structural pluralism,** in which minority ethnic group members remain socially apart from the dominant group. Assimilation and pluralism must be understood not as absolute conditions but as relative processes; that is, they occur in degrees and will vary from group to group and from individual to individual.

As explained in Chapter 10, all groups except Native Americans entered the society as immigrants, voluntarily or involuntarily. Most commonly, immigrants, following their arrival, begin to interact with out-group members and to adopt the ways of the dominant culture.[6] Obviously, groups and individuals experience this process at different rates. Some assimilate relatively quickly and without much difficulty, whereas others may remain apart from the societal mainstream for years, perhaps even for generations. Crucial to understanding assimilation are the cultural and physical differences between the minority ethnic group and the dominant group. Those groups more similar physically and culturally to the dominant group will be integrated into the mainstream more readily (Yinger, 1981).

The key measures of social integration are residence and intermarriage. In this aspect of the ethnic hierarchy, as with others, it is third-tier groups that are most negatively affected. As mentioned earlier, residential segregation remains persistent in American society, particularly the black-white pattern. For other groups, this phenomenon is evident but not nearly as tenacious (Farley and Frey, 1994; Langberg and Farley, 1985; Massey and Denton, 1993). As to marriage across ethnic lines, for Euro-American groups it has become so common as to be almost the norm (Alba, 1995; Lieberson and Waters, 1988; Waters, 1990). Hispanic Americans and Asian Americans are intermarrying

---

[6]As we earlier noted, rather than a unilateral process, there is actually an exchange of cultural traits between dominant and minority ethnic groups.

at lower, though increasing, rates. The intermarriage rate for African Americans is below that for all other ethnic groups, although it, too, is on the increase (Alba and Golden, 1986; Kitano and Daniels, 1995; Lieberson and Waters, 1988; U.S. Census Bureau, 1997d).

Stability and Change in the American Ethnic Hierarchy

As we have now seen, the American ethnic hierarchy consists of three tiers, with groups arranged according to where they stand in aggregate income and wealth, occupation, and political power, the degree to which they are the targets of prejudice and discrimination, and the extent to which they have been socially integrated into the mainstream society.

Clearly, the division between tier-one and tier-two groups is gradually evaporating, but the third tier of groups continues to maintain a markedly lower aggregate economic and social status. This is particularly the case for African Americans. But the status of ethnic minorities, especially African Americans, can be seen as a glass half full or a glass half empty.

Regarding the collective status of African Americans as well as other tier-three groups, it can be argued that greater progress has occurred in the past three decades than at any time in the society's history (Patterson, 1997). Stephan and Abigail Thernstrom (1997, 1998) explain that the persisting stereotype of African Americans as mostly being part of the economic underclass has contributed mightily to a failure to recognize the enormous changes that have taken place over the past five or so decades, especially the burgeoning of the African American middle class. In addition, studies have shown that whites are now less resistant to blacks in most areas of social life, and it is only in residence where resistance to black-white interaction remains strongly evident. This view of the hierarchy reflects a glass half full.

In another way, however, the glass can be viewed as half empty. Along with great progress, there is no denying that members of the third-tier groups remain disproportionately among the poor and the powerless. Moreover, in addition to economic disparities, the social boundaries separating the third tier from the first and second tiers, particularly African Americans from Euro-Americans, are dissolving only very slowly. Members of third-tier groups continue to encounter higher levels of prejudice and discrimination, and the extent to which they have been afforded entry into the full range of societal institutions remains lower than that afforded tier-one and tier-two groups. There are, then, significant economic and social gaps that remain evident between Euro-Americans and America's ethnic minorities.

Efforts at Changing the Hierarchy

The recognition of these economic and social gaps has given rise in recent decades to a number of highly controversial public policies. Recall (in Chapter

8) the ongoing societal debate in the United States between liberty and equity regarding the size and scope of the welfare state. American society, it was noted, is constantly engaged in a kind of battle between the forces of individual freedom and social equality. Those who feel that liberty should take precedence over equity argue that people must be left alone to lead their lives as they choose and to succeed or fail on their own efforts. This is to be done within the context of the free market. As was explained, however, the vagaries of the market unavoidably give rise to inequalities; as a result, there arises a counterforce in all modern capitalist societies that compels the state to intervene to some degree in the market in order to give people more opportunities to compete fairly. The end product of individualistic competition—inequality—is thus acceptable so long as there is assurance that the competition is fair and that everyone has an equal opportunity to win. It is the provision of those equal opportunities that therefore becomes critical.

Starting in the 1960s, it was recognized that the success of the civil rights movement, securing equal political and legal rights for African Americans, did not necessarily affect African American economic status. President Johnson, in announcing the federal government's intention to address this issue, put it this way: "You do not take a person hobbled by chains and liberate him, bring him up to the starting line of a race and then say, 'you are free to compete with all the others,' and still justly believe that you have been completely fair" (quoted in Skrentny, 1996:153).

It was acknowledged that African Americans had been systematically excluded from the mainstream society economically, politically, and socially and thus had been handicapped as a result of direct policies and customs. Other minority ethnic groups as well as women were subsequently added as target groups, the argument being that they, too, had been the victims of long-standing exclusion. Given generations of denied opportunities, was it fair to expect African Americans and other minorities to compete on an equal basis with the white—and essentially male—majority? How could these groups ever hope to catch up if they entered the competition burdened by decades of imposed disabilities and discrimination?

Affirmative Action

In response to the handicap imposed by past systematic discrimination, the federal government undertook sweeping measures to help bring about the economic improvement of African Americans and, later, that of other minority groups. These measures became known as **affirmative action.** As these policies evolved in the 1960s, they stipulated that those doing business with the federal government (universities as well as businesses) were required to take steps to increase their minority representation and to establish goals and timetables to meet that objective.

As with other aspects of affirmative action, there is disagreement about the effects these policies have had during the past three decades. One point about which most seem to agree is that affirmative action opened opportunities to qualified minorities to a degree and at a pace that would not have otherwise occurred. In particular, it is claimed, expansion of the African American middle class was stimulated. Even here, however, there is argument. Stephan and Abigail Thernstrom (1997) contend that economic opportunities for African Americans were opening quite rapidly even before the advent of affirmative action and in some ways actually slowed down once these policies were in place.

With more widespread and stringent application in the 1970s, affirmative action policies grew increasingly controversial (Skrentny, 1996). Public sentiment regarding these measures has been ambivalent, but in the 1990s, antipathy to affirmative action seemed to grow more popular and shrill. A 1995 national poll revealed that 79 percent of Euro-Americans opposed racial preferences in employment or college admissions (Fineman, 1995). Quite simply, most Euro-Americans had come to see such measures as "reverse racism" and in violation of the American creed. So negative was their view that, as political scientists Paul Sniderman and Thomas Piazza concluded, it had "led some whites to dislike blacks—an ironic example of a policy meant to put the divide of race behind us in fact further widening it" (1993:109). The lack of political support for affirmative action was abetted by the courts in a number of relevant decisions as well as by a referendum in California that called for the abolition of the use of affirmative action in all state hiring and university admissions.

The issue of affirmative action has prompted one of the most heated and politically volatile public debates in recent years, pitting those who favor the continuation of such policies against those who feel they should be abandoned. Let's examine the major points made by proponents and opponents of these policies.

Pro–Affirmative Action   Those who favor affirmative action build their case on a few critical points; namely, that these policies have accomplished what they were intended to do and that their need is still evident. Advancing the position of minorities through the use of goals and preferential hiring practices is necessary if the victims of past discrimination are eventually to attain equity with the majority (Kennedy, 1994; Taylor, 1997). Even if direct forms of discrimination no longer prevail, proponents point out, the indirect and institutional forms continue to perpetuate nonwhite (and female) disadvantages in the labor market and in higher education (Bergmann, 1996). Simply protecting minority individuals against ethnic or sex discrimination is therefore inadequate by itself. Hiring workers or admitting students without regard to ethnicity or sex will automatically preserve the disproportionate representation of white males because they enter the competition with background advantages accumulated over many generations. Artificial incentives for minorities are needed temporarily until the opportunity structure is made more truly equitable. Most important, proponents of affirmative action argue that without such policies, there is a risk of returning to an ethnic (and gender) norm of discrimination.

Some maintain that the critical importance of affirmative action lies in providing access for minorities to social networks that aid in securing better jobs and educational opportunities (Patterson, 1997). In this view, having education and skills is important, but even more important is being enmeshed in key networks, through which individuals find jobs, meet influential people, and learn bargaining skills (essentially much like the idea, explained in Chapter 6, of having social connections). Individuals may possess formal qualifications, but unless they are able to move into the inner circles of the educational and work worlds, their chances of moving into elite positions and top jobs are diminished. African Americans have lacked the connections, or what some have termed "social capital," ordinarily developed through ties made in universities, in the corporate world, or through intermarriage, that Euro-Americans have been able to avail themselves of more easily. Here is where affirmative action can play a role, casting African Americans and other minorities into networks that they otherwise would have little chance of penetrating (Loury, 1997; Patterson, 1998).

Anti–Affirmative Action   Those who oppose affirmative action programs or who strongly criticize the way they have been carried out argue that, in effect, these programs have become a kind of reverse discrimination in which those previously discriminated against are given preference over others merely on the basis of ethnicity (Glazer, 1975; Yates, 1994). Hence, opponents maintain, the very objective intended—reducing ethnic discrimination—has been undermined, the victims now being white males. Government is seen as re-creating racial and ethnic categories that had rightfully been abandoned. The effect of affirmative action in many cases has been to create quotas favoring minorities.

Another charge against affirmative action policies has been that they shift emphasis from equality of opportunity to equality of result, thus distributing social benefits on the basis of group membership, not individual merit. Less-qualified minority persons, as a consequence, may be promoted over better-qualified majority persons. Moreover, the targeted groups of affirmative action, it is argued, are stigmatized because of their special treatment, thus producing negative social and psychological effects on those who are supposedly the beneficiaries of these programs (Sowell, 1990). Shelby Steele (1991), for example, has suggested that affirmative action programs create a kind of implied inferiority. Whites commonly view blacks as having acquired their positions on the basis of special preference and, thus, as less than qualified or less than competent. This not only fuels negative stereotypes by whites, argues Steele, but also creates self-doubt among African Americans and other minorities.

In addition to charges of reverse discrimination and negative effects on employment and educational qualifications, affirmative action programs have been criticized as too sweeping in application and therefore unable to select out from among the various targeted minorities those who are in fact the past or present victims of discrimination (Schrag, 1995). For instance, although Latinos are covered under the principles of affirmative action, this broad panethnic category, as shown in Chapter 10, comprises several disparate components, each with different American experiences. Should Cuban Americans, who have not been discriminated against in work and education, be entitled to the benefits of these programs in the same way as Mexican Americans in the Southwest, who have been past victims of discrimination? Such problems suggest that minority group membership is no longer unambiguous. Moreover, many have pointed out that the major recipients of affirmative action benefits have been middle-class ethnic and gender minorities, not the "truly needy," that is, those in disadvantaged class positions. Filtering out those truly deserving of compensatory benefits has therefore become more complicated not only between various groups but within them as well.

Advocates of affirmative action have countered their detractors on these points. As to the lack of qualifications of those employed or admitted through preferential policies, proponents argue that "qualifications" can be variously interpreted, no matter how seemingly objective and valid tests or other sorting mechanisms may seem. They also point out that merit has never really been the sole criterion used in filling occupational and educational positions. Athletes have been given preference in university admission for decades, for example, as have veterans in applying for jobs. On the matter of quotas, it is argued that the objective of affirmative action is to facilitate the entrance of minorities into various institutions, not to keep them out, as was the purpose of earlier discriminatory quotas. And while opponents see racial minorities being stigmatized by affirmative action, defenders argue that their absence in jobs and schools would create an even greater stigma (Kennedy, 1994).

Affirmative Action and Societal Values   To see the issue of affirmative action as a fundamental split between Euro-Americans on the one hand and ethnic minorities on the other is too simple. National surveys have consistently indicated that a majority of Americans, regardless of ethnicity, support preferential policies as long as they are not perceived as "rigid quotas" (Harris, 1991a, 1991b; Morin, 1995). Even a significant percentage of African Americans are opposed to affirmative action measures when they take such form.

Opposition to affirmative action, then, must be seen as stemming not simply from prejudicial attitudes, but from a number of factors. People may oppose or feel resentment toward these policies not because they are antiminority or wish to keep things as they are (surely many *do* oppose these policies for such reasons), but because they see them as fundamentally in violation of the value of fairness. In a number of ways, affirmative action is incompatible with some basic tenets of the dominant American ideology, individual achievement in particular. Affirmative action creates a system in which rewards are distributed on the basis of group membership, not individual merit, and substitutes group rights for individual rights. It also contradicts the popular belief in personal effort as the key to upward mobility. Finally, as they have been implemented, affirmative action policies have at times seemed to violate the belief in equality of opportunity, substituting instead equality of result.

The Future of Compensatory Policies   Just as the implementation of affirmative action has stimulated much controversy, the future of these policies has been subject to political debate. Again, to think of the issue as either a clear and simple "favor" or "disfavor" is too simple. Much of the debate revolves around whether these policies can, or should, be made more fair.

Some maintain that social class—not race or ethnicity—should be the major criterion by which people are deemed eligible for compensatory advantages (Kahlenberg, 1996; Schrag, 1995) or that policies should be applied in a "race neutral" fashion (Wilson, 1994). Others maintain that such measures bring with them the same kinds of inherent problems as those based on race and ethnicity, that is, issues of determining who should be eligible and how they are to be chosen (Hacker, 1994; Kinsley, 1991).

Another confounding aspect of affirmative action concerns the very objective of such policies. They were originally intended to provide a temporary advantage to those ethnic minorities who had been the historic victims of systematic discrimination. As they evolved, however, their purpose was transformed into an effort to create schools and workplaces that resembled proportionately the ethnic makeup of the society, state, or community. So, is their purpose to help bring about greater equity among the society's diverse groups or is it to create more ethnic diversity within the society's major institutions? Efforts at attaining one of these objectives do not necessarily correspond to attainment of the other.

Rising political and social pressures seem to make it likely that the use of affirmative action will be scaled back and the actual content of these policies will be significantly reshaped. Yet it is unlikely that all forms of compensatory measures will be completely abandoned in the near future. Corporations, for example, recognize that recruiting more minority managers and workers is simply good business in an increasingly ethnically diverse society as well as a global economy (Glater and Hamilton, 1995). And most Americans seem to support some form of affirmative action so long as it does not involve special treatment to particular groups (Sniderman and Carmines, 1997).

Affirmative action, in sum, has emerged as one of the most vexing issues of ethnicity in America. Yet it is important to consider the widespread use of such measures in other multiethnic societies. Preferential policies designed to bring about more equity among diverse groups have been adopted in countries as divergent as Australia, India, Canada, and Malaysia. The problems revolving around this issue are not unique to the United States. As countries everywhere are transformed into multiethnic societies, ameliorating the inequitable distribution of societal resources among various ethnic groups has become an inescapable predicament.

Summary

Ethnic stratification systems are made up of dominant and minority groups. Minority groups receive fewer of the society's rewards on the basis of their physical or cultural traits. The dominant group is the group at the top of the ethnic hierarchy that disproportionately holds elite positions in government and the economy and generally possesses more of the society's valued resources. Also, the dominant group's norms and values become the society's standards.

Ethnic stratification is the product of contact between previously separate groups. The manner in which ethnic groups meet—through conquest, annexation, voluntary or involuntary immigration—is a critical factor in explaining the shape of the system of ethnic inequality that ordinarily ensues.

Ethnicity and social class are closely interrelated. In multiethnic societies, ethnicity becomes an important factor in the distribution of societal rewards and thus in the determination of people's class position. Members of minority ethnic groups are never randomly scattered throughout the economic and political class hierarchies but tend to cluster at specific points.

The American ethnic hierarchy can be viewed as divided into three comprehensive tiers: Euro-American Protestants constitute tier one, Euro-American Catholics and Jews of various national origins and many Asians make up tier two, and groups often defined in racial terms—African Americans, Native Americans, some Asians—as well as Hispanics make up tier three. Ethnicity is not a critical factor in social or economic life for those of tier one, but it remains important for those of tier two (though decreasingly so), and it has great social and economic consequences for those of tier three. The hierarchy is based on aggregate income and wealth, political power, extent to which prejudice and discrimination remain significant, and extent of participation in all societal institutions.

There is a wide gap between aggregate income and wealth of African Americans and Euro-Americans, for which there are several competing explanations. Hispanic Americans also generally lag behind Euro-Americans, but Asian Americans exceed Euro-Americans on most measures of social class. None of the three non–Euro-American ethnic categories have entered into political and corporate elites in proportion to their population.

Prejudice and discrimination are most consequential for non–Euro-American groups. Discrimination may take individual and institutional forms. The most persistent form of institutional discrimination today in the United States occurs in housing and affects groups of the third tier, particularly African Americans, more than others. Similarly, on key measures of social integration, third-tier groups are most affected, experiencing more persistent residential segregation and lower intermarriage rates.

Efforts to change the prevailing patterns of American ethnic inequality have centered on closing the economic gap between third-tier groups, particularly African Americans, and the larger society. Affirmative action measures have been the major public policy tool in addressing this issue. Proponents of affirmative action argue that such measures are necessary and productive and that there is much historic precedent for them. Opponents argue that they constitute a form of reverse discrimination, are too sweeping in application, stigmatize targeted groups, do not benefit those who most need help, and promote group rights over individual rights. Affirmative action policies appear to conflict with some basic elements of the American ideology, especially individual achievement.

12

Gender Inequality

If we want to assess and criticize women's disadvantages today, we usually compare their existing status with an imagined future when complete equality reigns . . . Alternatively, if we want to evaluate how women's social status has improved, we must turn in the other direction and face the past.
ROBERT MAX JACKSON

Real equality is going to come not when a female Einstein is recognized as quickly as a male Einstein, but when a female schlemiel is promoted as quickly as a male schlemiel.
BELLA ABZUG

Lee Un Kee lives in a tiny farming village in South Korea named Punsooilri, thirty miles from Seoul, the capital city. He has been married for twenty-four years. When asked if he has beaten his wife, he indignantly replies "How could I have been married all these years and not beaten my wife? Of course, you have to apologize afterward," he adds. "Otherwise, you can have bad feelings in your relationship with your wife." Chong Chin Suk, a fifty-six-year-old woman who runs Punsooilri's village store, admits that "Of course my husband beats me. But it was my fault because I scolded him." She explains, "Maybe there are some cases where it's just the man's fault. But ultimately the woman is to blame, because if she won't argue with her husband, he probably won't beat her." Speaking with other women in the village, it is apparent that wife-beating is quite commonplace in Punsooilri (Kristof, 1996b).

In 1996, a reactionary Islamic movement called the Taliban gained power in Afghanistan. Imposing what it interpreted as strict Islamic principles, the Taliban placed women into a state of virtual imprisonment. In Kabul, the country's major city, women were forbidden to work or to go to school. If they left their homes, they were ordered to wear garments that completely covered their bodies and concealed their eyes behind cloth mesh. If they did leave their homes, they ran the risk of being assaulted by militiamen who might deem their attire not sufficiently modest. "I'm very afraid to go out on the street," said a female surgeon. "It's terrible for a woman to be hit by a strange man" (Cooper, 1996).

Late one night in Lima, Peru, a group of drunken men in their twenties raped María Elena, a seventeen-year-old girl who was on her way home from work. In Peru, however, the law exonerates a rapist if he offers to marry the victim and she accepts. This creates a situation in which relatives of rape victims, particularly in poor and rural areas, put pressure on the girl to accept the rapist's offer. This course, they believe, will restore honor to the victim and her family. María Elena's family, though incensed by the attack, encouraged her to accept when one of the rapists offered to marry her. In some cases, the rapist threatens the victim if she refuses the offer. When María Elena first declined to marry one of her attackers, his two accomplices threatened to slash her face. Yielding to the threat and to pressure by her family, she finally relented. "What choice did I have?" she asked. "Everyone insisted that the way to solve the problem was for me to get married." Three months after the wedding, her husband abandoned her (Sims, 1997).[1]

In Jordan (and several other Arab countries), women or girls who have committed adultery or have had premarital sex are in some cases killed by their husbands, brothers, or fathers. These so-called "honor killings" are a means of restoring the family's status and dignity which, in the eyes of the community, have been severely tarnished by the woman's or girl's sexual behavior. The slayings are usually condoned by the society or punished only lightly. In Jordan, where more than twenty such incidents occur each year (one in four homicides in a country with a population of only four million), a man who is prosecuted and found guilty can be sentenced to as little as a few months in prison. The mother of one victim who was shot dead by her brother justified the killing: "We were the most prominent family, with the best reputation. Then we were disgraced. Even my brother and his family stopped talking to us. No one would even visit us. They would say only, 'You have to kill.' " Afterward, the slain woman's sister declared "Now we can walk with our heads held high" (Beyer, 1999; Jehl, 1999).

To most Americans these are shocking cases of discrimination against women. But such incidents are commonplace in much of the world. Most discrimination is not as blatant and abusive as these cases demonstrate, but male dominance, referred to as **patriarchy,** is virtually universal in the contemporary world.

This chapter looks at the nature of gender inequality and explores the ways in which men and women are treated differently in society. Examining gender inequality reveals an equivocal picture of both change and inertia. On the one hand, men everywhere outrank women and receive more of the

---

[1]There are similar laws pertaining to rape in fourteen other Latin American countries. In Costa Rica, the law exonerates a rapist if he offers to marry the victim, even if she does not accept.

society's rewards. In 1980 the United Nations reported that women, though one-half the world's population, did two-thirds of the world's work, earned one-tenth of the world's income, and owned one-hundredth of the world's property. Clearly, social, economic, and political inequality between men and women is a ubiquitous phenomenon. On the other hand, changes in women's subordinate status during the past three decades in the majority of the world's societies are equally obvious. In some cases the gap between men and women has narrowed dramatically in a relatively brief time. Both of these realities must be recognized.

Gender Differentiation

Sex and Gender

What is "gender"? And how does it differ from "sex"? These are commonly used terms, often without consideration for the important difference between them. Let's consider sex first. At birth, we are biologically male or female. Our sexual organs are different, our hormones and other aspects of body chemistry are different, and our biological functions are different: Women give birth; men do not. These relatively fixed physiological and biological differences are what define **sex.**

But the differences between men and women do not end here. They differ as well as a result of cultural, social, and psychological factors. These are differences acquired not through birth but through the socialization process. Every society establishes a set of accepted behaviors to which males and females are expected to conform. How are women expected to act, *qua* women? And, how are men expected to act, *qua* men? These are standards of femininity and masculinity and, as learned patterns of behavior, will vary from society to society; they are not fixed or constant. These socially and culturally determined differences are what constitute **gender.** In a very real sense, then, we are born male or female, but we must learn to be men and women.

Whether gender identity and gender roles stem from biological differences or are the product of historical, social, environmental, and technological circumstances, is a matter of intense debate among anthropologists and sociologists (Chafetz, 1978). Although few would hold that gender roles are entirely either biologically or socially determined, the prevailing social science position is that culture is the key to understanding most differences in male and female behavior. In this view, there is nothing "natural" about women playing nurturing occupational roles (like nurse or schoolteacher) or men playing more assertive and peremptory roles (like soldier or doctor). Gender differences are a product of socialization, discrimination, and other forms of social control (Epstein, 1988).

Proof of this position is found in the fact that women do not fill the same roles (spouse, mother, and so on) the same way from one society to another.

Moreover, the "correct" or expected behavior for males and females, that is, the standards that define masculinity and femininity, constantly undergo change. As social conditions change, gender roles will change accordingly. Anthropologist Marvin Harris points out that evidence from primate studies indicates that there is no hormonal barrier "that would prevent women from learning to be more aggressive than men if the exigencies of social life were to call for women to assume aggressive gender roles and for men to be more passive" (1989:266). This is already beginning to occur in modern societies as men take on more child-rearing responsibilities, calling for more nurturant behavior, and as women enter into highly competitive professional occupations.

Nonetheless, few would deny that biology imposes limits on the social roles that men and women play. Anthropologist Lionel Tiger (1969), for example, explains that human gender roles evolved naturally as males were physically equipped to be hunters and women were the bearers of children.

Biology and culture should not be seen as mutually exclusive in any case. What is generally understood is that the two are inextricably linked in determining male and female roles and behavior. Biologically derived characteristics are always processed by cultural influences. As Alice Rossi explains, men and women are biologically predisposed to certain roles, but those roles are subsequently refined by and fitted into various cultures (1977, 1984).

Gender Stratification

Whatever the basis of gender roles, it is quite evident that they are not evaluated or rewarded equally; in virtually all societies, women are subordinate to men (Chafetz, 1978; Friedl, 1978). There is, then, in all societies a gender hierarchy, just as there is a class hierarchy, an ethnic hierarchy, and so on. And as the subordinate stratum in this hierarchy, women have less access to wealth, power, and prestige. The gender hierarchy, however, is less complex and variegated than the others, simply because most societies have constructed only two genders.[2]

Why Gender Inequality?

Explanations of why men and women have, throughout human history, played different roles and why those roles have been unequally rewarded have been the focus of much social science research and remain strongly

---

[2]As Judith Lorber points out, however, neither gender nor sex are pure categories. "Combinations of incongruous genes, genitalia, and hormonal input are ignored in sex categorization, just as combinations of incongruous physiology, identity, sexuality, appearance, and behavior are ignored in the social construction of gender statuses" (Lorber, 1995:34). Alternative, or third, genders have been recognized in some societies, but these cases are uncommon (Nanda, 1990).

debated issues. The intention of this chapter is not to engage the debate but simply to explore the various forms of gender inequality in the United States and other contemporary societies. In brief, however, as with explanations for class inequality (Chapter 8), gender inequality has been explained from various theoretical perspectives, each offering a somewhat different account for the virtually universal feature of male dominance in human societies. What follows represents a small sample of theoretical attempts at explaining gender inequality.

Functional theories posit that gender differentiation and stratification contribute in some fashion to accomplishing critical tasks (Nielsen, 1990). These theories focus on the different roles that men and women play and the way each contributes to the society's survival. Gender inequality is seen not as the outgrowth of differential power but rather as functionally necessary.

In preindustrial societies, the role differentiation of men and women can be seen clearly. In hunting-and-gathering societies, which typified the economic structure of societies for most of human history, hunting was almost universally a male activity whereas foraging was mostly done by women. Friedl (1978) suggests that one of the major reasons for this specialization was that women were usually either pregnant or caring for young children. The particular skills required of hunting precluded women's participation since they could not be performed by a woman carrying a child, either in pregnancy or in her arms.

With the emergence of agrarian societies, preparing the soil and planting crops became mostly a male function, and tending and harvesting were assigned to women (Murdock, 1935). Although in industrial societies these role assignments no longer seem functionally necessary, certain roles, in the functionalist view, remain gender-specific. Women continue to fulfill roles like child rearing that require expressive qualities such as affection and compassion. Men, by contrast, fulfill instrumental roles as major breadwinners (Parsons and Bales, 1955).

Theorists using a conflict perspective see gender differentiation not as functionally necessary, but attribute it to some form of power that one gender—almost always men—derives from its social role. This power differential generates gender inequality.

Some theorists in this camp stress control over the distribution of material goods. Ernestine Friedl (1978) explains that in a few technologically simple societies, there is relative equality between men and women because both sexes work side by side in food production and what is produced is distributed equitably among workers. Gender inequality begins to emerge as societies become more productive and as women play a reduced economic role. In modern societies, so long as women do not exercise control over the investment of money—the key societal resource—they will have little power and social recognition. Within the home, too, women who work not in the labor force but as housewives, providing services to husbands and children without pay, are especially vulnerable to male dominance. Progress toward true gender equality is stimulated by the acquisition by women of positions of power in the economy and political system, as in the United States and other industrial societies.

A somewhat related theory suggests that gender inequality stems from the childbearing role of women. The essential argument is that women are encumbered for lengthy periods by pregnancy, nursing, and related activities. Logically, then, as human societies evolved, women assumed domestic roles, those that revolved around child care and household duties, and men assumed hunting and related activities that occasionally took them away from the family or community (Huber, 1990). The resources of knowledge, weaponry, and technology that derived from these activities provided men with economic power and prestige. Women's activities, on the other hand, were seen as routine and mundane.

Randall Collins (1971) theorizes that innate physical differences are the key to understanding the origins of gender inequality. He explains that since humans have a strong drive for sexual gratification and males are, on average, bigger and stronger than females, men can force themselves on the weaker sex. This element of coercion has thus shaped the fundamental features of the woman's role.

Sexism and Sexist Stereotypes

As with other forms of social inequality, an ideology has served to rationalize and stabilize male dominance. This ideology, **sexism,** is essentially the belief that women and men are innately different and that those innate differences translate into female inferiority. With sexism, sex differences are assumed to produce differences in social behavior. Women or men can be no other way because they are born that way. "Biology is destiny," as the expression goes.[3]

Over many generations, the sexist ideology has created a self-fulfilling prophecy. Male dominance in various spheres of social life led to the assumption that their superiority was natural. This, in turn, shaped people's expectations. One did not expect to see a woman military leader or a woman business executive or a woman politician. These were assumed to be "naturally" male-occupied positions, requiring skills and talents that women, by nature, did not possess. Hence, women were not trained to take such positions, which, as a result, continued to be filled primarily by men.

---

[3]Sexism has been variously defined. Some see it as any form of prejudice or discrimination against people based on their sex (Benokraitis, 1997). Others have defined it as "the subordination of women by men" (Rothenberg, 1998:132), and others as a synonym for gender stratification (Nielsen, 1990). The term as it is used here implies a belief in the biological grounding of social and behavioral differences between men and women.

Sexist Stereotypes   A set of stereotypes has developed historically that has served as the basis of the ideology of sexism. As with racism, members of the categories "male" and "female" are assumed to carry with them certain innate characteristics. Women are "ruled by emotion," they are "less intelligent" than men, and so on.[4] Women are commonly portrayed as being more compassionate, sensitive, and dependent than men, who are seen as mentally tough, decisive, and independent. These stereotypes are supported by various types of gendered language: sex-linked adjectives (for example, a "beautiful" woman, but a "handsome" man), occupational titles and forms of address, slang phrases, and so on (Chafetz, 1978).

Surprisingly, despite recent changes in gender relations and in women's family and occupational roles, many of these stereotypes remain persistent. In 1990 a national survey found that well over half of all Americans believed that there were basic personality and mental differences between men and women. More important, many of the standard stereotypes were used to describe each gender (DeStefano and Colasanto, 1990).

Sexist stereotypes continue to serve as justifications for gender inequality in different spheres of social life. Thus, if women are assumed to be more compassionate and sensitive, it is only logical that they continue to play occupational roles that complement these traits, such as nurse or social worker. And, by the same token, if they are not confident and decisive, they are not as capable as men of assuming important leadership positions in politics and the economy. These stereotypes have begun to lose their effectiveness, however, as women increasingly move into social roles previously dominated by males.

Gender Inequality in the Workforce: Continuity and Change

The gender division of labor in the workforce is a critical factor in understanding the more general system of gender stratification. As noted in earlier chapters, power is very much dependent on control of economic resources. Thus, to the extent that women do not play a role in the economy that would enable them to control or direct the distribution of those resources, their subordinate place is sustained (Friedl, 1978). A comparative study of 111 societies concluded that women's roles are less traditional where their economic power, as indicated by their labor force participation rate, is high (South, 1988).

---

[4]Nineteenth-century scientists assumed that since women's brains were smaller than men's, the superior male intellect was a given. We know today, however, that brain size differs with body weight and, when average disparity in body weight is taken into account, women's brains are actually a bit larger than men's.

Table 12-1 ■ Percentage of Women and Men in the U.S. Labor Force.

Year	Women in Labor Force as % of All Women	Men in Labor Force as % of All Men	Women as % of Total Labor Force
1900	20.0	85.7	18.1
1930	23.6	82.1	21.9
1950	33.9	86.4	29.6
1970	43.3	79.7	38.1
1990	57.5	76.1	45.2
1998	59.8	74.9	46.3
2015*	61.9	72.2	48.0

Sources: U.S. Census Bureau, *Historical Statistics of the U.S.: Colonial Times to 1970,* Part I, 1975; Fullerton, 1999.
*Projected.

Labor Force Participation

A powerful trend of the past several decades has been the vastly increasing number and percentage of women who have entered the workforce. This is especially evident in the United States, where a remarkable transformation has occurred within one generation in the occupational expectations of and for women (Bianchi and Spain, 1996). As can be seen in Table 12-1, women have steadily become a larger portion of the workforce over the past hundred years; today they constitute almost half of all workers. Figure 12-1 shows the dramatic change in labor force participation by women in almost all age groups since 1950.

Today, women from families of all social classes and ethnic groups are workers. To be sure, women in the past were also part of the labor force, particularly working-class, immigrant, and minority women, whose economic situation required that they contribute to their family's livelihood. In recent decades, however, women from the entire social spectrum have increasingly entered the mainstream labor force as full- or part-time workers. They also work a substantial number of hours while raising families. By 1996 almost three-quarters of married women with dependent children worked in the paid labor force and almost two-fifths worked full-time and year-round (Bianchi and Spain, 1996). Unlike in past generations, the expectation of most women is no longer that they will stay at home attending to domestic chores. Although they may see themselves in this traditional family role for a period of time, they fully expect to be working in the mainstream labor force at some point in their lives.

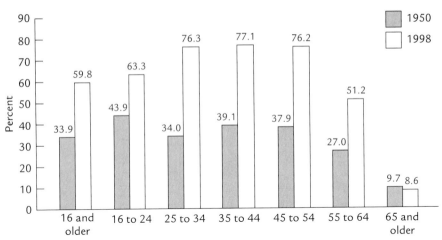

Figure 12-1 ■ Labor Force Participation Rates of Women by Age, 1950 and 1998.
Source: Fullerton, 1999.

The rate of labor force participation is not the same in all societies of the modern world. In less-developed societies and in societies where religion dictates most societal norms (particularly Muslim countries), there is less female participation than in Western industrialized countries. However, in recent decades, economic globalization has drawn many women in the underdeveloped world into the unskilled labor force. In those settings, multinational corporations manufacturing electronic products, shoes, clothing, and other consumer goods employ mainly women in their assembly plants. The low wages and often oppressive work conditions of these women have been well documented (Klein, 1999; Peterson and Runyan, 1999; Fuentes and Ehrenreich, 1983).

When considering the expanding participation of women in the workforce, remember that women have traditionally engaged in unpaid, or nonmarket, work. And the performance of such work by women remains very much in evidence. A United Nations study reported that worldwide, 66 percent of women's work is unpaid, compared with 34 percent of men's work (United Nations, 1996). Housework and child rearing are the major forms of women's unpaid labor. Think about the time and effort spent in meal preparation, cleaning, child care, shopping, and numerous other chores that are involved in maintaining a household. Even today in industrial societies, despite the vastly increased numbers of women in the general labor force, they continue to perform most of this work. In her interviews of working couples, sociologist Arlie Hochschild (1989) asked about how they juggled work and family responsibilities. One woman described her duties as homemaker with the metaphor of the "second shift": "You're on duty at work. You come home, and you're on duty. Then you go back to work and you're on duty" (7).

In addition to their sharply increased numbers, there are three outstanding trends in analyzing the place of women in the labor force: They are occupationally concentrated, they are more likely to be paid less than men, and they are less likely to occupy positions of authority.

Occupational Concentration

In virtually all societies, work is divided along sexual lines: Some roles are assigned to men and others to women. In the 1930s, anthropologist George Murdock surveyed over three hundred technologically simple societies around the world and found in all of them a gendered division of labor. In none did men and women share work roles (Murdock, 1937). Which particular roles are typically male and which typically female, however, will differ from society to society. That is, occupations ordinarily reserved for women in one society may be reserved for men in another. For example, in the United States, the overwhelming majority of physicians have traditionally been men; only in recent years have women begun to enter the medical profession in large numbers. In Russia, however, most physicians have been—and continue to be—women (Knaus, 1981; Ramer, 1990). In the United States, women have been clustered in traditionally female occupations such as nurse, schoolteacher, retail salesperson, and domestic service worker. Table 12-2 shows the extent of occupational concentration in some selected cases. Note how jobs with the highest percentage of women are those that involve interpersonal skills assumed to be natural to women. Likewise, those with the fewest women involve more physically active duties, assumed to be natural to men.

Much of the occupational segregation based on gender in the United States is evident in other societies. A United Nations study of twenty-four countries indicated that over 90 percent of typists and nurses were women, closely in line with U.S. patterns (United Nations, 1991).

Another consistent occupational pattern among societies is that traditional female roles are accorded less prestige than traditional male roles (Linton, 1936). As Friedl has explained, "Evidence of a society . . . in which women's activities are the most prestigious has never been found" (1978:69). Moreover, the kind of work done by women is usually considered less valuable and is rewarded accordingly (England, 1992). It is generally the case that, the more women who work in an occupation, the less both its female and male workers earn (Reskin and Padavic, 1994).

Gender stereotypes sustain and reinforce occupational clustering. If it is assumed that men are more aggressive and daring by nature, police officer or firefighter become "natural" male occupations. If women are assumed to be more compassionate and nurturing, nurse or schoolteacher become "natural" female occupations. (Consider Table 12-2 again in this light.) These stereotypes often lead to self-fulfilling prophecies. If women are believed to be less adept at math and science, they are apt to be counseled

Table 12-2 ■ Percentage of Women in Selected Occupations

Occupation	1983	1998
Secretaries	99.0	98.4
Dental hygienists	98.6	99.1
Preschool and kindergarten teachers	98.2	97.8
Registered nurses	95.8	92.5
Data entry keyers	93.6	81.8
Bank tellers	91.0	89.5
Telephone operators	90.4	85.8
Hairdressers and cosmetologists	88.7	90.8
Waiters and waitresses	87.8	78.3
Elementary school teachers	83.3	84.0
Social workers	64.3	68.4
High school teachers	51.8	56.9
Real estate sales representatives	48.9	53.0
Editors and reporters	48.4	51.0
Bartenders	48.4	54.6
College and university teachers	36.3	42.3
Lawyers and judges	15.8	28.6
Physicians	15.8	26.6
Police and detectives	9.4	16.3
Engineers	5.8	11.1
Clergy	5.6	12.0
Truck drivers	3.1	5.3
Airplane pilots	2.1	3.4
Carpenters	1.4	1.2
Firefighting occupations	1.0	2.3
Automobile mechanics	0.5	0.8

Source: U.S. Census Bureau, *Statistical Abstract of the United States 1999,* Table 675.

along those lines in high school, leaving them ill prepared for a rigorous engineering curriculum, for example, when they enter college. Women students themselves may see engineering as a male dominion and not as a field that they would find comfortable or appropriate. The overwhelming majority of engineers thus continue to be men, and engineering schools continue to struggle in attracting female students (U.S. Department of Education, 1998).

Examples abound of the ways in which gender stereotypes influence oc-cupational selection. Consider automobile sales, a field that is primarily male. Not only are automobile salespersons expected to be aggressive (a "natu-rally" male trait), but they are assumed to be more familiar with automobiles and things mechanical, and thus can be more effective in dealing with cus-tomers. Real estate sales, by contrast, is a relatively gender-neutral field, with virtually no obstacles to women. Again, consider the gender stereotypes that might account for this. Women are presumably no less "naturally" knowl-edgeable about homes and things that relate to them than men. In both cases, there is no validity to presumed natural gender differences, but stereotypes, reinforced in all spheres of social life, continue to influence our assumptions about who should fill these positions.

Although in the United States and other modern societies men and women remain concentrated in particular occupational roles, the sexual di-vision of labor is not as rigidly enforced as in the past, and in some cases dra-matic change has occurred in recent decades. Certain fields remain over-whelmingly female, but occupational sex segregation has steadily declined since the 1970s (Bowler, 1999; Reskin and Padavic, 1994; Wootton, 1997). Women can now be found in the entire range of occupations and are the ma-jority in some fields (e.g., pharmacist, editor, insurance adjuster) that were formerly male dominated. In the case of insurance adjusters, for example, in 1990, 72 percent were women, compared to 30 percent in 1970 (Bianchi and Spain, 1996).

Most important, American women are progressively moving into occu-pational areas involving managerial and professional roles that were previ-ously difficult, at best, to enter. These are precisely the kinds of positions—those involving control of valued resources and decisions regarding their distribution—that contribute to increased societal power. Women in 1970 were 18 percent of all managers; ten years later they were 30 percent, and twenty years later, 40 percent (Reskin and Padavic, 1994). This is a continu-ing trend (Bowler, 1999; Glater, 2001). At the very top of the managerial lad-der, however, women have not experienced a comparable degree of mobility. This point is addressed later in this chapter.

Earnings

As with occupational concentration, a mixed picture is evident regarding men's and women's earnings: Changes are occurring, but significant dis-crepancies remain. Over the past twenty years, women's earnings have in-creased as those of men have declined. Thus, the ratio of women's to men's earnings has narrowed considerably. Figure 12-2 shows that trend very clearly. Among the college-educated in particular, the growth in women's earnings far outpaced men's. Still, women earn, on average, slightly more

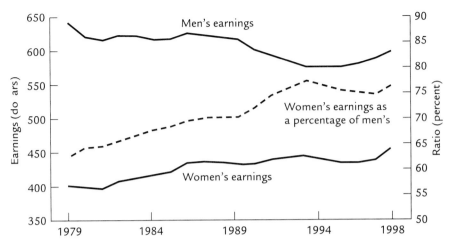

Figure 12-2 ■ Median Usual Weekly Earnings of Full-time Wage and Salary Workers in Constant (1998) Dollars by Sex, 1979–98 Annual Averages.
Source: Bowler, 1999.

than 75 percent of what men earn. This disparity is evident whether comparisons are made by education, occupation, age, or race/ethnicity.

In regard to earnings, the picture that emerges among women workers themselves is also mixed. As shown in Figure 12-3, the earnings of college-educated women rose substantially during the past two decades, while those with no college showed little or no advancement. In 1998, women with some college but no degree earned only 67 percent of what women with a four-year degree earned. Those with only a high school diploma earned considerably less, and those without even a high school diploma earned just 40 percent as much as women with a college degree. When race and ethnicity are factored in, however, the situation is somewhat different. Black and Hispanic women's earnings are closer to parity with their male peers. Whereas white women earn 76 percent of what white men earn, black and Hispanic women earn 86 percent of what black and Hispanic men earn (Bowler, 1999).

In the past, discrepancies in pay between men and women were the result largely of direct discrimination. Employers would routinely pay women less than men for doing the same job. Their rationale was that women were not breadwinners and therefore did not require the same salary as men. Moreover, it was assumed that women were working only as a temporary measure and were not reliant on their jobs for a living, as were men. Two measures destroyed the legal basis for gender discrimination in the workforce: the Equal Pay Act of 1963, and Title VII of the Civil Rights Act, passed in 1964. The former prohibited employers from paying women less than men for doing essentially the same job. Title VII prohibited discrimination in hiring or in wages on the basis of race or sex.

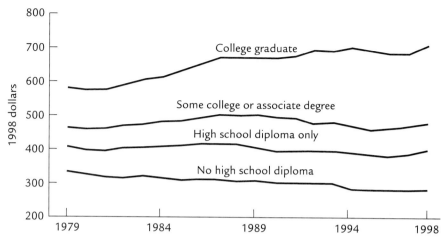

Figure 12-3 ■ Women's Median Usual Weekly Earnings in Constant (1998) Dollars by Educational Attainment, 1979–98 Annual Averages.
Source: Bowler, 1999.

What, then, accounts for the continued gender discrepancy in pay? Economists today explain that the differentials in pay between men and women are mostly the result of the particular occupational areas in which women find themselves concentrated (Reskin and Padavic, 1994). More are in unskilled, poor-paying jobs, particularly at the low end of the service sector. This includes restaurant workers, retail salespersons, and domestic service workers. Because of child-rearing responsibilities, women have often chosen less demanding or part-time jobs in order to assure flexibility. These jobs pay less and provide little in the way of training or skills acquisition that would lead to more demanding and better-paying jobs. Women must also take time away from work following childbirth, causing a further loss of opportunity to improve skills and wages (Bianchi and Spain, 1996). As women increase their investment in human capital (education, skills, and experience) and also delay childbirth, they should, in this view, increase their productivity and earnings vis-à-vis men. There is evidence to support this view. Among young, educated workers, the wage gap is close to disappearing (Ingrassia and Wingert, 1995).

Many sociologists, however, point to continuing discrimination, albeit in more subtle, institutional forms than in the past, as a factor in accounting for the wage gap between men and women. They emphasize that the increasing convergence of men's and women's wages is the result primarily of changes in societal views of women's abilities, as well as affirmative action and other legal measures, that have forced employers to hire more women. Also, they explain the narrowing gender gap in some part as simply a result of the decline in men's earnings. Sociologists also stress the power advantages that men continue to hold in gaining access to elite positions, enabling them to define how jobs are to be categorized and rewarded (Bianchi and Spain, 1996).

Comparable worth is an issue that emerged in the 1980s and is seen by some as a principal means of closing the pay gap between men and women. **Comparable worth** refers to the proposition that men and women should be paid the same for jobs of equal or comparable worth. This idea extends the notion of "equal pay for equal work," which merely holds that women and men should be paid the same wage for doing the same jobs (Goldin, 1990). Not only should male and female nurses, for example, be paid the same, but the pay of nurses should be comparable to the pay of workers in occupations that require a similar level of skills (airline pilots, perhaps). The question of how jobs are assessed in terms of skills and merit, of course, is highly problematic and has created wide disagreements about measurement and about whether the concept of comparable worth has any real meaning (Barko, 2000; England, 1992; Hutner, 1986). Presumably, implementing comparable worth would serve to increase the earnings of workers in occupations that are heavily dominated by women, which are currently undervalued.

It is of note that the earnings gap between men and women is not unique to the United States. Multinational firms in developing countries routinely pay women employees far less than they pay men. Indeed, this is one reason why women employees are preferred (Safa, 1990). In a number of countries, mostly in the industrialized world, the earnings gap is narrower than in the United States, but this is ordinarily not the case. Although women make up 41 percent of the European workforce, on average they continue to earn considerably less than men in both the manufacturing and service sectors (Dwyer, 1996).

Authority

It is obvious that women in all areas of the labor force work in jobs that not only pay less than men but in which authority is limited. In the same occupational fields, women tend to be in less authoritative positions than men. What is more striking is the finding that women are underrepresented in power positions even in fields that they numerically dominate, like nursing and librarianship (Reskin and Padavic, 1994; Williams, 1995).

Moreover, even where they have entered previously male-dominated fields, women often are relegated to specific positions that are lower in prestige and income. Women in the legal profession, for example, have advanced markedly in the past two decades (Epstein, 1993). In the early 1970s, only one of every thirty-three lawyers was a woman; today nearly one of every four lawyers and nearly half of all law students are women. Yet women lawyers continue to average less in salaries than their male counterparts, and they lag in attaining partnerships in large firms (Epstein, 1996). In medicine, too, the gender gap is obvious. Women physicians are clustered in less prestigious specialties such as pediatrics and family medicine. The more prestigious and higher-paying specialties, like surgery and cardiology, remain male-dominated (Steinhauer, 1999).

Opportunities for women to reach authoritative positions differ from industry to industry. A study of the United States and three other industrial societies found that women were more inclined to rise to managerial positions in service industries, such as publishing, and were less likely to do so in heavy industries, such as automobiles (Clement and Myles, 1994). Industries in which women did have easier access to the top were those in which women made up the bulk of the workforce.

Work and the Family

Traditionally, women have been expected to perform household duties centering on child rearing and domestic functions. Men, on the other hand, have been expected to leave the home to work, with primary responsibility for supporting the family economically and protecting its members. This traditional arrangement has been brought into question by the entrance of women—often as primary breadwinners—in significant numbers into the mainstream workforce in recent decades.

Despite the changed work role of women, the gender breakdown of traditional family roles has not changed radically. Today, although a majority of all adult women are in the labor force, women continue to do the bulk of child care and household tasks. Indeed, the actual number of hours they work in the home is not much different than it was in the early part of the twentieth century (Schor, 1992). A comparative study of Sweden and the United States found that in both countries, men did between 20 and 30 percent of housework (Wright et al., 1992). Although a majority of Americans believe that women today should work even if they are raising families, the prevailing view of "normal" gender roles still conforms to those of an earlier time. Consider how odd, even at the dawn of the twenty-first century, we find a family in which the wife is the major breadwinner while the husband remains at home caring for the children and attending to household chores.

The frequent conflicts women encounter between their family and work roles account in large part for the extent to which they lag behind in higher-status and higher-paying occupational positions. This is evident in medicine, for example, where, as noted earlier, women earn less than men and are concentrated in less prestigious specialties. Aside from lingering sexism in the profession, women cite the difficulties of combining family obligations (especially child care) with professional demands as the major hindrance to promotion in their fields. Trying to balance work and family, many young female doctors choose specialties that require less training, since most of that training coincides with their prime childbearing years. Others may work part-time or take positions that offer a less demanding and more flexible schedule. Their earnings and prestige suffer as a result (Steinhauer, 1999).

Patterns of Gender Inequality: Politics, the Corporation, and Education

The picture of women in the labor force reveals clearly that inequality in the world of work continues to prevail, but it reveals equally clearly that traditional patterns are undergoing fundamental change. In almost every other area of social, political, and economic life, the place of women in American society is decidedly different from what it was just a short time ago. This section examines patterns of gender inequality in three major institutional realms: the political world, the corporate world, and education.

Gender Inequality in the Political World

It is extremely important to examine the extent of gender inequality and the patterns of change in the political realm because it is here that power is most evident and where many critical decisions are made regarding changes in the structure of social inequality.

Political Participation   The United States and other modern societies have moved toward gender equality in politics only in the twentieth century. So taken for granted are equal political rights for men and women today that we often forget how thoroughly excluded women were from political participation just a short historical time ago. Not until ratification of the Nineteenth Amendment to the U.S. Constitution in 1920 were women nationwide able to vote. A few European countries, as well as Australia and New Zealand, had provided women's suffrage before that time, but many, such as France, Italy and Japan, did not give women the vote until the 1940s. Women's suffrage is by no means universal even today. In some Islamic countries, such as Kuwait and Saudi Arabia, women are still denied political participation.

Political Leadership   Voting in elections is only a small part of effective political participation. Occupying leadership positions is infinitely more critical. To what extent have women begun to play significant political roles in the United States and other modern societies?

At the top levels of government, women have made some significant inroads, far more than in the corporate world. Looking first at elective offices, we can see clearly that women office holders have increased their numbers substantially over the past few decades. Whereas women were little more than 2 percent of the U.S. Congress in 1970, in 2001 they were more than 13 percent. One must consider these figures, of course, in light of the fact that women constitute over half the total population. Moreover, in a few countries, the contrast with the United States is sharp. For example, more than 40 percent of national parliamentary seats are held by women in Sweden, the top-ranked country in women's political representation (UNDP, 2000).

At lower levels of government, however, American women have made some truly spectacular gains in numbers and in leadership posts since the 1970s. In 1997 women occupied 21.5 percent of the nation's state legislative seats, compared to 8 percent in 1975, and they held twenty-four top legislative posts, such as Speaker of the House or Senate president (Ayres, 1997). Moreover, an increasing number of women are winning election to governorships and other statewide executive offices, as well as mayorships, city councils, and county boards.

In other spheres of government, the role of women has also begun to change significantly. There are currently two women serving on the U.S. Supreme Court (there were none before 1981), and women are being appointed to federal judgeships in unprecedented numbers. At the state level, in 1997 nine women were chief justices of state supreme courts and 70 out of a total of 357 state supreme court members were women. This represented a more than threefold increase since 1985 (*New York Times*, 1997).

In presidential administrations through the 1970s, women were rarely members of the cabinet, the locus of greatest political influence in the executive branch of government. This began to change in the 1980s. Three women in the Reagan administration and two in the Bush administration served in the cabinet, though their positions carried relatively little political weight. In the first Clinton administration, three women were appointed to the cabinet, including the attorney general, a comparatively powerful post. In the second Clinton administration, four of the ten cabinet members were women, including, most importantly, the secretary of state, the government's top foreign policy position. Madeleine Albright's appointment as secretary of state in 1997 represented the first time a woman had ever served in that position and marked a watershed in the appointment of women to high political office. Indeed, in most countries, not only the United States, women in legislative or ministerial positions of high rank have rarely held office in the most "masculine" areas, like defense, foreign policy, or finance (Peterson and Runyan, 1993).

Finally, the possibility of a female American president is no longer as remote as it had seemed in previous eras. Geraldine Ferraro was nominated as the Democratic candidate for the vice presidency in 1984, and as women continue to play a more significant political role, achieving the highest office is an inevitability. Public opinion polls indicate the increasing public acceptance of this occurrence. More than 90 percent say they would vote for a qualified woman for president (Newport et al., 1999). In other parts of the world women have already achieved the highest offices of government. In fact, in thirty-four countries, both developed and developing, the president or prime minister for some period of time during the 1990s was a woman (United Nations, 2000).[5]

---

[5]Peterson and Runyan (1999) note that women who have held the highest-ranking office of government are typically perceived as exceptional women, who act "like men."

Gender Inequality in the Corporate World

In the world of work, women generally occupy fewer positions of authority, but their specific place in the corporate world, especially in posts at the top, presents a mixed picture. On the one hand, women, as already noted, continue to be severely underrepresented in top managerial positions. Moreover, the wage gap is as evident here as it is in the general workforce. On the other hand, when looked at in historical perspective, women have made substantial gains in recent decades and they continue to advance into power positions at an increasing rate.

Until the last ten or so years, women were scarcely present in top-ranking posts of the corporate world. In the mid-1970s women as a proportion of the boards of directors of the 250 largest corporations constituted only 1.8 percent (Herman, 1981; Robertson, 1973). Little change was evident by 1980, when only 36 of the 1,499 top positions in the 100 largest corporations were filled by women (Dye and Strickland, 1982). In addition, most of those few women were recruited from outside the corporate world, leading to speculation that they were serving as "window dressing." Ten percent of the most senior jobs at the 500 largest U.S. companies in 1996 were held by women, and at the very highest levels—CEO, president, executive vice president—2.4 percent were women (Himelstein, 1996). By 2000, 12.5 percent of the top officers in these firms were women, and 6.2 percent held positions at the highest executive level (Catalyst, 2000). Despite these increases, however, women undeniably still play a diminutive role at the top of the corporate world.

The question of why women continue to lag in achieving the highest corporate posts is not easily answered. As with the wage gap, some point to a continuation of sexist attitudes and blatant discrimination. Others explain it as a more subtle reluctance of male executives to accept women or ethnic minorities into a clubby environment in which these men feel comfortable with each other (Zweigenhaft, 1987).

A number of other explanations have been offered. Dye (1995) lists a few of these:

- Women are not aggressive in corporate politics.
- Women have lower expectations of earnings and positions.
- Because women must take time to have children, they fall further behind men in the competition for top positions.
- Affirmative action has helped women to secure more entry-level positions but has not had the same impact at the senior managerial level.
- Women choose staff assignments rather than fast-track, operating-head assignments.
- Women are more reluctant to change locations than are men and thus miss out on opportunities and are less valuable to the corporation.

Source: *Washington Post* National Weekly Edition, April 20, 1998, p. 9. Kirk Anderson. Reprinted by permission.

In addition, most women advance through corporate divisions that are traditionally "female" (such as human resources, community relations, or legal), which rarely lead to positions at the very top (Ghiloni, 1987; Himelstein, 1996; Glass Ceiling Commission, 1995).

A survey of 461 women executives of Fortune 1,000 companies found that male stereotyping and preconceptions of women continue to act as barriers to advancement at the top of the corporate world. The respondents in this study claimed that the most important factor in their own success was having consistently exceeded performance expectations—that is, they had to be not only good but exceptionally good. The second most important factor was adjusting their personal style so as not to appear threatening to male executives. This is quite different from the view of a majority of male executives who explained the low numbers for women at the top as a result of simply not having been on the executive trajectory long enough; eventually, in this view, women will catch up (Grimsley, 1996; Dobrzynski, 1996b).

Despite social impediments to upward movement in the corporate world, the number of female executives is rising, and it seems safe to assume that in the not too distant future even women CEOs will be unremarkable. A recent study showed that from 1995 to 2000, for example, the number of Fortune 500 companies in which more than 25 percent of corporate officers are women doubled from 25 to 50. The study projected that women would constitute 16.5

percent of top corporate officers by 2005, 20.1 percent by 2010, and 27.4 percent by 2020 (Catalyst, 2000). Companies are beginning to establish goals for placing more women in executive positions, some even creating quotas mandating minimum numbers of women in the senior ranks (Himelstein, 1997).

As increasing numbers of women are playing decision-making roles in the corporate world, women's earnings in top positions are changing as well. A recent study examined the compensation patterns of the top five executive officers of a large group of U.S. firms. It showed that the gender gap in pay virtually disappears once age and experience are accounted for. That is, female executives at the top level earn, on average, considerably less than their male counterparts, but this pay disparity is mostly a product of the fact that they are younger and have less seniority (Bertrand and Hallock, 2000).

Although American women are still severely underrepresented in the highest posts of the corporate world, their progress toward the top is actually more significant than that of women in most countries of the world, including European societies. Despite the protection of equal-opportunity laws, European women are not moving into middle and senior management jobs as quickly as American women, and the percentage of women on European corporate boards is far below that of the United States (Dwyer, 1996).

Dye and Strickland concluded in 1982 that "The major institutions of U.S. society are managed and directed almost exclusively by men" (340). Clearly, that is no longer the case. Nonetheless, it remains equally evident that women have far to go before they achieve parity with men in both the political and the corporate worlds.

Women and Education

Much of the explanation for the rapidly changing status of women in politics and the economy can be attributed to the changes in education that women have experienced over the past few decades. As discussed in Chapter 5, the key to entrance into the society's power elites today is access to higher education. And as women secure more education, their political and economic status has changed concomitantly.

Consider the number and percentage of women in higher education today compared to forty years ago. Whereas in 1960 almost twice as many males as females attended college, by 1980 females were a majority of college attendees. In 1997, of the 14.3 million students enrolled in college, 8 million were women (U.S. Department of Education, 2000). As is seen in Table 12-3, more women than men today earn bachelor's and master's degrees. Also significant is the marked change in the number and percentage of women earning doctoral and professional degrees.

Although the increase in higher education for women vis-à-vis men is clear and dramatic, the types of degrees they earn continue to be sex-typed. In 1993, while women were awarded almost 90 percent of undergraduate degrees in library science and home economics and 78 percent of undergrad-

Table 12-3 ■ Degrees Earned, by Level and Sex (in thousands)

Degree	1960		1970		1980		1990		1997		2001*	
	M	F	M	F	M	F	M	F	M	F	M	F
Bachelor's	254	138	451	341	474	456	492	560	521	652	505	645
Master's	51	24	126	83	151	147	154	171	181	238	161	221
First professional	NA	NA	33	2	53	17	44	27	46	33	41	32
Doctorate	9	1	26	4	23	10	24	14	27	19	26	18

Sources: U.S. Census Bureau, *Statistical Abstract of the U.S. 1997*, Table 303; U.S. Department of Education, *Digest of Education Statistics, 1999*.
* Projected.

uate education degrees, they earned only 16 percent of undergraduate engineering degrees. Nonetheless, even here there have been marked changes. In 1970 women earned only one out of one hundred engineering degrees (Bianchi and Spain, 1996).

It is of note that the educational level of women in elite positions is even higher than their male counterparts'. Dye's study of top institutional leaders in the United States (1995) showed that nearly half of the women leaders had earned master's or doctorate degrees and another quarter held law degrees. As Dye explains, "This strongly suggests that women need more education than men to compete effectively for top posts" (1995:185).

The Status of Women in Global Perspective

Although the general pattern of gender stratification in the United States is similar in other societies, the degree of women's subordinate status and the discrimination they encounter are far more severe, particularly in countries of the developing world.

Discrimination and Abuse

Despite the progress that women in the United States and other industrial societies have made in the past three decades in securing political rights and economic power, discrimination in the workplace is by no means a thing of the past. Moreover, in the realm of interpersonal relations, problems of harassment and physical abuse, sexual and otherwise, continue to be serious issues. Still, in looking at the status of women in a global context, the forms and degree of discrimination that American women face appear mild. In comparing their status with women in most of the remainder of the world, it could be argued that American women are an extremely privileged female population.

Women in the Developing World   In many developing societies, female subordination is especially harsh. Women in these societies continue to be treated in a fashion that would bewilder—and anger—most Americans. Bride burnings remain widespread today in India, for example, and rape is almost commonplace in South Africa (MacFarquhar, 1994a, 1994b). These are by no means extraordinary situations, as the vignettes at the outset of this chapter suggested. Much of the discrimination against women in these societies not only is based on tradition but is built into the legal structure. Consider that there are laws in some countries that prohibit women from traveling abroad without male permission. In other countries women are under the legal guardianship of their husbands and have no property rights (United Nations, 1995).

Consider the status of women in Brazil. A national study in 1992 reported an average of 337 assaults on women daily. Because male police rarely treated wife-beating as more than a domestic matter, in 1985 a number of women's police stations were established. Despite this measure, as well as laws that address the issue of discrimination and violence against women, in practice the penalties for such actions are relatively mild and ineffective (Robinson and Epstein, 1994). Anthropologist Richard Parker (1991) studied the Brazilian sexual culture and concluded that "The social, political, and economic institutions that work together to minimize the opportunities for choice and self-determination on the part of women from all walks of life in Brazil continue to function with ruthless efficiency" (169). The fact that some changes have begun to take place among the most privileged sectors of Brazilian society, Parker notes, should not be seen as indicative of a decline of oppression for the vast majority of Brazilian women. Brazil remains "a profoundly patriarchal social order" (170).

The circumstances of women in some Muslim societies of the Middle East are particularly arresting (Erturk, 1991). Women have virtually no political rights, they are not encouraged to enter the workforce but are expected to remain at home, they must cover their faces when they appear in public, and they remain strictly segregated from men in schools, mosques, and other social settings. Marriages are usually prearranged, and women may have no right to refuse the choice of a partner. Moreover, Islamic law permits men to have as many as four wives, although the right is not commonly exercised.[6]

Perhaps the most shocking aspect of women's subordination in the developing world is the widespread practice of female circumcision in at least twenty-eight African societies (Abusharaf, 1998). This involves the ritual excision of some or all of the female external genitalia (the clitoris, and small and large genital lips), resulting in diminished ability to experience sexual pleasure (Dugger, 1996). The procedure is usually performed on girls in their teens or younger and is done to assure their virginity for their future husbands. The cutting is ordinarily done in a crude fashion with a knife, razor blade, or broken bottle, using no anesthetic, and often results in serious health problems including hemorrhaging, infection, problems during childbirth, and even death.

Female circumcision, or genital mutilation, has come under attack in recent years from various sources, including governments and human rights groups. However, it is firmly entrenched in the culture of these societies, making change slow and difficult. Families insist on having female children circumcised since the honor of the girl and the family dictates it. Social pressures can be so great that some wives who have not been cut as children will choose to have the operation performed on them as adults (Abusharaf, 1998). Even when there is objection, cultural norms may prevail. In Ivory Coast, for example, the wife of a man who insists on having

---

[6]It is important to note that there are major differences among Muslim societies regarding women's rights.

his daughter circumcised says that she despises the practice. Yet she admits, "It is up to my husband. We live in Africa. The man makes the decisions about the children" (Dugger, 1996). Many of the girls themselves look forward to the cutting, understanding that the rite represents an entry into adulthood and makes them desirable marriage partners. In Sudan, 90 percent of women have been cut, and in Mali, 93 percent (Dugger, 1996).

Many of the societal norms of traditional societies that support what Americans would consider oppressive conditions for women are being challenged and changed. For example, in Qatar, a small Persian Gulf country strongly ruled by Islamic principles, an increasing number of women are going to college and then to work, some even with men, and some now drive cars of their own. Most no longer tolerate being one among several wives and strongly endorse the right of women to refuse a marriage proposal, something that was not acceptable just a few year earlier. Women have also been promised the right to vote (Jehl, 1997).

Nonetheless, change is coming piecemeal and only gradually. To the surprise of many Westerners, women themselves in these societies do not necessarily advocate quick and thorough change in their circumstances. This may reflect not only the perceived need to proceed slowly with what are radical social and political changes but also a commitment to traditional cultural ways. Recall the practice of female circumcision in Central Africa, which continues to be condoned and even desired by many women. In Qatar, much the same attitude toward change in women's roles is evident. "I think in our society we should cover our faces," says a twenty-six-year-old clerical worker who also wears a head scarf and a cloak that covers her entire body. She acknowledges that when she travels to Europe or the United States, she does not cover herself, but she believes there remain lines in Qatar that should not be crossed. Another working Qatari woman, a bank manager who was among the first women in the country to drive and to work with men, expresses the view that "It's part of our religion." Working and studying are accepted, she added, "but going to mixed parties and having contact with foreign men—these things cannot be done" (Jehl, 1997:A7).

Japanese Society   Japan presents an interesting comparison with American society in gender stratification. It is not a developing society, but rather one that rivals the United States in economic prosperity and productivity. Yet the place of women in Japan could not present a stronger contrast. "Japanese men are blatantly male chauvinists," wrote the noted Japan scholar Edwin Reischauer, "and women seem shamefully exploited and suppressed" (1988:175).

To begin with, until quite recently Japanese women were not a significant portion of the labor force. Today, however, about half of all Japanese women are employed, and they make up 40 percent of workers (Pollack, 1997). In the past, Japanese working women were rarely found in other than menial, often part-time, jobs and they continue to be concentrated in low-status positions. The glass ceiling blocking the movement of women into managerial positions is far more implacable than in the United States. What's more, once Japanese women workers marry or become pregnant, they are expected to quit their jobs (Xuewen et al., 1992). Thus, women workers have not been able to benefit from Japan's tradition of lifetime employment.

Sexual discrimination against women in Japan is, by American standards, blatant. In want-ads, companies often specify the sex of employees they seek and set an age limit for women applicants. In the workplace, women are commonly relegated to subservient roles, such as pouring tea for male colleagues (Pollack, 1996). Many Japanese women are hired in electronics assembly plants, where work is considered a more natural female setting. Very few women work in automobile factories, however. This contrasts with the workforce composition of Japanese firms in their U.S. plants. About 20 percent of workers at Nissan's plant in Tennessee and 30 percent of workers at Honda's plants in Ohio are women (Pollack, 1997). Not surprisingly, there is a wide earnings gap between Japanese men and Japanese women; women earn about 60 percent of men's income (recall that the comparable U.S. percentage is about 75).

Some of these conditions are undergoing slow but gradual change. Antidiscrimination laws have recently been enacted in Japan, requiring companies to provide equal opportunities for men and women. Also, the ban on women working at night has been lifted, opening up new job opportunities (Pollack, 1997).

If the place of women in the workforce seems harsh by American standards, the family provides no haven. Japanese families have traditionally been notoriously patriarchal, with women playing a mainly perfunctory role. As one Japanese husband put it, referring to his wife, "She's like air or water. You couldn't live without it, but most of the time, you're not conscious of its existence" (Kristof, 1996a). Traditionally, women have had virtually no social life outside the family, in contrast to their husbands, who usually spend much time with their co-workers (Reischauer, 1988).

Another view of Japanese women in the family, however, suggests that they are not as powerless as is often assumed. Although formally they may be subservient to their husbands, Japanese women are strongly influential within the family, though often in a behind-the-scenes manner (Kato, 1989).

Japanese marriages are consummated not so much on the basis of love and high expectations as on duty and children. This, in combination with the social pressures on women to make adjustments to an unhappy relationship, has resulted in a comparatively low rate of divorce. Also, the severe economic and social hardship that women encounter following a marital breakup serves as an additional disincentive to divorce (Vogel, 1979).

Women and Power

The gender patterns in the United States with regard to political and economic elites are very much the same in other comparable societies: The number and percentage of women in positions of power are disproportionately small, and they are advancing at a slow pace. Sociologist Gwen Moore (1988) found, for example, that the tiny number of women in elite positions in various societal institutions was similar in the United States, West Germany, and Australia. Also, women were found to be peripheral to the informal elite networks that are critical in leading to higher decision-making positions.

Table 12-4 shows the role of women in political and economic life in a range of contemporary societies. What is indicated is the percentage of powerful and prestigious political and occupational positions held by women. A strong relation is evident between the degree of economic development of the country and the percentage of women in important roles. With few exceptions, women in highly developed, industrialized countries occupy comparatively significant percentages of parliamentary seats, managerial and administrative posts, and professional and technical jobs. These percentages taper off sharply as the level of development drops.

Intimately related to women's subordinate status in political and economic life in most developing societies is the deprived status of women in education. Two-thirds of the world's illiterates are women, and most of these are in societies that are relatively underdeveloped economically and politically (United Nations, 2000). In these societies, it is often an economic decision to educate sons rather than daughters. It is not uncommon for girls to be taken out of school to work at home or to care for younger siblings. Usually there are more and better-paying jobs for men than for women. Early pregnancy, too, prevents many girls from staying in school.

Changes in women's educational status are occurring, however. The gender gap at the primary school level has narrowed significantly in the developing countries as a whole, though it persists in sub-Saharan Africa, North Africa, and South Asia. Women are an increasing percentage of secondary and post-secondary students as well, though the differences between males and females are still extremely wide (United Nations Population Fund, 2000).

The Feminist Movement

In every society today there is an active movement seeking to change the structure of gender stratification. And it is quite obvious that everywhere change is, in fact, occurring, albeit at noticeably different rates. Consider again the incidents described at the outset of this chapter, for example, in light of the changes that have been prompted by a global feminist movement. The routine abuse of women, as in Punsooilri, is no longer accepted as the norm, even in rural South Korea. The restrictions imposed on women by the Taliban

Table 12-4 ■ Positions Held by Women (percentages)

Country[1]	Seats Held in Parliament	Administrators and Managers	Professional and Technical Workers
Norway (1)	36.4	30.6	58.5
Sweden (3)	42.7	27.4	48.6
Germany (6)	33.6	26.6	49.0
Canada (8)	22.7	37.3	52.2
Australia (11)	25.1	24.0	44.4
United States (13)	12.5	44.4	53.4
Venezuela (20)	28.6	24.3	57.6
Israel (23)	12.5	22.4	52.9
Czech Republic (26)	13.9	23.2	54.1
Italy (31)	10.0	53.8	17.8
Botswana (32)	17.0	25.7	52.8
Mexico (35)	18.0	20.7	40.2
Japan (41)	9.0	9.5	44.0
Peru (50)	10.8	26.9	41.6
Russian Federation (53)	5.7	37.9	65.6
Eritrea (59)	14.7	16.8	29.5
Korea (63)	4.0	4.7	31.9
Sri Lanka (66)	4.9	17.3	27.2
Egypt (68)	2.0	16.4	28.4
Jordan (69)	2.5	4.6	28.7

Source: United Nations Development Programme (UNDP), *Human Development Report 2000* (New York: Oxford University Press, 2000): 165–168.
[1]The countries are arranged in the order of their "gender empowerment measure," an index developed by the United Nations Development Programme to measure gender inequality in key areas of economic and political participation and decision making in 70 countries. Each country's rank is shown in parentheses beside its name.

in Afghanistan have been recognized as exceedingly repressive even in the Muslim world. And the laws pertaining to rape in Peru are being fought by advocates of women's rights.

In the United States and in other Western industrial societies, women as a collectivity start from a more advanced position and thus the focus of the feminist movement in these countries has fallen more on securing equal political and economic opportunities rather than on preventing women's physical and mental abuse. But in all cases the objective in a broad sense is the same: the advancement of the status of women.

Feminism

The set of beliefs and actions that center on assuring the equality of men and women in various areas of social life is referred to as **feminism.** It is important to consider in the context of human social development how radically new is the idea of gender equality. Although sexist ideology has been successfully challenged in the past several decades, for most of human history the notion that men were intellectually as well as physically superior to women was taken for granted. Thus, thoughts of gender equality were always outside the mainstream. Until the past few decades, sexist ideology, like beliefs regarding racial superiority, was the accepted view among the overwhelming majority of people.

The Feminist Movement in the United States   Although the contemporary phase of the U.S. feminist movement stems from around 1960, an earlier movement began in the mid-nineteenth century and continued for over seven decades. The Seneca Falls Convention of 1848 marks a point at which women began to mobilize against discrimination in education and politics. The most important objective was the franchise, which was finally secured in 1920 with passage of the Nineteenth Amendment to the U.S. Constitution. Following the attainment of its major goal, the early feminist movement receded and did not experience a revival until the 1960s.

During the 1960s, a number of factors came together to give momentum to a resurgent feminist movement. First, a book of seminal importance was published, Betty Friedan's *The Feminine Mystique* (1963), whose message instilled a new consciousness among many women. Friedan spoke of an inchoate problem in which women of the post–World War II generation, despite their increasing prosperity, felt unfulfilled. As she put it, "We can no longer ignore that voice within women that says: 'I want something more than my husband and my children and my home' " (32).

Second, women piggybacked onto the civil rights movement of the 1960s, calling attention to the fact that, as a collectivity, they too were targets of blatant as well as subtle forms of discrimination. The civil rights movement provided a model for organizing and political action, and it was at this point that women were increasingly acknowledged as a sociological minority (Freeman, 1975).

A third factor concerns changes in women's reproductive rights. This took two forms. One was the introduction of birth control pills, which provided women with greater options regarding issues of childbearing. Another was the legalization of abortion in 1973, which provided further control over reproductive issues. Prior to this time, unwanted pregnancies were either carried to term or were aborted surreptitiously. These medical and legal innovations led to monumental changes in the role of women in the family and ultimately in the workforce.

The Feminist Ideological Spectrum

The current feminist movement is a complex array of organizations, individuals, and ideologies that is difficult to define with clarity. The very meaning of feminism today is subject to different definitions among different women. Sociologists Myra Marx Ferree and Beth Hess (1994) suggest that there are a few basic premises that, together, characterize a "feminist worldview":

- A claim that women are a special category of people based on biological features and cultural experiences.
- The belief that only women should define what is feminine.
- Recognition of and dissatisfaction with the fact that men create rules that women must live by.
- The belief that changing the subordinate status of women is possible and essential.

The feminist movement today encompasses a number of branches that maintain somewhat different agendas and, at times, conflicting objectives. Within these branches are further divisions, making it difficult to conveniently lump together into a few units the various perspectives. For our purposes (and at the risk of oversimplification), however, the spectrum can be roughly divided into two camps: *gender* feminism and *equity* feminism.

Equity Feminism   Gender neutrality may be seen as the basic goal of equity feminism or what Judith Lorber (1998) has called gender reform feminism. The focus of the efforts of equity feminists is the attainment of equal rights and opportunities for women in all areas of social and economic life (Kaminer, 1996; Wolf, 1994). As Christine Sommers (1995) describes her, an equity feminist "wants for women what she wants for everyone: fair treatment without discrimination" (22).

Equity feminism might be seen as mainstream feminism, embraced by a broad social spectrum. The target of the movement from this perspective is the reform of various societal institutions that continue to discriminate against women. Strong emphasis is placed on changing the workplace, where gender segregation remains prevalent, women's wages remain low, and a glass ceiling continues to bar women's entry into power positions. Though liberal feminists predominate among this branch of the movement, it also includes those who approach feminism from socialist and Marxist positions.

Gender Feminism   Gender feminism begins from the position that society is fundamentally patriarchal. All institutions—the school, the economy, the polity, religion—are dominated by men, and their dominance is supported by a gender ideology. In this view, men use various means, including aggression and violence, to maintain their societal power. Lorber (1998) refers to this branch of feminism as gender resistance feminism.

Gender neutrality, from this perspective, is not a meaningful goal since the domination of men is so comprehensive. The objectives, therefore, are to develop woman-centered institutions that speak to the unique needs and values of women (Lorber, 1998). Also sought are changes in the legal system to provide women with protection against a system that is viewed as discriminatory against women in its very essence. The view is that women are under attack and that the gains of the past couple of decades are threatened (Faludi, 1991).

Even within this branch of feminism there are divisions. At one extreme, for example, are radical feminists, who see men unavoidably as victimizers of women. Sexual harassment of women is defined very broadly so that almost any form of sex might qualify as male sexual exploitation (Dworkin, 1987; MacKinnon, 1993).

Gender feminism is prevalent among academicians and many feminist philosophers and leaders. Yet, as Sommers (1995) suggests, it "lacks a grass roots constituency" (22). That is, few women outside the university have subscribed to its version of feminist goals or to its victimization view of women's social status.[7]

The majority of American women today do not consider themselves part of an organized feminist movement, regardless of its branch, and some may even speak disparagingly of it, but nonetheless, they favor unquestioningly the basic goals of the movement: equality for women in various facets of social, economic, and political life. In sociologist Lillian Rubin's interviews of working-class women, she found such ambiguity in their responses to the notion of feminism. On the one hand, they saw feminists stereotypically as overly aggressive, demanding, and not sufficiently feminine. "I'd never be a feminist," explained a mother working as an insurance company claims adjuster, "because they want women to give up being feminine and soft." But on specific issues, like pay equity, sexual harassment, or women in politics, they voiced decidedly feminist opinions. The same woman who earlier said she would never be a feminist recognizes the significance of the movement in opening up occupational opportunities for women that previously didn't exist. "Yeah, I'm glad it [the women's movement] happened because otherwise I wouldn't have my job. My company didn't used to hire women to be adjusters before that" (Rubin 1994:73).

---

[7]Lorber (1998) identifies a third major feminist perspective, gender rebellion feminism, which draws from postmodernism and emphasizes the connections between various forms of stratification (race, class, gender).

Summary

Sex refers to the relatively fixed physiological and biological differences between men and women; gender refers to differences that are determined socially and culturally and that are manifest in the different roles played by men and women in all societies. The question of whether gender identity and gender roles are biologically rooted or are socially determined is a debatable issue, but the prevailing social science position strongly favors the latter.

Gender stratification is evident in all societies. The gender hierarchy is almost always one in which women are the subordinate stratum. The ideology of sexism holds that male and female differences are biological in origin and not subject to change. This belief, reinforced by a set of stereotypes, has traditionally helped to rationalize and stabilize male dominance.

Women have entered the workforce in unprecedented numbers in the past several decades, but they remain heavily concentrated in certain occupations, generally earn less than men, and do not often occupy positions of authority. Nevertheless, legal and traditional impediments to occupational mobility have been reduced enormously in the past several decades, and significant changes continue to occur in the status of women. In certain areas, namely education and the professions, change has come quite rapidly. In politics and the corporate world, the rate has been slower but gradual nonetheless. Women have begun to enter lower and middle managerial positions in greater numbers, but it is at the uppermost echelons that societal power remains overwhelmingly male.

Women in the developing world and even in some societies of the developed world experience a level of subordination that is far more profound and consequential than in the United States and most other Western industrial societies. In all societies, an active feminist movement seeks changes in the structure of gender stratification.

The feminist movement in the United States experienced a resurgence beginning in the 1960s, stimulating the push for women's rights and socioeconomic equality during the past thirty years. Although the feminist ideological spectrum is broad and complex, it can be roughly broken down into two very general perspectives, equity feminism and gender feminism.

13

Political Inequality

[The poor] have to labor in the face of the majestic equality of the law, which forbids the rich as well as the poor to sleep under bridges, to beg in the streets, and to steal bread.
ANATOLE FRANCE

We can have democracy in this country or we can have great wealth concentrated in the hands of a few, but we can't have both.
LOUIS D. BRANDEIS

The political philosopher Bertrand de Jouvenel described politics as "a systematic effort . . . to move other men in the pursuit of some design cherished by the mover" (1963:30). Max Weber defined power in much the same way as Jouvenel defined politics: "the possibility of imposing one's will upon the behavior of other persons" (1954:323). *Politics,* then, is about **power;** to speak of the pursuit and exercise of power is to imply the pursuit and exercise of politics.

Most often we think of politics as the actions of politicians and government officials, the comings and goings of people in Washington or in one of the state capitals. But politics, in a broad sense, is the exchange of power resources, that is, people using money, material goods, knowledge, fame, information, influence, beauty, authority, and so on in trying to affect other people's behavior. As such, power is inherent in all human relations, from the family to the society as a whole. This chapter focuses on the latter—power in the societal realm. In modern societies, societal power is attached to decision-making positions in organizations, particularly those that are part of the state, the economy, and the media. It is in those organizations that people in positions of authority make decisions having the broadest impact on the society.

Political Stratification

The Scope and Dimensions of Power

If power involves making decisions, we can begin to understand power inequality by thinking about the critical decisions that affect our lives and the extent to which we can influence those decisions. Essentially, decision-making power can be seen at two social levels, the interpersonal and the societal.

Interpersonal Power   At the interpersonal level, most of us can pretty much shape our lives as we choose. Shall I go to work, or shall I stay home and watch television? Shall I dress casually today, or more formally? Shall I have pizza or tacos for lunch? These are the kinds of decisions that may be important to us at the moment, but they have little or no impact on anyone but ourselves. It is decisions at this level, however, over which we have utmost personal control.

If we move up the power scale a notch, we find that our ability to influence decisions begins to decline. This level of power is apparent in the relationships between husbands and wives, parents and children, employers and employees, and teachers and students. In these situations, people seek to exert their will over others, but in none of these cases do the consequences of the actions of anyone extend much beyond the immediate group. You might fail to convince your friends that the movie you wish to see will be more entertaining than the one they want to see, but no one outside the circle of friends will feel the effects of this power act. Similarly, a teacher may wield significant power over her students in the classroom, but only her students will be directly affected.

Societal Power   Once we move beyond the relatively narrow range of personal actions that we take on a day-to-day basis, most of us have very little say. On major issues that profoundly affect us, decisions are made by others who are not subject to our direct influence. How much will we earn, and how much will we have to pay for the consumer goods we want and need? What will be the content of our formal education, and to what ends will we be able to apply it? What opportunities will the labor market offer? Will our society live in peace, or will it be at war with other nations? What will be the quality of the air we breathe or the water we drink? On these and other issues of the economy, government, education, international affairs, and the environment, most of us are simply observers, lacking the capacity to directly affect decisions in any meaningful way. However, a small number of people in the society—an elite—*do* have the power to decide these and other vital issues that fundamentally shape our lives. Thus, we can begin to see the outlines of political inequality.

Societal power is exercised when the effects of an organization's or an individual's decisions are felt, either directly or indirectly, by many—perhaps by all—people in the society. The actions of the state are the clearest example of such widespread power. Virtually no one is immune to the consequences of decisions made by government leaders. Issues of taxation, spending, welfare, war and peace, and a myriad of other vital concerns are decided by the political elite.

But societal power does not lie only within the sphere of government. Huge transnational corporations also exert a similar scope and depth of influence. The decision by one or a few oil companies to raise the price of oil, for example, will affect not only those who drive automobiles but the economy as a whole, given the importance of oil as a source of energy. Jobs, prices of consumer goods, and the fate of countless projects will be at stake. Or, consider the societal power of producers, editors, and owners of national television networks. As a source of information and entertainment, television in modern societies is unmatched. Hence, the power to choose what will be presented as news and other programming constitutes an enormous power. The policies and decisions of private organizations, like oil companies or TV networks, are therefore as public in their effect as the policies and decisions of government agencies.

Societal power ordinarily occurs only within institutions (like government, the corporation, and the mass media) or within specific large organizations that make up those institutions (such as the U.S. Congress, General Motors, and NBC). And it is exercised by key decision makers who occupy elite positions in those organizations.

Elites and Masses

In deciding those issues that affect all or great parts of the society, it is only the few at the top who are able to make their influence felt. Only on issues that affect limited and specific parts of the society (mostly at the interpersonal level) do most people have any input. To simplify matters, then, we can divide the society into two main power strata: elites and masses.

Elites are groups whose members occupy the society's top positions of power. They exercise authority, influence, and control of resources within the society's important organizations (Marger, 1987). Elite members formulate the policies, guide the activities, and decide the significant issues of the government, the corporation, education, and other major societal institutions. Moreover, they possess the authority and credibility to transmit and defend the explanation and justification for the prevailing political and economic systems, that is, the dominant ideology.

Masses, or non-elites, are those who make up the vast majority of the society's populace, those whose power is limited. Obviously, there are great differences in power among non-elites. A middle-level bureaucrat working for a state government agency has less power than the governor but more power than lower-level agency workers. However, in deciding the fundamental issues of the political and economic systems—in political scientist Harold Lasswell's (1936) oft-quoted phrase, "who gets what, when, how?"—these differences shrink in significance. The important distinction is basically between the few at the very top—the elites—and the remaining populace.

The Inevitability of Elite Rule   In studying political inequality, it is axiomatic that in every society a relatively small number of people—an elite—always rule. Recall from Chapter 8 Michels's notion of the "iron law of oligarchy." Once organizations—and societies—reach a certain level of size and complexity, it can be no other way. "The people" never rule. This does not mean that masses have no power. Particularly in democratic societies, there are opportunities for citizens to participate in the political process and to try to hold elites accountable. The key analytic questions, then, involve the relationship between elites and masses and the extent to which masses are able to influence decisions made by the elites. The following sections first examine the power structure in American society, along with some major theories, and then look at the extent of political inequality and how the power of elites may be checked by the political process.

Political and Other Forms of Inequality   Political inequality should not be seen as unrelated to other forms of social inequality. As will become evident in the discussion that follows, there is a strong and ineluctable linkage of political inequality with other forms of inequality, particularly class inequality. Indeed, as noted in Chapter 1, power is at the base of all forms of stratification. In the end, those who have more wealth and prestige than others are usually able to convert that wealth and prestige into power. Whether power precedes wealth and prestige or vice versa is a chicken-and-egg question. In any case, they are closely interrelated. This linkage has been observed by many philosophers and social observers. Marx maintained that "political power, properly so called, is merely the organized power of one class for oppressing another" (Tucker, 1972:352). Coming from the opposite side of the political spectrum, the conservative philosopher Edmund Burke similarly observed that "As wealth is power, so all power will infallibly draw wealth to itself by some means or other" (Baker, 1992:245).

Three Models of Power in America

Social scientists' analyses of political power in the United States have boiled down to a debate among three major theoretical schools: class, elitist, and pluralist. As with any of the theories explored in previous chapters, it is important to keep in mind that there are no clear "rights" and "wrongs." Theoretical perspectives in the social sciences, remember, do not provide definitive answers; rather, they enable us to look at social structures and processes in different ways, each providing elements that together lead to a more informed view.

Sociological models of the American power structure present different scenarios of *who* has power, *how* they exercise it, and *in whose interests* their power is wielded. On one key point there seems to be general agreement among the three theories: In no modern society, regardless of how democratic its system may be, do masses actually rule in the sense that they themselves make critical political decisions. Instead, they rely on leaders to make those decisions. But on other details of elite rule there is a wide range of thought. Do elites use their power for the society's welfare or for personal gain? Are elites necessary, or might their functions be assumed by other forms of leadership? Are elites closed and cohesive units, or are they open and diverse? Is there only one ruling elite, or are there several? Also, the social characteristics of elites themselves have been subject to much investigation and debate. From what social classes, ethnic groups, and other social categories do elite members come? And how do patterns of elite circulation change, enabling those of different social origins to enter into positions of power and privilege?

Finally, and perhaps most important, how much power can masses exert against the power of elites? Is democracy real, or is it merely an illusion, even in societies like the United States that are considered thoroughly democratic in their politics?

The Class Model

The class model of the American power structure derives from the Marxian theory of inequality, discussed in Chapter 8. Power is seen as originating in the society's institutions of property and the class relations that derive from them. Political power, in this view, is exercised by those who control the means of production, that is, the capitalist class. Societal power, therefore, is concentrated in the hands of a few and not subject to control by political institutions, no matter how democratic they may seem to be. This obviously does not conform to the common perceptions of the structure of power and political behavior held by most Americans.

The Instrumentalist View   There are two ways of viewing the power structure using a Marxian, or class, perspective. One view holds that members of the capitalist class do not necessarily govern, in the sense of occupying political offices, but they *rule,* by controlling political officials and institutions (Gold et al., 1975). The critical question in this view is, Who are the people in strategic positions? Theorists using this perspective have investigated the relations between top corporate and political decision makers, usually finding them to be of similar social backgrounds with a strong understanding of common purpose. Corporate leaders and the capitalist class act in concert with political and other institutional leaders to protect capitalist interests and to preserve the prevailing class system, from which, of course, they benefit most.

In addition to the direct political influence of the corporate elite through exchange of strategic positions with government leaders, capitalist control is effected through campaign financing and lobbying. As discussed later in this chapter, the major contributors to the campaigns of political office seekers are corporations and those who are independently wealthy, that is, the capitalist class. Lobbying is another tool used by capitalist interests to mold government policies in their favor. Through these means, then, the capitalist class is able to influence the decisions of politicians and their appointees in government agencies.

The Structuralist View   Another class, or Marxian-influenced, perspective on power contends that the interpersonal linkage between political and economic elites is of little importance in assuring the maintenance of capitalist class interests by the state. They argue that the structure of political and economic institutions in capitalist society makes it imperative that the state serve those interests regardless of whether capitalists directly or indirectly take part in state affairs. Attempts to influence government policymakers through campaign contributions, lobbying, and so on are merely "icing on the cake." Plainly, the state cannot carry through anticapitalist policies because of mechanisms built into the modern capitalist political economy (Block, 1977; Poulantzas, 1973). Politicians, therefore, come naturally to view the interests of dominant economic groups as fundamental to a prosperous socioeconomic system and are prepared to accede to their needs more readily than to those of other interest groups. Recall from Chapter 7 the preparedness of the federal government to assist weak sectors of the private economy through subsidies and other aids or to rescue failing corporations and banks.

In this view, social and strategic ties among corporate and government leaders are unimportant. Since the viability of the state is dependent on a healthy economy, state leaders *must* promote the interests of big business, that is, the large corporations, regardless of who they are or what their views may be. If the economy declines, tax revenues dry up, imperiling government programs and weakening public support for elected officials and other government leaders. Political scientist Charles Lindblom has neatly summarized this relationship:

> If business is not induced to perform, the result is economic distress. When the economy fails, the Government falls. . . . Hence, no category of persons is more attentive to the needs of business than the Government official. Businessmen consequently do not need to strain or conspire to win privileges already thrust on them by anxious legislators and administrators. (1978:A19)

In sum, whether because of influence on government leaders or because of the structural nature of the political economy, class theorists agree that the state sooner or later must weigh the interests of the capitalist class more heavily than others. Moreover, in modern capitalist societies the distinction between government leaders and corporate officials becomes less meaningful. With the active role of government in the making of economic policy, the various forms of public financial support given to private corporations, and the constant crossover of personnel from one sphere to the other, key economic and political decisions are often made by officials of government and corporations in concert. One of the more blatant examples of this came in 1995, when Republican Congress members invited corporate lobbyists to help them draft legislation dealing with the very issues on behalf of which the lobbyists had been working (Judis, 1995).

The Power Elite Model

The power elite model begins with the premise that societal power is concentrated in elite groups that control the resources of key societal institutions. Moreover, masses, though not completely powerless, can render little control over the decisions of elites. The presumption that societal power is concentrated in the hands of a few is, of course, also a fundamental premise of the class model. But the origins of societal power, in the power elite view, lie not in the institutions of property and the class relations that derive from them, but in the control of social organizations, particularly the state and the corporation.

This perspective, like the class model, runs counter to the common American view of how leaders relate to citizens and how the power of the former is kept in check by the latter. But in this view, the dominant relationship of elites to masses is prevalent in *all* societies, democratic or not. The composition of the elites and the basis of their power may vary at different times, but the essential fact of elite rule remains unchanged.

Mills and the Power Elite   In Chapter 5, C. Wright Mills's theory of the power elite was introduced (Mills, 1956). To briefly reiterate, Mills held that a small group of leaders made up of top corporate executives, key government officials, and the highest-ranking military officers constitute an American power elite. These are the persons who actually have the capacity to make basic decisions in their institutions and thus to determine the society's key policy issues, both public and private.

Aside from the power elite, what is the actual structure of power in American society, according to Mills? Do the masses have a role to play at all, or is the power elite beyond the control of citizens? Mills conceptualized the hierarchy of power in the United States as a trilevel arrangement: the power elite at the top, the masses at the bottom, and a middle level of power wherein less consequential political decisions are made (Figure 13-1). This middle level consists essentially of Congress, organized labor, important state and local political officials, and various pressure groups. There is a balance of power among the middle-level groups, but they are of little consequence in deciding the society's larger issues.

At the bottom, the bulk of the populace is relatively disorganized, inert, and in the process of becoming a "mass," that is, a society that responds with no countervoice to decisions made by a centralized power elite. The trans-

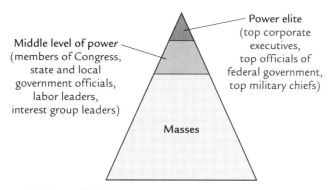

Middle level of power
(members of Congress,
state and local
government officials,
labor leaders,
interest group leaders)

Power elite
(top corporate
executives,
top officials of
federal government,
top military chiefs)

Masses

Figure 13-1 ■ Mills's Model of the American Power Structure

Source: Martin N. Marger, *Elites and Masses: An Introduction to Political Sociology,* 2d ed. (Belmont, CA: Wadsworth, 1987), 144. Copyright © 1987 Wadsworth Publishing Co. Reprinted with permission of Wadsworth, an imprint of the Wadsworth Group, a division of Thomson Learning. Fax 800-730-2215.

formation of the American public into a mass society is due largely to the nature of mass communications, in which most people only receive but cannot respond to opinions voiced by organized authorities. Political ends are accomplished through successful manipulation of the populace, using such primary means as television. According to Mills, "The public is merely the collectivity of individuals each rather passively exposed to the mass media and rather helplessly opened up to the suggestions and manipulations that flow from these media" (1956:305).

The reaction among social scientists and other social observers to Mills's description of power in the United States was at first mainly negative. *The Power Elite* was published in 1956, and power in the United States during the 1950s was seen by most as a balanced plurality of various interest groups, none of which was dominant. The idea that a small and relatively cohesive group could determine the basic shape of political and economic life in the society did not sit well with these pluralist assumptions. Not until the late 1960s, after the society had experienced the reality of bitter and often violent domestic conflict, as well as the arrogance of presidential power in Vietnam, was Mills's thesis reconsidered.

Perhaps the most important aspect of Mills's work is that it compelled political sociologists to rethink basic ideas about power in contemporary America. *The Power Elite* has become a classic work largely because of the controversy it initially aroused and still continues to provoke. Indeed, much of the research on power in the United States in the past several decades has been, by and large, a response to Mills's thesis.[1]

---

[1]For critiques of Mills's power elite thesis, see Domhoff and Ballard, 1968.

The Pluralist Model

The class and power elite models coincide on the notion that societal power is held by a small, self-serving group—either a ruling class or a power elite. Americans, however, are reluctant to think of politics as the conflict between social classes or the covert actions of elites. The pluralist model breaks sharply from these ideas.

Specifically, pluralism can be contrasted with the class and elite models on two major points. First, pluralists see societal power as fragmented rather than as resting in the hands of a relatively centralized and cohesive few. Whereas elite and class theorists see the power pie as uncut, pluralists see it divided into many pieces. Second, pluralists see average citizens as having meaningful input into decision making, thus exerting effective power over leaders; elite and class theorists see average citizens as having little real control over leaders and thus having little or no say in the shaping and resolution of the most important and far-reaching societal issues.

It is clear, then, why pluralism is more palatable to the American political mind: It is based on the democratic image of the sociopolitical system into which Americans are socialized from their earliest school experience. The distrust of an all-powerful government is also a fundamental part of the American political tradition, and again pluralism complements this belief quite well. Most simply, pluralist systems are usually seen as democratic systems, and there is a tendency to equate the two. A well-functioning pluralist system is one in which no single group among many diverse groups is able to impose its will on the society as a whole. This is contrasted to an oligarchic system, in which a single group rules with minimal accountability to the citizenry.

Interest Groups   Pluralists, unlike elite and class theorists, see a role for the masses in the power process. This is largely accomplished through the interest group system. The critical nature of interest groups as a democratizing force in politics was first suggested by Alexis de Tocqueville in the 1830s in his commentary on American society. Tocqueville pointed out that the ascendance of industrialization and the diffusion of democratic ideas in Europe in the late eighteenth and early nineteenth centuries caused the demise of a social aristocracy. This was a group that had traditionally served as an intermediary between the ruling monarch and the masses. In preindustrial societies an aristocracy stood as a stabilizing and generally benign force, acting as a filter of sorts through which the monarch's power was moderated as it passed down to the lower social levels. Tocqueville felt that without such an intermediate level of power, a society might easily be swept up by either an all-powerful tyrant or a "tyranny of the majority."

In modern democratic societies such as the United States, however, Tocqueville saw no aristocracy. What, then, substitutes for this important middle level of power? His answer: a network of well-organized voluntary associations, representing economic, political, and religious interests. Tocqueville was especially impressed with the American tendency to form innumerable autonomous and private organizations whose purposes were to further an almost endless variety of goals and activities. In Tocqueville's view this middle layer of organizations between rulers and masses serves a dual purpose. First, it prevents elites from exerting unmitigated power, and second, it provides the citizenry with a means of input into the power process. In other words, it is through these organizations that citizens are able to influence societal leaders and hold them accountable.

The existence of pluralism within government itself was also seen by Tocqueville as highly significant in the maintenance of political democracy. He was convinced that the American system of separation of powers and the proliferation of state and local units of government were additional safeguards against the growth of an all-powerful state. Thus, many competing power centers, he observed, typify the politics of American society both inside and outside its governmental institutions.

Modern Pluralism   Tocqueville's portrait of the American democratic system has become the theoretical groundwork of modern pluralism. Following a similar line of thought, political scientists in the 1950s developed an updated theory that took as its central theme the interplay of many varied interest or pressure groups (Truman, 1951). Interest groups are made up of people who share a particular objective—an "interest"—and act collectively to persuade government decision makers to act toward the group's benefit. People may choose any number of associational ties, depending on their needs and desires. Labor unions, church groups, civic organizations, environmental groups, business and professional associations, and the like all constitute interest groups. Through group efforts, people are more likely to be able to influence the political process than would be possible if they were to act alone. In the pluralist view, then, politics becomes a struggle of competing groups within an arena supervised by the state.

In sum, interest groups act as pressure groups on government, supporting issues and political actions of importance to their members. They serve as a means by which individuals with common interests can exert influence on decision makers by collective action. Voluntary associations are therefore vital to the functioning of the political system in enabling average citizens to exert at least some control over leaders. Through interest group activities, in combination with elections, political officials are held accountable and cannot favor the interests of only one or a few groups on all issues. The system remains relatively balanced and tranquil through compromise among the competing groups and their leaders.

Strategic Elites   Modern pluralists understand that, necessarily, elites play a critical role in societal decision making even in democratic societies like the United States. What is important, however, is that elites are, in this view, not a single integrated unit. Rather, there are numerous elites that do not agree on all issues. It is the competition between and within elites that holds the power of leaders in check (Dahl, 1967; Rose, 1967). Elites oppose one another (Democrats versus Republicans, labor leaders versus business leaders, and so on), and differing views are held by different members of any one particular elite (liberal Democrats versus conservative Democrats, Republicans who support free trade versus Republicans who oppose it, and so on). Unavoidably, then, elites make the society's important decisions. But there are multiple elites, not the single, overriding power elite or governing class that Mills had portrayed.

Sociologist Suzanne Keller has explained the role of a plurality of "strategic" elites in the power structure. She suggests that because of the complexity of modern societies, no single group of leaders can have the expertise or scope of influence to make critical decisions in every area of societal life. Numerous specialized or strategic elites therefore arise "whose judgments, decisions, and actions have important and determinable consequences for many members of society" (1963:20). Business leaders are competent to operate corporations but cannot run governments, which are the domain of political leaders; political leaders, in turn, know little about educational affairs, which is the specialty of an elite of professional educators; and so on. This view contrasts sharply with the notion of a relatively unified set of elites at the top of the power hierarchy that constitute a single "power elite" or "ruling class."

The American Power Structure: Unity and Division

The issue of whether a unified power elite or a diffuse power structure exists in the United States has absorbed the attention of sociologists and political scientists for several decades. Unfortunately, the issue is not easily resolved, because the actions of elites are never totally or even in large measure visible to non-elites. Rare are the occasions when the public actually gets a glimpse of what occurs behind the closed doors of congressional committees or corporate boards. The public speeches and pronouncements of politicians and business leaders are almost always scripted to create the most favorable image—they seldom reveal true motivations or objectives.

Another hindrance to a resolution of this long debate is the question of methodology. Using varying definitions of power as well as different strategies in discovering it, researchers have almost automatically been led to disparate findings. The picture of elite power in the United States or any other society as either totally unified or totally dispersed does not, of course, represent its true character. Realistically, the American power structure falls somewhere between these two extremes. Most class and elite theorists would not deny many elite divisions, nor would pluralists reject at least some degree of elite unity.

In addition, the shape of the elite structure and the nature of interrelations among its elements are not static. At certain times, pressures can bring elites of power together, and at other times, separate them. Some of these pressures are found in the society's class system; others are the result of the structural nature of political and economic institutions.

Power in America: An Integrated Model

Drawing on all three theoretical perspectives, it is possible to pick out key features of the American power structure that together define its essential character. On the one hand, societal power is limited to a small number of individuals whose functional and social ties are unavoidably close. This relative integration of political and economic decision makers at the top of the power structure supports the basic point of the class and elitist views. On the other hand, there is also evidence to support a basic pluralist tenet, that is, the lack of consensus among elites on many critical issues.

Elite Integration   As G. William Domhoff (1967, 1971, 1998) has shown, corporate and political elites come together in various policy-planning groups, advisory councils, and lobbying situations. Through these points of interaction, they exchange views, come to know one another, and lay out long-range policy plans. Given these common sites of decision making, a natural confraternity of power emerges. Business and government leaders also frequently exchange positions, especially at the upper levels of national power. They move back and forth between the private and public sectors as top advisers, cabinet officials, and lobbyists. This constant interplay of functional power contributes to the development of a common frame of reference and a consensus regarding basic societal issues.

As was shown in Chapter 5, those who dominate key societal institutions exhibit strikingly similar social backgrounds. Most important, their class origins are relatively narrow, with most coming from the upper or upper-middle classes. Even those who do move into power positions from lesser social ranks will have been exposed to similar socialization experiences later in life, such as higher education and corporate affiliations. Indeed, these may be more important than similar childhood experiences in molding common political interests (Putnam 1976).

Predominance of the Corporate Elite   Resources of power are varied, but it is economic resources that are paramount in modern capitalist societies. Thus economic leaders will generally, though not at all times, dominate the elite structure. Media coverage of news events leads one to assume that government leaders are the major decision makers who raise and settle issues. Power and politics, it seems, are limited to what occurs within the institutions of government: the presidency, the Congress, the bureaucracy, and so on. This view, however, seriously underestimates the ability of economic institutions and their leaders to influence the shaping of public policies.

The corporate elite may actually decide few public issues, but to a great extent they are able to set the agenda and boundaries of political debate. With

control of the society's productive resources, economic leaders set the framework within which political decisions makers must operate. Political leaders
are thus influenced by the long- and short-range interests of economically
powerful institutions (i.e., corporations) more than any other factor. As Kenneth Dolbeare has described the American political economy:

> The policies of government and of business are so intertwined and mutually
> supportive that no citizen can tell where one ends and the other begins. . . .
> Thus the first priority that underlies the entire pattern of government activity,
> social welfare and regulatory measures included, is the furtherance of the
> growth and other needs of the economic system. (1974:26–27)

Politicians at all levels of government understand that political actions can
never be completely divorced from economic consequences. Policies can be
enacted only to the extent that economic circumstances permit. And those circumstances are very much determined by individuals who, through their organizations, control the society's productive resources—that is, by the corporate elite.

The Commonality of Needs and Interests   Much interchange of personnel
occurs among elites. Although there is no question that a certain degree of
specialization makes it difficult for different elites to cross over from one institutional sphere to another (corporations, government bureaus, and universities all operate somewhat differently and have different objectives), the
skills needed to manage corporations are increasingly the same as those
needed to manage government bureaus and universities. When combined
with similar socialization experiences stemming from relatively common
class backgrounds, this makes for a natural coming together of elites.

There is also much interchangeability of government and corporate personnel. It is common for high corporate officials to leave the private sector
and assume top positions in government, and the movement occurs in the
opposite direction as well. When they finish their term of government service, most cabinet officers, for example, return to the corporate world or the
legal profession, from which they originally came before their appointment
to public office. With a mutual understanding of what constitutes a healthy
and progressive society, and with an agreement that a stable corporate system is necessary to maintain that condition, corporate and political elites can
interact with ease and can move back and forth between their two worlds
with little difficulty.

In addition to their back-and-forth movement between institutional sectors, top leaders commonly hold more than one position at a time. A corporate executive, for example, may also be a board member of other corporations, a member of a government commission, a trustee of a prestigious
university, and a director of a civic or cultural organization. Thomas Dye, in
his study of American institutional elites, found that approximately 15 percent of those identified as the nation's elite held multiple top positions. He

refers to this group as "interlockers," an inner group of top leaders who constitute a kind of "elite within the elite" (1995:153–158). Through their overlapping power positions, members of the inner group come to know each other socially, meeting not only in corporate boardrooms but at cultural and civic events, charitable functions, university trustee meetings, and alumni events. They are also members of the same exclusive social clubs. It is this inner group that links the corporate world with other major institutions, especially government, universities, and foundations (Dye, 1995; Useem, 1978).

Elite Divisions   Although elite integration is apparent, looking at the policy decisions of elites reveals that on many specific issues there are significant divisions among them. These policy differences are most evident among political elites, but even within the corporate world, decision makers are rarely unanimous in their views and actions. One need only glance at the front page of a daily newspaper or watch the national news on television to realize that there are deep and abiding disagreements on most issues, some of them quite basic. It is this lack of consensus on many issues to which pluralists point to support the view that elites are not socially cohesive, attitudinally unified, and dominated by business interests.

The fact that the power elites in American society come predominantly from the higher social classes does not automatically assure that they will at all times act on behalf of the interests of those classes. That upper-class origins do not automatically assure sympathy for upper-class political values and interests is exemplified by political figures such as Franklin D. Roosevelt and, more recently, the Kennedys. Though possessing unquestionable aristocratic credentials, they often displayed concern for the interests of the working class and ethnic minorities, who were their major base of electoral support.

There are noticeable interest differences and ideological conflicts among elites that are recognized not only by pluralists but even, in part, by those who emphasize the cohesiveness of institutional leaders. Consider, as an illustration, the issue of free trade. Despite the fact that they are all capitalists, corporate elites may differ as to whether they think it is beneficial for the United States to open its markets—with no controls—to foreign economies. The automobile industry, for example, has lobbied strongly during the past two decades to limit imports from Japan. Corporations such as retail merchandisers may approach this issue quite differently, seeing the benefits of open markets. Politicians will likewise view the issue with different perspectives, depending on their specific political interests and ideologies. Being strongly committed to laissez-faire principles, Republicans would be expected to adhere to the idea of free markets, with no tariffs or other controls on trade. But some Republicans may be fervent nationalists and thus oppose strong competition from other countries. Likewise, some Democrats support free trade, understanding that it will lower prices on consumer goods and therefore benefit middle- and working-class families. Other Democrats, however, will oppose free trade, fearing that it will cost some American workers their jobs. These kinds of disagreements play themselves out constantly in the give-and-take of national and lower-level politics regarding trade issues, tax policies, environmental controls, and so on.

Consensus on Basic Issues   The policy differences among elites are significant, but they do not represent basic disagreements on the most essential issues of the political economy and on the ways in which decisions are to be carried out. There is consensus on the fundamental shape of the capitalist political economy. Those who question or openly advocate systemic changes (introducing socialist elements, for example) are not likely to be taken seriously and are unlikely to enter the circle of political and economic power to begin with.

The Role of Masses in the System of Power

If elites always rule, no matter what kind of political system prevails, where does this leave the rest of the populace? Are the masses simply pawns to be duped, deceived, and manipulated by self-serving elites? Is democracy merely a sham, more symbolic than real? These are particularly important questions in the United States since the system of governance is a democracy, wherein citizens are assumed to have some power in settling important societal issues and where elites are assumed to be held accountable. This section examines when and how citizens can apply power and thus reduce the inequality between themselves and the power elites.

Political Participation: A Key Life Chance

Like education and health care, the ability to influence the political system by having one's interests addressed is, in a democratic society, a critical life chance. This means having access to and being able to hold accountable those who make decisions—the political elites. The electoral process is seen as the key to mass input in selecting and holding accountable political elites, and it is through this process that some degree of political equality is assured. "One person, one vote" is an axiom of electoral democracy, guaranteeing that everyone, regardless of wealth or social status, can exercise at least some political power on an equal basis. As Sam Rayburn, a Speaker of the U.S. House of Representatives, once earthily put it, "A whore's vote is just as good as a debutante's" (Baker, 1992).

Voting, however, is only one among a number of forms of political participation and is certainly not the most effective. The extent and scope of participation are strongly related to the class system. Those higher in income and wealth, occupation, and education are those who participate in the most meaningful and effective ways. The result is deep and abiding political inequality.

The Scale of Participation   The participation of citizens in the political process is assumed to be the most fundamental characteristic of democratic

Table 13-1 ■ The Hierarchy of Political Participation

Leaders	Persons directly involved in government	3%
Activists	Persons engaged in organized political action within private organizations	14%
Communicators	Persons who receive and communicate political information	13%
Citizens	Persons who have knowledge of the political system, hold opinions on issues, have a party preference, and usually vote	30%
Marginals	Persons who have minimal contacts with the political system	18%
Isolates	Persons who rarely or never participate in politics in any way	22%

Source: Marvin E. Olsen, "A Model of Political Participation Stratification," *Journal of Political and Military Sociology* 1(Fall 1973), 188.

systems. Yet the level of participation by non-elites in *any* form of political activity is relatively low. This has been true of American society for most of the twentieth century, despite the granting of voting rights and other political opportunities to previously disenfranchised groups such as women, African Americans, and other minorities.

Sociologist Marvin Olsen (1982) constructed a model of political roles that enables us to envision different forms and degrees of political participation. At one extreme are those who are maximally involved politically, whom Olsen calls *leaders*. They actually run for office or are government officials; they are a very small percentage. At the other extreme are the *isolates*, those who are politically unaware and apathetic and either acquiesce in or withdraw entirely from the political system; they constitute perhaps a fifth of the population. In between these two extremes are those who participate in varying degree. Close to the leaders are *activists* who exercise influence on government through lobbying and contributing to political campaigns. They are important and effective participants in the political system. Below activists are *communicators*, who are informed and knowledgeable about politics and discuss them with others. *Citizens* are somewhat aware of current political issues and vote but do little else in the way of political participation. Although they constitute the power base of the political system, they exert influence only collectively, not individually. *Marginals* are potentially available for mobilization by parties and candidates and may respond from time to time to particular issues that directly affect their lives. But their exposure to issues is minimal and short-lived, and thus their political activity is never sustained.

What this hierarchy of political activity reveals is that most of the citizenry is, at best, involved at a very superficial level (Table 13-1). The important players are the leaders and the activists. Comprising less than 20 percent of the population, it is these two categories that exercise influence—the former through authority in the formal political system and the latter through lob-bying, campaign financing, and the like.

Olsen's description is consistent with studies of political participation and with surveys of the American public (Davis and Smith, 1994). The level of cit-izen involvement in the political process is, quite simply, low. Voting is the simplest and least expensive form of citizen participation. Yet, even this act is practiced by only a minority of the eligible population. In no national U.S. election since 1932 have more than 63 percent of eligible voters actually cast their ballots. Only in presidential elections might the percentage of voters ever exceed 50 percent. In local elections, far less than half ever participate. In sum, most actions requiring time, energy, money, or information are engaged in by only a small fraction.

Low rates of participation are not limited to the United States. Although voting percentages in most other democratic societies are considerably higher, the percentages involved in other forms of political activity in those societies resemble the U.S. pattern (Verba and Nie, 1972; Milbraith and Goel, 1977; Olsen, 1982).

The Effective—and Costly—Forms of Participation

It is at the levels of leaders, activists, and, to a lesser degree, communicators that the effective forms of participation occur. These forms of participation are far more costly than others in terms of time, energy, and, especially, money. It is here that the most glaring evidence of political inequality occurs. A gulf separates those who can effectively make their interests known to the powerful and can expect them to respond and those who are relatively pow-erless. Two of the most important forms of participation are financial support of candidates for office and lobbying. In both cases, the connection between class inequality and political inequality is obvious. What is demonstrated is the inextricable link between money and political power. Quite simply, those with greater financial resources are far more able to exert their influence on decision makers.

Campaign Financing   Being elected to political office today generally re-quires a great deal of money. Campaign financing is, in itself, a major busi-ness. In 1952, the first year in which total political costs were calculated, $140 million was spent electing people to local, state, and federal offices (Alexander, 1992). By 1980, the figure was $2 billion (Rosenbaum, 1996). In 2000, about $3 billion was spent just on the congressional and presidential campaigns alone (Center for Responsive Politics, 2000). Consider the ex-pense of running for a U.S. House or Senate seat. In 2000, while the average winning House candidate spent $636,000, campaigns in some hotly con-tested races cost millions. In the twenty-seventh district of California, the

Table 13-2 ■ 2000 Federal Election Campaign Financing

	Raised	Spent
President		
George W. Bush	$184,228,804	$151,564,555
Al Gore	$133,308,785	$100,409,248
Senate		
Democrats	$204,159,912	$186,987,158
Republicans	$186,875,850	$171,450,952
House		
Democrats	$250,673,351	$206,104,298
Republicans	$277,345,794	$232,520,438

Source: Center for Responsive Politics, 2000.

two candidates spent a total of $9 million, as did the two running for the seat from the tenth district of Illinois. For a contested Senate seat in 2000, the average expenditure by a winning candidate was $5.6 million; in the two most expensive campaigns, the two candidates in New York spent $80 million, and the two in New Jersey spent $67 million (Center for Responsive Politics, 2000). Fund raising and campaign spending by the two parties in the 2000 federal election is shown in Table 13-2.

Candidates who are independently wealthy can use personal funds to help finance their campaigns for political office. The number of wealthy candidates funding their own campaigns has risen dramatically in recent years. In 1998, fifteen House and Senate candidates spent more than $1 million in personal funds (Center for Responsive Politics, 2000). H. Ross Perot spent $63 million of his own money running for the presidency in 1992 and another $37.2 million four years later. Another multibillionaire, Steve Forbes, publisher of *Forbes* magazine (and son of the late Malcolm Forbes), spent $37 million of his fortune in his unsuccessful campaign for the Republican nomination for president in 1996 and millions more again in his 2000 quest for the nomination. In the single most ambitious expenditure of personal funds to date running for political office (other than the presidency), Jon Corzine spent $60 million of his fortune in winning a U.S. Senate seat from New Jersey in 2000.

Given the costs of running for office, candidates who are not independently wealthy must turn to those who can provide them the financial aid they need. This is particularly true of positions at the federal level, where campaigns are of a broader scope than local ones, requiring costly television and other media advertising. So critical have campaign funds become to politicians that while in office they spend as much of their time raising money as attending to constituent and legislative matters. Although labor unions and other organizations contribute to political campaigns, the two major sources of wealth are the giant corporations along with wealthy

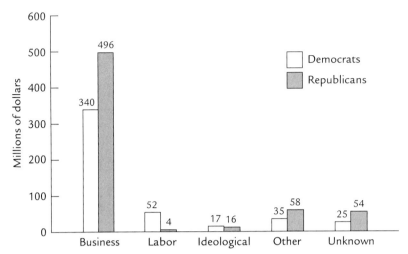

Figure 13-2 ■ Business-Labor-Ideology Split in PAC, Soft and Individual Donations to Candidates and Parties, 1999–2000 (in $ millions)
Source: Center for Responsive Politics, 2000.

individuals and families of the capitalist class. Figure 13-2 shows the total amounts given by business, labor, and ideological groups to candidates in federal elections in 2000. The dominance of the business sector is obvious.

One of the major forms of campaign contributions to candidates, particularly those running for Congress, is the PAC system. **Political action committees** (PACs) are organizations outside the official political parties that are designed to raise and distribute money to candidates. They are organized by particular interest groups, such as corporations, professional associations, and labor unions, or by groups that are concerned with a particular issue, such as abortion rights or gun control. The vast majority, however, are organized by big business, either by individual corporations or by trade and industry groups. Labor unions and ideological groups (the National Rifle Association, for example), while also heavily contributing to PACs, run a distant second to the corporate sector (Figure 13-2).

Soft money, another way in which political campaigns are financed, refers to funds that are given to the parties rather than to specific candidates. The advantage is that unlike individual contributions to candidates, there are no legal limits on how much can be given to a political party. This method has become the parties' primary means of raising tens of millions of dollars from wealthy contributors. Five, ten, or even one hundred times the amount of the legal limit on individual contributions is regularly donated to both parties in soft money (Center for Responsive Politics, 2000). As with PAC money, the soft money flow is dominated by corporations and affluent individuals and families. Together, Democrats and Republicans raised about $500 million in soft money for the 2000 elections, ten times more than they had raised in 1992 (Center for Responsive Politics, 2000).

Other forms of political contributions are even more unregulated and undisclosed than are PACs and soft money. For example, groups may run television ads or engage in other kinds of political campaigning that mention candidates by name and clearly promote a particular agenda but remain immune from federal election law because they do not explicitly call for a specific candidate's election or defeat. This means that elected officials may benefit from huge contributions, including those made by groups or individuals with important business before them, that the public has no way of discovering. In Montana a group calling itself Citizens for Better Medicare ran television ads accusing the Democratic Senate candidate of pushing for government price controls on drugs. The viewers of the commercials had no way of knowing that the group was sponsored by the pharmaceutical industry (Marcus, 2000).

The gap between the political "haves" and "have nots" could not be clearer. In 1992, only one-half of 1 percent of the population made a political contribution of greater than $200 (Schiff, 1996). This means that the electoral system, so tied to money, is overly supported and influenced by very wealthy individuals and families and corporate executives. The Republican Party's black-tie gala in 1997, for example, was attended by two thousand supporters who each paid $1,000 for the dinner. The party raised over $11 million in that single evening. Four donors—two corporations and two individuals—made contributions of $250,000 each (Clines, 1997). Several years ago, Trent Lott, the Senate majority leader, held a private luncheon with two hundred of his party's biggest patrons at a Palm Beach luxury resort. When asked about changing the way campaigns are financed, Lott defended unlimited donations as "the American way" (Seelye, 1997). As the political system is driven by money, the majority of the population is left on the margins of the process.

Those who contribute campaign moneys obviously do so with the expectation that they will realize a return on their investment. That is, they understand that there is a quid pro quo in which the recipient will remember them and will act in their interests on issues that affect them (Clawson et al., 1992). Money does not "buy" politicians; it buys access and influence. Who can phone his or her representative in Congress regarding a pressing issue and expect to speak directly with that person? Few constituents would expect, much less actually receive, such a personal response. Big campaign donors, however, regularly communicate and establish close relationships with elected officials who are expected to defend them when issues arise that are relevant to their interests. The money basis of the electoral system helps explain why, for example, the numerous tax bills enacted by Congress from 1977 to 1990 resulted in huge tax cuts to corporations and families at the top of the income hierarchy while middle- and working-class families experienced a rise in their federal tax burden (Barlett and Steele, 1992). As journalist William Greider describes it, "Behind all the confusion and complexity of the tax debate, democracy's natural inclinations were literally thrown into reverse—rewarding the few at the expense of the many" (1992:80).

Campaign spending has become a major political issue in recent years and, as with other issues of social inequality, evokes the confrontation of liberty and equity. Conservatives often defend the system as providing an opportunity for people to express themselves and to support their candidates as they choose. In this view, to limit campaign contributions would violate a basic liberty: free speech. Liberals, on the equity side, see excessive campaign spending as unfair to those on the lower rungs of the class hierarchy by skewing the political system toward the wealthy, who are the major campaign contributors.

Lobbying   Lobbying is an important means by which individuals and organizations, through their interest groups, seek access to public officials. As with the system of campaign financing, however, this is a part of the political process that is heavily biased in favor of those with great economic resources. Trying to persuade legislators and other government officials through direct efforts is a well-institutionalized practice in American politics. Indeed, the term "lobbyist" derives from the past in which representatives of interest groups would collar legislators in the lobby of the Capitol. But today lobbying efforts have become tools for groups whose wealth enables them to retain permanent staffs of lobbyists in Washington and in state capitals, constantly working to further their political interests. An estimated $1.2 billion is spent each year by organizations lobbying the U.S. Congress (Hosansky, 1998).

As might be expected, corporations, given their immense financial capacities, are predominant lobbying forces. They support industrial and trade associations, which lobby for particular industries or business groups collectively. The American Petroleum Institute, for example, will lobby for the entire oil industry; the American Insurance Association, for the insurance industry. One of the most powerful lobbies in Washington is the Business Roundtable, made up of chief executive officers of the very largest U.S. corporations. Rather than rely on paid lobbyists, these corporate CEOs themselves lobby members of Congress as well as meet with the president and cabinet members (Domhoff, 1998). Also, and perhaps more significant, individual firms have their own lobbying staffs. Public-interest groups, labor unions, and professional groups such as doctors, lawyers, and educators also actively lobby, but their efforts do not match those of the corporate sector (Abramson, 1998).

As the system works, lobbyists bestow monetary and material benefits on legislators and other government officials in hopes of favorable treatment on particular issues. In 1997, for example, Atlantic Richfield, one of the largest U.S.-based oil companies, paid for a five-day trip to London for then House Speaker Newt Gingrich, his wife, and two aides. During the trip, Gingrich spoke at the company's annual dinner. The group stayed at one of London's most upscale hotels where the room alone for Gingrich and his wife cost over $12,000. The full cost of the excursion was $42,000. Upon his return, Gingrich was quoted as saying that "every American should make this trip" (Kamen, 1998). In the same year, the Tobacco Institute, representing cigarette companies, flew eleven Congress members to an exclusive Scottsdale, Arizona, resort for a "legislative conference" at a cost of $63,000 (Carlson, 1998).

In addition to such material benefits, lobbyists influence government in another, and perhaps more important, way. They constitute a key source of information for legislators and other policymakers on general as well as specific issues. Speaking to a meeting of lobbyists, former Senator Alan Cranston put the matter bluntly: "Lobbyists are in fact an extension of our congressional staffs, providing information and ideas that are vital to the molding of legislation" (quoted in Green, 1984:61). Given this understanding of their role, lobbyists are able to supply input into the shaping of government policies that affect their interests. When legislation arises concerning, for example, the pharmaceutical industry or the trucking industry, necessary information is supplied by the companies themselves, usually through their lobbyists. Such information will, of course, be presented in a way that reflects the interests of the lobbying group. Government officials, however, come to see such efforts as helpful and even vital to their decision-making functions.

Corporations and other key economic groups have disproportionate capacity not only to lobby lawmakers and other government officials but also to influence public opinion. Through extensive public relations efforts, they can sell their political views to the society in a manner that is financially and organizationally prohibitive to most groups and individuals. Television and print media advertising are enormously costly, and therefore only those with adequate economic resources can use them. This means, essentially, the giant corporations.

Political Participation and Social Class

In a very broad sense, the political system is an open one in which equality of opportunity prevails: Everyone can follow the issues, become informed, and vote. All can participate. However, as pointed out, the political process entails a great deal more than voting. The issue, then, is not *whether* people can participate, but *in what ways* they can participate. There is clearly a class bias in the political system, one in which those with substantial economic resources have tremendous advantages over others. In effect, they are the serious participants (the "activists," in the participation hierarchy) who can exert influence on political elites. Most of the remainder of the populace are minimally involved or are merely spectators. Even the most conscientious citizens, as William Greider describes them, become disillusioned: "They have become 'citizens' of a purified form—free to speak frankly on the public issues they value, but utterly disconnected from the power structure where those issues are decided" (1992:202).

In terms of social class, the serious players in this system are a distinct subset of the general populace. They are higher than average in income, occupation, and education. The relationship between social class and political participation extends over the entire spectrum of participation. Even voting, the simplest form of participation, is class related; the higher the social class, the more likely one is to vote (Verba and Nie, 1972; Wolfinger and Rosenstone, 1980). In 1996, over 70 percent of citizens living in families with incomes of $50,000 or more reported that they voted, compared with less than 40 percent of those in families with incomes of less than $10,000 (U.S. Census Bureau, 1998b).

This would not pose serious problems if the needs and wishes of these upper- and upper-middle-class citizens coincided with those of subordinate classes. But as political scientists Sidney Verba and Norman Nie explain, "the participants differ substantially from the nonparticipants in the problems they consider salient and in the solutions they prefer" (1972:15). Those who participate most extensively bring their class perceptions and biases to the electoral process. As a result, to the extent that political leaders do respond to the electorate, they respond to the perceived needs of these classes rather than to the needs of the working and lower classes. Political scientist Richard Hamilton (1972) found that during the 1950s and 1960s, for example, the majority of Americans beneath the upper-middle class indicated consistently that they favored government efforts to establish various social welfare programs such as health care and guaranteed incomes. Yet throughout this period, legislators responded carefully with conservative policies that did not basically threaten the status quo.

In any case, most legislators at the national level are from upper-middle-class backgrounds themselves and are thus not likely to hold views that reflect the needs of groups lower in the class hierarchy. Their perceptions of social and economic problems will be consonant with those of the significant participants in the electoral process.

That corporations and the wealthy are more apt to have their interests protected by government policies does not mean that other groups and interests do not benefit from government functions; obviously they do. And it is equally clear that noncorporate sectors of the society often successfully pressure political decision makers much as do the affluent and the corporations. Labor unions, for example, have been an extraordinarily effective interest group during the past half century, and the demands of other groups, such as African Americans and women, have also been gradually responded to by government. Nonetheless, the basic structure of the political economy remains intact. And as the nucleus of that system, the giant corporations and the wealthy can apply resources that will, if not assure, certainly strongly influence political action that addresses their interests and concerns.

In addition, the corporations and the wealthy have the resources to persevere in the political system. Consider tax policies, which are critical to the capitalist class and the corporations in general. The passage of a tax bill, whether favorable to their interests or not, does not end the matter. These groups continue to fight the battle with money and lobbyists, either protecting the privileges they have won or seeking those they desire. "Thus," as Greider notes, "the monied interests are always mobilized and working toward better results, knowing that the continuum of legislative action does not stop with one victory or one setback. Citizens may grow weary and move on to something else, but for obvious reasons, the wealthy are always on the case" (1992:81).

Participation and Elite Accountability

We have now seen that electoral activities—the primary form of non-elite political participation—may be limited in actually holding elites responsive to public needs and desires. Focusing only on electoral politics, however, may cause us to overlook other ways in which elites elude public accountability.

The classical view of democracy rests on the assumption that participation is equated with citizen power. Political leaders are ultimately required by the electorate to answer for their actions and must therefore respond to its general will. This assumption seems ill founded, however, for several reasons. One is simply the class bias of the system. As already noted, the serious participants do not represent a broad spectrum of the class hierarchy; rather, they are concentrated at the upper levels. The connection between participation and control of political elites, however, is frayed for several additional reasons. These relate to the roles of interest groups, economic elites, and the mass media in the policymaking process.

Interest Groups   Pluralists have considered interest group activity one of the most important instruments of citizen input into the policymaking process. If elections are not always effective in communicating the needs and desires of the people to the political elite, interest groups, serving as intermediaries between people and government, may do so. This assumes, of course, that most of the populace will be active members of one or several interest groups. Studies have shown, however, that this is not ordinarily the case (Almond and Verba, 1963; Putnam, 1996).

 As with participation in the electoral process, there is a definite link between the scope and intensity of activism in interest groups and one's class position. Most simply, the higher one's class, the greater the number of memberships and the greater the extent of participation in such organizations. Thus, like the electoral process, the interest group system is heavily class biased. Furthermore, the most effective interest groups are those that are firmly part of the lobbying system, that do not come and go with changing issues. These mainly represent dominant economic interests.

Power without Participation   Focusing attention on electoral behavior may cause us to mistakenly accept this as the most significant wellspring of power. Electoral decisions, however, are only secondary to the establishment of the political agenda itself. Rather than deciding *who* will argue and act on particular issues, deciding *which* issues will become part of the political debate is a more primary act of power. Political scientists Robert Alford and Roger Friedland (1975) point out that the traditional pluralist perception of the political process assumes that the most important decisions are made at the point where legislation is proposed and debated. But this overlooks the more important preemptive development of policy options by dominant—principally economic—interest groups. In these decisions, nonelites do not participate.

 In any case, since the policymaking process is, in more cases than not, reliant on the cooperation of government and dominant economic groups, the latter are in a position to greatly influence the structure of political action, no matter what role they may play in participatory politics. Whatever government does is dependent on tax revenues, and the ability of government at all levels to raise revenues is, in turn, dependent on the production and investment decisions of dominant economic groups, specifically major corporations. Alford and Friedland call this "power without participation" (1975).

The Unaccountability of Economic Elites   Let's assume for the moment that elections do serve their intended purpose, to give citizens some input into the decisions of political leaders and to hold the latter accountable. At best they can only help control the actions of political officials. The capacity of the corporate elite to make public policy, however, through its interaction with government officials and through its own decision-making power is enormous. Indeed, when considered in total, the decisions made by corporate leaders in regard to investment of capital, location of factories and equipment, employment levels, and so on are often of greater public consequence than those made by public officials.

Despite these far-reaching public consequences, non-elites have virtually no control over the decision-making processes of corporations. Representatives of interest groups or of the general public neither sit on corporate boards nor participate in the selection of those boards. Corporate leaders do not seek input from the electorate; they are not required to maintain even the nominal public responsibility of elected or appointed government officials. The multifarious powers of the corporate elite are simply not publicly controlled. Even if we accept the most favorable picture of the role of the participatory process in democratic politics, it can affect only a part—and perhaps not the most critical part—of the mosaic of power in the United States and other advanced capitalist societies.

The Unaccountability of Media Elites   Although not formally a part of either government or the economy, the mass media are integrally tied to both, and both rely on the mass media to function as they do. Moreover, the mass media have substantial independent resources that make them a formidable institution of power in their own right. Perhaps most important, the mass media, as explained in Chapter 9, are, for most people, the major sources of information regarding politics and public policy. Despite their great power and major influence on the shape of politics, the media are private institutions that operate largely free of citizen input into their content and direction. Decisions regarding what to print or televise are made unilaterally by the media elite, who are not publicly accountable through the electoral process.

As discussed in Chapter 9, not only do the media elite determine the content of the information the public receives, but they monitor access to the media and thus are able to decide who will communicate their views to the society. Only those who are able to pay can send their messages to the widest audience through the mass media. This, again, means the largest corporations.

Mass Participation and the Class Structure

What impact can non-elite participation, particularly the electoral process, have on the distribution of the society's rewards? Can it, in Lasswell's terms, affect "who gets what, when, and how?" In short, can it change the shape of the society's class and status hierarchies?

As shown in earlier chapters, the class structure in the United States has remained amazingly stable during the past century. The distribution of wealth and power has not been fundamentally affected by the techniques of procedural democracy. Indeed, in some ways mass participation may actually serve to stabilize the system of inequality and assure the status quo by giving the illusion of power. Political scientist Murray Edelman has keenly described the symbolic functions of participatory politics:

> To quiet resentments and doubts about particular political acts, reaffirm belief in the fundamental rationality and democratic character of the system, and thus fix conforming habits of future behavior is demonstrably a key function of our persisting political institutions: elections, political discussions, legislatures, courts, and administration. Each of them involves motor activity (in which the mass public participates or which it observes from a distance) that reinforces the impression of a political system designed to translate individual wants into public policy. (1964:17)

If the electoral process has the effect of stabilizing the opportunity and reward structures of the society, it is not surprising that those of higher social class and status should be its main participants. Indeed, if participation through normal channels has little effect on government responses to the needs of subordinate groups, and if the party system and other aspects of electoral politics frustrate these groups' effective mobilization, then low rates of participation by those at the lower end of the class and status hierarchies are, in Alford and Friedland's words, "neither analytically surprising nor politically irrational" (1975:448). Verba and Nie (1972) contend that the upper-class bias of participatory politics is not easily overcome, even by lower-class citizens who do choose to become politically active; their numbers are too small and their organizational resources too limited for them to be an effective voice.

Political participation by non-elites, then, is simply not the same for all class groups since each has access to different resources that affect the ultimate payoff for participating. Participation is meaningful for those groups that bring to the political arena sufficient political and economic resources to make themselves heard. Those with the time, skills, organization, and, especially, money to participate convincingly—not simply by voting or joining an activist group—are likely to see the system working effectively, and indeed for them it *is* working effectively. It is to these groups that government leaders respond, thereby preserving the basic political economy and its attendant structure of inequality.

Noninstitutional Forms of Participation

What has been discussed to this point are institutional means by which masses can try to influence elites. These are legitimate ways in which, presumably, people can make their views known and pursue their interests through the prevailing political system. This is a system, however, that seems to work most effectively in the interests of the wealthy and powerful, giving ordinary citizens very limited ability to hold elites accountable or gain access to institutions of power.

When people find that their political objectives cannot be met by using the conventional institutions, that is, the electoral system with its attendant parties and interest groups, they may act outside the established political framework. Such nontraditional political behavior can be quite diverse, ranging from petitions, peaceful meetings, demonstrations, sit-ins, marches, or rallies to acts of civil disobedience, strikes, violent protests, or even armed confrontations with government authorities. Most actions are short-lived and have minimal subsequent impact on the political system, but others evolve into organized and prolonged sociopolitical movements that ultimately affect the society's dominant institutions.

Sociopolitical Movements   Sociopolitical movements may involve various class or minority groups seeking concessions from ruling elites, or they may involve groups seeking more fundamental changes in the society's institutional arrangement. In all cases they represent a challenge, in some degree, to the political or economic status quo. At certain moments, large numbers of people choose to use unconventional political tactics. They may also question the legitimacy of leaders and no longer feel that prevailing institutions are entirely just or unchangeable. In short, at such times people's political behavior and consciousness change (Piven and Cloward, 1978).

These collective attempts to alter the society's institutions of inequality differ, depending on the scope of change sought (sweeping or limited), the direction of change desired (progressive or regressive), and the methods used (persuasive and legitimate or coercive and unlawful). On the basis of these features, three general types of sociopolitical movements can be distinguished: reform, revolutionary, and reactionary.

Reform movements, the most common of the three, are relatively limited in terms of scope, direction of change, and methods. Their intent is the acquisition of social and political rights and economic benefits for certain disenfranchised or subordinate groups (workers, African Americans, gays, women) or the resolution of a certain issue to the benefit of some group (voting rights, welfare, health care). The objective is thus limited to making the prevailing system more responsive to the needs of such groups. Proposed changes are progressive in direction and actions are taken, for the most part, within the existing political framework. In a sense, the idea is for aggrieved groups to secure a piece of the action. The industrial labor movement of the 1930s is a good example. Traditionally, leaders of heavy industries with many unskilled workers had resisted efforts at collective bargaining. When automobile and steel workers, along with coal miners, challenged big industrial employers to recognize their labor unions, the workers eventually won by engaging in strikes, sit-downs, and at times violent confrontations with both company and public police. The industrial labor movement did not aim for a complete dismantling of the capitalist system but only for a greater role for workers within that system.

Whereas reform movements focus on specific issues or groups and do not seek to alter the society's institutional system in any fundamental way, **revolutionary movements** are sweeping in scope and aim for a restructuring of societal institutions and, ultimately, the class system itself. Franz Schurman (1971:20) has defined a revolution as "an overturning of fundamental hierarchical relationships in a society—what is below displaces what is above." Simply put, following revolution, those previously at the top of the social hierarchy may now be at the bottom.

Since a revolution's aim is basically to replace the existing social order, its adherents, of course, operate outside the established political framework. And their methods are bound to be coercive rather than persuasive; indeed, violence is usually assumed to be an integral element of revolution. Turning the social structure upside down obviously does not occur without the use of coercion by those seeking change and forceful retaliation by those resisting it. Ruling groups do not voluntarily relinquish their power. As Michels (1962[1915]:245) observed, "A class considered as a whole never spontaneously surrenders its position of advantage. It never recognizes any moral reason sufficiently powerful to compel it to abdicate in favor of its 'poorer brethren.' "

Given the scope and intensity of such change, it is not surprising that we have witnessed so few truly revolutionary movements in modern times. The first, and perhaps prototypical, social revolution occurred in France in 1789. Here the traditional ruling class, made up of the landowning aristocracy, was ultimately replaced by a new ruling class, the bourgeoisie, whose economic base was commerce and industry. An entirely new social order emerged based on the ideology of this now-dominant class. Other total revolutions that have basically altered class relations occurred in Russia in 1917, China in 1949, and Cuba in 1959.

Whereas both reform and revolutionary movements seek to establish new societal institutions and relations, **reactionary movements** are regressive, designed to resist progressive changes in the structure of inequality or perhaps even to re-create social hierarchies that existed in earlier times. The scope of change sought may be limited, as in reform movements, or quite broad, as in revolutionary ones. To explain and justify these goals, reactionary ideologies are often predicated on claims of cultural, physical, or moral superiority of some social groups and the inferiority of others. Racist, sexist, or homophobic movements are founded on such beliefs and thus aim to deny rights and privileges to their targeted groups.

Beginning in the late 1950s and early 1960s, a number of sociopolitical movements aimed at bringing about changes in the class, racial/ethnic, and gender hierarchies arose in the United States. Most were nonviolent and reformist in nature, but some were marked by violence, and a few even had revolutionary overtones. These movements focused on a diversity of groups and issues, including black civil rights, ending the Vietnam War, student rights, women's liberation, gay rights, consumerism, the environment, and protesting nuclear power and the proliferation of nuclear weapons. Some of these had a strong impact that led to profound societal changes. Then, in the late 1970s and 1980s, a number of conservative and reactionary sociopolitical movements emerged whose focus included a range of social, political, and moral issues such as abortion, prayer in public schools, educational curricula, and pornography. Led by rightist elements of the Republican Party and by Christian fundamentalists, these movements seemed to coalesce around a broad ideology whose theme called for the reversal of what was perceived as the political and social liberalization of American society during the previous two decades. These movements sought to impose a strict version of morality on the society and to return it to more traditional values.

Out of the broad array of sociopolitical movements of the past several decades has emerged a somewhat ambiguous picture. Undeniably, class, racial/ethnic, and gender hierarchies have been altered, in some cases quite significantly. Nonetheless, social inequality in numerous forms remains a fundamental societal feature. Those at the top of the society's hierarchies have great resources with which to resist mass challenges and thus to ensure stability and order in the stratification system: Most of the society's wealth and productive resources are owned and controlled by a relatively small number of persons and organizations; the dominant ideology works in an invidious fashion to instill support of the stratification system among most people, regardless of their class position; and, as explained in this chapter, the institutional means available to masses to influence political elites are in large part only symbolic. The result is that those with wealth, power, and status retain their privileges without serious challenge from below. Systems of inequality do undergo some alteration, but the changes are ordinarily slow, deliberate, and mild rather than radical and profound. Sociopolitical movements that do not pose a threat to dominant institutions and to the prevailing class system are likely to be more successful than those calling for sweeping and fundamental changes.

Summary

Political inequality essentially entails a hierarchy of decision-making power. On the significant societal issues, a few at the top—an elite—are able to make their influence felt. Elites are groups whose members occupy the society's top positions of power, exercising authority and control of resources within the government, the corporation, and other major societal institutions. Masses, or non-elites, are those who make up the vast majority of the society's populace, those whose power is limited.

Since it is elites that actually rule in any society, one of the key questions of sociology concerns the nature of leadership: Are leaders unified in thought and action, or are they sufficiently divided to assure at least some degree of mass control? Three general groups of theories have clustered around this issue, particularly as it pertains to the United States. Class (or Marxist) theorists and elite theorists posit a unified elite structure whose members have common social backgrounds and common ruling interests. Pluralist theorists, in contrast, see power at the top as diffuse, with no single group able to dominate.

There is some evidence to support each of these general views of the American power structure. Elites are integrated through the interweaving of their organizations (the corporation and the federal government, in particular), their interchange of positions, and their common social background. At the same time, there is no absolute unity of purpose and belief among them. Political and economic elites do not always see eye to eye on issues, and there are splits even within each of these two power groups.

An integrated model of power in America, combining elements of the three major theories, recognizes discord among elites but not basic disagreements on essential issues of the political economy. Within the power elite, corporate leaders, though not actually deciding most public issues, are able to set the agenda and boundaries of political debate.

There is a hierarchy of participation in the political system in which only a relative few participate in any significant way; these few tend to be mainly from the society's top class and status groups. The relationship between social class and participation is very strong: the higher one's social class, the higher the level and significance of participation. The most effective forms of participation are campaign financing and lobbying, both dominated by large corporations and wealthy individuals.

Electoral politics has limited impact on the policy decisions of political elites. In any case, elections can seek to hold accountable only those who are part of the political elite. Elections have no bearing on the selection or actions of decision makers of nongovernmental institutions, especially the corporation and the media. Thus, the electoral process represents only a limited aspect of the panorama of societal power in the United States and in other advanced capitalist societies.

Sociopolitical movements are forms of participation in which masses seek change in the distribution of economic and political power outside the conventional electoral system. They can range from reform movements, with limited objectives and tactics, to revolutions that seek complete transformation of the class hierarchy. Reactionary movements are aimed at resisting progressive changes in the system of inequality or reinstalling earlier forms of inequality.

Glossary

absolute poverty A socioeconomic condition in which people are unable, for whatever reason, to meet their fundamental necessities of life.

accident of birth Placement into a family of a particular class and ethnic status through birth.

affirmative action Public policies designed to provide, through preferential measures, wider opportunities in work and education for ethnic minorities and women.

apartheid The former system of caste in South Africa based on racial categorization.

assimilation The integration of a minority ethnic group into the societal mainstream. *See* **cultural assimilation; structural assimilation.**

authority Legitimate power.

blue-collar workers Those who work in manual occupations.

bourgeoisie The merchant class or, in Marxian theory, the capitalist class.

bureaucracy A type of social organization, typical of modern societies, that enables large numbers of people playing specialized roles to operate as a cohesive unit.

capitalism A system of economic production based on market principles and guided by the private ownership of property and the competitive pursuit of profit.

capitalist class The class at the pinnacle of the stratification system, whose members derive most of their income from investments and assets. In Marxian theory, the class that owns the means of production.

caste A type of social stratification in which status is acquired by heredity and in which mobility is severely constrained by law and custom.

charismatic authority As described by Weber, authority that derives from a leader's personal appeal.

class consciousness Awareness among members of a social class of their common economic and political interests vis-à-vis other classes.

closed societies Societies in which social mobility is uncommon and where political and cultural norms and values dictate against it.

comparable worth The idea that women and men should be paid equal wages for jobs that require comparable skill levels; sometimes referred to as *pay equity.*

corporate welfare Tax breaks, subsidies, and other government measures designed to benefit large corporations.

cultural assimilation The adoption by a minority ethnic group of the dominant group's norms and values.

cultural pluralism The maintenance of many varied ethnic cultural systems within the framework of a common economic and political system.

culture of poverty A theory that explains poverty as the result of a set of norms and values—a culture—that is uniquely characteristic of the poor.

cycle of poverty The idea that poverty is sustained by the entrapment of people in an array of social circumstances—low income, poor education, poor housing, poor health, etc.—that together operate in a circular process, making it improbable that individuals can break the cycle.

deindustrialization The departure of capital and industrial jobs from communities where they had been traditionally located.

demand-side policies Government efforts to reduce unemployment and stimulate economic demand by increasing public spending and imposing a greater tax burden on the wealthy.

deserving poor An element of the poor who are seen as poor through no apparent fault of their own.

discrimination Actions against minority ethnic groups that create disadvantages in various areas of social, economic, and political life. *See* **individual discrimination; institutional discrimination.**

dominant group In a multiethnic society, the group that exerts predominant economic, social, and political power and that has the greatest influence on shaping the society's cultural system.

dominant ideology An ideology that explains and justifies the prevailing power and reward structures.

downsizing The tendency for large corporations to reduce their workforce, with the objective of greater efficiency and profitability.

economic restructuring The radical shift in the past several decades from what had been a manufacturing-based economy to a service-based economy, eliminating, in the process, many traditional blue-collar jobs; related to the emergence of new technologies and the development of a global economy.

elite The tiny percentage of the population who occupy the society's top positions of power.

entitlement A government benefit that is automatically given to all who have reached a particular age (e.g., Social Security) or who otherwise qualify under the law for the benefit.

equity The distribution of the society's rewards in a just manner.

estate system A closed type of stratification, sometimes referred to as feudalism, based on land ownership; typical of agrarian societies.

ethnic group A group within a larger society that in some degree is set off from others by unique cultural traits.

ethnic minority A group singled out and treated differentially on the basis of its cultural or physical differences from the dominant group.

ethnic stratification A rank order of groups, each made up of people with presumed common cultural and/or physical characteristics, interacting in a system of dominance and subordination.

false consciousness A Marxian notion that refers to a belief on the part of non-ruling groups that the prevailing political and economic systems work in their interests, when in fact they work primarily in the interests of the ruling class.

family As it pertains to income and wealth data, two or more persons related by blood or marriage living together.

feminism The set of beliefs and actions that center on assuring the equality of men and women in various areas of social life.

feminization of poverty The tendency for women to comprise an increasingly large proportion of the poverty population, due in large measure to single parenthood.

fiscal policy Government measures involving taxation and public spending that influence the economy.

flat tax *See* **proportional tax.**

gender The socially and culturally defined roles of males and females.

gender stratification The hierarchical order of men and women in society.

global economy The interconnection of the economies of politically independent countries in trade, transfers of capital, labor, production, and distribution.

Horatio Alger myth The idea that anyone, regardless of social standing, can become wealthy and successful through hard work and perseverance.

horizontal mobility *See* **lateral mobility.**

household As it pertains to income and wealth data, all persons occupying a housing unit, that is, separate living quarters.

ideological hegemony A Marxian notion referring to the predominance of ruling class ideas.

ideology A set of beliefs and values that rationalizes a society's structure of power and privilege.

income Money received over a period of time.

individual achievement The belief that each member of society is responsible for his or her fate and that one's social position is a product of personal efforts and talents.

individual discrimination Actions against minorities carried out by individuals or small groups, usually in violation of the society's laws or norms.

inequality of condition Differences in people's living standards or life conditions.

inequality of opportunity Differences in people's opportunities to acquire the rewards offered by their society.

influence A form of power that entails the ability of some people to get other people to do what they want them to do voluntarily, without coercion.

institutional discrimination Actions, often unintentional, against minorities that are the result of the policies and structures of organizations and institutions.

intergenerational mobility Change of position in the class hierarchy from one generation to the next (e.g., father to son).

intragenerational mobility Change of position in the class hierarchy during an individual's lifetime.

Jim Crow The system of black-white segregation maintained in the U.S. southern states until the 1960s that constituted a caste-like form of stratification.

lateral mobility A change of position that in terms of socioeconomic status is neither better nor worse than the previous position.

legal-rational authority As described by Weber, authority that derives from specific duties and obligations assigned to a particular position in an organization.

legitimacy The willing acceptance by most members of the society of the prevailing institutional and stratification systems.

legitimation The process by which people come to accept willingly the society's institutional system and its attendant social inequality.

liberal capitalism A democratic political system in combination with a capitalist socioeconomic system.

liberalism, classical The philosophy that extols the worth of individuals and their right to control their destiny.

liberty Freedom to pursue one's interests as one desires and to reap the benefits of one's efforts.

life chances Opportunities that people have to acquire those things that are valued and desirable in their society.

lifestyle The behaviors and values common to members of a social class.

lobbying Efforts by individuals and organizations to access and influence public officials, usually through interest groups.

lower-middle class An occupationally diverse class comprised of middle managers, semiprofessionals, craftspersons, and many service workers.

macroeconomic policy The role of government in managing the national economy.

masses Non-elites, those who make up the vast majority of the society's populace and whose power is limited.

means of production In Marxian theory, productive resources, i.e., things that are necessary to supply the society's economic needs.

meritocracy A system in which rewards are yielded on the basis of performance and qualification.

middle-class squeeze The tendency for those of the middle, or intermediate, classes to be pushed either upward or, more commonly, downward in terms of wages, salaries, and family income.

minority group A group that, on the basis of members' physical or cultural traits, exerts less power and receives fewer of the society's rewards. *See also* **ethnic minority.**

mode of production In Marxian theory, the economic base, including the forces and relations of production; a society's system of economic production (e.g., feudalism, capitalism).

multiethnic society A society made up of various ethnic groups.

multinational corporation *See* **transnational corporation.**

official poverty Poverty as defined by government-imposed standards of measure.

oligarchy A form of rule in which the few, an elite, rule the many.

open societies Societies in which there are theoretically few impediments to social mobility.

opportunity structure The number and types of occupations relative to the number and qualifications of workers available to fill them.

panethnic group Several distinct ethnic groups lumped together into an inclusive category, usually based on the groups' world region of origin (e.g., Asian Americans).

patriarchy The dominance of men over women, especially within the family.

pluralism (1) The retention of ethnic cultures within the larger society; *see* **cultural pluralism; structural pluralism.** (2) A political system in which there are numerous competing centers of power, none capable of dominating at all times.

political action committees (PACs) Political organizations established by interest groups, which raise and distribute money for political candidates.

political economy The interrelationship of government and the economy.

post-industrial society A society characterized by the production mainly of services and information rather than finished goods, as in a traditional industrial society.

poverty *See* **absolute poverty, relative poverty,** and **official poverty.**

power The ability to realize one's will despite the resistance of others. *See also* **societal power.**

power elite Those who occupy positions of great importance in key institutions, especially the economy and government, and whose decisions have profound impact on the society.

power structure The relatively fixed distribution of power among groups and organizations that set the agenda of public policy.

prejudice Negative ideas regarding subordinate ethnic groups.

prestige The deference that people are given by others; social esteem.

progressive tax A tax in which those with higher incomes pay a higher percentage.

proletariat In Marxian theory, the industrial working class.

proportional tax A tax that levies the same percentage rate on all income earners; also called a flat tax.

public assistance programs Social welfare programs that are means-tested, requiring that recipients demonstrate a need in order to qualify for them.

race A socially created category of people who share a set of roughly similar genetic characteristics, or gene frequencies.

racism A belief system that avers the reality of races and the inherent behavioral differences between members of racial groups.

reactionary movement A sociopolitical movement designed to recreate conditions and institutions that prevailed in an earlier time.

reform movement A sociopolitical movement whose objectives are to obtain a greater share of power within the existing sociopolitical system and whose tactics are usually part of the legitimate system of rule.

regressive tax A tax that imposes a heavier relative burden as income declines.

relative poverty Poverty that is relative to the standards and expectations of people in a particular society at a particular time.

revolutionary movement A sociopolitical movement whose objective is to change radically the system of stratification.

ruling class In Marxian theory, the class that controls the means of production and, thereby, the political system as well.

sex The relatively fixed physiological and biological differences between men and women.

sexism A belief in the biological grounding of social and behavioral differences between men and women; implicit is the notion of male superiority.

social class A category of people with approximately similar incomes and occupations who share similar lifestyles.

social Darwinism A theory, based on the notion of "survival of the fittest," holding that one's wealth or poverty is the product of one's inherent capabilities.

social differentiation The division of the society into different roles; the horizontal dimension of social structure, implying no rank order.

social insurance programs Social welfare financed through payroll taxes, primarily Social Security and Medicare.

social mobility The ability of individuals or groups to change their position on a social hierarchy. *See also* **intergenerational mobility** and **intragenerational mobility.**

social resources What is valued and scarce, for which people in society compete.

social stratification The ranking of persons and groups on the basis of various social, and sometimes physical, characteristics; the vertical dimension of social structure, implying inequality.

socialization The process through which people learn their society's culture.

societal power Power exercised by individuals and organizations, public and private, whose scope of activity is broad enough to affect many, if not all, elements of the society.

socioeconomic status (SES) A combination of income and wealth, occupation, and education.

soft money Campaign contributions, unlimited by law, given to parties rather than to specific candidates.

status As described by Weber, differences in prestige that derive from a particular lifestyle, not from purely economic factors.

status communities As described by Weber, groupings of people who have similar cultural and social interests and common consumer patterns.

structural assimilation An increasing degree of social interaction among different ethnic groups of a multiethnic society.

structural mobility Changes in class position that are the result of changes in the society's labor force and economy as well as innovations in technology.

structural pluralism The continued social separation of minority ethnic groups from the dominant group.

structured inequality Stratification that is not random but is sustained by the society's institutional arrangement.

supply-side policies Government measures designed to stimulate economic production by giving tax breaks to corporations and the wealthy who, it is assumed, will subsequently increase investment in productive projects such as factories and machines.

tax expenditures Tax breaks that benefit mostly middle- and upper-income families.

traditional authority As described by Weber, authority that derives from custom or tradition.

transnational corporation A corporation that manufactures and sells products and services in numerous countries.

underclass That element of the poor who are chronically unemployed, largely dependent on social welfare, and socially isolated from the mainstream society.

underground economy Economic activities that occur outside the mainstream economy, untaxed and unregulated.

undeserving poor An element of the poor who are seen as able-bodied but who are unemployed and therefore not considered to merit public assistance.

universalism The notion that everyone should be treated the same regardless of ascribed personal characteristics.

upper class That class at the top of the society's stratification system, whose members earn the most income and own the most wealth.

upper-middle class That class whose members have above-average income and wealth and occupy critical managerial, professional, and technical positions.

vertical mobility The movement of people up or down the class hierarchy.

wealth One's assets, in particular those that are income-producing.

welfare state Government insurance, public assistance, education, and medical programs designed to maximize the economic and social welfare of the society's population.

white-collar workers Those who work in nonmanual occupations, ranging from low-skilled and low-status to highly skilled and high-status.

work ethic The notion that hard work is the key to success.

working class That class whose members occupy manual laboring jobs or work at low-status white-collar jobs.

References

Abramson, Jill. 1998. "The Business of Persuasion Thrives in Nation's Capitol." *New York Times* (September 29):A1–A22.

Abramson, Jill, and Barry Meier. 1997. "Tobacco Braced for Costly Fight." *New York Times* (December 15):A1, A12.

Abusharaf, Rogaia Mustafa. 1998. "Unmasking Tradition." *The Sciences* 38 (March/April):22–27.

Alba, Richard D. 1990. *Ethnic Identity: The Transformation of White America.* New Haven: Yale University Press.

———. 1995. "Assimilation's Quiet Tide." *The Public Interest* (Spring):3–18.

Alba, Richard D., and Reid M. Golden. 1986. "Patterns of Ethnic Marriage in the United States." *Social Forces* 65:202–223.

Alba, Richard D., and Gwen Moore. 1982. "Ethnicity in the American Elite." *American Sociological Review* 47:373–383.

Alexander, Herbert E. 1992. *Financing Politics: Money, Elections, & Political Reform.* 4th ed. Washington, DC: CQ Press.

Alford, Robert R., and Roger Friedland. 1975. "Political Participation and Public Policy." In *Annual Review of Sociology,* vol. 1, edited by A. Inkeles, 429–479. Palo Alto, CA: Annual Reviews.

Allen, Charles F., and Jonathan Portis. 1992. *The Comeback Kid: The Life and Career of Bill Clinton.* New York: Carol Publishing Group.

Allen, Michael Patrick. 1987. *The Founding Fortunes: A New Anatomy of the Super-Rich Families in America.* New York: E. P. Dutton.

Almond, Gabriel, and Sidney Verba. 1963. *The Civic Culture.* Princeton, NJ: Princeton University Press.

American Experience, The. 1997. *The Richest Man in the World* (January 20). <http://www.pbs.org/wgbh/pages/amex/carnegie>.

Amery, Elizabeth A. 1996. "Let Them Eat Caviar." *Forbes* (October 14):65–66.

Anderson, Charles H. 1970. *White Protestant Americans: From National Origins to Religious Group.* Englewood Cliffs, NJ: Prentice Hall.

Aoyagi, Kiyotaka, and Ronald P. Dore. 1964. "The Buraku Minority in Urban Japan." In *Transactions of the Fifth World Congress of Sociology,* vol. 3, 95–107. Louvain: International Sociological Association.

Aron, Raymond. 1968. *Main Currents in Sociological Thought,* vol. 1. Garden City, NY: Anchor.

Atkinson, A. T. 1975. *The Economics of Inequality.* Oxford: Clarendon Press.

Ayres, B. Drummond, Jr. 1997. "Women in Washington Statehouse Lead U.S. Tide." *New York Times* (April 14):A1, A12.

Bagdikian, Ben. 1971. *The Information Machines.* New York: Harper & Row.

_____. 1983. *The Media Monopoly.* Boston: Beacon.

_____. 1989. "Missing from the News." *The Progressive* 53(August):32–33.

Baker, Daniel B. 1992. *Power Quotes.* Detroit: Visible Ink Press.

Baker, Stephen. 1996. "The New Factory Worker." *Business Week* (September 30) :59–68.

Baltzell, E. Digby. 1958. *Philadelphia Gentlemen.* New York: Free Press.

_____. 1964. *The Protestant Establishment: Aristocracy and Caste in America.* New York: Vintage.

Banfield, Edward. 1968. *The Unheavenly City.* Boston: Little, Brown.

_____. 1974. *The Unheavenly City Revisited.* Boston: Little, Brown.

Banton, Michael. 1970. "The Concept of Racism." In *Race and Racialism,* edited by Sami Zubaida, 17–34. London: Tavistock.

Barber, Richard J. 1970. *The American Corporation.* New York: Dutton.

Baritz, Loren. 1982. *The Good Life: The Meaning of Success for the American Middle Class.* New York: Harper & Row.

Barlett, Donald L., and James B. Steele. 1992. *America: What Went Wrong?* Kansas City, MO: Andrews and McMeel.

———. 1998a. "Corporate Welfare." *Time* (November 9):36–54.

———. 1998b. "Sweet Deal." *Time* (November 23):81–82.

Barko, Naomi. 2000. "The Other Gender Gap." *The American Prospect* (June 19–July 3):61–63.

Barnet, Richard J., and Ronald E. Müller. 1974. *Global Reach.* New York: Simon & Schuster.

Barth, Ernest A. T., and Donald L. Noel. 1972. "Conceptual Frameworks for the Analysis of Race Relations." *Social Forces* 50:333–348.

Beard, Charles. 1913. *An Economic Interpretation of the Constitution.* New York: Macmillan.

Beck, Roy. 1996. *The Case against Immigration: The Moral, Economic, Social, and Environmental Reasons for Reducing U.S. Immigration Back to Traditional Levels.* New York: Norton.

Becker, Gary S. 1996. "What Makes the Welfare Bill a Winner." *Business Week* (September 23):22.

Bell, Daniel. 1973. *The Coming of Post-Industrial Society.* New York: Basic Books.

Bennett, H. S. 1969. *Life on the English Manor: A Study of Peasant Conditions 1150–1400.* Cambridge: Cambridge University Press.

Bennett, W. Lance. 1988. *News: The Politics of Illusion.* 2d ed. New York: Longman.

Benokraitis, Nijole V. 1997. *Subtle Sexism: Current Practice and Prospects for Change.* Thousand Oaks, CA: Sage.

Berger, Peter. 1963. *Invitation to Sociology: A Humanistic Perspective.* New York: Anchor Doubleday.

Bergmann, Barbara R. 1996. *In Defense of Affirmative Action.* New York: Basic Books.

Bernstein, Aaron. 1997. "Sharing Prosperity." *Business Week* (September 1):64–69.

Bernstein, Jared. 1996. "Growing Poverty in a Growing Economy." *Poverty & Race* 5 (November/December):1–2, 10.

Bernstein, Jared, and Lawrence Mishel. 2000. "Income Picture" (September 26). Washington, DC: Economic Policy Institute.

Berreman, Gerald D. 1961. "Caste in India and the United States." *American Journal of Sociology* 66:510–512.

_____. 1966. "Structure and Function of Caste Systems." In *Japan's Invisible Race: Caste in Culture and Personality,* edited by George De Vos and Hiroshi Wagatsuma, 277–307. Berkeley: University of California Press.

Bertrand, Marianne, and Kevin F. Hallock. 2000. "The Gender Gap in Top Corporate Jobs." NBER Working Paper No. W7931 (October) Cambridge, MA: National Bureau of Economic Research.

Béteille, André. 1969. *Castes Old and New: Essays in Social Structure and Social Stratification.* Bombay: Asian Publishing Home.

_____. 1996. *Caste, Class and Power: Changing Patterns of Stratification in a Tanjore Village.* 2nd ed. Delhi: Oxford University Press.

Beyer, Lisa. 1999. "The Price of Honor." *Time* (January 18):55.

Bianchi, Suzanne M., and Daphne Spain. 1996. *Women, Work, and Family in America.* Washington, DC: Population Reference Bureau.

Blackburn, Clare. 1991. *Poverty and Health: Working with Families.* Milton Keynes: Open University Press.

Blau, Joel. 1999. *Illusions of Prosperity: America's Working Families in an Age of Economic Insecurity.* New York: Oxford University Press.

Blau, Peter M., and Otis D. Duncan. 1967. *The American Occupational Structure.* New York: John Wiley & Sons.

Blauner, Bob. 1992. "Talking Past Each Other: Black and White Languages of Race." *American Prospect* 10(Summer):55–64.

Block, Fred. 1977. "The Ruling Class Does Not Rule: Notes on the Marxist Theory of the State." *Socialist Review* 7(May–June):6–28.

Bloom, David E., and Adi Brender. 1993. *Labor and the Emerging World Economy.* Washington, DC: Population Reference Bureau.

Bluestone, Barry, and Bennett Harrison. 1982. *The Deindustrialization of America.* New York: Basic Books.

_____. 2000. *Growing Prosperity: The Battle for Growth with Equity in the Twenty-first Century.* Boston: Houghton Mifflin.

Borjas, George J. 1994. "Tired, Poor on Welfare." In *Arguing Immigration,* edited by Nicolaus Mills, 76–80. New York: Touchstone.

Bouvier, Leon F. 1992. *Peaceful Invasions: Immigration and Changing America.* Lanham, MD: University Press of America.

Bowler, Mary. 1999. "Women's Earnings: An Overview." *Monthly Labor Review* (December):13–21.

Bowles, Samuel, and Herbert Gintis. 1976. *Schooling in Capitalist America: Educational Reform and the Contradictions of Economic Life.* New York: Basic Books.

Boxer, Charles R. 1962. *The Golden Age of Brazil.* Berkeley: University of California Press.

Bradsher, Keith. 1995. "Widest Gap in Incomes? Research Points to U.S." *New York Times* (October 27):C2.

Bragg, Rick. 1996a. "More Than Money, They Miss the Pride a Good Job Brought." *New York Times* (March 5): A17, A18.

_____. 1996b. "Big Holes Where the Dignity Used to Be." *New York Times* (March 5): A1, A16.

Braverman, Harry. 1974. *Labor and Monopoly Capital.* New York: Monthly Review Press.

Braverman, Marilyn. 1988. "English Yes; English Only, No." *Reconstructionist* 52(June):29–31.

Brimelow, Peter. 1995. *Alien Nation*. New York: HarperCollins.

Brittain, John A. 1977. *The Inheritance of Economic Status*. Washington, DC: The Brookings Institution.

_____. 1978. *Inheritance and the Inequality of Material Wealth*. Washington, DC: The Brookings Institution.

Bronfenbrenner, Urie et al. 1996. *The State of Americans: This Generation and the Next*. New York: Free Press.

Bryce, James. 1959. *The American Commonwealth,* vol. II. Edited by Louis Hacker. New York: G. P. Putnam's Sons.

Burch, Philip H., Jr. 1980. *Elites in American History. Vol. 3: The New Deal to the Carter Administration*. New York: Holmes and Meier.

Bureau of Labor Statistics. 2001. *Union Members Summary*. January 18. <http://stats. bls.gov/news.release/union2.nr0.htm>

Burma, John. 1954. *Spanish-speaking Groups in the United States*. Durham, NC: Duke University Press.

Business Week. 1994. "How the Gap between Rich and Poor Hurts the Economy." (August 15):78–83.

_____. 1996. "Low-Wage Lessons." (November 11):108–116.

_____. 1997. "Executive Compensation Scoreboard." (April 21):67–102.

_____. 2000. "Executive Pay." (April 17):100–142.

Butterfield, Fox. 1986. "Why Asians Are Going to the Head of the Class." *New York Times* (August 3):12, 18–23.

Byrne, John A. 1996. "How High Can CEO Pay Go?" *Business Week* (April 22): 100–106.

Camarillo, Albert. 1979. *Chicanos in a Changing Society*. Cambridge, MA: Harvard University Press.

Canedy, Dana. 1996. "Quality, Not Flash, Marks New Gain in Luxury Sales." *New York Times* (December 12):A1, C22.

Caplan, Nathan, Marcella H. Choy, and John K. Whitmore. 1991. *Children of the Boat People: A Study of Educational Success*. Ann Arbor: University of Michigan Press.

Caplan, Nathan, John K. Whitmore, and Marcella H. Choy. 1989. *The Boat People and Achievement in America*. Ann Arbor: University of Michigan Press.

Caplow, Theodore, and Howard M. Bahr. 1979. "Half a Century of Change in Adolescent Attitudes: Replication of a Middletown Survey by the Lynds." *Public Opinion Quarterly* 43 (Spring):1–17.

Carlson, Margaret. 1998. "The Gravy Train Never Stops." *Time* (January 19):14.

Carnoy, Martin, Hugh M. Daley, and Raul Hinajosa Ojeda. 1993. "The Changing Economic Position of Latinos in the U.S. Labor Market since 1939." In *Latinos in a Changing U.S. Economy,* edited by Rebecca Morales and Frank Bonilla, 28–54. Newbury Park, CA: Sage.

Castles, Stephen, Heather Booth, and Tina Wallace. 1984. *Here for Good: Western Europe's New Ethnic Minorities*. London: Pluto Press.

Catalyst. 2000. *2000 Catalyst Census of Women Corporate Officers and Top Earners of the Fortune 500*. New York: Catalyst.

Caute, David. 1978. *The Great Fear: The Anti-Communist Purge under Truman and Eisenhower*. New York: Simon & Schuster.

Center for Responsive Politics. 2000. *Who's Paying for This Election?* Washington, DC: The Center for Responsive Politics.

Chafetz, Janet Saltzman. 1978. *Masculine Feminine or Human?: An Overview of the Sociology of the Gender Roles.* 2d ed. Itasca, IL: F. E. Peacock.

Charlson, May E., John P. Allegrante, and Laura Robbins. 1993. "Socioeconomic Differentials in Arthritis and Its Treatment." In *Medical Care and the Health of the Poor,* edited by David E. Rogers and Eli Ginzberg, 77–89. Boulder, CO: Westview.

Chavez, Linda. 1991. *Out of the Barrio: Toward A New Politics of Hispanic Assimilation.* New York: Basic Books.

Chronicle of Higher Education. 1998. *Almanac Issue* (August 28).

Clawson, Dan, Alan Neustadtl, and Denise Scott. 1992. *Money Talks: Corporate PACs and Political Influence.* New York: Basic Books.

Clement, Wallace. 1975. *The Canadian Corporate Elite.* Toronto: McLelland & Stewart.

Clement, Wallace, and John Myles. 1994. *Relations of Ruling: Class and Gender in Postindustrial Societies.* Montreal: McGill-Queens University Press.

Clines, Francis X. 1996. "Washington's Troubles Hit Island of Affluence." *New York Times* (July 26):A1, A9.

_____. 1997. "G.O.P. Gathers Big Donors for Multimillion-Dollar Gala." *New York Times* (May 14):A1, A14.

Cohen, Stanley, and Jock Young, eds. 1973. *The Manufacture of News.* London: Constable.

Coleman, James S. 1965. *Education and Political Development.* Princeton, NJ: Princeton University Press.

_____. 1966. "Structure and Function of Caste Systems." In *Japan's Invisible Race: Caste in Culture and Personality,* edited by George De Vos and Hiroshi Wagatsuma, 277–307. Berkeley: University of California Press.

Coleman, James et al. 1966. *Equality of Educational Opportunity.* Washington, DC: U.S. Government Printing Office.

Coleman, Richard P., and Lee Rainwater. 1978. *Social Standing in America: New Dimensions of Class.* New York: Basic Books.

Collins, Randall. 1971. "A Conflict Theory of Sexual Stratification." *Social Problems* 19:3–21.

Comstock, George. 1980. "The Impact of Television on American Institutions." In *Readings in Mass Communication: Concepts and Issues in the Mass Media.* 4th ed, edited by M. Emery and T. C. Smyth, 28–44. Dubuque, IA: Wm. C. Brown.

Cooper, Kenneth J. 1996. "Women under Virtual House Arrest." *Washington Post* (October 7):A01.

Corak, Miles. 1998. "Does Your Parents' Income Count?" *Canadian Social Trends* (Summer):6–10.

Crawford, James. 1992. *Hold Your Tongue: Bilingualism and the Politics of "English Only."* Reading, MA: Addison-Wesley.

Critser, Greg. 2000. "Let Them Eat Fat: The Heavy Truths about American Obesity." *Harper's* (March):41–47.

Crockett, Roger O. 2000. "How to Bridge America's Digital Divide." *Business Week* (May 8):56.

Current Biography. 1943. "Lana Turner." 4(June):77–79.

Dahl, Robert A. 1967. *Pluralist Democracy in the U.S.: Conflict and Consensus.* Chicago: Rand McNally.

Dahrendorf, Ralf. 1959. *Class and Class Conflict in Industrial Society.* Stanford, CA: Stanford University Press.

Danziger, Sheldon, and Peter Gottschalk. 1993. "Introduction." In *Uneven Tides: Rising Inequality in America,* edited by Sheldon Danziger and Peter Gottschalk, 1–18. New York: Russell Sage Foundation.

_____. 1995. *America Unequal.* New York: Russell Sage Foundation.

Danziger, Sheldon, and Deborah Reed. 1999. "Winners and Losers: The Era of Inequality Continues." *Brookings Review* (Fall):14–17.

Davis, David Brion. 1966. *The Problem of Slavery in Western Culture.* Ithaca, NY: Cornell University Press.

Davis, Kingsley. 1949. *Human Society.* New York: Macmillan.

Davis, Kingsley, and Wilbert E. Moore. 1945. "Some Principles of Stratification." *American Sociological Review* 10:242–249.

Davis, James A., and Tom W. Smith. 1994. *The General Social Surveys: Cumulative Code Book, 1972–1994.* Chicago: National Opinion Research Center.

Dawson, Richard E., Kenneth Prewitt, and Karen S. Dawson. 1977. *Political Socialization.* 2d ed. Boston: Little, Brown.

deBroucker, Patrice, and Laval Lavallée. 1998. "Does Your Parents' Education Count?" *Canadian Social Trends* (Summer):11–15.

de Jouvenel, Bertrand. 1963. *The Pure Theory of Politics.* New Haven, CT: Yale University Press.

de la Garza, Rudolph O., Louis DeSipio, F. Chris Garcia, John Garcia, and Angelo Falcon. 1992. *Latino Voices: Mexican, Puerto Rican, and Cuban Perspectives on American Politics.* Boulder, CO: Westview.

DeParle, Jason. 1999. "Bold Effort Leaves Much Unchanged for the Poor." *New York Times* (December 30):1, 10.

DeStafano, Linda, and Diane Colasanto. 1990. "Unlike 1975, Today Most Americans Think Men Have It Better." *Gallup Poll Monthly* (February):25–31.

de Tocqueville, Alexis. 1966. *Democracy in America.* Edited by J. Mayer and M. Lerner. New York: Harper & Row. (original work published 1840)

De Vos, George, and Hiroshi Wagatsuma. 1966. *Japan's Invisible Race: Caste in Culture and Personality.* Berkeley: University of California Press.

Dewar, Heather. 1997. "Attitudes Changing in U.S., Poll Says." *Detroit Free Press* (June 16):1A, 8A.

Diamond, Robert S. 1970. "A Self-Portrait of the Chief Executive." *Fortune* 81(May):181, 320–323.

Dinnerstein, Leonard, Roger L. Nichols, and David M. Reimers. 1990. *Natives and Strangers: Blacks, Indians, and Immigrants in America.* 2d ed. New York: Oxford University Press.

Dobrzynski, Judith H. 1996. "Gaps and Barriers, and Women's Careers." *New York Times* (February 28):C2.

Dolbeare, Kenneth. 1974. *Political Change in the U.S.* New York: McGraw-Hill.

Domhoff, G. William. 1967. *Who Rules America?* Englewood Cliffs, NJ: Prentice Hall.

_____. 1971. *The Higher Circles.* New York: Vintage.

_____. 1974. *The Bohemian Grove.* New York: Harper & Row.

_____. 1979. *The Powers That Be.* New York: Vintage.

_____. 1983. *Who Rules America Now? A View for the 80s.* Englewood Cliffs, NJ: Prentice Hall.

_____. 1993. "The American Power Structure." In *Power in Modern Societies,* edited by Marvin E. Olsen and Martin N. Marger, 170–182. Boulder, CO: Westview.

_____. 1998. *Who Rules America? Power and Politics in the Year 2000.* 3d ed. Mountain View, CA: Mayfield.

Domhoff, G. William, and Hoyt Ballard. 1968. *C. Wright Mills and the Power Elite.* Boston: Beacon.

Dowd, Douglas. 1993. *Of, by, and for Which People? U.S. Capitalist Development Since 1776.* Armonk, NY: M. E. Sharpe.

Drozdiak, William. 1997. "Germany Finds Its Blood Lines Are No Longer Pure." *Washington Post Weekly Edition* (May 5):14.

Dugger, Celia W. 1996. "African Ritual Pain: Genital Cutting." *New York Times* (October 5):1, 4.

Duncan, Greg J., Johanne Boisjoly, and Timothy Smeeding. 1996. "Economic Mobility of Young Workers in the 1970s and 1980s." *Demography* 33:497–509.

Duncan, Greg J., Timothy M. Smeeding, and Willard Rodgers. 1993. "W(h)ither the Middle Class? A Dynamic View." In *Poverty and Prosperity in the USA in the Late Twentieth Century,* edited by Dimitri B. Papadimitriou and Edward N. Wolff, 240–271. London: Macmillan.

Dworkin, Andrea. 1987. *Intercourse.* New York: Free Press.

Dwyer, Paula. 1996. "Out of the Typing Pool, Into Career Limbo." *Business Week* (April 15):92–94.

Dye, Thomas R. 1990. *Who's Running America: The Bush Era.* 5th ed. Englewood Cliffs, NJ: Prentice Hall.

_____. 1995. *Who's Running America: The Clinton Years.* 6th ed. Englewood Cliffs, NJ: Prentice Hall.

Dye, Thomas R., and Julie Strickland. 1982. "Women at the Top: A Note on Institutional Leadership." *Social Science Quarterly* 63(June):333–341.

Easton, David, and Jack Dennis. 1969. *Children in the Political System.* New York: McGraw-Hill.

Economic Policy Institute. 2000. "Wage and Income Trends—Up the Down Escalator." Washington, DC: Economic Policy Institute.

Edelman, Murray. 1964. *The Symbolic Uses of Politics.* Urbana: University of Illinois Press.

Ehrenreich, Barbara. 1989. *Fear of Falling: The Inner Life of the Middle Class.* New York: HarperPerennial.

Elkins, Stanley M. 1976. *Slavery: A Problem in American Institutional and Intellectual Life.* 3d ed. Chicago: University of Chicago Press.

England, Paula. 1992. *Comparable Worth: Theories and Evidence.* New York: Aldine de Gruyter.

Epstein, Aaron. 1996. "Female Lawyers Move Up, Still Face Glass Ceiling." *Detroit Free Press* (January 8):5A.

Epstein, Cynthia Fuchs. 1988. *Deceptive Distinctions: Sex, Gender, and the Social Order.* New Haven, CT: Yale University Press.

_____. 1993. *Women in Law.* 2d ed. Urbana, IL: University of Illinois Press.

Epstein, Edwin Jay. 1974. *News from Nowhere.* New York: Vintage.

Epstein, Edwin M. 1969. *The Corporation in American Politics.* Englewood Cliffs, NJ: Prentice Hall.

Erturk, Yakin. 1991. "Convergence and Divergence in the Status of Moslem Women: The Cases of Turkey and Saudi Arabia." *International Sociology* 6:307–320.

Espiritu, Yen Le. 1992. *Asian American Panethnicity: Bridging Institutions and Identities.* Philadelphia: Temple University Press.

Faludi, Susan. 1991. *Backlash: The Undeclared War against American Women.* New York: Crown.

Farley, Reynolds. 1993. "The Common Destiny of Blacks and Whites: Observations about the Social and Economic Status of the Races." In *Race in America: The Struggle for Equality,* edited by Herbert Hill and James E. Jones Jr., 197–233. Madison: University of Wisconsin Press.

———. 1996. *The New American Reality: Who We Are, How We Got Here, Where We Are Going.* New York: Russell Sage Foundation.

Farley, Reynolds, and Walter R. Allen. 1987. *The Color Line and the Quality of Life in America.* New York: Russell Sage Foundation.

Farley, Reynolds, and William H. Frey. 1994. "Changes in the Segregation of Whites from Blacks during the 1980s: Small Steps toward a More Integrated Society." *American Sociological Review* 59:23–45.

Farrell, Christopher, Ann Therese Palmer, and Seanna Browder. 1998. "A Rising Tide." *Business Week* (August 31):72–75.

Feagin, Joe R., and Clairece Booher Feagin. 1978. *Discrimination American Style: Institutional Racism and Sexism.* Englewood Cliffs, NJ: Prentice Hall.

Featherman, David L., and Robert M. Hauser. 1978. *Opportunity and Change.* New York: Academic Press.

Federman, Maya, Thesia I. Garner, Kathleen Short, W. Boman Cutter IV, John Kiely, David Levine, Duane McGough, and Marilyn McMillen. 1996. "What Does It Mean to Be Poor in America?" *Monthly Labor Review* 119(May):3–17.

Ferree, Myra Marx, and Beth B. Hess. 1994. *Controversy and Coalition: The New Feminist Movement across Three Decades of Change.* Rev. ed. New York: Twayne.

Fidler, John. 1981. *The British Business Elite: Its Attitudes to Class, Status and Power.* London: Routledge and Kegan Paul.

Fineman, Howard. 1995. "Race and Rage." *Newsweek* (April 3):23–33.

Finnegan, William. 2000. "A Slave in New York." *The New Yorker* (January 24):50–61.

Fischer, Claude S., Michael Hout, Martin Sanchez Jankowski, Samuel R. Lucas, Ann Swidler, and Kim Voss. 1996. *Inequality by Design: Cracking the Bell Curve Myth.* Princeton, NJ: Princeton University Press.

Fitzpatrick, Joseph P. 1980. "Puerto Ricans." In *Harvard Encyclopedia of American Ethnic Groups,* edited by Stephen Thernstrom, 858–867. Cambridge, MA: Harvard University Press.

———. 1987. *Puerto Rican Americans: The Meaning of Migration to the Mainland.* 2d ed. Englewood Cliffs, NJ: Prentice Hall.

———. 1995. "Puerto Rican New Yorkers, 1990." *Migration World* 23(1):16–19.

Fletcher, Michael A. 1997. "Coming to Terms with the Racial Melting Pot." *Washington Post Weekly Edition* (May 5):31.

Fogel, Robert William, and Stanley L. Engerman. 1974. *Time on the Cross.* Boston: Little, Brown.

Forbes. 1988. "The 400 Richest People in America." (October 24):142–320.

———. 1992. "The Richest People in America." (October 19):90–254.

———. 1995. "The Billionaires." (July 17):110–111.

———. 1996. "The *Forbes* Four Hundred." (October 14):108–320.

———. 1997. "The 100 Largest U.S. Multinationals." (July 28):218–220.

———. 1998. "Who Gets Paid What." (May 18):234–299.

———. 2000a. "The 400 Richest People in America." (October 9):117–344.

———. 2000b. "The Celebrity 100." (March 20):162–244.

Fordham, Signithia, and John U. Ogbu. 1986. "Black Students' School Success: Coping with the "Burden of 'Acting White.' " *The Urban Review* 18:176–206.

Foreman, Christopher H., Jr. 1998. "Black America: The Rough Road to Racial Uplift." *Brookings Review* (Spring):8–11.

Frank, Robert H. 2000. "Why Living in a Rich Society Makes Us Feel Poor." *New York Times Magazine* (October 15):62–64.

Franklin, John Hope. 1980. *From Slavery to Freedom.* 5th ed. New York: Knopf.

Fraser, Steven, ed. 1995. *The Bell Curve Wars: Race, Intelligence, and the Future of America.* New York: Basic Books.

Fredrickson, George M. 1971. *The Black Image in the White Mind.* New York: Harper & Row.

Free, Lloyd A., and Hadley Cantril. 1968. *The Political Beliefs of Americans.* New York: Simon & Schuster.

Freeman, Jo. 1975. *The Politics of Women's Liberation: A Case Study of an Emerging Social Movement and Its Relation to the Policy Process.* New York: David McKay.

Freeman, Richard B. 1994. "How Labor Fares in Advanced Economies." In *Working under Different Rules,* edited by Richard B. Freeman, 1–28. New York: Russell Sage Foundation.

———. 1996. "Toward an Apartheid Economy?" *Harvard Business Review* (September–October):114–121.

———. 1998. "The Facts about Rising Economic Disparity." In *The Inequality Paradox: Growth of Income Disparity,* edited by James A. Auerbach and Richard S. Belous, 19–33. Washington DC: National Policy Association.

———. 1999. *The New Inequality: Creating Solutions for Poor America.* Boston: Beacon Press.

Freeman, Richard B., and Lawrence F. Katz. 1994. "Rising Wage Inequality: The United States vs. Other Advanced Countries." In *Working under Different Rules,* edited by Richard B. Freeman, 29–62. New York: Russell Sage Foundation.

French, Howard W. 1996. "Booming City, Flush with Rats and Dying Children." *New York Times* (September 30):A4.

Freyre, Gilberto. 1956. *The Masters and the Slaves.* New York: Knopf.

———. 1963. *New World in the Tropics: The Culture of Modern Brazil.* New York: Vintage.

Friedan, Betty. 1963. *The Feminine Mystique.* New York: Norton.

Friedl, Ernestine. 1978. "Society and Sex Roles." *Human Nature* (April):68–75.

Froman, Creel. 1984. *The Two American Political Systems: Society, Economics, and Politics.* Englewood Cliffs, NJ: Prentice Hall.

Fuentes, Annette, and Barbara Ehrenreich. 1983. *Women in the Global Factory.* Boston: South End Press.

Fullerton, Howard N., Jr. 1999. "Labor Force Participation: 75 Years of Change, 1950–98 and 1998–2025." *Monthly Labor Review* (December):3–12.

Galbraith, John Kenneth. 1992. *The Culture of Contentment.* Boston: Houghton Mifflin.

———. 1994. *A Journey through Economic Time: A Firsthand View.* Boston: Houghton Mifflin.

———. 1996. *The Good Society: The Humane Agenda.* Boston: Houghton Mifflin.

Gallup, George, Jr. 1982. *The Gallup Poll: Public Opinion 1981.* Wilmington, DE: Scholarly Resources.

———. 1988. *The Gallup Poll: Public Opinion 1987.* Wilmington, DE: Scholarly Resources.

Gans, Herbert J. 1967. "Some Comments on the History of Italian Migration and on the Nature of Historical Research." *International Migration Review* 1:5–9.

_____. 1968. *People and Plans: Essays on Urban Problems and Solutions.* New York: Basic Books.

_____. 1971. "The Uses of Poverty: The Poor Pay All." *Social Policy* 2:21–23.

_____. 1979. *Deciding What's News.* New York: Pantheon.

_____. 1988. *Middle American Individualism: The Future of Liberal Democracy.* New York: Free Press.

_____. 1994. "Positive Functions of the Undeserving Poor: Uses of the Underclass in America." *Politics and Society* 22(September):270.

_____. 1996. "The So-Called Underclass and the Future of Antipoverty Policy." In *Myths about the Powerless: Contesting Social Inequalities,* by M. Brinton Lykes et al., 87–101. Philadelphia: Temple University Press.

Garrett, J. T. 1994. "Health." In *Native America in the Twentieth Century,* edited by Mary B. Davis, 233–237. New York: Garland.

Garson, Barbara. 1988. *The Electronic Sweatshop: How Computers Are Transforming the Office of the Future into the Factory of the Past.* New York: Simon & Schuster.

Gates, Henry Louis, Jr. 1998. "The Two Nations of Black America." *Brookings Review* (Spring):4–7.

Gerbner, G. 1967. "An Institutional Approach to Mass Communications Research." In *Communication: Theory and Research,* edited by L. Thayer, 429–451. Springfield, IL: Charles C. Thomas.

Gerth, Hans, and C. Wright Mills. 1946. *From Max Weber.* New York: Oxford University Press.

Geschwender, James A. 1978. *Racial Stratification in America.* Dubuque, IA: W. C. Brown.

Ghiloni, Beth W. 1987. "The Velvet Ghetto: Women, Power, and the Corporation." In *Power Elites and Organizations,* edited by G. William Domhoff and Thomas R. Dye, 21–36. Newbury Park, CA: Sage.

Giddens, Anthony. 1975. *The Class Structure of the Advanced Societies.* New York: Harper & Row.

Gilbert, Dennis, and Joseph A. Kahl. 1993. *The American Class Structure: A New Synthesis.* 4th ed. Belmont, CA: Wadsworth.

Gitlin, Todd. 1980. *The Whole World Is Watching.* Berkeley: University of California Press.

Glass Ceiling Commission. 1995. *Good for Business: Making Full Use of the Nation's Human Capital.* Washington, DC: U.S. Government Printing Office.

Glater, Jonathan D. 2001. "Women Are Close to Being Majority of Law Students." *New York Times* (March 26):A1, A16.

Glater, Jonathan D., and Martha M. Hamilton. 1995. "Affirmative Action's Defenders." *Washington Post* (March 17–April 2):20.

Glazer, Nathan. 1958. "The American Jews and the Attainment of Middle-Class Rank: Some Trends and Explanations." In *The Jews: Social Patterns of an American Group,* edited by Marshall Sklare, 138–146. Glencoe, IL: Free Press.

_____. 1975. *Affirmative Discrimination: Ethnic Identity and Public Policy.* New York: Basic Books.

Glazer, Nathan, and Daniel P. Moynihan, 1970. *Beyond the Melting Pot.* 2d ed. Cambridge, MA: MIT Press.

Gleckman, Howard. 1998. "A Rich Stew in the Melting Pot." *Business Week* (August 31):76.

Glenn, Evelyn Nakano, and Roslyn L. Feldberg. 1977. "Degraded and Deskilled: The Proletarianization of Clerical Work." *Social Problems* 25:52–64.

Gold, David A., Clarence Y. H. Lo, and Erik Olin Wright. 1975. "Recent Developments in Marxist Theories of the Capitalist State." Parts 1 and 2. *Monthly Review* 27 (October/November):29–43, 35–51.

Goldberg, Carey. 1997. "Hispanic Households Struggle as Poorest of the Poor in U.S." *New York Times* (January 30):A1, A12.

Goldberg, David Theo, ed. 1994. *Multiculturalism: A Critical Reader.* Cambridge, MA: Basil Blackwell.

Goldberg, Steven. 1974. *The Inevitability of Patriarchy.* Rev. ed. New York: Morrow.

_____. 1986. "Reaffirming the Obvious." *Society* (September/October):4–7.

Goldsen, Rose K. 1977. *The Show and Tell Machine: How Television Works and Works You Over.* New York: Dell.

Goldin, Claudia. 1990. *Understanding the Gender Gap: An Economic History of American Women.* New York: Oxford University Press.

Gollin, Albert E. 1988. "Media Power: On Closer Inspection, It's Not That Threatening." In *Impacts of Mass Media,* 2d ed., edited by R. E. Hiebert and C. Reuss, 41–44. New York: Longman.

Gottschalk, Peter. 1997. "Inequality, Income Growth, and Mobility: The Basic Facts." *Journal of Economic Perspectives* 11 (Spring):21–40.

Gottschalk, Peter, and Sheldon Danziger. 1998. "Family Income Mobility—How Much Is There, and Has It Changed?" In *The Inequality Paradox: Growth of Income Disparity,* edited by James A. Auerbach and Richard S. Belous, 92–111. Washington, DC: National Policy Association.

Gouldner, Alvin. 1976. *The Dialectic of Ideology and Technology.* New York: Seabury.

Graham, Richard. 1970. "Brazilian Slavery Reexamined: A Review Article." *Journal of Social History* 3:431–453.

Gramsci, Antonio. 1971. *Selections from the Prison Notebooks.* New York: International.

Granovetter, Mark S. 1974. *Getting a Job: A Study of Contacts and Careers.* Cambridge, MA: Harvard University Press.

Grebler, Leo, Joan W. Moore, and Ralph C. Guzman. 1970. *The Mexican-American People: The Nation's Second Largest Minority.* New York: Free Press.

Green, Mark. 1984. *Who Runs Congress?* 4th ed. New York: Dell.

Greenberg, Edward S., and Benjamin I. Page. 1995. *The Struggle for Democracy.* 2d ed. New York: HarperCollins.

Greider, William. 1992. *Who Will Tell the People: The Betrayal of American Democracy.* New York: Touchstone.

Grimes, Michael D. 1991. *Class in Twentieth-Century American Sociology: An Analysis of Theories and Measurement Strategies.* New York: Praeger.

Grimsley, Kirstin Downey. 1996. "No Easy Path to the Top." *Washington Post Weekly Edition* (March 4–10):37.

_____. 1998. "Not Much in the Family Way." *Washington Post National Weekly Edition* (February 23):35.

Grobsmith, Elizabeth S. 1994. "Prisons and Prisoners." In *Native America in the Twentieth Century,* edited by Mary B. Davis, 481–483. New York: Garland.

Grusky, David B., and Robert M. Hauser. 1984. "Comparative Social Mobility Revisited: Models of Convergence and Divergence in 16 Countries." *American Sociological Review* 49:19–38.

Guttsman, W. L. 1963. *The British Political Elite.* New York: Basic Books.

Gwyn, Richard. 1985. *The 49th Paradox: Canada in North America.* Toronto: McClelland and Stewart.

Hacker, Andrew. 1994. "Education: Ethnicity and Achievement." In *Debating Affirmative Action: Race, Gender, Ethnicity, and the Politics of Inclusion,* edited by Nicolaus Mills, 214–229. New York: Delta.

_____. 1995. *Two Nations: Black and White, Separate, Hostile, Unequal.* Expanded and updated edition. New York: Ballantine.

_____. 1997. *Money: Who Has How Much and Why.* New York: Scribner.

Hall, D. J., H. C. de Bettignies, and G. Amado-Fischgrund. 1969. "The European Business Elite." *European Business* 23 (October):8–11.

Hamilton, Richard. 1972. *Class and Politics in the U.S.* New York: Wiley.

Hammonds, Keith H. 1997. "Rich School, Poor School: Can We Level the Field?" *Business Week* (October 13):42.

Handlin, Oscar. 1957. *Race and Nationality in American Life.* Boston: Little, Brown.

Harrington, Michael. 1962. *The Other America: Poverty in the United States.* New York: Macmillan.

_____. 1973. *Socialism.* New York: Bantam.

_____. 1976. *The Twilight of Capitalism.* New York: Simon & Schuster.

_____. 1984. *The New American Poverty.* New York: Holt, Rinehart and Winston.

Harris, Louis. 1991a. "Three-to-One Majority Backs Affirmative Action If No Strict Quotas." *The Harris Poll* (June 2).

_____. 1991b. "The Code Language That Now Pervades the Racial Issue." *The Harris Poll* (September 15).

Harris, Marvin. 1964. *Patterns of Race in the Americas.* New York: Norton.

_____. 1989. *Our Kind.* New York: HarperCollins.

Hauser, Robert M., Peter J. Dickinson, Harry P. Travis, and John N. Koffel. 1975. "Structural Changes in Occupational Mobility among Men in the United States." *American Sociological Review* 40:585–598.

Hauser, Robert M., and David L. Featherman. 1978. *Opportunity and Change.* New York: Academic Press.

Havemann, Judith. 1996. "Aiming for Zero—but Falling Short." *Washington Post* (December 2–8):29–30.

Heilbroner, Robert. 1993. *The Making of Economic Society.* 9th ed. Englewood Cliffs, NJ: Prentice Hall.

Heilbroner, Robert, and Lester Thurow. 1981. *Five Economic Challenges.* Englewood Cliffs, NJ: Prentice Hall.

_____. 1994. *Economics Explained.* Rev. ed. New York: Touchstone.

Herman, Edward S. 1981. *Corporate Control, Corporate Power.* Cambridge: Cambridge University Press.

Herman, Edward S., and Noam Chomsky. 1988. *Manufacturing Consent: The Political Economy of the Mass Media.* New York: Pantheon.

Herrnstein, Richard J., and Charles Murray. 1994. *The Bell Curve: Intelligence and Class Structure in American Life.* New York: Free Press.

Hershberg, Theodore et al. 1979. "A Tale of Three Cities: Blacks and Immigrants in Philadelphia: 1850–1880, 1930 and 1970." *Annals of the American Academy of Political and Social Science* 441:55–81.

Hershey, Robert D., Jr. 1997. "The Rise of the Working Class." *New York Times* (September 3):C1, C2.

Hess, Robert D., and Judith V. Torney. 1967. *The Development of Political Attitudes in Children.* Chicago: Aldine.

Himelstein, Linda. 1996. "Shatterproof Glass Ceiling." *Business Week* (October 28):55.

_____. 1997. "Breaking Through." *Business Week* (February 17):64–69.

Hirschfeld, Julie R. 2001. "Congress of Relative Newcomers Poses Challenge to Bush, Leadership." *CQ Weekly* (January 20):178–182.

Hispanic Business. 1995. "The Corporate Elite." (January):11–13.

Hochschild, Arlie, with Anne Machung. 1989. *The Second Shift: Working Parents and the Revolution at Home.* New York: Viking.

Hochschild, Jennifer L. 1981. *What's Fair? American Beliefs about Distributive Justice.* Cambridge, MA: Harvard University Press.

_____. 1995. *Facing Up to the American Dream: Race, Class, and the Soul of the Nation.* Princeton, NJ: Princeton University Press.

Hoffman, Constance A., and Martin N. Marger. 1991. "Patterns of Immigrant Enterprise in Six Metropolitan Areas." *Sociology and Social Research* 75:144–157.

Hoffman, Donna L., and Thomas P. Novak. 1998. "Bridging the Racial Divide on the Internet." *Science* 280(April 17):390–391.

Holusha, John. 1995. "First to College, Then the Mill." *New York Times* (August 22): D1, D7.

Holt, Douglas B. 2000. "Postmodern Markets." In Juliet Schor, *Do Americans Spend Too Much?* 69–74. Boston: Beacon Press.

Hornblower, Margot. 1995. "Putting Tongues in Check." *Time* (October 9):40–50.

Hosansky, David. 1998. "Taxes, Regulations Sought by Business Lobbyists." *CQ Weekly* (April 18):966–972.

Howe, Irving. 1976. *World of Our Fathers.* New York: Simon & Schuster.

Huber, Joan. 1990. "Micro-Macro Links in Gender Stratification." *American Sociological Review* 55:1–10.

Huber, Joan, and William H. Form. 1973. *Income and Ideology.* New York: Free Press.

Huff, Daniel D. 1992. "Upside-Down Welfare." *Public Welfare* (Winter):36–40.

Hutner, Frances C. 1986. *Equal Pay for Comparable Worth: The Working Woman's Issue of the Eighties.* New York: Praeger.

Ibrahim, Youssef M. 1996. "Welfare's Snug Coat Cuts Norwegian Cold." *New York Times* (December 13):A1, A8.

Ifill, Gwen. 1992. "Tenacity and Change in a Son of the South." *New York Times* (July 16):A1, A14.

Illich, Ivan. 1971. *Deschooling Society.* New York: Harper & Row.

Ingrassia, Michele, and Pat Wingert. 1995. "The New Providers." *Newsweek* (May 22):36–37.

Inhaber, Herbert, and Sidney Carroll. 1992. *How Rich Is Too Rich? Income and Wealth in America.* New York: Praeger.

Iyengar, Shanto, and Donald R. Kinder. 1987. *News That Matters: Television and American Opinion.* Chicago: University of Chicago Press.

Jackman, Mary R. 1994. *The Velvet Glove: Paternalism and Conflict in Gender, Class, and Race Relations.* Berkeley: University of California Press.

Jackman, Mary R., and Robert W. Jackman. 1983. *Class Awareness in the United States.* Berkeley: University of California Press.

Jackson, Robert Max. 1998. *Destined for Equality: The Inevitable Rise of Women's Status.* Cambridge, MA: Harvard University Press.

Jacobs, Charles, and Mohamed Athie. 1994. "Bought and Sold." *New York Times* (July 13):19.

Jacoby, Russell, and Naomi Glauberman, eds. 1995. *The Bell Curve Debate: History, Documents, Opinions.* New York: Times Books.

Jacoby, Tamar. 1998. *Someone Else's House: America's Unfinished Struggle for Integration.* New York: Free Press.

Jehl, Douglas. 1997. "In a Changing Islamic Land, Women Savor Options." *New York Times* (July 20):3.

———. 1999. "Arab Honor's Price: A Woman's Blood." *New York Times* (June 20):1, 9.

Jencks, Christopher. 1993. *Rethinking Social Policy: Race, Poverty, and the Underclass.* New York: HarperPerennial.

Jencks, Christopher et al. 1972. *Inequality: A Reassessment of the Effect of Family and Schooling in America.* New York: Harper.

Jencks, Christopher, and Meredith Phillips. 1998. "The Black-White Test Score Gap." *Brookings Review* (Spring):24–27.

Jiobu, Robert M. 1988. *Ethnicity and Assimilation.* Albany: State University of New York Press.

Johnson, Dirk. 1994. "Family Struggles to Make Do after Fall from Middle Class." *New York Times* (March 11):A1, A9.

Johnston, David Cay. 2000. "Study Finds That Many Large Companies Pay No Taxes." *New York Times* (October 20):C2.

Joint Center for Political and Economic Studies. 1994. *Black Elected Officials: A National Roster.* Washington, DC: Joint Center for Political and Economic Studies.

Jones, Edward W., Jr. 1986. "Black Managers: The Dream Deferred." *Harvard Business Review* (May–June):84–93.

Jordan, Winthrop. 1969. *White over Black.* Baltimore: Penguin.

Judis, John B. 1994. "Why Your Wages Keep Falling." *The New Republic* (February 14): 26–29.

———. 1995. "The Contract with K Street." *The New Republic* (December 4):18–25.

Kacapyr, Elia. 1996. "Are You Middle Class?" *American Demographics* (October):30–35.

Kahlenberg, Richard D. 1995. "Class, Not Race." *New Republic* (April 3):21-27.

———. 1996. *The Remedy: Class, Race, and Affirmative Action.* New York: Basic Books.

Kamen, Al. 1998. "A Ticket to Ride." *Washington Post National Weekly Edition* (January 12):14.

Kaminer, Wendy. 1996. *True Love Waits: Essays and Criticism.* Reading, MA: Addison-Wesley.

Kasarda, John. 1995. "Industrial Restructuring and the Changing Location of Jobs." In *State of the Union: America in the 1990s,* vol. 1, edited by Reynolds Farley, 215–267. New York: Russell Sage Foundation.

Kato, Ryoko. 1989. "Japanese Women: Subordination or Domination?" *International Journal of Sociology of the Family* 19:49–57.

Katz, Lawrence F., and Alan B. Krueger. 1999. "New Trend in Unemployment?" *Brookings Review* (Fall):4–8.

Kaus, Mickey. 1995. *The End of Equality.* 2d ed. New York: Basic Books.

Keister, Lisa A. 2000. *Wealth in America: Trends in Wealth Inequality.* New York: Cambridge University Press.

Keister, Lisa A., and Stephanie Moller. 2000. "Wealth Inequality in the United States." *Annual Review of Sociology* 26:63–81.

Keller, Suzanne. 1953. "The Social Origins and Career Lines of Three Generations of American Business Leaders." Ph.D. diss., Columbia University.

_____. 1963. *Beyond the Ruling Class.* New York: Random House.

Kennedy, Randall. 1994. "Persuasion and Distrust: The Affirmative Action Debate." In *Debating Affirmative Action: Race, Gender, Ethnicity, and the Politics of Inclusion,* edited by Nicolaus Mills, 48–67. New York: Delta.

Key, V. O. 1964. *Public Opinion and American Democracy.* New York: Knopf.

Kikumura, Akemi, and Harry H. L. Kitano. 1973. "Interracial Marriage: A Picture of the Japanese-Americans." *Journal of Social Issues* 29:67–81.

Kilborn, Peter T. 1992. "Lives of Unexpected Poverty in Center of a Land of Plenty." *New York Times* (July 7):A1, A14.

Killian, Lewis. 1975. *The Impossible Revolution, Phase II: Black Power and the American Dream.* New York: Random House.

Kim, Illsoo. 1981. *New Urban Immigrants: The Korean Community in New York.* Princeton, NJ: Princeton University Press.

_____. 1987. "The Koreans: Small Business in an Urban Frontier." In *New Immigrants in New York,* edited by Nancy Foner, 219–242. New York: Columbia University Press.

King, Martin Luther, Jr. 1964. *Why We Can't Wait.* New York: Harper & Row.

Kinsley, Michael. 1991. "Class, Not Race." *New Republic* (August 19–26):4.

Kitano, Harry H. L., and Roger Daniels. 1995. *Asian Americans: Emerging Minorities.* 2d ed. Englewood Cliffs, NJ: Prentice Hall.

Klausner, Samuel Z. 1988. *Succeeding in Corporate America: The Experience of Jewish M.B.A.'s.* New York: American Jewish Committee.

Klein, Naomi. 1999. *No Logo: Taking Aim at the Brand Bullies.* New York: Picador.

Kluegel, James R., and Eliot R. Smith. 1986. *Beliefs about Inequality: Americans' Views of What Is and What Ought to Be.* New York: Aldine de Gruyter.

Knaus, William A. 1981. *Inside Russian Medicine: An American Doctor's First-Hand Report.* New York: Everest House.

Kolenda, Pauline. 1985. *Caste in Contemporary India: Beyond Organic Solidarity.* Prospect Heights, IL: Waveland Press.

Kolko, Gabriel. 1967. *The Triumph of Conservatism.* Chicago: Quadrangle.

Konigsberg, Eric. 1993. "No Hassle." *The New Republic* (March 1):21–23.

Koretz, Gene. 1997. "Big Payoffs from Layoffs: How the Largest Downsizers Fared."*Business Week* (February 24):30.

Korman, Abraham K. 1988. *The Outsiders: Jews and Corporate America.* Lexington, MA: Lexington Books.

Kotlowitz, Alex. 1991. *There Are No Children Here: The Story of Two Boys Growing Up in the Other America.* New York: Anchor Books.

Kozol, Jonathan. 1991. *Savage Inequalities: Children in America's Schools.* New York: HarperPerennial.

_____. 1995. *Amazing Grace: The Lives of Children and the Conscience of a Nation.* New York: Crown.

Kraar, Louis. 1977. "How Lockheed Got Back Its Wings." *Fortune* 96(October): 199–210.

Kristof, Nicholas D. 1995. "Japanese Outcasts Better Off Than in Past but Still Outcast."*New York Times* (November 30):A1, A8.

_____. 1996a. "Welfare as Japan Knows It: A Family Affair." *New York Times* (September 10):A1, A10.

_____. 1996b. "Do Korean Men Still Beat Their Wives? Definitely." *New York Times* (December 5):A4.

Kristof, Nicholas, and Frank Bruni. 2000. "A Son of Politics, George W. Bush, Is Making an Uncommon Rise." *New York Times* (August 3):1, 14.

Kroll, Luisa. 1998. "Warning: Capitalism Is Contagious." *Forbes* (May 18):220–221.

Kuttner, Robert. 1996. "Tipping the Income Scales." *Washington Post* (July 1–7):5.

Ladd, Everett Carll. 1994. *The American Ideology: An Exploration of the Origins, Meaning, and Role of American Political Ideas.* Storrs, CT: The Roper Center for Public Opinion Research.

Landry, Bart. 1987. *The New Black Middle Class.* Berkeley: University of California Press.

Lane, Robert E. 1962. *Political Ideology.* New York: Free Press.

Langberg, Mark, and Reynolds Farley. 1985. "Residential Segregation of Asian Americans in 1980." *Sociology and Social Research* 70(October):71–75.

Langton, Kenneth P. 1969. *Political Socialization.* New York: Oxford University Press.

Lannoy, Richard. 1971. *The Speaking Tree: A Study of Indian Culture and Society.* New York: Oxford University Press.

Lasswell, Harold. 1936. *Politics: Who Gets What, When, How?* New York: McGraw-Hill.

Lau, Gloria, and Tim W. Ferguson. 1998. "Doc's Just an Employee Now." *Forbes* (May 18):162–172.

Laxer, James. 1998. *The Undeclared War: Class Conflict in the Age of Cyber Capitalism.* Toronto: Viking.

Lazarsfeld, Paul, Bernard Berelson, and H. Gaudet. 1948. *The People's Choice.* New York: Columbia University Press.

Leach, Edmund. 1967. "Caste, Class and Slavery: The Taxonomic Problem." In *Caste and Race: Comparative Approaches,* edited by Anthony de Reuck and Julie Knight, 5–16. Boston: Little, Brown.

Lee, Sharon M. 2001. *Using the New Racial Categories in the 2000 Census.* Washington, DC: Population Reference Bureau.

Leland, John. 1998. "Blessed by the Bull." *Newsweek* (April 27):50–53.

Lemann, Nicholas. 1991. *The Promised Land: The Great Black Migration and How It Changed America.* New York: Vintage.

Lenski, Gerhard. 1966. *Power and Privilege.* New York: McGraw-Hill.

Leonhardt, David. 1997. "Two-tier Marketing." *Business Week* (March 17):82–90.

Lerman, Robert I. 1999. *Retreat or Reform? New U.S. Strategies for Dealing with Poverty.* Washington, DC: The Urban Institute.

Levin, Murray. 1971. *Political Hysteria in America.* New York: Basic Books.

Levitan, Sar A., William B. Jonston, and Robert Taggart. 1975. *Still a Dream: The Changing Status of Blacks Since 1960.* Cambridge, MA: Harvard University Press.

Levy, Frank. 1995. "Incomes and Income Inequality." In *State of the Union: America in the 1990s. Vol. One: Economic Trends,* edited by Reynolds Farley, 1–58. New York: Russell Sage Foundation.

———. 1998. *The New Dollars and Dreams: American Incomes and Economic Change.* New York: Russell Sage Foundation.

Lewis, Hylan. 1967. "The Family: Resources for Change." In *The Moynihan Report and the Politics of Controversy,* edited by Lee Rainwater and William L. Yancey, 314–343. Cambridge, MA: MIT Press.

Lewis, John. 1972. *The Marxism of Marx.* London: Lawrence and Wishart.

Lewis, Oscar. 1961. *The Children of Sanchez.* New York: Random House.

———. 1965. *La Vida.* New York: Random House.

———. 1966. "The Culture of Poverty." *Scientific American* 215(October):19–25.

Lieberson, Stanley. 1961. "A Societal Theory of Race Relations." *American Sociological Review* 26:902–910.

Lieberson, Stanley, and Mary C. Waters. 1988. *From Many Strands: Ethnic and Racial Groups in Contemporary America.* New York: Russell Sage Foundation.

Light, Ivan, and Edna Bonacich. 1988. *Immigrant Entrepreneurs: Koreans in Los Angeles 1965–1982.* Berkeley: University of California Press.

Lindblom, Charles E. 1978. "The Business of America Is Still Business." *New York Times* (January 4):A19.

Linton, Ralph. 1936. *The Study of Man.* New York: Appleton-Century-Crofts.

Lippmann, Walter. 1922. *Public Opinion.* New York: Macmillan.

Lipset, Seymour Martin. 1963. *The First New Nation: The United States in Historical and Comparative Perspective.* New York: Basic Books.

———. 1982. "Social Mobility in Industrial Societies." *Public Opinion* (June/July): 41–51.

———. 1990. *Continental Divide: The Values and Institutions of the United States and Canada.* New York: Routledge.

———. 1996. *American Exceptionalism: A Double-Edged Sword.* New York: Norton.

Lipset, Seymour Martin, and Reinhard Bendix. 1959. *Social Mobility in Industrial Society.* Berkeley: University of California Press.

Lipset, Seymour Martin, and Earl Raab. 1995. *Jews and the New American Scene.* Cambridge, MA: Harvard University Press.

Lipsyte, Robert. 1996. "Knight: Can a Logo Conquer All?" *New York Times* (February 7):B7.

Litt, Edgar. 1963. "Civic Education, Community Norms, and Political Indoctrination." *American Sociological Review* 28:69–75.

Locke, John. 1960 [1690]. "Two Treatises of Government." In *Great Political Thinkers.* 3d ed., edited by W. Ebenstein, 393–413. New York: Rinehart.

Loprest, Pamela. 1999. "Families Who Left Welfare: Who Are They and How Are They Doing?" Washington, DC: The Urban Institute.

Lorber, Judith. 1995. "The Social Construction of Gender." In *Race, Class, and Gender in the United States: An Integrated Study.* 3d ed., edited by Paula S. Rothenberg, 33–45. New York: St. Martin's.

———. 1998. *Gender Inequality: Feminist Theories and Politics.* Los Angeles: Roxbury.

Loury, Glenn. 1997. "How to Mend Affirmative Action." *The Public Interest* (Spring):33–43.

Lowenstein, Roger. 1995. *Buffet: The Making of an American Capitalist.* New York: Random House.

Lyman, Rick. 1998. "Scene One: A Fire Escape." *New York Times* (February 13):B1, B14.

Lynd, Robert, and Helen Lynd. 1929. *Middletown.* New York: Harcourt, Brace and Co.

MacFarquhar, Emily. 1994a. "The War against Women." *U.S. News & World Report* (March 28):42–48.

———. 1994b. "The Echoes of Sita." *U.S. News & World Report* (March 28):54–55.

MacKinnon, Catharine A. 1993. *Only Words.* Cambridge, MA: Harvard University Press.

Maharidge, Dale. 1998. "The Sleeping Giant Awakes." *Mother Jones* (January/February):56–61.

Mandel, Michael J., and Toddi Gutner. 1999. "The Prosperity Gap." *Business Week* (September 27):90–92, 96–102.

Mann, Michael. 1970. "The Social Cohesion of Liberal Democracy." *American Sociological Review* 35:423–439.

Mannari, Hiroshi. 1974. *The Japanese Business Leaders.* Tokyo: University of Tokyo Press.

Mannheim, Karl. 1936. *Ideology and Utopia.* New York: Harcourt, Brace and World.

Manning, Wendy, and William O'Hare. 1988. "The Best Metros for Asian-American Business." *American Demographics* 10(August):34–37, 59.

Marcus, Ruth. 2000. " 'Soft' Money's Hard Impact." *Washington Post National Weekly Edition* (May 29):6–7.

Marger, Martin N. 1987. *Elites and Masses: An Introduction to Political Sociology.* 2d ed. Belmont, CA: Wadsworth.

_____. 1993. "The Mass Media as a Power Institution." In *Power in Modern Societies,* edited by Marvin E. Olsen and Martin N. Marger, 238–249. Boulder, CO: Westview.

_____. 2000. *Race and Ethnic Relations: American and Global Perspectives.* 5th ed. Belmont, CA: Wadsworth.

Marks, Jonathan. 1995. *Human Biodiversity: Genes, Race, and History.* New York: Aldine de Gruyter.

Marsden, Peter, and Joseph Swingle. 1994. "Conceptualizing and Measuring Culture in Surveys." *Poetics* 22:269–289.

Marx, Karl. 1920. *The Poverty of Philosophy.* Chicago: H. Kerr.

Marx, Karl, and Friedrich Engels. 1968. *Selected Works in One Volume.* New York: International.

Mason, Christopher. 1996. "West of Eden." *New York* (September 2):20–27.

Mason, Philip. 1970. *Patterns of Dominance.* London: Oxford University Press.

Massey, Douglas S. 1981. "Dimensions of the New Immigration to the United States and the Prospects for Assimilation." *Annual Review of Sociology* 7:57–85.

Massey, Douglas S., and Nancy A. Denton. 1993. *American Apartheid: Segregation and the Making of the Underclass.* Cambridge, MA: Harvard University Press.

Matthews, Donald. 1954. *The Social Background of Political Decision-Makers.* New York: Doubleday.

_____. 1973. *U.S. Senators and Their World.* New York: Norton.

Mayer, Kurt B. 1955. *Class and Society.* Rev. ed. New York: Random House.

Mayer, Susan. 1995. "A Comparison of Poverty and Living Conditions in the United States, Canada, Sweden, and Germany." In *Poverty, Inequality and the Future of Social Policy: Western States in the New World Order,* edited by Katherine McFate, Roger Lawson, and William Julius Wilson, 109–151. New York: Russell Sage Foundation.

McChesney, Robert W. 2000. *Rich Media, Poor Democracy: Communication Politics in Dubious Times.* New York: The New Press.

McClendon, McKee J. 1977. "Structural and Exchange Components of Vertical Mobility." *American Sociological Review* 42:56–74.

McComas, Maggie. 1986. "Atop the Fortune 500: A Survey of the C.E.O.s." *Fortune* 113(April 28):26–31.

McCombs, Maxwell, and Donald Shaw. 1972. "The Agenda-Setting Function of Mass Media." *Public Opinion Quarterly* 36:176–187.

McConnell, Sheila. 1996. "The Role of Computers in Reshaping the Work Force."*Monthly Labor Review* 119(August):3–5.

McCoy, George. 1994. "Mental Health." In *Native America in the Twentieth Century,* edited by Mary B. Davis, 330–335. New York: Garland.

McKinley, James C., Jr. 1996. "At a Ceremony in Kenya, a Brother and Sister Painfully Enter Adulthood." *New York Times* (October 5):4.

McNamee, Stephen J., and Robert K. Miller, Jr. 1998. "Inheritance and Stratification." In *Inheritance and Wealth in America,* edited by Robert K. Miller Jr. and Stephen J. McNamee, 193–213. New York: Plenum Press.

Mead, Lawrence M. 1992. *The New Politics of Poverty: The Nonworking Poor in America.* New York: Basic Books.

———. 1996. "Work Requirements Can Transform the System." *The Chronicle of Higher Education* (October 4):B6, B7.

Mead, Walter Russell. 1998. "The New Global Economy Takes Your Order." *Mother Jones* (March/April):32–41.

Meltzer, Milton. 1971. *Slavery: From the Rise of Western Civilization to the Renaissance.* New York: Cowles.

Meredith, Robyn. 1996. "Minimum Wage, Minimum Effect." *New York Times* (October 1): C1, C6.

Merton, Robert K. 1949. "Discrimination and the American Creed." In *Discrimination and National Welfare,* edited by R. H. MacIver, 99–126. New York: Harper & Row.

Meyer, Alfred G. 1970. *Marxism: The Unity of Theory and Practice.* Rev. ed. Cambridge, MA: Harvard University Press.

———. 1977. *Marxism and Politics.* New York: Oxford University Press.

Michels, Robert. 1962 [1915]. *Political Parties.* Translated by Eden and Cedar Paul. New York: Free Press.

Milbraith, Lester, and M. L. Goel. 1977. *Political Participation.* 2d ed. Chicago: Rand McNally.

Miliband, Ralph. 1969. *The State in Capitalist Society.* New York: Basic Books.

Mills, C. Wright. 1951. *White Collar.* New York: Oxford University Press.

———. 1956. *The Power Elite.* New York: Oxford University Press.

———. 1959. *The Sociological Imagination.* New York: Oxford University Press.

———. 1962. *The Marxists.* New York: Dell.

Milner, Murray, Jr. 1972. *The Illusion of Equality.* San Francisco: Jossey-Bass.

Min, Pyong Gap. 1988. *Ethnic Business Enterprise: Korean Small Business in Atlanta.* New York: Center for Migration Studies.

———. 1995. "Korean Americans." In *Asian Americans: Contemporary Trends and Issues,* edited by Pyong Gap Min, 199–231. Thousand Oaks, CA: Sage.

Mishel, Lawrence. 1995. "Rising Tides, Sinking Wages." *The American Prospect* (Fall):60–64.

Mishel, Lawrence, and Jared Bernstein. 1993. *The State of Working America, 1992–1993.* Armonk, NY: M. E. Sharpe.

Mishel, Lawrence, Jared Bernstein, and John Schmitt. 1999. *The State of Working America, 1998–99.* Ithaca, NY: Cornell University Press.

———. 2001. *The State of Working America, 2000–01.* Ithaca, NY: Cornell University Press.

Montagu, Ashley. 1972. *Statement on Race.* 3d ed. New York: Oxford University Press.

———. 1974. *Man's Most Dangerous Myth: The Fallacy of Race.* 5th ed. New York: Oxford University Press.

Montero, Darrel. 1980. *Japanese Americans: Changing Patterns of Ethnic Affiliation Over Three Generations.* Boulder, CO: Westview.

Moore, Gwen. 1988. "Women in Elite Positions." *Sociological Forum* 3:566–585.

Moore, Joan. 1975. *Mexican Americans.* 2d ed. Englewood Cliffs, NJ: Prentice Hall.

Moore, Stephen, and Dean Stansel. 1995. *Ending Corporate Welfare As We Know It.* Washington, DC: Cato Institute.

Morin, Richard. 1995. "Feelings That Aren't Set in Concrete." *Washington Post Weekly Edition* (March 13–19):37.

_____. 1996. "Tuned Out, Turned Off." *Washington Post Weekly Edition* (February 5–11):6–8.

_____. 1997. "Aging with an Attitude." *Washington Post* (June 9):35.

Morisi, Teresa L. 1996. "Commercial Banking Transformed by Computer Technology."*Monthly Labor Review* 119(August):30–36.

Morris, Michael. 1996. "Culture, Structure, and the Underclass." In *Myths about the Powerless: Contesting Social Inequalities,* edited by M. B. Lykes, A. Banuazizi, R. Liem, and M. Morris, 34–49. Philadelphia: Temple University Press.

Mullan Harris, Kathleen. 1996. "The Reforms Will Hurt, Not Help, Poor Women and Children." *The Chronicle of Higher Education* (October 4):B7.

Muller, Thomas, 1993. *Immigrants and the American City.* New York: New York University Press.

Murdock, George Peter. 1937. "Comparative Data and the Division of Labor by Sex," *Social Forces* 15:551–555.

Murr, Andrew. 1997. " 'Didn't Seem Like Much.' " *Newsweek* (December 1):37.

Murray, Charles. 1984. *Losing Ground: American Social Policy 1950–1980.* New York: Basic Books.

Murray, Robert K. 1955. *Red Scare: A Study in National Hysteria, 1919–1920.* Minneapolis: University of Minnesota Press.

Myrdal, Gunnar. 1944. *An American Dilemma: The Negro Problem and Modern Democracy.* New York: Harper & Row.

Nanda, Serena. 1990. *Neither Man nor Woman: The Hijras of India.* Belmont, CA: Wadsworth.

Nasar, Sylvia. 1992. "Those Born Wealthy or Poor Usually Stay So, Studies Say." *New York Times* (May 18):A1, C7.

Nash, Manning. 1962. "Race and the Ideology of Race." *Current Anthropology* 3: 285–288.

Nash, Nathaniel C. 1995. "Europeans Shrug As Taxes Go Up." *New York Times* (February 16):A4.

National Conference. 1995. *Taking America's Pulse: A Summary Report of the National Conference Survey on Inter-Group Relations.* New York: National Conference.

Newcomer, Mabel. 1955. *The Big Business Executive.* New York: Columbia University Press.

Newman, Katherine. 1993. *Declining Fortunes: The Withering of the American Dream.* New York: Basic Books.

_____. 1999. *Falling from Grace: Downward Mobility in the Age of Affluence.* Berkeley: University of California Press.

Newsweek. 1995. "Global Boom: It Could Last until 2000." (January 2):120.

New York Times. 1994. "Black Household Income Leads Whites' in Queens." (June 6): A1, B7.

_____. 1996. "Ball Changes Hands." (September 25):B8.

_____. 1997. "Idaho's New Chief Justice Helps Break Glass Ceiling." (February 23):20.

_____. 1998. "$13 Million an Hour." (January 15):A1.

Nichols, Roger L. 1992. "Indians in the Post-Termination Era." In *The American Indian: Past and Present,* 4th ed., edited by Roger L. Nichols, 289–301. New York: McGraw-Hill.

Nielsen, Joyce McCarl. 1990. *Sex and Gender in Society: Perspectives on Stratification.* 2d ed. Prospect Heights, IL: Waveland Press.

Niemi, Richard G., and Barbara I. Sobieszek. 1977. "Political Socialization." In *Annual Review of Sociology,* vol. 3, edited by A. Inkeles, 209–233. Palo Alto, CA: Annual Reviews.

Noble, Charles. 1997. *Welfare as We Knew It: A Political History of the American Welfare State.* New York: Oxford University Press.

Noel, Donald L. 1968. "A Theory of the Origin of Ethnic Stratification." *Social Problems* 16:157–172.

O'Hare, William. 1987. "Best Metros for Hispanic Businesses." *American Demographics* 9(November):30–32.

Oliver, Melvin L., and Thomas M. Shapiro. 1995. *Black Wealth/White Wealth: A New Perspective on Racial Inequality.* New York: Routledge.

Olsen, Marvin E. 1973. "A Model of Political Participation Stratification." *Journal of Political and Military Sociology* 1:183–200.

_____. 1982. *Participatory Pluralism.* Chicago: Nelson-Hall.

Orshansky, Mollie. 1969. "How Poverty Is Measured." *Monthly Labor Review* 92(February):12–19.

Ossowski, Stanislaw. 1963. *Class Structure in the Social Consciousness.* New York: Free Press.

Padilla, Felix. 1987. *Up from Puerto Rico.* New York: Columbia University Press.

Page, Benjamin I. 1978. *Choices and Echoes in Presidential Elections.* Chicago: University of Chicago Press.

Paletz, David L., and Robert M. Entman. 1981. *Media Power Politics.* New York: Free Press.

Pammett, Jon H. 1996. "Getting Ahead around the World." In, *Social Inequality in Canada,* edited by Alan Frizzell and Jon H. Pammett, 67–86. Ottawa: Carleton University Press.

Pappas, Ben. 1997. "Cathedrals to Sunglasses and Other Fantasies of the Very Rich." *Fortune* (October 13):53–57.

Parenti, Michael. 1986. *Inventing Reality: The Politics of the Mass Media.* New York: St. Martin's.

Parker, Richard G. 1991. *Bodies, Pleasures, and Passions: Sexual Culture in Contemporary Brazil.* Boston: Beacon.

Parkin, Frank. 1971. *Class Inequality and Political Order.* New York: Praeger.

Parsons, Talcott. 1953. "A Revised Analytical Approach to the Theory of Social Stratification." In *Class, Status and Power,* edited by R. Bendix and S. M. Lipset, 92–128. Glencoe, IL: Free Press.

_____. 1955. "Family Structure and the Socialization of the Child." In *Family, Socialization and Interaction Process,* edited by Talcott Parsons and Robert F. Bales, 3–9. Glencoe, IL: Free Press.

Parsons, Talcott, and Robert F. Bales. 1955. *Family Socialization and Interaction.* Glencoe, IL: Free Press.

Passell, Peter. 1996. "Asia's Path to More Equality and More Money for All." *New York Times* (August 25):E5.

Patterson, Orlando. 1982. *Slavery and Social Death: A Comparative Study.* Cambridge, MA: Harvard University Press.

_____. 1995. "The Paradox of Integration." *New Republic* (November 6):24–27.

_____. 1997. *The Ordeal of Integration: Progress and Resentment in America's "Racial" Crisis.* Washington, DC: Civitas/Counterpoint.

_____. 1998. "Affirmative Action: Opening Up Workplace Networks to Afro-Americans." *Brookings Review* (Spring):17–23.

Pear, Robert. 1992. "New Look at the U.S. in 2050: Bigger, Older and Less White." *New York Times* (December 4):A1, A10.

_____. 1997. "Academy's Report Says Immigration Benefits the U.S." *New York Times* (May 18):1, 12.

———. 2000. "Far More Single Mothers Are Taking Jobs." *New York Times* (November 5):22.

Pedraza-Bailey, Silvia. 1985. *Political and Economic Migrants in America: Cubans and Mexicans.* Austin: University of Texas Press.

Pessen, Edward. 1984. *The Log Cabin Myth: The Social Backgrounds of the Presidents.* New Haven: Yale University Press.

Peterson, V. Spike, and Anne Sisson Runyan. 1999. *Global Gender Issues.* 2nd ed. Boulder, CO: Westview.

Pettigrew, Thomas F. 1979. "Racial Change and Social Policy." *Annals of the American Academy of Political and Social Science* 441:114–131.

Phillips, Kevin. 1990. *The Politics of Rich and Poor: Wealth and the American Electorate in the Reagan Aftermath.* New York: Random House.

_____. 1994. *Boiling Point: Democrats, Republicans and the Decline of Middle-Class Prosperity.* New York: HarperCollins.

_____. 1995. "Rich Transforming U.S. Playgrounds." *USA Today* (August 23):11A.

Pinkney, Alphonso. 1984. *The Myth of Black Progress.* New York: Cambridge University Press.

Piven, Frances Fox, and Richard A. Cloward. 1978. *Poor People's Movements.* New York: Vintage.

Plamenatz, John. 1971. *Ideology.* London: Macmillan.

Polivka, Anne E. 1996. "A Profile of Contingent Workers." *Monthly Labor Review* 119(October):10–21.

Pollack, Andrew. 1992. "Asian Immigrants New Leaders in Silicon Valley." *New York Times* (January 14):A1, C5.

_____. 1996. "Few Women on Japan's Assembly Lines." *New York Times* (April 26):A8.

_____. 1997. "Opportunity at a Price." *New York Times* (July 8):C1, C4.

Porter, John. 1965. *The Vertical Mosaic: An Analysis of Social Class and Power in Canada.* Toronto: University of Toronto Press.

Portes, Alejandro. 1969. "Dilemmas of a Golden Exile: Integration of Cuban Refugee Families in Milwaukee." *American Sociological Review* 34:505–518.

Portes, Alejandro, J. M. Clark, and R. L. Bach. 1977. "The New Wave: A Statistical Profile of Recent Cuban Exiles to the United States." *Estudios Cubanos/Cuban Studies* 7:1–32.

Portes, Alejandro, J. M. Clark, and R. D. Manning. 1985. "After Mariel: A Survey of the Resettlement Experiences of 1980 Cuban Refugees in Miami." *Estudios Cubanos/Cuban Studies* 15:37–59.

Portes, Alejandro, and R. D. Manning. 1986. "The Immigrant Enclave: Theory and Empirical Examples." In *Competitive Ethnic Relations,* edited by S. Olzak, 47–68. New York: Academic Press.

Portes, Alejandro, and Rubén Rumbaut. 1990. *Immigrant America: A Portrait.* Berkeley: University of California Press.

Portes, Alejandro, and Alex Stepick. 1993. *City on the Edge: The Transformation of Miami.* Berkeley: University of California Press.

Portes, Alejandro, and Richard Schauffler. 1996. "Language and the Second Generation: Bilingualism Yesterday and Today." In *The New Second Generation,* edited by A. Portes, 8–29. New York: Russell Sage Foundation.

Postman, Neil. 1985. *Amusing Ourselves to Death: Public Discourse in the Age of Show Business.* New York: Penguin.

Poulantzas, Nicos. 1973. *Political Power and Social Classes.* London: NLB and Sheed and Ward.

Prewitt, Kenneth, and Alan Stone. 1973. *The Ruling Elites.* New York: Harper & Row.

Primus, Wendell, Lynette Rawlings, Kathy Larin, and Kathryn Porter. 1999. *The Initial Impacts of Welfare Reform on the Incomes of Single-Mother Families.* Washington, DC: Center on Budget and Policy Priorities.

Puddington, Arch. 1992. "Is White Racism the Problem?" *Commentary* (July):31–36.

Putnam, Robert D. 1976. *The Comparative Study of Political Elites.* Englewood Cliffs, NJ: Prentice Hall.

_____. 1996. "The Strange Disappearance of Civic America." *The American Prospect* (Winter):34–48.

Quinley, Harold E., and Charles Y. Glock. 1979. *Anti-Semitism in America.* New York: Free Press.

Ramer, Samuel C. 1990. "Feldshers and Rural Health Care in the Early Soviet Period." In *Health and Society in Revolutionary Russia,* edited by Susan Gross Solomon and John F. Hutchinson, 121–145. Bloomington: Indiana University Press.

Ratcliffe, R. G. 1998. "Governor Gets His Pot of Baseball Gold from Sale of Texas Rangers." *Houston Chronicle* (June 18):35.

Rawley, James A. 1981. *The Transatlantic Slave Trade: A History.* New York: North.

Reich, Robert B. 1989. "As the World Turns." *New Republic* 200(May 1):23, 26–28.

_____. 1992. *The Work of Nations: Preparing Ourselves for 21st Century Capitalism.* New York: Vintage.

_____. 1994. "Meet the Nimble New Middle Class." *Washington Post* (March 27):M5.

_____. 1998. "Working Class Dogged." *Mother Jones* (March/April):40.

———. 2001. *The Future of Success.* New York: Alfred A. Knopf.

Reischauer, Edwin O. 1988. *The Japanese Today: Change and Continuity.* Cambridge, MA: Harvard University Press.

Reskin, Barbara, and Irene Padavic. 1994. *Women and Men at Work.* Thousand Oaks, CA: Pine Forge Press.

Richard, Amy O'Neill. 2000. *International Trafficking in Women to the United States: A Contemporary Manifestation of Slavery and Organized Crime.* Washington, DC: Center for the Study of Intelligence.

Rifkin, Jeremy. 1995. *The End of Work: The Decline of the Global Labor Force and the Dawn of the Post-Market Era.* New York: G. P. Putnam's Sons.

_____. 2000. *The Age of Access: The New Culture of Hypercapitalism Where All of Life Is a Paid-for Experience.* New York: Tarcher/Putnam.

Roberts, Sam. 1995. *Who We Are: A Portrait of America Based on the Latest U.S. Census.* Rev. ed. New York: Times Books.

Robertson, Wyndham. 1973. "The Highest Ranking Women in Big Business." *Fortune* 90(April):81–89.

Robinson, Linda, and Jack Epstein. 1994. "Battered by the Myth of Machismo." *U.S. News & World Report* (April 4):41–42.

Rodriguez, Clara. 1989. *Puerto Ricans: Born in the U.S.A.* Boston: Unwin and Hyman.

Rose, Arnold. 1967. *The Power Structure.* New York: Oxford University Press.

Rosenbaum, David E. 1996. "In Political Money Game, The Year of Big Loopholes." *New York Times* (December 26):A1, A10.

Rosenblatt, Roger. 1999. "Introduction." In *Consuming Desires: Consumption, Culture, and the Pursuit of Happiness,* edited by Roger Rosenblatt, 1–22. Washington, DC: Island Press.

Rosenthal, Neal H. 1995. "The Nature of Occupational Employment Growth: 1983–93." *Monthly Labor Review* (June):45–54.

Rosentraub, Mark S. 1999. *Major League Losers: The Real Cost of Sports and Who's Paying for It.* Rev. ed. New York: Basic Books.

Rossi, Alice. 1977. "A Biosocial Perspective on Parenting." *Daedalus* 106:1–31.

———. 1984. "Gender and Parenthood." *American Sociological Review* 49:1–18.

Rothenberg, Paula S. 1998. *Race, Class, and Gender in the United States: An Integrated Study.* 4th ed. New York: St. Martin's.

Rubin, Lillian B. 1994. *Families on the Fault Line: America's Working Class Speaks About the Family, the Economy, Race and Ethnicity.* New York: HarperPerennial.

Rudolph, Lloyd, and Susanne Hoeker Rudolph. 1967. *The Modernity of Tradition: Political Development in India.* Chicago: University of Chicago Press.

Rudwick, Elliott. 1964. *Race Riot at East St. Louis.* Carbondale, IL: Southern Illinois University Press.

Rudwick, Elliott, and August Meier. 1969. "Negro Retaliatory Violence in the Twentieth Century." In *The Making of Black America: Essays in Negro Life and History,* vol. 2, edited by August Meier and Elliott Rudwick, 406–417. New York: Atheneum.

Russell, Cheryl, and Marcia Mogelonsky. 2000. "Riding High on the Market." *American Demographics* (April):44–54.

Ryan, William. 1975. *Blaming the Victim.* Rev. ed. New York: Vintage.

Saad, Lydia. 1995. "Immigrants See U.S. as Land of Opportunity." *Gallup Poll Monthly* (July):19–33.

Safa, Helen I. 1990. "Women and Industrialization in the Caribbean." In *Women, Employment, and the Family in the International Division of Labour,* edited by Sharon Stichter and Jane L. Parpart, 72–97. Philadelphia: Temple University Press.

Sagarin, Edward. 1971. *The Other Minorities.* Waltham, MA: Xerox.

Samuelson, Robert J. 1997. "The Rich and Deserving." *Washington Post National Weekly Edition* (August 18):24.

Sandefur, Gary. 1996. "Welfare Doesn't Cause Illegitimacy and Single Parenthood." *Chronicle of Higher Education* (October 4):B7–B8.

Saunders, Peter. 1990. *Social Class and Stratification.* London: Routledge.

Schiff, Bob. 1996. "Bogus Comparisons Trivialize Money Influence." *Public Citizen* (Spring):15.

Schlesinger, Arthur M., Jr. 1992. *The Disuniting of America: Reflections on a Multicultural Society.* New York: Norton.

Schmidhauser, John R. 1960. *The Supreme Court: Its Politics, Personalities, and Procedures.* New York: Holt, Rinehart and Winston.

Schor, Juliet B. 1992. *The Overworked American: The Unexpected Decline of Leisure.* New York: Basic Books.

———. 1998. *The Overspent American: Upscaling, Downshifting, and the New Consumer.* New York: Basic Books.

———. 1999. "What's Wrong with Consumer Society?" In *Consuming Desires: Consumption, Culture, and the Pursuit of Happiness,* edited by Roger Rosenblatt, 37–50. Washington, DC: Island Press.

———. 2000. *Do Americans Shop Too Much?* Boston: Beacon Press.

Schrag, Peter. 1995. "So You Want to Be Color Blind: Alternative Principles for Affirmative Action." *The American Prospect* (Summer):38–43.

Schuman, Howard. 1982. "Free Will and Determinism in Public Beliefs about Race." In *Majority and Minority: The Dynamics of Race and Ethnicity in American Life,* 3d ed., edited by Norman R. Yetman and C. Hoy Steele, 345–350. Boston: Allyn & Bacon.

Schuman, Howard, Charlotte Steeh, and Lawrence Bobo. 1985. *Racial Attitudes in America: Trends and Interpretations.* Cambridge, MA: Harvard University Press.

Schurman, Franz. 1971. "System, Contradictions, and Revolution in America." In *The New American Revolution,* edited by R. Aya and N. Miller, 18–96. New York: Free Press.

Seelye, Katharine Q. 1997. "Lott Calls Gifts the 'American Way'." *New York Times* (February 21):A15.

Sennett, Richard, and Jonathan Cobb. 1973. *The Hidden Injuries of Class.* New York: Vintage.

Shapiro, Isaac, and Robert Greenstein. 2000. *The Widening Income Gulf.* Washington, DC: Center on Budget and Policy Priorities.

Shaw, Donald L., and Maxwell E. McCombs. 1977. *The Emergence of American Political Issues: The Agenda-Setting Function of the Press.* St. Paul: West Publishers.

Sherden, William A. 1998. *The Fortune Sellers: The Big Business of Buying and Selling Predictions.* New York: Wiley.

Shils, Edward. 1968. "The Concept and Functions of Ideology." In *The International Encyclopedia of the Social Sciences,* vol. 7, edited by D. Sills, 66–76. New York: Macmillan.

Shostak, Arthur B. 1969. *Blue Collar Life.* New York: Random House.

Sidel, Ruth. 1996. *Keeping Women and Children Last: America's War on the Poor.* New York: Penguin.

Sigal, Leon V. 1973. *Reporters and Officials: The Organization and Politics of News Reporting.* Lexington, MA: Heath.

Silberman, Charles. 1985. *A Certain People: American Jews and Their Lives Today.* New York: Summit.

Sims, Calvin. 1997. "Justice in Peru: Rape Victim Is Pressed to Marry Attacker." *New York Times* (March 12):A1, A8.

Simon, Julian L. 1991. "The Case for Greatly Increased Immigration." *The Public Interest* 102(Winter):89–103.

Simpson, Glenn R. 1994. "Of the Rich, by the Rich, for the Rich: Are Congress's Millionaires Turning Our Democracy into a Plutocracy?" *Washington Post* (April 17):C4.

Sinha, Surajit. 1967. "Caste in India: Its Essential Pattern of Socio-Cultural Integration." In *Caste and Race: Comparative Approaches,* edited by Anthony de Reuck and Julie Knight, 92–105. Boston: Little, Brown.

Skocpol, Theda. 1996. "Delivering for Young Families: The Resonance of the GI Bill." *The American Prospect* (September/October):66–72.

Skrentny, John David. 1996. *The Ironies of Affirmative Action: Politics, Culture, and Justice in America.* Chicago: University of Chicago Press.

Sloan, Allan. 1997. "The New Rich." *Newsweek* (August 4):48–55.

Slomczynski, Kazimierz M., and Tadeusz K. Krauze. 1987. "Cross-National Similarity in Social Mobility Patterns: A Direct Test of the Featherman-Jones-Hauser Hypothesis."*American Sociological Review* 52:598–611.

Smeeding, Timothy M. 1998. "U.S. Income Inequality in a Cross-National Perspective: Why Are We So Different?" In *The Inequality Paradox: Growth of Income Disparity,* edited by James A. Auerbach and Richard S. Belous, 194–217. Washington, DC: National Policy Association.

Smith, David H. 1980. *Participation in Social and Political Activities: A Comprehensive Analysis of Political Involvement, Expressive Leisure Time, and Helping Behavior.* San Francisco: Jossey-Bass.

Sniderman, Paul M., and Edward G. Carmines. 1997. *Reaching beyond Race.* Cambridge, MA: Harvard University Press.

Sniderman, Paul M., and Thomas Piazza. 1993. *The Scar of Race.* Cambridge, MA: Belknap Press.

Soltow, Lee. 1984. "Wealth Inequality in the United States in 1798 and 1860." *Review of Economics and Statistics* 66:444–451.

Sommers, Christina Hoff. 1995. *Who Stole Feminism?: How Women Have Betrayed Women.* New York: Touchstone.

Sorokin, Pitirim. 1927. *Social Mobility.* New York: Harper & Brothers.

South, Scott J. 1988. "Sex Ratios, Economic Power, and Women's Roles: A Theoretical Extension and Empirical Test." *Journal of Marriage and the Family* 50:19–31.

Sowell, Thomas. 1990. *Preferential Policies: An International Perspective.* New York: William Morrow.

Spring, Joel H. 1972. *Education and the Rise of the Corporate State.* Boston: Beacon.

Srinivas, M. N. 1962. *Caste in Modern India and Other Essays.* New York: Asia Publishing House.

Stampp, Kenneth M. 1956. *The Peculiar Institution: Slavery in the Ante-Bellum South.* New York: Knopf.

Stanley, David T., Dean E. Mann, and Jameson W. Doig, 1967. *Men Who Govern.* Washington, DC: Brookings Institution.

Steele, Shelby. 1991. *The Content of Our Character: A New Vision of Race in America.* New York: HarperPerennial.

Stein, A. 1971. "Strategies for Failure." *Harvard Educational Review* 41:158–204.

Stein, Herbert, and Murray Foss. 1995. *The New Illustrated Guide to the American Economy.* Washington, DC: The AEI Press.

Steinberg, Stephen. 1995. *Turning Back: The Retreat from Racial Justice in American Thought and Policy.* Boston: Beacon Press.

Steinhauer, Jennifer. 1999. "For Women in Medicine, a Road to Compromise, Not Perks." *New York Times* (March 1):A1, A21.

Stevenson, Harold W., and James W. Stigler. 1992. *The Learning Gap: Why Our Schools Are Failing and What We Can Learn from Japanese and Chinese Education.* New York: Simon & Schuster.

Stoesz, David. 1999. "Unraveling Welfare Reform." *Society* (May/June):53–61.

Strobel, Fredrick R. 1993. *Upward Dreams, Downward Mobility: The Economic Decline of the American Middle Class.* Lanham, MD: Rowman and Littlefield.

Suro, Roberto. 1989. "Employers Are Looking Abroad for the Skilled and the Energetic."*New York Times* (July 16):IV–4.

Sweeney, John. 1996. *America Needs a Raise.* Boston: Houghton Mifflin.

Swidler, Ann. 1992. "Inequality and American Culture: The Persistence of Voluntarism." *American Behavioral Scientist* 35:606–629.

Syme, S. Leonard, and Lisa F. Berkman. 1997. "Social Class, Susceptibility, and Sickness." In *The Sociology of Health and Illness*, 5th ed., edited by Peter Conrad, 29–35. New York: St. Martin's.

Szabo, Joan C. 1989. "Opening Doors for Immigrants." *Nation's Business* 77 (August):48–49.

Taeuber, Karl E. 1975. "Racial Segregation: The Persisting Dilemma." *Annals of the American Academy of Political and Social Science* 422:87–96.

Tannenbaum, Frank. 1947. *Slave and Citizen: The Negro in the Americas*. New York: Knopf.

Taylor, William L. 1997. "Affirmative Action: The Questions to Be Asked." In *Double Exposure: Poverty and Race in America*, edited by Chester Hartman, 171–173. Armonk, NY: M. E. Sharpe.

TenBroek, Jacobus, Edward N. Barnhart, and Floyd W. Matson. 1968. *Prejudice, War and the Constitution*. Berkeley: University of California Press.

Terry, Don, and Karen De Witt. 1996. "Toll Is Even Greater in Forgotten Anacostia." *New York Times* (July 26):A1, A9.

Thernstrom, Abigail, and Stephen Thernstrom. 1998. "Black Progress: How Far We've Come—and How Far We Have to Go." *Brookings Review* (Spring): 12–16.

Thernstrom, Stephan, and Abigail Thernstrom. 1997. *America in Black and White: One Nation, Indivisible*. New York: Simon & Schuster.

Thomas, Evan, and Gregory L. Vistica. 1998. "Fallout from a Media Fiasco." *Newsweek* (July 20):24–26.

Thomas, Jo. 1997. "Satisfaction in Job Well Done Is Only Reward for E-Mail Software Inventor." *New York Times* (January 21):A6.

Thompson, Craig J. 2000. "A New Puritanism?" In Juliet Schor, *Do Americans Spend Too Much?* 63–68. Boston: Beacon Press.

Thornton, Russell. 1995. "North American Indians and the Demography of Contact." In *Race, Discourse, and the Origin of the Americas: A New World View*, edited by Vera Lawrence Hyatt and Rex Nettleford, 213–230. Washington, DC: Smithsonian Institution Press.

Thurow, Lester C.. 1975. *Generating Inequality: Mechanisms of Distribution in the U.S. Economy*. New York: Basic Books.

———. 1995. "Why Their World Might Crumble." *New York Times Magazine* (November 19):78–79.

———. 1996. *The Future of Capitalism: How Today's Economic Forces Shape Tomorrow's World*. New York: William Morrow.

———. 1999. *Building Wealth: The New Rules for Individuals, Companies, and Nations in a Knowledge-Based Economy*. New York: HarperCollins.

Tiger, Lionel. 1969. *Men in Groups*. London: Nelson.

Time. 1995. "The Rise of English Only." (October 9):49.

Toth, Jennifer. 1993. *Mole People: Life in the Tunnels Beneath New York City*. Chicago: Chicago Review Press.

Truman, David B. 1951. *The Governmental Process*. New York: Random House.

Tuchman, Gaye. 1978. *Making News*. New York: Free Press.

Tucker, Robert C., ed. 1972. *The Marx-Engels Reader*. New York: Norton.

Tumin, Melvin M. 1953. "Some Principles of Stratification: A Critical Analysis." *American Sociological Review* 18:387–394.

_____. 1964. "Ethnic Group." In *Dictionary of the Social Sciences,* edited by Julius Gould and William L. Kolb, 243. New York: Free Press.

Turner, Jonathan H., and Charles E. Starnes. 1976. *Inequality: Privilege and Poverty in America.* Pacific Palisades, CA: Goodyear.

Turner, Ralph. 1960. "Sponsored and Contest Mobility and the School System." *American Sociological Review* 25:855–867.

Tuttle, William M., Jr. 1970. *Race Riot: Chicago in the Red Summer of 1919.* New York: Atheneum.

Twitchell, James B. 1996. *ADCULTusa: The Triumph of Advertising in American Culture.* New York: Columbia University Press.

Tyler, Gus. 1975. "Introduction: A People on the Move." In *Mexican-Americans Tomorrow,* edited by Gus Tyler, 1–18. Albuquerque: University of New Mexico Press.

Uchitelle, Louis. 1997. "Welfare Recipients Taking Jobs Often Held by the Working Poor." *New York Times* (April 1):A1, A16.

————. 2000. "Who's Afraid Now That Big Is No Longer Bad?" *New York Times* (November 5):1, 12.

Uchitelle, Louis, and N. R. Kleinfield. 1996. "On the Battlefields of Business, Millions of Casualties." *New York Times* (March 3):1, 26.

UNDP (United Nations Development Programme). 1993. *Human Development Report 1993.* New York: Oxford University Press.

_____. 1995. *Human Development Report.* New York: United Nations Publications.

_____. 1997 *Human Development Report 1997.* New York: Oxford University Press.

————. 1999. *Human Development Report 1999.* New York: Oxford University Press.

————. 2000. *Human Development Report 2000.* New York: Oxford University Press.

United Nations. 1991. *The World's Women 1970–1990: Trends and Statistics.* New York: United Nations Publications.

————. 2000. *The World's Women 2000.* New York: United Nations.

United Nations, International Labor Organization. 1996. "More and Better Jobs for Women." Report issued July 29, 1996.

United Nations Population Fund. 2000. *The State of World Population 2000.* New York: United Nations Population Fund.

USA Today. 1994. "Ivy League Degrees Pay Off." (April 21):1.

Useem, Michael. 1978. "The Inner Group of the American Capitalist Class." *Social Problems* 25:225–240.

U.S. Census Bureau. 1975. *Historical Statistics of the U.S.: Colonial Times to 1970. Part I.* Washington, DC: U.S. Government Printing Office.

_____. 1993a. *1990 Census of Population: Asians and Pacific Islanders in the United States.* CP-3-5. Washington, DC: U.S. Government Printing Office.

_____. 1993b. *Ancestry of the Population in the United States, 1990.* CP-3-2. Washington, DC: U.S. Government Printing Office.

_____. 1995a. "The Black Population in the United States: March 1994 and 1993." *Current Population Reports,* Series P20-480. Washington, DC: U.S. Government Printing Office.

_____. 1995b. *Statistical Abstract of the United States 1995.* Washington, DC: U.S. Government Printing Office.

_____. 1996. *A Brief Look at Postwar U.S. Income Inequality.* Washington, DC: U.S. Government Printing Office.

_____. 1997a. "Poverty in the United States: 1996." *Current Population Reports,* Series P60-198. Washington, DC: U.S. Government Printing Office.

_____. 1997b. *Presence of Children under 18 Years Old—Families by Median and Mean Income, and Type of Family: 1974 to 1996.* <http://www.census.gov/hhes/income/histinc/f10.html>.

_____. 1997c. "Money Income in the United States: 1996." *Current Population Reports,* Series P60-197. Washington, DC: U.S. Government Printing Office.

_____. 1997d. *Statistical Abstract of the United States 1997.* Washington, DC: U.S. Government Printing Office.

_____. 1997e. *Race and Hispanic Origin of Householder—Families by Median and Mean Income: 1947–1996.* <http:www.census.gov/hhes/income/histinc/f05.html>.

_____. 1998a. *Median Net Worth by Race and Hispanic Origin of Householder and Monthly Household Income Quintile: 1993 and 1991.* <http//www.census.gov/hhes/www/wealth/wlth93+4.html>.

_____. 1998b. "Voting and Registration in the Election of November 1996." *Current Population Reports,* Series P20-504. Washington, DC: U.S. Government Printing Office.

_____. 1999. *Statistical Abstract of the United States: 1999.* Washington, DC: U.S. Government Printing Office.

_____. 2000a. "Poverty in the United States: 1999." *Current Population Reports,* P60-210. Washington, DC: U.S. Government Printing Office.

_____. 2000b. "Educational Attainment in the United States: March 1999." *Current Population Reports,* Series P20-528. Washington, DC: U.S. Government Printing Office.

_____. 2000c. "Money Income in the United States: 1999." *Current Population Reports,* P60-209. Washington, DC: U.S. Government Printing Office.

_____. 2000d. *The Black Population in the United States: March 1999.* Current Population Reports, Series P20-530. Washington, DC: U.S. Government Printing Office.

_____. 2000e. *The Changing Shape of the Nation's Income Distribution.* Current Population Reports P60-204. Washington, DC: U.S. Government Printing Office.

_____. 2000f. *The Hispanic Population in the United States: March 1999.* Current Population Reports, Series P20-527. Washington, DC: U.S. Government Printing Office.

_____. 2000g. *The Asian and Pacific Islander Population in the United States: March 1999.* Current Population Reports, Series P20-529. Washington, DC: U.S. Government Printing Office.

U.S. Commission on Civil Rights. 1992. *Civil Rights Issues Facing Asian Americans in the 1990s.* Washington, DC: U.S. Government Printing Office.

U.S. Department of Education. 1991. *Indian Nations at Risk: An Educational Strategy for Action.* Washington, DC: U.S. Government Printing Office.

_____. 1992. *Digest of Education Statistics.* Washington, DC: U.S. Government Printing Office.

_____. 1997. National Center for Education Statistics. *Degrees and Other Awards Conferred by Institutions of Higher Education: 1994–95.* Washington, DC: U.S. Government Printing Office.

_____. 1998. *Women and Men of the Engineering Path: A Model for Analyses of Undergraduate Careers.* Washington, DC: U.S. Government Printing Office.

_____. 2000. *Digest of Education Statistics.* Washington, DC: U.S. Government Printing Office.

U.S. Department of the Interior. 1991. *American Indians Today*. 3d ed. Washington, DC: Department of the Interior, Bureau of Indian Affairs.

U.S. Immigration and Naturalization Service. 2000. *Statistical Yearbook of the Immigration and Naturalization Service 1998*. Washington, DC: U.S. Government Printing Office.

Valentine, Charles A. 1971. "The 'Culture of Poverty': Its Scientific Significance and Its Implications for Actions." In *The Culture of Poverty: A Critique,* edited by Eleanor Burke Leacock, 193–225. New York: Simon & Schuster.

van den Berghe, Pierre L. 1967. *South Africa: A Study in Conflict*. Berkeley: University of California Press.

_____. 1978. *Race and Racism: A Comparative Perspective*. 2d ed. New York: Wiley.

Veblen, Thorstein. 1899. *The Theory of the Leisure Class*. New York: Macmillan.

Veltman, Calvin. 1983. *Language Shift in the United States*. Berlin: Mouton.

Verba, Sidney, and Norman H. Nie. 1972. *Participation in America*. New York: Harper & Row.

Verba, Sidney, and Garry R. Orren. 1985. *Equality in America: The View from the Top*. Cambridge, MA: Harvard University Press.

Vobejda, Barbara, and Judith Havemann. 1999. "Untouched by Reform." *Washington Post National Weekly Edition* (January 11):29–30.

Vogel, Ezra F. 1979. *Japan as Number 1: Lessons for America*. Cambridge, MA: Harvard University Press.

Waldman, Steven, and Rich Thomas. 1990. "How Did It Happen?" *Newsweek* (May 21): 27–28, 32.

Walker, Alan, and Carol Walker. 1995. "Poverty." In *The Social Science Encyclopedia,* 2d ed., edited by Adam Kuper and Jessica Kuper, 655–657. London: Routledge.

Wallace, James, and Jim Erickson. 1992. *Hard Drive: Bill Gates and the Making of the Microsoft Empire*. New York: Wiley.

Warner, W. Lloyd, and James Abegglen. 1963. *Big Business Leaders in America*. New York: Atheneum.

Warren, Christopher L., and John F. Stack, Jr. 1986. "Immigration and the Politics of Ethnicity and Class in Metropolitan Miami." In *The Primordial Challenge: Ethnicity in the Contemporary World,* edited by John F. Stack Jr., 61–79. New York: Greenwood.

Waters, Mary C. 1990. *Ethnic Options: Choosing Identities in America*. Berkeley: University of California Press.

Waters, Mary C., and Karl Eschbach. 1995. "Immigration and Ethnic and Racial Inequality in the United States." *Annual Review of Sociology* 21:419–446.

Wax, Murray L. 1971. *Indian Americans: Unity and Diversity*. Englewood Cliffs, NJ: Prentice Hall.

Weber, Max. 1954. *Max Weber on Law in Economy and Society*. Edited by Max Rheinstein. Cambridge, MA: Harvard University Press.

Weinstein, James. 1968. *The Corporate Ideal in the Liberal State: 1900–1918*. Boston: Beacon Press.

Williams, Christine L. 1995. *Still a Man's World: Men Who Do "Women's Work."* Berkeley: University of California Press.

Williams, David R. 1990. "Socioeconomic Differentials in Health: A Review and Redirection." *Social Psychology Quarterly* 53:81–99.

Williams, Lena. 1995. "Not Just a White Man's Game." *New York Times* (November 9): C1, C6.

Williams, Robin, Jr. 1970. *American Society: A Sociological Interpretation*. 3d ed. New York: Knopf.

Williamson, Jeffrey, and Peter H. Lindert. 1980. *American Inequality: A Macroeconomic History*. New York: Academic Press.

Wilson, Kenneth L., and Alejandro Portes. 1980. "Immigrant Enclaves: An Analysis of the Labor Market Experiences of Cubans in Miami." *American Journal of Sociology* 86:295–315.

Wilson, William Julius. 1980. *The Declining Significance of Race*. 2d ed. Chicago: University of Chicago Press.

———. 1987. *The Truly Disadvantaged: The Inner City, the Underclass, and Public Policy*. Chicago: University of Chicago Press.

———. 1991. "Studying Inner-City Social Dislocations: The Challenge of Public Agenda Research." *American Sociological Review* 56:1–14.

———. 1994. "Race Neutral Programs and the Democratic Coalition." In *Debating Affirmative Action: Race, Gender, Ethnicity, and the Politics of Inclusion*, edited by Nicolaus Mills, 159–173. New York: Delta.

———. 1996. *When Work Disappears: The World of the New Urban Poor*. New York: Knopf.

Wirth, Louis. 1945. "The Problem of Minority Groups." In *The Science of Man in the World Crisis*, edited by Ralph Linton, 347–372. New York: Columbia University Press.

Woellert, Lorraine. 1999. "Keeping Newt Flush and Center." *Business Week* (October 18):66–72.

Wolf, Naomi, 1994. *Fire with Fire: The New Female Power and How to Use It*. New York: Fawcett Columbine.

Wolfe, Alan. 1998. *One Nation, after All: What Middle-Class Americans Really Think about God, Country, Family, Racism, Welfare, Immigration, Homosexuality, Work, the Right, the Left, and Each Other*. New York: Viking.

Wolff, Edward N. 1995a. "How the Pie Is Sliced: America's Growing Concentration of Wealth." *The American Prospect* (Summer):58–64.

———. 1995b. *Top Heavy: A Study of the Increasing Inequality of Wealth in America*. New York: The Twentieth Century Fund Press.

Wolfinger, Raymond E., and Steven J. Rosenstone. 1980. *Who Votes?* New Haven, CT: Yale University Press.

Wong, Morrison. 1989. "A Look at Intermarriage among the Chinese in the United States in 1980." *Sociological Perspectives* 32:87–107.

Woodward, C. Vann. 1974. *The Strange Career of Jim Crow*. 3d ed. New York: Oxford University Press.

Wootton, Barbara H. 1997. "Gender Differences in Occupational Employment." *Monthly Labor Review* (April):15–24.

World Bank. 2000. *World Development Indicators 2000*. Washington, DC: The World Bank.

Worsnop, Richard. 1992. "Native Americans." *CQ Researcher* 2(May 8):385–408.

Wright, Erik Olin. 1978. *Class, Crisis, and the State*. London: Verso.

———. 1985. *Classes*. London: Verso.

———. 1997. *Class Counts: Comparative Studies in Class Analysis*. Cambridge: Cambridge University Press.

Wright, Erik Olin, Karen Shire, Shu-Ling Hwang, Maureen Dolan, and Janeen Baxter. 1992. "The Non-Effects of Class on the Gender Division of Labor in the Home: A Comparative Study of Sweden and the United States." *Gender and Society* 6:252–282.

Wright, Lawrence. 1994. "One Drop of Blood." *New Yorker* (July 25):46–50, 52–55.

Wright, Ronald. 1992. *Stolen Continents: The Americas through Indian Eyes Since 1492.* Boston: Houghton Mifflin.

Xuewen, Sheng, Norman Stockman, and Norman Bonney. 1992. "The Dual Burden: East and West (Women's Working Lives in China, Japan, and Great Britain)." *International Sociology* 7:209–223.

Yates, Steven. 1994. *Civil Wrongs: What Went Wrong with Affirmative Action.* San Francisco: ICS Press.

Yearwood, Lori Teresa. 1999. "Tough Struggle to Stay Afloat." *Miami Herald* (June 20):1, 14.

Yellen, Janet L. 1998. "Trends in Income Inequality." In *The Inequality Paradox: Growth of Income Disparity,* edited by James A. Auerbach and Richard S. Belous, 7–17. Washington, DC: National Policy Association.

Yinger, J. Milton. 1981. "Toward a Theory of Assimilation and Dissimilation." *Ethnic and Racial Studies* 4:249–264.

Zeigler, Harmon, and Wayne Peak. 1970. "The Political Functions of the Educational System." *Sociology of Education* 43:115–142.

Zweigenhaft, Richard L. 1975. "Who Represents America?" *Insurgent Sociologist* 5(Spring):119–130.

_____. 1984. *Who Gets to the Top? Executive Suite Discrimination in the Eighties.* New York: American Jewish Committee.

_____. 1987. "Minorities and Women of the Corporation: Will They Attain Seats of Power?" In *Power Elites and Organizations,* edited by G. W. Domhoff and T. R. Dye, 37–62. Newbury Park, CA: Sage.

Zweigenhaft, Richard L., and G. William Domhoff. 1998a. *Diversity in the Power Elite: Have Women and Minorities Reached the Top?* New Haven, CT: Yale University Press.

_____. 1998b. "The New Power Elite." *Mother Jones* (March/April):44–47.

Index

abject poor. *See* underclass
abolitionists, 145
abortion, legalization of, 342
absolute poverty, 49–50
Abzug, Bella, 314
access to education, 166–168
accident of birth, 161–162, 171
activists, political, 361, 362
Adidas, 103
administration, means of, 216
AFDC (Aid to Families with Dependent
    Children), 64, 71–73, 182, 184
affirmative action, 307–308, 313
    arguments in favor of, 308–309
    and creation of middle class, 174–175
    future of, 311–312
    opposition to, 309–310
    and societal values, 310–311
Afghanistan, 314
African Americans, 260, 268–272, 282
    change in ethnic hierarchy, 21, 292, 306
    in civil rights era, 270–271
    in corporate world, 301
    economic status relative to Euro-
        Americans, 292, 293–295, 312
    education, 292–293
    effect of ethnicity on class status, 287
    elected officials, 300
    ethnic diversity, 271–272
    family income, 37, 289
    family structure, 293
    gender gap in earnings, 327
    lack of job opportunities for poor, 294
    middle class, 271, 292, 306, 308
    Northward migration, 269–270
    overrepresentation in underclass, 34,
        53, 61
    in post–civil rights era, 271

    proportion of population, 261, 279
    relativity of status, 284
    and slavery, 144–145, 268
    socioeconomic status, 292
    and theories of urban poor, 65–66
Afrikaners, 149–150
age discrimination, 281
Age of Reason, 226
age stratification, 16
agrarian societies, 82, 151–154
Albright, Madeleine, 331
alcoholism, 65
Alford, Robert, 370, 372
Alger, Horatio, Jr., 131
Allen, Paul, 122
altruism, 222
American Dream, 42, 91, 234
American ethnic hierarchy, 261–262,
    287–288, 306, 312
American ideology, 253
    and affirmative action, 311
    ancillary beliefs, 241–243
    distrust of government, 189–190
    equality of opportunity, 234–235
    Horatio Alger myth, 131, 158, 171
    individualism, 10, 20, 70, 83, 188–189,
        231–234, 246, 253
    individualistic view of poverty, 70
    liberal capitalism, 189, 239–240, 253
    and lower-middle class, 32
    meritocracy and universalism, 235–238
    self-reliance, 75
    and welfare, 75
    work ethic, 238–239
American Indians. *See* Native Americans
Andreessen, Mark, 122
Angelou, Maya, 116
Anglo core group, 264–265

annexation, 284
anti-Asian attitudes, 275
antitrust legislation, 173, 192, 193
antiwelfare bias, 233
apartheid, 147, 149–150, 303
aristocracy, 354
Aristotle, 81
Aron, Raymond, 199
artisans, 152
Asian Americans, 260, 274–276, 279, 282
   education, 296
   explanations for high achievement of,
      297–298
   family income, 37, 296
   in government positions, 300
   proportion of population, 261
   socioeconomic status, 296–297
   underrepresentation in corporate
      positions, 302
Asian/Pacific Islander census category, 260
assimilation, 267–268, 305
authoritarianism, 65
authority
   as basis of class conflict, 217
   of elites, 348
   gender differences in, 328–329
   as legitimation of power, 226
   Weber on, 213–214, 215

baby boom, 90
Bagdikian, Ben, 249
Bahr, Howard M., 233
Baltzell, E. Digby, 119–120, 130–131
Bandar bin Sultan, 123
Banfield, Edward, 65
bank tellers, 89
Beard, Charles, 133
The Bell Curve (Herrnstein and Murray),
   63–64
Bendix, Reinhard, 139, 155
Bennett, Lance, 250
Berger, Peter, 4, 8
Bernstein, Jared, 43
Berreman, Gerald D., 150
bilingual classrooms, 278
birth control pills, 342
Black Boy (Wright), 269 n. 5
black power, 271
blacks. *See* African Americans
Blau, Peter, 157
blue-collar work, 32, 87, 89, 94–95, 112, 157
bourgeoisie, 82, 209, 374
   See also capitalist class
Boxer, Charles, 146
Brandeis, Louis D., 346
Brazil
   economic inequality in, 45

slavery in, 145–146
   status of women in, 336–337
bride burnings, 336
British immigrants, 264–265
Brittain, John, 124, 161–162
Brown v. Board of Education of Topeka, 270
Bryce, James, 236
Buffett, Warren, 124
Burakumin, 151
Burch, Philip, 133
bureaucracy, 213, 215, 217
Burke, Edmund, 349
Bush, George H., 132
Bush, George W., 132
business cycle, government efforts to
   influence, 192–194
business elite. *See* corporate elite
business power, 190, 347–348
Business Roundtable, 367

Cambodian Americans, 296
campaign financing, 350, 362–366, 376
Canada
   corporations in, 196
   and immigration, 284
   power elite in, 140
   trust in government in, 189–190
   union membership in, 106
   welfare state in, 188
   working-class party in, 88
Cantril, Hadley, 233
capital gains tax, 180
capitalism
   American-style, 189
   control of economic resources, 208–209
   versus democracy, 176
   end of, 224
   equality *versus* liberty in, 22, 24
   and government regulation, 192–194
   and inequality, 19, 23, 175–176
   liberal, 189, 239–240, 253
   Marx on, 83, 204–205
   and middle classes, 83–84
   political economy of, 68
   and poverty, 68
   and racial/ethnic stratification, 307
capitalist class, 116–117
   campaign financing, 364
   change in, 206
   as a ruling class, 202–203
   and societal power, 350–352
   See also elite; upper class
Caplow, Theodore, 233
Carnegie, Andrew, 84, 120
caste, 147–148, 171
   in India, 148–149
   in Japan, 151

caste *(continued)*
  in South Africa, 149–150
  in the United States, 150–151
Castro, Fidel, 214, 274
Catholic Church, 152
Catholics
  discrimination toward, 265
  underrepresentation in government
    positions, 299
celebrity rich, 115–116
charismatic authority, 214
charter group, 264
chief executive officers (CEOs), average
    income, 114–115
childbearing, and gender inequality, 319
childhood poverty, 53, 77–78
child rearing, 318, 319, 322, 327, 329
China, 207, 226
Chinese immigration, 275
Chinese Revolution, 374
Citigroup, 99
citizens, 361
civil disobedience, 270
Civilian Conservation Corps (CCC), 76
civil rights legislation, 174, 303, 327
civil rights movement, 21, 56, 243, 270–271,
    307, 342
class. *See* social class
class conflict, and societal change, 203–205
class consciousness, 27–28, 81, 203, 237–238
classical liberalism, 238–240
class inheritance, 161–162
classless society, 28, 204
class model, of the American power
    structure, 350–352
class theorists, 376
Clement, Wallace, 140
clergy, 152
Clinton, Bill, 131–132, 136
closed societies, 143, 154–155, 171
Coca-Cola, 99
coercion, and obedience to authority, 226
Cold War, 90, 177
Coleman, James, 170, 238–239
college attendance, and family income, 163
college graduates, by race/ethnicity, 291
college quality, 163
Collins, Randall, 319
colonialism, 284
communicators, 361
communism, 204, 205, 242
The Communist Manifesto (Marx), 202
comparable worth, 328
compensatory policies. *See* affirmative
    action

competition
  in the educational system, 246
  among ethnic groups, 285–286
compulsory education, 173
computer ownership, and social class, 168
computer technology, 97, 160
Comte, Auguste, 198
conditional lottery, 165
conflict theory, 218, 219–221, 224
Congress of Industrial Organizations (CIO),
    270
conquest, 284
conspicuous consumption, 123
consumerism, and middle classes, 109–112
consumer patterns, 84–85
contingent workers, 95
contradictory class locations, 209
corporate elite, 127, 128
  predominance of, 357–358
  unaccountability of, 371
Corporate Foreign Tax Credit, 185
corporate sector, 84
  advertising, 242, 248
  campaign financing, 363–364
  ethnic underrepresentation in, 301–302
  gender inequality in, 332–334
  as lobbying force, 367
  power without participation, 370
  societal power, 190, 347–348
corporate welfare, 185–187, 197
Corzine, Jon, 363
cost of living, 51
counterideologies, fear of, 242–243
Cranston, Alan, 367
credit card spending, 110
criminal justice system, 241
Cuba, 207
Cuban Americans, 273–274, 295, 301–302
Cuban Revolution, 374
cultural assimilation, 305
cultural capital, 74, 170
cultural pluralism, 305
culture. *See* American ideology
culture of dependency, 72
culture of poverty, 65–66, 294
cycle of poverty, 66–67

Dahrendorf, Ralf, 216–217
Danziger, Sheldon, 43, 44
Davis, Kingsley, 219
debt (negative wealth), 44, 110
deindustrialization, 68–69
de Jouvenel, Bertrand, 346
deliberate socialization, 245–246
demand-side policies, 194–195, 197

democracy
  versus capitalism, 176
  U.S. as political, 175–176
democratic ideology, in industrialized
    societies, 223
Democratic Republic of Congo, 76
Democrats, 197
demographic factors, affecting decline in
    middle classes, 108–109
Denton, Nancy, 293
description, sociological, 9
desegregation, 271
deserving poor, 70
de Tocqueville, Alexis, 82–83, 354–355
developing societies
  women in unskilled labor force, 322
  women's subordination in, 336–338, 340
dictatorship of the proletariat, 204
differential power, 286
digital divide, 168
discrimination, 302–303
  age, 281
  and black-white economic gap, 293–294
  against Catholics, 265
  and cycle of poverty, 67
  employment, 293, 295
  by gender, 281
  housing, 67, 164, 293–294, 304, 305, 313
  individual and institutional, 303–304,
      312–313
  against Mexican Americans, 272
  reverse, 308, 310, 313
  verbal, 303
  against women, 336–339
distribution, laws of, 222
division of labor, 208, 215
Dolbeare, Kenneth, 358
Domhoff, G. William, 127–128, 135, 302, 357
dominant group, 280, 312
  defined, 283
  relativity of, 283–284
dominant ideologies, 208, 228, 253, 348
  See also American ideology
downsizing, 106–108
downward mobility, 155–156, 157–158
Duncan, Otis Dudley, 157
Durkheim, Émile, 217, 224
Dye, Thomas R., 121, 125, 128–129, 135, 334,
    336, 358–359

earnings
  of CEOs, 114–115
  and decline of American labor unions,
      106
  decrease in, 57

by educational level, 92–93
effect of women workers on, 109
by gender, 325–328
stagnation of, 92
of women corporate managers, 334
  See also income distribution
economic base, 201
economic class, 26
economic expansion, lack of effect on
    wealth inequality, 44–45
economic inequality
  change and continuity in, 41–47, 48
  a comparative perspective, 45–47
  and discrimination, 293–294
  between whites and blacks, 293–295
economic institutions, predominance of in
    Marxian theory, 200–201
economic leaders, social-class origins, 135
economic restructuring, 45, 89
  and African Americans, 294
  downsizing, 106–108
  globalization, 97–105
  labor union decline, 105–106
  and the middle classes, 96–109
  in post-1973 period, 91
  and poverty, 56–57, 68–69
  and social inequality, 294
  and technological changes, 96–97
Edelman, Murray, 372
education
  access to quality, 166–168
  of African Americans, 292–293
  American view of, 235, 242
  of Asian Americans, 296
  competition and inequality, 19
  compulsory, 173
  effect of family environment on, 170
  financing, 166–168
  and gap between high- and low-wage
      workers, 92–93
  high school graduates, by race/ethnicity,
      290
  of Hispanic Americans, 295
  and individual mobility, 162–164
  of lower-middle class, 32, 86
  of Native Americans, 298
  political, 245
  and socialization, 244–246
  and social mobility, 165–170
  as training, 246
  of upper-middle class, 31
  of women, 334–336
  of women in underdeveloped nations,
      340
  of the working class, 32, 87

education *(continued)*
  of the working poor, 33
  See also higher education
"effortocracy," 239
egalitarianism, 235–236
Ehrenreich, Barbara, 85
electoral system, 240
Electronic Data Systems, 122
elite, 130, 215, 347
  commonality of needs and interests,
      358–359
  consensus on basic issues, 360
  corporate, 127, 128, 357–358, 371
  defined, 348, 375
  divisions among, 359–360
  integration, 357, 376
  media, 242, 249, 250, 371
  strategic, 355–356
  training and recruitment, 216
  view of ideology, 229
  See also power elite
elite rule, 348–350
elitist theory, 253, 376
empirical substantiation, 7, 23
employment discrimination, 293, 295
endogamy, 151
Engels, Friedrich, 199, 203, 204
Engerman, Stanley, 145
engineering, women in, 324, 336
English language, exclusive use movement,
      278, 283
Enlightenment, 226
entitlements, 184
Entman, Robert, 250
equality
  of condition, 16, 23, 71
  versus equity, 176 n. 2
  versus liberty, 22, 24
  of opportunity, 16–19, 23, 71, 234–235,
      253
  as a radical idea, 226
Equal Pay Act of 1963, 327
equity feminism, 343, 345
equity *versus* equality, 176 n. 2
establishment, 130
estate system, 151–154, 171, 203, 225–226,
      227
ethnic categories, 259–261
ethnic conflict, 207
ethnic groups, 256–257, 279
  American, 261–262
  changing, 259
  consequences of contact, 285–286
  forms of contact, 284–285
  minorities, 282–283
  self-identification, 27
  See also racial/ethnic stratification

ethnic nationalism, 207
ethnic slurs, 303
ethnocentrism, 285, 286
Euro-Americans, 260
  Anglo core group, 264–265, 279
  largest ancestry groups, 267
  median family income, 289
  new immigration, 266–268
  old immigration, 265–266
excise taxes, 179
expendables, 152
explanation, sociological, 9–10

false consciousness, 203, 229, 253
family
  census definition, 34
  female-headed, 65
  income, 34–35, 41–43, 289–290
  single-parent, 109
  structure of, and poverty, 53–54, 59
  two-wage-earner, 93
Farley, Reynolds, 94
farmworkers, 83
federal budget, fiscal year 2001, 182
Federal Communications Commission
      (FCC), 191
Federal Trade Commission (FTC), 192
female circumcision, 337–338
feminism
  defined, 342
  ideological spectrum, 343–344
feminist movement, 340–341, 342, 345
feminization of poverty, 54
Ferraro, Geraldine, 331
Ferree, Myra Marx, 343
feudalism. *See* estate system
financial assets, 40
fiscal policy, and the distribution of income
      and wealth, 178–179, 196
Fitzgerald, F. Scott, 27, 118
Fogel, Robert, 145
Food and Drug Administration (FDA), 191
food stamps, 71, 184
Forbes, Malcolm, 1, 39, 363
Forbes, Steve, 363
Forbes list, 44, 117–118, 124
force, use of, 226–227
Foreman, Christopher H., Jr., 280
Form, William, 228, 231
France, Anatole, 346
Frank, Robert, 110
Free, Lloyd A., 233
Freeman, Richard, 43, 46, 105
free market, 240, 307
free trade, 359–360
Freyre, Gilberto, 145–146
Friedan, Betty: *The Feminine Mystique*, 342

Friedl, Ernestine, 318, 323
Friedland, Roger, 370, 372
functionalism, 217–219, 224, 230,
    253, 318

Galbraith, John Kenneth, 25, 172, 178
Gandhi, Mohandas, 214
Gans, Herbert, 34, 69, 89, 250
Gates, Bill, 117, 118, 122–123
gender
    and sex, 316–317, 345
    and social mobility, 164
gender differentiation, 316–317
    in agrarian societies, 318
    in hunting-and-gathering societies, 318
    and occupational clustering, 323–325, 345
gender feminism, 343–344, 345
gender inequality, 3, 15, 281, 345
    in the corporate world, 332–334
    in earnings, 325–328
    explanations for, 317–319
    international, 314–316, 322–323, 330,
        336–338, 340–341
    in Japan, 338–339
    in the political world, 330–331
    in the workforce, 320–329
    See also women
gender rebellion feminism, 344 n. 7
gender reform feminism, 343
genital mutilation, 337–338
genocide, 303
German immigrants, 265
Germany
    ethnic discrimination, 285
    wages in, 95
    welfare state, 190
Getty, J. Paul, 114
G.I. Bill, 174, 197
Gilbert, Dennis, 29 n. 2
Gilded Age, 121
Gingrich, Newt, 116, 367
Gini index, 46
Gitlin, Todd, 252
glass ceiling, 302
globalization, 11, 97–105
Gottschalk, Peter, 44
Gouldner, Alvin, 229
governing class, 152
governing class theory (Domhoff),
    127–128
government
    distrust of, 189–190
    ethnic representation in, 299–301
    regulation, 191–194
    women in, 330–331
    See also political participation; public
        policy

government spending
    categories of, 181–182
    public perceptions of, 191
Gramsci, Antonio, 229
Great Depression, 90, 155–156, 194
Great Society, 64, 174, 182
Greider, William, 366, 368, 369
group mobility, 21
Gwyn, Richard, 189

Hacker, Andrew, 114, 117, 293
Hamilton, Richard, 368–369
Harrington, Michael, 208
    The New American Poverty, 56
    The Other America, 55–56
Harris, Marvin, 317
health, and social class, 17–18
hegemony, ideological, 228–229
Heilbroner, Robert, 152, 189
Helmsley, Leona, 172
Hemingway, Ernest, 27
Herrnstein, Richard J., 63–64
Hess, Beth, 343
hidden curriculum, 246
hidden welfare, 185, 191
higher education
    and family income, 163
    and race/ethnicity, 291
    state-supported, 184
    women and, 334–336
high school graduates, by race/ethnicity,
    290
Hilbert, Steve, 123
Hispanic Americans
    classification, 260
    in corporate world, 301
    Cuban Americans, 273–274
    economic gap relative to Euro-
        Americans, 295–296
    gender gap in earnings, 327
    median family income, 37, 289
    Mexican Americans, 272–273
    as minority group, 282
    political power, 301
    in poverty, 53
    Puerto Ricans, 273
    rapid growth of, 261, 279
historical materialism, 201
Hitler, Adolf, 214
Hochschild, Arlie, 322
Hochschild, Jennifer, 234, 237
Holmes, Oliver Wendell, 177
homeless, 56
home mortgage deduction, 184
home ownership, 174
Homestead Act of 1862, 173
Honda, 99

Horatio Alger myth, 131, 135, 158, 171
horizontal (lateral) mobility, 156
household, census definition, 34
household income, 35
    by race/ethnicity, 291
housework, as women's role, 322, 329
housing
    effect on education, 67
    segregation, 164, 293–294, 304, 305, 313
Housman, John, 124
Huber, Joan, 228, 231
human nature, view of as unchanging, 241

ideological hegemony, 202, 228–229, 253
ideology
    changing, 21–22, 243
    defined, 227–228
    dominant, 20, 228, 253
    elitist view of, 229
    and functionalist theory, 230
    and legitimation, 20
    Marx and, 228–229
    nature of, 227–228
    and reality, 230
    and structured inequality, 20
    See also American ideology; racist
        ideology; sexism
illegitimacy, 72
Illich, Ivan, 244
immigration
    Asian, 275
    Cuban, 274
    economic effects of, 108–109, 277
    effect on opportunity structure, 160–161
    involuntary, 285
    Irish, 265
    Mexican, 272
    newest, 276–279
    old and new, 265–268
    restrictive quotas, 266
    social issues, 277–279
    voluntary, 284–285
imperatively coordinated associations, 217
incidental socialization, 246
income distribution, 34–38
    family income, 34–35, 41–43, 289–290
    and fiscal policy, 179
    historical perspective, 36–37
    regional disparities, 37–38
    and social class, 26
    trends in, 41–44
    in U.S. compared to other industrialized
        nations, 46–47
    See also earnings
income quintiles, 36–38
income tax, 173, 178, 179–180, 196
indentured servitude, 144

India, caste system, 147, 212
individual discrimination, 303
individualism, 10, 20, 70, 83, 188–189,
    231–234, 246, 253
individual mobility, 161–166, 171
indoctrination, 245
industrialization, 83–84, 223
inequality
    of condition, 16, 23, 71
    of opportunity, 16–19, 23, 71, 234–235,
        253
    See also social inequality
information, control of, 253
information society, 160
inherited wealth, 39, 124
institutional discrimination, 303–304
interest groups
    as a democratizing force in politics, 354
    and social class, 370
intergenerational mobility, 155, 158, 171
interlockers, 359
intermarriage, 150, 262, 305–306
intermediate classes, 33
international comparisons
    economic inequality, 45–47
    income distribution, 46–47
    poverty, 76–79
    social inequality, 222–223
    taxation, 180–181
    welfare programs, 187
international gender inequality, 314–316,
    341
    discrimination and abuse, 336–338,
        340–341
    labor force participation, 322–323
    and power, 330, 340
internment, of Japanese Americans, 275
interpersonal power, 347
Interstate Commerce Commission, 191
intragenerational mobility, 155, 171
invisible hand, 192
involuntary immigration, 285
IQ, 63, 168, 229
Ireland, 77
Irish immigrants, 265
isolates, 361
Israel, 77
Ivy League universities, 163

Jackman, Mary R., 225, 227, 232
Jackson, Robert Max, 314
Japan, 88
    corporations in, 196
    postwar, 91
    power elite, 140
    status of women in, 338–339
Japanese Americans, internment, 275, 303

Jefferson, Thomas, 239
Jencks, Christopher, 62, 75
Jewish Americans, 284
    changing attitudes toward in
        government, 299–300
    in the corporate world, 301
    upward mobility, 267
Jim Crow, 145, 147, 150–151, 268–269, 270,
    272, 303
Johnson, Lyndon B., 51, 56, 64, 174, 307
Jones, Dan, 165 n. 3
Jordan, Winthrop, 315
justice, and social class, 18

Kahl, Joseph A., 29 n. 2
Keister, Lisa, 117
Keller, Suzanne, 356
Key, V. O., 245
Keynes, John Maynard, 193
Killian, Lewis, 265
King, Martin Luther, Jr., 270–271
klasse für sich, 204
Kluegel, James, 232, 235
Knight, Phil, 103
Konigsberg, Eric, 123–124
Korean Americans, 276
Kozol, Jonathan, 167
Ku Klux Klan, 269, 271
Kuttner, Robert, 25

labor force participation, by gender,
    321–323
labor market changes, and poverty, 57
labor mobility, 103–104
labor unions
    decline of, 105–106
    as forces of stabilization, 206, 207
    political lobbying, 369
    as reform movement, 373–374
    and social mobility, 21
    Wagner Act, 174
    weakness, 190–191
    and wealth inequality, 47
Ladd, Everett, 235
laissez-faire, 192, 193
land-grant colleges and universities, 173
language
    gendered, 320
    See also English language
Lasswell, Harold, 172, 225, 348, 371
Latinos. *See* Hispanic Americans
leaders
    economic, 135
    political, 133–335, 248, 330–331,
        361, 362
    See also elite; power elite
legal rational authority, 214

legitimacy, 226
legitimation, 20, 226–227, 247–253
Lenin, V. I., 204, 214
Lenski, Gerhard, 153, 221–223, 224
Leonhardt, David, 112
Letterman, David, 39
Levin, Murray, 245
Lewis, Oscar, 65, 66
liberal capitalism, 189, 239–240, 253
liberty
    versus equity, 22, 24, 168, 237, 307
    as natural right, 240
Lieberman, Joseph, 300
Lieberson, Stanley, 285
life chances, 16–19, 23, 210–211
lifestyle
    lower-middle class, 86
    new consumerism, 109–112
    and social class, 26–27
    upper class, 29–31, 114–125, 126–132
    upper-middle class, 85–86
    working class, 87–88
Lindblom, Charles, 351
Lippmann, Walter, 251
Lipset, Seymour Martin, 139, 155
lobbying, 350–351, 366–368, 376
Locke, John, 239, 240
Lorber, Judith, 317 n. 2, 343, 344
Lott, Trent, 366
lower-middle class, 32, 82, 86, 112. *See also*
    middle class
loyalty oaths, 246
luck, and social mobility, 165
Luddite movement, 96
lynching, 269
Lynd, Robert and Helen, 233

macroeconomic policy, 177–180
majority groups. *See* dominant group
male superiority, belief in, 65
managerial positions, women in, 325, 329,
    332–334, 345
Mandela, Nelson, 150
Mannheim, Karl, 228 n. 2
manumission, 146
Mao Tse-tung, 214
marginals, 361
Marx, Karl, theory of, 83, 198–199, 224, 253,
    349
    class conflict, 203–205, 218
    enduring points, 207–208
    failure of vision, 205–207
    hegemony of capitalist class, 202–203
    and ideology, 228–229
    industrial working class in, 83
    predominance of economic institutions
        in, 200–201

Marx, Karl, theory of *(continued)*
  revision of, 208–210
  social inequality, 199–210
Mason, Philip, 1, 143
masses, 215, 216, 348–349, 375
  and mass communication, 352–353
  political participation and the class
    structure, 371–372
  role of in system of power, 360–375
Massey, Douglas, 293
mass media
  content, 248–251
  economic context, 247–248
  effects, 251–253
  government access to, 248
  in the legitimation process, 247–253
  manipulation of the populace, 254, 353
  media elite, 242, 249, 250, 371
  and new consumerism, 110
  self-censorship, 250–251
  television, 247, 251, 348, 353
maternity leave, 187–188
Matthews, Donald, 134
Mauritania, 147
Mayer, Kurt B., 78 n. 5
McCarthy hearings, 246
McConnell, Sheila, 97
Mead, Lawrence, 61
Mead, Walter Russell, 109
means of production, 201, 202, 205,
  224, 350
media elite, 242, 249, 250, 371
median family income, 35
  between the mid-1970s and
    mid-1990s, 42
  by race/ethnicity, 1999, 289–290
Medicaid, 71, 174, 184
Medicare, 56, 71, 174, 177, 184, 197
merchant class (bourgeoisie), 152, 154
meritocracy, 235, 253
Mexican Americans, 272–273, 295
Mexican Revolution, 272
Mexican War, 272, 284
Miami, Florida, 274, 277, 301
Michels, Robert, 215–216, 348, 374
Microsoft, 122–123
middle class
  and economic restructuring, 89–109
  growth of, 42, 90–91, 206
  historical development of in U.S., 82–85,
    112
  new, 84
  and new consumerism, 109–112
  and occupational structure, 85–89
  "professional," 85
  public policy and growth of, 173–174
  shrinking of since 1970s, 91–96

  as a state of mind, 81
  See also lower-middle class; upper-
    middle class; working class
middle-class squeeze, 92–95, 157
middle-income jobs, decline of, 93–95
military spending, 90–91, 177
Mill, John Stuart, 239
Miller, Craig, 94
"Millionaire's Club," 193
Mills, C. Wright, 11, 114, 126–127, 133, 209,
  251, 352–353
minimum wage, 47, 58
Mining Act of 1872, 185
minority groups, 280-284, 287, 312. *See also*
  racial/ethnic stratification; *specific*
  minority groups
Mishel, Lawrence, 43
mixed-race people, 261 n. 2
mobility. *See* social mobility
mode of production, 200, 201
Montgomery bus boycott, 270
Moore, Demi, 123
Moore, Gwen, 340
Moore, Wilbert, 219
Morrill Act of 1854, 173
Morris, Michael, 62 n. 1
MTV, 99
muckrakers, 21
multiethnic societies, 255, 257, 280, 286
Murdock, George, 323
Murray, Charles
  The Bell Curve, 63–64
  Losing Ground, 64
Muse, Robert, 107
Muslim societies, status of women in, 337

national debt, 196
Native Americans, 260, 279, 282
  forced removal of, 263, 303
  median family income, 289
  population, 261, 263–264
  socioeconomic status, 298
natural rights, 240
negative stereotyping, 164
neo-Marxism, 208–210
Nestlé, 99
Netscape Navigator, 122
net worth, 38, 40
new class. *See* upper-middle class
new consumerism, 109–111, 113
New Economy, 95
new immigration, 266–268
Newman, Katherine, 93, 156
new middle class, 84
new poverty, 56–57
new rich, 118, 121–123
newspapers, 247

Nie, Norman, 368, 372
Nike, 98, 99, 103
Nineteenth Amendment, 330, 342
Nixon, Richard, 56
nobility, 151, 152
Noel, Donald, 285, 286
nonviolent protest, 270–271
North Korea, 226
Norway, 190

occupations
    of Asian Americans, 296
    as basis of class formation, 8, 211
    blurring of, 88–89
    concentration, by gender, 323–325
    and ethnicity, 288–289
    of lower-middle class, 86
    of middle classes, 85–89
    of upper-middle class, 31
    of working class, 87
official poverty, 50–52, 79
old economy, 95
old immigration, 265–266
old rich, 118, 212
old upper class, 120–121
oligarchy, 215–216, 348, 354
Olsen, Marvin, 361, 362
OPEC oil embargo, 91
open societies, 143, 154–155, 171, 237–238
Operation Wetback, 273
operatives, 87
opportunity, equality/inequality of, 71,
    234–235, 253
opportunity structure, 160
order theory. *See* functionalism
organizational authority, 217
organizational power, 213, 215
Orren, Garry, 167, 240
Ozzie and Harriet, 91

PACs, 364
Paletz, David, 250
panethnic groups, 257
pariahs, 147, 152
Parker, Richard, 337
Parkin, Frank, 208
participatory politics, symbolic functions, 372
part-time employment, 95
party (Weber), 212–213
paternalism, 144, 145
patriarchy, 315
Perot, H. Ross, 122, 363
Peru, 315, 341
Pessen, Edward, 133–134
petty bourgeoisie, 82, 209, 374
Phillips, Kevin, 44, 118
physically challenged, 281

Piazza, Thomas, 308
placement tests, and social class, 168–170
Plamenatz, John, 227
Plessy v. *Ferguson,* 269, 270
pluralism, 305, 354–356, 376
political action committees (PACs), 364
political attitudes, upper-middle class, 86
political democracy, United States as,
    175–176
political economy, 172–175, 207
political inequality, 346–349
political leaders, 361, 362
    access to the mass media, 248
    by gender, 330–331
    social-class origins of, 133–135
political participation
    as a critical life chance, 360
    effective forms of, 362–368
    and elite accountability, 369–371
    by gender, 330
    noninstitutional forms of, 372–375
    scale of, 360–361
    and social class, 368–369
    working class, 88
Political Parties (Michels), 215
political power, 346, 350
political rank, 212–213
political revolutions, 226
Porter, John, 140, 264
Portuguese, 145–146
post-capitalist society, 204
post-industrial society, 84–85
Postman, Neil, 250
post–World War II era
    expansion of the middle classes, 91
    prosperity, 90–91
poverty
    absolute, 49–50
    biological explanations, 63–65
    and capitalism, 68
    childhood, 53, 77–78
    chronic, 60
    in comparative perspective, 76–79
    culture of, 65–66
    cycle of, 66–67
    defining, 33, 49
    and deindustrialization, 68–69
    explanations of, 62–70, 233–234
    and family structure, 53–54
    feminization of, 54
    as functional, 69
    individualistic view of, 62–66, 70
    new, 56–57
    number of Americans living in, 52–53
    official, 50–52
    persistence, 57–58
    popular views of, 70–71

poverty *(continued)*
  and public policy, 70–76
  by race/ethnicity, 290
  rediscovery of in 1960s, 55–56
  relative, 50
  structure-focused explanations for, 66–69
  systemic origins of, 250
  trends, 55
poverty line, 51–52, 80
Powell, Colin, 116
power, 223
  authoritative, 217
  class model of, 350–352
  differences in, 3
  of dominant group, 283
  and ethnicity, 299–300
  as foundation of all forms of inequality,
      14–15, 19
  and gender inequality, 318–319
  instrumentalist view of, 350–351
  integrated model of, 357–360, 376
  legitimate, 227
  organizational, 213, 215
  paths to, 136–140
  pluralist model of, 354–356
  political, 346, 350
  and privilege and prestige, 222
  scope and dimensions of, 346–348
  and social inequality, 14–15, 220–221
  stability of, 19
  structuralist view of, 351–352
  three models of in America, 340–350
  Weber on, 213–214
  without participation, 370
  women and, globally, 340, 341
power elite, 126–127
  conservative elitist view, 130–131
  "inner group," 129
  Mills' theory of, 352–353
  model of, 352–353
  in other societies, 140
  recruitment process, 136–140
  relationship with upper class, 126–131
  and social class, 131–135
  and the upper class, 126–132
The Power Elite (Mills), 353
prejudice, 302–303, 312
prescriptive approach, 10
present orientation, 65
prestige. *See* status
Prewitt, Kenneth, 129, 135, 138
private property, 19
privilege, 222
probabilities, 8, 17 n. 1, 18, 37, 138
Procter and Gamble, 99
Professional Air Traffic Controllers
      Organization (PATCO), 106

professional-managerial sector, 206, 217
professional middle class, 85
Progressive Era, 193
progressive taxes, 173, 178, 196
proletariat, 202, 203, 204
propaganda, 229, 247
property rights, of women, 336
property taxes, 166–167
proportional (flat) taxes, 178, 196
public assistance programs, 71–73, 80,
      182–184, 197. *See also* welfare programs
public goods, 181–182, 197
public housing, 67
public policy, 165–167
  affirmative action, 307–312
  efforts at changing hierarchy, 307–312
  fiscal policy, 177–180, 194–196, 197
  influence of upper class on, 128
  market-oriented approach to, 57
  and the middle classes, 109, 173–174
  partisan differences in, 194–196
  and poverty, 70–76
  Reagan administration, 64, 106, 195
  role in stabilizing inequality, 3
  school financing, 166–168
public works programs, 76
Puerto Ricans, 273, 295

Qatar, 338
quintiles, income, 36–38
quotas, 277, 309, 310

race, 257–259, 279
  politics of, 261 n.2
  popular usage, 257
  as social creation, 258
race riots, 269–270
racial conflict, 207
racial endogamy, 150
racial/ethnic stratification, 3, 15, 280–313
  American ethnic hierarchy, 287–288
  and college graduation, 291
  discrimination, 67, 302–303
  dominant groups, 283
  and the economic hierarchy, 288–291
  and family income, 37
  and high school graduation rates, 290
  and median family income, 289–290
  minority groups, 280–283
  origins of, 284–286
  and poverty, 290
  and power, 299–300
  relativity of, 283–284
  and self-identification, 27
  and social class, 286–287, 312
  and social integration, 305–306
  and social mobility, 164

stability and change in, 306–312
and wealth, 291
racial segregation, 145, 147, 150–151,
268–269, 270, 303
racism, 228, 282, 302
racist ideology, 145, 150, 266, 269, 271, 282
radical feminists, 344
Rainwater, Lee, 238–239
Rayburn, Sam, 360
reactionary movements, 374, 375, 376
Reagan, Ronald, 57, 64, 106, 116, 195
antigovernment platform, 189
antilabor policies, 106
supply-side policies, 195
tradition of social Darwinism, 64
Red scare, 246
Reed, Deborah, 43
reform movements, 373–374, 376
regressive taxes, 178, 196
regulatory agencies, 191–192, 193, 197
Reich, Robert, 89, 104–105, 109
Reischauer, Edwin, 338
relative poverty, 50, 79
reproductive rights, 342
Republicans, 197
residence, and social integration, 305
residential segregation, 164, 293–294, 304,
305, 313
retainer class, 152
reverse discrimination, 308, 309, 310, 313
revolutionary movements, 204, 374, 376
Rifkin, Jeremy, 83 n. 1, 96, 97, 168
Roosevelt, Franklin D., 76, 193, 270, 359
Rosenblatt, Roger, 110
Rossi, Alice, 317
Rousseau, Jean Jacques, 239
routine personal service workers, 104, 105
routine production workers, 104
Rubin, Lillian, 156, 344
ruling class
simultaneous economic and
political/social power, 130,
224, 228
upper class as, 126, 127
Russia, 207
Russian Revolution, 374

sales taxes, 178, 179
Samuelson, Robert J., 237
Saunders, Peter, 34
savings and loan bailout, 187
Schlesinger, Arthur M., Jr., 255
school segregation laws, 270
Schor, Juliet, 110, 111, 112
Schurman, Franz, 374
scientific method, 10
Scorsese, Martin, 5

segregation, 268–269. *See also* racial
segregation
self-fulfilling prophecy, 169
self-interest, 240
self-reliance, 32, 75, 188, 232–234, 253
self-selection, 138, 216
Seneca Falls Convention of 1848, 342
separate but equal doctrine, 269, 270
serfs, 151, 152, 153, 227
service sector, 32, 57, 84, 94, 206
sex, and gender, 316–317, 345
sex discrimination. *See* gender inequality
sexism, 228, 319–320, 345
defined, 319 n. 3
stereotypes, 320
sexual harassment, 344
sexual slavery, 147
Sharlow, James, 107
single motherhood, 72
single-parent families, 59, 109
skepticism, 7–8, 23
slavery, 171, 203
in Brazil, 145–146
in modern form, 147
slave trade, 285
in the United States, 144–145, 268
Smith, Adam, 235, 239
The Wealth of Nations, 192
Smith, Eliot, 232
Sniderman, Paul, 308
social capital, 309
social class
and computer ownership, 168
defined, 15, 26
and ethnicity, 286–287, 312
and health, 17–18
and income distribution, 26
and interest group participation, 370
and justice, 18
as lifestyle, 26–27
for Marx, 201–202
and placement tests, 168–170
and political inequality, 349
and political participation, 368–369, 376
popular notions of, 27–28
and the power elite, 131–132
six-part model of, 29–34, 47
systems of, 154–155
two dimensions of, 25–27, 47
Weber's notion of, 210–211
social connections, 137–38
social Darwinism, 63, 266
social differentiation, 12, 23
social distance, 145
social esteem. *See* status
social forces, and inequality, 10–12
social hierarchy, 15, 19

social inequality
    change in systems of, 20–22
    comparative, 222–223
    of condition, 16, 23, 71
    and cultural norms and values, 19
    functional theory and, 218–219
    in industrialized societies, 223
    legitimation of, 226–227
    Lenski's theory of, 221–223
    major issues in the study of, 2–4
    Marx's theory of, 199–210
    of opportunity, 16–19, 23, 71, 234–235,
        253
    and power, 14–15, 220–221
    stability of, 19–20
    theories of, 198
    Weber's contribution to theory, 214
social insurance programs, 71
social integration, 305–306, 313
socialism, 204, 205, 207, 224
socialization, 243–244, 253
    deliberate, 245–246
    and mass media, 247–253
social mobility, 23, 82, 142–143
    determinants of, 160–170
    direction of, 155–156, 157–158
    downward, 107
    and education, 165–170
    expectations of, 32, 33
    group, 21–22
    in historical perspective, 158
    horizontal, 156
    individual, 20–21, 160–161
    inter-/intragenerational, 155
    patterns of, 155, 159
    range of, 158
    rate of, 156–157
    and social networks, 164
    structural determinants, 160–161
    trends, 156–158
    vertical, 155–156
social reality, and ideology, 230
Social Register, 121
social resources, 12
social revolutions, 226
social safety net, 189
Social Security, 71, 174, 177, 178, 184, 197
social stratification systems, 12–13,
        23, 143
    basis of, 15–16
    caste, 147–151
    class, 154–155
    estate, 151–154
    slavery, 144–147
    three dimensions of, 13–15
    See also gender inequality; racial/ethnic
        stratification; social class

social upper class. *See* upper class
societal institutions, neutrality of, 241–242
societal power, 347–348
socioeconomic status (SES)
    and six-part model of social class, 29
    See also social class
sociological approach, 23
    empirical substantiation, 7
    objectives of inquiry, 9–10
    objectivity, 6
    and probabilities, 8, 17, 18, 37, 138
    skepticism, 4–5, 7–8
sociological imagination, 11
sociopolitical movements, 373–375, 376
soft money, 364–365
Sommers, Christine, 343, 344
Sorokin, Pitirim A., 142
South Africa, apartheid system, 147,
        149–150, 303
Southeast Asian immigrants, 296
South Korea, 46, 314, 340
Soviet Union, 204
Spencer, Herbert, 63
SSI (Supplemental Security Income). *See*
        welfare programs
Stampp, Kenneth, 144
status, 14, 31, 124, 211–212, 222
status communities, 27, 212
Steele, Shelby, 309
stock options, 115, 122
stock ownership, 40, 206
Stone, Alan, 129, 135, 138
strategic elites, 355–356
Strickland, Julie, 334
strikes, labor, 106, 373
structural assimilation, 305
structuralist view, of power, 351–352
structural mobility, 160–161
structural pluralism, 305
structured inequality, 16
student placement, 168–170
subsidies, 185
suburbs, movement to, 90
Sudan, 147
super rich, the, 40
supply and demand, 192
supply-side policies, 195–196, 197
surplus, 223, 224
Sweden, 95
symbolic analysts, 104

talent pool, 136–37
Taliban, 314, 340
Tannenbaum, Frank, 146
tariffs, 187
taxation, 177–181
    capital gains tax, 180

corporate tax laws, 185
excise taxes, 179
income tax, 173, 178, 179–180, 196
progressive taxes, 173, 178, 196
property taxes, 166–167
proportional (flat) taxes, 178, 196
regressive taxes, 178, 196
sales taxes, 178, 179
U.S. compared to other industrial
    societies, 180–181
tax breaks, 195
tax expenditures, 184
technological changes, 96–97, 222–223
and emergence of inequality, 223
and restructuring, 96–97
telecommunications industries, 122
television, 247, 251, 348, 353
Thernstrom, Stephan and Abigail, 306, 308
third estate, 152
Third Industrial Revolution, 89, 96
Thurow, Lester, 38, 78–79, 93, 98, 117, 122,
    165, 176 n. 2, 189
Tiger, Lionel, 317
Title VII, Civil Rights Act of 1964, 327
Tobacco Institute, 367
Toth, Jennifer, 56
tracking, 169–170
trade restrictions, 187
traditional authority, 214
transfer payments, 182, 197
transnational corporations, 99–104, 100–102
trickle down policies, 195–196
Trollope, Anthony, 1
Tumin, Melvin M., 221
Turner, Lana, 165
Twitchell, James, 111
two-income families, 93, 109
two-tiered society, 92, 93
two-tier marketing, 111–112

Uncle Tom's Children (Wright), 269 n. 5
underclass, 33–34, 58, 60–62, 68–69, 69 n. 2,
    79, 271, 294
underground economy, 60
undeserving poor, 34, 69, 70
unemployment, 96
among African Americans, 292
among Hispanic Americans, 295
among Native Americans, 298
unemployment insurance, 174, 177, 184
United States
caste in, 150–151
historical development of middle class,
    82–85, 112
income distribution compared to other
    industrialized nations, 46–47
slavery in, 144–145, 268

taxation in compared to other
    industrialized societies, 180–181
universal health care, lack of, 188
universalism, 235–236
untouchables, 148
upper class, 29–31, 128, 130
income, 114–116
old rich and new rich, 118–123
and the power elite, 126–132
subculture, 120
wealth, 116–118
upper-middle class, 31-32, 82, 85, 104, 112,
    113. *See also* middle class
upside-down welfare, 195
upward mobility. *See* social mobility
urban ghettos, 53, 60, 61, 68, 69, 294
urban riots, 227, 269–270
U.S. Census Bureau, 260, 261
utopias, 204, 228 n. 2

value-laden framework, 6
values
and affirmative action, 310–311
consensus of, 230
of dominant class, 208
and social inequality, 19
varnas, 148
Veblen, Thorstein: *The Theory of the Leisure
    Class*, 123
Verba, Sidney, 167, 240, 368, 372
verbal discrimination, 303
vertical mobility, 155–156
Vietnamese Americans, 296, 297
Vietnam War, 56, 353
violence
in the family, 65
poor as victims of, 52
Voltaire, 239
voluntary associations. *See* interest groups
voluntary immigration, 284
Voting Rights Act of 1965, 271
voting rights legislation, 174, 271

wages. *See* earnings
Wagner Labor Relations Act of 1935, 174
Warner, Lloyd, 133
War on Poverty, 51, 56, 174, 197
wealth
acquisition of, 124–125
in American society, 39–41
defined, 14, 38–39
distribution of, 38–44
and effective political participation,
    362–366
expansion of, 118
forms of, 40
versus income, 38

wealth *(continued)*
 inequality, 43–44, 117
 inequality of in U.S. compared to other
  industrialized nations, 47
 inherited, 39, 124
 institutional *versus* personal, 129
 and perpetuation of class hierarchy, 39
 and power, 126
 privileges of, 123–124
 and racial/ethnic stratification, 289–291
 upper class, 116–118
"wealthfare," 185
wealthy, Americans' attitudes toward, 237
Weber, Max, 13, 14, 16, 26, 198–199, 224
 on authority, 213–214
 on bureaucracy, 213
 on class, 210–211
 on party, 212–213
 on power, 213–214, 346
 on status groups, 27, 124, 211–212
 theory of inequality, 210–217
welfare programs, 56, 57, 71–75
 bias against, 233
 corporate, 185
 lack of effect on poverty, 74
 for the middle classes, 184–185, 197
 for the poor, 182–184
 popular views of, 72, 75–76
 reform, 73–75, 76 n. 4
welfare state, 177–178, 187, 188–191
white-collar workers, 84, 85, 88–89, 112
Williams, Robin, 232
Willis, Bruce, 123
Wilson, William Julius, 58, 62 n. 1, 68–69, 70,
  294–295
Wirth, Louis, 281
Wolfe, Alan, 81
Wolff, Edward, 39, 40

woman-centered institutions, 344
women
 in corporate management, 325, 329,
  332–334, 345
 in the developing world, 336–338
 and education, 334–336
 increase of jobs for in middle and upper
  ranges, 94
 labor force participation, 109, 321–323
 occupational concentration, 323–325, 345
 and power, 340
 recruitment into industrial labor force in
  WWII, 90
 status of in global perspective, 336–340
 unpaid labor, 322
 work and family conflict, 329
 See also gender inequality
women's movement, 21, 243
women's suffrage, 330
Woods, Tiger, 262
work ethic, 238–239, 253
working class, 32–33, 82, 87–88, 112
 accommodation with the capitalist
  system, 206
 growth of, 83–84
 occupations, decline in, 206
 subculture, 87
working mothers, 93
working poor, 33, 58–59, 79
Works Projects Administration (WPA), 76
World Cup, 99, 103
Wright, Erik Olin, 208–209
Wright, Richard, 269 n. 5

yellow peril, 275

Zweigenhaft, Richard, 302